expert one-on-one
Visual Basic .NET Business Objects

Rockford Lhotka

Apress™

expert one-on-one
Visual Basic .NET Business Objects

expert one-on-one Visual Basic .NET Business Objects

ISBN (pbk): 1-59059-145-3

Printed and bound in the United States of America 2345678910

Technical Reviewers: Mark Horner, David Schultz Donald Xie

Editorial Directors: Dan Appleman, Gary Cornell, Martin Streicher, Jim Sumser, Karen Watterson, John Zukowski

Project Manager: Nicola Phillips

Proofreader: Helena Sharman

Production Editors: Sarah Hall, Paul Grove

Indexer: Martin Brooks

Artist and Cover Designer: Kurt Krames

Distributed to the book trade in the United States by Springer-Verlag New York, Inc., 175 Fifth Avenue, New York, NY, 10010 and outside the United States by Springer-Verlag GmbH & Co. KG, Tiergartenstr. 17, 69112 Heidelberg, Germany.

In the United States: phone 1-800-SPRINGER, email `orders@springer-ny.com`, or visit `http://www.springer-ny.com`. Outside the United States: fax +49 6221 345229, email `orders@springer.de`, or visit `http://www.springer.de`.

For information on translations, please contact Apress directly at 2560 Ninth Street, Suite 219, Berkeley, CA 94710. Phone 510-549-5930, fax 510-549-5939, email `info@apress.com`, or visit `http://www.apress.com`.

The source code for this book is available to readers at `http://www.apress.com` in the Downloads section.

Acknowledgements

Writing this book has been a big project, and I want to thank a number of people who helped make it come to fruition.

First, I'd like to thank my wife and sons for being patient with me over the past several months. Without your love and support this would have been impossible!

I'd also like to thank Greg Frankenfield and Paul Fridman for making Magenic such an awesome place to work. The support that you and the rest of Magenic have provided has been great, and I appreciate it very much!

The original editorial team and the reviewers put in a lot of time and effort, and really helped shape this book into what you see here. I owe them all a debt of gratitude for their fine work.

I want to thank Kevin Ford, Mike Amundsen, and Juan Carlos Fidalgo for all their help. I got a lot of good feedback, information, ideas, and support from each of you and I appreciate it very much. I am truly fortunate to have such good friends.

Additionally, I want to acknowledge Chris Kinsman and Chuck Macomber for their help with the `NetRun` utility. Of all the things in .NET that are cool, no-touch deployment is the most exciting to me. Both of you helped me resolve some sticky issues I was facing in getting it to work – thank you.
Finally, I'd like to thank the scores of people who've sent me e-mails of support, encouragement, or just plain asking when the book would be done! I hope you find this book to be as rewarding to read as it has been for me to write.

Code well and have fun!

About the Author

Rockford Lhotka

Rockford Lhotka is the Principal Technology Evangelist for Magenic Technologies, a company focused on delivering business value through applied technology, and one of the nation's premier Microsoft Gold Certified Partners. Rockford is also the author of several other titles, including *Fast Track Visual Basic .NET*, *Professional Visual Basic Interoperability – COM and VB6 to .NET*, and *Visual Basic 6 Distributed Objects*, and is a columnist for MSDN Online and a contributing author for Visual Studio Magazine. He regularly presents at major conferences around the world, including Microsoft PDC, Tech Ed, VS Live!, and VS Connections. He has over 16 years' experience in software development, and has worked on many projects in various roles, including software architecture, design and development, network administration, and project management.

For Teresa, Tim, and Marcus with love.

TABLE OF CONTENTS

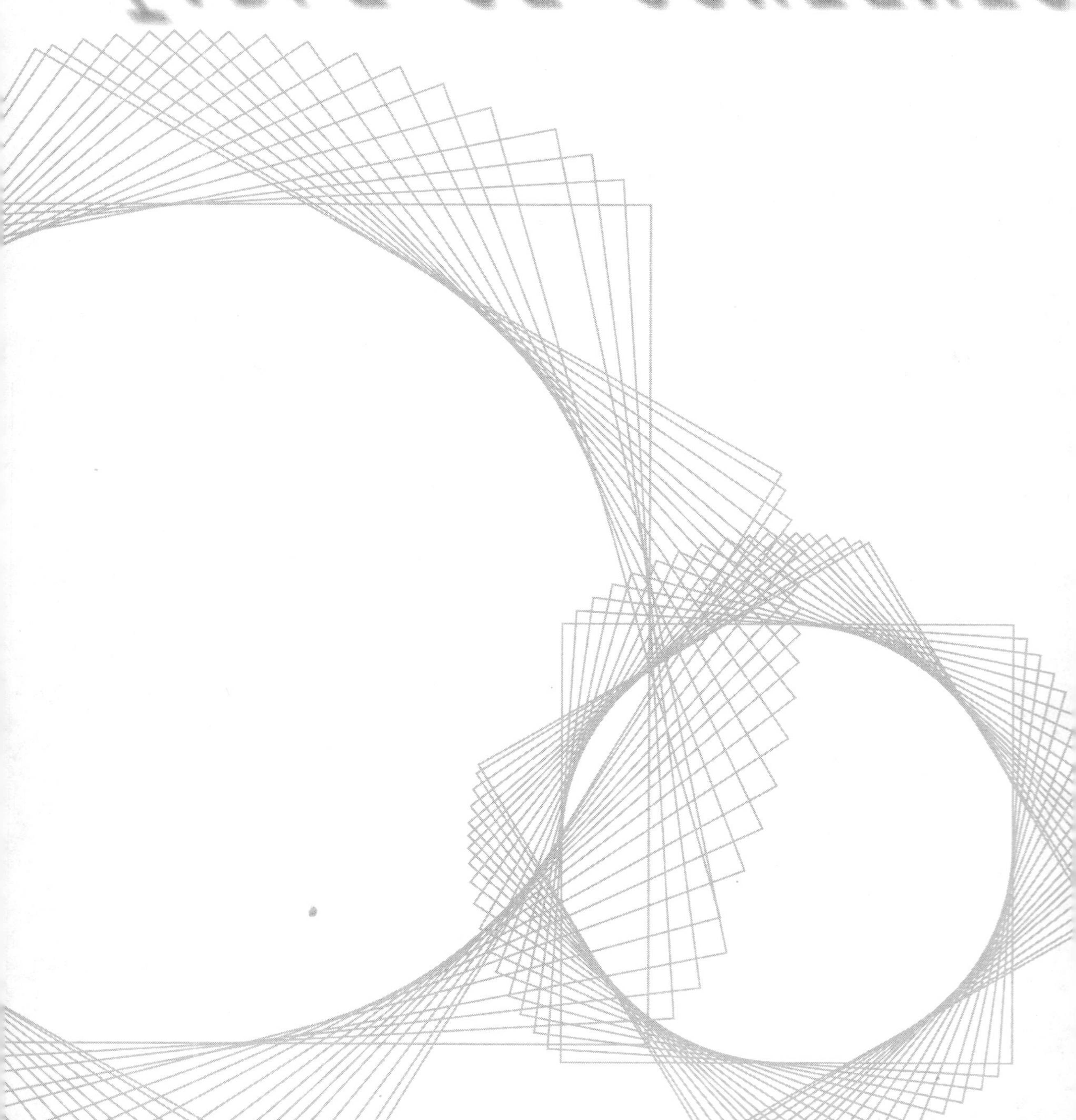

Table of Contents

INTRODUCTION

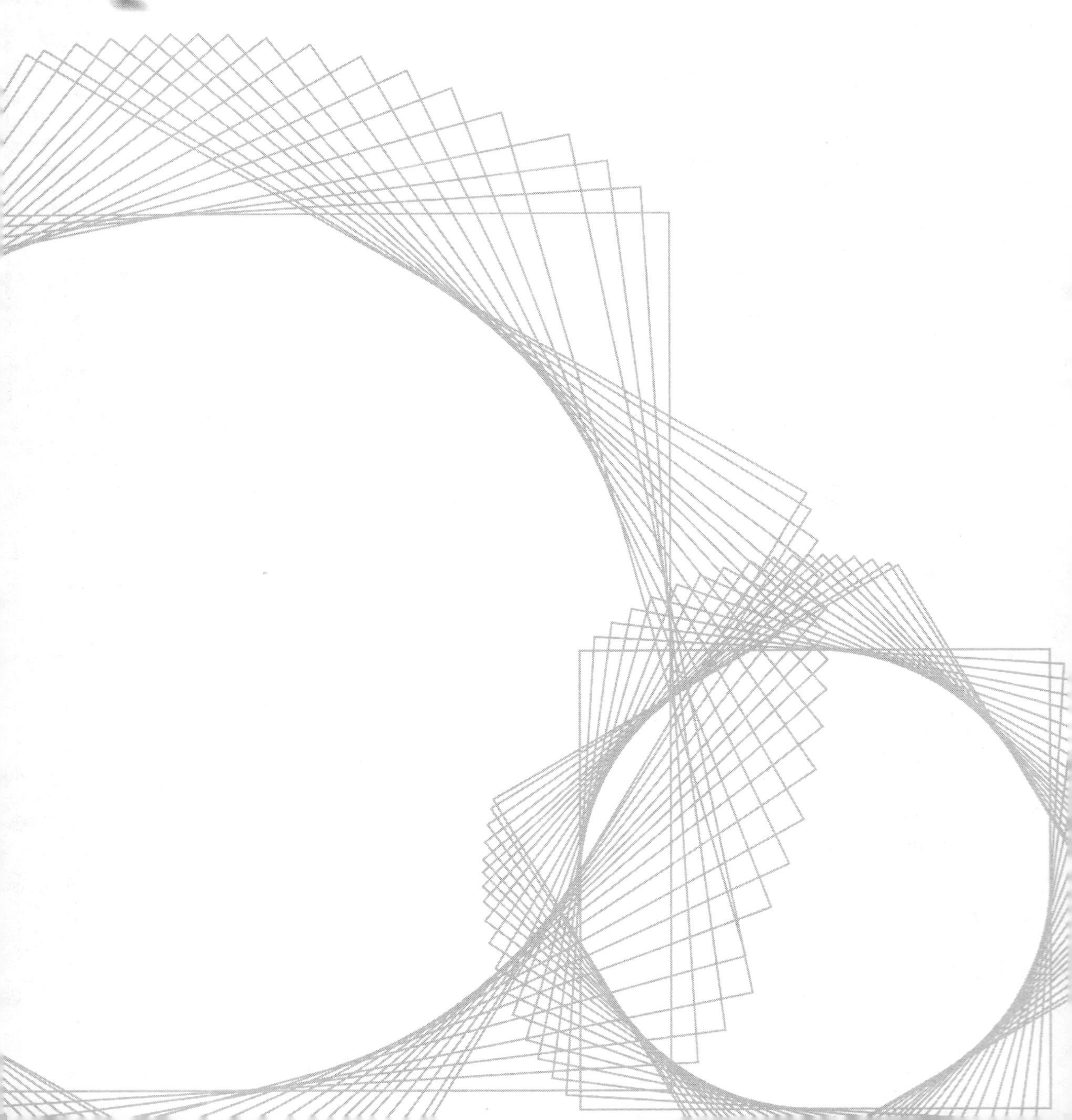

Introduction

This book is about application architecture, design, and development in .NET, using object-oriented concepts. Specifically, we'll be building business-focused objects called **business objects**, and we'll be implementing them in various distributed environments that include web and client-server configurations. To this end, we'll be making use of a great many .NET technologies, object-oriented design and programming concepts, and distributed architectures.

In the first half of the book, we'll walk through the process of creating a framework to support object-oriented application development in .NET. This will include a lot of architectural concepts and ideas. It will also involve some in-depth use of advanced .NET techniques as we create our framework.

In the second half of the book, I'll make use of the framework to build a sample application with several different interfaces. If you wish, it's perfectly possible to skip the first half of the book and simply make use of the framework to build object-oriented applications.

One of my primary goals in creating this framework was to simplify .NET development. Developers using the framework don't need to worry about the details of underlying technologies such as remoting, serialization, or auto-deployment. All of these are embedded in the framework, so that a developer using it can focus almost entirely on business logic and application design, rather than getting caught up in 'plumbing' issues.

From COM to .NET

This book is a follow-up to the popular *Professional Visual Basic 6 Business Objects* and *Visual Basic 6 Distributed Objects* books that I wrote two or three years ago, and looks at how the same powerful techniques can be applied to the .NET world.

The Visual Basic 6 books discussed how to use VB6, COM, DCOM, and COM+ to create applications using object-oriented techniques. (Or at least, they were as object-oriented as was possible in VB6 and COM.) They also covered the concept of **distributed objects**, where a given object is 'spread' over multiple machines in a physical n-tier environment. In COM, this is not a trivial thing to implement, and so these books included a fair amount of discussion relating to object state and state serialization techniques.

The end result was an architecture that I called **CSLA**, for Component-based, Scalable, Logical Architecture. Over the years, I've received hundreds of e-mails from people who have used CSLA as a basis for their own architecture as they've built applications ranging from small, single-user programs to full-blown enterprise applications that power major parts of their businesses.

I've also received a handful of e-mails from people for whom CSLA *wasn't* successful, but this is not surprising. To use CSLA effectively, one must become versed in object-oriented and component-based design, understand the concept of distributed objects, and develop a host of other skills. The distributed object architecture has many benefits, but it is not the simplest, or the easiest to understand.

Over the last couple of years, I've also received a steady stream of e-mails inquiring about a .NET version of my business objects books. Am I writing one, and if so, when will it be out? The answer is that I've been researching how to design a distributed, object-oriented architecture in .NET since I first received an early, quasi-working version of the .NET Framework. It was soon apparent to me that the change from COM to .NET was so great that I couldn't, in good conscience, write this book until I'd had enough time to make certain that my ideas were solid, and that I had found the right way to implement them in .NET.

Designing CSLA .NET

One of the characteristics of .NET is that it often provides several ways to solve the same problem. Some of the approaches available will be better than others, but which is the best may not be immediately obvious. I've spent a lot of time trying various approaches to distributing objects, and several of those have proven to work, but in the end I've arrived at the one that best matches my original goals.

Before I discuss those goals, I think it's important to talk about one other issue that I wrestled with before starting this book. Because .NET does so many things differently from the way COM does them, I found myself left with a choice between writing two rather different types of business objects book.

The first option was a book that showed how to translate or implement COM-based CSLA in the .NET environment. This would be useful to people who've built VB6 applications based on this architecture. Unfortunately, it wouldn't really show how to use the capabilities of .NET, since it would be focused on applying COM-style concepts in the .NET environment.

The other option was a book that focused on using .NET to build distributed object applications. This would be useful to *anyone* wishing to build object-oriented applications in the .NET environment, and could show how to take full advantage of the new technologies at our disposal.

In the end, I decided to go with the second option, and to create a fully .NET-based distributed object architecture that takes advantage of all that .NET has to offer. For readers of the VB6 books who would like to port their applications to .NET, I have some articles on my website at http://www.lhotka.net that offer some insight into the best ways to perform such a task. This book should also be useful, though, as it takes the same object-oriented and component-based concepts, and shows how they can be implemented far more easily in the .NET environment than was possible in COM.

As I started researching and writing toward this end, I developed a set of goals for the architecture and the book. These goals are important, as they're key to understanding why I made many of the choices I did in terms of which .NET technologies to use, and how to use them. They are:

- To support a fully object-oriented programming model
- To allow the developer to use the architecture without jumping through hoops
- To enable high scalability
- To enable high performance
- To provide all the capabilities and features of the original CSLA, namely:
    - n-Level undo on a per-object basis (Edit, Cancel, Apply)
    - Tracking of broken business rules
    - Support for many types of UI based on the same objects
    - Integration with MTS/COM+ for transactions
- To simplify .NET by handling complex issues like serialization and remoting
- To use the tools provided by Microsoft, notably IntelliSense and auto-completion in VS.NET

Of these, the goal that has probably had the largest impact is that of saving the developer from jumping through hoops – that is, to allow them to do 'normal' programming. In the COM-based CSLA, the developer had to write a lot of extra code to track business rules, implement n-level undo, and support serialization of object data. All this code was important, but it added nothing to the business value of the application.

Fortunately, .NET offers some powerful technologies that help to reduce or eliminate much of this 'plumbing' code. In several cases, my architectural decisions were driven by this goal. The end result is that the developer can, for the most part, simply write a normal Visual Basic .NET class, and have it automatically enjoy all the benefits of n-level undo, business rule tracking, and so forth.

It has taken a great deal of time and effort, but I've certainly enjoyed putting this architecture and this book together, and I hope that you, the reader, will find it valuable during development of your own applications.

What's covered in this book?

This book covers the thought process behind the CSLA .NET architecture, describes the construction of the framework that supports the architecture, and demonstrates how to create Windows Forms, Web Forms, and XML Web Services applications based on business objects written using the framework.

Chapter 1, *Distributed architecture*, is an introduction to some of concepts surrounding distributed architectures, including logical and physical architectures, business objects, and distributed objects. Perhaps more importantly, this chapter sets the stage, showing the thought process that resulted in the remainder of the book.

Chapter 2, *Framework design*, takes the architecture described at the end of Chapter 1 and uses it as the starting point for a code framework that enables the goals described above. By the end, you'll have seen the design process for the objects that we'll implement in Chapters 4 and 5, but before that we have some other business.

Chapter 3, *Key technologies*, is a quick overview of the .NET technologies used to implement the framework and application. There are many books available that dive into the specifics of each of these technologies, but in this book my focus is on pulling them all together to show how they can each be used as part of a larger whole. In Chapter 3, I'll introduce each of the technologies, and discuss how we'll be using them through the remainder of the book.

Chapter 4, *Business framework implementation*, and **Chapter 5**, *Data access and security*, are all about the construction of the framework itself. If you're interested in the code behind n-level undo, object distribution, auto-deployment, and object persistence, then these are the chapters for you. They make use of some of the more advanced and interesting parts of the .NET Framework as well, including remoting, serialization, reflection, .NET security, Enterprise Services, strongly named assemblies, dynamically loaded assemblies, application configuration files, and more. Chapter 3 provides an overview of each of these, but in Chapters 4 and 5 we'll make use of them to create the framework.

The rest of the book then focuses on creating an application that makes use of the architecture and framework. Even if you're not particularly interested in learning all the lower-level .NET concepts from Chapters 4 and 5, you can take the framework and build applications based on it by reading Chapters 6 thru 10.

In **Chapter 6**, *Object-oriented application design*, we'll discuss the requirements of our sample application and create its database. We'll be using SQL Server and creating not only tables but also stored procedures to enable retrieval and updating of data.

In **Chapter 7**, *Business object implementation*, we'll create the business objects for the application. This chapter really illustrates how the framework can be used to create a powerful set of business objects for an application rapidly and easily. The end result is a set of objects that not only model our business entities, but also support n-level undo and various physical configurations to optimize for performance, scalability, security and fault-tolerance, as discussed in Chapter 1.

Chapter 8, *Windows Forms UI*, will demonstrate how to create a Windows Forms interface to our business objects. **Chapter 9**, *Web Forms UI*, will cover the creation of a Web Forms, or ASP.NET, interface with comparable functionality. In **Chapter 10**, *Web services interface*, we'll use XML Web Services to provide a programmatic interface to our application that can be called by any SOAP client.

Most of this book focuses on OLTP (online transaction processing)-style applications and the object models that support those types of applications. However, for reporting or other functions that require manipulation of very large sets of data, we need to use different design patterns, and our object model requires adjustment or reworking. We'll discuss some of these issues and potential solutions in **Chapter 11**, *Reporting and batch processing*.

By the end, you'll have a framework that supports object-oriented application design in a practical, pragmatic manner. The framework implements a logical model that you can deploy in various physical configurations to support Windows, web, and web services clients optimally.

What you need to use this book

The code in this book has been verified to work against Microsoft Visual Studio .NET Professional and Microsoft Visual Studio .NET 2003 Professional, and therefore against versions 1.0 and 1.1 of the .NET Framework – any minor changes necessary to the code are noted in the text. The Enterprise version of Visual Studio .NET and the full version of SQL Server are useful but not necessary; the database work in the later chapters can be handled by MSDE, albeit without quite so much help from the IDE.

As a consequence of the above, you'll need at least one PC with Windows 2000 or Windows XP Professional Edition installed. To test CSLA .NET's support for multiple physical tiers, of course, you'll need an additional PC for each tier you wish to add!

Conventions

We've used a number of different styles of text and layout in this book to differentiate between different kinds of information. Here are some examples of the styles used, and an explanation of what they mean.

Code has several fonts. If we're talking about code in the body of the text, we use a fixed-width font like this: `For...Next`. If it's a block of code that can be typed as a program and run, on the other hand, then it will appear within a gray box:

```
If Thread.CurrentPrincipal.Identity.IsAuthenticated Then
  pnlUser.Text = Thread.CurrentPrincipal.Identity.Name
  EnableMenus()
End If
```

Sometimes, you'll see code in a mixture of styles, like this:

```
dgProjects.DataSource = ProjectList.GetProjectList()
DataBind()
```

```
' Set security
Dim user As System.Security.Principal.IPrincipal
user = Threading.Thread.CurrentPrincipal
```

When this happens, the code with a white background is code you're already familiar with, or which doesn't require immediate action. Lines highlighted in gray are new additions to the code since we last looked at it, or else they indicate something that we particularly want to draw your attention to.

Advice, hints, and background information come in this style.

> **Important pieces of information are placed inside boxes like this.**

Bullets appear indented, with each new bullet marked as follows:

- **Important words** are in a bold type font.
- Words that appear on the screen, or in menus like File or Window, are in a similar font to the one you would see on a Windows desktop.
- Keys that you press on the keyboard, such as *Ctrl* and *Enter*, are in italics.

Customer support

We always value hearing from our readers, and we want to know what you think about this book: what you liked, what you didn't like, and what you think we can do better next time. You can send us your comments by e-mail to info@apress.com. Please be sure to mention the book title in your message.

How to download sample code for this book

Visit www.apress.com, and go to the Downloads section. Download files are archived in a zipped format, and need to be extracted with a decompression program such as WinZip or PKUnzip. The code is typically arranged with a suitable folder structure, so ensure that your decompression software is set to use folder names before extracting the files.

Errata

We've made every effort to make sure that there are no errors in the text or in the code. However, no one is perfect and mistakes do occur. If you find an error in the book, such as a spelling mistake or a faulty piece of code, we would be very grateful to hear about it. By sending in errata, you may save another reader hours of frustration, and you will be helping us to provide ever-higher quality information. Simply submit the problem at the book's page on www.apress.com, and your information will be checked and posted on the errata page for the title, or used in subsequent editions of the book.

CHAPTER 1

1

Distributed architecture

Object-oriented design and programming are big topics – there are entire books devoted solely to the process of object-oriented design, and other books devoted to using object-oriented programming in various languages and on various programming platforms. My focus in this book is not to teach the basics of object-oriented design or programming, but rather to show how to apply them to the creation of distributed .NET applications.

It can be difficult to apply object-oriented design and programming effectively in a physically distributed environment. This chapter is intended to provide a good understanding of the key issues around distributed computing as it relates to object-oriented development. We'll cover a number of topics, including:

- How logical n-tier architectures help address reuse and maintainability
- How physical n-tier architectures impact performance, scalability, security and fault tolerance
- Data-centric vs. object-oriented application models
- How object-oriented models help increase code reuse and application maintainability
- Effective use of objects in a distributed environment, including the concepts of anchored and unanchored objects
- The relationship between an architecture and a framework

This chapter provides an introduction to the concepts and issues surrounding distributed, object-oriented architecture. Then, throughout this book, we'll be exploring an n-tier architecture that may be physically distributed across multiple machines. We'll also be using object-oriented design and programming techniques to implement a framework supporting this architecture. With that done, we'll create sample applications to demonstrate how the architecture and the framework support our development efforts.

Logical and physical architecture

In today's world, an object-oriented application must be designed to work in a variety of physical configurations. While the entire application *might* run on a single machine, it's more likely that the application will run on a web server, or be split between an intelligent client and an application server. Given these varied physical environments, we are faced with questions such as:

- Where do the objects reside?
- Are the objects designed to maintain state, or should they be stateless?
- How do we handle object-to-relational mapping when we retrieve or store data in the database?
- How do we manage database transactions?

Before we get into discussing some answers to these questions, it's important that we fully understand the difference between a **physical architecture** and a **logical architecture**. After that, we'll define objects and distributed objects, and see how they fit into the architectural discussion.

When most people talk about n-tier applications, they're talking about physical models where the application is spread across multiple machines with different functions: a client, a web server, an application server, a database server, and so on. And this is not a misconception – these are indeed n-tier systems. The problem is that many people tend to assume there's a one-to-one relationship between the tiers in a logical model and the tiers in a physical model, when in fact that's not always true.

A *physical* n-tier architecture is quite different from a *logical* n-tier architecture. The latter has nothing to do with the number of machines or network hops involved in running the application. Rather, a logical architecture is all about separating different types of functionality. The most common logical separation is into a UI tier, a business tier, and a data tier that may exist on a single machine, or on three separate machines – the logical architecture doesn't define those details.

> **There *is* a relationship between an application's logical and physical architectures: the logical architecture always has at least as many tiers as the physical architecture. There may be more logical tiers than physical ones (since one physical tier can contain several logical tiers), but never fewer.**

When you start looking around, the sad reality is that many applications have no clearly defined logical architecture – the logical architecture merely defaults to the number of physical tiers. This lack of formal logical design causes problems, since it reduces flexibility. If we design a system to operate in two or three physical tiers, then changing the number of physical tiers at a later date is typically very difficult. However, if we start by creating a *logical* architecture of three tiers, we can switch more easily between one, two, or three physical tiers later on.

The flexibility to choose your physical architecture is important because the benefits gained by employing a physical n-tier architecture are different from those gained by employing a logical n-tier architecture. A properly designed logical n-tier architecture provides the following benefits:

- Logically organized code
- Easier maintenance
- Better reuse of code
- Better team development experience
- Higher clarity in coding

On the other hand, a properly chosen physical n-tier architecture can provide the following benefits:

- Performance
- Scalability
- Fault-tolerance
- Security

It goes almost without saying that if the physical or logical architecture of an application is designed poorly, there's a risk of damaging the things that would have been improved had the job been done well.

Complexity

As experienced designers and developers, we often view a good n-tier architecture as a way of simplifying an application and reducing complexity, but this isn't necessarily the case. It's important to recognize that n-tier designs (logical and/or physical) are typically *more* complex than single-tier designs. Even novice developers can visualize the design of a form or a page that retrieves data from a file and displays it to the user, but novice developers often struggle with 2-tier designs, and are hopelessly lost in an n-tier environment.

With sufficient experience, architects and developers do typically find that the organization and structure of an n-tier model reduces complexity for large applications. However, even a veteran n-tier developer will often find it easier to avoid n-tier models when creating a simple form to display some simple data.

The point here is that n-tier architectures only simplify the process for large applications or complex environments. They can easily complicate matters if all we're trying to do is create a small application with a few forms that will be running on someone's desktop computer. (Of course, if that desktop computer is one of hundreds or thousands in a global organization, then the *environment* may be so complex that an n-tier solution provides simplicity.)

In short, n-tier architectures help to decrease or manage complexity when *any* of these is true:

- The application is large or complex
- The application is one of many similar or related applications that *when combined* may be large or complex
- The environment (including deployment, support, and other factors) is large or complex

On the other hand, n-tier architectures can increase complexity when *all* of these are true:

- The application is small or relatively simple
- The application isn't part of a larger group of enterprise applications that are similar or related
- The environment is not complex

Something to remember is that even a small application is likely to grow, and even a simple environment will often become more complex over time. The more successful our application, the more likely that one or both of these will happen. If you find yourself on the edge of choosing an n-tier solution, it's typically best to go with it, expecting and planning for growth.

This discussion illustrates why n-tier applications are viewed as relatively complex. There are a lot of factors, technical and non-technical, that must be taken into account. Unfortunately, it is not possible to say definitively when n-tier does and doesn't fit. In the end, it is a judgment call that we, as architects of our applications, must make, based on the factors that affect our particular organization, environment, and development team.

Relationship between logical and physical models

Architectures such as .NET's forebear, Windows DNA, represent a merger of logical and physical models. Such mergers seem attractive because they appear so simple and straightforward, but typically they're not good in practice – they can lead people to design applications using a logical or physical architecture that's not best suited to their needs.

> *To be fair, Windows DNA didn't* mandate *that the logical and physical models be the same. Unfortunately, almost all of the printed material (even the mouse mats) surrounding Windows DNA included diagrams and pictures that illustrated the 'proper' Windows DNA implementation as an intertwined blur of physical and logical architecture. While some experienced architects were able to separate the concepts, many more didn't, and created some horrendous results.*

The logical model

When we're creating an application, it's important to start with a logical architecture that clarifies the roles of all components, separates functionality so that a team can work together effectively, and simplifies overall maintenance of the system. The logical architecture must also include enough tiers so that we have flexibility in choosing a physical architecture later on.

Traditionally, we'd devise at least a 3-tier logical model that separates the interface, the logic, and the data management portions of the application. Today that is rarely sufficient, because the 'interface' tier is often physically split into two parts (browser and web server), and the 'logic' tier is often physically split between a client or web server and an application server. Additionally, there are various application models that break the traditional business tier up into multiple parts – model-view-controller and façade-data-logic being two of the most popular at the moment.

This means that our logical tiers are governed by the following rules:

- The logical architecture includes tiers to organize our components into discrete roles
- The logical architecture must have at least as many tiers as our anticipated physical deployment

Following these rules, most modern applications have four to six logical tiers. As we'll see, the architecture used in this book includes five logical tiers.

The physical model

By ensuring that the logical model has enough tiers to give us flexibility, we can configure our application into an appropriate physical architecture that will depend on our performance, scalability, fault-tolerance, and security requirements. The more physical tiers we include, the worse our performance will be – but we have the potential to increase scalability, security, and/or fault tolerance.

Performance and scalability

The more physical tiers there are, the *worse* the performance? That doesn't sound right, but if we think it through, it makes perfect sense: **performance** is the speed at which an application responds to a user. This is different from **scalability**, which is a measure of how performance changes as we add load (such as increased users) to an application. To get optimal performance – that is, the fastest possible response time for a given user – the ideal solution is to put the client, the logic, and the data on the user's machine. This means no network hops, no network latency, and no contention with other users.

If we decide that we need to support multiple users, we might consider putting application data on a central file server. (This is typical with Access and dBase systems, for example.) However, this immediately affects performance because of contention on the data file. Furthermore, data access now takes place across the network, which means we've introduced network latency and network contention too. To overcome this problem, we could put the data into a managed environment such as SQL Server or Oracle. This will help to reduce data contention, but we're still stuck with the network latency and contention problems. Although improved, performance for a given user is still nowhere near what it was when everything ran directly on that user's computer.

Even with a central database server, scalability is limited. Clients are still in contention for the resources of the server, with each client opening and closing connections, doing queries and updates, and constantly demanding the CPU, memory, and disk resources that are being used by other clients. We can reduce this load by shifting some of the work off to another server. An **application server** such as MTS or COM+ (sometimes referred to as Enterprise Services in .NET) can provide database connection pooling to minimize the number of database connections that are opened and closed. It can also perform some data processing, filtering, and even caching to offload some work from the database server.

These additional steps provide a dramatic boost to scalability, but again at the cost of performance. The user's request now has *two* network hops, potentially resulting in double the network latency and contention. For a given user, the system gets slower – but we are able to handle many times more users with acceptable performance levels.

In the end, the application is constrained by the most limiting resource. This is typically the speed of transferring data across the network, but if our database or application server is underpowered, they can become so slow that data transfer across the network is not an issue. Likewise, if our application does extremely intense calculations and our client machines are slow, then the cost of transferring the data across the network to a relatively idle high-speed server can make sense.

Security

Security is a broad and complex topic, but if we narrow our discussion solely to consider how it's affected by physical n-tier decisions, it becomes more approachable. We find that we're not talking about authentication or authorization as much as we're talking about controlling physical access to the machines on which portions of our application will run. The number of physical tiers in an application has no impact on whether we can authenticate or authorize users, but we *can* use physical tiers to increase or decrease physical access to the machines where our application executes.

Security requirements vary radically based on the environment and the requirements of your application. A Windows Forms application deployed only to internal users may need relatively little security, while a Web Forms application exposed to anyone on the Internet may need extensive security.

To a large degree, security is all about surface area: how many points of attack are exposed from our application? The surface area can be defined in terms of **domains of trust**.

Security and internal applications

Internal applications are totally encapsulated within our domain of trust – the client and all servers are running in a trusted environment. This means that virtually every part of our application is exposed to a potential hacker (assuming that the hacker can gain physical access to a machine on our network in the first place). In a typical organization, a hacker can attack the client workstation, the web server, the application server, and the database server if they so choose. Rarely are there firewalls or other major security roadblocks *within* the context of an organization's LAN.

> *Obviously, we do* have *security – we typically use Windows domain or Active Directory security on our clients and servers, for instance – but there's nothing stopping someone from attempting to communicate directly with any of these machines. What we're talking about here is* access, *and within a typical network, we have access to all machines.*

Because the internal environment is so exposed to start with, security should have little impact on our decisions regarding the number of physical tiers for our application. Increasing or decreasing the number of tiers will rarely have much impact on a hacker's ability to compromise the application from a client workstation on our LAN.

An exception to this rule comes when someone can use our own web services or remoting services to access our servers in invalid ways. This problem was particularly acute with DCOM, because there were browsers that could be used by end users to locate and invoke server-side services. Thanks to COM, users could use Excel to locate and interact with server-side COM components, bypassing the portions of our application that were *supposed* to run on the client. This meant that we were vulnerable to power users who could use our components in ways we never imagined!

> *The problem is likely to transfer to web services in the near future, as new versions of Microsoft Office and other end-user tools gain web service browsers. We can then expect to find power users writing macros in Microsoft Excel to invoke our web services in ways we never expected.*

The technology we'll be using in this book is .NET remoting, which is not geared toward the same ease of use as web services, and it's unlikely that end users will have browsers to locate remoting services. Even so, we'll be designing our remoting services to prevent casual usage of our objects, even if a power user were to gain access to the service from some future version of Microsoft Excel!

In summary, while security should not cause us to increase or decrease the number of physical tiers for internal applications, it *should* inform our design choices when we expose services from our server machines.

Security and external applications

For external applications, things are entirely different. To start with, we assume that there are at least two tiers: the client workstation is separate from any machines physically running within our environment. Typically, the client workstations are on the other side of a firewall from any of our servers, and we control the specific IP ports by which they gain entry to our network.

This means that the client workstations are outside our domain of trust, which in turn means that we must assume they are compromised and potentially malicious. If we actually run any code on those clients, we must assume that it ran incorrectly or not at all – in other words, we must completely validate any input from the client as it enters our domain of trust, even if we put code into the client to do the validation.

In many web applications, for instance, we'll include script code that executes on the browser to validate user input. When the user posts that data back to our Web Form, we must revalidate the data, because we must assume that the user somehow defeated or altered the client-side validation, and is now providing us with invalid data.

> *I've had people tell me that this is an overly paranoid attitude, but I've been burned this way too many times. Any time we are exposing an interface (Windows, web, XML, etc.) such that it can be used by clients outside our control, we* must *assume that the interface will be misused. Often, this misuse is unintentional – someone wrote a macro to automate data entry rather than doing it by hand – but the end result is that our application fails unless we completely validate the input as it enters our domain of trust.*

The ideal in this case is to expose only one server (or one type of server – a web server, say) to clients that are outside our domain of trust. That way, we only have one 'port of entry', at which we can completely control and validate any inbound data or requests. It also reduces the hacker footprint by providing only one machine with which a hacker can interact. At this stage, we've only dictated two physical tiers: the client, and our server.

Many organizations take this a step further, and mandate there to be a second firewall behind which all data must reside. Only the web server can sit between the two firewalls. The idea is that the second firewall prevents a hacker from gaining access to any sensitive data, even if they breach the first firewall and take control of the web server. Typically, a further constraint in configurations like this is that the web server can't interact directly with database servers. Instead, the web server must communicate with an application server (which is behind the second firewall), and that server communicates with the database server.

There's some debate as to how much security is gained through this approach, but it's a common arrangement. What it means to *us* is that we now have a minimum of four tiers: the client, the web server, an application server, and a data server – and as we discussed earlier, the more physical tiers we have, the worse our performance will be. As a general rule, switching from a 3-tier web model (client, web server, database server) to this type of 4-tier web model (client, web server, application server, database server) will result in a 50% performance reduction.

Some of this performance hit can be mitigated by special network configurations – using dual NICs and special routing for the servers, for example – but the fact remains that there's a substantial impact. That second firewall had better provide a lot of extra security, because we're making a big sacrifice in order to implement it.

Fault tolerance

Fault tolerance is achieved by identifying points of failure and providing redundancy. Typically, our applications have numerous points of failure. Some of the most obvious are:

- The network feed to our building or data center
- The power feed to our building or data center
- The network feed and power feed to our ISP's data center
- The primary DNS host servicing our domain
- Our firewall
- Our web server
- Our application server
- Our database server
- Our internal LAN

To achieve high levels of fault tolerance we need to ensure that if any one of these fails, some system will instantly kick in and fill the void. If our power goes out, a generator kicks in. If our network feed is cut by a bulldozer, we have a second network feed coming in from the other side of our building, and so forth.

Considering some of the larger and more well-known outages of major websites in the past couple of years, it's worth noting that most of them occurred due to construction work cutting network or power feeds, or because their ISP or external DNS provider went down or was attacked. That said, there are plenty of examples of websites going down due to local equipment failure. The reason why the high-profile failures are seldom due to this type of problem is because large sites make sure to provide redundancy in these areas.

Clearly, adding redundant power, network, ISP, DNS, or LAN hardware will have little impact on our application architecture. Adding redundant servers, on the other hand, *will* affect our n-tier application architecture – or at least, our application design. Each time we add a physical tier to our n-tier model, we need to ensure that we can add redundancy to the servers in that tier. The more physical tiers, the more redundant servers we need to configure and maintain. Thus, adding a tier always means adding at least *two* servers to our infrastructure.

Not only that, but to achieve fault tolerance through redundancy, all servers in a tier must also be identical at all times. In other words, at no time can a user be tied to a specific server – in other words, no server can ever maintain any user-specific information. As soon as a user is tied to a specific server, that server becomes a point of failure for that user, and we have lost fault tolerance (for that user, at least).

Achieving a high degree of fault tolerance is not easy. It requires a great deal of thought and effort to locate all points of failure and make them redundant. Having fewer physical tiers in our architecture can assist in this process by reducing the number of tiers that must be made redundant.

Ultimately, the number of physical tiers in our architecture is a trade-off between performance, scalability, security, and fault tolerance. Furthermore, the optimal configuration for a web application is not the same as that for an intranet application with intelligent client machines. If the framework we're going to create is to have any hope of broad appeal, we need flexibility in the physical architecture so that we can support web and intelligent clients effectively, and provide both with optimal performance and scalability.

A 5-tier logical architecture

In this book, I'll be exploring a 5-tier logical architecture, and showing how we can implement it using object-oriented concepts. Once we've created it, we'll configure the logical architecture into various physical architectures to achieve optimal results for Windows Forms, Web Forms, and web services interfaces.

If you get any group of architects into a room and ask them to describe their ideal architecture, each one will come up with a different answer. I make no pretense that this architecture is the only one out there, nor do I intend to discuss all the possible options. My aim here, as throughout the book, is to present a coherent, distributed, object-oriented architecture that supports Windows, web, and web services interfaces.

In our framework, the logical architecture comprises the five tiers shown in the following figure:

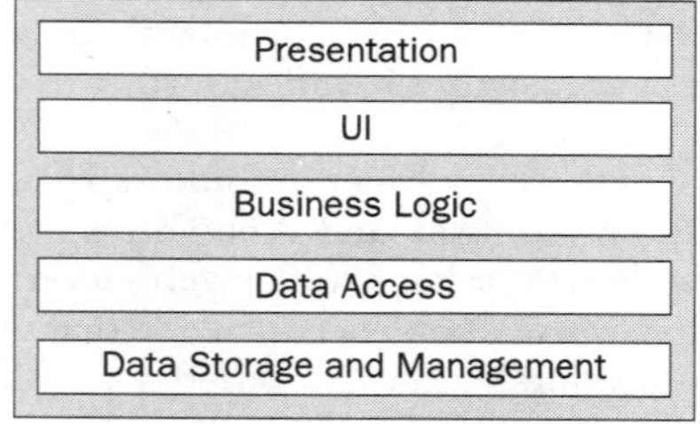

Remember that the benefit of a logical n-tier architecture is the separation of functionality into clearly defined roles or groups, in order to increase clarity and maintainability. Let's define each of the tiers more carefully.

Presentation

At first, it may not be clear why I've separated presentation from the user interface (UI). Certainly, from a Windows perspective, presentation and UI are one and the same: some GUI forms with which the user can interact. From a web perspective (or from that of terminal-based programming), however, the distinction is probably quite clear. The browser (or a terminal) merely presents information to the user, and collects user input. All of the actual interaction logic – the code we write to *generate* the output, or to *interpret* user input – runs on the web server (or mainframe), and not on the client machine.

Knowing that our logical model must support both intelligent and web-based clients (along with even more limited clients, such as cell phones or other mobile devices), it's important to recognize that in many cases, the presentation *will* be physically separate from the user interface logic. To accommodate this separation, we will need to design our applications around this concept.

The types of presentation tiers continue to multiply, and each comes with a new and relatively incompatible technology with which we must work. It's virtually impossible to create a programming framework that entirely abstracts presentation concepts. Because of this, our architecture and framework will merely support the creation *of varied presentations, not automate or simplify them. Instead, our focus will be on simplifying the other tiers in the architecture, where technology is more stable.*

UI

Now that we understand the distinction between presentation and UI, the latter's purpose is probably fairly clear. This tier includes the logic to decide what the user sees, the navigation paths, and how to interpret user input. In a Windows Forms application, this is the code behind the form. Actually, it's the code behind the form in a Web Forms application too, but here it can also include code that resides in server-side controls – *logically*, that's part of the same tier.

In many applications, the UI code is very complex. For a start, it must respond to the user's requests in a non-linear fashion. (We have little control over how users might click on controls, or enter or leave our forms or pages.) The UI code must also interact with logic in the business tier to validate user input, to perform any processing that's required, or to do any other business-related action.

Basically, what we're talking about here is writing UI code that accepts user input and then provides it to the business logic, where it can be validated, processed, or otherwise manipulated. The UI code must then respond to the user by displaying the results of its interaction with the business logic. Was the user's data valid? If not, what was wrong with it? And so forth.

In .NET, our UI code is almost always event-driven. Windows Forms code is all about responding to events as the user types and clicks on our form, and Web Forms code is all about responding to events as the browser round-trips the user's actions back to the web server. While both Windows Forms and Web Forms technologies make heavy use of objects, the code that we typically write into our UI is not object-oriented as much as it is procedural and event-based.

That said, there is great value in creating frameworks and reusable components to support a particular type of UI. If we're creating a Windows Forms UI, we can make use of visual inheritance and other object-oriented techniques to simplify the creation of our forms. If we're creating a Web Forms UI, we can use ASCX user controls and custom server controls to provide reusable components that simplify page development.

Because there's such a wide variety of UI styles and approaches, we won't spend much time dealing with UI development or frameworks in this book. Instead, we'll focus on simplifying the creation of the business logic and data access tiers, which are required for any type of UI.

Business logic

Business logic includes all business rules, data validation, manipulation, processing, and security for our application. One definition from Microsoft is, *"The combination of validation edits, logon verifications, database lookups, policies, and algorithmic transformations that constitute an enterprise's way of doing business."*

The business logic *must* reside in a separate tier from the UI code. I believe that this particular separation is the most important if we want to gain the benefits of increased maintainability and reusability for our code. This is because any business logic that creeps into the UI tier will reside within a *specific* UI, and will not be available to any other UIs that we might later create.

Any business logic that we write into (say) our Windows UI is useless to a web or web service UI, and must therefore be written into those as well. This instantly leads to duplicated code, which is a maintenance nightmare. Separation of these two tiers can be done through techniques such as clearly defined procedural models, or object-oriented design and programming. In this book, we'll be applying object-oriented concepts: encapsulating business data and logic in a set of objects is a powerful way to accomplish separation of the business logic from the user interface.

Data access

Data access code interacts with the data management tier to retrieve, update, and remove information. The data access tier doesn't actually manage or store the data; it merely provides an interface between the business logic and the database.

Data access gets its own logical tier for much the same reason that we split presentation from the user interface. In some cases, data access will occur on a machine that's physically separate from the one where the UI and/or business logic is running. In other cases, data access code will run on the same machine as the business logic (or even the UI) in order to improve performance or fault tolerance.

> *It may sound odd to say that putting the data access tier on the same machine as our business logic can* increase *fault tolerance, but consider the case of web farms, where each web server is identical to all the others. By putting the data access code on the web servers, we provide automatic redundancy of the data access tier along with the business logic and UI tiers.*
>
> *Adding an extra physical tier just to do the data access makes fault tolerance harder to implement, because it increases the number of tiers in which redundancy needs to be implemented. As a side-effect, adding more physical tiers also reduces performance, so it's not something that should be done lightly.*

By logically defining data access as a separate tier, we enforce a separation between the business logic and how we interact with a database (or any other data source). This separation gives us the flexibility to choose later whether to run the data access code on the same machine as the business logic, or on a separate machine. It also makes it much easier to change data sources without affecting the application. This is important because we may need to switch from one database vendor to another at some point.

This separation is useful for another reason: Microsoft has a habit of changing data access technologies every three years or so, meaning that we need to rewrite our data access code to keep up (remember DAO, RDO, ADO 1.0, ADO 2.0, and now ADO.NET?). By isolating the data access code into a specific tier, we limit the impact of these changes to a smaller part of our application.

Data access mechanisms are typically implemented as a set of services, with each service being a procedure that's called by the business logic to create, retrieve, update, or delete data. While these services are often constructed using objects, it's important to recognize that the designs for an effective data access tier are really quite procedural in nature. Attempts to force more object-oriented designs for relational database access often result in increased complexity or decreased performance.

> *If we're using an object database instead of a relational database, then of course our data access code may be very object-oriented. Few of us get such an opportunity, however, since almost all data is stored in relational databases.*

Sometimes, the data access tier can be as simple as a series of methods that use ADO.NET directly to retrieve or store data. In other circumstances, the data access tier is more complex, providing a more abstract or even metadata-driven way to get at data. In these cases, the data access tier can contain a lot of complex code to provide this more abstract data access scheme. The framework we'll create in this book will work directly against ADO.NET, but you could also use a metadata-driven data access layer if you prefer.

Another common role for the data access tier is to provide mapping between the object-oriented business logic, and the relational data in a data store – a good object-oriented model is almost never the same as a good relational database model. Objects often contain data from multiple tables, or even from multiple databases – or conversely, multiple objects in the model can represent a single table. The process of taking the data from the tables in our relational model and getting it into the object-oriented model is called **object-relational mapping**, and we'll have more to say on the subject in Chapter 2.

Data storage and management

Finally, we have the data storage and management tier. Database servers such as SQL Server or Oracle often handle these tasks, but increasingly other applications may provide this functionality too, via technologies such as web services.

What's key about this tier is that it handles the physical creation, retrieval, update, and deletion of data. This is different from the data access tier, which *requests* the creation, retrieval, update, and deletion of data. In the data management tier, we actually *implement* these operations within the context of a database or a set of files, etc.

The data management tier is invoked by our business logic (via the data access tier), but the former often includes additional logic to validate the data, and its relationship to other data. Sometimes, this is true relational data modeling from a database; other times, it's the application of business logic from an external application. What this means is that a typical data management tier will include business logic that we also implement in our business logic tier. This time, the replication is unavoidable, because relational databases are designed to enforce relational integrity – and that's just another form of business logic.

In any case, whether we're using stored procedures in SQL Server, or SOAP calls to another application, data storage and management is typically handled by creating a set of services or procedures that can be called as needed. Like the data access tier, it's important to recognize that the designs for data storage and management are typically very procedural.

The following table summarizes the five tiers and their roles:

Tier	Roles
Presentation	Renders display and collects user input.
UI	Acts as an intermediary between the user and the business logic, taking user input and providing it to the business logic, then returning results to the user.
Business Logic	Provides all business rules, validation, manipulation, processing, and security for the application.
Data Access	Acts as an intermediary between the business logic and data management. Also encapsulates and contains all knowledge of data access technologies (such as ADO.NET), databases, and data structures.
Data Storage and Management	Physically creates, retrieves, updates, and deletes data in a persistent data store.

Everything we've talked about to this point is part of a *logical* architecture. Now let's move on and see how it can be applied in various *physical* configurations.

Applying the logical architecture

Given this 5-tier logical architecture, we should be able to configure it into one, two, three, four, or five physical tiers in order to gain performance, scalability, security, or fault-tolerance to various degrees, and in various combinations.

In this discussion, we're assuming that we have total flexibility to configure what logical tier runs where. In some cases, there are technical issues that prevent physical separation of some tiers. Fortunately, there are fewer such issues with the .NET Framework than there were with COM-based technologies.

There are a few physical configurations that I want to discuss in order to illustrate how our logical model works. These are common and important setups that most of us encounter on a day-to-day basis.

Optimal performance intelligent client

When so much focus is placed on distributed systems, it's easy to forget the value of a single tier solution. Point-of-sale, sales force automation, and many other types of application often run in standalone environments. However, we still want the benefits of the logical n-tier architecture in terms of maintainability and code reuse.

It probably goes without saying that if we want to, we can install everything on a single client workstation. An optimal performance intelligent client is usually implemented using Windows Forms for the presentation and UI, with the business logic and data access code running in the same process and talking to a JET or MSDE (Microsoft SQL Server Desktop Engine) database. The fact that the system is deployed on a single physical tier doesn't compromise the logical architecture and separation.

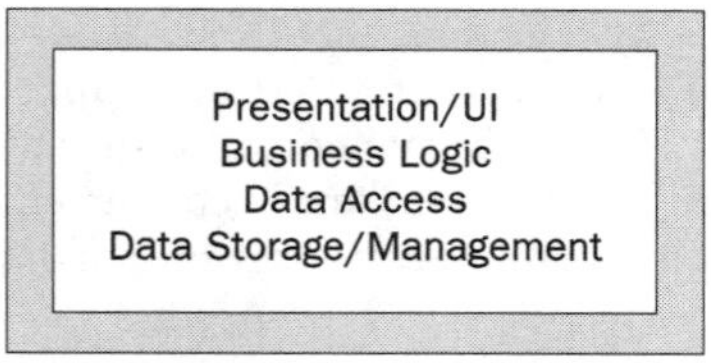

Presentation/UI
Business Logic
Data Access
Data Storage/Management

I think it's very important to remember that n-tier systems can run on a single machine in order to support the wide range of applications that require standalone machines. It's also worth pointing out that this is basically the same as 2-tier, 'fat client' physical architecture – the only difference in that case is that the data storage and management tier would be running on a central database server, such as SQL Server or Oracle:

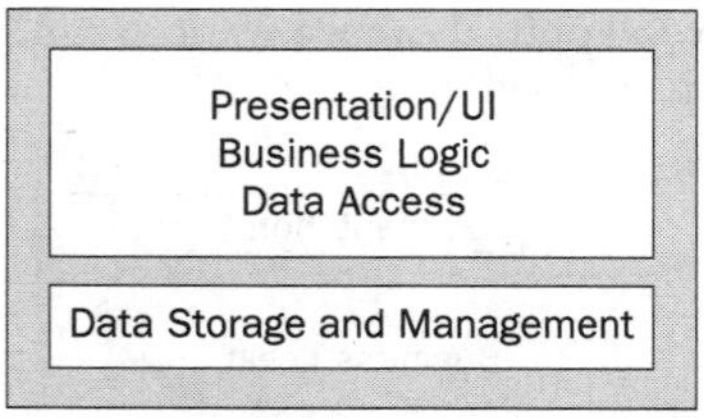

Presentation/UI
Business Logic
Data Access

Data Storage and Management

Other than the location of the data storage, this is identical to the single-tier configuration, and typically the switch from single-tier to 2-tier revolves around little more than changing the database configuration string for ADO.NET.

High scalability intelligent client

Single-tier configurations are good for standalone environments, but they don't scale well. To support multiple users, we often use 2-tier configurations. I've seen 2-tier configurations support more than 350 concurrent users against SQL Server with very acceptable performance.

Going further, we can trade performance to gain scalability by moving the data access tier to a separate machine. Single- or 2-tier configurations give the best performance, but they don't scale as well as a 3-tier configuration would do. A good rule of thumb is that if you have more than 50-100 concurrent users, you can gain by making use of a separate server to handle the data access tier:

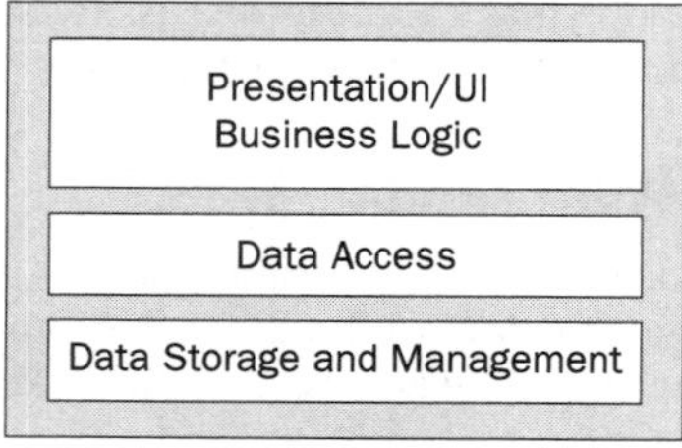

By doing this, we can centralize all access to the database on a single machine. In .NET, if the connections to the database for all our users are made using the same user ID and password, we'll get the benefits of **connection pooling** for all our users. What this means immediately is that there will be far fewer connections to the database than there would be if each client machine connected directly. The actual reduction depends on the specific application, but we're often looking at supporting 150-200 concurrent users with just 2 or 3 database connections!

Of course, all user requests now go across an extra network hop, causing increased latency (and therefore decreased performance). This performance cost translates into a huge scalability gain, however, since this architecture can handle many more concurrent users than a 2-tier physical configuration. If well designed, such an architecture can support *thousands* of concurrent users with adequate performance.

Optimal performance web client

As with a Windows Forms application, we get the best performance from a web-based application by minimizing the number of physical tiers. However, the tradeoff in a web scenario is different: in this case, we can improve performance and scalability at the same time, but at the cost of security, as we'll see shortly.

To get optimal performance in a web application, we want to run most of our code in a single process on a single machine, as shown in the following figure:

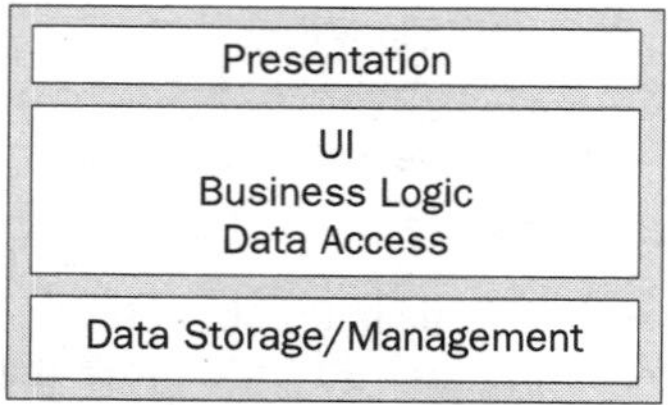

The presentation tier *must* be physically separate, because it's running in a browser, but the UI, the business logic, and the data access tier can all run on the same machine, in the same process. In some cases, we might even put the data management tier on the same physical machine, though this is only suitable for smaller applications.

This minimizes network and communication overhead, and optimizes performance. We also get very good scalability, since the web server can be part of a web farm in which all the web servers are running the same code:

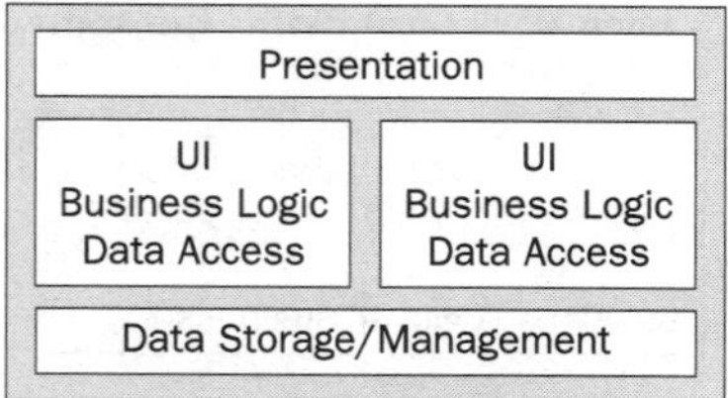

This setup gives us very good database connection pooling, since each web server will be (potentially) servicing hundreds of concurrent users, and all database connections on a web server are pooled.

> *With COM-based technologies such as ASP and Visual Basic 6, this configuration was problematic, because running COM components in the same process as ASP pages had drawbacks in terms of the manageability and stability of the system. Running the COM components in a COM+ Server Application addressed the stability issues, but at the cost of performance. These issues have been addressed in .NET, however, so this configuration is highly practical when using ASP.NET and other .NET components.*

Unless we notice that our database server is getting overwhelmed with connections from the web servers in our web farm, there will rarely be gains to be made in scalability by using a separate application server. If we *do* decide that we need a separate application server, we must realize that we'll reduce performance because we're adding another physical tier. (Hopefully, we'll gain scalability, since the application server can consolidate database connections across all the web servers.) We must also consider fault tolerance in this case, because we may need redundant application servers to avoid a point of failure.

Another reason for implementing an application server is to increase security, and that's the topic of the next section.

High security web client

As we discussed in the earlier section on security, there will be many projects in which it is dictated that a web server can never talk directly to a database. The web server must run in a 'demilitarized zone' or DMZ, sandwiched between the external firewall and a second, internal firewall. The web server must communicate with another server through the internal firewall in order to interact with the database or any other internal systems. This is illustrated by the following figure, where the dashed lines represent the firewalls:

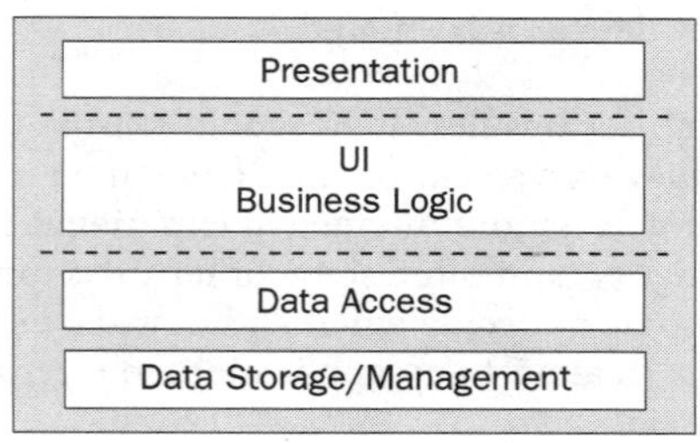

By splitting out the data access tier and running it on a separate application server, we are able to increase the security of the application. However, this comes at the cost of performance – as we discussed earlier, this configuration will typically cause a performance degradation of around 50%. Scalability, on the other hand, is fine: as with the first web configuration, we can achieve it by implementing a web farm in which each web server runs the same UI and business logic code.

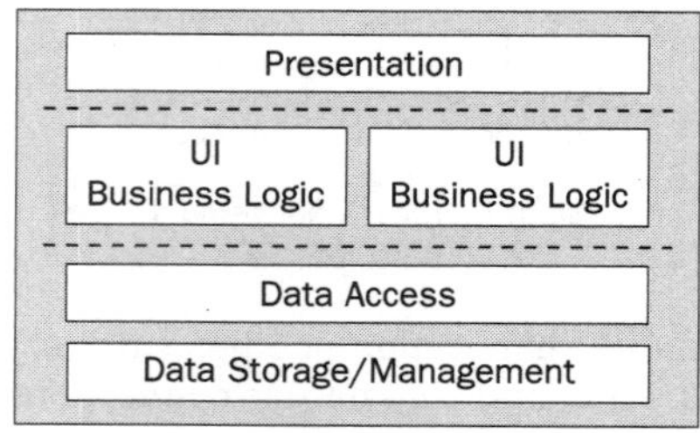

The way ahead

After we've implemented the framework to support this 5-tier architecture, we'll create a sample application with three different interfaces: Windows, web, and web services. This will give us the opportunity to see first hand how our framework supports the following models:

- High scalability intelligent client
- Optimal performance web client
- Optimal performance web client (variation to support web services)

Due to the way we'll implement our framework, switching to any of the other models we've just discussed will just require some configuration file changes, meaning that we can easily adapt our application to any of the physical configurations without having to change our code.

Managing business logic

At this point, you should have a good understanding of logical and physical architectures, and we've seen how a 5-tier logical architecture can be configured into various n-tier physical architectures. Now, in one way or another, all of these tiers will use or interact with our application's data. That's obviously the case for the data management and data access tiers, but the business logic tier must validate, calculate, and manipulate data; the UI transfers data between the business and presentation tiers (often performing formatting or using the data to make navigational choices); and the presentation tier displays data to the user, and collects new data as it is entered.

Similarly, it would be nice if all of our business logic would exist in the business logic tier, but in reality this is virtually impossible to achieve. In a web-based UI, we often include validation logic in the presentation tier, so that the user gets a more interactive experience in the browser. Similarly, most databases enforce referential integrity, and often some other rules too. Furthermore, the data access tier will very often include business logic to decide when and how data should be stored or retrieved from databases and other data sources. In almost any application, to a greater or a lesser extent, business logic gets scattered across all the tiers.

There is one key truth here that is important: for each piece of application data, there is a fixed set of business logic associated with that data. If the application is to function properly, the business logic must be applied to that data at least once. Why "at least"? Well, in most applications, some of the business logic is applied more than once – a validation rule, for example, can be applied in the presentation tier and then reapplied in the UI tier or business logic tier before being sent to the database for storage. In some cases, the database will include code to recheck the value as well.

Let's look at some of the more common options. We'll start with three popular (but flawed) approaches, and then discuss a compromise solution that is enabled through the use of distributed objects such as the ones we'll be supporting in the framework we'll create later in the book.

Potential business logic locations

The following figure illustrates common locations for validation and manipulation business logic in a typical application. Most applications have the same logic in at least a couple of these locations.

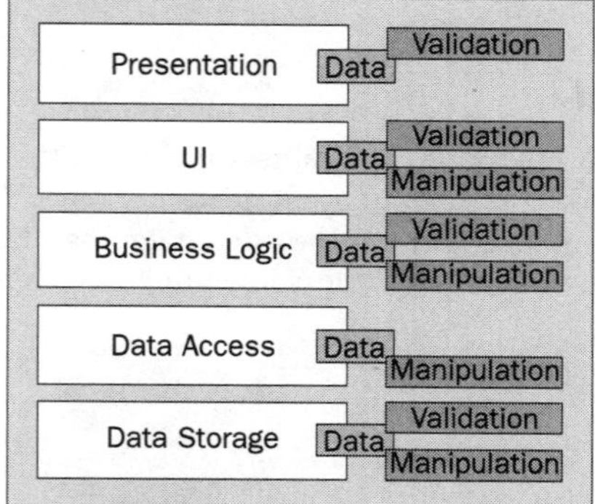

We put business logic in a web presentation tier to give the user a more interactive experience – and we put it into a Windows UI for the same reason. We recheck the business logic in the web UI (on the web server) because we don't trust the browser. And the database administrator puts the logic into the database (via stored procedures) because they don't trust any application developer!

The result of all this validation is a lot of duplicated code, all of which has to be debugged, maintained, and somehow kept in sync as the business needs (and thus logic) change over time. In the real world, the logic is almost never *really* kept in sync, and so we're constantly debugging and maintaining our code in a near-futile effort to make all of these redundant bits of logic agree with each other.

One solution is to force all of the logic into a single tier, making the other tiers as 'dumb' as possible. There are various approaches to this, although (as we'll see) none of them provides an optimal solution.

Business logic in the data management tier

The classic approach is to put all logic into the database as the single, central repository. The presentation and UI then allow the user to enter absolutely anything (since any validation would be redundant), and the business logic tier is essentially gone – it's merged into the database. The data access tier does nothing but move the data into and out of the database.

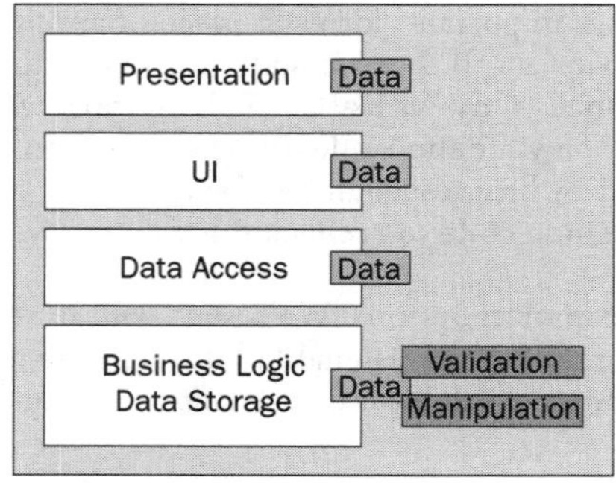

The advantage of this approach is that the logic is centralized, but the drawbacks are plentiful. For a start, the user experience is totally non-interactive. Users can't get any results, or even confirmation that their data is valid, without round-tripping the data to the database for processing. The database server becomes a performance bottleneck, since it's the only thing doing any actual work – and we have to write all of our business logic in SQL!

Business logic in the UI tier

Another common approach is to put all of the business logic into the UI. The data is validated and manipulated in the UI, and the data storage tier just stores the data. This approach is very common in both Windows and web environments, and has the advantage that the business logic is centralized into a single tier (and of course we can write our business logic in a language such as VB.NET or C#).

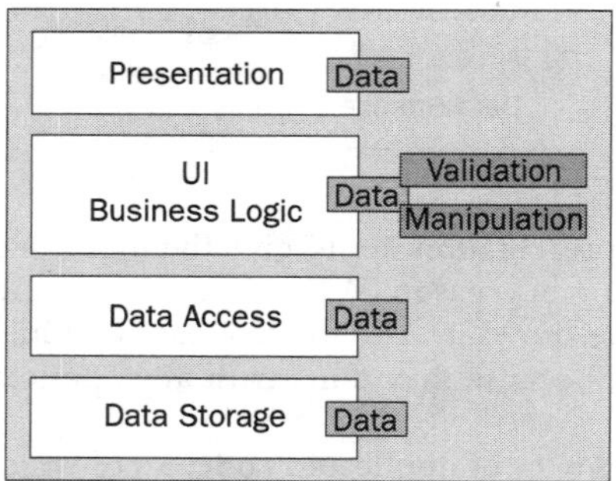

Unfortunately, in practice, the business logic ends up being scattered throughout the UI and intermixed with the UI code itself, decreasing readability and making maintenance more difficult. Even more importantly, business logic in one form or page is not reusable when we create subsequent pages or forms that use the same data. Furthermore, in a web environment, this architecture also leads to a totally non-interactive user experience, since no validation can occur in the browser. The user must transmit their data to the web server for any validation or manipulation to take place.

> *ASP.NET Web Forms' validation controls at least allow us to perform basic data validation in the UI, with that validation automatically extended to the browser by the Web Forms technology itself. While not a total solution, this is a powerful feature that does help.*

Business logic in the middle (business/data access) tier

Still another option is the classic UNIX client-server approach, where the business logic and data access tiers are merged, keeping the presentation, UI, and data storage tiers as 'dumb' as possible.

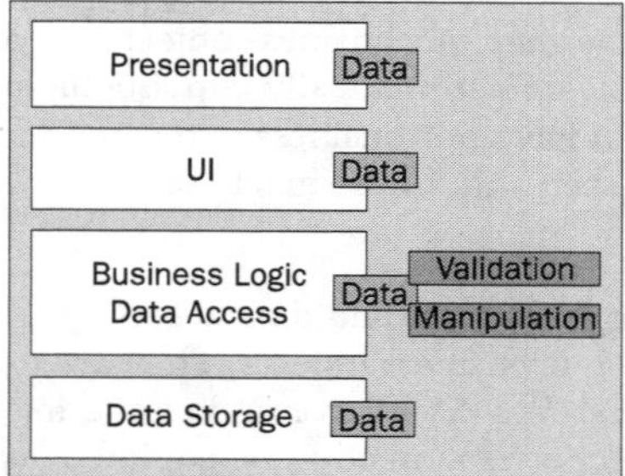

Unfortunately, once again, this approach falls foul of the non-interactive user experience problem: the data must be round-tripped to the data access tier for any validation or manipulation. This is especially problematic if the data access tier is running on a separate application server, since we're then faced with network latency and contention issues too. Also, the central application server can become a performance bottleneck, since it is the only machine doing any work for all the users of the application.

Business logic in a distributed business tier

I wish this book included the secret that allowed us to write all our logic in one central location and avoid all of these awkward issues. Unfortunately, that's not possible with today's technology: putting the business logic in the UI (or presentation) tier, the data access tier, or the data storage tier is problematic, for all the reasons given above. But we need to do something about it, so what have we got left?

What's left is the possibility of centralizing the business logic in a business logic tier that's accessible to the UI tier, to create the most interactive user experience possible. Also, the business logic tier needs to be able to interact efficiently with the data access tier, to achieve the best performance when interacting with the database (or other data source).

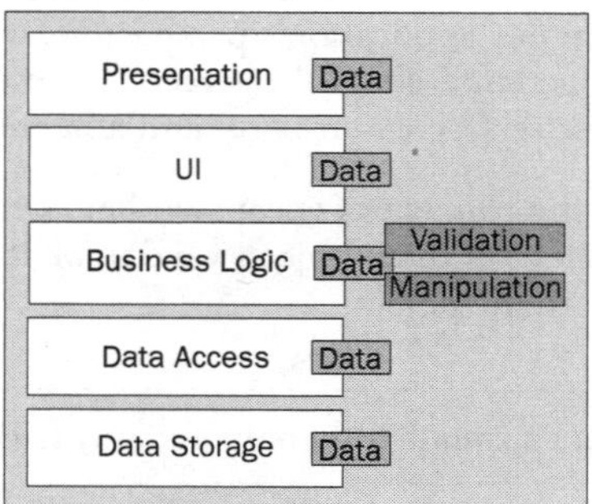

Ideally, this business logic will run on the same machine as the UI code when interacting with the user, but on the same machine as the data access code when interacting with the database. (As we discussed earlier, all of this could be on one machine or a number of different machines, depending on your physical architecture.) It must provide a friendly interface that the UI developer can use to invoke any validation and manipulation logic, and it must also work efficiently with the data access tier to get data into and out of storage.

The tools for addressing this seemingly intractable set of requirements are **business objects** that encapsulate our data along with its related business logic. It turns out that a properly constructed business object can move around the network from machine to machine with almost no effort on our part. The .NET Framework itself handles the details, and we can focus on the business logic and data.

By properly designing and implementing our business objects, we allow the .NET Framework to pass our objects across the network *by value*, automatically copying them from one machine to another. This means that with little effort, we can have our business logic and business data move to the machine where the UI tier is running, and then shift to the machine where the Data Access tier is running when data access is required.

At the same time, if we're running the UI tier and data access tier on the same machine, then the .NET Framework doesn't move or copy our business objects. They are used directly by both tiers with no performance cost or extra overhead. We don't have to do anything to make this happen, either – .NET automatically detects that the object doesn't need to be copied or moved, and takes no extra action.

The business logic tier becomes portable, flexible, and mobile, adapting to the physical environment in which we deploy the application. Due to this, we are able to support a variety of physical n-tier architectures with one code base, where our business objects contain no extra code to support the various possible deployment scenarios. What little code we need to implement to support the movement of our objects from machine to machine will be encapsulated in our framework, leaving the business developer to focus purely on the development of business logic.

Business objects

Having decided to use business objects and to take advantage of .NET's ability to move objects around the network automatically, we need to take a little time to discuss business objects in more detail. We need to see exactly what they are, and how they can help us to centralize the business logic pertaining to our data.

The primary goal when designing any kind of software object is to create an abstract representation of some entity or concept. In ADO.NET, for example, a `DataTable` object represents a tabular set of data. `DataTables` provide an abstract and consistent mechanism by which we can work with *any* tabular data. Likewise, a Windows Forms `TextBox` control is an object that represents the concept of displaying and entering data. From our application's perspective, we don't need to have any understanding of how the control is rendered on the screen, or how the user interacts with it. We're just presented with an object that includes a `Text` property and a handful of interesting events.

Key to successful object design is the concept of **encapsulation**. This means that an object is a black box: it contains data and logic, but as the user of an object, we don't know *what* data or *how* the logic actually works. All we can do is interact with the object.

> **Properly designed objects encapsulate both data and any logic related to that data.**

If objects are abstract representations of entities or concepts that encapsulate both data and its related logic, what then are **business objects**?

> **Business objects are different from regular objects only in terms of what they represent.**

When we create object-oriented applications, we are addressing problems of one sort or another. In the course of doing so, we use a variety of different objects. Now, while some of these will have no direct connection with the problem at hand (`DataTable` and `TextBox` objects, for example, are just abstract representations of computer concepts), there will be others that are closely related to the area or **domain** in which we're working. If the objects are related to the business for which we're developing an application, then they're business objects.

For instance, if we're creating an order-entry system, our business domain will include things such as customers, orders, and products. Each of these will likely become business objects within our order-entry application – the `Order` object, for example, will provide an abstract representation of the order being placed by a customer.

> **Business objects provide an abstract representation of entities or concepts that are part of our business or problem domain.**

Business objects as smart data

We've already discussed the drawbacks of putting business logic into the UI tier, but we haven't thoroughly discussed the drawback of keeping our data in a generic representation such as a `DataSet` object. The data in a `DataSet` (or an array, or an XML document) is unintelligent, unprotected, and generally unsafe. There's nothing to prevent us from putting invalid data into any of these containers, and there's nothing to ensure that the business logic behind one form in our application will interact with the data in the same way as the business logic behind another form.

A `DataSet` or an XML document might ensure that we don't put text where a number is required, or that we don't put a number where a date is required. At best, it might enforce some basic relational integrity rules. However, there's no way to ensure that the values match other criteria, or to ensure that calculations or other processing is done properly against the data, without involving other objects. The data in a `DataSet`, array, or XML document is not self-aware – it's not able to apply business rules, or to handle business manipulation or processing of the data.

The data in a business object, however, is what I like to call 'smart data'. The object not only contains the data, but also includes all the business logic that goes along with that data. Any attempt to work with the data must go through this business logic. In this arrangement, we have much greater assurance that business rules, manipulation, calculations, and other processing will be executed consistently everywhere in our application. In a sense, the data has become self-aware, and can protect itself against incorrect usage.

In the end, an object doesn't care whether it's used by a Windows Forms UI, or a batch processing routine, or a web service. The code using the object can do as it pleases; the object itself will ensure that all business rules are obeyed at all times.

Contrast this with the `DataSet` or an XML document, where the business logic doesn't reside in the data container, but somewhere else – typically, a Windows Form or a Web Form. If this `DataSet` is used by multiple forms or pages, we have no assurance that the business logic is applied consistently. Even if we adopt a standard that says that the UI developer must invoke methods from a `Module` to interact with the data, there's nothing preventing them from using the `DataSet` directly. This may happen accidentally, or because it was simply easier or faster to use the `DataSet` than to go through some centralized routine.

With business objects, there's no way to bypass the business logic. The only way to the data is through the object, and the object always enforces the rules.

So, a business object representing an invoice will include not only the data pertaining to the invoice, but also the logic to calculate taxes and amounts due. The object should understand how to post itself to a ledger, and how to perform any other accounting tasks that are required. Rather than passing raw invoice data around, and having our business logic scattered throughout the application, we are able to pass an `Invoice` object around. Our entire application can share not only the data, but also its associated logic. Smart data through objects can dramatically increase our ability to reuse code, and can decrease software maintenance costs.

Anatomy of a business object

Putting all of these pieces together, we get an object that has an interface (a set of properties and methods), some implementation code (the business logic behind those properties and methods), and state (the data). This is illustrated in the following diagram:

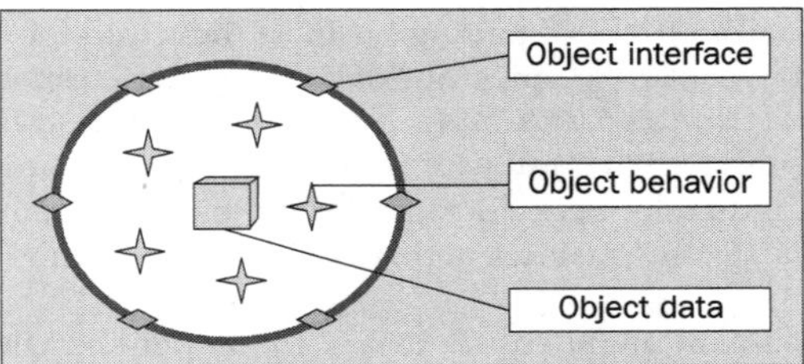

The hiding of the data and the implementation code behind the interface are keys to the successful creation of a business object. If we allow the users of our object to 'see inside' it, they will be tempted to cheat, and to interact with our logic or data in unpredictable ways. This danger is the reason why it will be important that we take care when using the `Public` keyword as we build our classes.

Any property, method, event, or variable marked as `Public` will be available to the users of objects created from the class. For example, we might create a simple class such as:

```
Public Class Project
  Private mID As Guid = Guid.NewGuid
  Private mName As String = ""

  Public ReadOnly Property ID() As Guid
    Get
      Return mID
    End Get
  End Property

  Public Property Name() As String
    Get
      Return mName
    End Get
    Set(ByVal Value As String)
      If Len(Value) > 50 Then
```

```
        Throw New Exception("Name too long")
      End If
      mName = Value
    End Set
  End Property
End Class
```

This defines a business object that represents a project of some sort. All we know at the moment is that these projects have an ID value, and a name. Notice though that the variables containing this data are `Private` – we don't want the users of our object to be able to alter or access them directly. If they were `Public`, the values could be changed without our knowledge or permission. (The `mName` variable could be given a value that's longer than the maximum of 50 characters, for example.)

The `Property` methods, on the other hand, are `Public`. They provide a controlled access point to our object. The `ID` property is read-only, so the users of our object can't change it. The `Name` property allows its value to be changed, but enforces a business rule by ensuring that the length of the new value doesn't exceed 50 characters.

> *None of these concepts is unique to business objects – they are common to all objects, and are central to object-oriented design and programming.*

Distributed objects

Unfortunately, directly applying the kind of object-oriented design and programming we've been talking about so far is often quite difficult in today's complex computing environments. Object-oriented programs are almost always designed with the assumption that all the objects in an application can interact with each other with no performance penalty. This is true when all the objects are running in the same process on the same computer, but it's not at all true when the objects might be running in different processes, or – worse still – on different computers.

Earlier in this chapter, we discussed various physical architectures in which different parts of our application might run on different machines. With a "high scalability intelligent client" architecture, for example, we'll have a client, an application server, and a data server. With a "high security web client" architecture, we'll have a client, a web server, an application server, and a data server. Parts of our application will run on each of these machines, interacting with each other as needed.

In these distributed architectures, we can't use a straightforward object-oriented design, because any communication between classic fine-grained objects on one machine and similar objects on another machine will incur network latency and overhead. This translates into a performance problem that simply can't be ignored. To overcome it, most distributed applications haven't used object-oriented designs. Instead, they consist of a set of procedural code running on each machine, with the data kept in a `DataSet`, an array, or an XML document that's passed around from machine to machine.

This isn't to say that object-oriented design and programming is irrelevant in distributed environments – just that it becomes complicated. To minimize the complexity, most distributed applications are object-oriented *within a tier*, but between tiers they follow a procedural or service-based model. The end result is that the application as a whole is neither object-oriented nor procedural, but is a blend of both.

Perhaps the most common architecture for such applications is to have the data-access tier retrieve the data from the database into a `DataSet`. The `DataSet` is then returned to the client (or the web server), where we have code in our forms or pages that interacts with the `DataSet` directly.

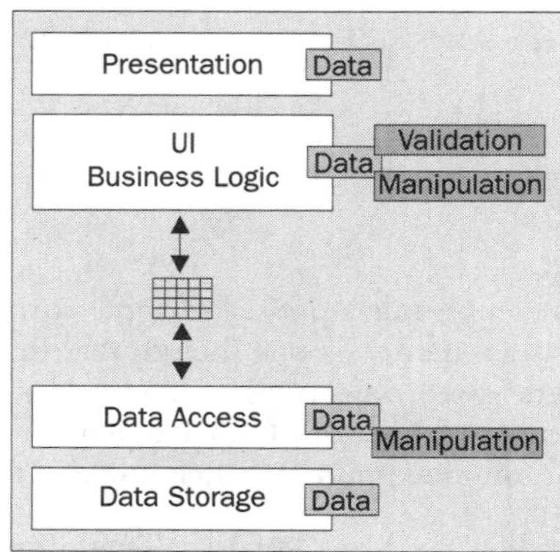

This approach has the flaws in terms of maintenance and code reuse that we've talked about, but the fact is that it gives pretty good performance in most cases. Also, it doesn't hurt that most programmers are pretty familiar with the idea of writing code to manipulate a `DataSet`, so the techniques involved are well understood, speeding development.

If we do decide to stick with an object-oriented approach, we have to be quite careful: it's all too easy to compromise our OO design by taking the data out of the objects running on one machine, sending the raw data across the network, and allowing other objects to use that data outside the context of our objects and business logic. **Distributed objects** are all about sending smart data (objects) from one machine to another, rather than sending raw data and hoping that the business logic on each machine is being kept in sync.

Through its remoting, serialization, and auto-deployment technologies, the .NET Framework contains direct support for the ability to have our objects move from one machine to another. (We'll discuss these technologies in more detail in Chapter 3, and make use of them throughout the remainder of the book.) Given this ability, we can have our data access tier (running on an application server) create a business object and load it with data from the database. That business object can then be sent to the client machine (or web server), where the UI code can use the object.

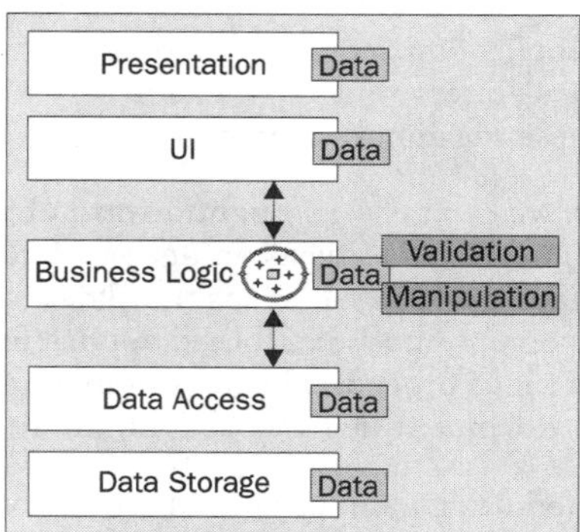

In this architecture, we're sending smart data to the client rather than raw data, so the UI code can use the same business logic as the data access code. This reduces maintenance, since we're not writing some business logic in the data access tier, and some other business logic in the UI tier. Instead, we've consolidated all of the business logic into a real, separate tier composed of business objects. These business objects will move across the network just like the `DataSet` did above, but they'll include the data *and* its related business logic – something the `DataSet` can't offer.

In addition, our business objects will move across the network more efficiently than the `DataSet`. *We'll be using a binary transfer scheme that transfers data in about 30% the size of data transferred using the* `DataSet`. *Also, our objects will contain far less metadata than the* `DataSet`, *further reducing the number of bytes transferred across the network.*

Effectively, we're sharing the business logic tier between the machine running the data access tier, and the machine running the UI tier. As long as we have support for moving data *and logic* from machine to machine, this is an ideal solution: it provides code reuse, low maintenance costs, and high performance.

A new logical architecture

Sharing the business logic tier between the data access tier and the UI tier opens up a new way to view our logical architecture. Though the business logic tier remains a separate concept, it is directly used by and tied into both the UI and data access tiers.

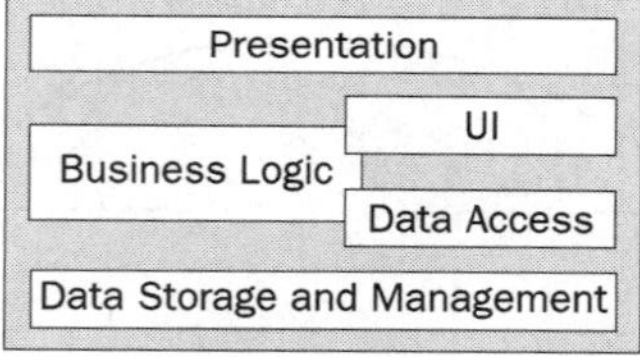

The UI tier can interact directly with the objects in the business logic tier, relying on them to perform all validation, manipulation, and other processing of the data. Likewise, the data access tier can interact with the objects as the data is retrieved or stored.

If all the tiers are running on a single machine (such as an intelligent client), then these parts will run in a single process and interact with each other with no network or cross-process overhead. In many of our other physical configurations, the business logic tier will run on both the client *and* the application server.

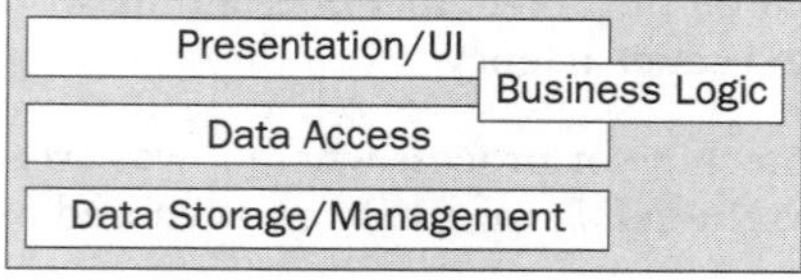

High scalability intelligent client

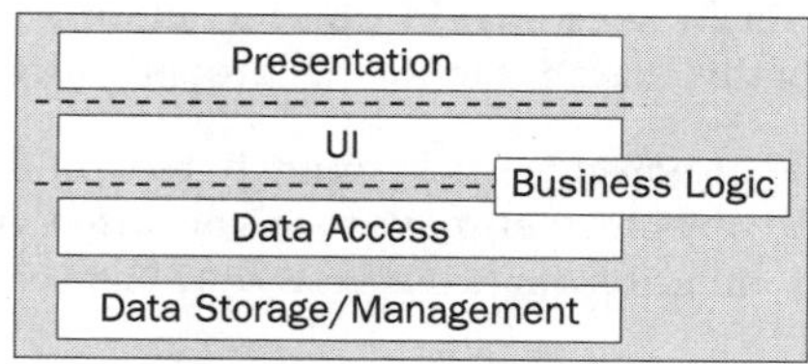

High security web client

Local, anchored, and unanchored objects

Normally, we think of objects as being part of a single application, running on a single machine in a single process. In a distributed application, we need to broaden our perspective. Some of our objects might only run in a single process on a single machine. Others may run on one machine, but be called by code running on another machine. Others still may move from machine to machine.

Local objects

By default, .NET objects are *local*. This means that ordinary objects are not accessible from outside the process in which they were created. It is not possible to pass them to another process or another machine (a procedure known as **marshaling**), either by value or by reference. Since this is the default behavior for all .NET objects, we must take extra steps to allow any of our objects to be available to another process or machine.

Anchored objects

In many technologies, including COM (Microsoft's Component Object Model), objects are always passed **by reference**. This means that when you 'pass' an object from one machine or process to another, what actually happens is that the object remains in the original process, while the other process or machine merely gets a pointer, or reference, back to the object.

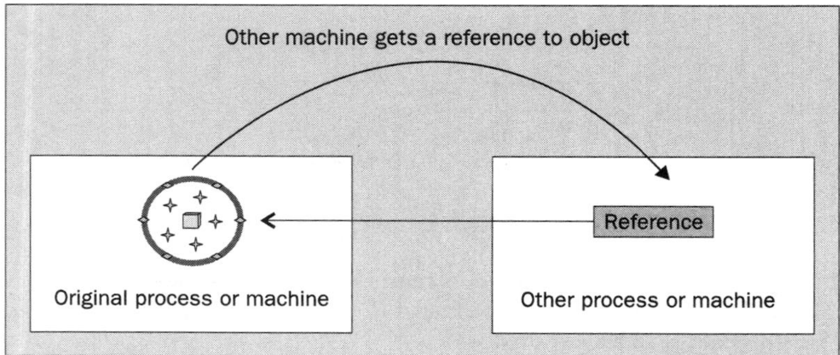

By using this reference, the other machine can interact with the object. Because the object is still on the original machine, however, any property or method calls must be sent across the network and processed by the object, and the results returned back across the network. This scheme is only useful if we design our object so that it can be used with very few method calls – just one is ideal! The recommended designs for MTS or COM+ objects call for a single method on the object that does all the work for precisely this reason, sacrificing 'proper' design in order to reduce latency.

This type of object is stuck, or **anchored**, on the original machine or process where it was created. An anchored object never moves – it's accessed via references. In .NET, we create an anchored object by having it inherit from `MarshalByRefObject`:

```
Public Class MyAnchoredClass
  Inherits MarshalByRefObject

End Class
```

From this point on, the .NET Framework takes care of the details. We can use remoting to pass an object of this type to another process or machine as a parameter to a method call, for example, or to return it as the result of a function.

Unanchored objects

The concept of distributed objects relies on the idea that we can pass an object from one process to another, or from one machine to another, **by value**. This means that the object is physically copied from the original process or machine to the other process or machine.

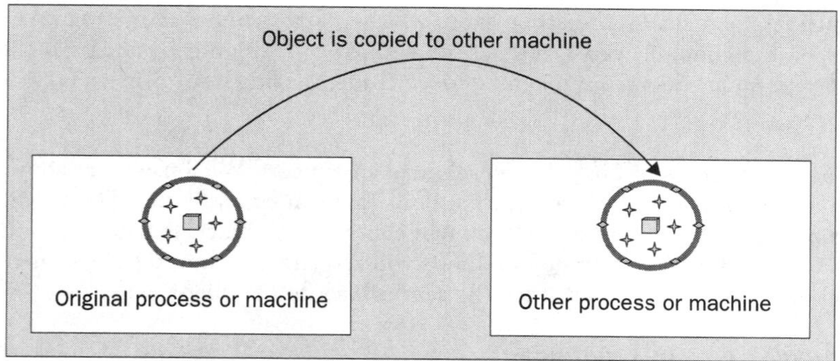

Since the other machine gets a copy of the object, it can interact with the object locally. This means that there is effectively no performance overhead involved in calling properties or methods on the object – the only cost was in copying the object across the network in the first place.

> *One caveat here is that transferring a large object across the network can cause a performance problem. As we all know, returning a `DataSet` that contains a great deal of data can take a long time. This is true of all unanchored objects, including our business objects. We need to be careful in our application design to ensure that we avoid retrieval of very large data sets.*

Objects that can move from process to process or from machine to machine are **unanchored**. Examples of unanchored objects include the `DataSet`, and the business objects we'll be creating in this book. Unanchored objects are not stuck in a single place, but can move to where they are most needed. To create one in .NET, we use the `<Serializable()>` attribute, or we implement the `ISerializable` interface. We'll discuss this further in Chapter 2, but the following illustrates the start of a class that is unanchored:

```
<Serializable()> _
Public Class MyUnanchoredClass

End Class
```

Again, the .NET Framework takes care of the details, so we can simply pass an object of this type as a parameter to a method call or as the return value from a function. The object will be copied from the original machine to the machine where the method is running.

When to use which

The .NET Framework supports all three of the mechanisms we just discussed, so we can choose to create our objects as local, anchored, or unanchored, depending on the requirements of our design. As you might guess, there are good reasons for each approach.

Windows Forms and Web Forms objects are all local – they're inaccessible from outside the processes in which they were created. The assumption is that we don't want other applications just reaching into our programs and manipulating the UI objects.

Anchored objects are important, because we can guarantee that they will always run on a specific machine. If we write an object that interacts with a database, we'll want to ensure that the object always runs on a machine that has access to the database. Because of this, we'll typically use anchored objects on our application server.

Many of our business objects, on the other hand, will be more useful if they *can* move from the application server to a client or web server, as needed. By creating our business objects as unanchored objects, we can pass smart data from machine to machine, reusing our business logic anywhere we send the business data.

Typically, we use anchored and unanchored schemes in concert. We'll use an anchored object on the application server to ensure that we can call methods that run *on that server.* Then we'll pass unanchored objects as parameters to those methods, which will cause those objects to move from the client to the server. Some of the anchored server-side methods will return unanchored objects as results, in which case the unanchored object will move from the server back to the client.

Passing unanchored objects by reference

There's a piece of terminology here that can get confusing. So far, we've loosely associated anchored objects with the concept of passing by reference, and unanchored objects as being passed by value. Intuitively, this makes sense, since anchored objects provide a reference, while unanchored objects provide the actual object (and its values). However, the terms "by reference" and "by value" have come to mean other things over the years.

The original idea of passing a value "by reference" was that there would be just one set of data – one object – and any code could get a reference to that single entity. Any changes made to that entity by any code would therefore be immediately visible to any other code.

The original idea of passing a value "by value" was that a copy of the original value would be made. Any code could get a copy of the original value, but any changes made to that copy were not reflected in the original value. That makes sense, since the changes were made to a copy, not to the original value.

In distributed applications, things get a little more complicated, but the definitions above remain true: we can pass an object by reference, so that all machines have a reference to the same object on some server; and we can pass an object by value, so that a copy of the object is made. So far, so good. However, what happens if we mark an object as `<Serializable()>` (that is, mark it as an unanchored object), and then *intentionally* pass it by reference? It turns out that the object is passed by value, but the .NET Framework attempts to give us the illusion that it was passed by reference.

To be more specific, in this scenario the object is copied across the network just as if it were being passed by value. The difference is that the object is then returned back to the calling code when the method is complete, and our reference to the original object is replaced with a reference to this new version.

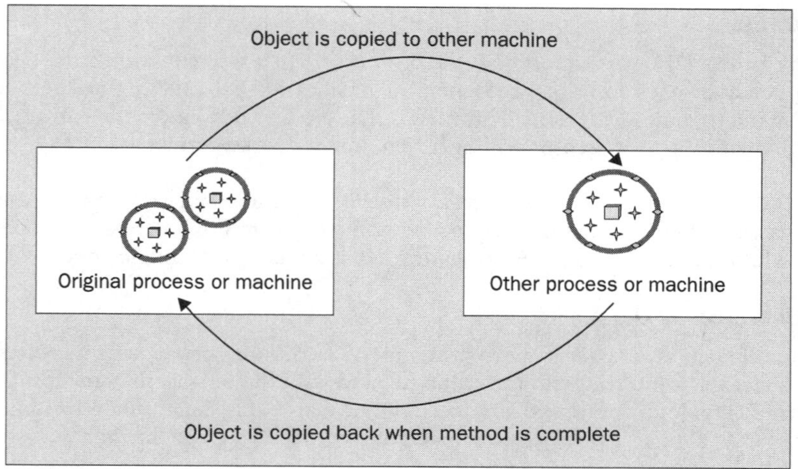

This is potentially very dangerous, since *other* references to the original object continue to point to that original object – only our particular reference is updated. We can potentially end up with two different versions of the same object on our machine, with some of our references pointing to the new one, and some to the old one.

> **If we pass an unanchored object by reference, we must always make sure to update *all* our references to use the new version of the object when the method call is complete.**

We can choose to pass an unanchored object by value, in which case it is passed one way, from the caller to the method. Or we can choose to pass an unanchored object by reference, in which case it is passed two ways, from the caller to the method, and from the method back to the caller. If we want to get back any changes the method makes to the object, we'll use by reference. If we don't care about, or don't want, any changes made to the object by the method, then we'll use by value.

Note that passing an unanchored object by reference has performance implications – it requires that the object be passed back across the network to the calling machine, so it's slower than passing by value.

Complete encapsulation

Hopefully, at this point, your imagination is engaged by the potential of distributed objects. The flexibility of being able to choose between local, anchored, and unanchored objects is very powerful, and opens up new architectural approaches that were difficult to implement using older technologies such as COM.

We've already discussed the idea of sharing the business logic tier across machines, and it's probably obvious that the concept of unanchored objects is exactly what we need to implement such a shared tier. But what does this all mean for the *design* of our tiers? In particular, given a set of unanchored or distributed objects in the business tier, what's the impact on the UI and data access tiers with which the objects interact?

Impact on the UI tier

What it means for the UI tier is simply that the business objects will contain all the business logic. The UI developer can code each form or page using the business objects, relying on them to perform any validation or manipulation of the data. This means that the UI code can focus entirely on displaying the data, interacting with the user, and providing a rich, interactive experience.

More importantly, since the business objects are distributed (unanchored), they'll end up running in the same process as the UI code. Any property or method calls from the UI code to the business object will occur locally without network latency, marshaling, or any other performance overhead.

Impact on the data access tier

The impact on the data access tier is more profound. A traditional data access tier consists of a set of methods or services that interact with the database, and with the objects that encapsulate data. The data access code itself is typically outside the objects, rather than being encapsulated within the objects. If we now encapsulate the data access logic inside each object, what is left in the data access tier itself?

The answer is twofold. First, for reasons we'll examine in a moment, we need an anchored object on the server. Second, we'll eventually want to utilize Enterprise Services (COM+), and we need code in the data access tier to manage interaction with Enterprise Services.

> *We'll discuss Enterprise Services in more detail in Chapters 2 and 3, and we'll use them throughout the rest of the book.*

Our business objects, of course, will be unanchored, so that they can move freely between the machine running the UI code and the machine running the data access code. However, if the data access code is inside the business object, we'll need to figure out some way to get the object to move to the application server any time we need to interact with the database.

This is where the data access tier comes into play. If we implement it using an anchored object, it will be *guaranteed* to run on our application server. Then we can call methods on the data access tier, passing our business object as a parameter. Since the business object is unanchored, it will physically move to the machine where the data access tier is running. This gives us a way to get the business object to the right machine before the object attempts to interact with the database.

> *We'll discuss this in much more detail in Chapter 2, when we lay out the specific design of the distributed object framework, and in Chapter 5, as we build the data access tier itself.*

Architectures and frameworks

Our discussion so far has focused mainly on architectures: logical architectures that define the separation of roles in our application, and physical architectures that define the locations where our logical tiers will run in various configurations. We've also discussed the use of object-oriented design and the concepts behind distributed objects.

While all of these are important and must be thought through in detail, we really don't want to have to go through this process every time we need to build an application. It would be preferable by far to have our architecture and design solidified into reusable code that we could use to build all our applications. What we want is an application **framework**.

A framework codifies our architecture and design to promote reuse and increase productivity.

The typical development process starts with analysis, followed by a period of architectural discussion and decision-making. After that, we start to design the application: first, the low-level concepts to support our architecture, and then the business-level concepts that actually matter to the end users. With the design done, we typically spend a fair amount of time implementing the low-level functions to support the business coding that comes later.

All of that architectural discussion, decision-making, design, and coding can be a lot of fun. Unfortunately, it doesn't directly contribute anything to the end goal of writing business logic and providing business functionality. This low-level supporting technology is merely 'plumbing' that must exist in order for us to create actual business applications. It's an overhead that in the long term we should be able to do once, and then reuse across many business application development efforts.

In the software world, the easiest way to reduce overhead is to increase reuse, and the best way to get reuse of our architecture (both design and coding) is to codify it into a framework.

This doesn't mean that *application* analysis and design are unimportant – quite the reverse! We typically spend far too little time analyzing our business requirements and developing good application designs to meet those business needs. Part of the reason is that we often end up spending substantial amounts of time analyzing and designing the 'plumbing' that supports the business application, and we run out of time to analyze the business issues themselves.

What I'm proposing here is that we can reduce the time spent analyzing and designing the low-level plumbing by creating a framework that can be used across many of our business applications. Is the framework that we'll create in this book ideal for every application and every organization? Certainly not! You'll have to take the architecture and the framework and adapt them to meet your organization's needs. You may have different priorities in terms of performance, scalability, security, fault-tolerance, reuse, or other key architectural criteria. At the very least, though, the remainder of this book should give you a good start on the design and construction of a distributed, object-oriented architecture and framework.

Conclusion

In this chapter, we've focused on the theory behind distributed systems – specifically, those based on distributed objects. The key to success in designing a distributed system is to keep clear the distinction between a logical and a physical architecture.

Logical architectures exist to define the separation between the different types of code in our application. The goal of a good logical architecture is to make our code more maintainable, understandable, and reusable. Our logical architecture must also define enough tiers to enable any physical architectures that we may require.

A physical architecture defines the machines on which our application will run. An application with several logical tiers can still run on a single machine. That same logical architecture might also be configured to run on various client and server machines. The goal of a good physical architecture is to achieve the best trade-off between performance, scalability, security, and fault tolerance within our specific environment.

The tradeoffs in a physical architecture for an intelligent client application are very different from those for a web application. A Windows application will typically trade performance against scalability, while a web application will typically trade performance against security.

In this book, we'll be using a 5-tier logical architecture consisting of presentation, UI, business logic, data access, and data storage. We'll be using this architecture to create Windows, web and Web services applications, each with a different physical architecture. In the next chapter, we'll start to design the framework that will make this possible.

CHAPTER 2

2

Framework design

In Chapter 1, we discussed some general concepts around physical and logical n-tier architecture, including laying out a 5-tier model for describing systems logically. In this chapter, we'll take that 5-tier logical model and expand it into a framework design. Specifically, we'll be mapping the logical tiers against the technologies illustrated in the following diagram:

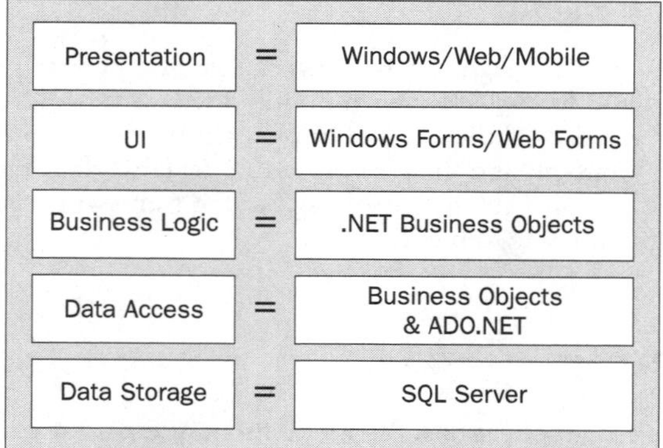

The framework itself will focus on the business logic and data access tiers. This is primarily due to the fact that there are already powerful technologies for building Windows, web, and mobile user interfaces and presentations. Also, there are already powerful data storage options available, including SQL Server, Oracle, DB2, XML documents, and so forth.

Recognizing that these pre-existing technologies are ideal for building the presentation and UI layers, and for handling data storage, allows us to focus on the parts of the application that have the least technological support, and where the highest return on investment occurs through reuse. Analyzing, designing, implementing, testing, and maintaining business logic is incredibly expensive. The more reuse we can achieve, the lower our long-term application costs become. The easier it is to maintain and modify this logic, the lower our costs over time.

When I set out to create the architecture and framework discussed in this book, I started with a set of high-level guidelines:

- Simplify the task of creating object-oriented applications in a distributed .NET environment.
- The Windows/web/web services interface developer should never see or be aware of SQL, ADO.NET, or other raw data concepts, relying instead on a purely object-oriented model of the problem domain.
- Business object developers should be able to use 'natural' coding techniques to create their classes – that is, they should employ everyday coding using variables, properties, and methods. Little or no extra knowledge should be required.
- The business classes should provide total encapsulation of business logic, including validation, manipulation, calculation, security, and data access. Everything pertaining to an entity in the problem domain should be found within a single class.
- Provide an n-tier logical architecture that can be easily reconfigured to run on one to four physical tiers.
- Complex features in .NET should be used, but largely hidden and automated: remoting, serialization, security, no-touch deployment, and so forth.
- The concepts present in the framework I created for VB6 should carry forward, including object undo capabilities, broken rules tracking, and object state tracking (`IsNew`, `IsDirty`, `IsDeleted`).

In this chapter, we'll focus on the design of a framework that allows us to make use of object-oriented design and programming with these guidelines in mind. Once we've walked through the design of the framework, in Chapters 4 and 5 we'll dive in and implement the framework itself, focusing first on the parts that support UI development, and then on providing scalable data access and object-relational mapping for our objects. Before we get into the design of the framework, however, let's discuss some of the specific goals I was attempting to achieve.

Basic design goals

When creating object-oriented applications, the ideal situation is that any non-business objects will already exist, so that we can just make use of them. In that case, all we need to do is focus on creating, debugging, and testing our business objects themselves, ensuring that each one encapsulates the data and business logic needed to make our application work.

As rich as the .NET Framework is, however, it doesn't provide all the non-business objects that we'll need in order to create most applications. All the basic tools are there, but there's a fair amount of work to be done before we can just sit down and write business logic. There's a set of higher-level functions and capabilities that we often need, but which aren't provided by .NET right out of the box.

These include:

- n-Level undo capability
- Tracking broken business rules to determine whether an object is valid
- Tracking whether an object's data has changed (is it 'dirty'?)
- Support for strongly typed collections of child objects
- A simple and abstract model for the UI developer
- Full support for data binding in both Windows Forms and Web Forms
- Saving objects to a database and getting them back again
- Table-driven security
- Other miscellaneous features

In all of these cases, the .NET Framework provides all the pieces of the puzzle, but we need to put them together so that they match our specialized requirements. What we *don't* want to do, however, is to have to put them together for every business object we create. We want to put them together *once*, such that all these extra features are automatically available to all our business objects.

Moreover, since our goal is to enable the implementation of *object-oriented* business systems, we must also preserve the core object-oriented concepts:

- Abstraction
- Encapsulation
- Polymorphism
- Inheritance

What we'll end up with is a framework consisting of a number of classes. The following diagram shows the end result – and don't worry; we'll break it down into digestible parts as we go through the chapter!

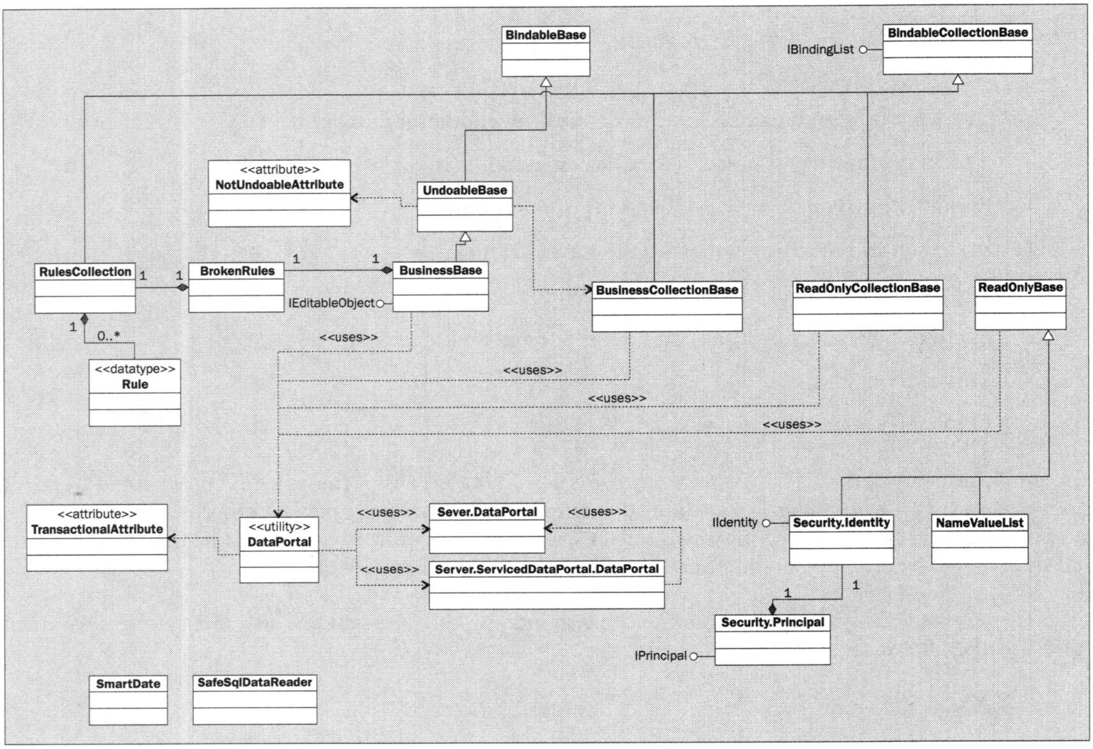

These classes will end up being divided into a set of assemblies, or DLLs. These are illustrated in the following component diagram:

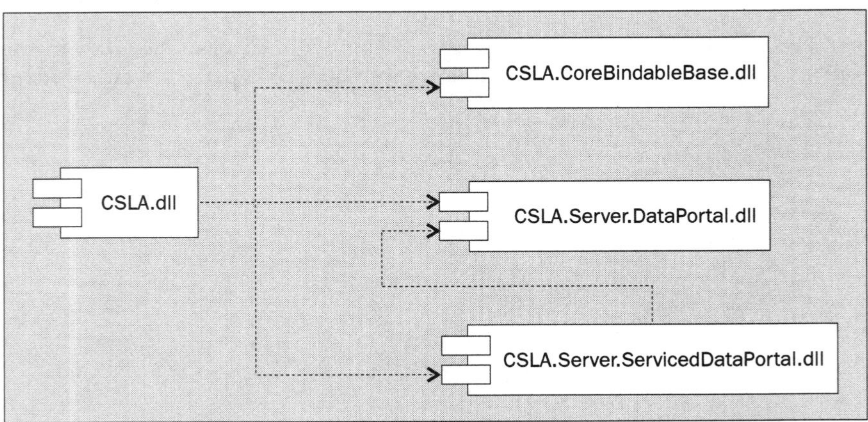

Again, don't worry too much about the details here – we'll be discussing them throughout the chapter. These diagrams are provided just to give a glimpse of what's coming, and for convenient reference as we discuss each of the classes and components in turn. Before we start to get into the details of the framework's design, let's discuss our desired set of features in more detail.

n-Level undo capability

Many Windows applications provide their users with an interface that includes OK and Cancel buttons (or some variation on that theme). When the user clicks an OK button, the expectation is that any work the user has done will be saved. Likewise, when the user clicks a Cancel button, they expect that any changes they've made will be reversed, or undone.

In simple applications, this functionality can often be delivered by saving the data to a database when OK is clicked, and discarding the data when Cancel is clicked. For slightly more complex applications, we may need to be able to undo any editing on a single object when the user presses the *Esc* key. (This is the case for a row of data being edited in a `DataGrid`: if the user presses *Esc*, the row of data should restore its original values.)

When applications become *much* more complex, however, these approaches won't work. Instead of simply undoing the changes to a single row of data in real time, we may need to be able to undo the changes to a row of data at some later stage.

Consider the case where we have an `Invoice` object that contains a collection of `LineItem` objects. The `Invoice` itself contains data that can be edited, plus data that's derived from the collection. The `TotalAmount` property of an `Invoice`, for instance, is calculated by summing up the individual `Amount` properties of its `LineItem` objects. The following class diagram illustrates this arrangement:

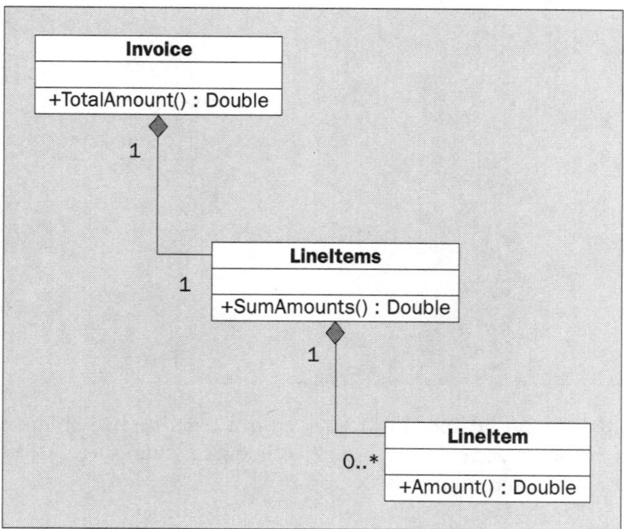

Typically, the methods on the collection and child object would be `Friend` in scope. Unfortunately, UML has no way to notate this particular scope, so the diagram shows them as `Public`.

Our user interface may allow the user to edit the `LineItem` objects, and then press *Enter* to accept the changes to the item, or *Esc* to undo them. However, even if the user chooses to accept changes to some `LineItem` objects, they can still choose to cancel the changes on the `Invoice` itself. Of course, the only way to reset the `Invoice` object to its original state is to restore the states of the `LineItem` objects as well – including any changes that were 'accepted' by the user for specific `LineItem` objects.

As if this weren't enough, many applications have more complex hierarchies of objects and sub-objects (which we'll call 'child objects'). Perhaps our individual `LineItem` objects each have a collection of `Component` objects beneath them, each representing one of the components sold to the customer that make up the specific line item.

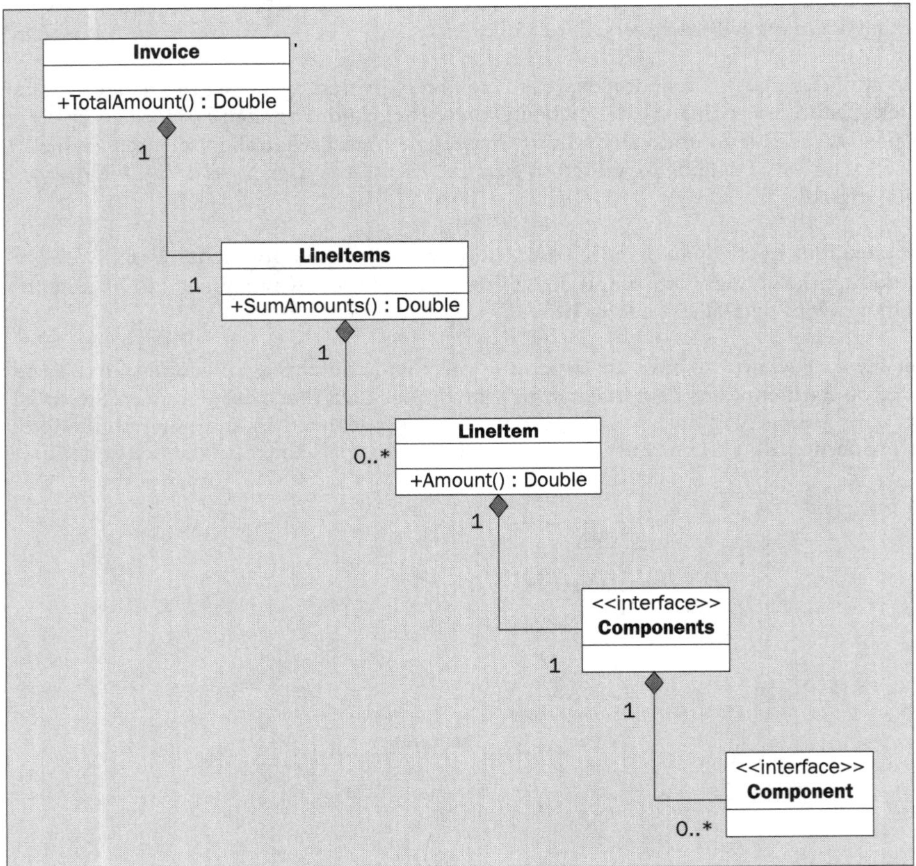

Now things get even more complicated. If the user edits a `Component` object, those changes ultimately impact upon the state of the `Invoice` object itself. Of course, changing a `Component` also changes the state of the `LineItem` object that owns the `Component`.

The user might accept changes to a `Component`, but cancel the changes to its parent `LineItem` object, forcing an undo operation to reverse *accepted* changes to the `Component`. Or in an even more complex scenario, the user may accept the changes to a `Component`, and its parent `LineItem`, only to cancel the `Invoice`. This would force an undo operation that reverses all those changes to the child objects.

Implementing an undo mechanism to support such n-level scenarios is not trivial. We must implement code to 'trap' or 'snapshot' the state of each object before it is edited, so that we can reverse the changes later on. We might even need to take more than one snapshot of an object's state at different points in the editing process, so that we can have the object revert to the appropriate point, based on when the user chooses to accept or cancel any edits.

> *This multi-level undo capability flows from the user's expectations. Consider a typical word processor, where we can undo multiple times to restore the content to ever-earlier states.*

And the collection objects are every bit as complex as the business objects themselves. We must handle the simple case when a user edits an existing `LineItem`, but we must also handle the case where a user adds a new `LineItem` and then cancels changes to the parent or grandparent, resulting in the new `LineItem` being discarded. Equally, we must handle the case where the user *deletes* a `LineItem` and then cancels changes to the parent or grandparent, causing that deleted object to be restored to the collection as though nothing had ever happened.

n-Level undo is a perfect example of complex code that we don't want to write into every business object. Instead, this functionality should be written *once*, so that all our business objects support the concept, and behave the way we want them to. We'll incorporate this functionality directly into our business object framework – but at the same time, we must be sensitive to the different environments in which our objects will be used. While n-level undo is of high importance when building sophisticated Windows user experiences, it is virtually useless in a typical web environment.

In web-based applications, the user typically doesn't have a Cancel button. They either accept the changes, or they navigate away to another task, allowing us simply to discard the changed object. In this regard, the web environment is much simpler – and if n-level undo is not useful to the web UI developer, they shouldn't be forced to deal with it! Our design will take into account that some user interface types will use the concept, while others will simply ignore it.

Tracking broken business rules

A lot of business logic involves the enforcement of **business rules**. The fact that a given piece of data is required is a business rule. The fact that one date must be later than another date is a business rule. Some business rules are the result of calculations, while others are merely toggles – when they're broken, the object is invalid. There's no easy way to abstract the entire concept of business rules, but we *can* easily abstract the concept of business rules that act like a toggle – that is, the rule is broken, or not broken.

> *There are commercial business rule engines and other business rule products that strive to take the business rules out of our software and keep it in some external location. Some of these may even be powerful and valuable. For most business applications, however, we end up coding the business rules directly into our software. If we're object-oriented, this means coding them into our objects.*

A fair number of business rules are of the toggle variety: required fields, fields that must be a certain length (no longer than, no shorter than), fields that must be greater than or less than other fields, and so forth. The common theme is that they are rules that, when broken, immediately make our object invalid. Combined, we can say that an object is valid if *none* of these rules is broken, but invalid if *any* of the rules is broken.

Rather than trying to implement a custom scheme in each business object to keep track of which rules are broken and whether the object is or isn't valid at any given point, we can abstract this behavior. Obviously, the rules *themselves* must be coded into our objects, but the tracking of which rules are broken and whether the object is valid can be handled by the framework. The result will be a standardized mechanism by which all business objects can be checked for validity, and the user interface developer is able to retrieve a list of currently broken rules to display to the user (or for any other purpose).

The list of broken rules is obviously linked to our n-level undo capability. If the user changes an object's data such that the object becomes invalid, but then cancels the changes, the original state of the object must be restored. The reverse is true as well: an object may start out invalid (perhaps because a required field is blank), so the user must edit data until it becomes valid. If the user later cancels the object (or its parent, grandparent, etc.), then the object must become *invalid* once again, since it will be restored to its original invalid state.

Fortunately, this is easily handled by treating the broken rules and validity of each object as part of that object's state. When an undo operation occurs, not only is the object's core state restored, but so too is the list of broken rules associated with that state. The object and its rules are restored together.

Tracking whether the object has changed

Another concept is that an object should keep track of whether its state data has been changed. This is important for the performance and efficiency of data updates. Typically, we only want to update data to the database if the data has changed – it's a waste of effort to update the database with values it already has! While the UI developer *could* keep track of whether any values have changed, it's simpler to have the object take care of this detail.

This can be implemented in a number of ways, ranging from keeping the previous values of all fields (so that we can make comparisons to see if they've changed), to saying that *any* change to a value (even 'changing' it to its original value) will result in us treating the object as being changed.

Obviously, there's more overhead involved in keeping all the original state values for comparison. On the other hand, a simpler model will often mark an object as being changed when actually it hasn't. This often has its own cost, because we'll typically only save 'dirty' objects to the database. An erroneous dirty flag will cause us to interact with the database to update columns with the values they already possess!

Rather than having our framework dictate one cost over the other, we'll simply provide a generic mechanism by which our business logic can tell the framework whether each object has been changed. This scheme supports both extremes of implementation, allowing us to make a decision based on the requirements of a specific application.

Strongly-typed collections of child objects

The .NET Framework includes the `System.Collections` namespace, which contains a number of powerful, *generic*, collection-based objects, including `ArrayList`, `Hashtable`, `Queue`, `Stack`, and `NameValueCollection`. For the most part, these collections accept any type of object – they provide no mechanism by which we can ensure that only objects of a specific type (such as a business object) are in the collection.

> *There is also a* `Collection` *object in the* `Microsoft.VisualBasic` *namespace. This type of collection is designed to emulate the behavior of the VB6* `Collection` *object for backwards compatibility. Unfortunately, it is missing some key functionality that will be required by our framework – namely, it is not* `<Serializable()>`*. Thus, the only collection objects we'll be using here are those from* `System.Collections`*.*

Fortunately, the .NET Framework also includes base collection classes from which we can inherit to create our own collection objects. These can be restricted to hold only the specific types of object we choose.

Sadly, the basic functionality provided by the collection base classes isn't enough to integrate fully with our framework. As mentioned previously, our business objects need to support some relatively advanced features, such as undo capabilities. Following this line of reasoning, the n-level undo capabilities that we've talked about must extend into the collections of child objects, ensuring that child object states are restored when an undo is triggered on the parent object. Even more complex is the support for adding and removing items from a collection, and then undoing the addition or removal if an undo occurs later on.

Also, a collection of child objects needs to be able to indicate if any of the objects it contains is dirty. While we *could* force business object authors to write code to loop through the child objects to discover whether any is marked as dirty, it makes a lot more sense to put this functionality into the framework's collection object, so that the feature is simply available for use. The same is true with validity: If any child object is invalid, then the collection should be able to report that it's invalid. If all child objects are valid, then the collection should report itself as being valid.

As with our business objects themselves, the goal of our business framework will be to make the creation of a strongly typed collection as close to normal .NET programming as possible, while allowing our framework to provide extra capabilities that we want in all our objects. What we're actually defining here are two sets of behaviors: one for business objects (parent and/or child), and one for *collections* of business objects. Though business objects will be the more complex of the two, our collection objects will also include some very interesting functionality.

Simple and abstract model for the user interface developer

At this point, we've discussed some of the business object features that we want to support. One of the key reasons for providing these features is to make the business object support Windows- and web-style user experiences with minimal work on the part of the UI developer. In fact, this should be an overarching goal when you're designing business objects for a system. The UI developer should be able to rely on the objects to provide business logic, data, and related services in a consistent manner.

Beyond all the features we've already covered is the issue of creating new objects, retrieving existing data, and updating objects in some data store. We'll discuss the *process* of object persistence later in the chapter, but first we need to consider this topic from the UI developer's perspective. Should the UI developer be aware of any application servers? Should they be aware of any database servers? Or should they simply interact with a set of abstract objects? There are three broad models that we can choose from:

- User interface in charge
- Object in charge
- Class in charge

To a greater or lesser degree, all three of these options hide information about how objects are created and saved, and allow us to exploit the native capabilities of .NET. Ideally, we'll settle on the option that hides the most information (keeping development as simple as possible), and best allows us to exploit the features of .NET.

> *Inevitably, the result will be a compromise. As with many architectural decisions, there are good arguments to be made for each option. In your environment, you may find that a different decision would work better. Keep in mind, though, that this particular decision is fairly central to the overall architecture of the framework we're building, so choosing another option will likely result in dramatic changes throughout the framework.*

To make this as clear as possible, the following discussion will assume that we have a physical n-tier configuration, where the client or web server is interacting with a separate application server, which in turn interacts with the database. The following diagram illustrates the Web Forms (on the left) and Windows Forms (on the right) versions of such an architecture:

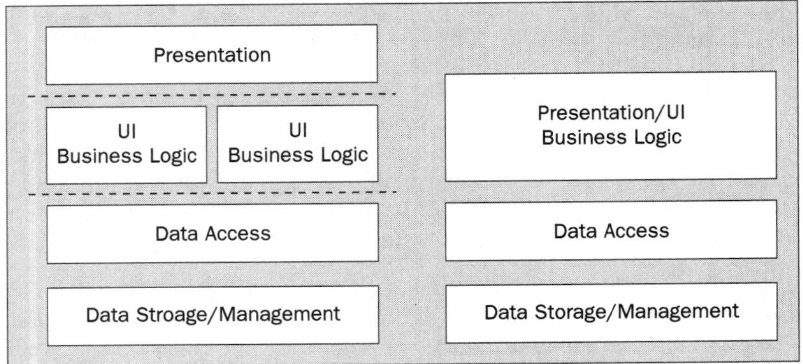

While not all applications will run in such configurations, we'll find it much easier to discuss object creation, retrieval, and updating in this context.

UI in charge

One common approach to creating, retrieving, and updating objects is to put the UI in charge of the process. This means that it's the UI developer's responsibility to write code to contact the application server in order to retrieve or update objects.

In this scheme, when a new object is required, the UI will contact the application server and ask it for a new object. The application server can then instantiate a new object, populate it with default values, and return it to the UI code. The code might be something like this:

```
Dim svr As AppServer = _
                Activator.GetObject("http://myserver/myroot/appserver.rem")

Dim objCust As Customer = svr.CreateCustomer()
```

Here, the object of type `AppServer` is anchored, so it always runs on the application server. The `Customer` object is unanchored, so while it is created on the server, it is returned to the UI by value.

> *This code uses .NET's remoting technology to contact a web server and have it instantiate an object (`svr`) on our behalf. If you're not familiar with remoting, there's an introduction in the next chapter.*

This may seem like a lot of work just to create a new, empty object, but it's the retrieval of default values that makes it necessary. If your application has objects that don't need default values, or if you're willing to hard-code the defaults, some of the work can be avoided by having the UI simply create the object on the client workstation. However, many business applications have configurable default values for objects, and those default values *must* be loaded from the database – and that means the application server must load them.

When retrieving an *existing* object, we follow largely the same procedure. The UI passes criteria to the application server, which uses the criteria to create a new object and load it with the appropriate data from the database. The populated object is then returned to the UI for use. The UI code might be something like this:

```
Dim svr As AppServer = _
               Activator.GetObject("http://myserver/myroot/appserver.rem")

Dim objCust As Customer = svr.GetCustomer(myCriteria)
```

Moving on, updating an object happens when the UI calls the application server, passing the object to the server. The server can then take the data from the object and store it in the database. Since the update process may result in changes to the object's state, the newly saved and updated object is then returned to the UI. The UI code might be something like this:

```
Dim svr As AppServer = _
               Activator.GetObject("http://myserver/myroot/appserver.rem")

objCust = svr.UpdateCustomer(objCust)
```

Overall, this model is straightforward: the application server must simply expose a set of services that can be called from the user interface to create, retrieve, and update objects. Each object can simply contain its business logic, without having to worry about application servers or other details.

The drawback to this scheme is that the UI code must know about and interact with the application server. If we move the application server, or decide to have some objects come from a different server, then the UI code must be changed. Moreover, if we create a Windows UI to use our objects, and then later create a web UI that uses those same objects, we'll end up with duplicated code. Both types of UI will need to include the code to find and interact with the application server.

The whole thing is complicated further when we consider that the physical configuration of our application should be flexible. It should be possible to switch from using an application server to running the data access code *on the client* just by changing a configuration file. If there is code scattered throughout our UI to contact the server any time we use an object, then we have a lot of points where we might introduce a bug that prevents simple configuration file switching.

Object in charge

Another option is to move the knowledge of the application server into our objects themselves. Now, the UI can just interact with our objects, allowing them to load defaults, retrieve data, or update themselves. In this model, creating a new object is done simply by using the `New` keyword:

```
objCust = New Customer()
```

Within the object's constructor, we would then write the code to contact the application server and retrieve default values. It might be something like this:

```
Public Sub New()
  Dim svr As AppServer = _
                 Activator.GetObject("http://myserver/myroot/appserver.rem")
```

```
    Dim values() As Object = svr.GetCustomerDefaults()

    ' Copy the values into our local variables

  End Sub
```

Notice here that we're *not* taking advantage of the built-in support for passing an object by value across the network. What we'd *like* to do is this:

```
  Public Sub New()
    Dim svr As AppServer = _
                  Activator.GetObject("http://myserver/myroot/appserver.rem")

    Me = svr.CreateCustomer()
  End Sub
```

> *In C#, code like this would result in a compiler error, since it's not legal to attempt to provide a value to the* `this` *variable. This actually compiles and runs in VB.NET, but as we'll see, the result is not very useful.*

But it won't work. While the `Me` reference is updated *inside the object*, the user interface retains its reference to the original, completely empty, object:

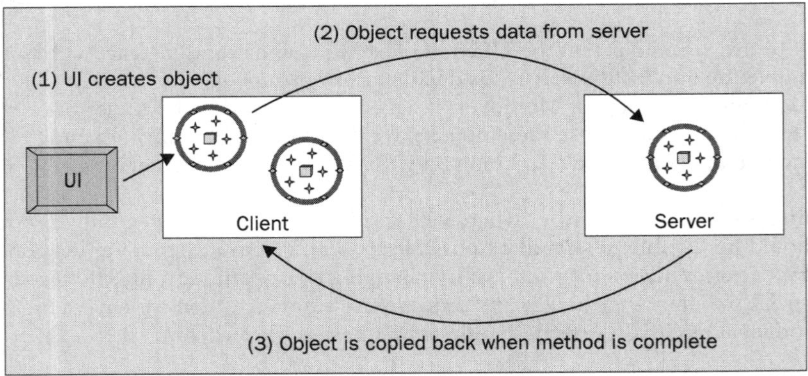

As you can clearly see, the UI doesn't get a reference to the fully populated object that's returned from the server. Because of this, we're left to implement the data transfer code manually, as we did in the first code sample above.

The problem becomes even more painful when we're retrieving an existing object. The UI code remains nicely simple:

```
    objCust = New Customer(myCriteria)
```

But in this case, we'll be retrieving all the data for the object – but not as an object! As when we were populating the object with default values, we must retrieve the data in some other manner (array, hash table, dataset, or some other data structure), and then load it into our object's variables.

Given that both the UI-in-charge and class-in-charge techniques avoid all this extra coding, let's just abort the discussion of this option and move on.

Class in charge

The UI-in-charge approach allowed us to use .NET's ability to pass objects by value, but required the UI developer to know about and interact with the application server. The object-in-charge approach enabled a very simple set of UI code, but made our object code prohibitively complex by making it virtually impossible to pass our objects by value.

The class-in-charge option gives us a good compromise by providing reasonably simple UI code that's unaware of application servers, while also allowing us to use .NET's ability to pass objects by value, thus reducing the amount of 'plumbing' code that we need to write in each object. By hiding more information from the UI, we are creating a more abstract and loosely coupled implementation, thus yielding better flexibility.

In this model, we'll be making use of the concept of `Shared` methods on a class. A `Shared` method can be called directly, without requiring an instance of the class to be created first. For instance, suppose that our `Customer` class contains the following code:

```
<Serializable()>
Public Class Customer
  Public Shared Function NewCustomer()
    Dim svr As AppServer = _
               Activator.GetObject("http://myserver/myroot/appserver.rem")

    Return svr.CreateCustomer()
  End Function
End Class
```

Then, the UI code could use this method without first creating a `Customer` object:

```
  Dim objCust As Customer = Customer.NewCustomer()
```

A common example of this tactic within the .NET Framework itself is the `Guid` class, where a `Shared` method is used to create new GUID values:

```
Dim myGuid As Guid = Guid.NewGuid()
```

We've accomplished the goal of making the UI code reasonably simple, but what about that `Shared` method and passing objects by value? Well, the `NewCustomer()` method contacts the application server and asks it to create a new `Customer` object with default values. The object is created on the server, and then returned back to our `NewCustomer()` code, which is running *on the client.* Now that the object has been passed back to the client by value, we can simply return it to the UI for use.

Likewise, we can create a `Shared` method on our class to load an object with data from the data store:

```
Public Shared Function GetCustomer(ByVal Criteria As String)
  Dim svr As AppServer = _
             Activator.GetObject("http://myserver/myroot/appserver.rem")

  Return svr.GetCustomer(Criteria)
End Function
```

Again, the code contacts the application server, providing it with the criteria necessary to load the object's data and create a fully populated object. That object is then returned by value to the `GetCustomer()` method running on the client, and then back to the UI code.

As before, the UI code remains simple:

```
    Dim objCust As Customer = Customer.GetCustomer(myCriteria)
```

The class-in-charge model requires that we write some `Shared` methods in each class, but keeps the UI code simple and straightforward. It also allows us to take full advantage of .NET's ability to pass objects across the network by value, minimizing the plumbing code we must write. Overall, therefore, it provides the best solution, and we'll be using it (and explaining it further) in the chapters ahead.

Supporting data binding

For nearly a decade, Microsoft has included some kind of data binding capability in its development tools. Data binding allows us as developers to create forms and populate them with data with almost no custom code – the controls on a form are 'bound' to specific fields from a data source (such as a `DataSet` object).

For almost the same amount of time, data binding has largely been a joke. Originally, it offered performance far below what we could achieve by hand-coding the link between controls and the data source. And even after many of the performance issues were addressed, the data binding implementations offered too little control to the developer, restricting the types of user experience we could offer. In VB6, for example, the primary issues blocking widespread use of data binding included:

- We couldn't easily validate the last field the user was editing if they pressed *Enter* to trigger the default button's click event on a form
- We couldn't bind controls to anything but a `Recordset` – it wasn't possible to bind controls to the properties of a business object
- We could only bind to one property on a given control – typically, the `Text` or `Value` property

The only place where data binding has been consistently useful is in displaying large amounts of data within a grid, as long as that data didn't need updating. In most cases, the weak performance and loss of control was worth it in order to save us from writing reams of boilerplate code. With the .NET Framework, however, Microsoft has dramatically improved data binding for Windows Forms. Better still, we can use data binding when creating web applications, since Web Forms support it too. The primary benefits or drivers for using data binding in .NET development include:

- Microsoft resolved the performance, control, and flexibility issues of the past
- We can now use data binding to link controls to properties of business objects
- Data binding can dramatically reduce the amount of code we write in the UI
- Data binding is sometimes *faster* than manual coding, especially when loading data into list boxes, grids, or other complex controls

Of these, the biggest single benefit is the dramatic reduction in the amount of UI code we need to write and maintain. Combined with the performance, control, and flexibility of .NET data binding, the reduction in code makes it a very attractive technology for UI development.

In Windows Forms, data binding is read-write, meaning that we can bind an element of a data source to an editable control such that changes to the value in the control will be updated back into the data source as well. In Web Forms, data binding is read-only, meaning that when we bind a control to the data source, the value is copied from the data source into the control, but we must update values from our controls back to the data source manually.

The reason why Web Forms data binding is read-only is down to the nature of web development in general: it's unlikely that our data source will be kept in memory on the server while the page is being displayed in the browser. When the updated values are posted from the browser back to the server, there is no longer a data source available for binding, so there's no way for the binding infrastructure to update the values automatically.

In both Windows Forms and Web Forms, data binding is now very powerful. It offers good performance with a high degree of control for the developer, overcoming the limitations we've faced in the past. Given the coding savings we gain by using data binding, it's definitely a technology that we want to support as we build our business framework.

Enabling our objects for data binding

While data binding can be used to bind against any object, or any collection of homogeneous objects, there are some things that we can do as object designers to make data binding work better. If we implement these 'extra' features, we'll enable data binding to do more work for us, and provide the user with a superior experience. The .NET `DataSet` object, for instance, implements these extra features to provide full data binding support to both Windows and web developers.

The IEditableObject interface

All of our editable business objects should implement the `IEditableObject` interface. This interface is designed to support a simple, one-level undo capability, and is used by simple forms-based data binding and complex grid-based data binding alike.

> *The `IEditableObject` interface is part of the .NET Framework, and can be found in the `System.ComponentModel` namespace.*

In the forms-based model, `IEditableObject` allows the data-binding infrastructure to notify our object before the user edits it, so that it can take a snapshot of its values. Later, we can tell the object whether to apply or cancel those changes, based on the user's actions. In the grid-based model, each of our objects is displayed in a row within the grid. In this case, the interface allows the data-binding infrastructure to notify our object when its row is being edited, and then whether to accept or undo the changes based on the user's actions. Typically, grids perform an undo operation if the user presses the *Esc* key, and an accept operation if the user moves off that row in the grid by any other means.

The IBindingList interface

All of our business *collections* should implement the `IBindingList` interface.

> *The `IBindingList` interface is part of the .NET Framework, and can be found in the `System.ComponentModel` namespace.*

This interface is used in grid-based binding, where it allows the control that's displaying the contents of the collection to be notified by the collection any time an item is added, removed, or edited, so the display can be updated. Without this interface, there is no way for the data-binding infrastructure to notify the grid that the underlying data has changed, so the user won't see changes as they happen.

Property change events

Finally, we need to add events to our editable business objects, so that they can notify the form any time their data values change. Changes that are caused directly by the user editing a field in a bound control are supported automatically, but if the object updates a property value through *code*, rather than it being due to direct user editing, we need to notify the data-binding infrastructure that a refresh of the display is required.

> *Interestingly, this feature has nothing to do with the* `IEditableObject` *or* `IBindingList` *interfaces. Those exist primarily to support grid or other complex controls, while these events exist primarily to support the binding of a control to a specific property on our object.*

We implement this by raising events for each property on the object, where the event is the property name with the word "`Changed`" appended. For instance, a `FirstName` property should raise a `FirstNameChanged` event any time the property value is changed. If any control is bound to the `FirstName` property of our object, this will be automatically intercepted by the data-binding infrastructure, which will trigger a refresh of *all* the data-bound controls on the form.

Since these events are simply `Public` events raised by our object, they are accessible not only to a form, but also to the UI developer, if they choose to receive and handle them.

Events and serialization

The events that are raised by our business collections and business objects are all valuable: events support the data-binding infrastructure, and enable us to utilize its full potential. Unfortunately, there's a conflict between the idea of objects raising events, and the use of .NET serialization via the `<Serializable()>` attribute.

When we mark an object as `<Serializable()>`, we're telling the .NET Framework that it can pass our object across the network by value. This means that the object will be automatically converted into a byte stream by the .NET runtime – a topic we'll cover in more detail in Chapter 3. It also means that any object *referenced* by our object will be serialized into the same byte stream, unless the variable representing it is marked with the `<NonSerialized()>` attribute. What may not be immediately obvious is that *events create an object reference behind the scenes.*

When our object declares and raises an event, that event is delivered to *any* object that has a handler for the event (because they're using either the `WithEvents` keyword or the `AddHandler` method). We often have a form handle events from objects, as illustrated in the following diagram:

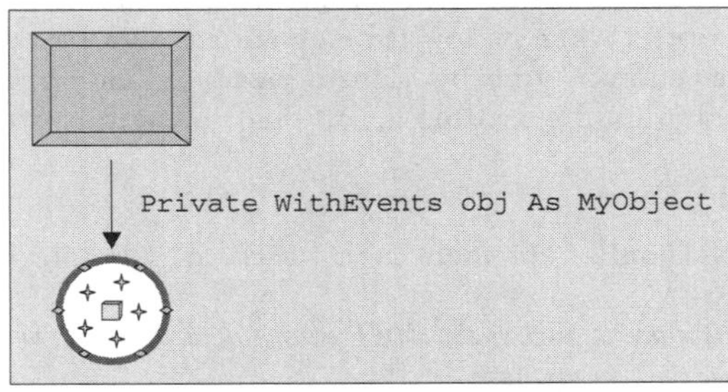

How does the event get delivered to the handling object? Well, it turns out that behind every event is a **delegate** – a strongly typed object that points back to the handling object. This means that any time we use events, we have bi-directional references between our object and the object handling our events:

Even though this back-reference is not visible to developers, it's completely visible to the .NET serialization infrastructure. When we go to serialize our object, the serialization mechanism will trace this reference, and attempt to serialize any objects (including forms) that are handling our events! Obviously, this is rarely desirable. In fact, if the handling object is a form, this will fail outright with a runtime error, because forms aren't `<Serializable()>`. Rather, they are anchored objects.

> **If any anchored object handles events that are raised by our `<Serializable()>` object, we will be unable to serialize our object, because the .NET runtime serialization process will error out.**

What we need to do is mark the events as `<NonSerialized()>`, but it's at this point that we run into a serious catch. It turns out that VB.NET doesn't support this concept. It is not possible to mark an *event* as `<NonSerialized()>`, which kind of makes sense: what we want to mark as `<NonSerialized()>` isn't the event, it's the underlying delegate.

In C#, this is handled by using the `field` target within an attribute (`[field: NonSerialized()]`), which marks the underlying delegate to be not serialized. Unfortunately, VB.NET doesn't support this particular attribute target (though it does support `Assembly` and `Module`). Without support for the `field` target, we need to come up with an alternate approach that *does* allow us to implement `IBindingList` and property "`Changed`" events.

The basic answer lies in the language-agnostic nature of the .NET platform. We can easily create a class in C# and inherit from it in VB.NET (or vice versa). This means that we can create a class in C# that declares and raises our events, and then inherit from that class to create our business objects and collections.

Object persistence and object-relational mapping

One of the biggest challenges facing a business developer building an object-oriented system is that a good object model is almost never the same as a good relational model. Since most of our data is stored in relational databases, using a relational model, this poses us the significant problem of translating that data into an object model for processing, and then changing back to a relational model later on, when we want to store the data from our objects back into the data store.

Relational vs. object modeling

Before we go any further, let's make sure we're in agreement that object models are not the same as relational models. Relational models are primarily concerned with efficient storage of data, such that replication is minimized. Relational modeling is governed by the rules of normalization, and almost all databases are designed to meet at least the third normal form. In this form, it's quite likely that the data for any given business concept or entity is split between multiple tables in the database, so as to avoid any duplication of data.

Object models, on the other hand, are primarily concerned with modeling *behavior*, not data. It's not the data that defines the object, but what the object represents within our business domain. In many cases, this means that our objects will contain data from multiple tables, or that multiple objects may represent a single table.

At the simplest level, consider a `Customer` object. In many organizations, customer data resides in multiple data stores. Sales data may be in a SQL Server database, while shipping data resides in Oracle, and invoicing data is in an AS400. Even if we're lucky enough to have only one type of database engine to deal with, it's very likely that our data will be in various tables in different databases.

Each of these data stores might be relational, but when we design our `Customer` object, we really don't care. Some of the data to construct our `Customer` object will come from each location, and when we update the `Customer` object, all three data stores may be updated. In even more complex cases, we may have interesting relationships between objects that bear little resemblance to a relational model. An invoice, for instance, will certainly have data from an `Invoice` table, but is likely to also include some customer information, and possibly some product or shipping information too.

A classic example of where object models and relational models often differ is in a many-to-many relational model. In such a model – and we'll take the example here of physicians and services – we have three tables, reflecting the fact that a physician provides many services, and any given service may be provided by many physicians:

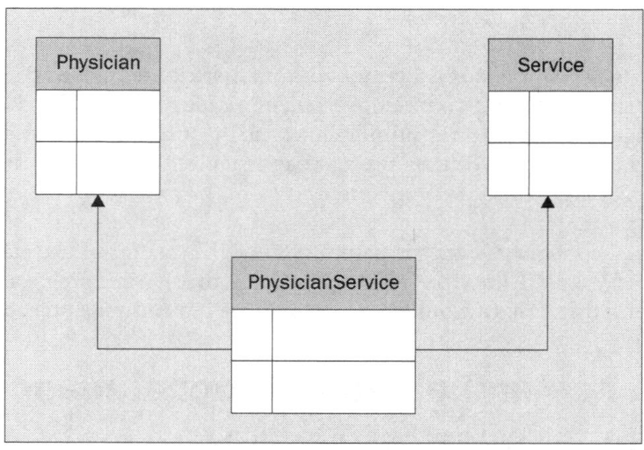

This relationship is constructed by creating a **link** (or **bridge**) **table** that contains keys from both the `Physician` and `Service` tables, providing a bi-directional, many-to-many link between the two entities. Now, while it's *possible* to construct the same model using objects, it is more natural to implement the object model with two types of link object – one for each type of parent entity.

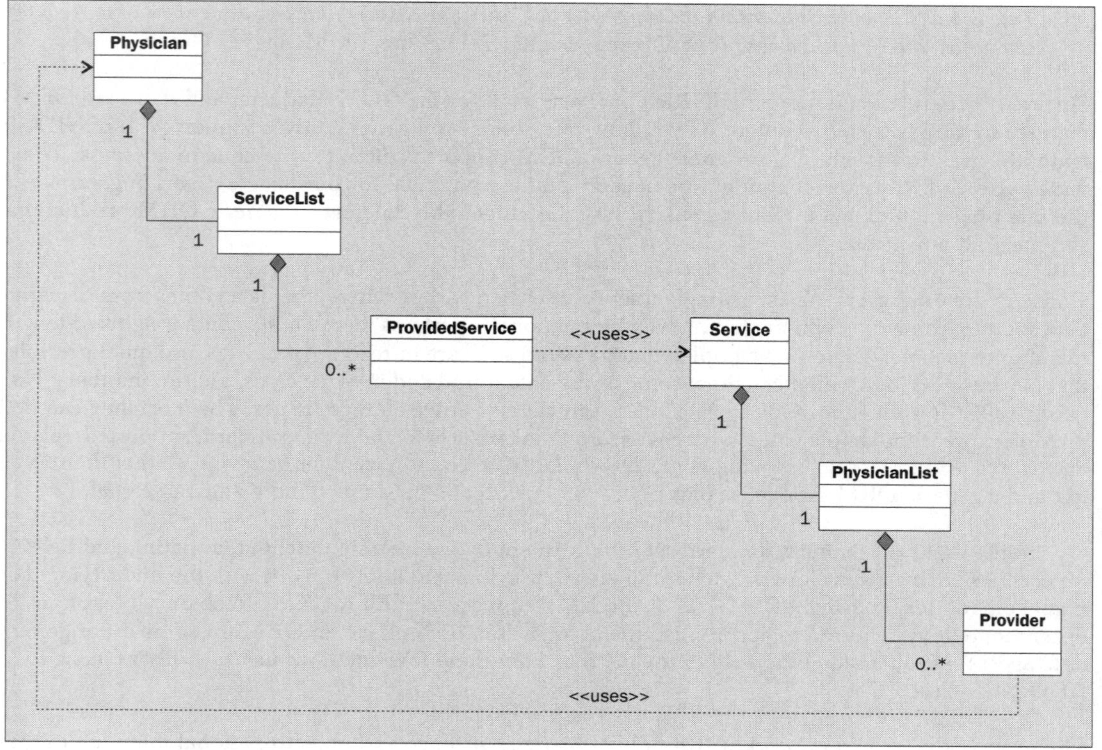

This object model provides a collection-based view of the entities, allowing us to retrieve a `Physician` object, along with a collection of child objects that represent the specific services provided by the doctor. Each of these child objects provides *access* to an actual `Service` object, but the child object is an entity in its own right, possibly not only providing information about the service, but also perhaps indicating how long the physician has been providing this service, or other pertinent data.

Note that this is conceptually an infinite loop. Given a physician, we could navigate to a provided service, and retrieve an actual `Service` object from there. As one of its child objects, that `Service` object would contain a `Provider` object that links back to the original `Physician` object. While this is obviously not a relational model, it's perfectly acceptable (and intuitive) from an object-oriented perspective.

> *We're replacing the underlying relational database with our object model. What we're trying to do is provide an object model that more accurately represents the business entities, so that we can work with a subset of the data in an object-oriented fashion. When we're not using the objects, the actual data is stored within relational databases.*

Object-relational mapping

If object models are not the same as relational models (or some other data models that we might be using), we'll need some mechanism by which we can translate our data from the data storage and management tier up into our object-oriented business logic tier.

> *This is a well-known issue within the object-oriented community. One of the best discussions of it can be found in David Taylor's book,* Object-oriented Technology: A Manager's Guide.

Several object-relational mapping (ORM) products exist for the COM platform, and there are ORM features in the J2EE environment. As yet, however, there is no generic ORM support within .NET. In truth, this isn't too much of a nuisance: generic ORM support is often problematic in any case. The wide variety of mappings that might be needed, and the potential for business logic driving variations in the mapping from object to object, make it virtually impossible to create a generic ORM product that can meet all our needs.

Consider the `Customer` object example that we discussed earlier. There, the data comes from disparate data sources, some of which might not even be relational – perhaps there's a file containing fixed-length mainframe records, where we've implemented custom software to read the data? It's also quite possible that our business logic will dictate that some of the data is updated in some cases, but not in others. No existing ORM product, for COM or for J2EE, can claim to solve all these issues. The most they can do is provide support for simple cases, where we're updating objects to and from standard, supported, relational data stores. At most, they'll provide hooks by which we can customize their behavior. Rather than trying to build a generic ORM product as part of this book, we'll aim for a much more attainable goal.

Our framework will define a standard set of four methods for creating, fetching, updating and deleting objects. As business developers, we'll implement these four methods to work with the underlying data management tier by using ADO.NET, or the XML support in .NET, or XML Web Services, or any other technology required to accomplish the task. In fact, if you have an ORM (or some other generic data access) product, you'll be able to invoke that from these four methods just as easily as using ADO.NET directly.

The point is that our framework will simplify object persistence and object-relational mapping to the point where all we need to do is implement these four methods to retrieve or update data. This places no restrictions on our ability to work with data, and provides a standardized persistence and mapping mechanism for all objects.

Preserving Encapsulation

As I noted at the beginning of the chapter, one of my key goals was to design this framework to provide powerful features while following the key object-oriented concepts, including **encapsulation**.

Encapsulation is the idea that all of the logic and data pertaining to a given business entity is held within the object that represents that entity. Of course, there are various ways in which one can interpret the idea of encapsulation – nothing is ever simple!

One approach is to say that we can encapsulate business data and logic in our object, and then encapsulate data access and ORM behavior in some other object. This provides nice separation between the business logic and data access, and encapsulates both types of behavior.

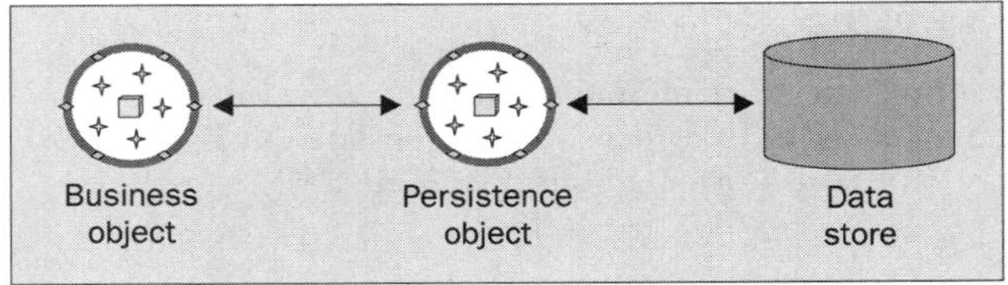

While there are certainly some advantages to this approach, there are drawbacks too. The most notable of these is that there's no easy or efficient way to get the data from the persistence object into or out of the business object. For the persistence object to load data into the business object, it must be able to bypass business and validation processing in the business object, and somehow load raw data into it directly. If our persistence object tries to load data into the object using our standard properties, we'll run into a series of issues:

- The data already in the database is presumed valid, so we're wasting a lot of processing time unnecessarily revalidating data. This can lead to a serious performance problem when loading a large group of objects.
- There's no way to load read-only property values. We often have read-only properties for things such as the primary key of the data, and we obviously need to load that into the object, but we can't load it via the normal interface (if that interface is properly designed).
- Sometimes, properties are interdependent due to business rules, which means that some properties must be loaded before others, or errors will result. The persistence object would need to know about all these conditions so that it could load the right properties first. The result is that the persistence object would become *very* complex.

On the other hand, having the persistence object load raw data into the business object breaks encapsulation in a big way, since we have one object directly tampering with the internal variables of another. We could do it by using reflection (which we'll discuss in more detail in Chapter 3), or by designing the business object to expose its private variables for manipulation. But the former is slow, and the latter is just plain bad object design: it allows the UI developer (or any other code) to manipulate these variables too, so we're asking for abuse of our objects, which will invariably lead to code that's impossible to maintain.

A much better approach, therefore, is to view encapsulation to mean that *all* the logic for the business entity should be in the object – that is, the logic to support the UI developer (validation, calculation, etc.), *and* the data access logic. This way the object encapsulates all responsibility for its data – it has sole control over the data from the moment it leaves the database, until the time when it returns to the database.

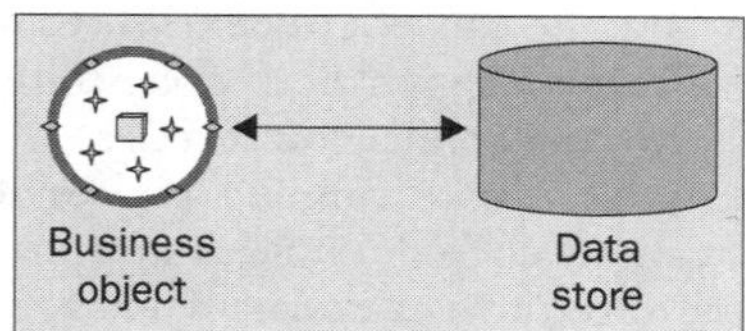

This is a simpler way of doing things, since it keeps all of the logic for our entity within the boundaries of a single object, and all of our code within the boundaries of a single class. Any time we need to alter, enhance, or maintain the logic for an entity, we know *exactly* where to find it. There is no ambiguity regarding whether the logic is in the business object, the persistence object, or possibly both – there is only one object.

The new approach also has the benefit of providing optimal performance. Since the data access and ORM code is *inside* the object, that code can interact directly with the object's private instance variables. We don't need to break encapsulation, nor do we need to resort to trickery such as reflection (or deal with the resulting performance issues).

The drawback to this approach is that we are including code inside our business class to handle data access – that is, we are blurring the line between the business logic tier and the data access tier in our n-tier logical model. Our framework will help to mitigate this by formally defining four methods into which the data access code will be written, so there will still be a substantial barrier between our business logic and our data access code.

On balance, then, I prefer this second view, since we achieve total encapsulation of all data and logic pertaining to a business entity with very high performance. Better still, we can accomplish this using techniques and technologies that are completely supported within the .NET Framework, so we don't need to resort to any complex or hard-to-code workarounds (such as using reflection to load the data).

> *If you're interested, my goal when writing my* Visual Basic 6 Business Objects *book was to achieve exactly this model. Unfortunately, there was no realistic way to accomplish it with the COM platform, and so I compromised and created UI-centric and data-centric objects to implement the model. With .NET, the technology* does *exist to reach this goal, and the next section will explain this in more detail.*

Supporting physical n-tier models

The question that remains, then, is how we're to support n-tier physical models if the UI-oriented and data-oriented behaviors reside in *one* object?

UI-oriented behaviors almost always involve a lot of properties and methods – a very fine-grained interface with which the user interface can interact in order to set, retrieve, and manipulate the values of an object. Almost by definition, this type of object *must* run in the same process as the UI code itself, either on the Windows client machine with our Windows Forms, or on the web server with our Web Forms.

Conversely, data-oriented behaviors typically involve very few methods: create, fetch, update, delete. They must run on a machine where they can establish a physical connection to the database server. Sometimes, this is the client workstation or web server, but often it means running on a physically separate application server.

This point of apparent conflict is where the concept of **distributed objects** enters the picture. It's possible to pass our business object from an application server to the client machine, work with the object, and then pass the object back to the application server so that its data can be stored in the database. To do this, we need some generic code running as a service on the application server with which the client can interact. This generic code does little more than accept the object from the client, and then call methods on the object to retrieve or update data as required – the object itself does all the real work. The following diagram illustrates this concept, showing how the *same physical business object* can be passed from application server to client, and vice versa, via a generic router object running on the application server.

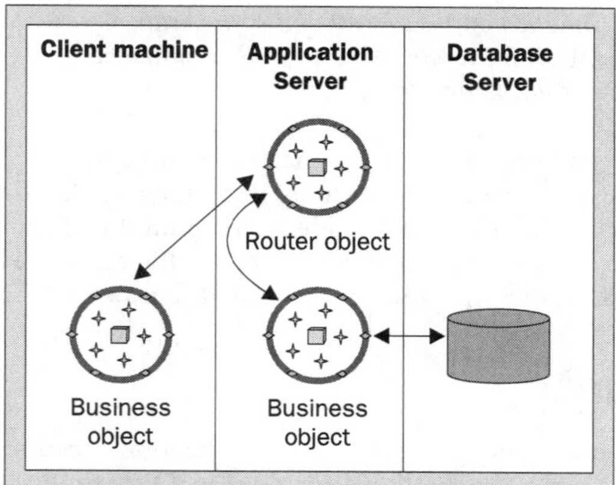

In Chapter 1, we discussed anchored and unanchored objects. In this model, the business object is unanchored, meaning that it can be passed around the network by value. The router object is anchored, meaning that it will always run on the machine where it is created.

In our framework, we'll refer to this router object as a **data portal**. It will act as a portal for all data access on all our objects. Our objects will interact with this portal to retrieve default values (create), fetch data (read), update or add data (update), and remove data (delete). This means that the data portal will provide a standardized mechanism by which all CRUD operations can be performed.

The end result will be that our business class will include a method that can be called by the UI to load an object based on data from the database:

```
Public Shared Function GetCustomer(ByVal CustomerID As String) As Customer
  Return DataPortal.Fetch(New Criteria(CustomerID))
End Function
```

The actual data access code will be contained within each of our business objects. The data portal will simply provide an anchored object on a machine with access to the database server, and will invoke the appropriate CRUD methods on our business objects themselves. This means that the business object will also implement a method that will be called by the data portal to actually load the data. That method will look something like this:

```
Protected Sub DataPortal_Fetch(ByVal Criteria As Object)
  ' Code to load the object's variables with data goes here
End Sub
```

The UI won't know (or need to know) how any of this works, so to create a `Customer` object, the UI will simply write code along these lines:

```
Dim obj As Customer = Customer.GetCustomer("ABC")
```

Our framework, and specifically our data portal, will take care of all the rest of the work, including figuring out whether the data access code should run on the client workstation or on an application server.

For more background information on the concept of a data portal, refer to my Adventures in VB.NET *column titled* A Portal for My Data *on MSDN online at* *http://msdn.microsoft.com/columns/vbnet.asp.*

By using a data portal, we can keep all our logic encapsulated within the business objects, and still support physical n-tier configurations. Better still, by implementing the data portal correctly, we'll be able to switch between having the data access code running on the client machine and placing it on a separate application server just by changing a configuration file setting. The ability to change between different physical configurations with no changes to code is a powerful, valuable feature.

Table-based security

Application security is often a challenging issue. Our applications need to be able to **authenticate** the user, which means that we need to know the user's identity. Our applications also need to be able to **authorize** the user to perform (or not to perform) certain operations, or to view (or not to view) certain data. Such authorization is typically handled by placing users into groups, or by defining roles to which a user can belong.

Authorization is just another type of business logic. The decisions about what a user can and can't do or can and can't see within our application are business decisions. While our framework will work with the .NET Framework to support authentication, it is up to our business objects to implement the rules themselves.

Sometimes, we can rely on our environment to authenticate the user. Windows itself can require a user to provide a user ID and password, and third party products also may be used for this purpose. Authorization, however, is something that belongs to our application. While we may rely on our environment (Windows, COM+, or another product) to manage the user and the groups or roles to which they belong, it's always up to us to determine what they can and cannot do within our application itself.

The association of users or roles with specific behaviors or data within our application is part of our business logic. The definition of who gets to do what is driven by business requirements, not technical requirements.

The .NET Framework directly supports Windows' integrated security. This means that we can use objects within the Framework to determine the user's Windows identity and any domain or Active Directory groups to which they belong. In some organizations, this is enough: all the users of the organization's applications are in the Windows NT domain or Active Directory (AD), and by having them log into a workstation or a web site using integrated security, our applications can determine the user's identity and roles (groups).

In other organizations, however – possibly the *majority* of organizations – applications are used by at least some users who are *not* part of the organization's NT domain or AD. They may not even be members of the organization in question. This is very often the case with web and mobile applications, but it's surprisingly common with Windows applications as well. In these cases, we *can't* rely on Windows' integrated security for authentication and authorization.

To complicate matters further, we really want a security model that provides role information not only to server-side code, but also to the code in our UI. Rather than allowing the user to attempt to perform operations that will generate errors due to security at some later time, we should gray out the options, or not display them at all. To do this requires the UI developer to have access to the user's identity and roles, just as the business object author does.

Arranging this state of affairs isn't too hard as long as we're using Windows' integrated security, but it's often problematic when we rely solely on (say) COM+ role-based security, since there's no easy way to make the COM+ role information for our user available to the UI developer.

> *In May 2002, Juval Lowy wrote an article for MSDN Magazine in which he described how to create custom .NET security objects that merge NT domain or AD groups and COM+ roles so that both are available to the application for use. You can find the article at* *http://msdn.microsoft.com/msdnmag/issues/02/05/RoleSec/RoleSec.asp.*

For our business framework, we'll provide support for both Windows' integrated security *and* custom, table-based security, where the user ID, password, and roles are managed in a simple set of SQL Server tables. This custom security is a model that can be adapted to use any existing security tables or services that already exist in your organization.

Framework Design

So far, we've been focused on the major goals for our framework. Now that we've covered the guiding principles, we can move on to discuss the design of the framework that we'll be creating to meet these goals. In the rest of this chapter, we'll walk through the various classes that will be combined to create the framework. We'll also discuss how they will be divided into assemblies (DLLs) to support our goal of enabling both n-tier logical and n-tier physical architectures. Once we've got our design down, in Chapters 4 and 5 we'll dive into the implementation of the framework code.

A comprehensive framework can be a large and complex entity. There are usually many classes that go into the construction of a framework, even though the end users of the framework, our business developers, only use a few of those classes directly. The framework we're discussing here and building through the rest of the book accomplishes the goals we've just discussed, along with enabling the basic creation of object-oriented, n-tier business applications. For any given application or organization, this framework will likely be modified and enhanced to meet specific requirements. This means that the framework will grow as you use and adapt it to your environment.

Let's start by taking a second look at our basic UML class diagram for the framework:

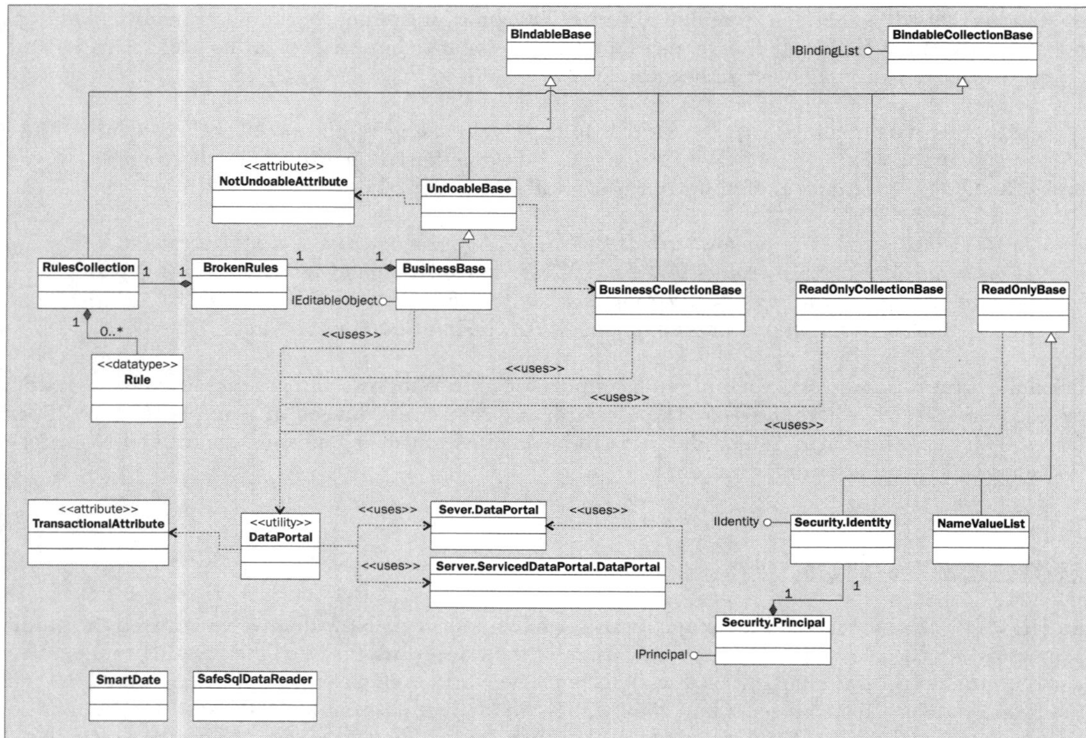

Obviously, there's a lot going on here, but we can break things down into smaller units of functionality, so that we can understand how it all fits together more easily. Specifically, we can divide the framework into functional groups:

- Business object creation
- n-Level undo functionality
- Data binding support
- Business rule tracking
- A data portal enabling various physical configurations
- Transactional and non-transactional data access
- Table-based security

For each functional group, we'll look at a subset of the overall class diagram, breaking it down into more digestible pieces.

Business Object Creation

First of all, it's important to recognize that the key classes in the framework are those that will be used by business developers as they create business objects, but that these are a small subset of those available. In fact, many of the framework classes are *never* used directly by business developers. The following diagram shows only those classes the business developer will typically use:

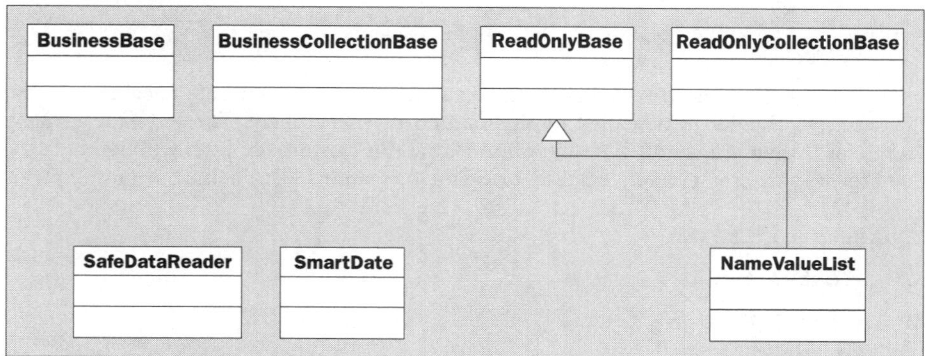

Obviously, the business developer may periodically interact with other classes as well, but these are the ones that will be at the center of most activity. Classes or methods that the business developer shouldn't have access to will be scoped to prevent accidental use.

BusinessBase

The `BusinessBase` class is the base from which all editable (read-write) business objects will be created. In other words, to create a business object, we'll inherit from this class:

```
<Serializable()> _
Public Class Customer
  Inherits BusinessBase

End Class
```

`BusinessBase` and the classes from which it inherits provide all the functionality that we've discussed earlier in this chapter, including n-level undo, tracking of broken rules, 'dirty' tracking, object persistence, and so forth. It supports the creation of root (top-level) objects and child objects. Root objects can be retrieved directly from and updated or deleted within our database, while child objects can only be retrieved or updated in the context of their parent object.

> *Throughout this book, I'm assuming we're building business applications, in which case almost all objects are ultimately stored in the database at one time or another. Even if your object is not persisted to a database, you can still use `BusinessBase` to gain access to the n-level undo, broken rule tracking, and 'dirty' tracking features built into the framework.*

For example, an `Invoice` is typically a root object, while the `LineItem` objects contained by an `Invoice` object are child objects. It makes perfect sense to retrieve or update an `Invoice`, but it makes no sense to create, retrieve, or update a `LineItem` without having an associated `Invoice`. To make this distinction, `BusinessBase` includes a method that we can call to indicate that our object is a child object: `MarkAsChild()`. By default, business objects are assumed to be root objects, unless this method is invoked. This means that a child object might look like this:

```
<Serializable()> _
Public Class Child
  Inherits BusinessBase

  Private Sub New()
    MarkAsChild()
  End Sub

End Class
```

The BusinessBase class provides default implementations of the four data access methods that exist on all root business objects, to be called by the data portal mechanism. These default implementations all raise an error if they are called. The intention is that our business objects will override these methods if they need to support create, fetch, update, or delete operations. The names of these four methods are:

- DataPortal_Create()
- DataPortal_Fetch()
- DataPortal_Update()
- DataPortal_Delete()

BusinessBase provides a great deal of functionality to our business objects, whether root or child. In Chapter 4, we'll build BusinessBase itself, and in Chapter 7 we'll implement a number of business objects that illustrate how BusinessBase is used.

BusinessCollectionBase

The BusinessCollectionBase class is the base from which all editable *collections* of business objects will be created. If we have an Invoice object with a collection of LineItem objects, this will be the base for creating that collection:

```
<Serializable()> _
Public Class LineItems
  Inherits BusinessCollectionBase

End Class
```

Of course, we'll have to implement Item(), Add(), and Remove() methods as appropriate in order to create a strongly typed collection object. The process is the same as though we'd inherited from System.Collections.CollectionBase, except that *our* collection will include all the functionality required to support n-level undo, object persistence, and the other business object features.

> *BusinessCollectionBase will ultimately inherit from System.Collections.CollectionBase, so we'll start with all the core functionality of a .NET collection.*

The BusinessCollectionBase class also defines the four data access methods that we discussed in BusinessBase. This will allow us to retrieve a collection of objects directly (rather than retrieving a single object at a time), if that's required by our application design.

ReadOnlyBase

Sometimes, we don't want to expose an editable object. Many applications have objects that are read-only or display-only. Read-only objects need to support object persistence only for retrieving data, not for updating data. Also, they don't need to support any of the n-level undo or other editing-type behaviors, since they are created with read-only properties.

For editable objects, we created `BusinessBase`, which has a property that we can set to indicate whether it is a parent or child object. The same base supports both types of objects, allowing us to switch dynamically between parent and child at runtime. Making an object read-only or read-write is a bigger decision, because it impacts the *interface* of our object. A read-only object should only include read-only `Property` methods as part of its interface, and that isn't something that we can toggle on or off at runtime. By implementing a specific base class for read-only objects, we allow them to be more specialized, and to have fewer overheads.

The `ReadOnlyBase` class is used to create read-only objects:

```
<Serializable()> _
Public Class StaticContent
  Inherits ReadOnlyBase

End Class
```

We shouldn't implement any read-write properties in classes that inherit from `ReadOnlyBase` – were we to do so, it would be entirely down to us to handle any undo, persistence, or other features for dealing with the changed data. If an object has editable fields, it should subclass from `BusinessBase`.

ReadOnlyCollectionBase

Not only do we sometimes need read-only business objects, but also we occasionally require immutable *collections* of objects. The `ReadonlyCollectionBase` class allows us to create strongly typed collections of objects where the object and collection are both read-only.

```
<Serializable()> _
Public Class StaticList
  Inherits ReadOnlyCollectionBase

End Class
```

As with `ReadOnlyBase`, this object supports only retrieval of data. It has no provision for updating data or handling changes to its data.

NameValueList

The `NameValueList` class is a specific implementation of `ReadOnlyBase` that provides support for read-only, name-value pairs. This reflects the fact that most applications use lookup tables, or lists of read-only data such as categories, customer types, product types, and so forth.

Rather than forcing business developers to create read-only, name-value collections for every type of such data, they can just use the `NameValueList` class. It allows the developer to retrieve a name-value list by specifying the database name, table name, name column, and value column. The `NameValueList` class will use those criteria to populate itself from the database, resulting in a read-only collection of values.

NameValueList can be used to populate combo box or list box controls in the user interface, or to validate changes to property values to ensure that they match a value in the list.

As implemented for this book, this class only supports SQL Server.

SafeSqlDataReader

Most of the time, we don't care about the difference between a null value and an empty value (such as an empty string or a zero), but databases often do. When we're retrieving data from a database, we need to handle the occurrence of unexpected null values with code such as this:

```
If dr.IsDBNull(idx) Then
  myValue = ""
Else
  myValue = dr.GetString(idx)
End If
```

Clearly, doing this over and over again, throughout our application, can get very tiresome. One solution is to fix the database so that it doesn't allow nulls where they provide no value, but that is often impractical for various reasons.

> *This is one of my pet peeves. Allowing nulls in a column where we care about the difference between a value that was never entered and the empty value ("", or 0, or whatever) is fine. Allowing nulls in a column where we* don't *care about the difference merely complicates our code to no good purpose, decreasing developer productivity and increasing maintenance costs.*

As a more general solution, we can create a utility class that uses SqlDataReader in such a way that we never have to worry about null values again. Unfortunately, the SqlDataReader class is not inheritable, so we can't subclass it directly, but we *can* wrap it using containment and delegation. The result is that our data access code works the same as always, except that we never need to write checks for null values. If a null value shows up, SafeDataReader will automatically convert it to an appropriate empty value.

Obviously, if we *do* care about the difference between a null and an empty value, we can just use a regular SqlDataReader to retrieve our data.

SmartDate

Dates are a perennial development problem. Of course, we have the Date data type, which provides powerful support for manipulating dates, but it has no concept of an 'empty' date. The trouble is that many applications allow the user to leave date fields empty, so we need to deal with the concept of an empty date within our application.

On top of this, date formatting is problematic. Or rather, formatting an ordinary date value is easy, but again we're faced with the special case where an 'empty' date must be represented by an empty string value for display purposes. In fact, for the purposes of data binding, we often want any date properties on our objects to be of type String, so the user has full access to the various data formats, as well as the ability to enter a blank date into the field.

Dates are also a challenge when it comes to the database: the date values in our database don't understand the concept of an empty date any more than .NET does. To resolve this, date columns in a database typically *do* allow null values, so a null can indicate an empty date.

Technically, this is a misuse of the null value, which is intended to differentiate between a value that was never entered, and one that is empty. Unfortunately, we're typically left with no choice, since there's no way to put an empty date value into a date data type.

The `SmartDate` class is an attempt to resolve this issue. Repeating our problem with `SqlDataReader`, the `Date` data type is not inheritable, so we can't just subclass `Date` and create a more powerful data type. We can, however, use containment and delegation to create a class that provides the capabilities of the `Date` data type while also supporting the concept of an empty date.

This isn't as easy at it might at first appear, as we'll see when we implement this class in Chapter 4. Much of the complexity flows from the fact that we often need to compare an empty date to a real date, but an empty date might be considered very small, or very large. If we have a `MinimumDate` property on an object, and the object's value is empty, then it probably represents the smallest possible date. If we have a `MaximumDate` property on an object, its empty value property represents the largest possible value.

The `SmartDate` class is designed to support these concepts, and to integrate with the `SafeSqlDataReader` so that it can properly interpret a null database value as an empty date.

n-Level undo functionality

The implementation of n-level undo functionality is quite complex, and involves heavy use of reflection. Fortunately, we can use inheritance to place the implementation in a base class, so that no business object needs to worry about the undo code. In fact, to keep things cleaner, this code is in its *own* base class, separate from any other business object behaviors:

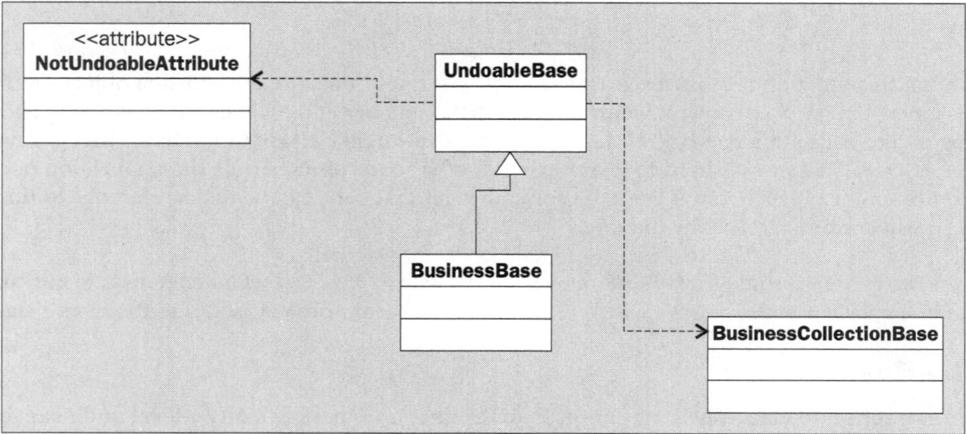

At first glance, it might appear that we could use .NET serialization to implement undo functionality: what easier way to take a snapshot of an object's state than to serialize it into a byte stream? Unfortunately, this isn't as easy as it might sound, at least when it comes to restoring the state of our object.

Taking a snapshot of a `<Serializable()>` object is easy – it can be done with code similar to this:

```
<Serializable()> _
Public Class Customer

  Public Function Snapshot() As Byte()
    Dim m As New MemoryStream()
    Dim f As New BinaryFormatter()

    f.Serialize(m, Me)
    m.Position = 0
    Return m.ToArray
  End Function

End Class
```

This converts the object into a byte stream, returning that byte stream as an array of type `Byte`. That part is easy – it's the restoration that's tricky. Suppose that the user now wants to undo their changes, requiring us to restore the byte stream back into our object. The code to deserialize a byte stream looks like this:

```
<Serializable()> _
Public Class Customer

  Public Function Deserialize(ByVal State() As Byte) As Customer
    Dim m As New MemoryStream(State)
    Dim f As New BinaryFormatter()

    Return CType(f.Deserialize(m), Customer)
  End Function

End Class
```

Notice that this function returns *a new customer object*. It doesn't restore our existing object's state; it creates a new object. Somehow, it would be up to us to tell any and all code that has a reference to our existing object to use this new object. In some cases, that might be easy to do, but it isn't always trivial. In complex applications, it's hard to guarantee that other code elsewhere in the application doesn't have a reference to our object – and if we don't somehow get that code to update its reference to this new object, it will continue to use the old one.

What we really want is some way to restore our object's state *in place*, so that all references to our current object remain valid, but the object's state is restored. This is the purpose of the `UndoableBase` class.

UndoableBase

Our `BusinessBase` class inherits from `UndoableBase`, and thereby gains n-level undo capabilities. Since all business objects subclass `BusinessBase`, they too gain n-level undo. Ultimately, the n-level undo capabilities are exposed to the business object and to UI developers via three methods:

- BeginEdit() tells the object to take a snapshot of its current state, in preparation for being edited. Each time BeginEdit() is called, a new snapshot is taken, allowing us to trap the state of the object at various points during its life. The snapshot will be kept in memory so that we can easily restore that data to the object if CancelEdit() is called.
- CancelEdit() tells the object to restore the object to the most recent snapshot. This effectively performs an undo operation, reversing one level of changes. If we call CancelEdit() the same number of times as we called BeginEdit(), we'll restore the object to its original state.
- ApplyEdit() tells the object to discard the most recent snapshot, leaving the object's current state untouched. It accepts the most recent changes to the object. If we call ApplyEdit() the same number of times as we called BeginEdit(), we'll have discarded all the snapshots, essentially making any changes to the object's state permanent.

We can combine sequences of BeginEdit(), CancelEdit(), and ApplyEdit() calls to respond to the user's actions within a complex Windows Forms UI. Alternatively, we can totally ignore these methods, taking no snapshots of the object's state, and therefore not providing for the ability to undo changes. This is common in web applications, where the user typically has no option to cancel changes. Instead, they simply navigate away to perform some other action or view some other data.

Supporting child collections

As shown in the previous diagram, the UndoableBase class also uses BusinessCollectionBase. As it traces through our business object to take a snapshot of the object's state, it may encounter collections of child objects. For n-level undo to work for complex objects as well as for simple objects, any snapshot of object state must extend down through all child objects, as well as the parent object.

We discussed this earlier with our Invoice and LineItem example. When we BeginEdit() on an Invoice, we must *also* take snapshots of the states of all LineItem objects, since they're technically part of the state of the Invoice object itself. To do this while preserving encapsulation, we make each individual object take a snapshot of its own state, so that no object data is ever made available outside the object.

Thus, if our code in UndoableBase encounters a collection of type BusinessCollectionBase, it will call a method on the collection to cascade the BeginEdit(), CancelEdit(), or ApplyEdit() call to the child objects within that collection.

NotUndoableAttribute

The final concept we need to discuss regarding n-level undo is the idea that some of our data might not be subject to being in a snapshot. Taking a snapshot of our object's data takes time and consumes memory, so if our object includes read-only values, there's no reason to take a snapshot of them. Since they can't be changed, there's no value in restoring them to the same value in the course of an undo operation.

To accommodate this scenario, the framework includes a custom attribute named NotUndoableAttribute, which can be applied to variables within our business classes.

```
<NotUndoable()> Private mReadonlyData As String
```

The code in UndoableBase simply ignores any variables marked with this attribute as the snapshot is created or restored, so the variable will always retain its value regardless of any calls to BeginEdit(), CancelEdit(), or ApplyEdit() on the object.

Data binding support

As we discussed earlier in the chapter, the .NET data binding infrastructure directly supports the concept of data binding to objects and collections. However, we can help to provide more complete behaviors by implementing a couple of interfaces and raising some events. Since VB.NET doesn't support the `field` target for attributes, we can use C# base classes to declare and raise any events that we'll need.

This technique works well for `IBindingList`, which is a well-defined interface that raises a single event. We'll create a C# class to implement the event, marking it as `[field: NonSerialized()]`. For the property "`Changed`" events, however, this scheme appears to be problematic. We don't want to be in a position where we need to implement a different C# base class for every business class we ever write, just so that it can raise events. Fortunately, there's a generic solution.

Earlier, when we discussed the property "`Changed`" events, we mentioned how the raising of a *single* such event triggers the data-binding infrastructure to refresh *all* bound controls. This means that we only need *one* property "`Changed`" event, as long as we can raise that event when *any* property is changed. Now, one of the elements of our framework is the concept of tracking whether an object has changed, or is 'dirty' – all editable business objects will expose this status as a read-only `IsDirty` property, along with a `Protected` `MarkDirty()` method that our business logic can use to set it. This value will be set any time a property or value on the object is changed, so it's an ideal indicator for us.

If we implement an `IsDirtyChanged` event on *all* our editable business objects, our UI developers can get full data binding support by binding a control to the `IsDirty` property. When any property on our object changes, the `IsDirtyChanged` event will be raised, resulting in all data-bound controls being refreshed to display the changed data.

> *Obviously, we won't typically want to display the value of* `IsDirty` *to the end user, so this control will typically be hidden from the user, even though it's part of the form.*

Following on from all of the above, we'll implement an `IsDirtyChanged` event in a C# base class using the `[field: NonSerialized()]` attribute. `BusinessBase` will subclass this C# class, and therefore all editable business objects will support this event. Ultimately, what we're talking about here is creating one C# base class (`BindableBase`) to raise the `IsDirtyChanged` event, and another (`BindableCollectionBase`) to implement the `IBindingList` interface, so that the `ListChanged` event can be fired. These classes are linked to our core `BusinessBase` and `BusinessCollectionBase` classes:

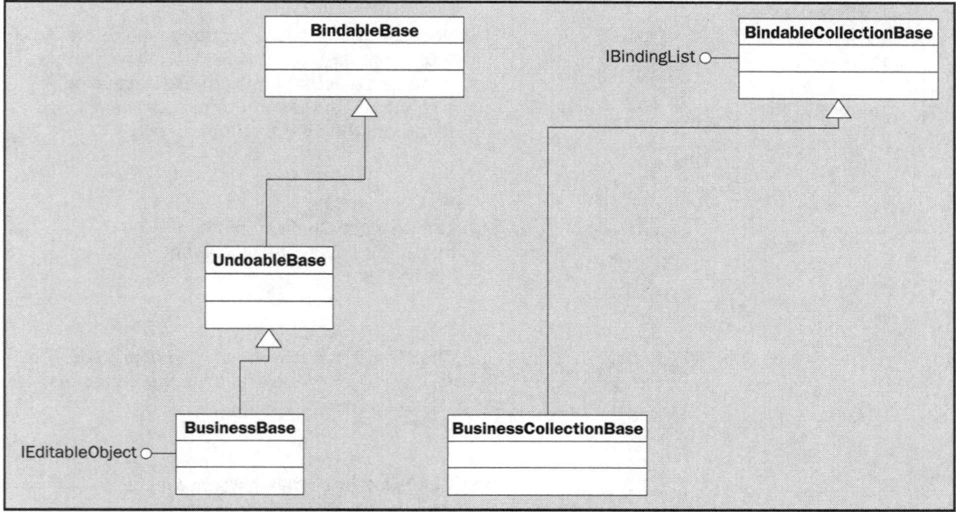

Combined with implementing `IEditableObject` in `BusinessBase`, we can now fully support data binding in both Windows Forms and Web Forms. `IEditableObject` and `IBindingList` are both part of the .NET Framework, as is the support for *`property`*`Changed` events. All we're doing here is designing our framework base classes to take advantage of this existing functionality, so the business developer doesn't have to worry about these details.

BindableBase

The `BindableBase` class just declares the `IsDirtyChanged` event, and implements a `protected` method named `OnIsDirtyChanged()` that raises the event. `BusinessBase` will call this method any time its `MarkDirty()` method is called by our business logic. Our business logic *must* call `MarkDirty()` any time the internal state of the object changes. Any time the internal state of the object changes, the `IsDirtyChanged` event will then be raised. This event can then be used by UI code to trigger a data-binding refresh:

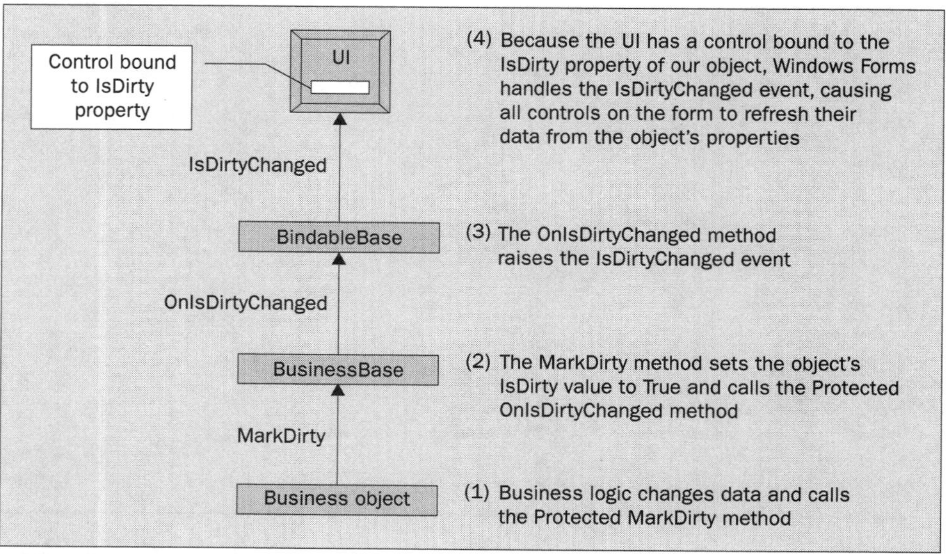
Control bound to IsDirty property
UI
(4) Because the UI has a control bound to the IsDirty property of our object, Windows Forms handles the IsDirtyChanged event, causing all controls on the form to refresh their data from the object's properties
IsDirtyChanged
BindableBase
(3) The OnIsDirtyChanged method raises the IsDirtyChanged event
OnIsDirtyChanged
BusinessBase
(2) The MarkDirty method sets the object's IsDirty value to True and calls the Protected OnIsDirtyChanged method
MarkDirty
Business object
(1) Business logic changes data and calls the Protected MarkDirty method

BindableCollectionBase

The `BindableCollectionBase` class just provides an implementation of the `IBindingList` interface, which includes a `ListChanged` event that is to be raised any time the content of the collection is changed. This includes adding, removing, or changing items in the list.

The interface also includes methods to support sorting, filtering, and searching within the collection. We won't be implementing these features in our framework. Obviously, they are supported concepts that could be implemented as an extension to the framework, if so desired.

Again, by implementing `BindableCollectionBase` in C#, we can mark the `ListChanged` event as `[field: NonSerialized()]`, which will cause the underlying delegate reference not to be serialized.

IEditableObject

The `IEditableObject` interface is defined in the `System.ComponentModel` namespace of the .NET Framework; it defines three methods and no events. Respectively, the methods indicate that the object should prepare to be edited (`BeginEdit()`), that the edit has been canceled (`CancelEdit()`), and that the edit has been accepted (`EndEdit()`). This interface is automatically invoked by the Windows Forms data binding infrastructure when our object is bound to any control on a form.

One of our requirements for `BusinessBase` is that it should support n-level undo. The requirement for the `IEditableObject` interface, however, is a *single* level of undo. Obviously, our n-level undo capability can be used to support a single level of undo, so implementing `IEditableObject` is largely a matter of 'aiming' the three interface methods at the n-level undo methods that implement this behavior.

The only complexity is that the `BeginEdit()` method from `IEditableObject` can (and will) be *called* many times, but it should only be *honored* on its first call. Our n-level edit capability would normally allow `BeginEdit()` to be called multiple times, with each call taking a snapshot of the object's state for a later restore operation. We'll need to add a bit more code to handle the difference in semantics between these two approaches.

Business rule tracking

As we discussed earlier, one of the framework's goals is to simplify the tracking of broken business rules – or at least, those rules that are a 'toggle', where a broken rule means that the object is invalid. An important side benefit of this is that the UI developer will have read-only access to the list of broken rules, which means that the descriptions of the broken rules can be displayed to the user, explaining what's making the object invalid.

The support for tracking broken business rules will be available to *all* editable business objects, so it's implemented at the `BusinessBase` level in the framework. Since all business objects subclass `BusinessBase`, they'll all have this functionality.

To provide this functionality, each business object will have an associated collection of broken business rules:

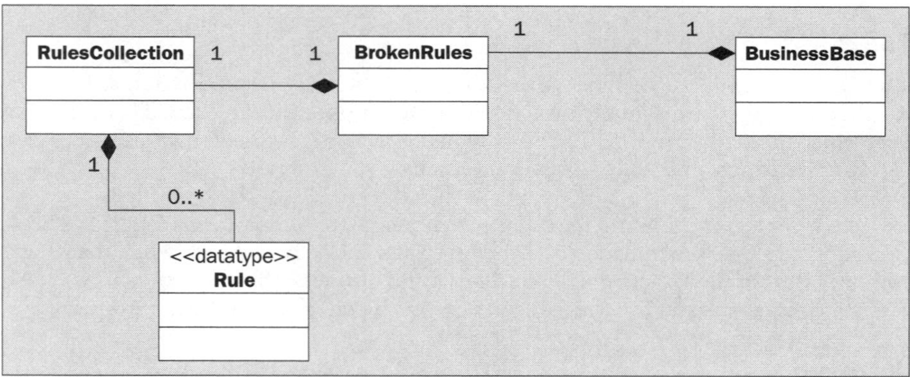

This is implemented such that rules can be marked as 'broken' by the business object, and a read-only list of the currently broken rules can be exposed to the UI code.

If all we wanted to do was keep a list of the broken rules, we could do that directly within `BusinessBase`. However, we also want to have a way of exposing this list of broken rules to the UI as a read-only list. For this reason, we'll implement a specialized collection object that our business object can change, but which the UI sees as being read-only. On top of that, we'll have the collection implement support for data binding so that the UI can display a list of broken rule descriptions to the user by simply binding the collection to a list or grid control.

> *The reason why the list of broken rules is exposed to the UI is due to reader feedback from my previous business objects books. Many readers wrote me to say that they'd adapted my COM framework to enhance the functionality of broken rule tracking in various ways, the most common being to allow the UI to display the list of broken rules to the user.*

To use the broken rule tracking functionality, within a business object, we might write code such as this:

```
  Public Property Quantity() As Integer
    Get
      Return mQuantity
    End Get
```

```
        Set(ByVal Value As Integer)
          mQuantity = Value
          MarkDirty()
          BrokenRules.MarkIfBroken("BadQuantity", _
                   "Quantity must be a positive number", mQuantity < 0)
          BrokenRules.MarkIfBroken("BadQuantity", _
                   "Quantity can't exceed 100", mQuantity > 100)
        End Set
      End Property
```

It's up to us to decide on the business rules, but the framework takes care of tracking which ones are broken, and whether the business object as a whole is valid at any given point in time. We're not creating a business rule engine or repository here – we're just creating a collection that we can use to track a list of the rules that are broken.

BrokenRules

Though the UML diagram above displays the `RulesCollection` and the `Rule` structure as independent entities, they are actually nested within the `BrokenRules` class. This simplifies the use of the concept, since the `BusinessBase` code only needs to interact directly with `BrokenRules`, which uses the `RulesCollection` and `Rule` types internally.

The `BrokenRules` class includes methods for use by `BusinessBase` to mark rules as broken or not broken. Marking a rule as broken adds it to the `RulesCollection` object, while marking a rule as not broken removes it from the collection. To find out if the business object is valid, all we need to do is see if there are any broken rules in the `RulesCollection` by checking its `Count` property.

RulesCollection

The `RulesCollection` is a strongly typed collection that can only contain `Rule` elements. It's constructed so that it can be manipulated by the `BrokenRules` code, and yet safely provided to UI code. There are no `Public` methods to alter the contents of the collection, so the UI is effectively given a reference to a read-only object. All the methods to manipulate the object are scoped as `Friend`, so they're unavailable to our business objects or to the UI.

Rule structure

The `Rule` structure contains the name and description of a rule, and it's a bit more complex than a normal structure in order to support data binding in Web Forms. A typical `Structure` consists of `Public` fields (variables) that are directly accessible from client code, but it turns out that Web Forms data binding won't bind to `Public` fields in a class or structure; it can only bind to `Public` properties. Because of this, our structure contains `Private` variables, with `Public` properties to expose them. This allows both Windows Forms and Web Forms to use data binding to display the list of broken rules within the UI.

The reason why `Rule` is a `Structure` instead of a `Class` is down to memory management. As our application runs, we can expect that business rules will be constantly broken and 'un-broken', resulting in the creation and destruction of `Rule` entities each time. There's a higher cost to creating and destroying an object than there is for a `Structure`, so we're minimizing this effect as far as we can.

Data portal

Supporting object persistence – the ability to store and retrieve an object from a database – can be quite complex. We discussed this earlier in the chapter, covering not only basic persistence, but the concept of object-relational mapping (ORM).

In our framework, we'll encapsulate data access logic within our business objects, allowing each object to handle its ORM logic, along with any other business logic that might impact data access. This is the most flexible approach to handling object persistence. At the same time, however, we don't want to be in a position where a change to our physical architecture requires every business object in the system to be altered. What we *do* want is the ability to switch between having the data access code run on the client machine and having it run on an application server, driven by a configuration file setting.

On top of this, if we're using an application server, we don't want to be in a position where every different business object in our application has a different remoting proxy exposed by the server. This is a maintenance and configuration nightmare, since it means that adding or changing a business object would require updating proxy information on all our client machines.

> *We'll discuss the technical details in Chapter 3, as part of our overview of remoting. This problem is also discussed more thoroughly in my MSDN Online article covering the data portal concept at* *http://msdn.microsoft.com/columns/vbnet.asp.*

Instead, it would be ideal if there was one consistent entry point to the application server, so that we could simply export that proxy information to every client, and never have to worry about it again. This is exactly what the `DataPortal` class provides:

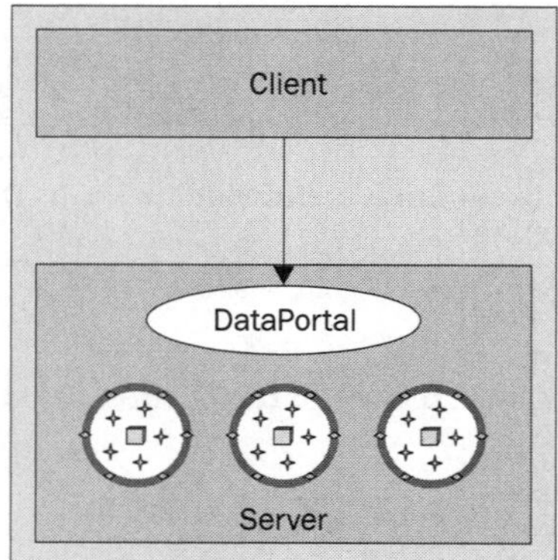

`DataPortal` provides a single point of entry and configuration for the server. It manages communication with our business objects while they are on the server running their data access code. Additionally, the data portal concept provides some other key benefits:

- Centralized security when calling the application server
- A consistent object persistence mechanism (all objects persist the same way)
- One point of control to toggle between running the data access code locally, or via remoting

The DataPortal class is designed in two parts. There's the part that supports business objects on the client side, and there's the part that actually handles data access. Depending on our configuration file settings, this second part might run on the client machine, or on an application server.

In this part of the chapter, we'll focus on the client-side DataPortal behavior. In the next section, where we discuss transactional and non-transactional data access, we'll cover the server-side portion of the data portal concept.

The client-side DataPortal is implemented as a class containing only Shared methods, which means that any Public methods it exposes become available to our code without the need to create a DataPortal object. The methods it provides are Create(), Fetch(), Update(), and Delete(). All four of these methods are used by editable business objects and editable collections, but our read-only objects and collections only use the Fetch() method.

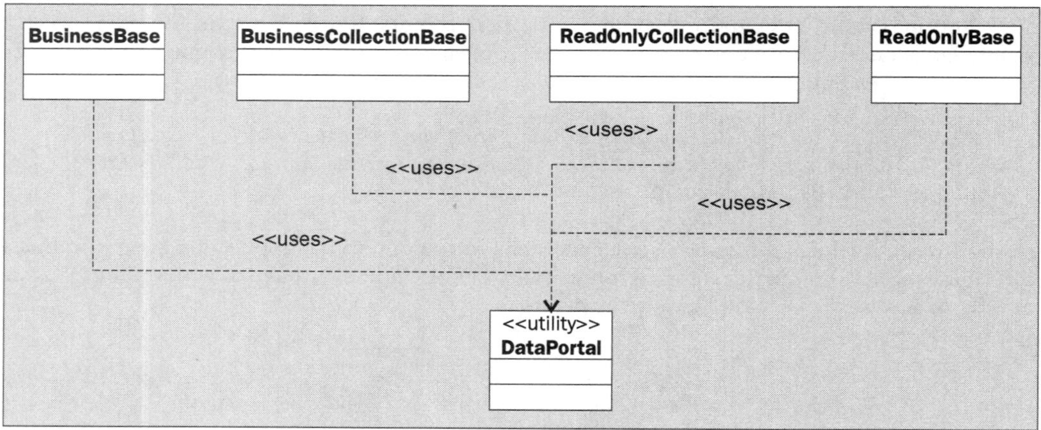

As we create our business objects, we'll implement code that uses DataPortal to retrieve and update our object's information.

The client-side DataPortal

The core of the client-side functionality resides in the client-side DataPortal class, which supports the key features of our data portal:

- Local or remote data access
- Table-based or Windows security
- Transactional and non-transactional data access

Let's discuss how each feature is supported.

Local or remote data access

When data access is requested (by calling the Create(), Fetch(), Update(), or Delete() methods), the client-side DataPortal checks the application's configuration file to see if the server-side DataPortal should be loaded locally (in-process), or remotely via .NET remoting.

If the server-side `DataPortal` is configured to be local, an instance of the server-side `DataPortal` object is created and used to process the data access method call. If the server-side `DataPortal` is configured to be remote, we use the `GetObject()` method of `System.Activator` to create an instance of the server-side `DataPortal` object on the server. Either way, the server-side `DataPortal` object is cached so that subsequent calls to retrieve or update data just use the object that has already been created.

> *The reality is that when the server-side* `DataPortal` *is on a remote server, we're only caching the client-side proxy. On the server, a new server-side* `DataPortal` *is created for each method call. This provides a high degree of isolation between calls, increasing the stability of our application. The server-side* `DataPortal` *will be configured as a* `SingleCall` *object in remoting.*

The powerful part of this is that the UI code *always* looks something like this:

```
Dim obj As Customer = Customer.GetCustomer(myID)
```

And the business object code *always* looks something like this:

```
Public Shared Function GetCustomer(ByVal ID As String) As Customer
  Return DataPortal.Fetch(New Criteria(ID))
End Function
```

Neither of these code snippets changes, regardless of whether we've configured the server-side `DataPortal` to run locally, or on a remote server. All that changes is the application's configuration file.

Table-based or Windows security

The client-side `DataPortal` also understands the table-based security mechanism in the business framework. We'll discuss this security model later in the chapter, but it's important to recognize that when table-based security is being used, the client-side `DataPortal` includes code to pass the user's identity information to the server along with each call.

Since we're passing our custom identity information to the server, the server-side `DataPortal` is able to configure the server environment to impersonate the user. This means that our business objects can check the user's identity and roles on both client *and* server, with assurance that both environments are the same.

If the application is configured to use Windows security, the `DataPortal` does not pass any security information. It is assumed in this case that we are using Windows' integrated security, and so Windows itself will take care of impersonating the user on the server. This requires that the server be configured to disallow anonymous access, forcing the user's security credentials to be used on the server as well as on the client.

Transactional or non-transactional data access

Finally, the client-side `DataPortal` has a part to play in handling transactional and non-transactional data access. We'll discuss this further as we cover the server-side `DataPortal` functionality, but the actual decision point as to whether transactional or non-transactional behavior is invoked occurs in the client-side `DataPortal` code.

The business framework defines a custom attribute named `TransactionalAttribute` that can be applied to methods within our business objects. Specifically, it can be applied to any of the four data access methods that our business object might implement to create, fetch, update, or delete data. This means that in our business object, we may have an update method (overriding the one in `BusinessBase`) marked as being `<Transactional()>`:

```
<Transactional()> _
Protected Overrides Sub DataPortal_Update()

  ' Data update code goes here
End Sub
```

At the same time, we might have a fetch method in the same class that's *not* transactional:

```
Protected Overrides Sub DataPortal_Fetch(ByVal Criteria As Object)

  ' Data retrieval code goes here
End Sub
```

This facility means that we can control transactional behavior at the method level, rather than at the class level. This is a powerful feature, as it means that we can do our data retrieval outside of a transaction to get optimal performance, and still do our updates within the context of a transaction to ensure data integrity.

The client-side `DataPortal` examines the appropriate method on our business object before it invokes the server-side `DataPortal` object. If our method is marked as `<Transactional()>`, then the call is routed to the transactional version of the server-side object. Otherwise, it is routed to the non-transactional version:

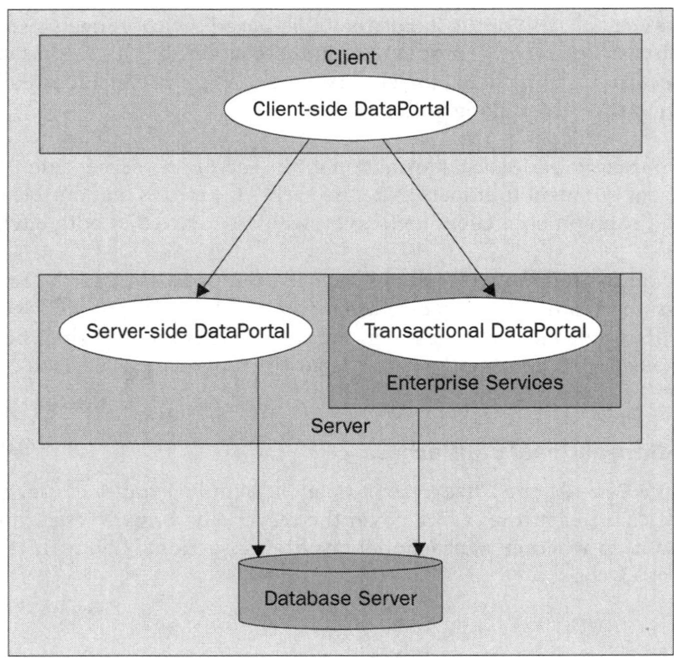

The server-side DataPortal

In the previous section, we discussed the behavior of the client-side `DataPortal`. This is the code that's invoked by our business objects as they create, fetch, update, or delete themselves. However, the client-side `DataPortal` is merely a front-end that routes all data access calls to the server-side `DataPortal` object.

> *I say 'server-side' here, but keep in mind that the server-side `DataPortal` object may run either on the client workstation, or on a remote server. Refer to the previous section for a discussion on how this selection is made.*

There are actually two different server-side `DataPortal` objects. One is designed as a normal .NET class, while the other is a serviced component, which means that it runs within Enterprise Services (otherwise known as COM+).

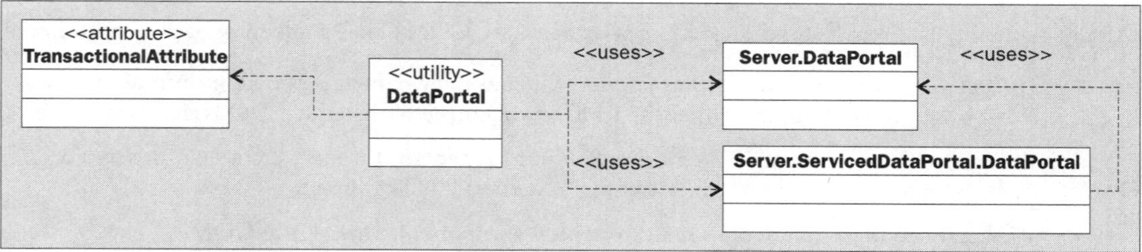

The client-side `DataPortal` examines the methods of our business object to see if they are marked as `<Transactional()>`. When the client-side `DataPortal`'s `Fetch()` method is called, it checks our business object's `DataPortal_Fetch()` method; when the `Update()` method is called, it checks our business object's `DataPortal_Update()` method; and so forth. Based on the presence or absence of the `<Transactional()>` attribute, the client-side `DataPortal` routes the method call to either the transactional or the non-transactional server-side `DataPortal`.

Transactional or non-transactional

If our business object's method is *not* marked as `<Transactional()>`, then the client-side `DataPortal` calls the corresponding method on our server-side `DataPortal` object. The object itself can be installed on a server and exposed via remoting as a `SingleCall` object. This means that each method call to the object results in remoting creating a new server-side `DataPortal` object to run that method.

If our business object's method *is* marked as `<Transactional()>`, then the client-side `DataPortal` calls the corresponding method on our *transactional* server-side `DataPortal`, which we'll call `ServicedDataPortal`. `ServicedDataPortal` runs in Enterprise Services and is marked as requiring a COM+ transaction, so any data access will be protected by a two-phase distributed transaction.

`ServicedDataPortal` uses the `<AutoComplete()>` attribute (which we'll discuss in Chapter 3) for its methods, so any data access is assumed to complete successfully, unless an error is raised. This simplifies the process of writing the data access code in our business objects. If they succeed, then great: the changes will be committed. To indicate failure, all we need to do is raise an error, and the transaction will be automatically rolled back by COM+.

The ServicedDataPortal itself is just a shell that's used to force our code to run within a transactional context. It includes the same four methods as the client-side DataPortal – all of which are marked with the <AutoComplete()> attribute, as noted above – but the code in each method merely delegates the method call to a regular, server-side DataPortal object.

This regular, server-side DataPortal object is automatically loaded into the same process, application domain, and COM+ context as the ServicedDataPortal object. This means that it will run within the context of the transaction, as will any business object code that it invokes. We only have one component to install physically into COM+, and yet all of our components end up being protected by transactions!

The flexibility we provide by doing this is tremendous. We can create applications that don't require COM+ in any way by avoiding the use of the <Transactional()> attribute on any of our data access methods. Alternatively, we can *always* use COM+ transactions by putting the <Transactional()> attribute on all our data access methods. Or we can produce a hybrid where some methods use two-phase distributed transactions in COM+, and some don't.

All this flexibility is important, because Enterprise Services (COM+) has some drawbacks. Most notably:

- Using two-phase distributed transactions will cause our data access code to run about 50% slower than if we'd implemented the transactions directly through ADO.NET
- Enterprise Services requires Windows 2000 or higher, so if we use COM+, our data access code can only run on a machine running Windows 2000 or higher
- We can't use no-touch deployment to deploy components that run in COM+

On the other hand, if we're updating two or more databases and we need those updates to be transactional, then we really need COM+ to make that possible. Also, if we run our data access code in COM+, we don't need to 'begin', 'commit' or 'roll back' our transactions manually using ADO.NET.

Criteria objects

Before we discuss the design of the server-side DataPortal object any further, we need to explore the mechanism that we'll be using to identify our business objects when we want to create, retrieve, or delete an object.

It is impossible to predict ahead of time all the possible criteria that might be used to identify all the possible business objects we'll ever create. Some objects might be identified by an integer, others by a string, others by a GUID, and so on. Others may require multiple parameters, and others still may have variable numbers of parameters. The permutations are almost endless.

Rather than expecting to be able to define Fetch() methods with all the possible permutations of parameters for selecting an object, we'll define a Fetch() method that accepts a single parameter. This parameter will be a Criteria object, consisting of the fields required to identify our specific business object. This means that for each of our business objects, we'll define a Criteria object that will contain specific data that's meaningful when selecting that particular object.

Having to create a Criteria class for each business object is a bit of an imposition on the business developer, but one way or another the business developer *must* pass a set of criteria data to the server in order to retrieve data for an object. Doing it via parameters on the Fetch() method is impractical, because we can't predict the number or types of the parameters – we'd have to implement a Fetch() method interface using a parameter array, or accepting an arbitrary array of values. Neither of these approaches provides a strongly typed way of getting the criteria data to the server.

Another approach would be to use the object itself as criteria – a kind of query-by-example (QBE) scheme. The problem here is that we'd have to create an instance of the whole business object on the client, populate some of its properties with data and then send the whole object to the server. Given that we typically only need to send one or two fields of data as criteria, this would be incredibly wasteful – especially if our business object has many fields that *aren't* criteria.

Typically then, a `Criteria` class will be a very simple class containing the variables that act as criteria, and a constructor that makes it easy to set their values. A pretty standard one might look something like this:

```
<Serializable()> _
Public Class Criteria

  Public SSN As String

  Public Sub New(ByVal SSN As String)
    Me.SSN = SSN
  End Sub

End Class
```

We can easily create and pass a `Criteria` object any time that we need to retrieve or delete a business object. This allows us to create a generic interface for retrieving objects, since all our retrieval methods can simply require a single parameter through which the `Criteria` object will be passed. At the same time, we have near-infinite options as to what the actual criteria might be for any given object.

There is another problem lurking in here, though. If we have a generic `DataPortal` that we call to retrieve an object, and if it only accepts a single `Criteria` object as a parameter, how does the `DataPortal` know which *type* of business object to load with data? How does the server-side `DataPortal` know which particular business class contains the code for the object we are trying to retrieve? We could pass the assembly and name of our business class as data elements within the `Criteria` object, or we could use custom attributes to provide the assembly and class name, but in fact there's a simpler way.

If we *nest* the `Criteria` class within our business object's class, then the `DataPortal` can use reflection to determine the business object class by examining the `Criteria` object. This takes advantage of existing .NET technologies, allowing us to use those, rather than developing our own mechanism to tell the `DataPortal` the type of business object we need. For instance:

```
<Serializable()> _
Public Class Employee
  Inherits BusinessBase

  <Serializable()> _
  Friend Class Criteria

    Public SSN As String

    Public Sub New(ByVal SSN As String)
      Me.SSN = SSN
    End Sub

  End Class

End Class
```

Now when the `Criteria` object is passed to our `DataPortal` to retrieve an `Employee` object, the server-side `DataPortal` code can simply use reflection to determine the class within which the `Criteria` class is nested. We can then create and populate an instance of that outer class (`Employee` in this case) with data from the database, based on the criteria information in the `Criteria` object.

To do this, the server-side `DataPortal` will use reflection to ask the `Criteria` object for the type information (assembly name and class name) of the class it is nested within. Given the assembly and class names of the outer class, the server-side `DataPortal` code can use reflection to create an instance of that class, and it can then use reflection on that object to invoke its `DataPortal_Fetch()` method.

Note that the `Criteria` class is scoped as `Friend`. The only code that creates or uses this class is the business object within which the class is nested, and our framework's `DataPortal` code. Since the `DataPortal` code will only interact with the `Criteria` class via reflection, scope is not an issue. By scoping the class as `Friend`, we reduce the number of classes the UI developer sees when looking at our business assembly, which makes our library of business classes easier to understand and use.

DataPortal behaviors

Regardless of whether we're within a transaction, the server-side `DataPortal` object performs a simple series of generic steps to get our business object to initialize, load, or update its data. The code for doing this, however, is a bit tricky, as it requires the use of reflection to create objects and invoke methods that normally couldn't be created or invoked.

In a sense, we're cheating by using reflection. A more 'pure' OO approach might be to expose a set of `Public` methods that the server-side `DataPortal` can use to interact with our object. While this might be great in some ideal world, we mustn't forget that those same `Public` methods would also then be available to the UI developer, even though they aren't intended for use by the UI. At best, this would lead to some possible confusion as the UI developer learned to ignore those methods. At worst, the UI developer might find ways to misuse those methods – either accidentally or on purpose. Because of this, we're using reflection so that we can invoke these methods privately, without exposing them to the UI developer, or any other code besides the server-side `DataPortal` for which they are intended.

Fortunately, our architecture allows this complex code to be isolated into the `DataPortal` class. It exists in just one place in our framework, and no business object developer should ever have to look at or deal with it.

Security

Before we cover the specifics of each of the four data access operations, we need to discuss security. As we stated earlier, the business framework will support either table-based or Windows' integrated security.

If we're using Windows' integrated security, the framework code totally ignores security concerns, expecting that we've configured our Windows environment and network appropriately. One key assumption here is that if our server-side `DataPortal` is being accessed via remoting, then IIS will be configured to disallow anonymous access to the web site that's hosting `DataPortal`, thus forcing Windows' integrated security to be active. Of course, this means that all users must have Windows accounts on the server, or in the NT domain to which the server belongs.

> *This also implies that we are dictating that IIS be used to host the server-side* `DataPortal` *if we are running it on a remote server. In fact, IIS is only* required *if we need to use Windows security. If we're using table-based security, it's possible to write a Windows service to host the* `DataPortal` *– but even in that case, IIS is recommended as a host because it is easier to configure and manage. We'll discuss remoting host options a bit more in Chapter 3.*

We might instead opt to use the business framework's custom, table-based security, which we'll discuss in detail later in this chapter. In that case, the client-side `DataPortal` will pass our custom security object for the current user as a parameter to the server-side `DataPortal` object. The first thing the server-side `DataPortal` object does then is to make this security object the current security object for the server-side thread on which the object is running.

The result of this is that our server-side code will always be using the same security object as the client-side code. Our business objects, in particular, will have access to the same user identity and list of roles on both client and server. Because of this, our business logic can use the same standard security and role checks regardless of where the code is running.

Create

The 'create' operation is intended to allow our business objects to load themselves with values that must come from the database. Business objects don't need to support or use this capability, but if they do need to initialize default values, then this is the mechanism to use.

There are many types of application where this is important. For instance, order entry applications typically have extensive defaulting of values based on the customer. Inventory management applications often have many default values for specific parts, based on the product family to which the part belongs. And medical records too often have defaults based on the patient and physician involved.

When the `Create()` method of the `DataPortal` is invoked, it is passed a `Criteria` object. As we've explained, the `DataPortal` will use reflection against the `Criteria` object to find out the class within which it is nested. Using that information, the `DataPortal` will then use reflection to create an instance of the business object itself. However, this is a bit tricky, since all our business objects will have `Private` constructors to prevent direct creation by the UI developer:

```
<Serializable()> _
Public Class Employee
  Inherits BusinessBase

  <Serializable()> _
  Friend Class Criteria

    Public SSN As String

    Public Sub New(ByVal SSN As String)
      Me.SSN = SSN
    End Sub

  End Class

  Private Sub New()
    ' Prevent direct creation
  End Sub

End Class
```

To fix this, our business objects will expose `Shared` methods to create or retrieve objects, and those `Shared` methods will invoke the `DataPortal`. (We discussed this 'class in charge' concept earlier in the chapter.) As an example, our `Employee` class may have a `Shared` factory method such as:

```
Public Shared Function NewEmployee() As Employee
  Return DataPortal.Create(New Criteria(""))
End Function
```

Notice that no `Employee` object is created on the client here. Instead, we ask the client-side `DataPortal` for the `Employee` object. The client-side `DataPortal` passes the call to the server-side `DataPortal`, so the business object is created on the server. Even though our business class only has a `Private` constructor, the server-side `DataPortal` uses reflection to create an instance of the class.

Again, we're 'cheating' by using reflection to create the object, even though it only has a `Private` constructor. However, the alternative is to make the constructor `Public` – in which case the UI developer will need to learn and remember that they must use the `Shared` factory methods to create the object. By making the constructor `Private`, we provide a clear and direct reminder that the UI developer *must* use the `Shared` factory method, thus reducing the complexity of the interface for the UI developer.

Once the business object has been created, the server-side `DataPortal` will call the business object's `DataPortal_Create()` method, passing the `Criteria` object as a parameter. At this point, we're executing code *inside* the business object, so the business object can do any initialization that's appropriate for a new object. Typically, this will involve going to the database to retrieve any configurable default values.

When the business object is done loading its defaults, the server-side `DataPortal` will return the fully created business object back to the client-side `DataPortal`. If the two are running on the same machine, this is a simple object reference; but if they are configured to run on separate machines, then the business object is automatically serialized across the network to the client (that is, it's passed by value), so the client machine ends up with a local copy of the business object.

The following UML sequence diagram illustrates this process:

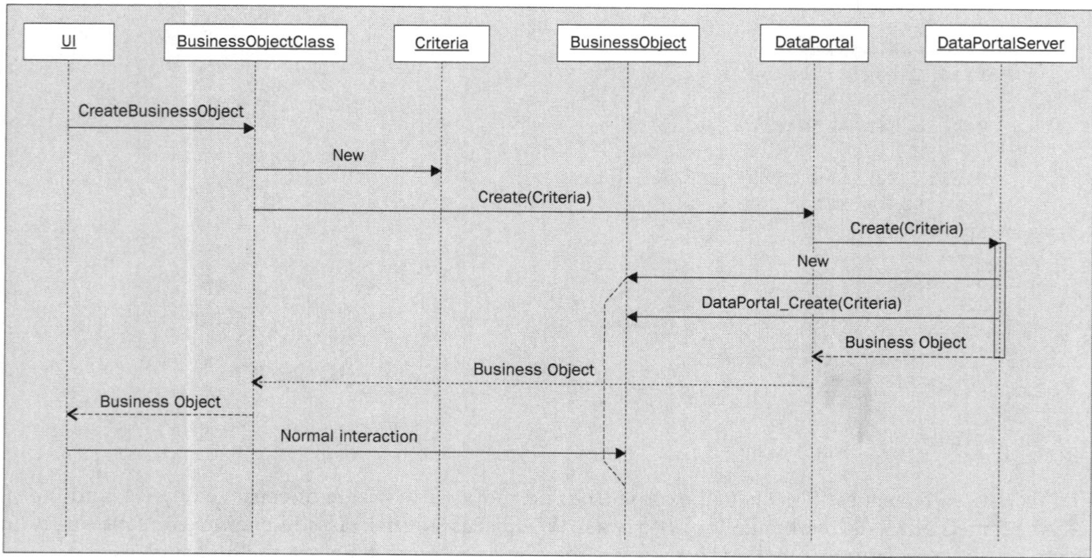

Here, you can see how the UI interacts with the business object *class* (the `Shared` factory method), which then creates a `Criteria` object and passes it to the client-side `DataPortal`. The `DataPortal` then delegates the call to the server-side `DataPortal` (which may be running locally or remotely, depending on configuration). The server-side `DataPortal` then creates an instance of the business *object* itself, and calls the business object's `DataPortal_Create()` method so it can populate itself with default values. The resulting business object is then returned ultimately to the UI.

In a physical n-tier configuration, remember that the `Criteria` object starts out on the client machine, and is passed by value to the application server. The business object itself is created on the application server, where it is populated with default values. It is then passed back to the client machine by value. Through this architecture we are truly taking advantage of distributed object concepts.

Fetch

Retrieving a pre-existing object is very similar to the creation process we just discussed. Again, we make use of the `Criteria` object to provide the data that will be used by our object to find its information in the database. The `Criteria` class is nested within the business object class, so the generic server-side `DataPortal` code can determine the type of business object we want, and then use reflection to create an instance of the class.

The following UML sequence diagram illustrates all of this:

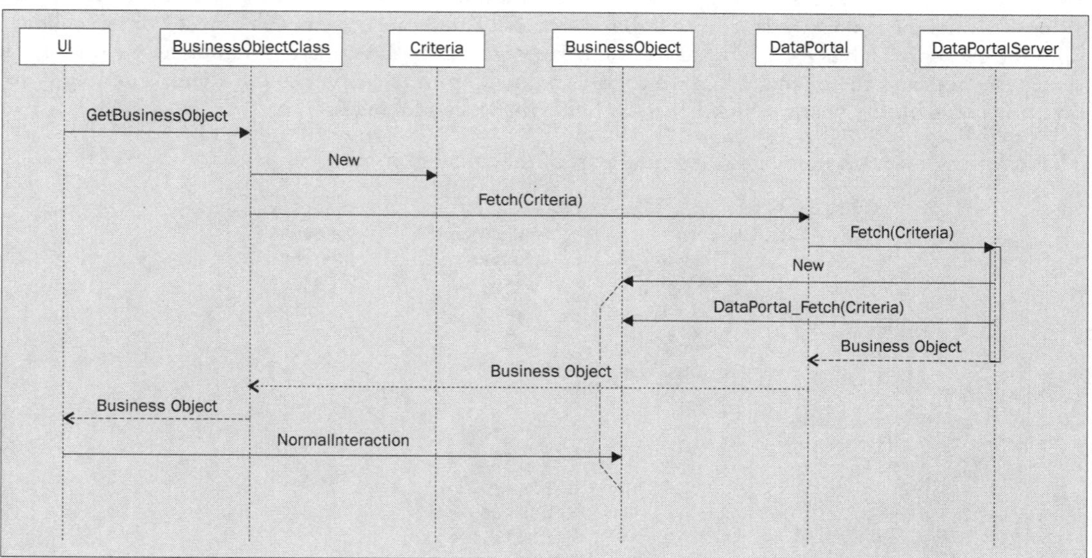

Here, the UI interacts with the business object class, which in turn creates a `Criteria` object and passes it to the client-side `DataPortal` code. The client-side `DataPortal` determines whether the server-side `DataPortal` should run locally or remotely, and then delegates the call to the server-side `DataPortal`.

The server-side `DataPortal` uses reflection to determine the assembly and type name for the business class and creates the business object itself. After that, it calls the business object's `DataPortal_Fetch()` method, passing the `Criteria` object as a parameter. Once the business object has populated itself from the database, the server-side `DataPortal` returns the fully populated business object to the UI.

As with the create process, in an n-tier physical configuration, the `Criteria` object and business object move by value across the network, as required. We don't have to do anything special beyond marking the classes as `<Serializable()>` – the .NET runtime handles all the details on our behalf.

Update

The update process is a bit different from what we've seen so far. In this case, the UI already has a business object with which the user has been interacting, and we want this object to save its data into the database. To achieve this, our business object has a `Save()` method (as part of the `BusinessBase` class from which all business objects inherit). The `Save()` method calls the `DataPortal` to do the update, passing the business object itself, `Me`, as a parameter.

The thing to remember when doing updates is that the object's data might change as a result of the update process (the most common scenario for this is that a new object might have its primary key value assigned by the database at the same time as its data is inserted into the database). This newly created key value must be placed back into the object.

This means that the update process is *bi-directional*. It isn't just a matter of sending the data to the server to be stored, but also a matter of returning the object *from* the server after the update has completed, so that the UI has a current, valid version of the object.

Due to the way .NET passes objects by value, this introduces a bit of a wrinkle into our overall process. When we pass our object to the server to be saved, .NET makes a copy of the object from the client onto the server, which is exactly what we want. However, after the update is complete, we want to return the object to the client. When we return an object from the server to the client, a new copy of the object is made on the client, which is *not* the behavior we're looking for.

The following diagram illustrates the initial part of the update process:

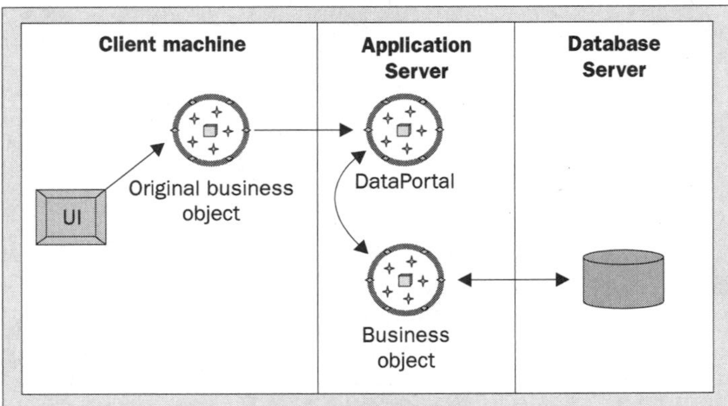

The UI has a reference to our business object, and calls its `Save()` method. This causes the business object to ask the `DataPortal` to save the object. The result is that a copy of the business object is made on the application server, where it can save itself to the database. So far, this is pretty straightforward.

> *Note that our business object has a `Save()` method, while the `DataPortal` infrastructure has methods named `Update()`. While this is a bit inconsistent, remember that the business object is being called by UI developers, and I have found that it is more intuitive for the typical UI developer to call `Save()` than `Update()`.*

However, once this part is done, the updated business object is returned to the client, and the UI must update its references to use the *newly updated* object instead:

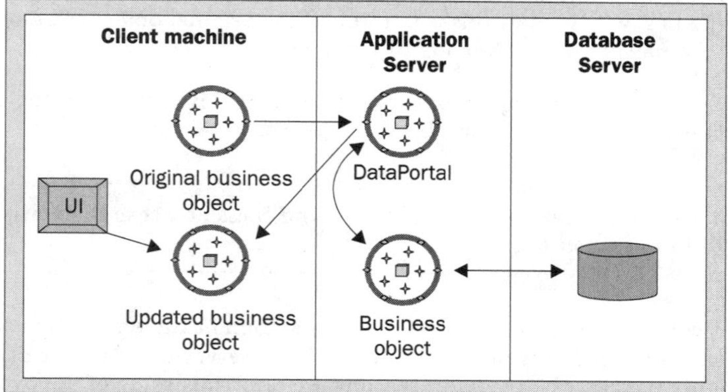

This is fine too, but it's important to keep in mind that we can't continue to use the old business object – we must update our references to use the newly updated object. The following UML sequence diagram illustrates the overall update process:

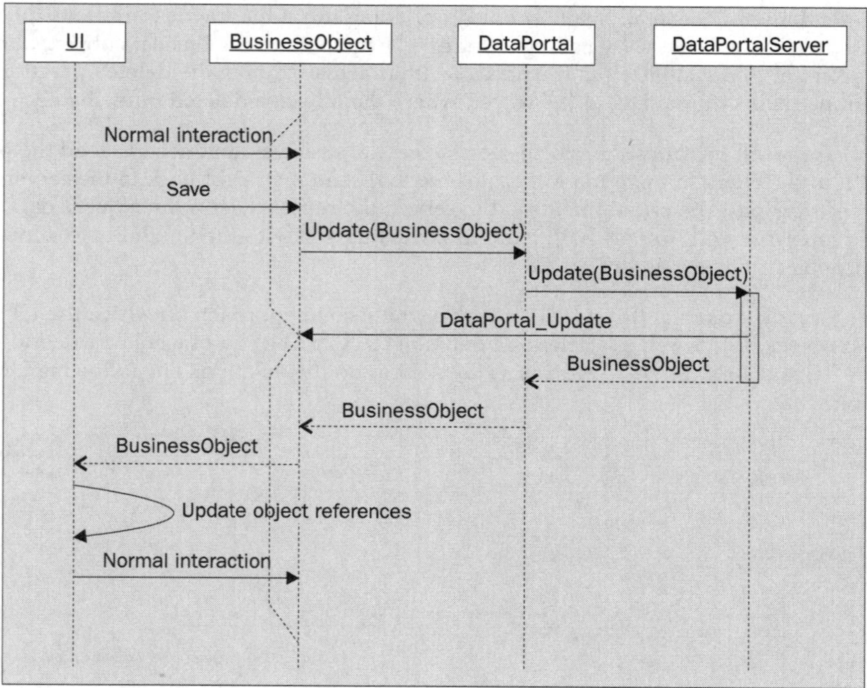

Here, we can see how the UI calls the `Save()` method on the business object, which causes the latter to call the `DataPortal`'s `Update()` method, passing itself as a parameter. As usual, the client-side `DataPortal` determines whether the server-side `DataPortal` is running locally or remotely, and then delegates the call to the server-side `DataPortal`.

The server-side DataPortal then simply calls the DataPortal_Update() method on the business object, so the object can save its data into the database. At this point, we have two versions of the business object: the original version on the client, and the newly updated version on the application server. However, the best way to view this is to think of the original object as being obsolete and invalid at this point. Only the newly updated version of the object is valid.

Once the update is done, the new version of the business object is returned to the UI; the UI can then continue to interact with the new business object as needed.

> **The UI must update any references from the old business object to the newly updated business object at this point.**

In a physical n-tier configuration, the business object is automatically passed by value to the server, and the updated version is returned by value to the client. If the server-side DataPortal is running locally, however, we're simply passing object references, and we don't incur any of the overhead of serialization and so forth.

Delete

The final operation, and probably the simplest, is to delete an object from the database – although by the time we're done, we'll actually have two ways of doing this. One way is to retrieve the object from the database, mark it as deleted by calling a Delete() method on the business object, and then calling Save() to cause it to update itself to the database (thus actually doing the delete operation). The other way is to simply pass criteria data to the server, where the object is deleted immediately.

This second approach provides superior performance, because we don't need to load the object's data and return it to the client, only to mark it as deleted and send it straight back to the server again. Instead, we simply pass the criteria fields to the server, the server deletes the object's data, and we're done. Our framework will support both models, providing you with the flexibility to allow either or both in your object models, as you see fit.

Since we've already looked at Save(), let's look at the second approach, in which the UI simply calls the business object class to request deletion of an object. A Criteria object is created to describe the object to be deleted, and the DataPortal is invoked to do the deletion. The following UML diagram illustrates this:

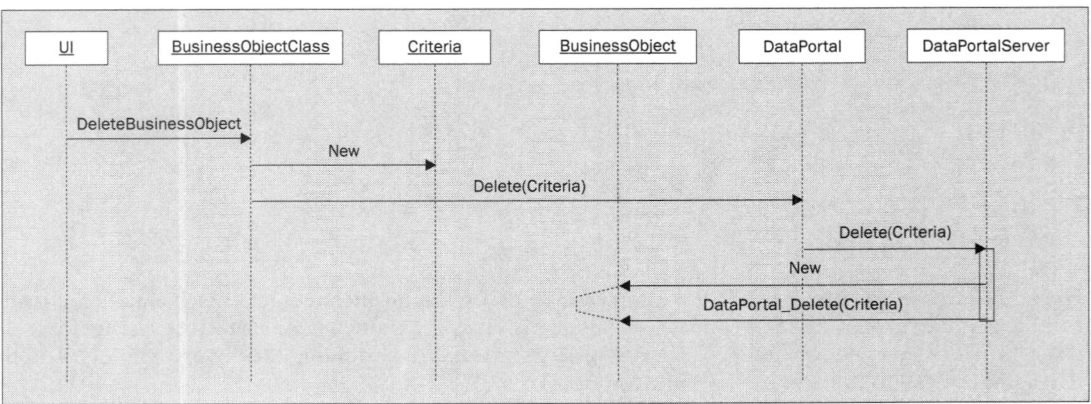

Since the data has been deleted at this point, we have nothing to return to the UI, so the overall process remains pretty straightforward. As usual, the client-side `DataPortal` delegates the call to the server-side `DataPortal`. The server-side `DataPortal` creates an instance of our business object and invokes its `DataPortal_Delete()` method, providing the `Criteria` object as a parameter. The business logic to do the deletion itself is encapsulated within the business object, along with all the other business logic relating to the object.

Table-based security

As we discussed earlier in the chapter, many environments include users who are not part of an integrated Windows domain or Active Directory. In such a case, relying on Windows' integrated security for our application is problematic at best, and we are left to implement our own security scheme. Fortunately, the .NET Framework includes several security concepts, along with the ability to customize them to implement our own security as needed.

Custom principal and identity objects

As you may know (and as we'll discuss in detail in the next chapter), the .NET Framework includes a couple of built-in **principal** and **identity** objects that support Windows' integrated security or generic security. We can also create our own principal and identity objects by creating classes that implement the `IPrincipal` and `IIdentity`. That is exactly what we'll do to implement our table-based security model. This is illustrated in the following UML diagram:

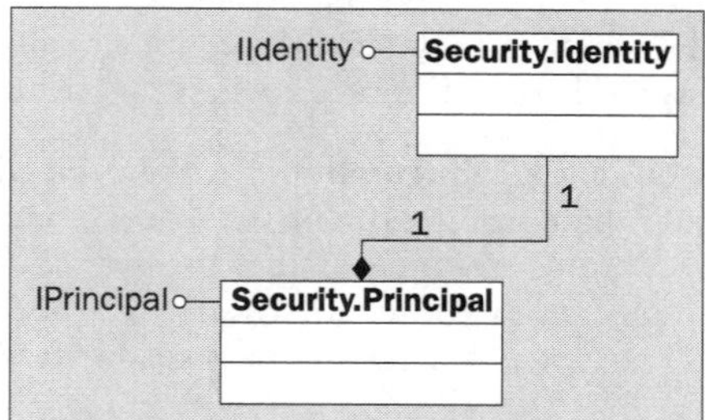

What we have here is a containment relationship, where the principal object contains an identity object. The principal object relies on the underlying identity object to obtain the user's identity. In many cases, the user's identity will incorporate the list of groups or roles to which the user belongs.

The .NET Framework includes `GenericPrincipal` and `GenericIdentity` classes that serve much the same purpose. However, by creating our own classes, we can directly incorporate them into our framework. In particular, our `BusinessIdentity` object will derive from `ReadOnlyBase`, and thus can be loaded with data via the `DataPortal` mechanism just like any other business object.

Using DataPortal

In our implementation, we'll be making the identity object derive from `ReadOnlyBase`, so it will be a read-only business object that can be retrieved from the database using the normal `DataPortal` mechanism we discussed earlier in the chapter. This relationship is shown in the following diagram:

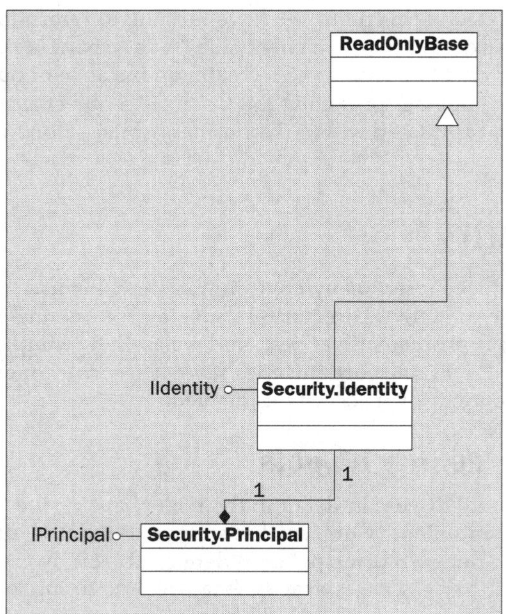

Our framework will support the use of either this table-based security model, or Windows' integrated model, as provided by the .NET Framework. The choice of models can be made by altering the application's configuration file, as we'll see in Chapter 7 when we start to implement our business objects.

If the table-based model is chosen in the configuration file, then the UI must log into our application before any business objects (other than our identity object) can be retrieved from the `DataPortal`. In other words, the `DataPortal` will refuse to operate until the user has been authenticated by retrieving an identity object. This is accomplished by calling a `Login()` method that we'll implement in our principal class. This method will accept a user ID and password that will be verified against a table in the database.

> *The model we're implementing in this book is overly simplistic. This is intentional, as it will allow for easy adaptation into your specific environment, whether that be table-based, encrypted, LDAP-based, or using any other back-end store for user ID and password information.*

Integration with our application

Once the login process is complete, the main UI thread will have our custom principal and identity objects as its security context. From that point forward, the UI code and our business object code can make use of the thread's security context to check the user's identity and roles, just as we would if we were using Windows' integrated security. Our custom security objects integrate directly into the .NET Framework, allowing us to employ normal .NET programming techniques.

Additionally, the principal and identity objects will be passed from the client-side `DataPortal` to the server-side `DataPortal` any time we create, retrieve, update, or delete objects. This allows the server-side `DataPortal` and our server-side objects all to run within the same security context as the UI and client-side business objects. Ultimately, we have a seamless security context for our application code, regardless of whether it is running on the client or server.

Namespace organization

At this point, we've walked through all the classes that will make up our business framework. Shortly, we'll discuss how to group them into components or assemblies, but first we should give some thought to the use of **namespaces**.

Namespaces allow us to group classes together in meaningful ways so that we can program against them more easily. Additionally, namespaces allow us to have different classes with the same name, as long as they are in different groups. From a business perspective, we might use a scheme like the following:

```
MyCompany.MyApplication.FunctionalArea.Class
```

A convention like this immediately tells us that the class belongs to a specific functional area within an application and organization. It also means that we could have multiple classes with the same names:

```
MyCompany.MyApplication.Sales.Product
MyCompany.MyApplication.Manufacturing.Product
```

It's quite likely that the concept of a 'product' in sales is different from that in manufacturing, and this approach allows us easily to reuse class names to make each part of our application as clear and self-documenting as possible.

The same is true when you're building a framework. We want to group our classes in meaningful ways so that they're comprehensible to the end developer. Additionally, we want to help the end developer by putting little-used or obscure classes in separate namespaces, so the business developer doesn't typically see them via IntelliSense.

Consider our `UndoableBase` class, which is not intended for use by a business developer – it exists for use within our framework. Ideally, when a business developer is working with our framework, they won't see `UndoableBase` via IntelliSense unless they go looking for it by specifically navigating to the namespace where we put it. To accomplish this, we can have some namespaces that are to be used by end developers, and others that are intended for internal use.

We'll prefix all our namespaces with `CSLA`, for **Component-based Scalable Logical Architecture**.

CSLA was the name of the COM-based business object framework about which I wrote in the mid to late 90s. In many ways, this book is an attempt to bring the basic concepts and capabilities of that architecture into the .NET environment. In fact, .NET enables the CSLA concepts, while COM often hindered them.

Our core objects – the ones intended for use by business developers – will go into the `CSLA` namespace itself:

```
CSLA.NotUndoableAttribute
CSLA.BusinessBase
CSLA.BrokenRules
CSLA.RulesCollection
CSLA.Rule data type
CSLA.BusinessCollectionBase
CSLA.ReadOnlyBase
CSLA.ReadOnlyCollectionBase
CSLA.DataPortal
CSLA.TransactionalAttribute
CSLA.NameValueList
CSLA.SmartDate
CSLA.SafeSqlDataReader
```

The `UndoableBase` class, which is for internal use only, will go into a separate namespace that won't typically be imported by business developers. This is also true of the `BindableBase` and `BindableCollectionBase` classes, which are primarily for internal use and shouldn't clutter the day-to-day coding of business developers:

```
CSLA.Core.UndoableBase
CSLA.Core.BindableBase
CSLA.Core.BindableCollectionBase
```

Following the lead of the .NET Framework itself, we'll group our security-related classes into their own namespace. This is useful because the business developer might choose to use Windows' integrated security rather than our custom security, and this approach means they'll only see these classes if they import this specific namespace:

```
CSLA.Security.Principal
CSLA.Security.Identity
```

Notice that we already have the client-side `DataPortal` class in the `CSLA` namespace, which makes sense since it's the client-side `DataPortal` that will be used by business developers. However, we've got two other `DataPortal` concepts that are used *within* our framework: the server-side `DataPortal`, and the transactional, serviced `DataPortal`. Here's where the ability to have duplicate names in different namespaces is ideal. We'll create namespaces for the server-side `DataPortal` classes to indicate their use:

```
CSLA.Server.DataPortal
CSLA.Server.ServicedDataPortal.DataPortal
```

The client-side `DataPortal` will use these two namespaces so that it can correctly invoke the transactional or non-transactional version of the `DataPortal` as appropriate.

The end result is that a typical business developer can simply import the `CSLA` namespace:

```
Imports CSLA
```

And all they'll see are the classes intended for use during business development. All the other classes and concepts within the framework are located in other namespaces, and therefore won't appear in IntelliSense by default unless the developer specifically imports those namespaces as well. If we're using the custom table-based security, we'll likely import the `CSLA.Security` namespace. But if we're not using that feature, we can ignore those classes and they won't clutter up our development experience.

Component design

Now that we've seen the overall design, and the classes that will comprise our business framework, we need to decide how to break them into components or assemblies. The framework will consist of a set of DLLs that can be referenced as we build our business objects and applications. The questions are: How do we decide how many DLLs (assemblies) there should be, and what should go into each?

The thing to remember about an assembly is that it is a *unit of deployment*. We can't deploy classes or objects; we can only deploy assemblies. Equally, *everything* in an assembly gets deployed – we don't get to pick and choose.

Due to the various physical configurations we want to support, we know that we have several deployment requirements. The server-side `DataPortal`, for instance, needs to have the option of being installed on a client or on an application server. The `BusinessBase` class needs to reside anywhere that business objects will be running – typically on both client *and* application server. The `ServicedDataPortal` runs in Enterprise Services, and can only be deployed on machines where COM+ exists (Windows 2000 or higher).

> *I understand that there are some hacks you can use to get Enterprise Services code to run in MTS under Windows NT 4.0. This is not supported by Microsoft, and may not work with future versions of the .NET Framework, so if you choose to pursue such a route you are on your own. I certainly don't recommend such a course of action.*

Also, a given assembly can only contain code from a single programming language. We have a couple classes that must be constructed in C#, so they will obviously end up in a separate assembly from our VB.NET code. Let's break this down systematically by deployment requirements:

Deployment details	Class	Assembly
Client *or* server	server-side `DataPortal`	`CSLA.Server.DataPortal`
Enterprise services required	serviced `DataPortal`	`CSLA.Server.ServicedDataPortal`

Client *and* server	`NotUndoableAttribute`
	`Core.UndoableBase`
	`BusinessBase`
	`BrokenRules`
	`RulesCollection`
	`Rule` data type
	`BusinessCollectionBase`
	`ReadOnlyBase`
	`ReadOnlyCollectionBase`
	Client-side `DataPortal`
	`TransactionalAttribute`
	`Security.Pricipal`
	`Security.Identity`
	`NameValueList`
	`SmartDate`
	`SafeSqlDataReader`
		`CSLA`

C# required	`Core.BindableBase` `Core.BindableCollectionBase`	`CSLA.Core.BindableBase`

The following component diagram illustrates these components and their dependencies graphically:

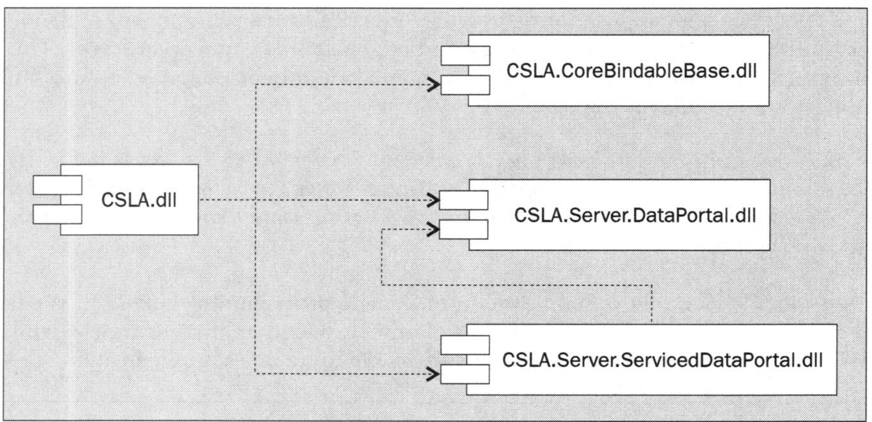

As you can see, `CSLA.dll` depends on all three of the other components. It contains classes that inherit from those in `CSLA.Core.BindableBase.dll` and which call into the server-side `DataPortal` components. Additionally, `CSLA.Server.ServicedDataPortal.dll` depends on `CSLA.Server.DataPortal.dll`, because our transactional `DataPortal` class makes use of the non-transactional server-side `DataPortal` class.

In Chapter 4, we'll implement the `CSLA` and `CSLA.Core.BindableBase` assemblies. In Chapter 5, we'll implement the `CSLA.Server.DataPortal` and `CSLA.Server.ServicedDataPortal` assemblies, along with a `DataPortal` web project that will act as the remoting host on our application server.

Conclusion

In this chapter, we've examined some of the key design goals for the business framework – **CSLA .NET** – that we'll be building in Chapters 4 and 5. These include:

- n-Level undo capability
- Tracking broken business rules to tell if our object is valid
- Tracking whether our object's data has changed (is it 'dirty')
- Support for strongly typed collections of child objects
- Providing a simple and abstract model for the UI developer
- Full support for data binding in both Windows and Web Forms
- Saving our objects to a database and getting them back again
- Table-driven security
- Other miscellaneous features

We've also walked through the design of the framework itself, providing a high-level glimpse into the purpose and rationale behind each of the classes that will make it up. With each class, we discussed how it relates back to our key goals to provide the features and capabilities we're looking for in the framework.

Finally, we wrapped up the chapter by organizing our classes into namespaces so they are easily understood and used, and we determined how to group them into components or assemblies to avoid circular dependencies and to enable the physical deployment scenarios we're after.

In Chapter 4, we'll implement much of the framework, and then in Chapter 5, we'll implement the rest. From there, we'll walk through the implementation of a sample application using the framework, during which process we'll more fully explore how the framework functions and meets the goals we set forth in this chapter. Before then, in Chapter 3, we'll take a quick tour of some of the .NET technologies that we've mentioned already, but with which you may not be entirely familiar.

CHAPTER 3

3

Key technologies

In Chapters 1 and 2, we've discussed some concepts of distributed, object-oriented architecture, and the specific architecture that we'll be implementing in this book. In Chapter 2, we also designed a framework to support our n-tier architecture.

The framework that we designed in Chapter 2 relies on some key technologies in the .NET Framework. These technologies are the building blocks necessary to implement web and client-server applications, to interact with databases, to pass objects around the network, and more. In particular, we'll be tapping into some of the deeper capabilities of .NET, including:

- Remoting
- Serialization
- Enterprise Services (COM+)
- Reflection
- Attributes
- .NET role-based security
- ADO.NET

As we've been working through our explanations so far, I've assumed that you've known at least a little about these technologies – or at least that you could pick enough up from the context. As we move forward to implementation, however, it becomes more important that you're comfortable with using them, and that's the aim of this chapter. If you've not had much experience of any or all of the technologies in this list, you'll find what you need here.

Of course, most of the technologies have entire books devoted to them, and it would be impractical for us to cover them in great detail here. Instead, we'll focus on each technology as it pertains to the creation of our distributed, object-oriented framework. Feel free to pick and choose the sections you read, and to come back here if you need a quick reminder.

Later in the book, we'll be using interface-oriented .NET technologies as well, including Windows Forms, Web Forms, and web services. These technologies don't apply to our framework, but they are used to create applications based on the business objects that we'll create using our framework. We'll devote entire chapters to demonstrating how to create interfaces using each of these three technologies.

Remoting

The .NET Framework includes the **remoting** subsystem, which is the technology that allows .NET applications to interact with each other. (This includes both cross-process communication and communication across the network from machine to machine.) Remoting is also intended for use when creating client-server applications, as it enables efficient communication between the various tiers of an n-tier application. Furthermore, remoting enables distributed object architectures, since it's capable of passing unanchored objects across the network.

As we discussed in Chapters 1 and 2, we'll rely on the concepts of anchored and unanchored objects, and the ability of remoting to support them, as we create our framework.

Basic concepts

To understand remoting, we need to cover some basic concepts and terms. Remoting is all about allowing code running in one process to communicate with code running in a different process – even if that different process is on another machine across the network.

Technically, remoting enables communication between code running in two different scopes, which can mean different contexts, different application domains, different Windows processes, or different machines.

Remoting allows a client application to communicate with a server object running in a different process. To do this, the client has an **object proxy** that represents the server object. To the client, the proxy *is* the server object, but in reality the object proxy takes each client method call and uses remoting to route it through to the server, where the server object can process the request:

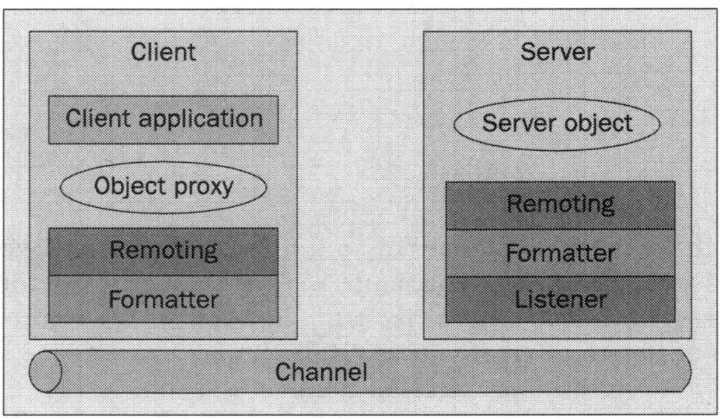

On the client, remoting invokes a **formatter object** to convert the method call and its parameters into a single blob of data that can be efficiently transferred to the server. Remoting then invokes a **channel object** that's responsible for physically transferring the blob of data to the server. The client-side channel contacts the server's remoting **listener object**, which accepts the blob of data and invokes the remoting subsystem on the server. The server-side remoting subsystem then invokes a formatter to unpack the blob back into meaningful data, including the method to be called and all its parameters. It then calls the actual server object's method, passing the parameter data.

Once the server object's method completes, remoting takes any return values from the method, packs them up using the formatter, and returns them to the client via the channel. On the client, the remoting subsystem uses the formatter to unpack the results and returns them to the proxy object. The proxy then returns the results to the client application. The end result is that the client application has the illusion that the object proxy *is* the server object.

Channels

So, to communicate between the two processes (or machines), the remoting subsystem in .NET uses a channel. In fact, .NET provides two channels: an HTTP channel, and a TCP channel. If required, it's also possible to create custom channels, though doing so is a far from trivial task.

Both built-in channels provide the same basic functionality, in that they allow remoting to send messages from the client to the server, and to retrieve any results from the server:

- The HTTP channel uses the standard HTTP protocol, so works it well with firewalls and proxy servers. However, it incurs more overhead than the TCP channel, because the message *header* data is in plain text.
- The TCP channel uses a proprietary binary message protocol that's smaller than the standard HTTP header. It's therefore faster, but it may have issues with firewalls and/or proxy servers.

While the TCP channel is slightly faster than the HTTP channel, the HTTP channel will work in more networking environments. As we'll see later in this section, the only way to use the TCP channel is to create our own remoting host application on the server. If we use IIS as the host, then HTTP is our only option. Using IIS as a host is often preferable, so the HTTP channel is the more commonly used of the two.

Note that the *body* of the message might be XML or binary, regardless of which channel we choose. How the body of the message is formatted is controlled by which formatter object we choose.

Formatters

The messages sent over a channel are formatted such that remoting can understand them at both ends of the connection. The .NET Framework provides two formatters: a SOAP/XML formatter, and a binary formatter. Again, it's possible to create our own formatters, though that too is non-trivial:

- The SOAP (Simple Object Access Protocol) formatter encodes the data into SOAP's XML format, so it's human-readable, but has a lot of overhead.
- The binary formatter encodes the data into a proprietary binary format that results in messages that are about 30% as big as those sent using the SOAP formatter. Also, encoding with the binary formatter is more efficient than converting the data into XML, so there's less overhead on both client and server.

The SOAP formatter is very nice for debugging during development, because we can navigate to our remoting service using a browser to see if it returns XML. For production deployment, however, the binary formatter is typically preferable, because it transfers so much less data across the network on each remoting call. Because of this, I typically *develop* using the SOAP formatter, and then switch to the binary formatter once I've got everything working properly.

Listener

The previous diagram shows a listener as part of the remoting process. The listener comes from the channel we choose, though, so while it's always involved, we don't have the option of choosing it.

Object proxies and location transparency

The last item from the diagram that we need to cover is the **object proxy**, the function of which is to allow the client to interact with an object that's anchored on the server. We'll be using this capability as we create our data portal mechanism.

One of our design goals for the data portal is that we should be able to switch between running the server-side data portal object in the local process on the client, or on a remote server. As mentioned in Chapter 2, this switch should be possible by simply changing a configuration file setting.

The reason why this is possible is that remoting supports the concept of **location transparency**, which means that when we write code on the client to invoke an object, the location of that object has no effect on the client code. Just by looking at the following (which you may remember from our "object in charge" discussion), it's impossible to tell whether `MyObject` is running in the local process, or on a remote server:

```
Dim objCust As New Customer()
objCust.DoSomething()
```

Thanks to location transparency, this code will work just fine whether `MyObject` is local or remote. This is very powerful, since it reduces the learning curve when we are working with remote objects – we use them just like we'd use a local object.

In order to *achieve* location transparency, the client needs information about the object it's going to interact with, and this is where the object proxy comes into play. The proxy looks just like the anchored server-side object, giving the code on the client the illusion that it's interacting with the remote object. The proxy takes care of interacting with the remoting subsystem to get each method call formatted and sent through the channel to the actual remote object.

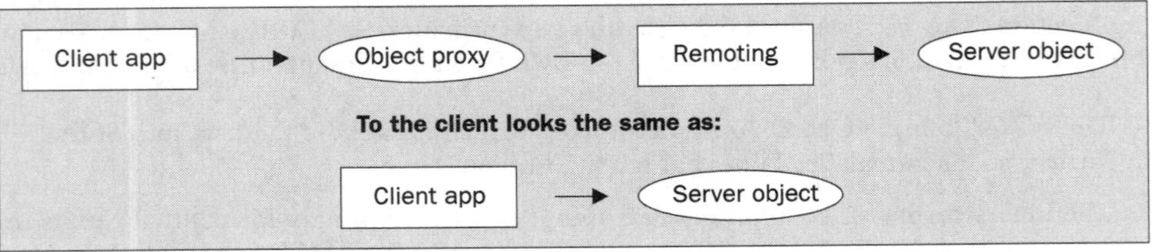

But how does the .NET runtime itself know how to find this remote object? Even if *our* code is unaware of the location of the object, .NET must know!

Remoting configuration

The discovery of remote objects is handled through remoting configuration. The remoting subsystem can be configured in two different ways: via an XML configuration file, or programmatically. On the server side, we configure remoting so that it knows which classes are to be made available to remote clients. On the client side, we configure remoting by identifying which classes are to be accessed remotely, along with the URL of the remoting server.

One very important side effect of this client-side approach is that if we *don't* configure a class to be remote, it will be invoked locally. This means that changing an application to use a local object rather than a remote object can be as simple as changing a configuration file on the client! We'll use this feature so that we can reconfigure our server-side data portal to run locally or remotely, without requiring any changes to UI or business logic code.

Remoting servers

Ultimately, a remoting server or host is just a program that exposes one or more classes so that they can be instantiated and used by other applications, via remoting. In most cases, the class will be in a DLL that was created by a class library project, though technically that's not essential. For the purposes of our discussion here, we'll assume that any such class *will* be in a DLL.

In Chapter 1, we discussed local, anchored, and unanchored objects. The following table summarizes these types:

Object Type	Availability	Creation
Local	Available only within the process where they are created	This is the default behavior
Anchored	Available via remoting, but the object always stays in the process where it was created	To create, inherit from `MarshalByRefObject`
Unanchored	Available via remoting, and the object will be copied across the network when passed as a parameter or returned as the result of a function	To create, use the `<Serializable()>` attribute and optionally also implement `ISerializable`

> *In the .NET documentation, an* anchored *object is referred to as an MBRO (marshal by reference object), and an* unanchored *object is referred to as an MBVO (marshal by value object). I find that such acronyms are not nearly as intuitive as the terms "anchored" and "unanchored", which is why we're avoiding the use of the acronyms in this book.*

The objects that run in a remoting server are *anchored* objects. This means that they inherit `MarshalByRefObject`, which makes them available to other applications via remoting, and ensures that they are anchored to the scope in which they are created – in this case, our remoting server process.

When we choose to run our server-side data portal on a remote server, we'll need to have some host application running on the server within which the data portal DLL is loaded. This is because all DLLs must be hosted in a process that's created by running some executable. There are two ways to create a remoting server process. We can host the DLL in a regular .NET program (EXE), or we can host it in IIS (Internet Information Server).

Hosting a DLL in IIS:

- Makes it easier to develop and configure, which is ideal for client-server scenarios
- Allows us to use Windows' integrated security
- Supports only the HTTP channel
- Means that the server class must be in a DLL

Creating a custom host executable (which can be *any* .NET executable):

- Makes it harder to develop and configure, but offers the potential of superior performance and support for peer-to-peer scenarios
- Has no support for Windows' integrated security
- Supports both the HTTP and TCP channels
- Means that the server class can be in a DLL, or in the host EXE itself

When creating client-server applications such as our data portal, the easiest and most powerful approach is to use IIS as the host, because it provides us with authentication, security, and management features for free. It enables the use of Windows authentication to ensure that only valid users can call our server-side code, and it allows us to use SSL to encrypt the remoting messages that are sent between client and server.

If we create our own custom host, we'll have to do quite a lot more work. We'd probably construct it as a Windows service, which would mean writing the service application, managing our own security, and creating our own monitoring and management tools.

> *The primary benefit to using a custom host for our server-side data portal is that we could run it on a Windows NT 4.0 server, while the use of an IIS host requires Windows 2000 or higher.*
>
> *Another possible benefit of creating a custom host is performance. If we create our own host, we can use a TCP channel for our remoting calls, avoiding some of the overhead of HTTP. In most cases, however, IIS will provide sufficient performance. Given the savings in development time and easier management, it's better to try IIS first, and only resort to a custom host if you must.*

In this book, we'll use IIS to host the remoting server (that is, the server-side data portal) in order to benefit from its ease of development and management, and its support for Windows' integrated security. To see how it's going to work, let's run through a simple example of creating a remoting server using IIS.

Creating the DLL

Having chosen to use IIS as the host, any class that we want to expose via remoting must be in a DLL. In VS.NET, we build a DLL by creating a Class Library project, so open up the IDE and create a new one named `TestServer`.

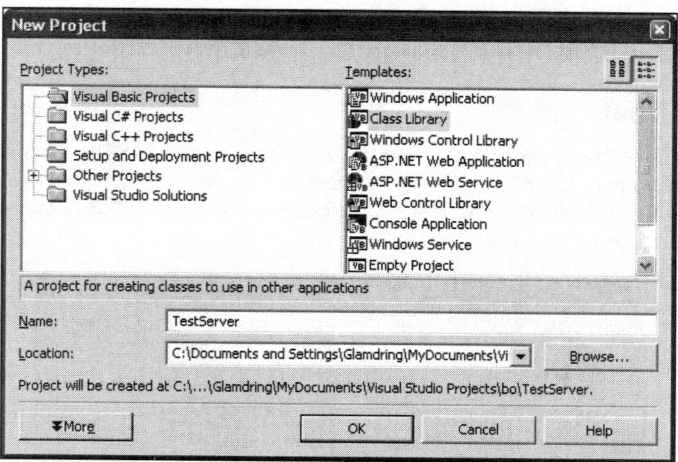

As you'd expect, this project will start with a class named `Class1`, containing the following simple code:

```
Public Class Class1

End Class
```

From our discussions so far, you know that at the moment this is just a local class that won't be available via remoting. To change it to an anchored class whose services we'll be able to use remotely, it must inherit from `MarshalByRefObject`. While we do this, let's also change its name to `TestService`:

```
Public Class TestService
  Inherits MarshalByRefObject

End Class
```

If this class is instantiated in the same process as the program using it, it will act normally – inheriting from `MarshalByRefObject` has no tangible impact in that case. If the `TestService` class is made available to clients via remoting, however, it will be an anchored object – it will run on the server, and the client will get an object proxy. All method calls from a client to the object will be transferred across the network to the server on which they can be run.

Let's add a couple of methods for our clients to call. For testing purposes, we'll make the methods return information about the machine and process in which the object is running:

```
Public Class TestService
  Inherits MarshalByRefObject

  Public Function GetServerName() As String
    Return System.Environment.MachineName
  End Function

  Public Function GetProcessID() As Integer
    Return System.Diagnostics.Process.GetCurrentProcess.Id
  End Function
End Class
```

We should be able to compare the values returned by these functions to our client's machine and process information, and thereby prove that the server code really is running on the server.

Creating the IIS host

Having created the DLL, we now need to create a remoting host using IIS. (Remember, the server DLL must have a process to run in.) While creating a custom host for remoting isn't difficult, using IIS makes the job almost trivial. With the `TestServer` solution still open in VS.NET, choose File | Add Project | New Project, and add an Empty Web Project named `TestService`:

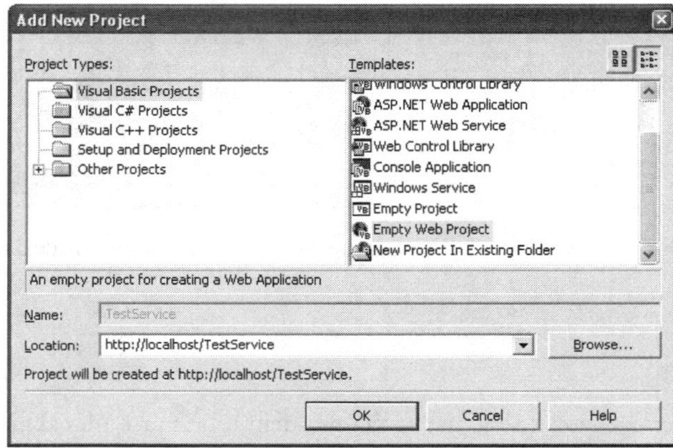

When you click OK, VS.NET will create a new web application named `TestService`. Since it's an *empty* project, however, there won't be any web forms or web service files included – not even a `Web.config` file!

To turn this empty project into a remoting host, all we need to do is add a reference to the DLL containing our server-side class, and set up a `Web.config` file to configure remoting. Right-click on the References entry for `TestService` in the Solution Explorer, and select Add Reference. Using the Projects tab, select `TestServer`, and click OK:

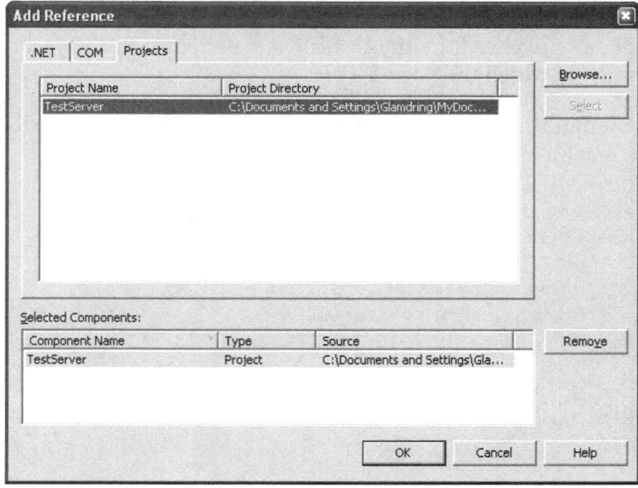

This will add a reference to our DLL. More importantly, when we build the solution, VS.NET will automatically build and copy the DLL into the `bin` directory under the virtual root (that is, http://localhost/TestService/bin), so that the DLL will be available to the remoting subsystem.

All that remains now is to set up a `Web.config` file with appropriate entries to configure remoting. Add one to the project by right-clicking on the `TestService` entry in the Solution Explorer and choosing Add | Add New Item, and then selecting a Web Configuration File:

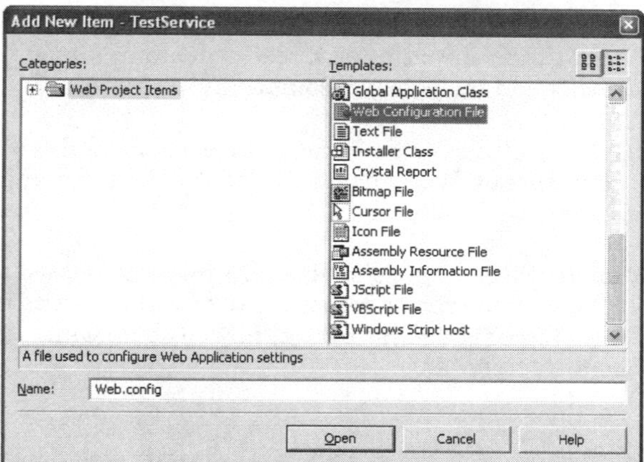

When you click Open, a `Web.config` file will be added to the project, complete with the default settings that we'd find in any new web project. All we need to do is add a section to the file to configure remoting:

```
<?xml version="1.0" encoding="utf-8" ?>
<configuration>
  <system.runtime.remoting>
    <application>
      <service>
        <wellknown mode="SingleCall"
                   objectUri="TestServer.rem"
                   type="TestServer.TestService, TestServer" />
      </service>
    </application>
  </system.runtime.remoting>

  <system.web>

  ...
```

The `<system.runtime.remoting>` element includes all the configuration information for the remoting subsystem. In this case, we're identifying a single class that's to be exposed to client applications via remoting.

> *There are many different options for configuring remoting. We won't be covering them all here, choosing instead to focus only on those that we'll use through the rest of the book.*

In this new XML code, the `<wellknown>` element identifies a server-side (anchored) class that can be used by clients. When we use it, our first dilemma is to decide between the two different operation modes:

- If the `mode` attribute is set to `SingleCall`, each method call from any client will cause the server to create a new object that will handle just that one method call. The object is not reused in any way after that, and is destroyed automatically via the .NET garbage collection mechanism.
- If the `mode` attribute is set to `Singleton`, all method calls from all clients will be handled by a single object running on the server. Many method calls may be handled on different threads at the same time, meaning that our code would have to be entirely safe for multithreading.

Implementing an object for the `Singleton` mode can be very complex, since we have to deal with multithreading issues. Typically, this means using thread synchronization objects, which will almost always reduce our performance and increase our complexity.

For most server-side behavior, `SingleCall` is ideal, since each method call is handled by a newly created object that has its own thread. We don't need to worry about threading issues, or about one client interfering with another in some way.

Once we've selected our mode, we need to define the URI that will be used to access the server-side object. This URI is combined with the server name and virtual root to construct a URL that our clients can use. In this case, the virtual root is `TestService`, so we end up with http://localhost/testservice/testserver.rem.

> **The `.rem` extension is important. When ASP.NET is installed on a server, it configures IIS to route `.rem` and `.soap` extensions to the remoting subsystem. Either extension will work, as they are configured to do the same thing.**

Finally, we need to tell the remoting subsystem which specific class and DLL this URL refers to. The `type` attribute is somewhat cryptic, since it accepts a string that contains the full name (including namespaces) of the class, a comma, and then the name of the assembly (DLL) that contains the class. Note that the assembly name doesn't include the `.dll` extension.

Note that the URI name (with the `.rem` extension) does not have to be the same as the name of our assembly or class. The two names are totally independent. Typically, however, we'll use a URI name that is somewhat similar to the class name, to make it clear which class will be invoked via the URI.

Now build the solution by using the Build | Build Solution menu option. This compiles the `TestService` project into a DLL, and copies it into the `bin` directory of the virtual root.

Testing with the browser

At this point, our remoting server is ready for use. If we want to, we can even test it directly from a browser by asking for its WSDL (web services definition language) specification. Open Internet Explorer and browse to http://localhost/testservice/testserver.rem?wsdl:

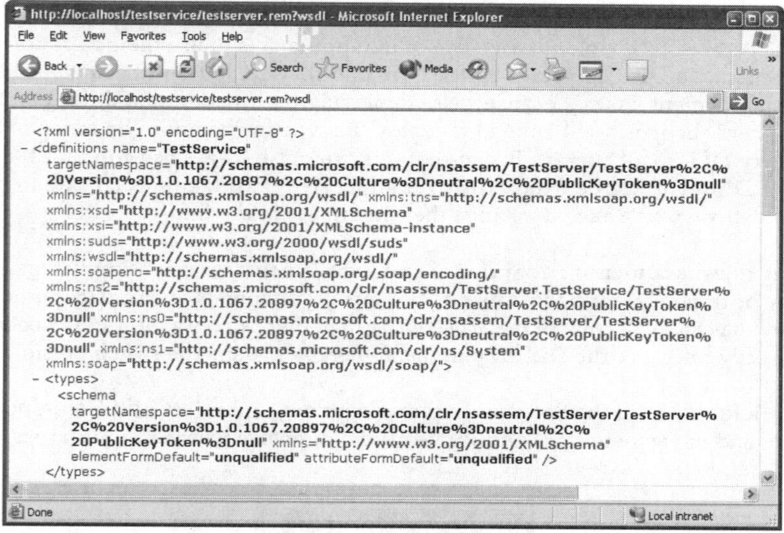

As long as you get the result that you can see here, this remoting server is ready to be called by clients.

Remoting clients

The way remoting works in general is that the client application is simply created to interact with the object. To make the object run remotely, we configure remoting on the client. To make the object run locally, we *don't* configure remoting on the client. It's that easy. To test this, create a new Windows Application project in a new solution in VS.NET. Predictably, we'll give it the name `TestClient`:

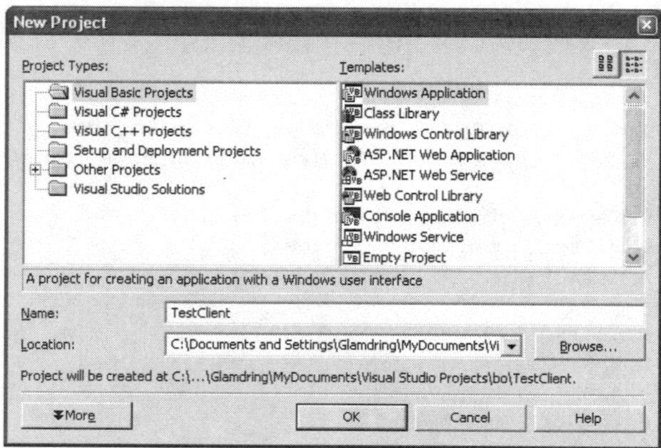

Before we can use the class in our new Windows Form via remoting, we need its **type information**: a complete description of the class, including its assembly, its name, a list of its properties and methods and events, and so forth. We need this information so that VS.NET can create the object proxy that enables our client application to interact with the remote class.

We can get type information in a couple of ways. The easier is to simply reference the DLL containing the class – `TestServer.dll` in our case. The other approach is to use the `soapsuds.exe` command-line utility to generate a DLL that contains the type information, but not the actual code. Either way, we face potential deployment issues, because we're deploying information that describes the remote object. If the remote object changes, we'll have to redeploy the type information (by redeploying the updated DLL or the proxy DLL to all clients). Because of this, we must always use good DLL design practices when creating a DLL that will be exposed via remoting. We must take special care to design the classes in that DLL so that we won't have to change their interfaces in the future.

There is one big drawback to using `soapsuds.exe`, which is that we can't simply toggle between running the code locally or remotely – and that's one of our core requirements for the data portal mechanism! If the client doesn't have a local copy of the *actual* DLL, then there's no way to run the code locally. Because of this, we'll directly reference the DLL in our client, thereby making the switch possible.

Right-click on **References** in the Solution Explorer window, and select **Add Reference**. Then, click the **Browse** button, and navigate to the `TestServer\bin` directory where `TestServer.dll` resides. Select this DLL, and click **OK**:

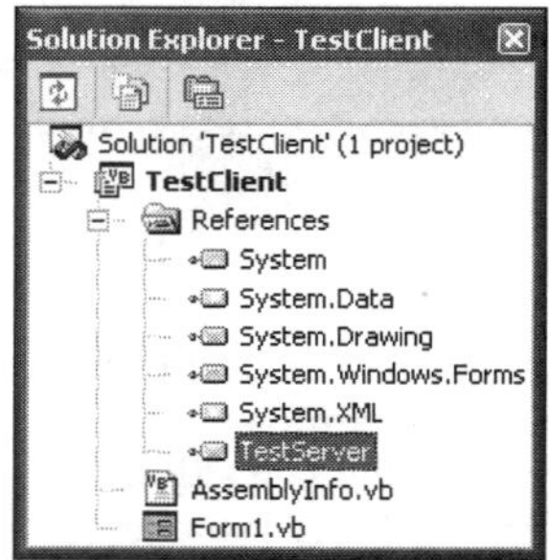

We can now write code to interact with the DLL. Add a button to the form, and write the following code behind the button:

```
Private Sub Button1_Click(ByVal sender As System.Object, _
                          ByVal e As System.EventArgs) Handles Button1.Click
```

```
  Dim output As New System.Text.StringBuilder()
  Dim test As New TestServer.TestService()

  With output
    .Append("TestServer values")
    .Append(vbCrLf)
    .Append("Machine: ")
    .Append(test.GetServerName)
    .Append(vbCrLf)
    .Append("Process: ")
    .Append(test.GetProcessID)
    .Append(vbCrLf)

    .Append(vbCrLf)
```

```
        .Append("Client values")
        .Append(vbCrLf)
        .Append("Machine: ")
        .Append(System.Environment.MachineName)
        .Append(vbCrLf)
        .Append("Process: ")
        .Append(System.Diagnostics.Process.GetCurrentProcess.Id)
        .Append(vbCrLf)
      End With

      MsgBox(output.ToString)

    End Sub
```

This code creates an instance of the `TestService` class, and then displays the machine and process ID from that object. It also displays the machine and process ID for the client itself. At this point, we can run the program, using the `TestService` class to create a local object that's no different from any other local object we might use. The result should be similar to the following:

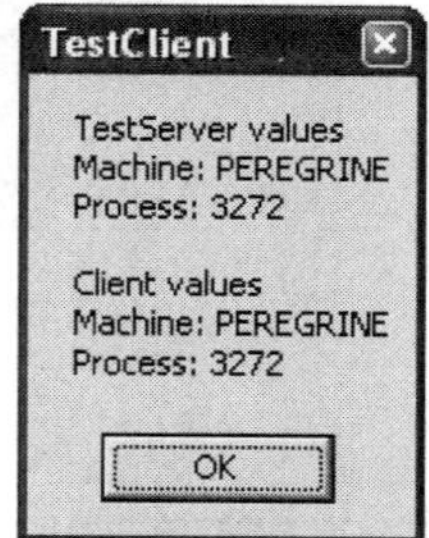

The machine name and process ID are the same for both client and server, which is not surprising given that the object is running in the same process as the client! Now let's see what happens when we change the code to use remoting.

Configuring remoting

When it comes to changing our client to use the object via remoting, we have two options. First, we can configure the remoting subsystem so that it knows that the `TestServer.TestService` class is to be invoked via remoting, rather than locally. If we take this approach, then any time we create a `TestService` object, the .NET runtime will automatically use remoting on our behalf.

To configure remoting this way, we need to add a reference to `System.Runtime.Remoting.dll`, and call a couple of methods in the remoting subsystem as our application is loaded. This approach is particularly nice if we will be creating `TestService` objects throughout our code, because it means that we can simply use the regular `New` keyword to create the objects.

The other approach is to do what we illustrated in Chapter 2, which is to use the `Activator` class from the .NET Framework. This has a `GetObject()` method that allows us to create an instance of an object by supplying a URL to the server. The advantage of *this* approach is that we don't need to reference the remoting DLL or worry about configuring remoting. The drawback is that we can't use the `New` keyword to create our objects – instead, we use `Activator.GetObject()`.

The `Activator.GetObject()` approach is nice if we're only creating our server-side object in one location in our code. It's often simpler just to use `Activator.GetObject()` than it is to reference an extra DLL and call the configuration methods to configure remoting. In general, however, the recommended approach is to configure remoting and simply use the `New` keyword, so that's what we'll do here and in the client-side `DataPortal` code.

With that decided, the first thing we need to do is add a reference to `System.Runtime.Remoting.dll` in our client project.

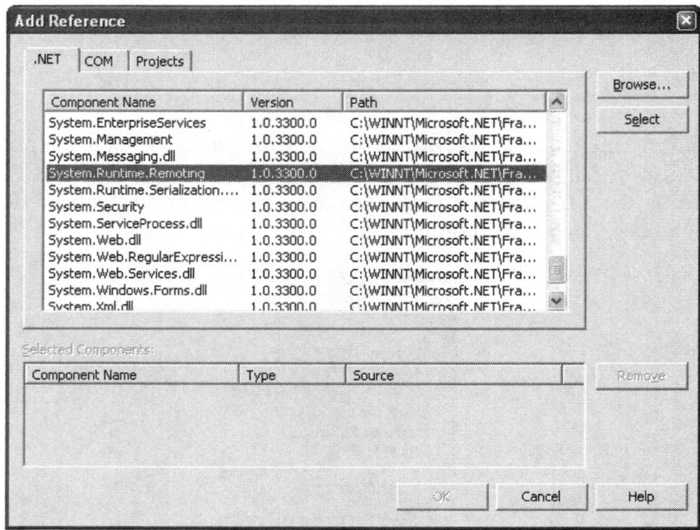

At the top of our form, we can import the remoting namespace:

```
Imports System.Runtime.Remoting
```

The following code shows how to configure remoting to create the object remotely:

```
  Private Sub Form1_Load(ByVal sender As System.Object, _
    ByVal e As System.EventArgs) Handles MyBase.Load

    RemotingConfiguration.RegisterWellKnownClientType( _
      GetType(TestServer.TestService), _
      "http://localhost/testservice/testserver.rem")

  End Sub
```

Note that this is done in the form's `Load` event handler, so it only happens once, as the application starts up. We are telling remoting that any requests for `TestServer.TestService` should be routed to a server identified by the provided URL. The .NET runtime takes care of the details on our behalf.

> *This example does assume that anonymous access is enabled for the virtual root we've created in our `TestServer` web project.*

No other changes are required. Remoting's intrinsic support for location transparency means that none of the code that actually *uses* the object has to change at all. When you run the program, you'll get a result similar to this:

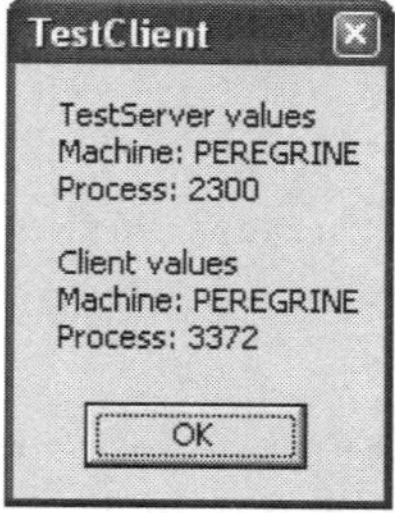

The fact that the process ID values are different proves that the object is running in a different process from the server. (The machine names are the same because I'm running the client on the same machine as the server.) If we ran the client program on another machine (having updated the URL), the machine names would be different as well.

What's really compelling about this is that we can choose to run the `TestService` object locally or remotely by whether or not we configure remoting in our form's `Load` event handler. If we configure remoting, we'll invoke the object remotely; otherwise we'll invoke it locally in the client process. We'll use this capability when we create our client-side data portal in Chapter 5.

Using the binary formatter

Though our client is running quite happily, there's something we need to address. Earlier, we discussed channels and formatters, and since we're using IIS as our remoting host, we *must* use the HTTP channel. By default, the HTTP channel uses the SOAP formatter, which converts the messages going across the network into SOAP's XML format, but in terms of bandwidth and processing requirements it's far more efficient to use the binary formatter.

IIS supports both the SOAP formatter and the binary formatter – it's up to the client to choose which one remoting should use. To make this choice, all we need to do is run a bit of extra code as we configure remoting in the form's `Load` event handler. To start the ball rolling, add a couple more `Imports` statements to the top of the form that will give us easier access to the namespaces we'll be using:

```
Imports System.Runtime.Remoting
Imports System.Runtime.Remoting.Channels
Imports System.Runtime.Remoting.Channels.Http
```

With that done, we can write code in the form's `Load` event handler to configure remoting to use the binary formatter over the HTTP channel:

```
  Private Sub Form1_Load(ByVal sender As System.Object, _
                         ByVal e As System.EventArgs) Handles MyBase.Load

    Dim properties As New Hashtable()
    properties("name") = "HttpBinary"
```

```
    Dim formatter As New BinaryClientFormatterSinkProvider()

    Dim channel As New HttpChannel(properties, formatter, Nothing)

    ChannelServices.RegisterChannel(channel)

    RemotingConfiguration.RegisterWellKnownClientType( _
      GetType(TestServer.TestService), _
      "http://localhost/testservice/testserver.rem")

  End Sub
```

The goal of this code is to call the `RegisterChannel()` method, providing it with an HTTP channel configured the way we'd like. To configure this channel, we must first create a `Hashtable` object with the properties of the channel. At a minimum, we must give the channel a name, as shown above.

With the `Hashtable` in place, we create our binary formatter object, which is of type `BinaryClientFormatterSinkProvider`. This enables remoting to perform binary formatting on the client side. Given the formatter, we can create an instance of an HTTP channel object that's configured the way we want it:

```
    Dim channel As New HttpChannel(properties, formatter, Nothing)
```

Finally, we call `RegisterChannel()` to register this properly configured channel with the remoting subsystem:

```
    ChannelServices.RegisterChannel(channel)
```

With this done, any remoting calls that use the http:// prefix will be handled by the channel object we just created, which means that they'll be using the binary formatter. This includes using any objects we've registered with the `RegisterWellKnownClientType()` method, or any objects that we create using the alternative `Activator.GetObject()` approach.

Since the IIS host already understands the binary formatter, all of our communication with the server will now be handled using the more efficient binary format. If you run the program now, you'll see exactly the same behavior as before – there's no visible or behavioral difference between the SOAP and binary formatters. All the changes are behind the scenes.

We'll be making heavy use of the remoting server and client concepts that we've discussed here in Chapters 4 and 5. For now, let's move on and discuss how .NET supports the serialization of objects.

Serialization

Serialization is the process of converting a complex set of data, such as that contained in an object, into a single blob that's often called a **byte stream**. The reverse, **deserialization**, is the process of unpacking the byte stream to recreate the complex set of data.

The term "byte stream" can refer to many things. It might refer to an XML document in a `String` *variable, a* `String` *variable containing comma-delimited values, an actual* `Stream` *object (such as a* `MemoryStream`*), or any other scheme through which a complex set of data values can be treated as a single entity for transfer across the network.*

Serialization is important when we talk about distributing objects. Most objects contain a complex set of data, and that data is typically stored in a set of variables. If we want to transfer that data across the network, we really can't do it one variable at a time, as doing so would mean incurring a network overhead for each and every one. Performance would become totally unacceptable. Instead, we need some way to send all the data across the network at once. By serializing the complex data into a single byte stream, we simplify the task to that of transferring that one stream across the network. We've efficiently transferred all of the data in one network call.

However, serialization is useful for more than just transferring objects across the network. We can also use it to clone objects efficiently. To do this, we simply serialize an object into a memory buffer, and then deserialize it to create an exact clone of the original object. The ASP.NET `Session` object, for example, uses this cloning technique to store objects between page calls, and to recreate objects as the next page is processed. (This only occurs when the `Session` object is configured to run outside the ASP.NET process, but it's a practical example of serialization within the .NET Framework itself.)

As you know from Chapters 1 and 2, the remoting subsystem makes use of serialization as well. When the SOAP and binary formatters need to prepare an object for transmission across the remoting channel, they use serialization to convert the object's data into a single byte stream. The "unanchored" objects that we've been discussing can also correctly be called "serializable" objects.

Types of serialization

Before we discuss how to code for serialization, we need to make a distinction between the two types of serialization employed by remoting and web services respectively.

Remoting uses a type of serialization that finds all the *variables* contained within an object, and converts their values into a byte stream. If we wish to do so, we can suppress serialization of specific variables by marking them with the `<NonSerialized()>` attribute.

Now, some objects will contain variables that are references to other objects. When we serialize such an object, not only is that object serialized, but the resulting byte stream will also include the variable data from any objects that it references. When objects reference other objects, the result is called an **object graph**, and when one of these byte streams is deserialized, the entire object graph is recreated. The original objects *and its references* are effectively cloned.

Web services uses a different serialization scheme. Rather than copying the *variables* within an object, web services serialization just scans the object to find any property methods and fields that are `Public` in scope, and read-write. Read-only and write-only properties are ignored, as are any non-`Public` variables. The web services serialization scheme will also serialize an object graph, but because of its limitations, we can't guarantee that web services will serialize all our objects.

Under the covers, web services uses the `XmlSerializer` object, which provides this more limited form of serialization. If we return an object from a web service, we get only the information that's accessible via the object's `Public`, read-write properties and fields. Additionally, this information is always generated in XML; there is no option to generate the data in a more compact binary format. Remoting, on the other hand, uses either a SOAP formatter or a binary formatter object to handle serialization, both of which serialize entire object graphs. The SOAP formatter generates XML output containing the data, while the binary formatter generates much more compact binary output of the same data.

> *In this book, we'll be making heavy use of remoting's serialization to implement distributed objects. In Chapter 10, we'll also make use of web services' serialization, as we implement an XML web services interface for our sample application.*

We do have to write a bit of extra code to make our object *support* serialization for remoting. This involves applying the `<Serializable()>` attribute to our class, and possibly also implementing the `ISerializable` interface. Happily, implementing `ISerializable` is only necessary if the default behavior of serialization is unacceptable, which is not usually an issue. In our case, we'll stick with the default serialization behavior, meaning that we can just use the `<Serializable()>` attribute.

> *One of my design goals for this book was to decrease the amount of plumbing code a business developer would have to write, or even see. While there are some interesting things we could do by implementing `ISerializable`, it would mean that every business object would include a fairly large amount of non-business code. In fact, it would basically mean that we'd be stuck writing the `GetState()` and `SetState()` methods from my VB6 Business Objects book. Luckily, the `<Serializable()>` attribute does all of this work for us, so we don't have to write it manually.*

The <Serializable()> Attribute

As stated above, applying the `<Serializable()>` attribute to a class tells the .NET runtime to allow the serialization of our object. Rather than writing a bunch of code by hand, we get the desired serialization behavior with one simple attribute:

```
<Serializable()> _
Public Class MyBusinessClass

End Class
```

We can get the same effect by applying the `<Serializable()>` attribute and implementing the `ISerializable` interface along with a special constructor, but it's far easier just to use the `<Serializable()>` attribute!

The <NonSerialized()> Attribute

Once a class is marked as `<Serializable()>`, all of its member variables will be automatically serialized into a byte stream when the object is serialized. Sometimes, however, we may have variables that *shouldn't* be serialized. In most cases, these will be references to other objects.

Consider an `Invoice` object, for instance. It contains a collection of `LineItem` objects, and we'd probably want to serialize those along with the `Invoice`, because they are essentially *part of* the `Invoice` object. However, it might also reference a `Customer` object. The `Customer` object is *used by* `Invoice`, but it is not *part of* `Invoice`.

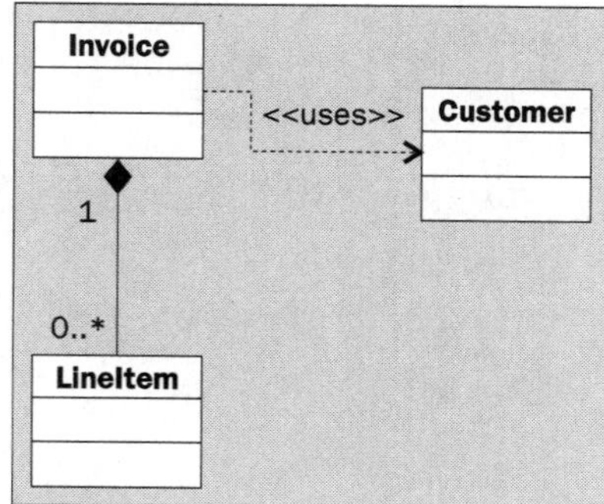

In such a case, we wouldn't want to serialize the `Customer` object as part of the `Invoice`, so our class might look like this:

```
<Serializable()> _
Public Class Invoice

  Private mLineItems As LineItemCollection

  <NonSerialized()> _
  Private mCustomer As Customer

End Class
```

The `<NonSerialized()>` attribute marks the `mCustomer` variable so that the serialization process will ignore it. The one caveat with doing this is that any code that interacts with `mCustomer` must assume that `mCustomer` could be `Nothing`. If the object is serialized and deserialized, the `mCustomer` variable will have the value `Nothing` in the newly created object.

Serialization and Remoting

From the explanations in this chapter so far, it's clear that serialization and remoting have a close relationship. As stated in Chapters 1 and 2, when an object that's available via remoting has the `<Serializable()>` attribute applied, the remoting subsystem will automatically copy our object across the network. By applying the attribute, we've created an unanchored object.

To see how this works, let's return to our earlier example application, where we created a `TestServer` assembly that was exposed via remoting from a `TestService` website. Add a serializable class named `Customer` to the `TestServer` project:

```
<Serializable()> _
Public Class Customer

  Private mName As String
  Private mThreadID As Integer

  Public Sub New()
    mThreadID = AppDomain.GetCurrentThreadId
  End Sub
```

```
  Public Property Name() As String
    Get
      Return mName
    End Get
    Set(ByVal Value As String)
      mName = Value
    End Set
  End Property

  Public ReadOnly Property CreatedID() As Integer
    Get
      Return mThreadID
    End Get
  End Property

  Public ReadOnly Property CurrentID() As Integer
    Get
      Return AppDomain.GetCurrentThreadId
    End Get
  End Property

End Class
```

Because this class is marked as `<Serializable()>`, it is unanchored and will be passed across the network by value automatically. Notice that when the object is created, it records the thread ID where it is running, and includes properties to return that value and the thread where the object is *currently* running. We'll use this to prove that it has been copied back to the client.

We can then add a method to our anchored `TestService` class so that the client can ask for `Customer` objects:

```
Public Class TestService
  Inherits MarshalByRefObject

  Public Function GetServerName() As String
    Return System.Environment.MachineName
  End Function

  Public Function GetProcessID() As Integer
    Return System.Diagnostics.Process.GetCurrentProcess.Id
  End Function

  Public Function GetCustomer() As Customer
    Dim obj As New Customer
    obj.Name = "Rockford Lhotka"
    Return obj
  End Function

End Class
```

Now we have an *anchored* server-side object, `TestService`, which returns *unanchored* `Customer` objects on request. The `Customer` object will be *created* on the server, and then passed by value back to the client. In the end, the `Customer` object will physically be in the client process.

We can add a button to our `TestClient` application's form to retrieve the `Customer` object:

```
Private Sub Button2_Click(ByVal sender As System.Object, _
    ByVal e As System.EventArgs) Handles Button2.Click

  Dim output As New System.Text.StringBuilder()
  Dim svc As New TestServer.TestService()
  Dim cust As TestServer.Customer()

  cust = svc.GetCustomer()
  With output
    .AppendFormat("Got customer: {0}", cust.Name)
    .Append(vbCrLf)
    .AppendFormat("Customer created on:   {0}", cust.CreatedID)
    .Append(vbCrLf)
    .AppendFormat("Customer currently on: {0}", cust.CurrentID)
    .Append(vbCrLf)
  End With

  MsgBox(output.ToString)

End Sub
```

When the application is run and the button clicked, you should get a result similar to this:

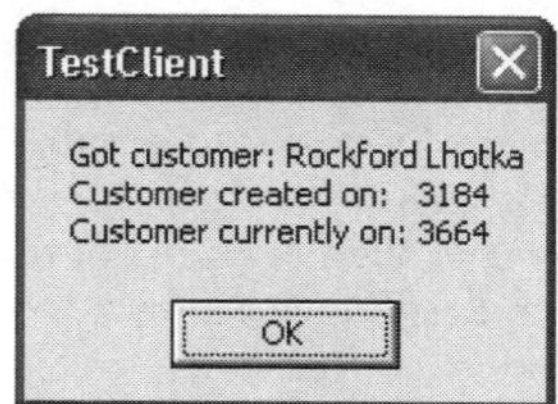

Notice that the `Customer` object was created on a different thread from the one where it's currently running. It was created in the server process, passed by value to the client, and is now running in the client process. Remoting serialized the `Customer` object's data into a byte stream, transferred it to the client, and then deserialized the byte stream into a new `Customer` object on the client – an exact clone of the original.

Be aware that remoting does not transfer the *code*, but only the data. For this mechanism to work, the DLL containing the `Customer` class must be on the client machine along with the client application. In order to deserialize the byte stream on the client, remoting loads the DLL containing the `Customer` class, creates an empty `Customer` object and then populates it with the deserialized data.

Thankfully, due to the support for no-touch deployment built into .NET, this is not as serious a drawback as it might appear. No-touch deployment can be used to ensure that the client has the DLL containing the business class, and that remoting and serialization will work together to copy individual objects from the server to the client, and vice versa. As long as the DLL containing the unanchored *class* is deployed to the client workstation, remoting can be used to pass *objects* based on that class back and forth between client and server.

For more information on using no-touch deployment in .NET, please refer to Appendix A.

Manually invoking serialization

Though we'll typically rely on remoting to invoke the appropriate serialization on our behalf, there are times when we might want to serialize and deserialize an object manually. One good example of this is that we might want to write a `Clone()` method for a class, and the easiest way to do it is via serialization:

```
<Serializable()> _
Public Class TheClass

  Private mName As String
  Private mID As Guid

  Public Function Clone() As Object

    Dim buffer As New IO.MemoryStream
    Dim formatter As _
              New Runtime.Serialization.Formatters.Binary.BinaryFormatter

    formatter.Serialize(buffer, Me)
    buffer.Position = 0
    Return formatter.Deserialize(buffer)

  End Function

End Class
```

The `Clone()` method here uses the binary formatter to serialize the object into a `MemoryStream`, which is just a memory buffer – a byte stream in memory. Once the object's data is in memory, we reset the 'cursor' within the `MemoryStream` object to the beginning of the stream, so that we can read the data it contains. Finally, we use the formatter to deserialize the byte stream to create a new, identical, object.

> *Technically, the resulting object may not be identical to the original. For instance, we may have marked some variables with the* `<NonSerialized()>` *attribute, in which case some variable values may not have been copied. Alternatively, had we implemented the* `ISerializable` *interface, we could have chosen to serialize some or none of the object's actual data.*

The .NET Framework even defines a formal interface for objects that know how to clone themselves, and we can use this technique to implement it – it's called `ICloneable`:

```
<Serializable()> _
Public Class TheClass

  Implements ICloneable

  Private mName As String
  Private mID As Guid

  Public Function Clone() As Object _
    Implements System.ICloneable.Clone

    Dim buffer As New IO.MemoryStream
```

```
      Dim formatter As _
              New Runtime.Serialization.Formatters.Binary.BinaryFormatter

      formatter.Serialize(buffer, Me)
      buffer.Position = 0
      Return formatter.Deserialize(buffer)

    End Function

  End Class
```

Alternatively, we can manually invoke the `XmlSerializer` object to serialize an object using web services-style serialization:

```
    Public Function GetData() As String
      Dim buffer As New IO.MemoryStream()
      Dim formatter As New Xml.Serialization.XmlSerializer(GetType(TheClass))

      formatter.Serialize(buffer, Me)
      buffer.Position = 0

      Return buffer.ToString
    End Function
```

This is *not* a clone method. We can't use web services serialization to clone an object, and since our current class doesn't include any `Public`, read-write properties, this method won't actually serialize any data at all right now! However, if we use this method in an object that *does* have some `Public`, read-write properties, it will return an XML string containing the values of those properties. This is exactly what would be returned as the result of an XML web service that returned the same object as a result.

Enterprise Services (COM+)

Enterprise Services is the set of .NET services known previously as COM+. In this section, I'll be providing an overview of Enterprise Services and its features as they relate to our CSLA .NET framework. We'll also discuss some of the background concepts necessary to understand how Enterprise Services work.

Some of the more commonly used services provided by COM+ include:

- Two-phase distributed transactions
- Object pooling
- Queued components
- Role-based security

Enterprise Services includes all the functionality of COM+, so it's a very large topic all by itself. The discussion that follows is far from complete, as we'll only focus on topics of immediate interest for this book – specifically, the two-phase distributed transactions that allow us to protect data access when multiple databases are involved.

Enterprise Services and COM+ contexts

Because Enterprise Services and COM+ are essentially one and the same, Enterprise Services' features can only be used by code running on a machine where COM+ is installed – which means Windows 2000 or higher. It also means that any of our code that uses Enterprise Services' features will be running in a **COM+ context**.

So what is a COM+ context, and how does it relate to Windows or .NET? To understand that, we need to take a quick step backwards and remind ourselves that *all* .NET code runs in a .NET **application domain** – an isolated environment that fulfils a role comparable to the one that's fulfilled by a Windows process for regular Windows applications. Since everything in Windows – including .NET code – must run within a Windows process, the result is that a .NET application domain must run within a Win32 process. In fact, a Win32 process can contain multiple application domains.

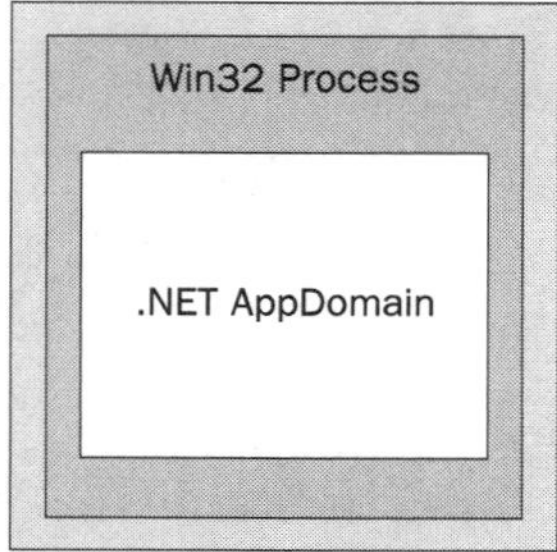

As we know, code running in one Windows process is isolated from code in any other Windows process. .NET simply adds a new layer to this by saying that code in one application domain is isolated from code in any other application domain. (This is true regardless of whether those application domains are in the same Windows process.)

When our code is running within Enterprise Services, things are even more complex. In that case, our code will also be running within an Enterprise Services (COM+) context, where a context groups objects that have the same Enterprise Services environment properties (such as transactional requirements). If we are updating some databases and have several objects involved, they'll all be part of that context.

So: a .NET application domain runs within a Windows process, and within our application domain we may have code running within an Enterprise Services context:

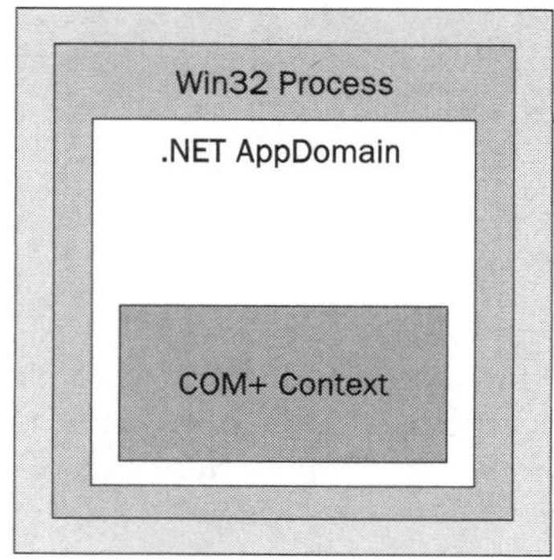

In fact, within a single application domain, we may have some code running with no Enterprise Services context, and other code running within an Enterprise Services context. There may even be several Enterprise Services contexts running within the same application domain!

Running code in Enterprise Services

To use any Enterprise Services feature, we must do some extra work in our code, and in our deployment. First, there are some steps that we must take when creating our project and class in order to gain access to Enterprise Services. With that done, we must then consider how our DLL will get installed into a COM+ application from which it can run.

There are two ways to get our code to run within an Enterprise Services context. We can program specifically to use Enterprise Services by subclassing `ServicedComponent`, or we can have code that's already running in Enterprise Services call a 'normal' .NET assembly, in which case the latter will be loaded into Enterprise Services as well.

> *If we're using .NET 1.1 and running under Windows Server 2003, we can also use a new capability that allows us to enter and leave COM+ transactional protection programmatically. We call a method to enter the transactional context, do our data access, and then call a method to indicate we're done with our transaction. Because the technologies involved were not widely deployed at the time of writing, however, we won't use that technique in our architecture.*

Using Enterprise Services directly

The direct (and most common) way to use Enterprise Services is to reference `System.EnterpriseServices` via the Add References dialog, and then inherit from `ServicedComponent` as we create our class:

```
Public Class MyEntSvc
  Inherits ServicedComponent

End Class
```

We also need to add some attributes to the `AssemblyInfo.vb` file of any project that contains a class inheriting from `ServicedComponent`. First, we need to give the assembly a **strong name**, which uniquely identifies an assembly by name, version number, culture, and a publisher key. All assemblies have a name and a version number, so it's the publisher key that makes the difference. If you already have a key file with your publisher key, you're all set. If you don't, you can use the .NET command line utility `sn.exe` to create a key file with this command:

```
> sn -k mykey.snk
```

The resulting file contains a unique key that you can use to sign your assemblies. Keep this key file safe, as it uniquely identifies you or your organization as the publisher. Once you have a key file, you need to reference it within the `AssemblyInfo.vb` file by adding lines like this:

```
' Strong name
<Assembly: AssemblyKeyFile("h:\rdl\mykey.snk")>
```

Next time the assembly is compiled, the public key from the key file will be incorporated into the DLL, giving the DLL a strong name.

We also need to provide some Enterprise Services information. Remember that our code will end up running in a COM+ application, or container. We can provide some attributes that help to define the nature of this application; at a minimum, we should provide an application name, a description, and an activation type:

```
' Enterprise Services attributes
<Assembly: ApplicationName("TestService")>
<Assembly: Description("My test service")>
<Assembly: ApplicationActivation(ActivationOption.Library)>
```

When using Enterprise Services in .NET, we'll typically want to use a COM+ Library Application. This gives us access to the Enterprise Services features we want, but causes the code to run in the calling process – be that a Web Forms page, an XML Web Service, or a remoting host.

> *The alternative is to use a COM+ Server Application, which would cause COM+ to host our component in a separate process. By running the Enterprise Services components in the calling process, we avoid the overhead of making cross-process calls.*

Note that nothing we've done so far actually *uses* any Enterprise Services features. All we've done is to engineer our class and assembly such that they run within the Enterprise Services environment – when we create an object of type `MyEntSvc`, it will always run within a COM+ context. To use any specific feature, we must apply attributes to the assembly, class, and methods (as appropriate) that identify the features we want to use:

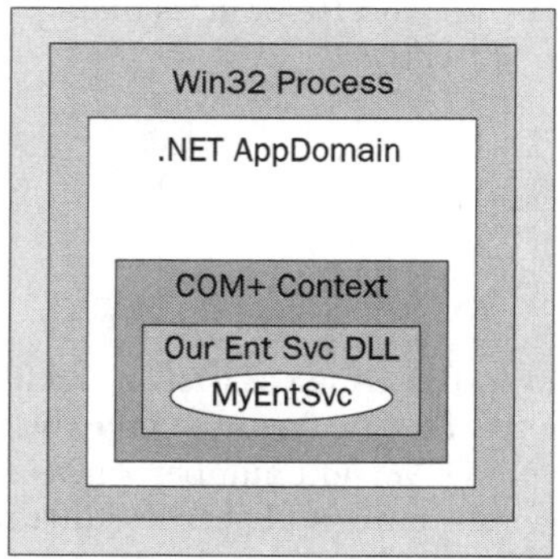

Installing the assembly into COM+

At this point, we've coded our DLL to use Enterprise Services by creating a class that inherits from `ServicedComponent`. For it to work, it must run within a COM+ context, which means that it must be installed into a COM+ application. As stated above, there are two ways to get a .NET assembly into a COM+ application: automatically, and manually.

If any .NET code attempts to interact with a serviced component that we've written but not yet installed in COM+, the .NET runtime will automatically attempt to put that component into COM+, based on the information we put in the `AssemblyInfo.vb` file. If the calling code is running under a user account with the Windows privileges required to create a COM+ application and install a component into that application, this will succeed. However, if the user account running the code doesn't have enough privileges, it will fail.

The default ASP.NET user account doesn't have the security required to install Enterprise Services components.

Because of the potential for problems arising from the automatic approach, it's usually better to use manual installation before running the application. This way, we can do the installation while logged in under an administrator account, and make sure that it's successful! Manual installation is done via the .NET `regsvcs.exe` command line utility. For instance, if we have a .NET assembly called `testservice.dll` that contains a serviced component, we could install it like this:

```
> regsvcs testservice.dll
```

We can't simply drag-and-drop .NET assemblies into the Component Services console like we can with COM components. COM+ and the Component Services console predate .NET, and don't understand how to deal with .NET assemblies.

This command will create a COM+ application (if it doesn't already exist) by using the information from the attributes we added to the `AssemblyInfo.vb` file. In our example, it would create a Library Application. (If the COM+ application already exists, the `regsvcs.exe` utility *doesn't* change its settings.) The command then registers our assembly with COM+, placing the assembly into the COM+ application.

Using Enterprise Services indirectly

The less obvious way to get our code to run within a COM+ context is to write a 'normal' DLL, and then call it from another DLL that *does* use Enterprise Services. For example, we could create a new DLL containing a new class:

```
Public Class MyWorker
  Public Sub DoWork()

  End Sub
End Class
```

This project doesn't reference `System.EnterpriseServices`, and nor does the class inherit from `ServicedComponent`. Code like this always runs within the application domain of the code that invokes it. Normally, we'd think of that being a Windows Forms executable or a Web Forms page, but it could also be that this component is invoked from another DLL that's already running in Enterprise Services. Suppose, for example, that our `MyEntSvc` class had the following code:

```
Public Class MyEntSvc
  Inherits ServicedComponent

  Public Sub CallWorker()
    Dim obj As New MyWorker()
    obj.DoWork()
  End Sub
End Class
```

Because the calling code is running in a COM+ context within the application domain, any DLLs that it invokes will run within that same COM+ context.

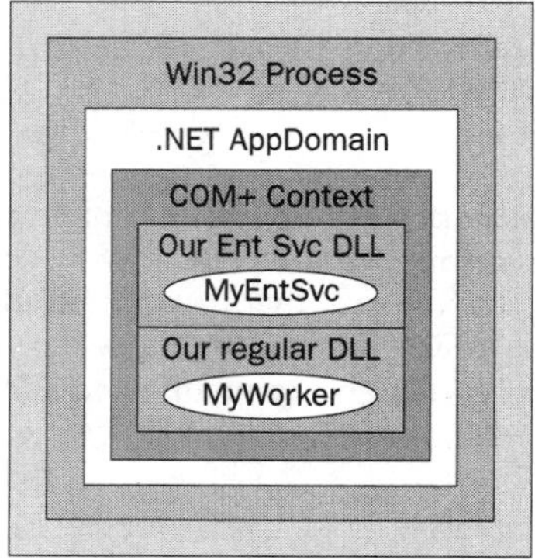

This is a powerful feature, as it means that we can write much of our code 'normally', but still be able to run it from within Enterprise Services if we need to do so. We'll make use of this feature in Chapter 5, when we'll write some components for dealing with data access.

Two-phase distributed transactions

Enterprise Services includes a wide variety of features and capabilities, but the one that we need to support in our n-tier framework is two-phase distributed transactions. **Two-phase transactions** are designed to provide transactional protection when we update two or more transactional resources (where a "transactional resource" means something like a database or a message queue).

> *Enterprise Services uses the Distributed Transaction Coordinator (DTC) to manage its distributed transactions. The DTC supports a variety of transactional resource types, including SQL Server, MSMQ, and any XA-compliant database.*

The other reason for using Enterprise Services transactions is when we're creating a number of server-side objects that all interact with the database as part of a single transaction. Enterprise Services transactions can be valuable here, even when we're talking to only one database, because the resulting code is much simpler. If we tried to do this by hand, we'd have to pass a transaction or connection object around manually from component to component in order to coordinate the transaction.

Keep in mind, however, that designing a set of server-side components to update a single database, and then relying on Enterprise Services transactions to simplify your code, will cause a performance hit: we're still incurring the overhead of COM+ and the DTC. We should always question the value of breaking server processing into multiple components, and weigh the benefits of componentization against the performance cost of Enterprise Services transactions. If we are not updating two or more transactional resources or trying to include many components in a single transaction, then Enterprise Services transactions are probably not the right solution.

> *The performance difference is clearly documented in the MSDN Library article* Performance Comparison: Transaction Control. *The article documents a set of performance tests in which we see that manual transactions via ADO.NET are about twice as fast as automatic transactions in COM+.*

To use Enterprise Services transactions, we must add the `<Transaction()>` attribute to our class. We'll also add the `<EventTrackingEnabled()>` attribute so that we can use the Component Services console to view statistics about our component as it is running:

```
<Transaction(TransactionOption.Required), EventTrackingEnabled(True)> _
Public Class DataService
  Inherits ServicedComponent

End Class
```

The `<Transaction()>` attribute indicates that instances of this class must run in a context that's protected by transactions. It accepts an argument – one of the values of the `TransactionOption` enumeration – that indicates exactly how the object treats transactions:

Value	Description
`Required`	The object must run in a transaction. If the calling object already has one, it will join that transaction. Otherwise, a new transaction will be created.
`RequiresNew`	The object will always run in a new transaction.
`Supported`	The object will participate in an existing transaction. If there is no existing transaction, it will run in a non-transactional context.
`Disabled`	The object will run in the context of any other transactional components, but it will not participate in the transaction.
`NotSupported`	The object will run in a separate, non-transactional context, and is thus isolated from any transactional components.

Each method in a transactional object can include an attribute to indicate whether it will be using the **auto-complete** feature. Auto-complete is the idea that the transaction is assumed to succeed, unless the method raises an error. If an error is raised, the transaction will be rolled back. If we omit the `<AutoComplete()>` attribute or set its value to `False`, we must indicate manually whether our code completed successfully.

Auto-complete is the easiest way to use Enterprise Services transactions, and is the approach we'll use in our transactional data portal implementation. To use auto-complete, we write our method this way:

```
<AutoComplete(True)> _
Public Sub UpdateData()

End Sub
```

Within our method, all we need to do now is ensure that any failure to update the data results in an error being raised. If an error *is* raised, COM+ will automatically roll back the transaction for any databases and any components involved. Typically, what this means is that we can simply write our data access code such that we don't catch any errors ourselves. By allowing any error simply to occur, we get COM+ to handle the rollback for us. (We should still use a `Try...Finally` block to close the database connection, however.)

```
<AutoComplete(True)> _
Public Sub UpdateData()
  Dim cn As New SqlConnection()
```

```
        ' Open connection here

        Try

            ' Do data updates here

        Finally
            cn.Close()
        End Try
    End Sub
```

We're not catching any errors, so they'll propagate up to COM+, where they'll cause the transaction to roll back. However, we do have a `Finally` block, so we're sure to close the connection object whether there was an error or not.

COM+ doesn't alter or stop the error; it just uses it as an indicator that our transaction should be rolled back. The error itself is automatically raised back to the client code that called our component. In the case of our transactional data portal, the calling code will be the client-side data portal.

Reflection

Reflection is a technology built into the .NET Framework that allows us to write code that can examine and interact with other code. We can use reflection to get a list of all the classes in an assembly, and all the methods or properties on each class. We can use reflection to get a list of all the instance variables in an object, and then we can use reflection to retrieve or alter the values of those variables.

Reflection is very powerful – so powerful, in fact, that it's incredibly dangerous. Reflection can be used to circumvent application designs, to break object encapsulation, and generally to misuse virtually any bit of code or data in an application. For all its danger, however, reflection is also very useful. It can be used to implement systems that would be virtually impossible without it. We'll be making use of reflection in several places as we build the framework in Chapters 4 and 5; in this chapter, we'll just take a quick look at how it's used in general.

Working with types

Before we get into reflection itself, we need to remind ourselves that everything in .NET has a type, and that all types ultimately come from the base type, `System.Object`. This includes simple value types such as `Integer` or `Single`, more complex types such as `String` or `Date`, and other types such as an `Enum` or `Structure`. It also includes any types that we may create using classes.

Getting a Type object

The .NET Framework includes a class named `System.Type`, which represents type information about any type. We can use the `Shared GetType()` function to retrieve the `Type` object representing a specific data type:

```
    Dim TypeData As Type = GetType(String)
```

or:

```
Dim TypeData As Type = GetType(Customer)
```

Alternatively, we can get type information for a specific *object* by calling the `GetType()` method on that object:

```
Dim TypeData As Type = objCustomer.GetType()
```

`System.Object` provides the `GetType()` method, and since all objects in .NET ultimately flow from `System.Object`, they too have a `GetType()` method that returns the type information about the object.

Getting information from a Type object

Once we have a `Type` object that represents the type data for either a data type or an object, we can use reflection to get information from that object. For example, we can get a list of the methods, properties, or fields (variables) contained within that type:

```
Public Class Customer
  Private mID As Guid = Guid.NewGuid()
  Private mName As String
  Private mSales As Single

  Public ReadOnly Property ID() As Guid
    Get
      Return mID
    End Get
  End Property

  Public Property Name() As String
    Get
      Return mName
    End Get
    Set(ByVal Value As String)
      mName = Value
    End Set
  End Property

  Public ReadOnly Property Sales() As Single
    Get
      Return mSales
    End Get
  End Property

  Public Sub Buy(ByVal Quantity As Integer)
    mSales += Quantity * 1.99
  End Sub
End Class
```

This is a pretty basic class, but it has the important elements we're interested in: some variables (fields), some properties (read-only and read-write), and a method. Given an object of this type, we can get hold of a `Type` object that contains information about it, and then use the facilities of the `System.Reflection` namespace to retrieve that information. For example, we can get a list of all the `Public` members (methods, properties, events, and variables) of our object:

```
Dim TypeInfo As Type = objCustomer.GetType()
Dim Members() As MemberInfo = TypeInfo.GetMembers()

Dim Member As MemberInfo
For Each Member In Members
  Debug.WriteLine(Member.Name)
Next
```

First, we get a `Type` object for our `Customer` object, and then we call the `Type` object's `GetMembers()` method. This returns an array of `MemberInfo` objects, each corresponding to one of the `Public` members on our object. With that data in hand, we can loop through the array to find information about each member in turn. (In this case, we're printing each member's name to the debug window.)

The `Type` object has other methods for retrieving only method, property, or field information, but perhaps more importantly we can return not only the `Public` members of an object, but its `Private`, `Friend`, or `Protected` members as well. For instance, we can get a list of the `Private` fields and their values from our object with code such as:

```
Dim Fields() As FieldInfo = _
      TypeInfo.GetFields(BindingFlags.Instance Or BindingFlags.NonPublic)

Dim Field As FieldInfo
For Each Field In Fields
  Debug.WriteLine(Field.Name & ": " & Field.GetValue(objCustomer).ToString)
Next
```

Notice that we're passing some values to the `GetFields()` method to indicate that we want only instance variables that are not `Public`. Once we get the array of non-`Public` variables, we can loop through them to display their names. We can also call the `GetValue()` method on the `FieldInfo` object, passing it our object reference, to retrieve the value in the variable. The result in the debug window will be something like this:

```
mID: 60a09fc2-b0c1-4e87-b175-5e499c02a973
mName: Fred
mSales: 0
```

At this point, it's probably apparent just how dangerous reflection can be. Using this technique, we can peek inside *any* object to see its private data! Even more dangerous is that we can use a similar technique to reach in and *alter* data. For instance, we can directly change the `mSales` variable:

```
Dim Sales As FieldInfo = _
  TypeInfo.GetField("mSales", _
                    BindingFlags.Instance Or BindingFlags.NonPublic)

Sales.SetValue(objCustomer, 42)
```

We first use the `GetField()` method to retrieve a `FieldInfo` object representing the `Private` field `mSales`. The `SetValue()` method then allows us to change the value of that variable by providing a reference to the `Customer` object, and the new value.

Along this same line, we can use reflection to invoke methods both `Public` and non-`Public`. Doing so is much slower than just calling a method normally, but we'll find a use for this technique in Chapter 5, when we implement a data service that works with any object. To call a method via reflection, we can write code such as:

```
Dim Method As MethodInfo = TypeInfo.GetMethod("Buy")
Dim params() As Object = {5}

Method.Invoke(objCustomer, params)
```

First, the method information is retrieved into a `MethodInfo` object. (If required, we could use flags here to indicate that we want to get at a non-`Public` method.) Once we have the `MethodInfo` object, we can call its `Invoke()` method to invoke the method. We provide a reference to our object, and an array of type `Object` that contains the parameters to be passed to the method as it is invoked.

At this point, we've seen how we can get information about a type or an object, and then interact with it by altering its variables and calling its methods – whether they are `Public` or not. There's one more trick we should cover here. Normally, we can only create objects from a class that has a `Public` constructor. If we don't write a constructor in a class, the compiler creates an empty `Public Sub New` on our behalf. On the other hand, if we create a `Private Sub New`, we can prevent the creation of an object.

Suppose that we add such a method to our `Customer` class:

```
Public Class Customer
  Private mID As Guid = Guid.NewGuid
  Private mName As String
  Private mSales As Single

  Private Sub New()

  End Sub
```

All of a sudden, our client code will fail to compile, due to the fact that we can no longer create an instance of the `Customer` class. This line will result in a compilation error:

```
Dim objCustomer As New Customer()
```

The .NET Framework provides a backdoor, however, that we can use to create an instance of the class *even with a `Private` constructor.* We can write the following:

```
Dim objCustomer As Customer
objCustomer = Activator.CreateInstance(GetType(Customer), True)
```

This will create an instance of the object by calling its `Private` constructor, but note that it only works if there's a default constructor – that is, a constructor that requires no parameters. However, it can be used to create instances of an object where the `New` keyword would fail to compile.

We'll be using this technique as we build our framework, because it allows us to create our business objects such that the UI developer is forced to use `Shared` factory methods to create them. However, we still need to be able to create them from our `DataPortal` code, bypassing the restrictions we're placing on the UI developer. Using reflection in this way allows us to do just that.

Attributes

If you've done much .NET programming, you've probably used .NET **attributes**. If nowhere else, you've already seen them used a few times in this book! Attributes are metadata that can be applied to an assembly, a class, a method, or a variable. This metadata can be used by Visual Studio .NET, the compiler, or the .NET runtime to alter how our code is used or acts.

The .NET Framework uses attributes extensively, and we'll use them as we create our framework. We'll also be creating our own `<Transactional()>` attribute, so that we can tell our `DataPortal` whether to run our data access methods in a context that's protected by transactions. Attributes are perfect for this sort of thing, because they're easy for developers to use, and they help to make business code self-documenting.

As we've seen, using them is pretty straightforward. For instance:

```
<Serializable()> _
Public Class TheClass
```

It's immediately obvious that this class is serializable. Suitably named attributes are intuitive, both to the initial developer and to any maintenance developers who may work with the code in the future.

Creating custom attributes

To augment the built-in attributes, and as suggested above, we can create our own custom attributes. To do this, we just need to create a class that inherits from the `System.Attribute` base class in the .NET Framework.

Simple attributes

The simplest kind of attribute we can create is one that takes no parameters. For instance:

```
Public Class TransactionalAttribute
  Inherits Attribute
End Class
```

We can then apply this attribute to anything we like. Note that our attribute's full name is `TransactionalAttribute`, but we only use `<Transactional()>` when applying it to our code:

```
<Transactional()> _
Public Class Test

  < Transactional()> _
  Private mName As String

  < Transactional()> _
  Public Sub DoWork()
```

Restricting attribute usage

In many cases, we'll want to place restrictions on where the attribute can be applied. To do this, we need to add an attribute to our attribute code!

```
<AttributeUsage(AttributeTargets.Method)> _
Public Class TransactionalAttribute
  Inherits Attribute
End Class
```

With this change, our attribute can no longer be applied to anything but a method. Placing it elsewhere will cause a compile-time error.

Detecting custom attributes

Creating and applying custom attributes is novel, but it doesn't really get us anywhere – we also need a way to determine whether an attribute has been applied. It turns out that this is yet another trick that can be performed by reflection. Earlier, we discussed the use of reflection to get information about methods and fields, but retrieving attribute information is just an extension of those concepts. For example, suppose that we've defined a simple attribute that can be applied to methods:

```
<AttributeUsage(AttributeTargets.Method)> _
Public Class TransactionalAttribute
  Inherits Attribute
End Class
```

Given this, we can write code to find out if any method has this attribute applied to it:

```
  Private Function IsTransactional(ByVal Method As MethodInfo) As Boolean

    Dim attrs() As Object = _
          Method.GetCustomAttributes(GetType(TransactionalAttribute), True)

    Return (UBound(attrs) > -1)

  End Function
```

All we need to do is pass this function a `MethodInfo` object corresponding to a method, and it will return `True` if the method has the `<Transactional()>` attribute applied. To achieve this, it calls the `GetCustomAttributes()` method on the `MethodInfo` object to get an array containing the custom attributes that match the provided attribute type. In other words, we'll get back an array containing all the `<Transactional()>` attributes applied to this method. All we need to do then is determine whether the array contains any elements – if it does, we know that the attribute was applied to the method.

On a total tangent, you might have noticed that I'm using the `UBound()` function rather than some new .NET technique. The reason for this is that I've been writing programs in one BASIC language or another for over 20 years. I used `UBound()` (or an equivalent) on the Apple II, CYBER, VAX/VMS, Amiga, Mac, under DOS and in Windows. .NET is just another in a long line of platforms to support BASIC. The VAX, for instance, had an alternative way to get the size of an array, but everyone used normal BASIC syntax rather than resorting to the platform-specific technique. .NET is no different – I'm programming in BASIC, *not some weird platform/language blur.*

Defining and detecting custom attributes is a powerful technique for building frameworks and other reusable code in .NET. Once a custom attribute is defined, we can construct code that checks for its presence or absence, and then we can alter behavior based on that knowledge. From that point forward, anyone wishing to use our framework can simply apply attributes to their code to achieve the desired behavior.

.NET role-based security

Role-based security is nothing new. Every Windows NT, Windows 2000, and Windows XP machine has the concepts of users and groups. A user belongs to one or more groups, and each group defines the role that the user plays on the computer: administrator, user, power user, etc.

These same concepts extend to the Windows domain system and the Microsoft Active Directory system. In both cases, users and groups are defined, with groups essentially defining the roles that each user plays within the network.

The .NET Framework itself supports the general concept of role-based security, and can interact with these existing technologies to provide the underlying implementation. The support for this concept comes from .NET **principal** and **identity** objects:

- An **identity** object defines the identity of the current user. It provides the user ID, and the type of authentication that was used to identify the user.
- A **principal** object defines the current user's identity, and the user's associated roles or groups. This means that the principal object contains an identity object, and a list of roles for the user.

There are three main categories of principal and identity objects:

- `WindowsPrincipal` and `WindowsIdentity`
- `GenericPrincipal` and `GenericIdentity`
- Custom principal and identity

The `WindowsPrincipal` object contains a `WindowsIdentity` object, along with the list of Windows groups that the user belongs to. These objects correspond to the Windows account our application is running under. They are automatically populated by the .NET Framework on our behalf.

The `GenericPrincipal` object contains a `GenericIdentity` object. These objects are very basic implementations of the .NET security scheme, and they can be loaded with a user identity and a list of roles by our code. They are designed to make it easy to implement custom security. For instance, we may want to identify the user and roles based on some tables in a database, and these objects make that relatively easy to do.

We can also implement our own custom principal and identity objects. To create a principal object, we need to create a class that implements the `System.Security.Principal.IPrincipal` interface, which includes the `Identity` property to retrieve the user's identity, and an `IsInRole()` method that's used to determine whether the user is in a given role. To create an identity object, we need to create a class that implements the `IIdentity` interface, which includes methods to retrieve the user's ID and the authentication scheme used to authenticate the user.

In many cases, we can use `GenericPrincipal` and `GenericIdentity` to provide simple, custom security implementations. In other cases, we may need to create a custom implementation. As part of our framework, we'll choose the second option. Specifically, we'll be creating a `BusinessIdentity` class that inherits from our framework's `ReadOnlyBase` class. By doing this, we'll be able to authenticate the user and retrieve their list of roles by using our `DataPortal` mechanism.

ADO.NET

The final technology we need to discuss here is **ADO.NET**, the core data access technology provided by the .NET Framework. It allows us to interact with relational databases such as SQL Server or Oracle, and provides XML support that allows us to treat XML data as a data source in its own right.

Obviously, ADO.NET is a very large and complex technology that we can't cover in a comprehensive manner in this chapter. However, there are some key concepts around ADO.NET that we do need to deal with, along with some of the techniques that we'll be using through the rest of the book.

ADO.NET architecture

To start with, it's important to understand the basic architecture of ADO.NET itself, so that we can see how best to use it when manipulating data in a distributed environment. ADO.NET is designed following a 2-tier model.

Data providers

At the bottom tier, ADO.NET provides interaction with databases via **data providers**. A data provider allows us to connect to a data source, and to execute commands that add, update, delete, or read data. To retrieve data, data providers include a **data reader** object. The objects that compose a data provider are shown in the following diagram:

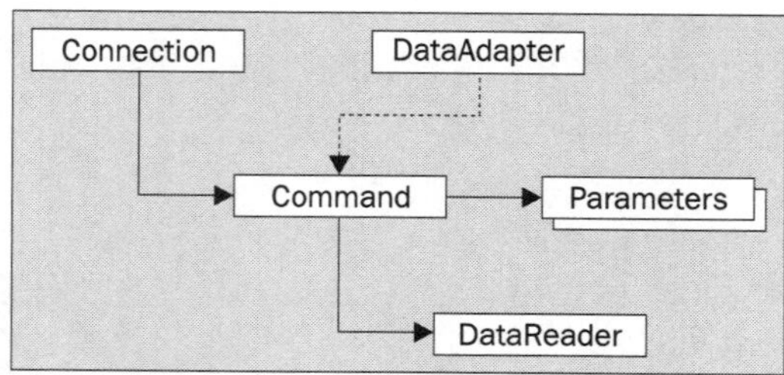

Microsoft supplies data providers to interact with various database engines, including:

- Microsoft SQL Server
- Oracle
- Databases with an OLEDB driver that's supported by .NET
- Databases with an ODBC driver that's supported by .NET

The SQL Server and Oracle providers are very fast, as they interact directly with the database. Be aware that the OLEDB and ODBC providers rely on OLEDB and ODBC to do the actual data interaction, so they involve an extra layer of overhead in order to reach the underlying database.

The DataSet object

A data provider only provides *interaction* with the data source, not any form of data *representation*. ADO.NET provides a separate tier to represent data: the `DataSet`. The `DataSet` and its related objects provide a powerful and abstract representation of tabular data:

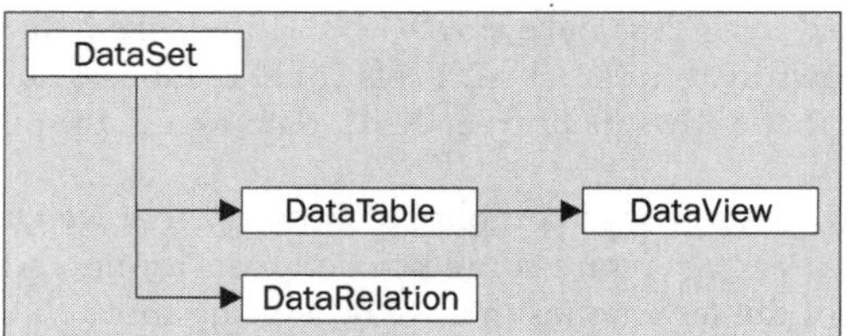

Each `DataSet` can contain multiple `DataTable` objects that can be related to each other via `DataRelation` objects. Each `DataTable` object represents a set of tabular data. That data can be accessed directly from the `DataTable` object, or we can construct `DataView` objects to provide different views of that data based on filters, sorts, and so forth.

The `DataSet` is entirely decoupled from any concept of a data source or provider. If we wish, we can use a `DataSet` by itself to represent *any* tabular data – it can be thought of as an in-memory scratchpad for data.

Data provider and DataSet interaction

The link between a `DataSet` and a data provider is the **data adapter** object, which understands how to get data into and out of a `DataSet`. A data adapter is linked to four command objects – one each for reading, updating, adding, and deleting data.

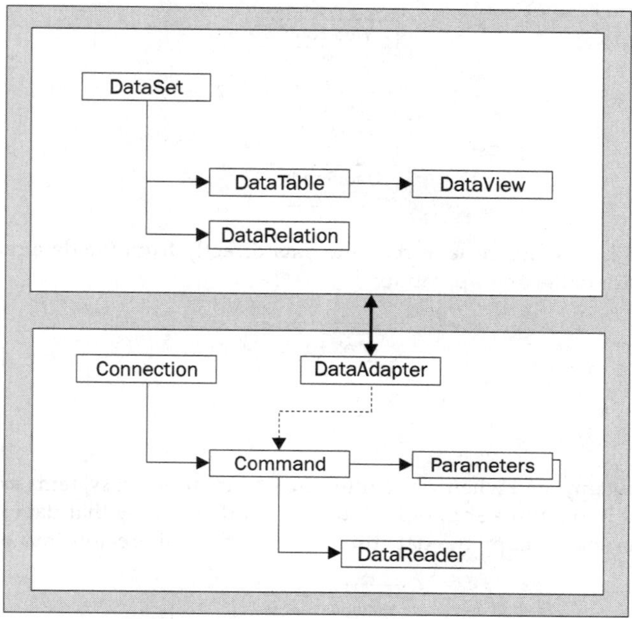

When we load a `DataSet` with data from a data provider, the data adapter invokes the appropriate command object to retrieve the data, and then uses a data reader object to pump the data from the data source into a `DataTable` object within the `DataSet`. In short, this means that a `DataSet` is populated via a data reader object:

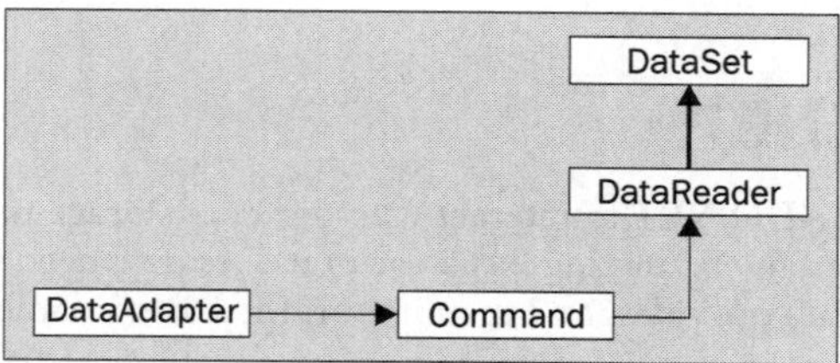

The separation between the interaction with a data source and the representation of the data in memory is very powerful. It means that the `DataSet` is totally disconnected from any data source – we can pass the `DataSet` object around a network, from machine to machine, without worrying about database connections and so forth. It also means, however, that there is some obvious overhead involved. Not only does the `DataSet` end up containing our data, but it also contains a lot of metadata that describes the data types, constraints, and relationships of our data. Depending on exactly what we intend to do with the data, the `DataSet` may or may not be the right choice.

Consider a typical web application that generates a display of data in the browser. We could build such a page using a `DataSet` – the data reader will copy the data into the `DataSet`, and we can then copy the data from the `DataSet` into our page.

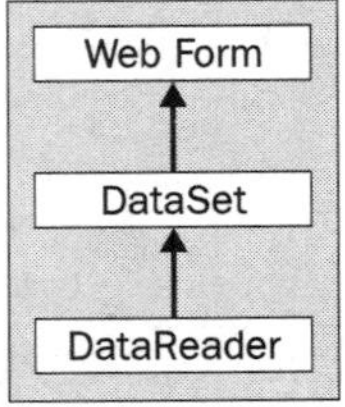

Alternatively, we could write our code to read the data directly from the data reader and put it into our page, avoiding an entire data copy operation:

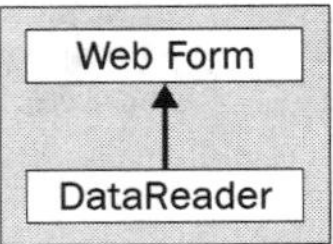

We can skip this extra copy step when we're building object-oriented systems as well. It may not make sense to copy the data into a `DataSet`, only to turn around and copy that data into a set of objects. It will often make more sense to copy the data directly from the data reader into our objects:

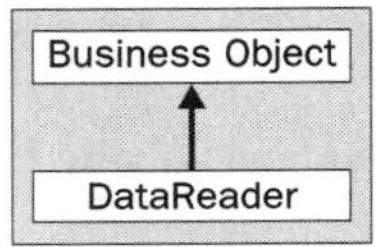

The flexibility inherent in the architecture of ADO.NET is powerful, and we'll exploit it as we design our overall architecture in this book.

Basic use of ADO.NET

Since we'll be making use of ADO.NET to interact with our data storage tier throughout this book, it's worth spending some time briefly examining basic use of it. First, we need to reference the assembly containing the appropriate data provider, and then import the latter's namespace to keep our code simple.

> *If we're using SQL Server or an OLEDB database, then most project types in VS.NET already reference the appropriate assembly. If we're using Oracle or an ODBC database, then we'll need to add a reference manually.*

Throughout this book, we'll be using Microsoft SQL Server 2000, but while you're developing you may also choose to use MSDE, which is a subset of SQL Server 2000. MSDE is included with some versions of VS.NET, and is also downloadable from MSDN. The following URLs contain information about licensing and downloading MSDE:

- http://support.microsoft.com/default.aspx?scid=KB;EN-US;Q324998
- http://www.microsoft.com/sql/howtobuy/msdeuse.asp?LN=en-us&gssnb=1

The data provider for SQL Server 2000 (and therefore for MSDE) is in `System.Data.dll`, and its namespace is `System.Data.SqlClient`. If it isn't already referenced in our project, we'll need to use the Add References dialog to add a reference to the assembly, and then add an `Imports` statement to the top of our code:

```
Imports System.Data.SqlClient
```

Connecting to a database

Connecting to a SQL Server database involves creating and initializing a `SqlConnection` object, and then calling its `Open()` method. When we're done with the connection, we should always call its `Close()` method. To ensure that the `Close()` method is always called, we should employ a `Try...Finally` block.

Initializing the `SqlConnection` object can be done via its properties, or by providing a connection string. The latter is the most common approach, mainly because it allows us to place the string in a configuration file, a registry entry, or some other location where we can change it without having to recompile the application.

> *In .NET, the recommended location for database connection strings is in the application configuration file. That is the technique we'll be using throughout this book.*

At a minimum, the connection string consists of the server name, the database name, and security information. For instance, a connection string for using Windows' integrated security to access the sample `pubs` database would look something like:

```
data source=myserver;initial catalog=pubs;integrated security=SSPI
```

Alternatively, we can provide a user ID and a password:

```
data source=myserver;initial catalog=pubs;user=myuser;password=mypassword
```

ADO.NET data providers implement database connection pooling inherently, so it's always available to us. However, database connections can *only* be pooled if they are identical. This means that all connections to the same database with the exactly the same connection string are pooled – so if we use integrated security in an environment where all code runs under the same user account, then we'll get connection pooling. However, if we use integrated security in an environment where our code runs under different user accounts, we'll get little or no pooling.

The key lies in whether the server impersonates the client's identity. For instance, if each client connects to the server anonymously, then all our server-side code will run under one identity for all users. This means that integrated security will result in all the database connections being under that identity, and so we'll get pooling. On the other hand, if all our clients connect to the server using integrated security, then the server-side code will run under the same account as each client. In this case, integrated security will result in database connections being established under the identities of the various users. The result will be that we'll have little or no database connection pooling.

Once we've decided on our database connection string, we can open the connection. The following code illustrates how this is done, and includes a `Try...Finally` block to ensure that the connection is closed, whether or not we encounter any errors:

```
Dim dbConn As String = _
        "data source=myserver;initial catalog=pubs;integrated security=SSPI"

  Dim cn As New SqlConnection(dbConn)
  cn.Open()

  Try
    ' Do database interaction here
  Finally
    cn.Close()
End Try
```

We'll use this basic structure throughout our code as we interact with the database.

Reading data with a data reader

Earlier, we discussed how data adapter objects use a data reader to populate a `DataSet` object. This is great when we're building a data-centric application where we'll be making use of the `DataSet` object. However, if we're trying to populate a set of object-oriented business objects, we'll probably want to use a data reader directly. This will provide the best performance when working with objects.

A data reader object is generated from a command object. The command object will execute either a stored procedure that returns data, or a text SQL `SELECT` statement. It's preferable to use stored procedures for this purpose, as they provide better performance, and also keep the data storage tier better separated from the data access tier within our logical model, as we discussed in Chapter 1.

In either case, the basic process is to open a database connection, create and initialize a command object, and then execute the command object to create a data reader object. We can then retrieve the data from the data reader and use it as we see fit.

Using Dynamic SQL

The following code illustrates the basic flow of operation when using a text SQL statement:

```
Dim dbConn As String = _
        "data source=myserver;initial catalog=pubs;integrated security=SSPI"

Dim cn As New SqlConnection(dbConn)
cn.Open()

Dim cm As New SqlCommand()

Try
  Dim dr As SqlDataReader
  With cm
    .Connection = cn
    .CommandText = "SELECT au_lname FROM authors WHERE Name=@name"
    .Parameters.Add("@name", myCriteria)

    dr = .ExecuteReader()
  End With
```

```
    ' Read the data here

  Finally
    cn.Close()
  End Try
```

Notice how we use the command object's `Parameters` collection to add a parameter for use within the SQL statement. While we could have used string concatenation to insert the parameter value directly, this technique is far superior. By using the parameter approach, we avoid having to worry about formatting the value properly based on data type – that's handled for us automatically. Also, this approach means that we can switch to calling a stored procedure with very little change to our code.

It's almost always preferable to call a stored procedure in a production application. That said, it's often faster and easier to debug if you use dynamic SQL statements – they make it easier for the developer to experiment, and to tweak the statement to get everything right. The SQL can be placed in a stored procedure prior to going into production.

Be aware that there are differences between dynamic SQL and the SQL you may put into your stored procedures, so there will be some work involved in converting to stored procedures and debugging them and the application. Using formal parameters in our dynamic SQL statements, as shown above, helps to minimize this effort.

Calling a stored procedure

The code to call a stored procedure is similar. Were we to have a stored procedure similar to this:

```
CREATE PROCEDURE getAuthorName
  (
    @Name varchar(20)
  )
AS
  SELECT au_lname
  FROM authors
  WHERE Name=@Name;
RETURN
```

We could call it with the following code:

```
Dim dbConn As String = _
          "data source=myserver;initial catalog=pubs;integrated security=SSPI"

Dim cn As New SqlConnection(dbConn)
cn.Open()

Dim cm As New SqlCommand()

Try
  Dim dr As SqlDataReader
  With cm
    .Connection = cn
    .CommandType = CommandType.StoredProcedure
    .CommandText = "getAuthorName"
    .Parameters.Add("@name", myCriteria)
```

```
      dr = .ExecuteReader()
    End With

      ' Read the data here

  Finally
    cn.Close()
  End Try
```

As you can see, we just need to set the `CommandType` property to indicate that we're calling a stored procedure, and then supply the stored procedure name as the `CommandText`.

Reading the data

In both cases, the result of the `ExecuteReader()` method is a new `SqlDataReader` object that we can use to read the resulting data. This object has a lot of properties to support the various ways we might choose to use it. The most basic (though not ideal) approach is to use the `GetValue()` method to retrieve all values as type `Object`. A loop to retrieve all the values from a data reader could look like this:

```
Dim field As Integer

While dr.Read()
  For field = 0 to dr.FieldCount - 1
    Debug.WriteLine(dr.GetValue(field))
  Next
End While
```

The reason why this is not ideal is that the `GetValue()` method *always* returns values as type `Object`, which is not particularly fast. This code also has another potential flaw, in that it doesn't handle null values from the database. The one *positive* thing about this code is that we're using a numeric index to select the field to retrieve. We do have the option of using field names instead, so that rather than `GetValue(0)`, we might use `GetValue("au_lname")`. The numeric option provides better performance, but it obviously decreases the readability of our code.

Instead of using `GetValue()`, we should be using the set of type-specific methods available on the data reader object, although this does require that we know the data types of the fields ahead of time. Consider the following code:

```
While dr.Read()
  mName = dr.GetString(0))
  mBirthDate = dr.GetDateTime(1))
  mSales = dr.GetDouble(2))
End While
```

We're now retrieving the values using type-specific methods. This is faster because .NET doesn't need to typecast the data as we put it into our variables. This is the approach we'll be using in our code throughout this book.

Using output parameters

Sometimes, we'll have an output parameter from a stored procedure that provides us with data along with the result set that we get from the data reader. When this is the case, you need to be aware that the output parameter values will not be available until after we've read through *all* the data in the data reader. As an example, consider the following code, which calls a stored procedure that has an output parameter:

```
Dim dbConn As String = _
      "data source=myserver;initial catalog=pubs;integrated security=SSPI"

Dim cn As New SqlConnection(dbConn)
cn.Open()

Dim cm As New SqlCommand()

Try
  Dim dr As SqlDataReader
  Dim param As SqlParameter
  With cm
    .Connection = cn
    .CommandType = CommandType.StoredProcedure
    .CommandText = "getAuthor"
    param = New SqlParameter
    With param
      .ParameterName = "@au_id"
      .Direction = ParameterDirection.Output
    End With
    .Parameters.Add(param)
    .Parameters.Add("@name", myCriteria)

    dr = .ExecuteReader()
  End With

  ' Read the data here

Finally
  cn.Close()
End Try
```

This shows how to define the parameter to *accept* an output value from the stored procedure. The following code illustrates how to get at the output parameter value:

```
' Read the data here
While dr.Read
  ' Work with each row of data
End While
Dim result As String = param.Value
```

We don't read the output parameter value from the `SqlParameter` object until after we've finished retrieving all the data from the data reader.

Handling null values

So far, none of our code handles any possible null values in the data. Exactly how we handle nulls will depend on what they mean to us. In the case that we don't really care about the difference between a value that has never been entered and one that is just empty, we must do extra work to deal with the null values. In our framework, we'll be creating a `SafeDataReader` class to encapsulate these details, so that our business code doesn't have to worry about nulls at all. Here though, let's discuss the options at our disposal via ADO.NET.

In the case that we *do* care about the difference between a value that has never been entered and one that is just empty, we'll need to use data structures within our application to make that distinction. The easiest data structure is the Object data type, which can hold a null value. In that case, we'll need to use the IsDBNull() method throughout our code to display (or otherwise deal with) our values appropriately. For instance:

```
Dim value As Object
value = dr.GetValue(0)

...

If IsDBNull(value) Then
  ' Handle null value appropriately
Else
  ' Handle regular value appropriately
End if
```

More common is the case where the difference between a null value and an empty value is not important, but where the database was not properly designed, and is allowing nulls where they don't belong. In such a case, we'll need to detect the fact that a field is null, and convert that null into an appropriate empty value. The basic scheme for doing so centers on the data reader's (rather than the Object's) IsDBNull() method. For a given field, we can do the following:

```
If dr.IsDBNull(0) Then
  mName = ""
Else
  mName = dr.GetString(0))
End If
```

Reading multiple result sets

It's possible for a stored procedure or a SQL statement to return *multiple* data sets. This is a powerful feature when our data contains relationships: we can retrieve, for example, an invoice and all of its line item data with a single stored procedure call. The invoice data and the line item data would be returned as two different result sets from the same call.

A data reader object supports this concept through the NextResult() method. Given our invoice example, we might have code that looks something like this:

```
dr = cm.ExecuteReader()
dr.Read()

' Read invoice data

dr.NextResult()

While dr.Read()
  ' Read this line item's data
End While
```

This reads the first row of the first result set, presumably containing our invoice header data. We then call the NextResult() method to move to the second result set, where we can loop through and read all the line item data.

Updating data

Updating data is done using a command object with an appropriate `INSERT`, `UPDATE`, or `DELETE` statement, or by calling a stored procedure that handles the operation. As with data retrieval, it's preferable to use stored procedures in a production setting, though dynamic SQL is often used in development.

Calling a stored procedure to update data is similar to calling one to retrieve data, though instead of calling `ExecuteReader()` on the command object, we'll be calling `ExecuteNonQuery()`. Suppose that we have a stored procedure such as:

```
CREATE PROCEDURE updateAuthorName
  (
    @ID uniqueidentifier,
    @Name varchar(50)
  )
AS
  SET NOCOUNT ON

  UPDATE authors SET au_lname=@Name
  WHERE au_id=@ID;
RETURN
```

We could call it with the following code:

```
Dim dbConn As String = _
          "data source=myserver;initial catalog=pubs;integrated security=SSPI"

Dim cn As New SqlConnection(dbConn)
cn.Open()

Dim cm As New SqlCommand()

Try
  With cm
    .Connection = cn
    .CommandType = CommandType.StoredProcedure
    .CommandText = "updateAuthorName"
    .Parameters.Add("@id", myID)
    .Parameters.Add("@name", newName)

    .ExecuteNonQuery()
  End With

Finally
  cn.Close()
End Try
```

As you can see, using a command object to update data is pretty straightforward. Something a little more complex is when we call a stored procedure that not only updates data, but also returns values via output parameters.

Suppose that we have an `authors` table with an auto-incrementing `id` column. The following stored procedure could add a record into that table, returning the newly created identity value via an output parameter:

```
CREATE PROCEDURE addOrder
  @id int output, @Name varchar(50)
AS

  INSERT INTO authors
  (au_lname)
  VALUES
  (@Name)

  SET @id = @@Identity

RETURN
```

The code to set up a parameter to accept an output value is a bit different from the code for simply sending a value into the stored procedure:

```
Dim dbConn As String = _
          "data source=myserver;initial catalog=pubs;integrated security=SSPI"

Dim cn As New SqlConnection(dbConn)
cn.Open()

Dim cm As New SqlCommand()

Try
  With cm
    .Connection = cn
    .CommandType = CommandType.StoredProcedure
    .CommandText = "updateAuthorName"

    Dim param As New SqlParameter("@id", 0)
    param.Direction = ParameterDirection.Output
    .Parameters.Add(param)

    .Parameters.Add("@name", newName)

    .ExecuteNonQuery()

    newID = .Parameters.Item("@id").Value
  End With

Finally
  cn.Close()
End Try
```

Rather than allowing the `Add()` method to create a `SqlParameter` object for us using its defaults, we create a `SqlParameter` object ourselves. This allows us to set the `Direction` property to indicate that it's an output parameter. The `SqlParameter` object is then added to the `Parameters` collection so that it can transfer the data from the stored procedure back to our code.

After the stored procedure has been executed, we can retrieve the value from the parameter object, and then use it as needed within our application.

ADO.NET transactions

Earlier in the chapter, we discussed Enterprise Services transactions, or two-phase transactions. ADO.NET itself supports a simpler form of transactions that can be used to protect updates made to a single database. We can write code to update multiple tables in a single database, or make multiple changes to a single table, using ADO.NET transactions to ensure that the update will be rolled back in case of error, or when our business logic decides that the operation must be cancelled.

To support this concept, ADO.NET includes transaction objects. These objects are part of the data provider tier in the ADO.NET architecture, so the transaction object for Microsoft SQL Server is called `SqlTransaction`.

The transaction object is associated with the connection object: we use a connection object to create a transaction object. From that point forward, any command objects to be run against this connection must first be associated with the active transaction object. The following code illustrates the changes from our previous data update code to utilize an ADO.NET transaction object:

```
Dim dbConn As String = _
          "data source=myserver;initial catalog=pubs;integrated security=SSPI"

Dim cn As New SqlConnection(dbConn)
cn.Open()

Dim cm As New SqlCommand()
Dim tr As SqlTransaction

Try
  tr = cn.BeginTransaction()

  With cm
    .Connection = tr.Connection
    .Transaction = tr
    .CommandType = CommandType.StoredProcedure
    .CommandText = "updateAuthorName"
    .Parameters.Add("@name", myCriteria)

    .ExecuteNonQuery()
  End With
  tr.Commit()

Catch
  tr.Rollback()

Finally
  cn.Close()
End Try
```

First, we begin a transaction by calling the `BeginTransaction()` method on the connection object. This results in an active transaction object. The transaction object itself has a `Connection` property; we must link our command objects to both the transaction object and the connection property from the transaction. If these are out of sync, we'll get a runtime error.

When implementing manual transactions, we also need to implement a `Catch` block in our error handler so we can call the `Rollback()` method in case of error. Otherwise, we call the `Commit()` method to commit the transaction.

Conclusion

In this chapter, we've looked briefly at all the key .NET technologies that we'll be using to create our n-tier framework. Obviously, we'll also be using Windows Forms, Web Forms, and various other technologies, but they are generally more mainstream and well understood.

Remoting enables efficient client-server or server-server communication. Serialization allows us to convert an object graph into a byte stream, and then to deserialize that byte stream back into a clone of the original graph of objects. We can do this on a single machine, or we can use this technology along with remoting to move objects from machine to machine on a network.

Enterprise Services provide access to COM+ features from within .NET. This is a large and complex technology that has a lot of implications for our architecture, code, and deployment. We'll be using Enterprise Services' transactional support as we create our data access code.

Reflection allows our code to examine classes, methods, and other code structures. We can use reflection to discover information about these structures, but more importantly we can use reflection to manipulate the variables of an object and to call its methods – even ones that are not `Public`. When building a framework, we'll find that there are times when we want to interact with parts of an object that are not publicly exposed, so we'll be using this technique in our framework.

.NET supports the concept of attributes that can be applied to assemblies, classes, methods, and variables. We'll be using custom attributes in our framework, and we've covered the basics of their creation and use in this chapter.

We also discussed .NET's own role-based security, and how the latter interacts with Windows or allows us to build custom security. Finally, we discussed ADO.NET, which we'll be using to read and write data from SQL Server.

At this point, we've covered the theory of distributed architecture and distributed objects, as well as the technologies we'll use to put it all together. Over the next two chapters, we'll construct a distributed object framework using these technologies, and also based on the theory from Chapter 1 and the design from Chapter 2.

CHAPTER 4

4

Business framework implementation

In Chapter 1, we discussed the concepts behind the use of business objects and distributed objects. In Chapter 2, we explored the design of our business framework. In the last chapter, we walked through the key .NET Framework technologies that we need to implement distributed object-oriented systems. In this chapter, we're going to combine all these things together as we create many of the classes in the CSLA .NET framework, using .NET technologies to support the creation of distributed, object-oriented, business applications. Specifically, we'll create the following components:

- `CSLA.Core.BindableBase.dll`
- `CSLA.dll` (or at least, the greater part of it)

Why these two? Well, as we've already seen, a number of the classes in our framework are dependent on other framework classes. For instance, `BusinessBase` is dependent on `Core.BindableBase`. At a component level, we defined these dependencies in Chapter 2.

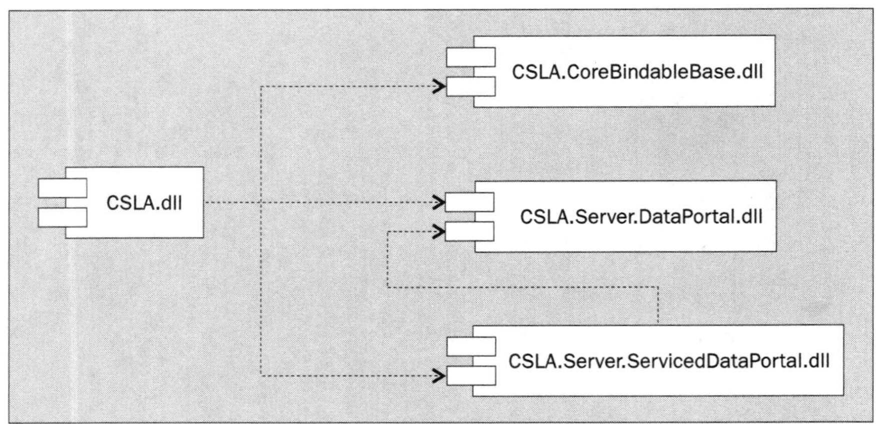

Each of these components contains the various classes that comprise our framework. Before we can create `BusinessBase` and `BusinessCollectionBase`, we must create their base classes in `CSLA.Core.BindableBase.dll`. We can then move on to create most of the classes within `CSLA.dll`, except those that are data-related, so we'll defer the creation of the data portal mechanism and any classes that require it to Chapter 5. Also, there are a handful of framework classes (including those for custom security) that require the data portal code to exist, so we'll create those in Chapter 5 as well.

> *In Chapter 7, we'll create a set of objects using the framework, based on the application and data design that we'll put together in Chapter 6.*

More specifically, the classes that we'll create in this chapter are:

- `Core.BindableBase`
- `Core.BindableCollectionBase`
- `NotUndoableAttribute`
- `Core.UndoableBase`
- `BusinessBase`
- `BrokenRules`
- `RulesCollection`
- `Rule` data type
- `BusinessCollectionBase`
- `ReadOnlyBase`
- `ReadOnlyCollectionBase`
- `SmartDate`

The reasoning behind the existence of each of these classes, and the explanation of how they are organized into namespaces and assemblies, was covered in Chapter 2. In this chapter, we'll focus mostly on the actual implementation of each assembly and class.

Setting up the CSLA .NET solution

Any time we're creating a VS.NET solution that will contain multiple projects (as is the case here), it's best to create the solution before creating any of the projects. The reason for this is that otherwise, VS.NET will name the solution after the name we give to the first project we create.

Open VS.NET and choose File | New | Blank Solution. Give it the name `CSLA`, because that's the name of our framework:

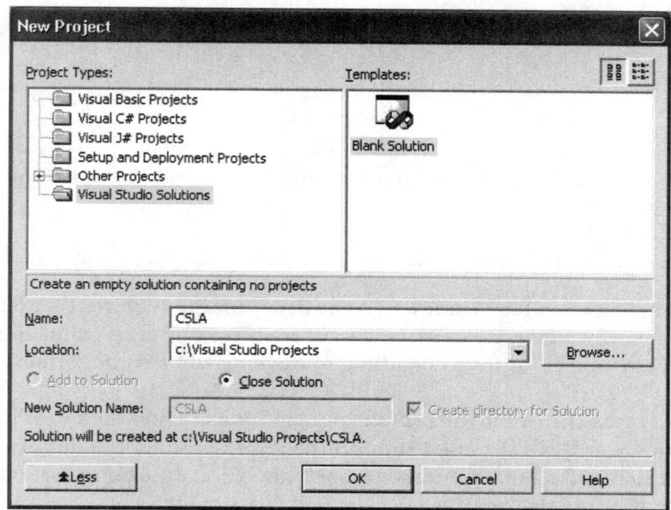

Notice that the solution is created in its own directory within our `Visual Studio Projects` directory. Any projects we add to this solution will, by default, be placed in sub-directories beneath this `CSLA` directory. This provides automatic organization of all our framework projects into a nice directory tree on the disk, and also into a single solution within VS.NET.

CSLA.Core.BindableBase

The `CSLA.Core.BindableBase` assembly contains two classes that are written in C#: `BindableBase` and `BindableCollectionBase`. These will be the bases from which our `BusinessBase` and `BusinessCollectionBase` classes inherit. Notice that `BindableCollectionBase` also inherits from `System.Collections.CollectionBase` so that it's a base *collection* class:

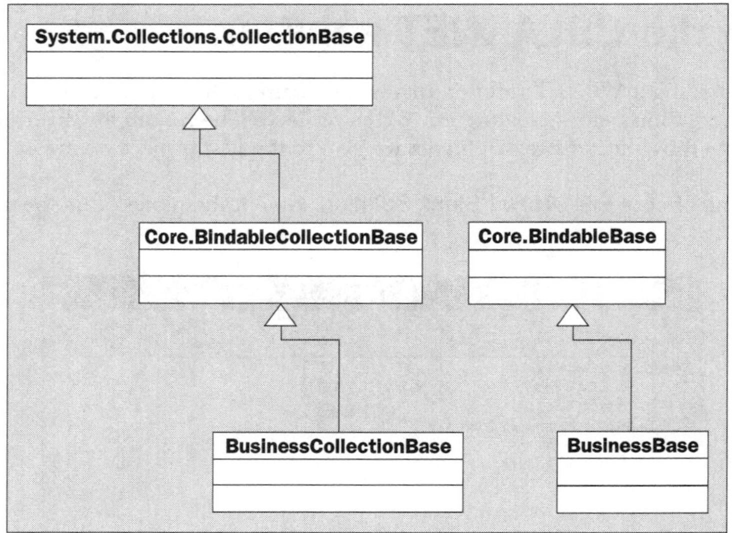

As we've discussed, full support for Windows Forms data binding requires that our business objects and collections raise events. If we then try to serialize our business object or collection (or pass it by value across the network), any object (or form) handling our events will also be serialized, which is a problem.

To solve this, we can mark the event with an attribute to indicate that the event handlers should not be serialized. Unfortunately, VB.NET doesn't support the attribute syntax to do this, since it doesn't allow the `field` target within an attribute. C# *does* support this syntax, meaning that we must create some base classes in C# in order to declare our events using this attribute.

With our `CSLA` solution open in VS.NET, use File | Add Project | New Project to add a new C# Class Library project named `CSLA.Core.BindableBase`:

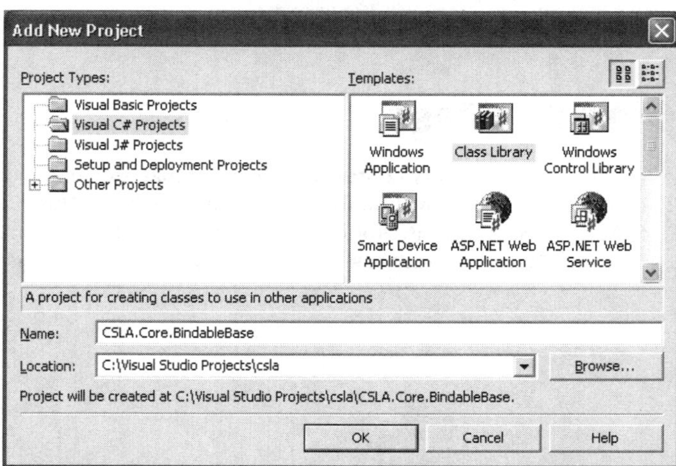

Core.BindableBase

First, let's create the base class that will safely declare our IsDirtyChanged event, which will be raised when *any* property is changed. Rename Class1.cs to BindableBase.cs, and then change its code to the following:

```
using System;

namespace CSLA.Core
{
  /// <summary>
  /// This base class declares the IsDirtyChanged event
  /// to be NonSerialized so serialization will work.
  /// </summary>
  [Serializable()]
  public abstract class BindableBase
  {
    [field: NonSerialized]
    public event EventHandler IsDirtyChanged;

    protected void OnIsDirtyChanged()
    {
      if (IsDirtyChanged != null)
        IsDirtyChanged(this, EventArgs.Empty);
    }
  }
}
```

Notice here that we're declaring this class to be in the CSLA.Core namespace, as discussed in Chapter 2. We might as well change the default namespace that VS.NET will use for any further C# code files we add to the project. Right-click on the project in Solution Explorer, and choose Properties. Change the default namespace to CSLA.Core. Note that changing this won't affect any code we may already have in the project.

It's important that this class is marked as [Serializable()]. We want our business objects to be serializable, and that means that any classes they inherit from must also be marked as such. BindableBase will be the ultimate base class for all our business objects.

Also, the class is declared as abstract, which is the same as MustInherit in VB.NET. This means that an instance of this class can't be created directly. Instead, it must be subclassed to create other classes from which we *can* create objects. In our case, these will be our business objects.

The key lines here, and the reason we're using C# in the first place, occur at the declaration of the event:

```
[field: NonSerialized]
public event EventHandler IsDirtyChanged;
```

By applying the attribute to the event, we're telling .NET that any delegate references that are used to raise the event to other objects should not be serialized. This means that the serialization process won't try to serialize the objects that are receiving and handling our IsDirtyChanged event.

The thing about events and inheritance is that an event can only be raised by code in the class where it is declared. It *can't* be raised by code in classes that inherit from this class. This means that our business objects can't raise the `IsDirtyChanged` event directly, even though we'll want them to do just that. To solve this, we're following a standard .NET design pattern by creating a `protected` method that in turn raises the event:

```
virtual protected void OnIsDirtyChanged()
{
  if (IsDirtyChanged != null)
    IsDirtyChanged(this, EventArgs.Empty);
}
```

Any classes that inherit from our base class can call this method when they want to raise the event. The code above is functionally equivalent to the following VB.NET code:

```
Protected Overridable Sub OnIsDirtyChanged()
  RaiseEvent IsDirtyChanged(Me, EventArgs.Empty)
End Sub
```

The result is that we now have a base class that allows our business objects to raise the `IsDirtyChanged` event, thereby supporting data binding.

Core.BindableCollectionBase

To support Windows Forms data binding fully, collection objects should implement the `System.ComponentModel.IBindingList` interface. This is a fairly complex interface that can be used to enable searching, sorting, and notification of changes to the collection; and to provide control over whether elements can be added, removed, or edited through data binding.

The reason we're discussing this here is that the notification of changes is handled through an event that's part of the `IBindingList` interface. To implement the interface, we must declare and raise a `ListChanged` event – and, of course, that event must have the attribute that prevents it from being serialized.

> *We won't implement the searching or sorting capabilities of this interface in this book. If these features are important to your business collections, you can enhance this code to provide that support for your framework. We'll hard-code the methods for these features of the interface to indicate that the features are not supported.*

Add a new class to the project, named `BindableCollectionBase`. Since this will act as our base collection class, it needs to inherit from `System.Collections.CollectionBase`, and of course it needs to implement the `IBindingList` interface as well. This means that we'll declare the class with the following code:

```
using System;
using System.Collections;
using System.ComponentModel;

namespace CSLA.Core
{
  /// <summary>
```

```
    /// This is a base class that exposes an implementation
    /// of IBindableList that does nothing other than
    /// create a nonserialized version of the listchanged
    /// event.
    /// </summary>
    [Serializable]
    public abstract class BindableCollectionBase : CollectionBase, IBindingList
    {

    }
}
```

When building a framework, it is always wise to think ahead to what future developers might want to do with it. Wherever possible, we should build in flexibility so that business developers can override or alter the behavior of our framework in meaningful ways. For instance, we can allow business developers to have their actual business collection objects control whether data binding can add, remove, or edit items in the collection. While we won't support those concepts by default, we'll add code in our framework so that the business developer can support the features if they desire.

To do this, we'll expose a set of `protected` variables that can optionally be altered by our business classes. Add the highlighted lines to the `BindableCollectionBase` class:

```
    [Serializable]
    public abstract class BindableCollectionBase : CollectionBase, IBindingList
    {
      protected bool AllowNew = false;
      protected bool AllowEdit = false;
      protected bool AllowRemove = false;
```

Since these values default to `false`, we are indicating that by default, these features are not supported by business collections. Because they are `protected` in scope, a business developer can set their values to `true` in order to enable the features for a specific business collection object. This is ideal, because the business collection class will need to implement extra code to support addition of new objects, and may also want to do extra processing to properly support the editing or removal of child objects.

Next, we'll declare the `ListChanged` event to be `NonSerialized`:

```
      [field: NonSerialized]
      public event ListChangedEventHandler ListChanged;
```

As with the `BindableBase` class, this event declaration creates an event that is safe for use with serialization. Once again, we also need to provide a way for our business collections to raise this event, so we create a `protected` method:

```
      virtual protected void OnListChanged(ListChangedEventArgs e)
      {
        if (ListChanged != null)
          ListChanged(this, e);
      }
```

This method can be called to raise the `ListChanged` event by any code that inherits from our base class. Much of the remaining code in the class then provides a very simple implementation of the `IBindingList` interface:

```
    void IBindingList.AddIndex(PropertyDescriptor property) { }

    object IBindingList.AddNew() { return OnAddNew(); }

    void IBindingList.ApplySort(PropertyDescriptor property,
                                ListSortDirection direction) { }

    int IBindingList.Find(PropertyDescriptor property, object key) { return 0; }

    void IBindingList.RemoveIndex(PropertyDescriptor property) { }

    void IBindingList.RemoveSort() { }

    bool IBindingList.AllowEdit { get { return AllowEdit; } }

    bool IBindingList.AllowNew { get { return AllowNew; } }

    bool IBindingList.AllowRemove { get { return AllowRemove; } }

    bool IBindingList.IsSorted { get { return false; } }

    ListSortDirection IBindingList.SortDirection
    { get { return ListSortDirection.Ascending; } }

    PropertyDescriptor IBindingList.SortProperty { get { return null; } }

    bool IBindingList.SupportsChangeNotification { get { return true; } }

    bool IBindingList.SupportsSearching { get { return false; } }

    bool IBindingList.SupportsSorting { get { return false; } }

    virtual protected object OnAddNew() { return null; }
  }
}
```

Since we're not supporting searching or sorting, this code provides no real functionality – it merely returns simple values, or performs no operation. Even so, an important element of the code here is the implementation of the `OnAddNew()` method:

```
virtual protected object OnAddNew() { return null; }
```

This translates to this VB.NET code:

```
Protected Overridable Function OnAddNew() As Object
  Return Nothing
End Function
```

This function is called if data binding tries to add a new object to the collection. It's up to our business implementation to override this OnAddNew() method with a version that actually does return a new, valid object.

Because the AllowNew variable defaults to false, our default behavior is to *not* support adding new items to the collection. This is why the VB.NET declaration for the OnAddNew() method shown above does not use the MustOverride keyword. MustOverride would force the business developer to provide an implementation of this method – which is pointless given that the method typically won't be called.

> **If the business developer changes the AllowNew value to true in their business collection class, then they must provide an implementation of the OnAddNew() method.**

Finally, the BindableCollectionBase class needs to override some methods from CollectionBase itself. When an item is inserted, removed, or changed, or the collection is cleared, a method is run that we can override. In each of these cases, we know that the content of the collection has changed, so we want to raise the ListChanged event:

```
    override protected void OnInsertComplete(int index, object value)
    {
      OnListChanged(
        new ListChangedEventArgs(ListChangedType.ItemAdded, index));
    }

    override protected void OnClearComplete()
    {
      OnListChanged(
        new ListChangedEventArgs(ListChangedType.Reset, 0));
    }

    override protected void OnRemoveComplete(int index, object value)
    {
      OnListChanged(
        new ListChangedEventArgs(ListChangedType.ItemDeleted, index));
    }

    override protected void OnSetComplete(int index,
                                    object oldValue, object newValue)
    {
      OnListChanged(
        new ListChangedEventArgs(ListChangedType.ItemChanged, index));
    }
  }
}
```

Now, any time the collection's contents change, our event will be raised automatically.

CSLA

At this point, we've created the two base classes that safely declare our events for data binding. We're now ready to move on and implement the bulk of the business framework that we described in Chapter 2. This code will make use of what we've already done in this chapter, and will be enhanced when we implement the DataPortal and data access code in Chapter 5.

Here, we'll implement the classes in order of dependence. The following diagram illustrates the dependencies of the classes:

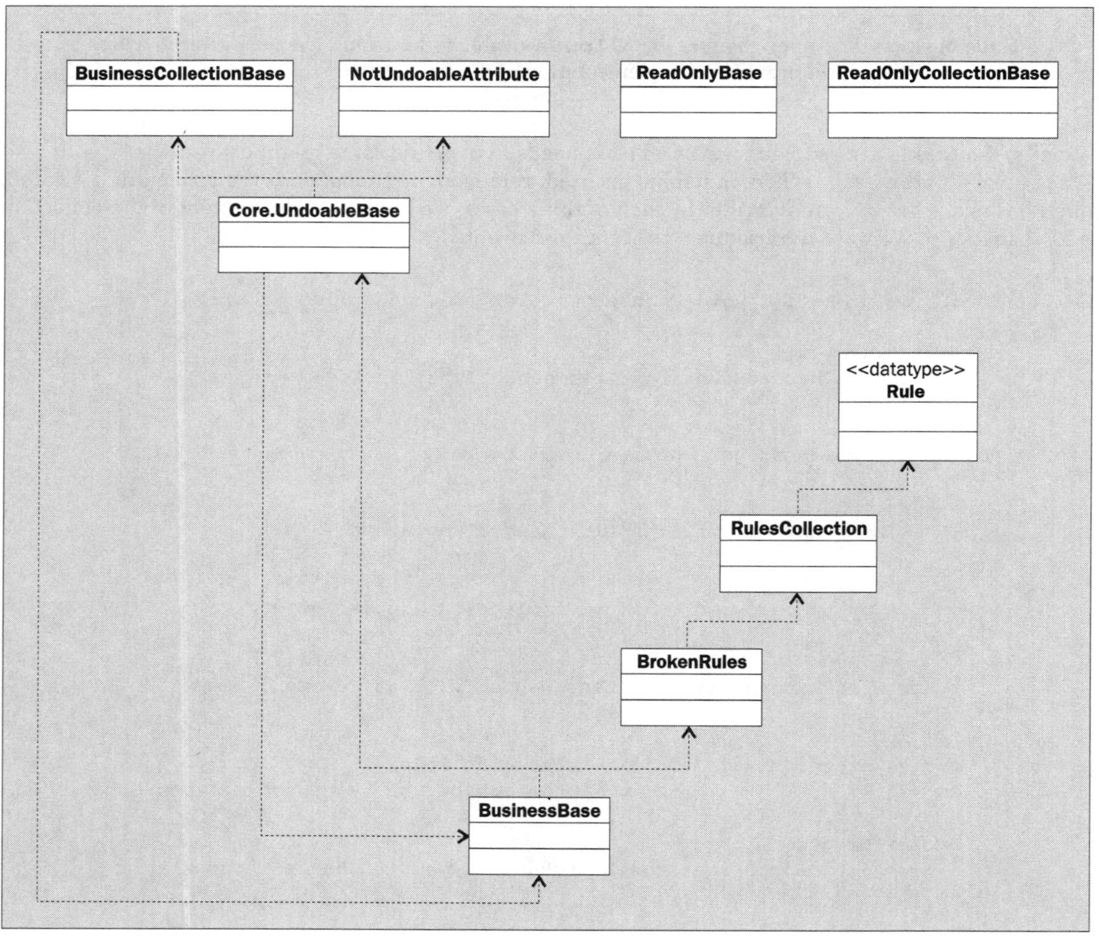

You can see clearly that before we can implement the BusinessBase class, we must implement a number of other classes. Also, notice that we have a circular dependency between UndoableBase and BusinessBase, and another among UndoableBase, BusinessCollectionBase, and BusinessBase. This is not a problem in any technical sense, since all three of these classes are in the same assembly. However, it does mean that as we create UndoableBase, we'll have to write some code that will give us compiler errors until after we've created BusinessBase and BusinessCollectionBase.

Our general plan of attack, then, will be to focus on getting the dependent classes done first, and then we'll wrap up by implementing the `ReadOnlyBase` and `ReadOnlyCollectionBase` classes. As an initial step, add a new VB.NET Class Library project to our solution by right-clicking the solution in Solution Explorer, and choosing Add | New Project. Name it `CSLA`, and make sure that it's in the `CSLA` directory:

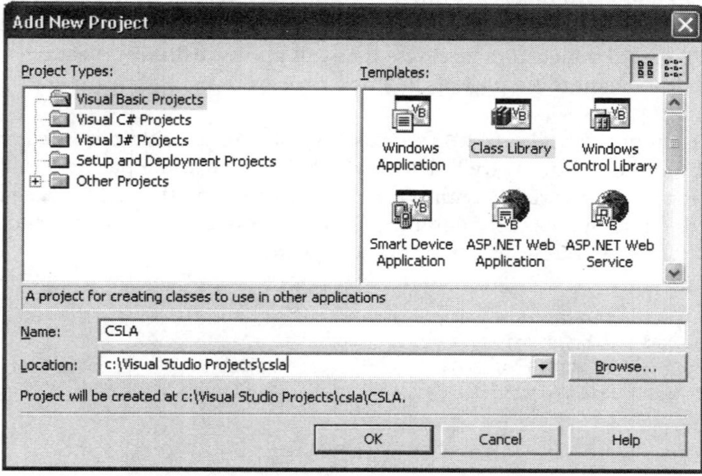

When the project has been created, open its Properties window and make sure that Option Strict is On by default for this project. Then, right-click on `Class1.vb` and delete it from the project. This time, we'll be adding our own classes as and when we need them.

Much of the code we'll be writing will rely on the classes we created in the `CSLA.Core.BindableBase` assembly. Use the Add Reference dialog to add a reference to this project:

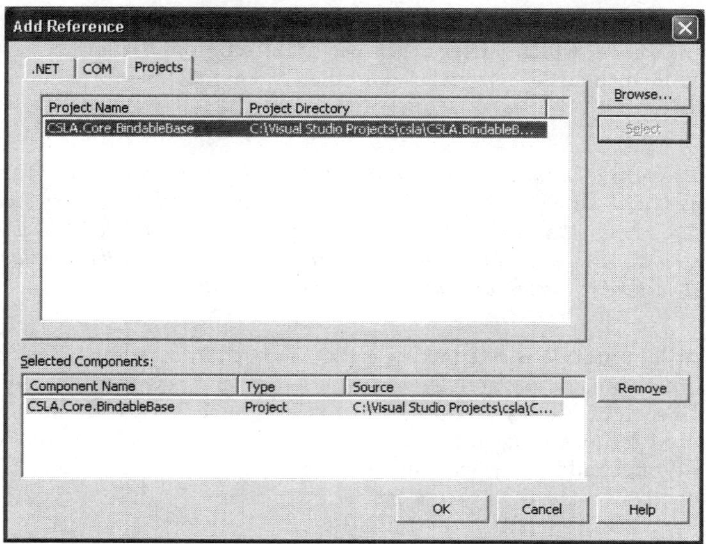

NotUndoableAttribute

As you know, we'll be supporting n-level undo capabilities for our business objects and collections. Sometimes, however, we may have values in our objects that we don't want to be included in the snapshot that's taken before an object is edited. (These may be read-only values, or recalculated values, or values – large images, perhaps – that are simply so big that we choose not to support undo for them.) In this section, we'll create the custom attribute that will allow business object developers to mark any variables that they don't want to be part of the undo process.

In our implementation of the `UndoableBase` class, which will provide our `BusinessBase` class with support for n-level undo operations, we'll detect whether this attribute has been placed on any variables. If so, we'll simply ignore that variable within the undo process, neither taking a snapshot of its value, nor restoring it in the case of a cancel operation. To create the attribute, add a class to the project named `NotUndoableAttribute`, with the following code:

```
' This attribute allows us to mark fields that should
'  not be copied as part of the undo process
<AttributeUsage(AttributeTargets.Field)> _
Public Class NotUndoableAttribute
  Inherits Attribute

End Class
```

The `<AttributeUsage()>` attribute allows us to specify that this attribute can only be applied to fields, or variables, within our code. Beyond that, our attribute is merely a marker to indicate that certain actions should (or should not) be taken by our `UndoableBase` code, so there's no real code here at all.

Core.UndoableBase

The `UndoableBase` class is where all the work to handle n-level undo for an object will take place. This is pretty complex code, which makes heavy use of reflection to find all the instance variables in our business object, take snapshots of their values, and then (potentially) restore their values later in the case of an undo operation.

> *Typically, a snapshot of a business object's variables is taken before the user or an application is allowed to interact with the object. That way we can always undo back to that original state. When we're done, the `BusinessBase` class will include a `BeginEdit()` method that will trigger the snapshot process, a `CancelEdit()` method to restore the object's state to the last snapshot, and an `ApplyEdit()` method to commit any changes since the last snapshot.*

The reason this snapshot process is so complex is that we need to copy the values of *all* variables in our object, and our business object is essentially composed of several classes all merged together through inheritance. As we'll see, this causes problems when classes have fields with the same names as fields in the classes they inherit from; and particular problems if a class inherits from another class in a different assembly. For now though, add a new class named `UndoableBase` to the VB.NET project, and import some namespaces that will make the process easier:

```
Imports System.Reflection
Imports System.IO
Imports System.Runtime.Serialization
Imports System.Runtime.Serialization.Formatters.Binary

Public Class UndoableBase
```

This class should also be in the CSLA.Core namespace, and since our project is already named CSLA, all our classes will be in the CSLA namespace by default. We can use the Namespace keyword to place the class in a sub-namespace named Core:

```
Namespace Core

  Public Class UndoableBase

  End Class

End Namespace
```

Since this will be a base class from which our business objects will ultimately derive, it must be marked as <Serializable()>. It should also be declared with MustInherit, so that no one can create an instance of this class directly – they must create business object classes instead. Finally, we know that we want all our business objects to support the IsDirtyChanged event as implemented by our BindableBase class, so we'll inherit from that too:

```
Namespace Core

  <Serializable()> _
  Public MustInherit Class UndoableBase
    Inherits CSLA.Core.BindableBase

  End Class

End Namespace
```

With that base laid down, we can start to discuss how we're actually going to implement the undo functionality. There are three operations involved: taking a snapshot of the object state, restoring the object state in case of an undo, and discarding stored object state in case of an accept operation.

Additionally, if this object has a collection of child objects, that collection must also perform the store, restore and accept operations. To achieve this, any time we encounter a variable that's derived from the BusinessCollectionBase type, we'll cascade the operation to that object so it can take appropriate action.

The three operations will be implemented by a set of three methods:

- CopyState()
- UndoChanges()
- AcceptChanges()

Helper Functions

To implement the three principal methods, we'll need some helpers that will simplify our use of reflection. More specifically, they simplify the process of determining whether a variable has the <NotUndoable()> attribute attached, and whether a given class inherits from another class. Add the following code to the UndoableBase class:

```
#Region " Helper Functions "

    Private Function NotUndoableField(ByVal Field As FieldInfo) As Boolean

      Return Attribute.IsDefined(Field, GetType(NotUndoableAttribute))

    End Function

    Private Function TypeInheritsFrom( _
       ByVal TypeToCheck As Type, ByVal CheckAgainst As Type) As Boolean

      Dim base As Type = TypeToCheck

      ' Scan up through the inheritance hierarchy, checking each
      '  class to see if it is the one we're looking for
      While Not base.BaseType Is Nothing

        ' If we find the target class, return True
        If base Is CheckAgainst Then Return True

        base = base.BaseType
      End While

      ' The target class is not in the inheritance hierarchy so return False
      Return False

    End Function

#End Region
```

The NotUndoableField Function

The NotUndoableField() function in the above listing returns a Boolean to indicate whether the specified field has the <NotUndoable()> attribute. If the attribute has been applied to the field, the function returns True. We'll use this method as we walk through the variables in our object to snapshot their values, and we'll only snapshot the values of variables *without* this attribute.

The TypeInheritsFrom Function

In everyday VB.NET code, given an *object*, we can discover inheritance information with the `Is` keyword, like this:

```
If myObject Is BusinessBase Then
```

However, this doesn't work if you're given a *type*. For instance, this won't do what you'd like it to:

```
Dim myType As Type = myObject.GetType
If myType Is BusinessBase Then
```

The trouble is that a lot of the code in `UndoableBase` will use `Type` objects, rather than the objects themselves, because we're breaking the business object's variables into groups based on the *class* in which they were defined. Also, we really do need to know whether a given `Type` object represents a class that's a subclass of `BusinessBase` or `BusinessCollectionBase`.

The `TypeInheritsFrom()` function returns a `Boolean` indicating whether the `Type` specified in its first parameter is a subclass of the `Type` specified in its second parameter. We make this determination by using the `BaseType` property to walk up the inheritance chain of the first parameter, checking for a match with the second at each stage.

We'll end up doing this comparison against three types: `UndoableBase`, `BusinessBase`, and `BusinessCollectionBase`. To make things more efficient, let's declare some `Shared` variables that will retrieve these `Type` objects just once, so that we can reuse them throughout our application:

```
<Serializable()> _
Public MustInherit Class UndoableBase
  Inherits CSLA.Core.BindableBase

  ' Variables containing type info for comparisons
  Private Shared UndoableType As Type = GetType(UndoableBase)
  Private Shared BusinessType As Type = GetType(BusinessBase)
  Private Shared CollectionType As Type = GetType(BusinessCollectionBase)
```

Since these are `Shared`, they'll be initialized the first time any business object is created, and reused by all business objects subsequent to that point.

CopyState

The `CopyState()` method will take a snapshot of our object's current data, and store it in a `System.Collections.Stack` object.

Stacking the data

Since we're supporting n-level undo capability, each of our objects could end up storing a number of snapshots. As each undo or accept operation occurs, we'll get rid of the most recent snapshot we've stored; this is the classic behavior of a 'stack' data structure. Fortunately, the .NET Framework includes a pre-built `Stack` class that we can use. Let's declare that now:

```
<Serializable()> _
Public MustInherit Class UndoableBase
  Inherits CSLA.Core.BindableBase

  ' Keep a stack of object state values
  <NotUndoable()> _
  Private mStateStack As New Stack
```

This variable is marked as `<NotUndoable()>` because we certainly don't want to take a snapshot of our snapshots! We just want the variables that contain actual business data. Once we've taken a snapshot of our object's data, we'll serialize the data into a single byte stream, and put that byte stream on the stack. From there, we can retrieve it to perform an undo operation if needed.

Taking a snapshot of data

The process of taking a snapshot of each variable value in our object is a bit tricky. First, we need to use reflection to walk through all the variables in our object. Then, we need to check each variable to see if it has the `<NotUndoable()>` attribute – if so, we need to ignore it. Finally, we need to be aware that variable names may not be unique within our object.

In fact, it's the last part that complicates matters the most. To see what I mean, consider the following two classes:

```
Public Class BaseClass
  Private mID As Integer
End Class

Public Class SubClass
  Inherits BaseClass

  Private mID As Integer
End Class
```

Here, each class has its own variable named `mID`, and in most circumstances that's not a problem. However, if we use reflection to walk through all the variables in a `SubClass` object, we'll find *two* `mID` variables – one for each of the classes in the inheritance hierarchy.

In order to get an accurate snapshot of our object's data, we need to accommodate this scenario. In practice, this means that we need to prefix each variable name with the name of the class to which it belongs. Instead of two `mID` variables, we have `BaseClass!mID` and `SubClass!mID`. The exclamation point is arbitrary, but we do need *some* character to separate the class name from the variable name.

As if this weren't complex enough, reflection works differently with classes that are subclassed from other classes in the *same* assembly, from when a class is subclassed from a class in a *different* assembly. If our example `BaseClass` and `SubClass` are in the same assembly, we can use one technique, but if they're in different assemblies, we need to use a different technique. Of course, our code should deal with both scenarios, so the business developer doesn't have to worry about these details.

The following `CopyState()` method deals with all of the above issues; we'll walk through how it works after the listing:

```
Protected Friend Sub CopyState()

  Dim currentType As Type = Me.GetType
  Dim state As New Hashtable()
  Dim fields() As FieldInfo
  Dim field As FieldInfo
  Dim fieldName As String

  Do
    ' Get the list of fields in this type
    fields = currentType.GetFields(BindingFlags.NonPublic Or _
                                   BindingFlags.Instance Or _
                                   BindingFlags.Public)

    For Each field In fields
      If field.DeclaringType Is currentType Then

        ' See if this field is marked as not undoable
        If Not NotUndoableField(field) Then

          ' The field is undoable, so it needs to be processed
          If TypeInheritsFrom(field.FieldType, CollectionType) Then

            ' This is a child collection, cascade the call
            CType(field.GetValue(Me), BusinessCollectionBase).CopyState()

          ElseIf TypeInheritsFrom(field.FieldType, BusinessType) Then

            ' This is a child object, cascade the call
            CType(field.GetValue(Me), BusinessBase).CopyState()

          Else

            ' This is a normal field, simply trap the value
            fieldName = field.DeclaringType.Name & "!" & field.Name
            state.Add(fieldName, field.GetValue(Me))
          End If
        End If
      End If
    Next

    currentType = currentType.BaseType

  Loop Until currentType Is UndoableType

  ' Serialize the state and stack it
  Dim buffer As New MemoryStream()
  Dim formatter As New BinaryFormatter()
  formatter.Serialize(buffer, state)
  mStateStack.Push(buffer.ToArray)

End Sub
```

This method is scoped as Protected Friend, which is a bit unusual. The method needs Protected scope because BusinessBase will subclass UndoableBase, and its BeginEdit() method will need to call CopyState(). That part is fairly straightforward.

The method also needs Friend scope, however, because business objects will be contained within business collections. When a collection needs to take a snapshot of its data, what that really means is that the objects *within* the collection need to take snapshots of their data. BusinessCollectionBase will include code that goes through all the business objects it contains, telling each business object to take a snapshot of its state. This will be done via the CopyState() method – which means that BusinessCollectionBase needs the ability to call this method too. Since it's in the same project, we can accomplish this with Friend scope.

In order to take a snapshot of data, we need somewhere to store the various field values before we push them onto the stack. For this purpose, we're using a Hashtable, which allows us to store name-value pairs. It also provides high-speed access to values based on their name, which will be important for our undo implementation. Finally, the Hashtable object supports .NET serialization, which means that we can serialize the Hashtable and pass it by value across the network as part of our overall business object.

The routine we've written here is essentially a big loop that starts with the outermost class in our inheritance hierarchy, and walks back up through the chain of classes until it gets to UndoableBase. At that point, we can stop: we know that we've got a snapshot of all our business data.

Get a list of fields

It's inside the loop that we do all the real work. First, we get a list of all the fields corresponding to the current class:

```
' Get the list of fields in this type
fields = currentType.GetFields(BindingFlags.NonPublic Or _
                               BindingFlags.Instance Or _
                               BindingFlags.Public)
```

We don't care whether the fields are Public – we want all of them anyway! What's more important is that we only want instance variables, not those declared as Shared. The result of this call is an array of FieldInfo objects, each of which corresponds to a variable in our object.

Avoiding double-processing of fields

As we discussed earlier, our array could include variables from the base classes of the current class. Due to the way the JIT compiler optimizes code within the same assembly, if some of our base classes are in the same assembly as our actual business class, we may find the same variable listed in multiple classes! As we walk up the inheritance hierarchy, we could end up processing those variables twice, so as we loop through the array we only look at the fields that *directly* belong to the class we're currently processing:

```
For Each field In fields
  If field.DeclaringType Is currentType Then
```

Skip <NotUndoable()> fields

At this point in the proceedings, we know that we're dealing with a field (variable) within our object that's part of the current class in the inheritance hierarchy. However, we only want to take a snapshot of the variable if it doesn't have the <NotUndoable()> attribute, so we need to check for that:

```
' See if this field is marked as not undoable
If Not NotUndoableField(field) Then
```

Having got this far, we know that we have a variable that needs to be part of our snapshot, so there are three possibilities: we may have a regular variable, we may have a reference to a child object, or we may have a reference to a collection of child objects.

Cascading the call to child objects or collections

If we have a reference to a child object (or a collection of child objects), we need to cascade our `CopyState()` call to that object, so that it can take its own snapshot:

```
If TypeInheritsFrom(field.FieldType, CollectionType) Then

  ' This is a child collection, cascade the call
  CType(field.GetValue(Me), BusinessCollectionBase).CopyState()

ElseIf TypeInheritsFrom(field.FieldType, BusinessType) Then

  ' This is a child object, cascade the call
  CType(field.GetValue(Me), BusinessBase).CopyState()
```

For our object to 'reach into' these objects and manipulate their state would break encapsulation. Instead, therefore, we call the (collection) object's own `CopyState()` method (which in turn loops through all its child objects calling *their* `CopyState()` methods).

> *Of course, the `GetValue()` method returns everything as type `Object`, so we need to use the `CType()` function to convert the object to `Business(Collection)Base`, so we can call the method.*

Later on, when we implement methods to undo or accept any changes, they'll work the same way – that is, they'll cascade the calls through the collection object to all the child objects. This way, all the objects handle undo the same way, without breaking encapsulation.

Taking a snapshot of a regular variable

If we have a regular variable, we can simply store its value into our `Hashtable` object, associating that value with the combined class name and variable name:

```
' This is a normal field, simply trap the value
fieldName = field.DeclaringType.Name & "!" & field.Name
state.Add(fieldName, field.GetValue(Me))
```

Note that these 'regular' variables might actually be complex types in and of themselves. All we know is that the variable doesn't contain an object derived from `BusinessCollectionBase` or `BusinessBase`. It could be a simple value such as an `Integer` or `String`, or it could be a complex object (as long as that object is marked as `<Serializable()>`).

After we've gone through every variable for every class in our inheritance hierarchy, our `Hashtable` will contain a complete snapshot of all the data in our business object.

> *Note that this snapshot will include some variables that we'll be putting into the* `BusinessBase` *class to keep track of the object's status (such as whether it's new, dirty, deleted, etc.). The snapshot will also include the collection of broken rules that we'll implement later. An undo operation will restore the object to its previous state in* every *way.*

Serializing and stacking the hash table

At this point, we have our snapshot, but it's in a complex data type: a `Hashtable`. To further complicate matters, some of the elements contained in the `Hashtable` might be references to more complex objects. In that case, the `Hashtable` just has a reference to the existing object – not a copy or a snapshot at all.

Fortunately, there's an easy answer to both issues. We can use .NET serialization to convert the `Hashtable` to a byte stream, reducing it from a complex data type into a very simple one for storage. Better yet, the very process of serializing the `Hashtable` will *automatically* serialize any objects to which it has references.

This does require that all objects referenced by our business objects must be marked as `<Serializable()>`, so that they can be included in the byte stream. If we don't do that, the serialization attempt will result in a runtime error. Alternatively, we can mark any objects that can't be serialized as `<NotUndoable()>`, so that the undo process simply ignores them.

The code to do the serialization is fairly straightforward:

```
' Serialize the state and stack it
Dim buffer As New MemoryStream()
Dim formatter As New BinaryFormatter()
formatter.Serialize(buffer, state)
```

The `MemoryStream` object is our byte stream in memory. The `BinaryFormatter` object does the actual serialization, converting the `Hashtable` (and any objects to which it refers) into a stream of bytes. Once we have the byte stream, we can simply convert it to a byte array and put that on the stack:

```
mStateStack.Push(buffer.ToArray)
```

Converting a `MemoryStream` to a byte array is a non-issue, since the `MemoryStream` already contains a byte array with its data. It just provides us with a reference to that existing array, so no data is copied.

The act of conversion to a byte array is important, however, because a byte array is serializable, while a `MemoryStream` object is not. If we need to pass our object across the network by value *while it is being edited*, we need to ensure that the snapshots in our stack can be serialized by .NET.

> *We don't* anticipate *passing our objects across the network while in the middle of being edited, but since our business object is* `<Serializable()>`*, we can't prevent the business developer from doing just that. If we were to reference a* `MemoryStream`*, the business application would get a runtime error as the serialization failed, and that's not acceptable. By converting the data to a byte array, we avoid accidentally crashing the application in the off chance that the business developer does decide to pass our object across the network as it is being edited.*

At this point, we're a third of the way through. We can create a stack of snapshots of our object's data, so now we need to move on and implement the undo and accept operations.

UndoChanges

The `UndoChanges()` method is the reverse of `CopyState()`. It takes a snapshot of data off the stack, deserializes it back into a `Hashtable`, and then takes each value from the `Hashtable` and restores it into the appropriate object variable.

We've already solved the hard issues of walking through the types in our inheritance hierarchy and retrieving all the fields in the object – we had to deal with those when we implemented `CopyState()`. The structure of `UndoChanges()` will therefore be virtually identical, except that we'll be restoring variable values rather than taking a snapshot.

The EditLevel property

Before we get underway, the one thing we do need to keep in mind is that we need to program defensively. The business developer might accidentally write code to call our `UndoChanges()` method at times when we have no state to restore! In that case, we obviously can't do any work, so to detect it we can implement an `EditLevel` property to indicate how many snapshot elements are on our `Stack` object:

```
Protected ReadOnly Property EditLevel() As Integer
  Get
    Return mStateStack.Count
  End Get
End Property
```

The property is declared as `Protected` because we'll also use it in the `BusinessBase` class, later in the chapter.

The UndoChanges method

Here's the code for the `UndoChanges()` method itself:

```
Protected Friend Sub UndoChanges()

  ' If there are no stacked states, do nothing
  If EditLevel > 0 Then
    Dim buffer As New MemoryStream(CType(mStateStack.Pop(), Byte()))
    buffer.Position = 0
    Dim formatter As New BinaryFormatter()
    Dim state As Hashtable = CType(formatter.Deserialize(buffer), Hashtable)

    Dim currentType As Type = Me.GetType
    Dim fields() As FieldInfo
    Dim field As FieldInfo
    Dim fieldName As String

    Do
      ' Get the list of fields in this type
      fields = currentType.GetFields(BindingFlags.NonPublic Or _
                                     BindingFlags.Instance Or _
                                     BindingFlags.Public)
```

```
        For Each field In fields
          If field.DeclaringType Is currentType Then

            ' See if the field is undoable or not
            If Not NotUndoableField(field) Then

              ' The field is undoable, so restore its value
              If TypeInheritsFrom(field.FieldType, CollectionType) Then

                ' This is a child collection, cascade the call
                CType(field.GetValue(Me), _
                      BusinessCollectionBase).UndoChanges()

              ElseIf TypeInheritsFrom(field.FieldType, BusinessType) Then

                ' This is a child object, cascade the call
                CType(field.GetValue(Me), BusinessBase).UndoChanges()

              Else

                ' This is a regular field, restore its value
                fieldName = field.DeclaringType.Name & "!" & field.Name
                field.SetValue(Me, state.Item(fieldName))
              End If
            End If
          End If
        Next

        currentType = currentType.BaseType

      Loop Until currentType Is UndoableType
    End If
  End Sub
```

Recreating the Hashtable object

First, we check to make sure that there's data on the stack for us to restore. Once that's done, we pop the most recently added snapshot off the stack and deserialize it to recreate the Hashtable object containing the detailed values:

```
Dim buffer As New MemoryStream(CType(mStateStack.Pop(), Byte()))
buffer.Position = 0
Dim formatter As New BinaryFormatter()
Dim state As Hashtable = CType(formatter.Deserialize(buffer), Hashtable)
```

This is the reverse of the process that we used to put the Hashtable onto the stack in the first place. We take the byte array off the stack and use it to create a new MemoryStream object. We then make sure that the MemoryStream's internal cursor is set to the start of the data, at which point we can use a BinaryFormatter object to deserialize the data. The result of that process is a Hashtable, which is what we started with in the first place.

Restoring the object's state data

Now that we have the Hashtable that contains the original object values, we can implement the same kind of loop as we did for CopyState() to walk through the variables in our object. If we encounter child business objects or business object collections, we cascade the UndoChanges() call to those objects so that they can do their own restore operation. Again, this is done to preserve encapsulation – only the code within a given object should manipulate that object's data.

When we encounter a 'normal' variable, we restore its value from the Hashtable:

```
' This is a regular field, restore its value
fieldName = field.DeclaringType.Name & "!" & field.Name
field.SetValue(Me, state.Item(fieldName))
```

At the end of this process, we'll have totally reversed any changes made to the object since the most recent snapshot was taken. All we have to do now is implement a method to *accept* changes, rather than to undo them.

AcceptChanges

AcceptChanges() is actually the simplest of the three methods. If we're accepting changes, it means that the current values in the object are the ones we want to keep, and that the most recent snapshot is now meaningless.

In concept, this means that all we need to do is discard the most recent snapshot. However, we also need to remember that our object may have child objects, or collections of child objects – and they need to know to accept changes as well. This means that we need to loop through our object's variables to find any such children, and cascade the method call to them too. Here's the code for the method:

```
  Protected Friend Sub AcceptChanges()
    If EditLevel > 0 Then
      mStateStack.Pop()

      Dim currentType As Type = Me.GetType
      Dim fields() As FieldInfo
      Dim field As FieldInfo
      Dim fieldName As String

      Do
        ' Get the list of fields in this type
        fields = currentType.GetFields(BindingFlags.NonPublic Or _
                                       BindingFlags.Instance Or _
                                       BindingFlags.Public)

        For Each field In fields
          If field.DeclaringType Is currentType Then

            ' See if the field is undoable or not
            If Not NotUndoableField(field) Then

              ' The field is undoable so see if it is a collection
              If TypeInheritsFrom(field.FieldType, CollectionType) Then
```

```
                ' It is a collection so cascade the call
                CType(field.GetValue(Me), _
                  BusinessCollectionBase).AcceptChanges()

              ElseIf TypeInheritsFrom(field.FieldType, BusinessType) Then

                ' It is a child object so cascade the call
                CType(field.GetValue(Me), BusinessBase).AcceptChanges()
              End If
            End If
          End If
        Next

        currentType = currentType.BaseType

      Loop Until currentType Is UndoableType
    End If
  End Sub
```

First, we ensure that there is data on the stack. If there is, we then remove and discard the most recent snapshot:

```
mStateStack.Pop()
```

Then all that remains is to implement the same basic looping structure as before, so that we can scan through all the variables in our object to find any child objects or child collections. If we find them, the `AcceptChanges()` call is cascaded to that object so it can accept its changes as well.

BusinessBase

With `UndoableBase` complete, we can implement almost all of the `BusinessBase` class. (The only bits we'll have to defer are those to do with tracking business rules via the `BrokenRules` class, and we'll discuss that next!)

> *Of course, there will also be a fair amount of code in `BusinessBase` to support data access – a topic we'll discuss in Chapter 5. In this chapter, we're focusing on the behaviors that support the creation of the user interface, and the implementation of non-data-access business logic.*

To get underway, add a new class to the `CSLA` project, and name it `BusinessBase`. We know that it needs to inherit from `UndoableBase` (and therefore also from `BindableBase`), so we can start with this code:

```
<Serializable()> _
Public MustInherit Class BusinessBase
  Inherits Core.UndoableBase

End Class
```

Notice that the class is marked as `MustInherit`. It's meaningless to create an unadorned `BusinessBase` object. Instead, this class will be used as a base from which business classes and objects can be created.

Tracking basic object status

All business objects have some common behaviors that we can implement in `BusinessBase`. At the very least, we need to keep track of whether the object has just been created, whether its data has been changed, or whether it has been marked for deletion. We'll also want to keep track of whether it is valid, but we'll implement that later on, when we build the `BrokenRules` class.

By tracking whether an object is new, we enable the business developer to implement fields that can be changed as an object is being created, but not after it's been saved to the database. For instance, a property on the object that's a primary field in the database can be changed by the user up until the data is actually stored in the database. After that point, it must become read-only. While the business developer could keep track of whether the object is new, it is simpler for our framework to deal with that detail on their behalf.

We'll also use the knowledge of whether the object is new to decide whether to do an insert or an update operation in the data access code. If the object is new, then we're inserting the data; otherwise, we're updating existing data.

As we discussed in Chapter 2, it is also important to keep track of whether the object's data has been changed – we can use this knowledge to optimize our data access. When the UI code asks the object to save its data to the database, we can choose to do the save operation only if the object's data has been changed. If it hasn't been changed, there's no reason to update the database with the values it already contains.

Also in Chapter 2, we discussed the two ways of deleting object data from the database. One way is to pass criteria data that identifies the object to the server, so that the server can simply delete the data. The other way is to retrieve the data from the database to construct the object on the client. The UI code can then mark the object as deleted, and save it to the server. In this case, our data access code will detect that the object was marked for deletion, and remove its data from the database.

These different approaches are valid in different business scenarios, and we're supporting both in our framework so that the business developer can choose between them as appropriate. By tracking whether an object is marked as deleted, we enable the second scenario.

To track these three pieces of information, we'll need some variables. To help keep everything organized, we'll put them, along with their related code, in a new region:

```
<Serializable()> _
Public MustInherit Class BusinessBase
  Inherits Core.UndoableBase

#Region " IsNew, IsDeleted, IsDirty "

  ' Keep track of whether we are new, deleted or dirty
  Private mIsNew As Boolean = True
  Private mIsDeleted As Boolean = False
  Private mIsDirty As Boolean = True

#End Region
```

Notice that these variables are *not* marked as `<NotUndoable()>`, so they *will* be stored and restored in the course of any `CopyState()`, `UndoChanges()`, or `AcceptChanges()` method calls. This is important, as these are all elements of our object's state that need to be restored in the case of an undo operation.

Also notice that as a business object is created, we default it to being 'new'. If we then load it with data from the database, we'll set the mIsNew variable to False, but to start with we assume that it's new. Given this, it's also reasonable to assume that a new object is not marked for deletion. It can be marked for deletion later on, but to start with it's assumed that we don't want to delete this new object!

The object also starts out marked as dirty. This may sound a bit surprising, but the data in a new object doesn't match anything in the database, and in our terms that means that it's 'dirty'. This is important, because we want to make sure that any new object will be saved to the database when requested by the business or UI code. Later on, we'll ensure that we don't try to update an object *unless* it is dirty, so here we're simply making sure that any new object will get saved appropriately.

IsDirty

Now we can implement the code that uses these variables, the most straightforward piece of which just keeps track of whether any data in our object has changed. There's no way to detect automatically when a variable within our object has been changed, so we must rely on the business developer to tell us when an object has become dirty.

However, there's no way that code from *outside* the business object should be able to alter this value – whether we are dirty should be controlled entirely from within that object. To this end, we'll implement a Protected method that allows the business logic within the object to mark the object as dirty.

```
  Protected Sub MarkDirty()
    mIsDirty = True
    OnIsDirtyChanged()
  End Sub

#End Region
```

The call to OnIsDirtyChanged() refers back to the code we created in BindableBase – it causes the IsDirtyChanged event to be raised. Since the MarkDirty() method should be called by our business logic any time that the object's internal state is changed, this means that the IsDirtyChanged event will be raised any time the object's data changes.

The next thing to realize is that there's never reason for the *business logic* in an object to mark the object as being 'not dirty'. If the user requests an undo operation, the object's state will be restored to its previous values – including the mIsDirty variable. This means that mIsDirty will be restored to False if the object is completely restored to its original state. However, we *will* need to mark the object as 'clean' from within BusinessBase, when the data is updated into the database. We'll create a Private method to support this functionality:

```
  Private Sub MarkClean()
    mIsDirty = False
    OnIsDirtyChanged()
  End Sub

#End Region
```

Again, we not only set the variable's value, but also call OnIsDirtyChanged() to cause the IsDirtyChanged event to be raised.

Finally, we need to expose a property so that business and UI code can get the value of the flag:

```
    Public Overridable ReadOnly Property IsDirty() As Boolean
      Get
        Return mIsDirty
      End Get
    End Property

  #End Region
```

Notice that this method is marked as `Overridable`. This is important, because sometimes our business objects aren't simply dirty because their own data has changed. For instance, consider a business object that contains a collection of child objects. Even if the business object's data hasn't changed, it will be dirty if any of its child objects has changed. In that case, the business developer will need to override the `IsDirty` property to provide a more sophisticated implementation. We'll see an example of this in Chapter 6, when we implement our example business objects.

IsDeleted

As we've said a couple of times already, deletion of an object can be done in a couple of ways: deferred, or immediate. The deferred approach allows us to load the object into memory, view its data, and manipulate it. At that point, the user may decide to delete the object, in which case we'll mark it for deletion. When the object is then saved to the database, instead of an `UPDATE` operation, we'll perform a `DELETE` operation. This approach is particularly useful for child objects, where we may be adding and updating some child objects at the same time as deleting others.

The immediate approach is entirely different. In that case, we don't load the object into memory at all – we simply pass criteria data to the `DataPortal`, which invokes our business logic to delete the data from the database directly. Immediate deletion is commonly employed where the UI presents the user with a large list of information, such as a list of customers. The user can select one or more customers from the list and then press a Delete button. In that case, there's no reason to retrieve the complete customer objects – we can simply remove them using criteria information.

Support for the immediate approach is provided by the `DataPortal`, which we'll be discussing in the next chapter. The deferred approach, on the other hand, is something that we'll implement here by using the `mIsDeleted` variable. First, let's create a property to expose the value:

```
    Public ReadOnly Property IsDeleted() As Boolean
      Get
        Return mIsDeleted
      End Get
    End Property

  #End Region
```

Unlike the `IsDirty` property, this one is not `Overridable`, because there's no reason for the business object to change this behavior.

Then, as with `mIsDirty`, we'll expose a `Protected` method so that our business logic can mark the object as deleted when necessary:

```
    Protected Sub MarkDeleted()
      mIsDeleted = True
      MarkDirty()
    End Sub

  #End Region
```

Of course, marking the object as deleted is another way of changing its data, so we also call the MarkDirty() method to indicate that the object's state has been changed. Later on, we'll implement a Public method named Delete() that can be called by the UI code. That method will call the MarkDeleted() method to actually mark the object for deletion.

As with mIsDirty, there's no reason for our business logic ever to mark an object as 'not deleted'. If that behavior is desired, an undo operation can be invoked, which will restore our object to its previous state – including resetting the mIsDeleted variable to its original False value.

IsNew

The third of our basic object status-tracking properties keeps track of whether the object is new. By "new", we simply mean that the object exists in memory, but not in the database or other persistent store. If the object's data resides in the database, then the object is classed as "old".

Having this piece of information around will allow us to write our data access code very easily later on – it encapsulates the decision surrounding whether to perform an INSERT or an UPDATE operation on the database. Sometimes, it can be useful to the UI developer as well, since some UI behaviors may be different for a new object, as compared to an existing object. The ability to edit the object's primary key data is a good example: this is often editable only up to the point that the data has been stored in the database. When the object becomes "old", the primary key is fixed.

To provide access to this information, we can implement a property:

```
    Public ReadOnly Property IsNew() As Boolean
      Get
        Return mIsNew
      End Get
    End Property

  #End Region
```

We also need to allow the business developer to indicate whether the object is new or old. However, neither the UI code nor any other code outside our business object should be able to change the value, so we'll create a couple of Protected methods:

```
    Protected Sub MarkNew()
      mIsNew = True
      mIsDeleted = False
      MarkDirty()
    End Sub

    Protected Sub MarkOld()
      mIsNew = False
      MarkClean()
    End Sub

  #End Region
```

After an object has been saved to the database, for instance, the `MarkOld()` method would be called, since at that point the object's data resides in the database and not just in memory. Notice, however, that we are not *only* altering the `mIsNew` variable.

The scenario for marking an object as being *new* is right after we've completed a delete operation, thereby removing the object's data from the database. This means that not only is the object now new (where it was old before), but also the object in memory is no longer marked for deletion – it has, in fact, already been deleted and is now like a brand new object.

Also, whether we're marking the object as new or old, we need to indicate that its data has been changed. If an object was old and is now marked as new, the object has changed. By definition, the data in the object no longer matches any data in a database, so the `MarkNew()` method calls `MarkDirty()`. On the other hand, if we're marking an object as old, it means that we've just synchronized the database and the object – typically because we've just performed an `INSERT` operation. In this case, the object is now both 'old' and 'clean' – all our data matches the data in the database. To this end, the `MarkOld()` method calls `MarkClean()` to mark the object as unchanged.

Object editing

Moving on from basic state-handling, in `UndoableBase` we implemented the basic functionality to take snapshots of our object's data, and then perform undo or accept operations using those snapshots. Those methods were implemented as `Protected` methods, so they're not available for use by code in the user interface. In `BusinessBase`, we can implement three standard methods for use by the UI code:

Method	Description
`BeginEdit()`	Initiate editing of the object – triggers a call to `CopyState()`
`CancelEdit()`	Indicates that the user wants to undo their recent changes – triggers a call to `UndoChanges()`
`ApplyEdit()`	Indicates that the user wants to keep their recent changes – triggers a call to `AcceptChanges()`

We'll also implement the `System.ComponentModel.IEditableObject` interface in order to support data binding. The `IEditableObject` interface is used by Windows Forms data binding to control the editing of objects.

BeginEdit, CancelEdit and ApplyEdit methods

First, let's implement the basic edit methods. Once again, we'll put them in a region to keep them organized:

```
#Region " Begin/Cancel/ApplyEdit "

  ' Allow the UI to start a nested edit on the object
  Public Sub BeginEdit()
    CopyState()
  End Sub

  ' Allow the UI to cancel a nested edit on the object
  Public Sub CancelEdit()
    UndoChanges()
  End Sub
```

```
    ' Allow the UI to apply a nested edit on the object
    Public Sub ApplyEdit()
      AcceptChanges()
    End Sub

  #End Region
```

These methods can be called by our UI code as needed. Before allowing the user to edit the object, the UI should call `BeginEdit()`. If the user then clicks a Cancel button, the `CancelEdit()` method can be called. If the user clicks a Save or Accept button, then `ApplyEdit()` can be called.

Calling `BeginEdit()` multiple times will cause stacking of states. This allows complex hierarchical interfaces to be created, in which each form has its own Cancel button that triggers a call to `CancelEdit()`.

Nothing *requires* the use of `BeginEdit()`, `CancelEdit()`, or `ApplyEdit()`. In many web scenarios, as we'll see in Chapter 9, there's no need to use these methods at all. A flat UI with no Cancel button has no requirement for undo functionality, so there's no reason to incur the overhead of taking a snapshot of our object's data. On the other hand, if we're creating a complex Windows Forms UI that involves modal dialog windows to allow editing of child objects (or even grandchild objects), we may choose to call these methods manually to support OK and Cancel buttons on each of the dialog windows.

IEditableObject interface

As we've described, we also want to support the `IEditableObject` interface. This interface is used by the Windows Forms data binding infrastructure in two cases:

- First, if our object is a child of a collection, and is being edited in a `DataGrid` control, the `IEditableObject` interface will be used so that the user can start editing a row of the grid (that is, one of our objects), and then press *Esc* to undo any edits they've made on the row.
- Second, if we bind controls from a Windows Form to our object's properties, the `IEditableObject` interface will be used to tell us that editing has *started.* It will *not* be used to tell us when editing is complete, or if the user requests an undo. It's up to our UI code to handle these cases.

If we *are* using data binding to bind our object to a form, we can allow the data binding infrastructure to tell us that editing has started. I typically don't rely on that feature, preferring to call `BeginEdit()` myself. Since I have to call `CancelEdit()` and `ApplyEdit()` manually anyway, I prefer simply to control the entire process.

`IEditableObject` is most important when our object is being edited within a `DataGrid` control. In that case, this interface is the *only* way to get the editing behavior that's expected by users. The `IEditableObject` interface comes from the `System.ComponentModel` namespace, so we'll import that first:

```
Imports System.ComponentModel
```

Then we can indicate that we want to implement the interface:

```
<Serializable()> _
Public MustInherit Class BusinessBase
  Inherits Core.UndoableBase
  Implements IEditableObject
```

Clearly, implementing the interface requires that we understand how it works! The interface defines three methods:

Method	Description
`BeginEdit()`	This is called to indicate the start of an edit process. However, it may be called *many times* during the same edit process, and only the first call should be honored.
`CancelEdit()`	This is called to indicate that any changes since the first `BeginEdit()` call should be undone.
`EndEdit()`	This is called to indicate that the edit process is complete, and that any changes should be kept intact.

While these methods are certainly *similar* to our existing edit methods, there are some key differences in the way `BeginEdit()` works. *Every* call to our existing `BeginEdit()` method will result in a new snapshot of our object's state, while only the *first* call to `IEditableObject.BeginEdit()` should be honored. Any subsequent calls (and they do happen during data binding) should be ignored.

> *When we bind an object's properties to controls on a Windows Form, we'll get many calls to `IEditableObject.BeginEdit()` from the Windows Forms data binding infrastructure. In the .NET Framework documentation, it's made quite clear that only the first such call should be honored, so that's what we'll implement here.*

So that we can implement the behavior of `IEditableObject.BeginEdit()` properly, we need to keep track of whether the edit process has been started, and when it ends. At the same time, though, we want to preserve our existing `BeginEdit()` functionality. To this end, we'll implement a separate method to implement `IEditableObject.BeginEdit()` that makes use of a variable to keep track of the editing status:

```
#Region " Begin/Cancel/ApplyEdit "

  <NotUndoable()> _
  Private mBindingEdit As Boolean = False

  ' Allow data binding to start a nested edit on the object
  Private Sub BindingBeginEdit() Implements IEditableObject.BeginEdit
    If Not mBindingEdit Then
      BeginEdit()
    End If
  End Sub

  ' Allow the UI to start a nested edit on the object
  Public Sub BeginEdit()
    mBindingEdit = True
    CopyState()
  End Sub

  ' Allow the UI to cancel a nested edit on the object
  Public Sub CancelEdit() Implements IEditableObject.CancelEdit
    mBindingEdit = False
```

```
      UndoChanges()
    End Sub

    ' Allow the UI to apply a nested edit on the object
    Public Overridable Sub ApplyEdit() Implements IEditableObject.EndEdit
      mBindingEdit = False
      AcceptChanges()
    End Sub

  #End Region
```

The `mBindingEdit` variable is set to `True` when an edit process is started, and to `False` when either `CancelEdit()` or `ApplyEdit()` (or `IEditableObject.EndEdit()`) is called. With this mechanism in place, the implementation of `IEditableObject.BeginEdit()` only calls the real `BeginEdit()` method if no edit session is currently underway.

Notice that `mBindingEdit` is declared with the `<NotUndoable()>` attribute. This variable controls interaction with the UI, not internal object state, and because of this there's no reason to make it part of the object's snapshot data – that would just waste memory.

With the implementation of the edit methods and `IEditableObject`, we now provide full control over our object's editing and undo capabilities, both to the UI developer and to Windows Forms data binding.

Object cloning

Since all business objects created with our framework must be marked as `<Serializable()>`, and they can only reference other serializable objects, we can easily implement a `Clone()` method that will completely copy any of our business objects. This will use the same technology that remoting uses to pass objects across the network by value: .NET serialization.

> *The primary reason I'm including this cloning implementation is to reinforce the concept that our objects and any objects they reference must be `<Serializable()>`. Having implemented a `Clone()` method as part of our framework, we make it very easy to create a test harness that attempts to clone each of our business objects, clearly establishing that they are, in fact, totally serializable.*

The .NET Framework formally supports the concept of cloning through the `ICloneable` interface, so we'll implement that here:

```
<Serializable()> _
Public MustInherit Class BusinessBase
  Inherits Core.UndoableBase
  Implements IEditableObject
  Implements ICloneable
```

This will require that we implement a `Clone()` method to make a copy of our object. To use serialization more easily, we need to import a couple of namespaces:

```
Imports System.IO
Imports System.Runtime.Serialization.Formatters.Binary
```

Then we can write a generic Clone() method that will make an exact copy of our business object (and any objects it references):

```
#Region " Clone "

  ' All business objects _must_ be serializable, and can
  '  therefore be cloned - this just clinches the deal
  Public Function Clone() As Object Implements ICloneable.Clone
    Dim buffer As New MemoryStream()
    Dim formatter As New BinaryFormatter()

    formatter.Serialize(buffer, Me)
    buffer.Position = 0
    Return formatter.Deserialize(buffer)
  End Function

#End Region
```

By implementing the ICloneable interface, we not only provide for easy testing to ensure that our object is serializable, but also potentially allow other parts of the .NET Framework to make copies of our object as needed.

Root and child objects

As we discussed in Chapter 2, a business object can be a root object, which means (for our purposes) that it can be retrieved from or stored in a database. Alternatively, it might be a child object, which relies on its parent object to initiate any database retrieval or storage. An example of a root object is an Invoice, while a child object would be a LineItem object within that Invoice.

Child objects are related to root objects via a containment relationship, as illustrated by the following UML diagram:

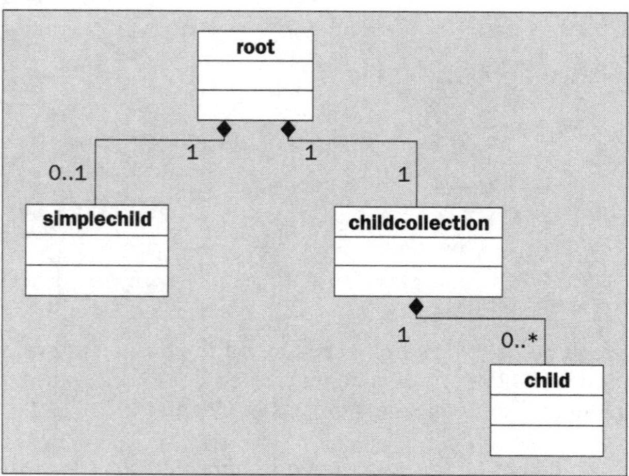

As we hinted when describing `BusinessBase` in Chapter 2, there are some objects that act as a root object for some of the time, and as a child object for some of the time. Consider, for instance, a `Posting` object that represents a quantity to be posted to a customer's account. Sometimes, we may have a single `Posting` object that's created and saved. At other times, we may have a broader `Adjustment` object that contains many child `Posting` objects.

We'll support all three scenarios – root, child, and combination – in `BusinessBase` by allowing the business programmer to make the choice through code. The key will lie in a `MarkAsChild()` method. If this method is not called, the object will be a root object. If it *is* called, the object will be a child object. The business developer can choose when and if they should call `MarkAsChild()`, thus giving them complete control over this feature.

Sometimes, we'll have objects that are loaded directly from the database as root objects on some occasions, but loaded as part of another object on others. This is entirely driven by the business requirements. For instance, consider an `OpenOrder` object. There are times when a user will need to be able to create and interact with an `OpenOrder` object directly, in which case it would be a root object. At other times, the user will be working with a `Customer` object that contains a collection of that customer's `OpenOrder` objects – each of which would then be a child object. This is a "combination" object – one that can be set to root or child, depending on how it is created.

If an object is configured as a root object, we'll allow certain behaviors that apply to root objects, and disable some that only apply to child objects. Conversely, if the object is configured as a child object, we'll disable root-level features such as data access, while enabling child-only behaviors. We'll control whether an object is a root or a child with a simple flag, property, and `Protected` method, much as we did with `mIsDirty` earlier on:

```
  #Region " IsChild "

    <NotUndoable()> _
    Private mIsChild As Boolean = False

    Protected ReadOnly Property IsChild() As Boolean
      Get
        Return mIsChild
      End Get
    End Property

    Protected Sub MarkAsChild()
      mIsChild = True
    End Sub

  #End Region
```

By default, objects are assumed to be root objects. Only if the business developer calls the `MarkAsChild()` method while the object is being created does it become a child object. We'll see how this works when we implement some business objects in Chapter 7.

The reason why we're implementing this as a method rather than as a read-write `Property` is because this is a one-time thing. As the object is created, we either mark it as a child or we don't – the value can't be changed later in the object's life.

Note that the `mIsChild` variable is marked with the `<NotUndoable()>` attribute. This is because it can't be changed after the object is created (that is, the code object, rather than the object in the database), so there's no reason to take a snapshot of its value. Since the value can't change, we'd be copying the value just so that we could undo it to the same value later – which is a waste of memory.

The `IsChild` property will be used within other `BusinessBase` code, and may be useful to the business developer, so it is declared as `Protected`.

Deleting objects

Earlier, we implemented an `IsDeleted` property to support the idea of deferred deletion – that is, when an object is marked as deleted, but isn't *actually* deleted until it's 'stored' to the database. The `MarkDeleted()` method we implemented was `Protected` in scope, for use by the business logic in the object to mark the object as being deleted.

We also need to provide a `Public` method named `Delete()` for the UI to call on our root business object to mark it for deletion. The root object will need to also mark any child objects as deleted, so we'll provide a `DeleteChild()` method with `Friend` scope for that purpose. The process is illustrated by the following sequence diagram:

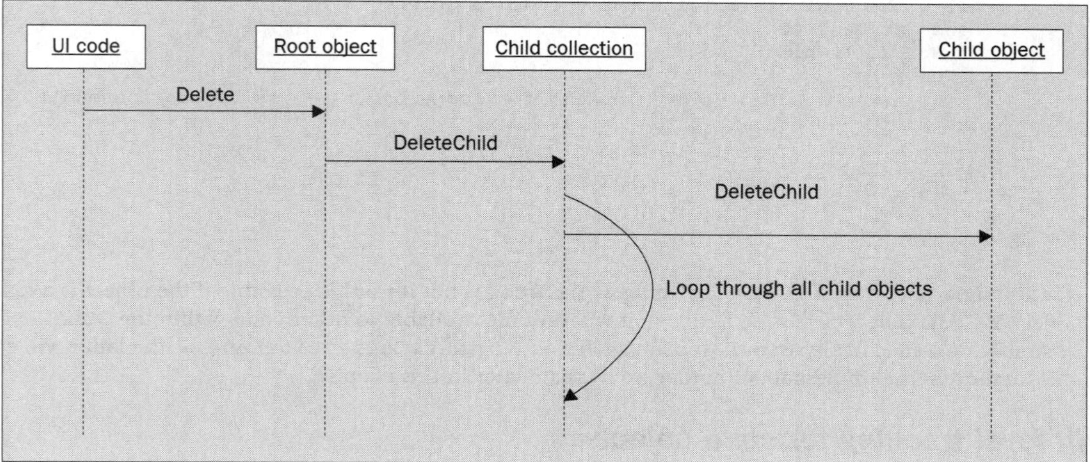

We can see that the UI code calls the root object's `Delete()` method, thus marking it for deletion. This also causes the root object to call a `DeleteChild()` method on its collection of child objects. The collection then loops through all the child objects, calling each of their `DeleteChild()` methods so that they can mark themselves for deletion as well.

For root objects, we provide a `Delete()` method that's for use by the UI code:

```
#Region " Delete "

  ' Allow the UI to mark the object for deletion if this is a root object
  Public Sub Delete()
    If Me.IsChild Then
```

```
      Throw New NotSupportedException("Cannot directly mark a child object " & _
                               "for deletion - use its parent collection")
    End If

    MarkDeleted()
  End Sub

#End Region
```

First, we check to ensure that this is not a child object. If it *is* a child object, we throw an exception to indicate that this method is not valid in that scenario. If it's a root object, then we simply call the `MarkDeleted()` method to mark the object for deletion. It's then up to our data access code to notice that `mIsDeleted` is `True` and actually perform the delete.

Child objects can be marked for deletion as well, but they can't be marked for deletion *directly*. Instead, they must be deleted by their parent object. Typically, the parent is a collection object that inherits from `BusinessCollectionBase`, and we're not really 'deleting' the child object as much as we're 'removing it from the collection'. The deletion is just a side-effect of the object being removed from the collection.

To support this, we'll also implement a `DeleteChild()` method:

```
  ' Allow the BusinessCollectionBase code to delete us
  Friend Sub DeleteChild()
    If Not Me.IsChild Then
      Throw New _
        NotSupportedException("Invalid for root objects - use Delete instead")
    End If

    MarkDeleted()
  End Sub

#End Region
```

This method does basically the same thing as `Delete()`, but it's only accessible if the object is a child object. Also, it is declared as `Friend`, so it will only be available to other code within the `CSLA` assembly. We specifically want it to be available to `BusinessCollectionBase`, as the latter will call this method in the implementation that we'll create later in this chapter.

Edit level tracking for child objects

When we implement `BusinessCollectionBase`, our code will make certain demands of each child business object. We've already seen something like this in action with the `DeleteChild()` method, but we need to support one other feature, too.

As we'll see in the implementation of `BusinessCollectionBase`, n-level undo of collections of child objects is pretty complex. The biggest of several problems arises when a new child object is added to the collection, and then the collection's parent object is 'cancelled'. In that case, the child object must be removed from the collection as though it were never there – the collection must be reset to its original state. To support this, child objects must keep track of the *edit level* at which they were added.

Earlier, as we implemented `UndoableBase`, we implemented a very short `EditLevel` property that returned a number corresponding to the number of times the object's state had been copied for later undo. From a UI programmer's perspective, the edit level is the number of times `BeginEdit()` has been called, minus the number of times `CancelEdit()` or `ApplyEdit()` have been called.

An example might help. Suppose that we have an `Invoice` object with a collection of `LineItem` objects. If we call `BeginEdit()` on the `Invoice`, then its edit level is 1. Since it cascades that call down to the child collection, the collection and all child objects are also at edit level 1.

If we then added a new child object, it would be added at edit level 1 – but if we then *cancel* the `Invoice`, we expect its state to be restored to what it was originally – effectively, back to the level 0 state. Of course, this includes the child collection, which means that the collection somehow needs to realize that our new child object should be discarded. To do this, the `BusinessCollectionBase` code will loop through its child objects looking for any that were added at an edit level that's higher than the current edit level.

In our example, when `Invoice` is canceled, its edit level immediately goes to 0. It cascades that call to the child collection, which then also has an edit level of 0. The collection scans its child objects looking for any that were added at an edit level greater than 0 – and finds our new child object that was added at edit level 1.

This implies that our business objects – if they are child objects – must keep track of the edit level at which they were added. To do this, we'll add a simple variable, with a `Friend` property to retrieve its value. We'll also add a `Friend` method that will be used by `BusinessCollectionBase` to set the child object's initial edit level:

```
#Region " Edit Level Tracking (child only) "

  ' We need to keep track of the edit level when we were added,
  ' so if the user cancels below that level we can be destroyed
  Private mEditLevelAdded As Integer

  ' Allow the collection object to use the edit level as needed (Friend scope)
  Friend Property EditLevelAdded() As Integer
    Get
      Return mEditLevelAdded
    End Get
    Set(ByVal Value As Integer)
      mEditLevelAdded = Value
    End Set
  End Property

#End Region
```

The purpose and use for this functionality will become much clearer as we implement the `BusinessCollectionBase` class later in this chapter, but at this point the `BusinessBase` class is complete – except for one major feature. We also want to automate the tracking of simple business rules to make it easy for the business developer to determine whether the object is valid at any given time.

BrokenRules

As we discussed in Chapter 2, most business objects will be validating data based on various business rules. In many cases, if any of those rules are broken, the business object is in an invalid state. Typically, this means that the object shouldn't be saved to a database until the data has been changed so that the rule is no longer broken.

Obviously, our framework can't implement the actual business rules and validation code – that will vary from application to application – but we *can* simplify the business developer's life by keeping track of whether there are any rules currently broken. We can keep a list of the rules that are broken, and we can prevent the object from being saved to the database via our data portal mechanism if that list has any entries. Also, if we have a list of broken rules, we can expose a read-only version of that list to the UI, so the UI can display the descriptions of the broken rules to the user.

> *This last bit – displaying the list of broken rules to the user – was a common enhancement to the architecture from my VB 5 and 6 Business Objects books. So many readers wrote in that they'd done this that I've included it directly into the framework in this book.*

It's important to realize that the `BrokenRules` collection doesn't *enforce* any rules. It merely allows the business logic to maintain a list of the business rules that are broken. It is entirely up to the business developer to implement those rules, and to tell the `BrokenRules` collection when each rule is broken or unbroken. This will be done by writing logic within a business object that goes something like this:

```
BrokenRules.Assert("NameReq", _
                   "Name is a required field", Len(Value) = 0)
```

If the length of the `String` variable called `Value` is zero, then the rule will be marked as broken and it will be added to the list. Otherwise, it will be considered unbroken, and if it is in the list it will be removed.

The `BrokenRules` object is a container for a collection of elements. Each element corresponds to a business rule that is currently broken, and includes a key name and a description for that rule. At first, this seems like a pretty simple concept – just a collection of elements. However, we have some special requirements, in that the collection should be read-write for our business object, but read-only for the UI code.

> *There's great value in exposing a read-only list to the UI code, because this makes it very easy for the UI developer to display descriptions of all broken rules to the user. In fact, since this is a collection, we can even use data binding to display the information in a control.*

The challenge is that there's no easy way to make a regular collection object that's read-only in one case, and read-write in another. To solve this problem, we'll create a special `RulesCollection` class that implements this behavior. We'll also define a `Rule` data type that defines the data we want to keep about each broken rule. Finally, the `BrokenRules` class itself will provide an easy interface for use by our business logic to mark rules as broken and unbroken.

To keep our `CSLA` namespace from becoming cluttered, we'll nest the `Rule` data type and the `RulesCollection` within the `BrokenRules` class. This means that they'll be addressed as follows:

```
CSLA.BrokenRules.Rule
CSLA.BrokenRules.RulesCollection
```

Add a new class to the `CSLA` project, and name it `BrokenRules`. Mark it as being `<Serializable()>` – `BusinessBase` will be referring to an object of this type, and since we'll be serializing our business objects, any other objects to which they refer must also be serializable:

```
<Serializable()> _
Public Class BrokenRules

End Class
```

This means that our business objects can be passed across the network by value, bringing their list of broken rules along for the ride. It also means that the list of broken rules is considered to be part of our object's state, so it will be serialized when `BeginEdit()` is called, and restored in the case of `CancelEdit()`.

Rule data type

We'll start the real work by creating the `Rule` data type. This could be a simple structure, but for one problem: Web Forms data binding can't bind to a regular structure. The data binding in Web Forms only binds to `Public` read-write properties, not to `Public` fields. Windows Forms doesn't have this limitation, but we want to support data binding in either environment.

> *The reason we're using a structure here instead of a class is that a structure is stored differently in memory. It's cheaper to create and destroy many structures than it is to create and destroy many objects. We can expect that business rules will be frequently broken and unbroken as the user works with our object, so we'll be creating and destroying* `Rule` *entities constantly. We're using a structure here to minimize the cost of that process.*

To put this issue into code, we *can't* simply create the data type like this:

```
#Region " Rule structure "

  Public Structure Rule
    Public mRule As String
    Public mDescription As String
  End Structure

#End Region
```

Instead, we need to declare the fields as `Private`, and implement `Property` methods to expose them for use. In the end, this works out well, since we want more control over the process anyway. If we simply expose the fields, then the UI code could change them. By implementing properties, we ensure that the UI can't change the data values.

We can also implement a `Friend` constructor, which achieves two things. First, since it's of `Friend` scope, it prevents the UI code (or our business object code) from creating a `Rule` directly – the only way to do that from 'outside' will be through our `BrokenRules` class. Second, implementing this constructor will simplify the code that we write in `BrokenRules`, allowing us to create and insert a new rule in a single line.

Here's the code for the `Rule` data type. Place it inside the `BrokenRules` class:

```
Public Class BrokenRules

#Region " Rule structure "

  <Serializable()> _
  Public Structure Rule
    Private mRule As String
    Private mDescription As String
```

```
    Friend Sub New(ByVal Rule As String, ByVal Description As String)
      mRule = Rule
      mDescription = Description
    End Sub

    Public Property Rule() As String
      Get
        Return mRule
      End Get
      Set(ByVal Value As String)

        ' The property must be read-write for Web Forms data binding
        ' to work, but we really don't want to allow the value to be
        ' changed dynamically so we ignore any attempt to set it
      End Set
    End Property

    Public Property Description() As String
      Get
        Return mDescription
      End Get
      Set(ByVal Value As String)

        ' The property must be read-write for Web Forms data binding
        ' to work, but we really don't want to allow the value to be
        ' changed dynamically so we ignore any attempt to set it
      End Set
    End Property
  End Structure

#End Region

End Class
```

Note that the structure is marked as `<Serializable()>`, which is important for the same reasons that `BrokenRules` itself is marked as such. Also note that the two `Property` methods are read-write, but they don't implement the `Set` portion of the method:

```
Set(ByVal Value As String)
  ' The property must be read-write for Web Forms data binding
  ' to work, but we really don't want to allow the value to be
  ' changed dynamically so we ignore any attempt to set it
End Set
```

This is *important.* Data binding requires that these properties should be read-write, but at the same time we don't want to allow the UI code (or data binding) to alter the values of our variables. The workaround we've used meets both criteria – it allows data binding to work, while totally ignoring any attempt by the UI or data binding code to alter the values.

RulesCollection

The .NET Framework makes it relatively easy to create a strongly typed collection object. All we need to do is subclass `CollectionBase`, implement our own `Item()`, `Add()`, and `Remove()` methods, and we're on our way. When we subclass `CollectionBase`, we gain access to a `Protected` variable called `List`, which gives us access to the underlying collection of values that's managed by the .NET Framework base class.

In our case, we also want to support data binding, so we'll subclass from our own `BindableCollectionBase` instead, but the process is the same.

Unfortunately, our requirements have posed us something of a problem on this occasion. The collection we need here is very different: it needs to be read-write when called by our internal `BrokenRules` code, but read-only when called by the UI. This requires some extra coding on our part. To start with, let's create the basic collection functionality by inserting the following code *inside* the `BrokenRules` class:

```
#Region " RulesCollection "

  <Serializable()> _
  Public Class RulesCollection
    Inherits CSLA.Core.BindableCollectionBase

    Friend Sub New()
      AllowEdit = False
      AllowRemove = False
      AllowNew = False
    End Sub

    Default Public ReadOnly Property Item(ByVal Index As Integer) As Rule
      Get
        Return CType(List.Item(Index), Rule)
      End Get
    End Property

    Friend Sub Add(ByVal Rule As String, ByVal Description As String)
      Remove(Rule)
      List.Add(New Rule(Rule, Description))
    End Sub

    Friend Sub Remove(ByVal Rule As String)
      Dim index As Integer

      ' We loop through using a numeric counter because
      ' the base class Remove requires a numeric index
      For index = 0 To List.Count - 1
        If CType(List.Item(index), Rule).Rule = Rule Then
          List.Remove(List.Item(index))
          Exit For
        End If
      Next
    End Sub

    Friend Function Contains(ByVal Rule As String) As Boolean
      Dim index As Integer
```

```
      For index = 0 To List.Count - 1
        If CType(List.Item(index), Rule).Rule = Rule Then
          Return True
        End If
      Next
      Return False
    End Function

  End Class

#End Region
```

The `New()`, `Add()`, `Remove()`, and `Contains()` methods are all declared here with `Friend` scope. This means that they won't be available to our business object code or UI code, but they *will* be available to the `BrokenRules` code that we'll implement shortly.

The `Item()` property is read-only and `Public`, so it provides read-only access to the list of `Rule` objects to both our business object code and the UI code. Also notice that the `New()` method sets the three values we defined in `BindableCollectionBase`, so data binding will know that it can't add, remove or edit items in this collection.

The trouble is that none of these steps will stop the UI developer from calling `Clear()` or `RemoveAt()` on our collection. Unfortunately, these two methods are exposed by the `CollectionBase` class, and they're available at all times. We need some way to prevent these methods from working, and yet still allow `BrokenRules` to use our `Add()` and `Remove()` methods.

To solve the problem, we'll override some special methods on the base class that allow us to intercept any attempt to remove items or clear the collection. Of course, we only want to block those activities when they are attempted by the UI code, not when *our* code is working with the collection. This means we need to be able to lock and unlock the collection, so that we can unlock it when we want to use it, and lock it the rest of the time.

To lock the collection, we'll add a variable to indicate whether adding, removing, or changing collection values is legal. Essentially, it will be legal if the request is made through our `Add()` or `Remove()` methods, otherwise it will be illegal:

```
<Serializable()> _
Public Class RulesCollection
  Inherits CSLA.Core.BindableCollectionBase

  Private mLegal As Boolean = False

  Friend Sub New()
    AllowEdit = False
    AllowRemove = False
    AllowNew = False
  End Sub

  Default Public ReadOnly Property Item(ByVal Index As Integer) As Rule
    Get
      Return CType(List.Item(Index), Rule)
    End Get
  End Property
```

```
Friend Sub Add(ByVal Rule As String, ByVal Description As String)
  Remove(Rule)
  mLegal = True
  List.Add(New Rule(Rule, Description))
  mLegal = False
End Sub

Friend Sub Remove(ByVal Rule As String)
  Dim index As Integer

  mLegal = True
  For index = 0 To list.Count - 1
    If CType(List.Item(index), Rule).Rule = Rule Then
      List.Remove(List.Item(index))
      Exit For
    End If
  Next
  mLegal = False
End Sub

Friend Function Contains(ByVal Rule As String) As Boolean
  Dim index As Integer

  For index = 0 To List.Count - 1
    If CType(List.Item(index), Rule).Rule = Rule Then
      Return True
    End If
  Next
  Return False
End Function
```

This allows us to solve the problem. The `CollectionBase` class will call a method before any insert, remove, clear, or change operation. We can override these methods, raising an error if the operation is invalid:

```
Protected Overrides Sub OnClear()
  If Not mLegal Then
    Throw New NotSupportedException("Clear is an invalid operation")
  End If
End Sub

Protected Overrides Sub OnInsert(ByVal index As Integer, _
                                 ByVal value As Object)
  If Not mLegal Then
    Throw New NotSupportedException("Insert is an invalid operation")
  End If
End Sub

Protected Overrides Sub OnRemove(ByVal index As Integer, _
                                 ByVal value As Object)
  If Not mLegal Then
    Throw New NotSupportedException("Remove is an invalid operation")
  End If
End Sub
```

```
    Protected Overrides Sub OnSet(ByVal index As Integer, _
                                  ByVal oldValue As Object, _
                                  ByVal newValue As Object)
      If Not mLegal Then
        Throw New _
          NotSupportedException("Changing an element is an invalid operation")
      End If
    End Sub
  End Class

#End Region
```

If our collection is locked and an attempt to change it is made, we throw a NotSupportedException to indicate that the operation is not supported by our object.

This scheme means that BrokenRules can call our Add() and Remove() methods, and yet we can still provide the UI with a reference to our RulesCollection object without the risk of UI code changing the collection's contents.

Since we're subclassing BindableCollectionBase, the UI can employ data binding to display the rule descriptions, or it can include code to loop manually through the collection to process or display the data.

BrokenRules

We now have everything we need to keep a collection of broken rules. Rather than having our business logic work directly with the collection, however, we'll implement a more abstract BrokenRules class that provides an easy-to-use interface through which rules can simply be marked as broken or unbroken.

The methods of BrokenRules will only be available to code in our business objects, so our goal here is to create a simple interface that business developers can use to keep track of their business rule status. First off, let's declare the collection object and create a method to allow the marking of a rule as broken or unbroken. Add the following to the BrokenRules class:

```
  Private mRules As New RulesCollection()

  Public Sub Assert(ByVal Rule As String, _
                    ByVal Description As String, _
                    ByVal IsBroken As Boolean)
    If IsBroken Then
      mRules.Add(Rule, Description)
    Else
      mRules.Remove(Rule)
    End If

  End Sub
```

This method will be used by our business logic, so we can write code in our business objects that looks something like this:

```
Public Property Name() As String
  Get
    Return mName
  End Get
  Set(ByVal Value As String)
    BrokenRules.Assert("NameReq", _
              "Name is a required field", Len(Value) = 0)
    mName = Value
  End Set
End Property
```

Obviously, the key line here is the call to `Assert()`, which will set the rule as broken if the new value is of zero length, or as unbroken if a longer value is supplied. This makes the implementation of many business rule checks very simple for the business developer.

We should also allow the business object to determine quickly whether any rules are broken. If not, the object is assumed to be valid. To do this, we'll add an `IsValid` property to the `BrokenRules` class:

```
Public ReadOnly Property IsValid() As Boolean
  Get
    Return mRules.Count = 0
  End Get
End Property
```

We'll also allow the business logic to ask if a specific rule is currently broken:

```
Public Function IsBroken(ByVal Rule As String) As Boolean
  Return mRules.Contains(Rule)
End Function
```

Both the business logic and the UI logic should have access to the collection – we went to great lengths to make the `RulesCollection` object read-write for `BrokenRules`, but read-only for everyone else. This means that we can simply provide a reference to the `RulesCollection` object, knowing that it will be read-only:

```
Public Function GetBrokenRules() As RulesCollection
  Return mRules
End Function
```

Finally, in case the UI developer wants a simple text representation of the list of broken rules, let's override the `ToString()` method with our own implementation that returns the list of broken rule descriptions as delimited text that can be displayed in a message box or a multi-line text display control:

```
Public Overrides Function ToString() As String
  Dim obj As New System.Text.StringBuilder()
  Dim item As Rule

  For Each item In mRules
    obj.Append(item.Description)
    obj.Append(vbCrLf)
  Next
  Return obj.ToString
End Function
```

At this point, we have a `BrokenRules` object that will enable `BusinessBase` and the business object author to manipulate the list of broken rules, and allow a business object to expose the collection of broken rules to the UI, if so desired.

Exposing BrokenRules from BusinessBase

We can now return to the `BusinessBase` class and enhance it to make use of `BrokenRules`. By incorporating `BrokenRules` support directly into `BusinessBase`, we are making this functionality available to all business objects created using our framework.

Every business object will have an associated `BrokenRules` object to keep track of that object's rules. `BusinessBase` will include the code that declares and configures this object, so add the following to `BusinessBase`:

```
#Region " BrokenRules, IsValid "

  ' Keep a list of broken rules
  Private mBrokenRules As New BrokenRules()

#End Region
```

We'll expose the `RulesCollection` collection from the `BrokenRules` object to the UI directly, as a `Public` property. We can do this because we've taken precautions to ensure that the UI code can't change the contents of the collection. We'll also need to implement an easy way for the business developer to access the `BrokenRules` object, so they can mark rules as broken or unbroken.

To do this, we'll expose a set of `Public` and `Protected` methods in `BusinessBase` that expose the appropriate functionality. The following diagram illustrates which objects will be exposed:

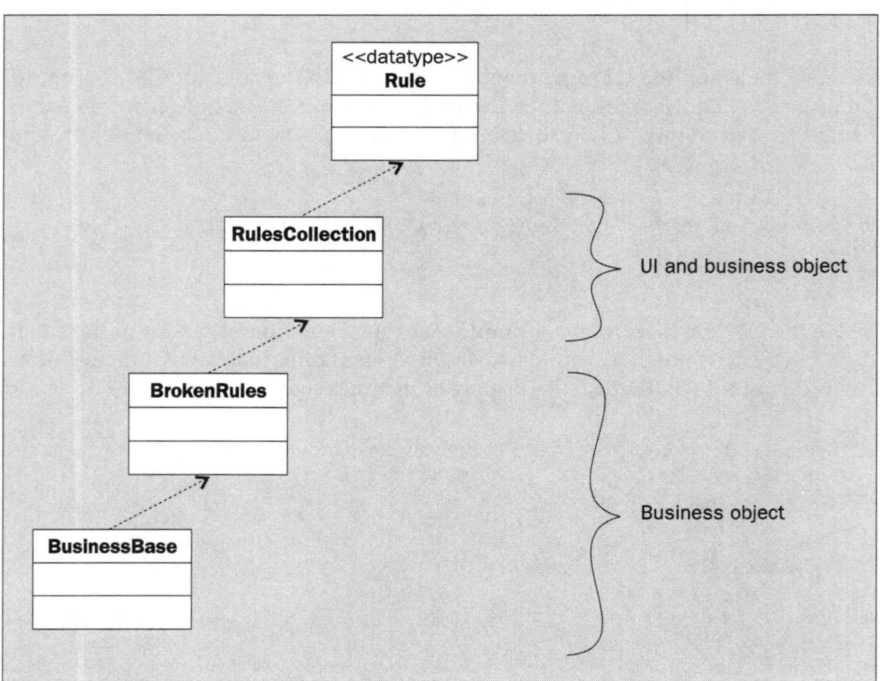

First, let's expose BrokenRules to the business object itself by adding this code within our new Region:

```
' Support broken rules tracking
Protected ReadOnly Property BrokenRules() As BrokenRules
  Get
    Return mBrokenRules
  End Get
End Property
```

All business objects should expose an IsValid property that can be used to determine whether the object is currently valid. By default, this will simply rely on BrokenRules, but we'll make it Overridable so that the business object author can enhance this behavior if required by their specific application:

```
Public Overridable ReadOnly Property IsValid() As Boolean
  Get
    Return mBrokenRules.IsValid
  End Get
End Property
```

Finally, we'll expose read-only data for use by the business logic or user interface code. We can expose both the RulesCollection itself, and the text version of the rules from BrokenRules.ToString():

```
Public Function GetBrokenRulesCollection() As BrokenRules.RulesCollection
  Return mBrokenRules.GetBrokenRules
End Function

Public Function GetBrokenRulesString() As String
  Return mBrokenRules.ToString
End Function
```

Data binding to the collection can be used to populate list or grid controls with a list of broken rules, while the GetBrokenRulesString() method will return a simpler text representation of all the broken rule descriptions. Again, all business objects will support this functionality.

At this point, we're done with the BusinessBase class: we can use it as a base to create business objects that support basic state management, n-level undo, cloning, parent/child functionality, and tracking of broken rules. In Chapter 5, we'll further enhance BusinessBase to understand object persistence and data access.

BusinessCollectionBase

While BusinessBase is the primary class in our framework for building business objects, we also need to support *collections* of business objects. As we built both UndoableBase and BusinessBase, we made accommodations for collections of type BusinessCollectionBase, which is what we'll build now.

BusinessCollectionBase needs to support many of the same features as we've implemented for business objects. These include n-level undo functionality, IsDirty, IsValid, and acting as either a root or a child object. Of course, the implementation of each of these is quite different for a collection of objects from what it is for a single object. In some ways, this class will be more complex than BusinessBase.

For a start, the n-level undo functionality must integrate with what we've written in `UndoableBase`. This means that the class must implement `CopyState()`, `UndoChanges()`, and `AcceptChanges()` methods that store and restore the collection's state as appropriate. Because a collection can also be a root object, it needs to implement `BeginEdit()`, `CancelEdit()`, and `ApplyEdit()` methods, just as we did in `BusinessBase`. In either scenario, the process of taking a snapshot of the collection's state is really a matter of having all the child objects snapshot their individual states.

The undo operation for a collection is where things start to get more complicated. Undoing all the child objects isn't too hard, since we can cascade the request to each object, and they can reset their state. At the collection level, however, an undo means restoring any objects that were deleted, and removing any objects that were added, so the collection's list of objects ends up the same as it was in the first place.

The `IsDirty` and `IsValid` concepts are relatively easy to implement. A collection is 'dirty' if it contains child objects that are dirty, added, or removed. A collection's 'validity' can be determined by finding out if all its child objects are valid. An invalid child object means that the entire collection is in an invalid state.

The idea that a collection can be a root object or a child object is particularly important. It's fairly obvious that a collection can be a child object – an `Invoice` root object will have a `LineItems` collection that contains `LineItem` objects, so the `LineItems` collection is itself a child object. However, collection objects can also be root objects.

We may have a root object called `Categories`, which contains a list of `Category` objects. It's quite possible that there's no root object to act as a parent for `Categories` – it may simply be an editable list of objects. To support this concept, our `BusinessCollectionBase`, like `BusinessBase` itself, must support these two modes of operation. In root mode, some operations are legal while others are not; in child mode, the reverse is true.

The code to implement all these features is somewhat intertwined, so be aware that at some points in the writing of the code, we'll end up relying on methods that haven't yet been implemented.

Creating the class

Add a new class to the `CSLA` project and name it `BusinessCollectionBase`. Let's start with the basics:

```
<Serializable()> _
Public MustInherit Class BusinessCollectionBase
  Inherits CSLA.Core.BindableCollectionBase

End Class
```

As with all our base classes, this one must be `<Serializable()>`. It also inherits from `BindableCollectionBase`, so it gains the implementation of `IBindingList` and the `ListChanged` event. This automatically grants all our business collection objects full support for Windows Forms data binding.

Note that our business collection objects *don't* inherit from `UndoableBase`, because they don't need to. `UndoableBase` enables an object to take a snapshot of its own state, but the 'state' of a collection is quite different from the state of a regular object. A collection has no intrinsic state of its own – rather, its state is the state of all the objects it contains. This means that `UndoableBase` does us no good, and we'll need to implement our own state management to deal with the unique nature of collections.

Clone method

Because the class is marked as `<Serializable()>`, we can implement a `Clone()` method just like we did in `BusinessBase`. First, add the `Implements` statement to the class:

```
<Serializable()> _
Public MustInherit Class BusinessCollectionBase
  Inherits CSLA.Core.BindableCollectionBase
  Implements ICloneable
```

Then, import a couple of useful namespaces:

```
Imports System.IO
Imports System.Runtime.Serialization.Formatters.Binary
```

Then, implement the method:

```
#Region " Clone "

  ' All business objects _must_ be serializable and
  ' thus can be cloned - this just clinches the deal
  Public Function Clone() As Object Implements ICloneable.Clone
    Dim buffer As New MemoryStream()
    Dim formatter As New BinaryFormatter()

    formatter.Serialize(buffer, Me)
    buffer.Position = 0
    Return formatter.Deserialize(buffer)
  End Function

#End Region
```

This method can be used to create a clone of the collection *and all its child objects* in a single step.

Contains method

We can also easily implement a `Contains()` method, so that business or UI code can see if the collection contains a specific object. This is a typical function provided by collection objects, and while it's not strictly necessary, it's a good feature to support any time we implement a collection:

```
#Region " Contains "

  Public Function Contains(ByVal Item As BusinessBase) As Boolean
    Dim element As BusinessBase

    For Each element In list
      If element.Equals(Item) Then
        Return True
      End If
    Next
    Return False
  End Function

#End Region
```

Root or child

Next, as we did in BusinessBase, we need to allow our collection object to know whether it is a root or a child object:

```
#Region " IsChild "

  Private mIsChild As Boolean = False

  Protected ReadOnly Property IsChild() As Boolean
    Get
      Return mIsChild
    End Get
  End Property

  Protected Sub MarkAsChild()
    mIsChild = True
  End Sub

#End Region
```

This functionality is the same as we implemented in BusinessBase, and it allows the business developer to mark the object as a child object when it is first created. We can now use the IsChild property in our code to adjust the behavior of our object (such as exercising control over deletion) accordingly.

Edit level tracking

The hardest part of implementing n-level undo functionality is that we can't just add or delete a child object. We always need to be able to 'un-delete' or 'un-add' those child objects in case of an undo operation.

In BusinessBase and UndoableBase, we implemented the concept of an **edit level**. The edit level allows us to keep track of how many BeginEdit() calls have been made to snapshot our state without corresponding CancelEdit() or ApplyEdit() calls. More specifically, it tells us how many states we have stacked up for undo operations.

In BusinessCollectionBase, we need the same edit level tracking as in BusinessBase. However, a collection won't actually stack its states. Rather, it cascades the call to each of its child objects, so that they can stack their *own* states. Because of this, we'll use a simple numeric counter to keep track of how many unpaired BeginEdit() calls have been made:

```
#Region " Edit level tracking "

  ' Keep track of how many edit levels we have
  Private mEditLevel As Integer

#End Region
```

As we implement CopyState(), UndoChanges(), and AcceptChanges(), we'll alter this value accordingly.

Reacting to insert, remove, or clear operations

Collection base classes don't implement `Add()` or `Remove()` methods directly, since those are to be implemented by the collection object's author. However, we *do* need to perform certain operations any time that an insert, remove, or clear operation occurs. To accommodate this, the `CollectionBase` class invokes certain overridable methods when these events occur. We can override these methods in our code:

```
#Region " Insert, Remove, Clear "
  Protected Overrides Sub OnInsert(ByVal index As Integer, _
                                   ByVal value As Object)
    ' When an object is inserted we assume it is a new object
    ' and so the edit level when it was added must be set
    CType(value, BusinessBase).EditLevelAdded = mEditLevel
    MyBase.OnInsert(index, value)
  End Sub

  Protected Overrides Sub OnRemove(ByVal index As Integer, _
                                   ByVal value As Object)
    ' When an object is 'removed' it is really
    ' being deleted, so do the deletion work
    DeleteChild(CType(value, BusinessBase))
    MyBase.OnRemove(index, value)
  End Sub

  Protected Overrides Sub OnClear()

    ' When an object is 'removed' it is really being deleted,
    ' so do the deletion work for all the objects in the list
    While List.Count > 0
      DeleteChild(CType(List(0), BusinessBase))
    End While
    MyBase.OnClear()
  End Sub
End Region
```

The `OnInsert()` method is called when an item is being added to the collection. We assume that it's a new child object, and tell the object at what edit level it is being added by changing the `EditLevelAdded` property. As we implemented it in `BusinessBase`, this merely records the value so that it can be checked later, during undo operations. We'll use this value when we implement the `UndoChanges()` and `AcceptChanges()` methods later on.

The `OnRemove()` method is called when an item is being removed from the collection. Since we need to support the concept of undo, we can't *actually* allow the object to be removed – we might need to restore it later. To resolve this, we'll call a `DeleteChild()` method, passing the object being removed as a parameter. We'll implement this method shortly – for now, it's enough to know that it keeps track of the object in case we need to restore it later.

Similarly, the `OnClear()` method is called when the entire collection is being cleared. What this really means is that we need to keep track of *all* the objects in the collection, in case they need to be restored later as part of an undo operation, so we loop through all the child objects, calling the `DeleteChild()` method on each.

Deleted object collection

To ensure that we can properly 'un-delete' objects in case of an undo operation, we need to keep a list of the objects that have been 'removed' from the collection. The first step in accomplishing this goal is to maintain an internal list of deleted objects.

Along with implementing this private collection object, we'll also provide a `ContainsDeleted()` method so that the business or UI logic can find out whether the collection contains a specific deleted object.

As with the `Contains()` method earlier, there is no specific requirement for such a method on a collection. However, it's often very useful to be able to ask a collection if it contains a specific item. Since our collection is unusual in that it contains two lists of objects, it is appropriate that we allow client code to ask whether we contain an object in our deleted list, as well as in our non-deleted list:

```
#Region " DeletedCollection "

  ' Here's the list of deleted child objects
  Protected deletedList As New DeletedCollection()

  ' This is a simple collection to store all of the deleted child objects
  <Serializable()> _
  Protected Class DeletedCollection
    Inherits CollectionBase

    Public Sub Add(ByVal Child As BusinessBase)
      List.Add(Child)
    End Sub

    Public Sub Remove(ByVal Child As BusinessBase)
      List.Remove(Child)
    End Sub

    Default Public ReadOnly Property Item(ByVal index As Integer) _
        As BusinessBase
      Get
        Return CType(List.Item(index), BusinessBase)
      End Get
    End Property
  End Class

  Public Function ContainsDeleted(ByVal Item As BusinessBase) As Boolean
    Dim element As BusinessBase

    For Each element In deletedList
      If element.Equals(Item) Then
        Return True
      End If
    Next
    Return False
  End Function

#End Region
```

The collection of deleted objects is `Protected`, to match the collection of regular objects. The root `CollectionBase` class exposes a `List` variable, which is a `Protected` collection of the values we contain. We're just following this precedent by exposing our internal `deletedList` variable as well.

Notice that `DeletedCollection` is a nested class that implements a simple, strongly typed collection of `BusinessBase` objects. Technically, we could just have used a native .NET collection type, but it's preferable to build a strongly typed collection for performance and ease of debugging.

Deleting and undeleting child objects

Now that we have a collection for storing deleted child objects, we can implement methods to delete and undelete objects as needed.

Deleting a child object is really a matter of marking the object as deleted, and moving it from `List` (the active list of child objects) to `deletedList`. Undeleting occurs when a child object has restored its state so that it's no longer marked as deleted. In that case, we must move it from `deletedList` back to `List`, and it becomes an active child object once again.

The permutations here are vast. The ways in which combinations of calls to `BeginEdit()`, `Add()`, `Remove()`, `CancelEdit()`, and `ApplyEdit()` can be called are probably infinite. Let's look at some relatively common scenarios, though, so we can see what happens as we delete and undelete child objects.

First, let's consider a case where we've loaded the collection object from a database, and the database included one child object: `A`. Then, we called `BeginEdit()` on the collection, and added a new object to the collection: `B`. The following diagram shows what happens if we remove those two objects, and then call `CancelEdit()` on the collection.

> *EL is the value of `mEditLevel` in the collection; ELA is the `mEditLevelAdded` value in each child object; and DEL is the `IsDeleted` value in each child object.*

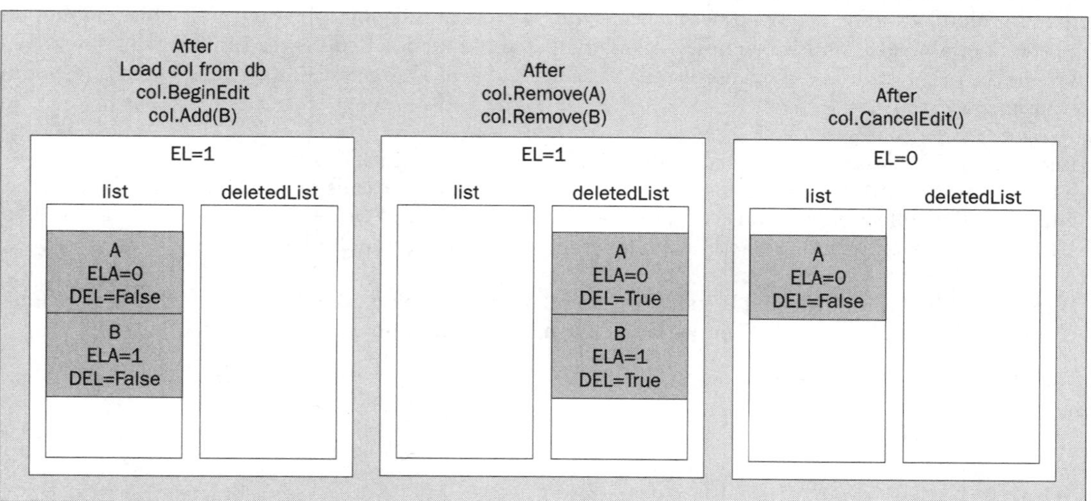

We can see that after both objects have been removed from the collection, they are marked for deletion and moved to the `deletedList` collection. This way they *appear* to be gone from the collection, but we still have access to them if needed.

After we call `CancelEdit()` on the collection, its edit level goes back to 0. Since child `A` came from the database, it was 'added' at edit level 0, so it sticks around. Child `B`, on the other hand, was added at edit level 1, so it goes away. Also, child `A` has its state reset as part of the `CancelEdit()` call (remember that `CancelEdit()` causes a cascade effect, so each child object restores its snapshot values). The result is that because of the undo operation, child `A` is no longer marked for deletion.

Another common scenario is where we do the same thing, but call `ApplyEdit()` at the end:

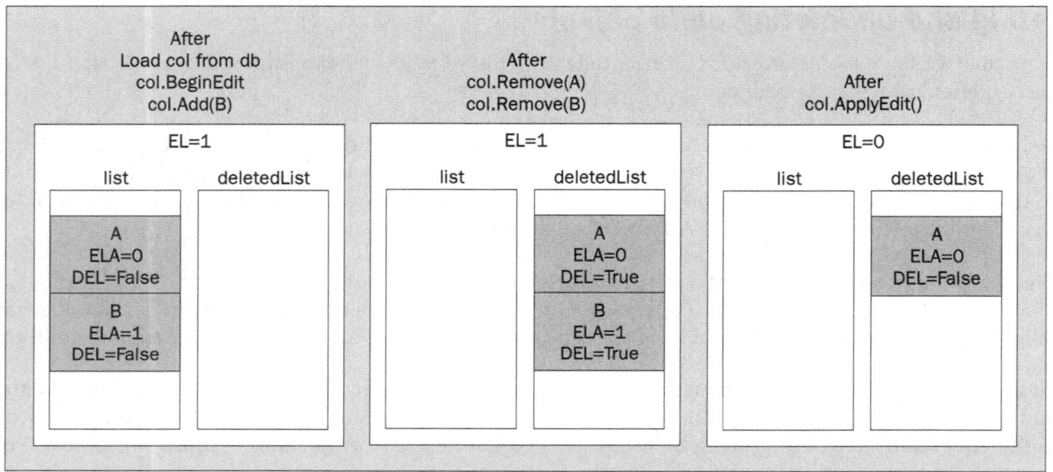

The first two steps are identical of course, but after we call `ApplyEdit()` things are quite different. Since we accepted the changes to the collection rather than rejecting them, the changes became permanent. Child `A` remains marked for deletion, and if the collection is saved back to the database, the data for child `A` will be removed. Child `B` is actually gone at this point. It was a new object added *and deleted* at edit level 1, and we've now accepted all changes made at edit level 1. Since we know that `B` was never in the database (because it was *added* at edit level 1), we can simply discard the object entirely from memory.

Let's look at one last scenario. Just to illustrate how rough this gets, this will be more complex – we'll have nested `BeginEdit()`, `CancelEdit()`, and `ApplyEdit()` calls on the collection. This can easily happen if the collection contains child or grandchild objects, and we've implemented a Windows Forms UI that uses dialog windows to edit each level (parent, child, grandchild, etc.).

Again, we'll have child `A` being loaded from the database, `B` being added at edit level 1, and we'll have child `C` added at edit level 2. Then we'll remove all three child objects:

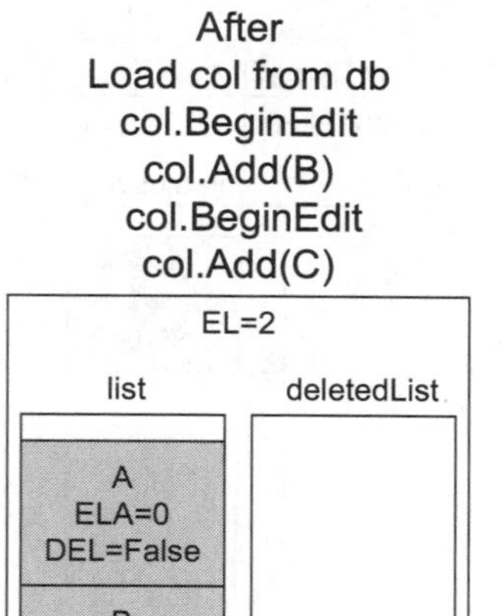

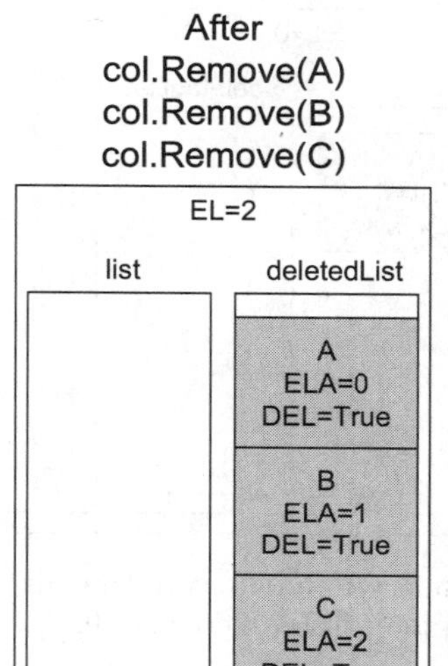

Suppose that we then call `ApplyEdit()` on the collection. This will apply all edits made at edit level 2, putting us back to edit level 1. Since child `C` was added at edit level 2, it simply goes away, but child `B` sticks around because it was added at edit level 1, which is where we're at now:

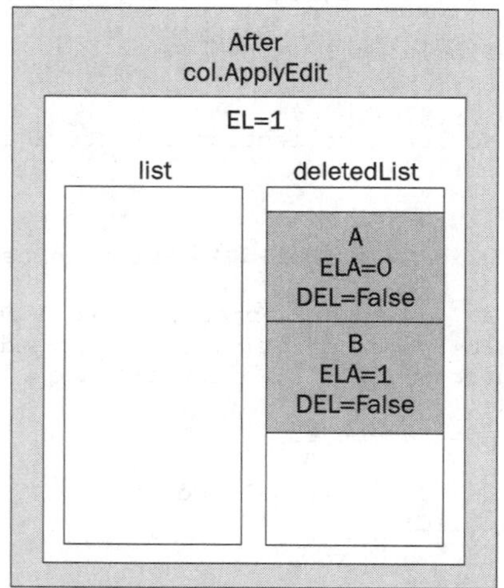

Both objects remain marked for deletion because we *applied* the changes made at edit level 2. Were we now to call `CancelEdit()`, we'd return to the point we were at when the first `BeginEdit()` was called, meaning that all that would be left is child `A`, not marked for deletion. Alternatively, we could call `ApplyEdit()`, which would commit all changes made at edit level 1: child `A` would continue to be marked for deletion, and child B is totally discarded since it was added and deleted at edit level 1. Both of these possible outcomes are illustrated by the following diagram:

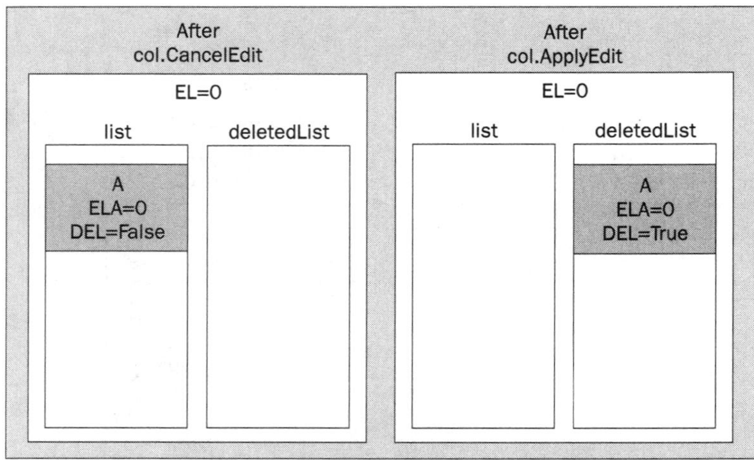

Which of the above results we end up with depends on whether we call `CancelEdit()` or `ApplyEdit()` to bring the edit level down to 0.

Having gone through all that, let's take a look at the code that will implement these behaviors. We'll create `DeleteChild()` and `UnDeleteChild()` methods to deal with marking the child objects as deleted and moving them between the `List` and `deletedList` collections:

```
#Region " Delete and Undelete child "

  Private Sub DeleteChild(ByVal Child As BusinessBase)

    ' Mark the object as deleted
    Child.DeleteChild()

    ' And add it to the deleted collection for storage
    deletedList.Add(Child)
  End Sub

  Private Sub UnDeleteChild(ByVal Child As BusinessBase)

    ' We are inserting an _existing_ object, so we need to preserve the object's
    ' EditLevelAdded value, because it will be changed by the normal add process
    Dim SaveLevel As Integer = Child.EditLevelAdded
    List.Add(Child)
    Child.EditLevelAdded = SaveLevel

    ' Since the object is no longer deleted, remove it from the deleted list
    deletedList.Remove(Child)
  End Sub

#End Region
```

On the surface, this doesn't seem too complicated, but look at the code that deals with the child's `EditLevelAdded` property in the `UnDeleteChild()` method. Earlier, we implemented the `OnInsert()` method, in which we assumed that any child being added to our collection was a new object, and therefore that its edit level value should be set with the collection's current value. However, the `OnInsert()` method will be run as we insert this *pre-existing* object as well, altering *its* edit level – which isn't what we want.

Here, we're not dealing with a new object – we're just restoring an old object. To solve this, we first store the object's edit level value, then we re-add the object to the collection, and then we restore the edit level value – effectively leaving it unchanged.

CopyState

Now we're at the point where we can implement the n-level undo functionality. This means implementing the `CopyState()`, `UndoChanges()`, and `AcceptChanges()` methods, making use of the plumbing that we've put in place so far.

The `CopyState()` method needs to take a snapshot of our collection's current state. It is invoked when the `BeginEdit()` method is called on our root object. At that time, the root object takes a snapshot of its own state and calls `CopyState()` on any child objects or collections so they can take snapshots of their state as well.

```
#Region " N-level undo "

  Friend Sub CopyState()
    Dim Child As BusinessBase

    ' We are going a level deeper in editing
    mEditLevel += 1

    ' Cascade the call to all child objects
    For Each Child In List
      Child.CopyState()
    Next

    ' Cascade the call to all deleted child objects
    For Each Child In deletedList
      Child.CopyState()
    Next
  End Sub
```

Each time we take a snapshot of our collection's state, we increase the edit level by one. In `UndoableBase`, we relied on the `Stack` object to track this for us, but here we're just using a simple numeric counter. Remember: a collection has no state of its own, so there's nothing to add to a stack of states. Instead, a collection is only responsible for ensuring that all the objects it *contains* take snapshots of their states. All we need to do is keep track of how many times we've asked our child objects to store their state, so we can properly implement the adding and removing of child objects that we described earlier.

Notice that we also stack the states of the objects in `deletedList`. This is important, because those objects might, at some point, get restored as active objects in our collection. Even though they're not active at the moment (because they're marked for deletion), we need to treat them the same as we treat regular objects.

Overall, this process is *fairly* straightforward: we're just cascading the method call down to the child objects. The same can't be said for `UndoChanges()` or `AcceptChanges()`.

UndoChanges

The `UndoChanges()` method is more complex. It too cascades the call down to the child objects, deleted or not, but it also needs to find any objects that were added since the latest snapshot. Those objects must be removed from the collection and discarded, since an undo operation means that it must be as though they were never added. Furthermore, it needs to find any objects that were deleted since the latest snapshot – those objects must be re-added to the collection.

Here's the complete method:

```
Friend Sub UndoChanges()
  Dim Child As BusinessBase
  Dim Index As Integer

  ' We are coming up one edit level
  mEditLevel -= 1
  If mEditLevel < 0 Then mEditLevel = 0

  ' Cancel edit on all current items
  For Index = List.Count - 1 To 0 Step -1
    Child = CType(List.Item(Index), BusinessBase)
    Child.UndoChanges()

    ' If item is below its point of addition, remove
    If Child.EditLevelAdded > mEditLevel Then List.Remove(Child)
  Next

  ' Undelete all deleted items
  For Index = deletedList.Count - 1 To 0 Step -1
    Child = deletedList.Item(Index)
    Child.UndoChanges()

    ' If item is below its point of addition, remove
    If Child.EditLevelAdded > mEditLevel Then deletedList.Remove(Child)

    ' If item is no longer deleted move back to main list
    If Not Child.IsDeleted Then UnDeleteChild(Child)
  Next
End Sub
```

First of all, we decrement `mEditLevel` to indicate that we're countering one call to `CopyState()`. Then, we loop through the list of active child objects, calling `UndoChanges()` on each of them so that they can restore their individual states.

Notice that we're looping through the `List` and `deletedList` collections backwards, from bottom to top, using a numeric index value. This is important, because it allows us to remove items from the collection safely as we go through each list. If we used `For...Each`, or even a forward-moving numeric index, we would be unable to remove items from the collection as we went without causing a runtime error.

After a child object has been restored, we can check the edit level when it was added to the collection. If we're undoing the collection to a point prior to that edit level, then we know that this is a new child object that now must be discarded.

```
' If item is below its point of addition, remove
If Child.EditLevelAdded > mEditLevel Then List.Remove(Child)
```

The same process occurs for the objects in `deletedList` – again, we call `UndoChanges()` on each of them, and also see if the child object was a newly added object that can now be discarded:

```
' If item is below its point of addition, remove
If Child.EditLevelAdded > mEditLevel Then deletedList.Remove(Child)
```

With the deleted child objects, we also need to see if they should still be deleted. Remember that the `IsDeleted` flag can be reset by `UndoChanges()`, so if we've now restored a deleted object to a state where it was no longer marked for deletion, then we need to put it back into the active list:

```
' If item is no longer deleted, move it back to main list
If Not Child.IsDeleted Then UnDeleteChild(Child)
```

At the end of the process, our collection object and all its child objects will be in the state they were when `CopyState()` was last called – we'll have undone any changes, additions, or deletions.

AcceptChanges

The `AcceptChanges()` method isn't nearly as complicated. It also decrements the `mEditLevel` variable to indicate that we're moving down our list of stacked state data. It then cascades the `AcceptChanges()` method call to each child object, so that child object can accept its own changes. The only complex bit of code is that we also need to alter the 'edit level added' value of each child:

```
    Friend Sub AcceptChanges()
      Dim Child As BusinessBase

      ' We are coming up one edit level
      mEditLevel -= 1
      If mEditLevel < 0 Then mEditLevel = 0

      ' Cascade the call to all child objects
      For Each Child In list
        Child.AcceptChanges()

        ' If item is below its point of addition, lower point of addition
        If Child.EditLevelAdded > mEditLevel Then _
           Child.EditLevelAdded = mEditLevel
      Next

      ' Cascade the call to all deleted child objects
      For Each Child In deletedList
        Child.AcceptChanges()

        ' If item is below its point of addition, lower point of addition
        If Child.EditLevelAdded > mEditLevel Then _
           Child.EditLevelAdded = mEditLevel
      Next
    End Sub

  #End Region
```

Here, we're making sure that no child object maintains an `EditLevelAdded` value that's higher than our collection's current edit level.

Think back to our `LineItem` example, and suppose that we were at edit level 1, and we *accepted* the changes. In that case, we're saying that the newly added `LineItem` object is to be kept – it is valid. Because of this, its edit level added value needs to be the same as the collection object – so it needs to be set to 0 as well.

This is important, because there's nothing to stop the user from starting a *new* edit session and raising the collection's edit level to 1 again. If they *then* cancel the operation, we don't want to remove that new `Category` object accidentally – it was already accepted once, and it should *stay* accepted.

Notice that here we're looping through the `List` and `deletedList` collections using `For...Each` loops. Since we won't be removing any items from either collection as we accept our changes, we can use this simpler looping structure rather than the bottom-to-top numeric looping structure we had to use in the `UndoChanges()` method.

At this point, we've implemented all the functionality we need to support n-level undo, so our `BusinessCollectionBase` is at pretty much at the same level as our `UndoableBase` class.

BeginEdit, CancelEdit, and ApplyEdit

Now we can implement the methods that the UI will need in order to control the edit process on our collection. Remember, though, that this control is only valid if the collection is a root object. If it's a child object, then its edit process should be controlled by its parent object. To that end, we'll check to ensure that the object isn't a child before allowing these methods to operate:

```
#Region " Begin/Cancel/ApplyEdit "

  Public Sub BeginEdit()
    If Me.IsChild Then
      Throw New NotSupportedException("BeginEdit not valid on a child object")
    End If

    CopyState()
  End Sub

  Public Sub CancelEdit()
    If Me.IsChild Then
      Throw New NotSupportedException("CancelEdit not valid on a child object")
    End If

    UndoChanges()
  End Sub

  Public Sub ApplyEdit()
    If Me.IsChild Then
      Throw New NotSupportedException("ApplyEdit not valid on a child object")
    End If

    AcceptChanges()
  End Sub

#End Region
```

These methods allow us to create a UI that starts editing a collection with `BeginEdit()`, lets the user interact with the collection, and then either cancels or accepts the changes with `CancelEdit()` or `ApplyEdit()` respectively.

IsDirty and IsValid

Finally, we can implement `IsDirty` and `IsValid` properties. To determine if our collection has changed (is dirty), all we need to do is determine whether we've added or removed any objects, or if any of our child objects themselves are dirty. To determine if the collection is valid, we merely need to see if any of our child objects are invalid:

```
#Region " IsDirty, IsValid "

  Public ReadOnly Property IsDirty() As Boolean
    Get
      ' Any deletions make us dirty
      If deletedList.Count > 0 Then Return True

      ' Run through all the child objects. If any
      ' are dirty then the collection is dirty
      Dim Child As BusinessBase

      For Each Child In list
        If Child.IsDirty Then Return True
      Next
      Return False
    End Get
  End Property

  Public ReadOnly Property IsValid() As Boolean
    Get
      ' Run through all the child objects. If any
      ' are invalid then the collection is invalid
      Dim Child As BusinessBase

      For Each Child In list
        If Not Child.IsValid Then Return False
      Next
      Return True
    End Get
  End Property

#End Region
```

In both cases, we're relying on our child objects to keep track of whether they've been changed or are valid, and then just summarizing to get the state of the collection itself.

At this point, the `BusinessCollectionBase` class is complete, insofar as we've implemented all the functionality that's demanded by `UndoableBase` and `BusinessBase`. You should be able to build the assembly at this point without errors.

> *In Chapter 5, we'll finish `BusinessCollectionBase` by enhancing it with support for data access, but for now it is complete.*

ReadOnlyBase

With BusinessBase and BusinessCollectionBase finished – at least for the time being – we are providing the tools that a business developer needs in order to build editable objects and collections. However, most applications also include a number of read-only objects and collections. We might have a read-only object that contains system configuration data, or a read-only collection of ProductType objects that are used just for lookup purposes.

The ReadOnlyBase class will provide a base on which business developers can build a read-only object. Once we're done with this, we'll implement a ReadOnlyCollectionBase to support read-only *collections* of data.

By definition, a read-only object is quite simple – it's just a container for data, possibly with some security or formatting logic to control how that data is accessed. It doesn't support editing of the data, so there's no need for n-level undo, change events, or much of the other complexity we built into UndoableBase and BusinessBase. In fact, other than data access logic, the only thing our base class can implement is a Clone() method.

Add a new class to the CSLA project and name it ReadOnlyBase. Then, add the following code:

```
Imports System.IO
Imports System.Runtime.Serialization.Formatters.Binary

<Serializable()> _
Public MustInherit Class ReadOnlyBase

  Implements ICloneable

#Region " Clone "

  ' All business objects _must_ be serializable and thus
  '  can be cloned - this just clinches the deal
  Public Function Clone() As Object Implements ICloneable.Clone
    Dim buffer As New MemoryStream()
    Dim formatter As New BinaryFormatter()

    formatter.Serialize(buffer, Me)
    buffer.Position = 0
    Return formatter.Deserialize(buffer)
  End Function

#End Region

End Class
```

As with all our business base classes, ReadOnlyBase is marked as <Serializable()> and MustInherit. The former enables the use of serialization as we construct the standard Clone() method, while the latter ensures that to use this class, the business developer will create their own specific business object.

Presumably, any business object based on this class would consist entirely of read-only properties, or methods that just return values. In Chapter 5, we'll implement data access functionality for this class, supporting only the reading of data from the database, with no update possible.

ReadOnlyCollectionBase

Like the `ReadOnlyBase` class, our `ReadOnlyCollectionBase` is quite simple to create. However, it does need a little extra code to ensure that the contents of the collection can't be altered, except by our data access logic as we load the collection with data from the database.

Add a new class to the `CSLA` project and name it `ReadOnlyCollectionBase`, with the following code:

```
<Serializable()> _
Public MustInherit Class ReadOnlyCollectionBase
  Inherits CSLA.Core.BindableCollectionBase

  Public Sub New()
    AllowEdit = False
    AllowNew = False
    AllowRemove = False
  End Sub

End Class
```

Since this class inherits from `BindableCollectionBase`, it fully supports data binding in Windows Forms. This also means that our constructor can set the values controlling data binding, so that data binding knows the collection can't be altered.

Clone method

As with our other business base classes, we support the concept of cloning the object, so add the `Implements` statement:

```
  Implements ICloneable
```

Import the required namespaces:

```
Imports System.IO
Imports System.Runtime.Serialization.Formatters.Binary
```

And then write the (now familiar) `Clone()` method:

```
#Region " Clone "

  ' All business objects _must_ be serializable and
  '  thus can be cloned - this just clinches the deal
  Public Function Clone() As Object Implements ICloneable.Clone
    Dim buffer As New MemoryStream
    Dim formatter As New BinaryFormatter

    formatter.Serialize(buffer, Me)
    buffer.Position = 0
    Return formatter.Deserialize(buffer)
  End Function

#End Region
```

Preventing changes

Finally, we need to override the OnInsert(), OnRemove(), OnClear(), and OnSet() methods from CollectionBase to prevent any chance of the contents of the collection being altered. Remember that *all* collection objects have RemoveAt() and Clear() methods, even if we don't implement them, and we need to make sure that they're useless.

At the same time, we do need to allow items to be added to the collection in the first place. To resolve this, we'll include a Protected variable named Locked that defaults to True. When our business logic needs to alter the contents of the collection, it can set Locked to False, do the changes, and then set it back to True to prevent any other code from changing the contents of the collection:

```
#Region " Insert, Remove, Clear, Set "

  Protected Locked As Boolean = True

  Protected Overrides Sub OnInsert(ByVal index As Integer, _
                                   ByVal value As Object)
    If Locked Then
      Throw New _
        NotSupportedException("Insert is invalid for a read-only collection")
    End If
  End Sub

  Protected Overrides Sub OnRemove(ByVal index As Integer, _
                                   ByVal value As Object)
    If Locked Then
      Throw New _
        NotSupportedException("Remove is invalid for a read-only collection")
    End If
  End Sub

  Protected Overrides Sub OnClear()
    If Locked Then
      Throw New _
        NotSupportedException("Clear is invalid for a read-only collection")
    End If
  End Sub

  Protected Overrides Sub OnSet(ByVal index As Integer, _
                                ByVal oldValue As Object, _
                                ByVal newValue As Object)
    If Locked Then
      Throw New _
     NotSupportedException("Items can not be changed in a read-only collection")
    End If
  End Sub

#End Region
```

Other than the data access code that we'll implement in Chapter 5, this completes the read-only collection base class for our framework.

SmartDate

The final class that we'll implement in this chapter is `SmartDate`. Date handling is often quite challenging because the standard `Date` data type doesn't have any comprehension of an 'empty' or 'blank' date.

In many applications, we have date fields that are optional, or where an empty date is not only valid but also has special meaning. For instance, we might have a `StartDate` field on an object to indicate the date on which something started. If it has not yet started, the field should be empty. For the purposes of manipulation, this 'empty' date should probably be considered to represent the *largest* possible date value. In other cases, an empty date might represent the *smallest* possible date value.

We *could* force the user to enter some arbitrary far-future date to indicate an 'empty' date, and indeed many systems have done this in the past, but it's a poor solution from both a programmatic and an end-user perspective. Ideally, we'd have a situation in which the user could just leave the field blank, and the program could deal with the concept of an 'empty' date and what that means.

> *In the early 90s, I worked at a company where they entered all 'far-future' dates as 12/31/99. Guess how much trouble they had around Y2K, when all of their 'never-to-be-delivered' orders started coming due!*

The `Date` data type in VB.NET is marked `NotInheritable` (`sealed` in C#), meaning that we can't inherit from it to create our own, smarter, data type. However, we *can* use containment and delegation to 'wrap' a `Date` value with extra functionality. That's exactly what we'll do here as we create a `SmartDate` data type that understands empty dates.

Not only will we make `SmartDate` understand empty dates, but also we'll give it extra capabilities to support a rich UI, including easy conversion of date values from `Date` to `String`, and vice versa. When we implement our data access code in Chapter 5, we'll enhance it to tie right into the data access mechanism so that we can easily store and retrieve both regular and empty date values.

Add a new class to the `CSLA` project and name it `SmartDate`. Like all our classes, it will be `<Serializable()>` so that it can be passed across the network by value:

```
<Serializable()> _
Public NotInheritable Class SmartDate

End Class
```

Since we'll be containing a regular `Date` value, we'll declare a variable for that purpose. We'll also declare a variable to control whether an empty value represents the largest or smallest possible date:

```
<Serializable()> _
Public NotInheritable Class SmartDate
  Private mDate As Date
  Private mEmptyIsMin As Boolean

End Class
```

Now we can implement some constructors to allow easy creation of a `SmartDate` object. At its simplest, we just want to be able to create an empty `SmartDate` with no extra work, so we have a default constructor. At the same time, we want to be able to control whether an empty date is the largest or smallest date possible, so this is an optional parameter that defaults to empty, meaning the smallest date:

```
#Region " Constructors "

  Public Sub New(Optional ByVal EmptyIsMin As Boolean = True)

    mEmptyIsMin = EmptyIsMin
    If mEmptyIsMin Then
      mDate = Date.MinValue
    Else
      mDate = Date.MaxValue
    End If
  End Sub

  Public Sub New(ByVal Value As Date, _
                 Optional ByVal EmptyIsMin As Boolean = True)

    mEmptyIsMin = EmptyIsMin
    mDate = Value
  End Sub

  Public Sub New(ByVal Value As String, _
                 Optional ByVal EmptyIsMin As Boolean = True)

    mEmptyIsMin = EmptyIsMin
    Me.Text = Value
  End Sub

#End Region
```

The other two constructor methods allow us to create a `SmartDate` object, initializing it with an existing date in either text or `Date` format. In both cases, we optionally allow control over how to treat an empty date.

If we set the value of `SmartDate` with a `String` value, our code turns around and sets `Me.Text`, which we'll implement later. `Me.Text` intelligently converts the text to a `Date` value, honoring our concept of empty dates.

Supporting empty dates

We've already defined a variable to control whether an empty date represents the largest or smallest possible date. We can expose that variable as a property, so that other code can determine how we handle dates:

```
#Region " Empty Dates "

  Public ReadOnly Property EmptyIsMin() As Boolean
    Get
      Return mEmptyIsMin
    End Get
  End Property

#End Region
```

We should also implement an `IsEmpty` property, so that code can ask us if we represent an empty date. Add this to the same region:

```
Public ReadOnly Property IsEmpty() As Boolean
  Get
    If mEmptyIsMin Then
      Return mDate.Equals(Date.MinValue)
    Else
      Return mDate.Equals(Date.MaxValue)
    End If
  End Get
End Property
```

Notice how we use the `mEmptyIsMin` flag to determine whether an empty date is to be considered the largest or smallest possible date for comparison purposes. If it is the smallest date, then we are empty if our date value equals `Date.MinValue`, while if it is the largest date, we are empty if our value equals `Date.MaxValue`.

Conversion functions

Given this understanding of empty dates, we can create a couple of functions to convert dates to text (or text to dates) intelligently. We'll implement these as `Shared` methods so that they can be used even without creating an instance of our `SmartDate` class. Using these methods, we could write business logic such as:

```
Dim userDate As Date = SmartDate.StringToDate(userDateString)
```

The following table shows the results of this function, based on various user text inputs.

User text input	**EmptyIsMin**	Result of **StringToDate()**
""	`True` (default)	`Date.MinValue`
""	`False`	`Date.MaxValue`
Any text that can be parsed as a date	`True` or `False` (ignored)	A date value

`StringToDate()` converts a `String` value containing a date into a `Date` value. It understands that an empty `String` should be converted to either the smallest or the largest date, based on an optional parameter:

```
#Region " Conversion Functions "

  Public Shared Function StringToDate(ByVal Value As String, _
                     Optional ByVal EmptyIsMin As Boolean = True) As Date

    If Len(Value) = 0 Then
      If EmptyIsMin Then
        Return Date.MinValue
```

```
      Else
        Return Date.MaxValue
      End If

    Else
      Return CDate(Value)
    End If

  End Function

#End Region
```

Given a String of non-zero length, this function attempts to convert it directly to a Date variable. If that fails, the CDate() function will throw an exception; otherwise a valid date is returned.

We can also go the other way, converting a Date variable into a String, while understanding the concept of an empty date. Again, an optional parameter controls whether an empty date represents the smallest or the largest possible date. Another parameter controls the format of the date as it's converted to a String. The following table illustrates the results for various inputs:

User date input	EmptyIsMin	Result of DateToString()
Date.MinValue	True (default)	""
Date.MinValue	False	Date.MinValue
Date.MaxValue	True (default)	Date.MaxValue
Date.MaxValue	False	""
Any other valid date	True or False (ignored)	String representing the date value

Add the following code to the same region:

```
  Public Shared Function DateToString(ByVal Value As Date, _
                                      ByVal FormatString As String, _
                      Optional ByVal EmptyIsMin As Boolean = True) As String

    If EmptyIsMin AndAlso Value = Date.MinValue Then
      Return ""

    ElseIf Not EmptyIsMin AndAlso Value = Date.MaxValue Then
      Return ""

    Else
      Return Format(Value, FormatString)
    End If

  End Function
```

This functions as a mirror to our first method. If we start with an empty String, convert it to a Date, and then convert that Date back to a String, we'll end up with an empty String.

Text functions

We can now move on to implement functions in our class that support both text and Date access to our underlying Date value. When business code wants to expose a date value to the UI, it will often want to expose it as a String. (Exposing it as a Date precludes the possibility of the user entering a blank value for an empty date, and while that's great if the date is required, it is not good for optional date values.)

Exposing a date as text requires that we have the ability to format the date properly. To make this manageable, we'll include a variable in our class to control the format used for outputting a date. We'll also implement a property so the business developer can alter this value if they don't like the default:

```
#Region " Text Support "

  Private mFormat As String = "Short date"

  Public Property FormatString() As String
    Get
      Return mFormat
    End Get
    Set(ByVal Value As String)
      mFormat = Value
    End Set
  End Property

#End Region
```

Given this information, we can use the StringToDate() and DateToString() methods to implement a Text property. This property can be used to retrieve or set our value using String representations of dates, where an empty String is appropriately handled. Add this to the same region:

```
  Public Property Text() As String
    Get
      Return DateToString(mDate, mFormat, mEmptyIsMin)
    End Get
    Set(ByVal Value As String)
      mDate = StringToDate(Value, mEmptyIsMin)
    End Set
  End Property
```

This property was used in one of our constructors as well, meaning that the same rules for dealing with an empty date apply during object initialization, as when setting its value via the Text property.

There's one other text-oriented method that we should implement: ToString(). All objects in .NET have a ToString() method, and ideally it returns a useful text representation of the object's contents. In our case, it should return the formatted date value:

```
  Public Overrides Function ToString() As String
    Return Me.Text()
  End Function
```

Since we've already implemented all the code necessary to render our Date value as text, this is easy to implement.

Date functions

We need to be able to treat a `SmartDate` like a regular `Date` – as much as possible, anyway. Since we can't inherit from `Date`, there's no way to be treated *just* like a regular `Date`, so the best we can do is to implement a `Date` property that returns our internal value:

```
#Region " Date Support "

  Public Property [Date]() As Date
    Get
      Return mDate
    End Get
    Set(ByVal Value As Date)
      mDate = Value
    End Set
  End Property

#End Region
```

The brackets around `[Date]` are required because `Date` is a reserved word. The brackets allow us to use a reserved word as a property name.

Beyond that, this property simply allows the business code to set or retrieve the date value arbitrarily. Of course, our text-based functionality will continue to treat either `Date.MinValue` or `Date.MaxValue` as an empty date, based on our configuration.

Date manipulation

We should also provide arithmetic manipulation of the date value. Since we're trying to emulate a regular `Date` data type, we should provide at least `CompareTo()`, `Add()`, and `Subtract()` methods:

```
#Region " Manipulation Functions "

  Public Function CompareTo(ByVal Value As SmartDate) As Integer
    If Me.IsEmpty AndAlso Value.IsEmpty Then
      Return 0
    Else
      Return mDate.CompareTo(Value.Date)
    End If
  End Function

  Public Sub Add(ByVal Value As TimeSpan)
    mDate.Add(Value)
  End Sub

  Public Sub Subtract(ByVal Value As TimeSpan)
    mDate.Subtract(Value)
  End Sub

#End Region
```

These are easily implemented by delegating each call down to the actual `Date` value we contain. It already understands how to compare, add, and subtract date values, so we don't have to do any real work at all.

Database format

The final thing we'll do is implement a method that allows our date value to be converted to a format suitable for writing to the database. Though we've got functions to convert a date to text, and text to a date, we don't have any good way of getting a date formatted properly to write to a database. Specifically, we need a way to either write a valid date, or write a null value if the date is empty.

In ADO.NET, a null value is expressed as `DBNull.Value`, so we can easily implement a function that returns either a valid `Date` object or `DBNull.Value`. If our `SmartDate` object contains an empty date value, we'll return null:

```
#Region " DBValue "

  Public ReadOnly Property DBValue() As Object
    Get
      If Me.IsEmpty Then
        Return DBNull.Value

      Else
        Return mDate
      End If
    End Get
  End Property

#End Region
```

Since we've already implemented an `IsEmpty()` property, our code here is pretty straightforward. If we are empty, we return `DBNull.Value`, which can be used to put a null value into a database via ADO.NET. Otherwise, we contain a valid date value, so we return that instead.

> *This routine could be altered to provide a different value from* `DBNull` *to represent an empty date in the database. Some people arbitrarily choose a far-future date such as 12/31/9999 to represent empty dates in the database, and in that case they'd alter this method to return that value instead of* `DBNull`*. I typically prefer to use a null value to represent an empty date in the database to avoid any chance of confusing it for a real date, and so that's the implementation I'm showing here.*

At this point, we've got a `SmartDate` class that business developers can use (if desired) to handle dates that must be represented as text, and where we need to support the concept of an empty date. In Chapter 5, we'll add a little data access functionality, so that a `SmartDate` can be easily saved and restored from a database.

Conclusion

In this chapter, we've combined the concepts from Chapter 1 with many of the technologies from the last chapter to implement about half of the framework that we designed in Chapter 2! At this point, we've got enough functionality for a business developer to build object-oriented systems that support useful concepts such as:

- n-Level undo
- Business rule tracking
- Data binding
- Change tracking
- Strongly typed collections
- Editable and read-only objects
- Root and child objects

In Chapter 5, we'll finish the business framework by implementing a `DataPortal` and then enhancing the classes we created in this chapter to understand the `DataPortal` and data access concepts. From Chapter 6 on, we'll focus on designing and building a simple business application that illustrates how the classes in our framework can be used to build distributed, object-oriented systems.

CHAPTER 5

5

Data access and security

In Chapter 4, we combined the concepts from Chapter 1, the framework design from Chapter 2, and the technologies from Chapter 3 to create about half of the CSLA .NET framework. In this chapter, we'll continue the process, completing implementation of the remaining classes. This will entail making some minor changes to some of the classes we created in Chapter 4 as well.

Specifically, we'll create the following components, as discussed in Chapter 2:

- `CSLA.Server.DataPortal.dll`
- `CSLA.Server.ServicedDataPortal.dll`

And we'll need to add some methods to the base classes that can interact with our data access framework:

- `BusinessBase`
- `BusinessCollectionBase`
- `ReadOnlyBase`
- `ReadOnlyCollectionBase`

Also, we'll create a host application that will run on an application server to host the server-side `DataPortal` components. This will be a simple ASP.NET application that's configured to act as a .NET remoting host. We'll follow the same process here that we walked through in Chapter 3 when we introduced the concept of using IIS as a remoting host.

Once we've enabled data access within the business framework, we'll employ that functionality to create our custom security infrastructure. This will include the creation of principal and identity objects as part of the .NET security framework. It will also include their integration directly into the overall `DataPortal` mechanism, so that our business objects can have the same security context on the application server as they do on a client workstation or a web server.

Finally, we'll close the chapter by creating a generic list class to support almost *any* read-only name-value list. Not only is this type of object invaluable – it's used by almost every application – but also it will give us a glimpse into how collection objects are populated through the `DataPortal` mechanism.

The classes we'll create in this chapter are:

- `TransactionalAttribute`
- `Server.DataPortal`
- `Server.ServicedDataPortal.DataPortal`
- `DataPortal` (client-side class)
- `Data.SafeDataReader`
- `Security.Principal`
- `Security.Identity`
- `NameValueList`

The reasoning behind each of these classes, and how they are organized into namespaces and assemblies, was covered in Chapter 2. We'll be reprising those discussions as we work our way through this chapter.

A note about object-oriented programming

One of the primary goals of object-oriented programming is to encapsulate all the functionality (data and implementation) for a domain entity into a single class. This means, for instance, that all the data and implementation logic for the concept of a customer should be in a `Customer` class.

A corollary to this is that an object should avoid externalizing its data, so that other code can interact with that data. Any time an object makes its internal data available to other code, the object loses control over that data. The end result is decreased maintainability, and the increased likelihood of unexpected results, because we no longer are sure that all our business logic is contained within that single class.

It has always been difficult to achieve strong encapsulation at the same time as distributing an application over physical tiers. If the data access code must run on an application server, but the object must run on the client or web server, we've typically created two different classes. One class is the business object itself that runs on the client, while the other contains the data access code and runs on the application server.

By definition, this breaks encapsulation, since we have two different objects (the business object and the data access object) that both externalize their data. Now, we can argue that this isn't too bad, because they're only externalizing their data to each other – and we might even argue that the objects are two halves of the same 'virtual' object – but in the end, we *are* breaking encapsulation. We're also making maintenance more complex, because we now have business logic split between two classes, and we need to maintain it in both – we end up trying to avoid duplication of logic, and yet provide good performance and functionality.

I used these arguments in my Visual Basic 6 Business Objects and Visual Basic 6 Distributed Objects books. They are reasonably valid, and result in a perfectly workable architecture, but the end result isn't ideal – it's far preferable to preserve encapsulation by having just one class. This wasn't practical in VB6 and COM, but since .NET enables this approach, it is the one I pursued in the creation of CSLA .NET.

A better solution is to preserve encapsulation entirely by keeping all of the business logic for an entity in a single class. This can be accomplished if it is practical to move the object physically from client to server and back again. As we discussed in Chapter 1, we can achieve this by making our business objects unanchored, so that they move from machine to machine. However, this also implies that we have an object that *is* anchored on the application server, so that our client-side code can pass our objects to it.

This requirement is the purpose behind the server-side `DataPortal` object. It acts as the anchored object on the application server, receiving business objects from our clients:

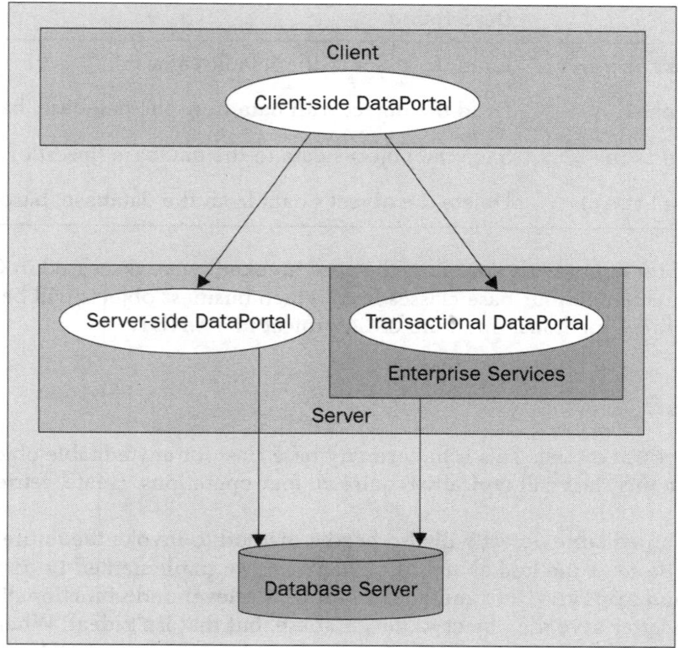

Once our object is physically on the server, it's the job of the server-side `DataPortal` to invoke the appropriate methods to create, retrieve, update, or delete the object's data. Remember that the data access code itself is *inside* our business object; the server-side `DataPortal` merely invokes the appropriate method.

On the client-side, we *also* have a `DataPortal` object, which exists to simplify how the server-side `DataPortal` is called. Instead of writing the remoting code into each of our business objects, we can write it into a centralized, client-side `DataPortal`, and our business object code can use this more abstract mechanism to interact with the server-side `DataPortal`.

CSLA

Before we implement the data portal mechanism itself, we need to make sure that the server-side DataPortal can properly interact with our business objects. Once again, the server-side DataPortal just invokes the appropriate methods on our business object to create, retrieve, update, or delete the object's data. This implies that the server-side DataPortal somehow knows what methods our object has implemented to perform these operations.

To ensure that all our business objects have a consistent set of methods, we'll implement some overridable methods in our base classes. This ensures that *all* business objects will have these methods, even if we choose not to override them in a particular implementation. To simplify debugging, however, the default implementations will simply raise errors – that way, we'll quickly discover that we need to override them! The methods will be Protected in scope so that they're not available to any UI code. They'll be named as follows:

Method	Description
DataPortal_Create()	Load the object with default values
DataPortal_Fetch()	Load the object with data from the database, based on criteria
DataPortal_Update()	Save the object's data to the database (insert or update)
DataPortal_Delete()	Delete the object's data from the database, based on criteria

The details behind these methods (and how they are invoked) were discussed in Chapter 2. In Chapter 4, we implemented four base classes from which business objects will be created. Let's update each of them with these methods; open the CSLA project in VS.NET.

BusinessBase

Open the BusinessBase class. This is the primary base class for any editable object, which means that any object based on this class will typically require all four operations: create, retrieve, update, and delete.

Not only that, but an editable object will also need a method to invoke the entire update process, so we'll implement a Save() method as well. In Chapter 4, we implemented BeginEdit(), CancelEdit(), and ApplyEdit() methods to support n-level undo functionality, and it might seem logical to have the latter save the object to the database, but that isn't ideal. When developing web applications, we may never use BeginEdit(), CancelEdit(), or ApplyEdit(), since n-level undo capabilities aren't typically important in the web environment. Because of this, we need a new method that explicitly causes the object to save its data into the database – hence Save().

Finally, note that no matter how much help we provide, it's the business developer who will need to write the specific data access code for their objects. That code will need to open database connections, which means that it will need access to database connection strings. There are many ways to store that piece of configuration data, but a good technique in .NET is to put the connection string into the application's configuration file. We'll add a utility function here to simplify the process of reading that file, so that the business developer has easy access to the connection string.

If you intend to use the configuration file to store connection strings, this utility function will be helpful. If not, you could change this implementation to suit your specific environment.

DataPortal methods

First, let's implement the four methods that will be invoked by the server-side `DataPortal` code. In all cases, we'll raise an error in our default implementation. If the business developer wants to support the function, they'll need to override the method in their actual business class.

```
#Region " Data Access "

  Protected Overridable Sub DataPortal_Create(ByVal Criteria As Object)
    Throw New NotSupportedException("Invalid operation - create not allowed")
  End Sub

  Protected Overridable Sub DataPortal_Fetch(ByVal Criteria As Object)
    Throw New NotSupportedException("Invalid operation - fetch not allowed")
  End Sub

  Protected Overridable Sub DataPortal_Update()
    Throw New NotSupportedException("Invalid operation - update not allowed")
  End Sub

  Protected Overridable Sub DataPortal_Delete(ByVal Criteria As Object)
    Throw New NotSupportedException("Invalid operation - delete not allowed")
  End Sub

#End Region
```

DataPortal_Create

The `DataPortal_Create()` method is called by the server-side `DataPortal` when our business object is to be initialized with default values. The use of this functionality is entirely optional, and in Chapter 7 we'll build some business objects that use it, and some that don't.

The code in our business object to implement `DataPortal_Create()` will typically go to the database and retrieve the appropriate default values for the object. Those values will be loaded into the object's variables, and then the fully populated object is returned to the client.

This method receives a `Criteria` object as a parameter, allowing us to provide criteria that might alter the ways the default values are loaded, as we discussed in Chapter 2. For instance, if we're loading a `Customer` object's default values, we might load different defaults depending on the user's profile, or some other information.

The code in this method may use ADO.NET to retrieve the default values from a database, or the default values may be retrieved from some other source (such as an XML file). It is up to the business developer to provide the implementation of this method to retrieve the default values properly.

DataPortal_Fetch

The `DataPortal_Fetch()` method is called to tell our object to populate itself with existing data from the database. It gets a `Criteria` object as a parameter, which should contain enough information for us to locate and load the appropriate data.

The code in this method will typically use ADO.NET to interact with the database to retrieve the data. Values from the database are placed into the object's variables, and the object is then returned to the client.

DataPortal_Update

The `DataPortal_Update()` method is called to tell our object to save its data to the database. If our object is new (`IsNew` is `True`), then it will insert itself into the database. Otherwise, it will update the existing data in the database with the values in the object itself.

The `DataPortal_Update()` method might also perform a delete operation. In Chapter 4, we discussed the fact that there are two approaches to deleting objects: deferred and immediate. In the deferred scenario, an object is marked for deletion, but the actual operation doesn't occur until later, when the object is updated into the database. Because of this possibility, the `DataPortal_Update()` code needs to check the `IsDeleted` flag of the object. If that flag is `True`, then the object is to be *deleted* from the database, rather than inserted or updated. We'll see how this works when we implement some actual business objects in Chapter 7.

DataPortal_Delete

The scenario where an object is immediately deleted is the purpose behind the `DataPortal_Delete()` method. Sometimes, we don't want to have to retrieve the object from the database, just to mark it as deleted and then call the update process. That can amount to a lot of overhead if we already know the object's key value and could simply invoke a delete process.

The `DataPortal_Delete()` method is passed a `Criteria` object, just like `DataPortal_Fetch()`, except that it uses this criteria data to delete the object, rather than to retrieve it. This approach is highly efficient and can be used any time the client or a client-side object has the key value for the object to be deleted.

The approach is typically only valid for root objects, and it's up to us to ensure that we delete not only the root object's data, but also the data of all its child objects. Child objects are deleted using the deferred approach, because we haven't designed them to be manipulated directly via the data portal mechanism.

Save method

By implementing the `DataPortal_Create()`, `DataPortal_Fetch()`, `DataPortal_Update()`, and `DataPortal_Delete()` methods in a business object's class, we allow full manipulation of the object via the server-side `DataPortal`. What we haven't discussed since Chapter 2 is what starts the whole process. How does the UI code actually create, retrieve, update, or delete a business object?

The create, retrieve, and (immediate) delete processes will be started by `Shared` methods in the business object class – a concept called 'class in charge' that we introduced in Chapter 2. We'll implement examples of this in Chapter 7 when we build our business classes. The update process, however, is a bit different. It's *not* invoked from a `Shared` method, because we have a *specific* business object that we want to update. That object itself should have a method that we can call to cause the object to save its data to the database.

The `Save()` method will perform this function. At a minimum, it must invoke the client-side `DataPortal`, which in turn invokes the server-side `DataPortal`, which finally invokes the object's `DataPortal_Update()` method. This flow of events was diagrammed and discussed in Chapter 2.

Because this method makes use of the client-side DataPortal, which we haven't written yet, the code we're about to add won't compile at this stage. Nevertheless, add the following code to the *Data Access* region of BusinessBase:

```
' Add/Save object
Public Overridable Function Save() As BusinessBase
  If Me.IsChild Then
    Throw New Exception("Cannot directly save a child object")
  End If

  If EditLevel > 0 Then
    Throw New Exception("Object is still being edited and cannot be saved")
  End If

  If Not IsValid Then
    Throw New Exception("Object is not valid and cannot be saved")
  End If

  If IsDirty Then
    Return CType(DataPortal.Update(Me), BusinessBase)
  Else
    Return Me
  End If
End Function
```

There are a number of checks in this method to ensure that the object is a root object; that it is not in the middle of an edit process; that it has no broken rules; and finally that it contains changed data.

If any of the first three checks fails, then the object cannot be saved, and an error is raised. If we get past those checks and the object has changed data (IsDirty is True), then the client-side DataPortal is invoked and the resulting object is returned by the Save() method. On the other hand, if the object is *not* dirty, then we simply return the object itself as a result of the method.

Returning an object as a result of the method is important. Remember that DataPortal_Update() might change the object's data during the update process, so it returns the object as a result. We, in turn, need to return that object to the UI code so that it can use this new, updated object. Even if the object wasn't dirty and we didn't do an actual update, we need to return the object so the UI can always count on getting back a reference to a valid business object. In Chapter 8, we'll implement a UI that makes use of the Save() method.

DB Method

At this point, we're basically ready to go: we can create, retrieve, update, and delete our business objects. However, we're leaving our business developers to write the four DataPortal_xxx() methods, and to do that they'll typically use ADO.NET. Let's add a method here to make it easier for them to get the connection string they need in order to do so.

> *Note that all we're doing here is providing an easy and standard way to get the connection string. We are not creating or opening the connection object or anything like that. It is up to the business developer to implement that code as appropriate for their particular database or data source. In fact, this 'connection string' could just as easily be a file path that the business developer uses to open an XML file.*

> *By providing centralized access to connection strings for typical database access, we help ensure that the application always uses a consistent connection string. This is important, because database connections are pooled based on the connection string, so we want all our connection strings to be identical whenever possible.*

The `DB()` method will take the name of the database as a parameter, and will return the connection string as a result. It will look in the application's configuration file for the information, expecting that the database name will be prefixed with "`DB:`". If we're after the `pubs` database, for example, it would expect an entry in the configuration file such as:

```
<add key="DB:Pubs"
   value="data source=(local);initial catalog=pubs;integrated security=SSPI" />
```

Since we're reading this from the application's configuration file, add the following `Imports` statement to the top of the `BusinessBase` code to make the classes of the `System.Configuration` namespace available to our code:

```
Imports System.Configuration
```

Then we can add the `DB()` function to the *Data Access* region:

```
  Protected Function DB(ByVal DatabaseName As String) As String
    Return ConfigurationSettings.AppSettings("DB:" & DatabaseName)
  End Function
```

This is just the regular code for retrieving a value from the application's configuration file.

At this point, we're done with `BusinessBase`. The server-side `DataPortal` can now properly interact with any business objects that subclass `BusinessBase`. Of course, it is up to the business developer to provide meaningful implementations of the four `DataPortal_xxx()` methods, but we've provided a framework into which the business logic can easily be inserted.

BusinessCollectionBase

In many ways, the `BusinessCollectionBase` class is similar to `BusinessBase`. It too can act as either a root or a child, and if the collection is a root object, then it can be created, retrieved, updated, or deleted by the data portal mechanism.

Because of the similarities in functionality, the code we'll insert into `BusinessCollectionBase` is identical to the code we added to `BusinessBase`. Obviously, the *business logic* in the four `DataPortal_xxx()` methods will be quite different when working with a collection than when working with a simple object, but that has no impact on our *framework*.

First, we import the `System.Configuration` namespace so that we can read from the application configuration file:

```
Imports System.Configuration
```

Then, we add the *Data Access* region:

```
#Region " Data Access "

  ' Add/save object
  Public Overridable Function Save() As BusinessCollectionBase
    If Me.IsChild Then
      Throw New Exception("Cannot directly save a child object")
    End If

    If mEditLevel > 0 Then
      Throw New Exception("Object is still being edited and cannot be saved")
    End If

    If Not IsValid Then
      Throw New Exception("Object is not valid and cannot be saved")
    End If

    If IsDirty Then
      Return CType(DataPortal.Update(Me), BusinessCollectionBase)
    Else
      Return Me
    End If

  End Function

  Protected Overridable Sub DataPortal_Create(ByVal Criteria As Object)
    Throw New NotSupportedException("Invalid operation - create not allowed")
  End Sub

  Protected Overridable Sub DataPortal_Fetch(ByVal Criteria As Object)
    Throw New NotSupportedException("Invalid operation - fetch not allowed")
  End Sub

  Protected Overridable Sub DataPortal_Update()
    Throw New NotSupportedException("Invalid operation - update not allowed")
  End Sub

  Protected Overridable Sub DataPortal_Delete(ByVal Criteria As Object)
    Throw New NotSupportedException("Invalid operation - delete not allowed")
  End Sub

  Protected Function DB(ByVal DatabaseName As String) As String
    Return ConfigurationSettings.AppSettings("DB:" & DatabaseName)
  End Function

#End Region
```

Other than adjusting the data type of the object returned from the `Save()` method, this code is identical to that from `BusinessBase`. This means that the business developer can implement comparable functionality to create, retrieve, update, or delete a collection, to what they can implement for a simpler business object.

ReadOnlyBase

The `ReadOnlyBase` class is used as a base for creating read-only business objects. Read-only objects obviously can't be updated or deleted. It also makes little sense to load a new read-only object with default values. This means that the only valid operation we can perform, *from a data access perspective*, is to retrieve such an object.

Having said that, the data portal mechanism assumes that all four `DataPortal_xxx()` methods exist on all business objects, so we need to provide implementations for all of them – not just `DataPortal_Fetch()`. However, because only `DataPortal_Fetch()` is actually valid, it will be the only one we create as `Overridable`. The other three will not be `Overridable`, and will simply return an error if invoked.

The above provisions also mean that there's no need for a `Save()` method, so we won't implement one of those either. On the other hand, the business developer *will* use ADO.NET to implement the `DataPortal_Fetch()` method, and they'll need a database connection string for that purpose, so we'll implement a `DB()` method.

Once again, import the `System.Configuration` namespace:

```
Imports System.Configuration
```

And then add the following code to `ReadOnlyBase`:

```
#Region " Data Access "

  Private Sub DataPortal_Create(ByVal Criteria As Object)
    Throw New NotSupportedException("Invalid operation - create not allowed")
  End Sub

  Protected Overridable Sub DataPortal_Fetch(ByVal Criteria As Object)
    Throw New NotSupportedException("Invalid operation - fetch not allowed")
  End Sub

  Private Sub DataPortal_Update()
    Throw New NotSupportedException("Invalid operation - update not allowed")
  End Sub

  Private Sub DataPortal_Delete(ByVal Criteria As Object)
    Throw New NotSupportedException("Invalid operation - delete not allowed")
  End Sub

  Protected Function DB(ByVal DatabaseName As String) As String
    Return ConfigurationSettings.AppSettings("DB:" & DatabaseName)
  End Function

#End Region
```

The server-side `DataPortal` will be using reflection to invoke both the `Protected` and `Private` methods. More accurately, it will use reflection to invoke non-`Public` methods, so there's no problem with declaring these three methods as `Private`.

By only exposing the one method for overriding by the business developer, we are employing a form of self-documentation. It isn't possible for the business developer to see the other three methods as being available for overriding accidentally, because the business developer simply won't see those methods at all.

ReadOnlyCollectionBase

Like `ReadOnlyBase`, the `ReadOnlyCollectionBase` class is intended to act as a base on which we can easily build read-only collections. It will have the same data access methods as `ReadOnlyBase`.

As usual, import the `System.Configuration` namespace:

```
Imports System.Configuration
```

Then implement the *Data Access* region:

```
#Region " Data Access "

  Private Sub DataPortal_Create(ByVal Criteria As Object)
    Throw New NotSupportedException("Invalid operation - create not allowed")
  End Sub

  Protected Overridable Sub DataPortal_Fetch(ByVal Criteria As Object)
    Throw New NotSupportedException("Invalid operation - fetch not allowed")
  End Sub

  Private Sub DataPortal_Update()
    Throw New NotSupportedException("Invalid operation - update not allowed")
  End Sub

  Private Sub DataPortal_Delete(ByVal Criteria As Object)
    Throw New NotSupportedException("Invalid operation - delete not allowed")
  End Sub

  Protected Function DB(ByVal DatabaseName As String) As String
    Return ConfigurationSettings.AppSettings("DB:" & DatabaseName)
  End Function

#End Region
```

Again, the only method that's `Protected` and `Overridable` is the `DataPortal_Fetch()` method. To the business developer, it's therefore very clear that this object only supports the retrieval operation. Any attempt to ask the data portal mechanism to create, update, or delete a read-only collection will result in an error being raised.

At this point, our four primary base classes, from which all business objects will be derived, support data access functionality and can interact appropriately with the data portal mechanism. Specifically, we've now ensured that the server-side `DataPortal` will be able to invoke our business objects as needed.

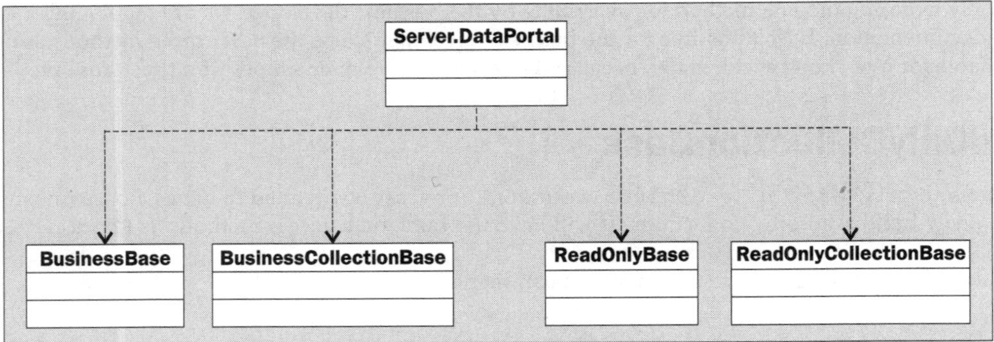

We can now move on to implementing the data portal mechanism itself. We'll start with the client-side `DataPortal` class, and then move on to the server-side `DataPortal` that actually invokes the four `DataPortal_xxx()` methods we've just been implementing.

Client-side DataPortal

The client-side `DataPortal` class is designed to simplify and centralize the code needed to interact with the server-side `DataPortal`. The methods in the client-side `DataPortal` are invoked by our business logic to create, retrieve, update, and delete business objects.

In Chapter 2, we discussed the 'class in charge' scheme that we'll be using, in which a business class will implement `Shared` methods to create, retrieve, and delete an object. These methods will call the client-side `DataPortal` in order to make those processes happen.

The following diagram shows the basic process flow when the UI code wants to get a new business object, or to load a business object from the database:

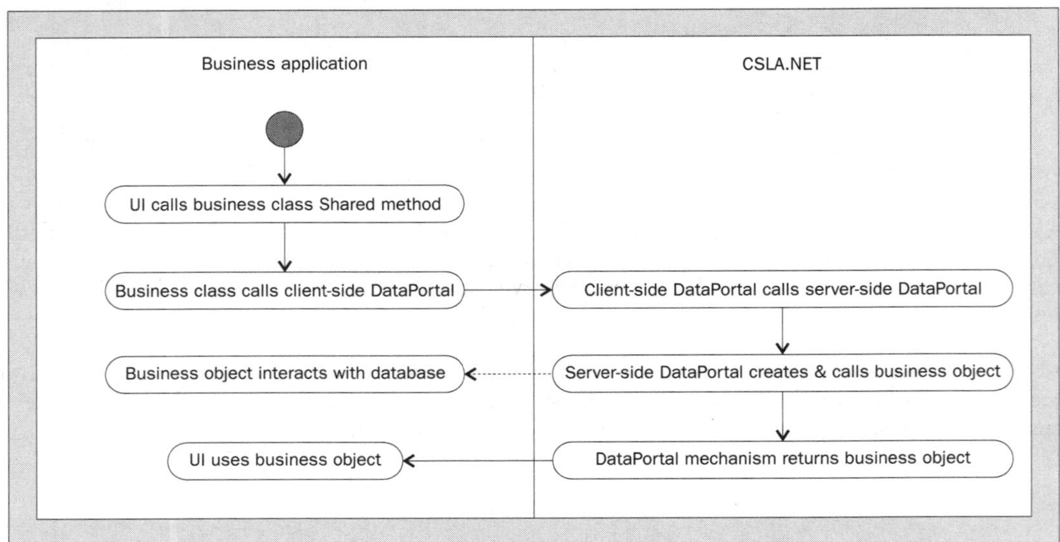

Following the class-in-charge model, you can see that the UI code calls a `Shared` method on the business class. The `Shared` method then calls the data portal mechanism to get the business object. The data portal mechanism creates the object and invokes the appropriate data access method (`DataPortal_Create()` or `DataPortal_Fetch()`). The populated business object is then returned to the UI, which can then use it as needed by the application.

We've already implemented a `Save()` method on the `BusinessBase` and `BusinessCollectionBase` classes. This makes the update process work, as illustrated by the next diagram:

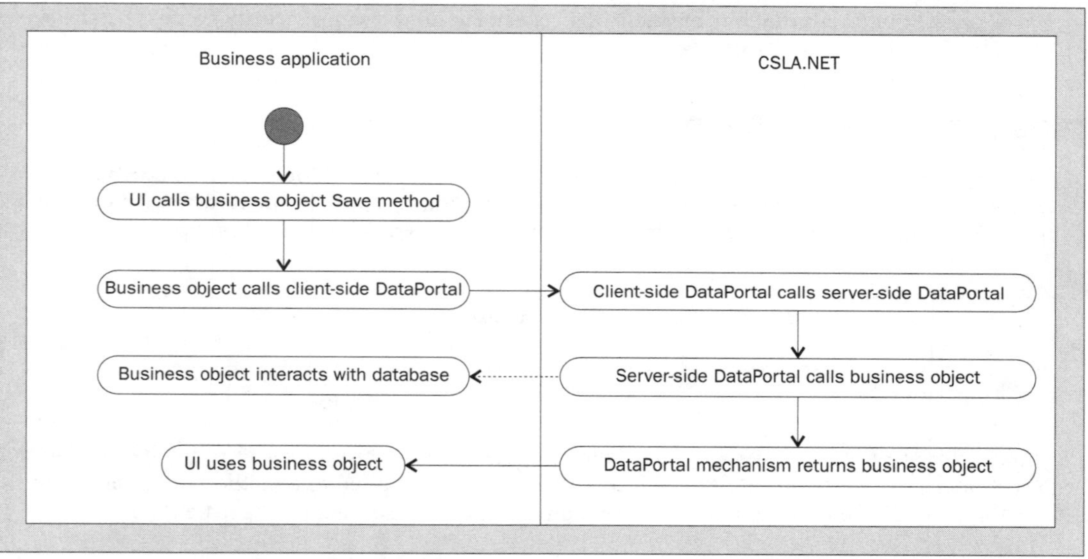

The process is almost identical, except that the UI starts off by calling the `Save()` method *on the object to be saved*, rather than invoking a `Shared` method on the business class. Likewise, immediate deletion follows the same basic process, with the exception that no business object is returned to the UI as a result.

In each case, the process relies entirely on the client-side `DataPortal`. As we described in Chapter 2, the client-side `DataPortal` does some interesting things, including the following three key features:

- Detecting whether the server-side `DataPortal` should run locally, or via remoting.

  Our application configuration file will control whether the server-side `DataPortal` is to run directly in the client process, or on another machine via remoting. By making this easily configurable, we enable various n-tier physical architectures without any need to change our application logic. The client-side `DataPortal` code will read the configuration file to determine how to invoke the server-side `DataPortal`.

- Invoking the transactional or non-transactional server-side `DataPortal`, as appropriate.

  Ultimately, we'll be implementing *two* server-side `DataPortal` classes. One of these will be designed to run 'normally', while the other will run within Enterprise Services, as a transactional serviced component. The client-side `DataPortal` will decide which of these two server-side objects to invoke on a method-by-method basis.

This means that our business developers can choose to have DataPortal_Fetch() work in non-transactional fashion for performance, and yet have the *same* object's DataPortal_Update() method use transactions to ensure data integrity. To achieve this, we'll implement a custom attribute named TransactionalAttribute.

- Integrating with our custom security.

  It's the job of the client-side DataPortal to determine whether we're using the custom security objects that we'll be implementing later in this chapter. If we *are* using our table-driven security, then the user's security objects will automatically be passed to the server-side DataPortal, so that our business objects can run in the same security context on the server as they do on the client.

TransactionalAttribute

Let's start by creating the TransactionalAttribute class. This will define a new attribute – <Transactional()> – that can be applied to the DataPortal_xxx() methods within our business objects. For instance, we'll be able to do this within a business class such as Customer:

```
<Transactional()> _
Protected Overrides Sub DataPortal_Update()

  ' Update the Customer data with full two-phase transactional protection
End Sub
```

Applying this attribute to a method will trigger the client-side DataPortal to route the method to the transactional server-side DataPortal. If this attribute is not applied to a method, then the client-side DataPortal will route the call to the faster, non-transactional server-side DataPortal.

Add a new class to the CSLA project named TransactionalAttribute. Enter the following code:

```
' This attribute allows us to mark DataPortal methods
'  as transactional to trigger use of Enterprise Services
<AttributeUsage(AttributeTargets.Method)> _
Public Class TransactionalAttribute
  Inherits Attribute
End Class
```

We use the <AttributeUsage()> attribute to indicate that this attribute can only be applied to methods. Beyond that, this attribute has no real functionality – it's just a tag that we can place on a method, rather like the <NotUndoable()> attribute that we implemented in Chapter 4.

DataPortal

The client-side DataPortal class will provide simple access to the underlying data portal mechanism, as described above. Add a new class to the CSLA project named DataPortal. VS.NET will create the empty class like so:

```
Public Class DataPortal

End Class
```

Before we get any further into the code, we need to reference and import the remoting subsystem for our CSLA project. Use the Add Reference dialog to add a reference to the remoting assembly:

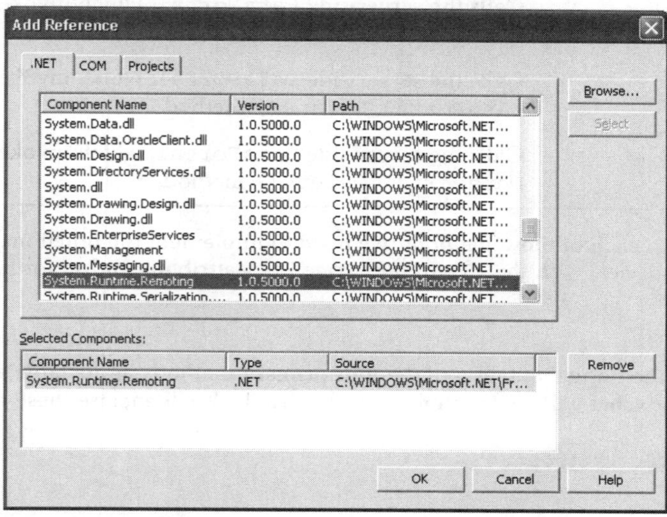

Next, it makes sense to import the namespaces that we'll need. We'll be using reflection and a couple of namespaces from the remoting assembly:

```
Imports System.Reflection
Imports System.Runtime.Remoting
Imports System.Runtime.Remoting.Channels
Imports System.Runtime.Remoting.Channels.Http
Imports System.Configuration
```

We discussed these technologies in Chapter 3, including the meanings of the namespaces.

Notice that in this implementation, we're using the HTTP channel for remoting. This is because we'll be using IIS to host the server-side DataPortal classes. Even though we'll use the HTTP channel, however, we'll still implement code to make sure that we're using the more efficient binary formatter to encode the data.

If you choose to implement a custom remoting host, you could opt instead to use the faster TCP channel. This would preclude the use of Windows' integrated security, but it would work fine with our custom, table-driven security implementation. Typically, such a host would be created as a Windows Service. We won't be implementing such a custom host in this book, since the IIS approach is much easier to implement, configure, and manage.

The client-side DataPortal will expose four methods that can be called by our business logic:

Method	Description
Create()	Calls the server-side DataPortal, which invokes our DataPortal_Create() method
Fetch()	Calls the server-side DataPortal, which invokes our DataPortal_Fetch() method
Update()	Calls the server-side DataPortal, which invokes our DataPortal_Update() method
Delete()	Calls the server-side DataPortal, which invokes our DataPortal_Delete() method

Behind the scenes in each of these methods, we need to implement the functionality to create the server-side DataPortal, to deal with the <Transactional()> attribute, and so forth.

Helper methods

Before we get into the implementation of the four primary methods in the table above, let's implement some helper methods that will deal with most of the details. We'll enclose these methods in a region:

```
  #Region " Helper Methods "

  #End Region
```

IsTransactionalMethod

Within a business class, the business developer may choose to mark any of our four DataPortal_xxx() methods as transactional, using code like this:

```
<Transactional()> _
Protected Overrides Sub DataPortal_Update()
```

To detect this, we'll need to write a method to find out whether the <Transactional()> attribute has been applied to a specified method. This is very similar to the NotUndoableField() method that we implemented in UndoableBase in Chapter 4:

```
Private Shared Function IsTransactionalMethod(ByVal Method As MethodInfo) _
    As Boolean

  Dim attribs() As Object = _
      Method.GetCustomAttributes(GetType(TransactionalAttribute), True)
  Return (UBound(attribs) > -1)
End Function
```

Here, we're passed a MethodInfo object – which provides access to the information describing a method – as a parameter. Using its GetCustomAttributes() method, we can get an array containing any attributes of type TransactionalAttribute. If that array ends up containing any elements, then we know that the attribute was applied to the method in question, so we return True.

GetMethod

Before we can find out if one of the `DataPortal_xxx()` methods on the business object has the `<Transactional()>` attribute applied, we need to get the `MethodInfo` object that describes the method in question. This requires the use of reflection, so that we can query the business object's type for a method of a particular name:

```
Private Shared Function GetMethod(ByVal ObjectType As Type, _
                                  ByVal Method As String) As MethodInfo

  Return ObjectType.GetMethod(Method, BindingFlags.FlattenHierarchy Or _
                                      BindingFlags.Instance Or _
                                      BindingFlags.Public Or _
                                      BindingFlags.NonPublic)
End Function
```

We provide qualifiers to the `GetMethod()` call to indicate that we don't care if the method is `Public` or non-`Public`. Either way, we'll get a `MethodInfo` object describing the method on the business object, which we can then use as a parameter to `IsTransactionalMethod()`.

Creating the server-side DataPortal

Next, we need to write methods that create the simple and transactional server-side `DataPortal` objects locally or using remoting, as required.

Reading the configuration file

To do this, we need to read the application's configuration file:

```
#Region " Server-side DataPortal "

  Private Shared Function PORTAL_SERVER() As String
    Return ConfigurationSettings.AppSettings("PortalServer")
  End Function

  Private Shared Function SERVICED_PORTAL_SERVER() As String
    Return ConfigurationSettings.AppSettings("ServicedPortalServer")
  End Function

#End Region
```

If we wanted the server-side `DataPortal` to run via remoting, we'd include lines in our application configuration file such as:

```
<add key="PortalServer"
     value="http://appserver/DataPortal/DataPortal.rem" />
<add key="ServicedPortalServer"
     value="http://appserver/DataPortal/ServicedDataPortal.rem" />
```

The URLs will point to the `DataPortal` website that we'll create later in this chapter as a remoting host. If these lines are not present in the application configuration file, the requests for the `PortalServer` and `ServicedPortalServer` entries will return empty `String` values. We can easily test these to see if local or remote configuration is desired.

If we do *supply URLs for our server-side* `DataPortal` *objects, the .NET remoting subsystem will automatically invoke the objects on the server we specify. This 'server' could be a web farm, because we're using the HTTP protocol. The reality isn't quite as pretty, however, because remoting caches the IP connection to the server after it is established. This results in better performance, because subsequent calls via remoting can reuse that connection, but it means that subsequent remoting requests are not load balanced, since they always go back to the same server. If that server can't be reached, remoting will automatically create a new connection – and if our servers are in a web farm, that could mean a different server. This means we do get good fault tolerance, but we don't really get ideal load balancing.*

Configuring remoting

Now that we have methods to retrieve the URL values (if any) from the configuration file, we can configure remoting. The easiest way to do this is in a `Shared Sub New` method. The .NET runtime will automatically call this method before any other code in our client-side `DataPortal` class is executed, so we are guaranteed that remoting will be configured before anything else happens.

Since we're using the HTTP channel, which defaults to using the SOAP formatter, this is a bit tricky – we want to use the binary formatter instead, because it sends a lot less data across the network. We also need to register the `Server.DataPortal` and `Server.ServicedDataPortal.DataPortal` classes as being remote, if the application configuration file contains URLs for them.

Add the following code to the *Helper Methods* region:

```
Shared Sub New()
  ' See if we need to configure remoting at all
  If Len(PORTAL_SERVER) > 0 OrElse Len(SERVICED_PORTAL_SERVER) > 0 Then

    ' Create and register our HTTP channel that uses the binary formatter
    Dim properties As New Hashtable
    properties("name") = "HttpBinary"

    Dim formatter As New BinaryClientFormatterSinkProvider

    Dim channel As New HttpChannel(properties, formatter, Nothing)

    ChannelServices.RegisterChannel(channel)

    ' Register the data portal types as being remote
    If Len(PORTAL_SERVER) > 0 Then
      RemotingConfiguration.RegisterWellKnownClientType( _
        GetType(Server.DataPortal), PORTAL_SERVER)
    End If

    If Len(SERVICED_PORTAL_SERVER) > 0 Then
      RemotingConfiguration.RegisterWellKnownClientType( _
        GetType(Server.ServicedDataPortal.DataPortal), SERVICED_PORTAL_SERVER)
    End If
  End If

End Sub
```

The first thing we do here is create an HTTP channel that uses the binary formatter, so we transfer less data across the network than if we used the default SOAP formatter. You've seen code like this before, back in Chapter 3. The outcome is that we create a custom HTTP channel object, and then register it with remoting. After that's done, remoting will use our custom channel for all HTTP remoting requests.

We then check to see if the application configuration file contains a URL for the non-transactional server-side `DataPortal`. If it does, we register the `Server.DataPortal` class as being remote, using that URL as the location. Then we do the same thing for the `ServicedDataPortal`. If there's a URL entry in the configuration file, we configure the class to be run remotely.

By taking this approach, we can configure the transactional and non-transactional server-side `DataPortal` objects to run on different servers if needed, providing a lot of flexibility.

Creating the server-side DataPortal objects

Now we're ready to create the server-side `DataPortal` objects themselves. Actually, we'll cache these objects, which will speed up performance, since it means that the client only needs to go through the creation process once. Declare a couple of variables to hold the cached references:

```
Public Class DataPortal
  Private Shared mPortal As Server.DataPortal
  Private Shared mServicedPortal As Server.ServicedDataPortal.DataPortal
```

Now let's add a method to create the simple server-side `DataPortal` object. Add this to the *Server-side Data Portal* region:

```
  Private Shared Function Portal() As Server.DataPortal

    If mPortal Is Nothing Then
      mPortal = New Server.DataPortal
    End If

    Return mPortal

  End Function
```

First, we see if we already have a server-side `DataPortal` object in the `mPortal` variable. If not, we proceed to create the object.

As I've said before, we're going to configure the IIS remoting host such that the server-side `DataPortal` object is a `SingleCall` object. This means that a new `Server.DataPortal` object will be created for each method call across the network. Such an approach provides optimal isolation between method calls, and is the simplest programming model we can use.

> *This is also the approach that will likely give us optimal performance. Our other option is to use a `Singleton` configuration, which would mean that all calls from all clients would be handled by a single server-side `DataPortal` object. Since concurrent client requests would be running on different threads, we'd have to write extra code in our server-side `DataPortal` to support multithreading, which would mean the use of synchronization objects. Any time we use synchronization objects, we tend to reduce performance - as well as radically increasing the complexity of our code for both development and debugging!*

We can create a similar method to return a reference to the transactional, serviced `DataPortal`:

```
Private Shared Function ServicedPortal() As _
                             Server.ServicedDataPortal.DataPortal

  If mServicedPortal Is Nothing Then
    mServicedPortal = New Server.ServicedDataPortal.DataPortal
  End If

  Return mServicedPortal

End Function
```

Again, we check whether a cached transactional `DataPortal` object already exists. If it doesn't, then create an instance of the transactional `DataPortal` object:

```
mServicedPortal = New Server.ServicedDataPortal.DataPortal
```

At this point, we have easy access to both the transactional and non-transactional server-side `DataPortal` objects from within our code.

Handling security

The last thing we need to do before implementing the four data access methods is to handle security. Remember that we're intending to support either Windows' integrated security, or our custom table-driven security.

If we're using Windows' integrated security, we're assuming the environment to be set up so that the user's Windows identity is automatically passed to the server through IIS. This means that our server-side code will run within an impersonated Windows security context, and the server security will match the client security automatically, without any effort on our part.

If we're using our custom security, we need to do this impersonation ourselves by ensuring that the server has the same .NET security objects as the client. We'll implement the table-driven security objects later in this chapter when we create our own principal and identity objects.

Our custom principal object will be set as our thread's `CurrentPrincipal` on the client, making it the active security object for our client-side code. When we invoke the server-side `DataPortal`, we need to pass the `CurrentPrincipal` value to the server, so that it can make the server-side `CurrentPrincipal` match the one on the client.

As is our habit, we'll use an application configuration entry to indicate whether we're using Windows security – the default will be to use our custom table-driven security. To use Windows' integrated security, our application configuration file would have an entry like this:

```
<add key="Authentication" value="Windows" />
```

Though we'll default to CSLA table-based security, we could also explicitly indicate we're using that security model with an entry like this:

```
<add key="Authentication" value="CSLA" />
```

To read this entry, let's implement a helper function in the `DataPortal` class:

```
#Region " Security "

  Private Shared Function AUTHENTICATION() As String
    Return ConfigurationSettings.AppSettings("Authentication")
  End Function

#End Region
```

With this in place, we can implement another helper function to return the appropriate security object to pass to the server. If we're using Windows security, this will be `Nothing`; if not, it will be the principal object from the current thread's `CurrentPrincipal` property. Add this to the same region:

```
  Private Shared Function GetPrincipal() As System.Security.Principal.IPrincipal
    If AUTHENTICATION() = "Windows" Then

      ' Windows integrated security
      Return Nothing
    Else

      ' We assume that we're using the CSLA framework security
      Return System.Threading.Thread.CurrentPrincipal
    End If
  End Function
```

We can use this `GetPrincipal()` method to retrieve the appropriate value to pass to the server-side `DataPortal`. If we're using CSLA .NET's table-based security, we'll be passing the user's identity objects to the server so that the server-side `DataPortal` and our business logic on the server can run within the same security context as we do on the client.

Data access methods

At last, we can implement the four primary methods in the client-side `DataPortal`. Since we've done all the hard work in our helper methods, implementing these will be pretty straightforward! All four will have the same structure of determining whether the business object's method has the `<Transactional()>` attribute, and then invoking either the simple or the transactional server-side `DataPortal` object.

Create

Let's look at the `Create()` method first:

```
#Region " Data Access methods "

  Public Shared Function Create(ByVal Criteria As Object) As Object

    If IsTransactionalMethod( _
          GetMethod(Criteria.GetType.DeclaringType, "DataPortal_Create")) Then
```

```
      Return ServicedPortal().Create(Criteria, GetPrincipal)
    Else
      Return Portal().Create(Criteria, GetPrincipal)
    End If

  End Function

#End Region
```

The method accepts a `Criteria` object as a parameter. As we discussed in Chapter 2, all business classes will contain a nested `Criteria` class. To create, retrieve, or delete an object we'll create an instance of this `Criteria` class, initialize it with criteria data, and pass it to the data portal mechanism. The server-side `DataPortal` code can then use the `Criteria` object to find out the class (data type) of the actual business object with the expression `Criteria.GetType.DeclaringType`.

In the client-side `DataPortal` code, we're using the `DeclaringType` property to get a `Type` object for the business class, and passing that `Type` object to the `GetMethod()` helper function that we created earlier. We're indicating that we want to get a `MethodInfo` object for the `DataPortal_Create()` method from the business class.

That `MethodInfo` object is then passed to `IsTransactionalMethod()`, which tells us whether the `DataPortal_Create()` method from our business class has the `<Transactional()>` attribute. All of this is consolidated into the following line of code:

```
    If IsTransactionalMethod( _
          GetMethod(Criteria.GetType.DeclaringType, "DataPortal_Create")) Then
```

And based on this, we either invoke the transactional server-side `DataPortal`:

```
      Return ServicedPortal().Create(Criteria, GetPrincipal())
```

Or else we invoke the non-transactional server-side `DataPortal`:

```
      Return Portal().Create(Criteria, GetPrincipal())
```

In both cases, we're calling our helper functions to create (if necessary) either the serviced or the simple server-side `DataPortal` object. We then call the `Create()` method on the server-side object, passing it both the `Criteria` object and the result from our `GetPrincipal()` helper function.

The end result is that the appropriate (transactional or non-transactional) server-side `DataPortal`'s `Create()` method runs (either locally or remotely, based on configuration settings), and can act on the `Criteria` object to create and load a business object with default values. The fully populated business object is returned from the server-side `Create()` method, and then we return it as a result of our function as well.

Fetch

The `Fetch()` method is almost identical to `Create()`, since it also receives a `Criteria` object as a parameter. Add this to the same `Region`:

```
Public Shared Function Fetch(ByVal Criteria As Object) As Object

  If IsTransactionalMethod( _
         GetMethod(Criteria.GetType.DeclaringType, "DataPortal_Fetch")) Then

    Return ServicedPortal().Fetch(Criteria, GetPrincipal())
  Else
    Return Portal().Fetch(Criteria, GetPrincipal())
  End If

End Function
```

Once again, we go through the process of retrieving a `MethodInfo` object, this time for the `DataPortal_Fetch()` method of our business class. This is passed to `IsTransactionalMethod()`, so that we know whether to invoke the transactional or the non-transactional server-side `DataPortal`.

In this case, we're calling the `Fetch()` method of the server-side `DataPortal` object, passing it the `Criteria` object and the result from `GetPrincipal()`. In response, the server-side `DataPortal` creates a business object and has it load its data based on the `Criteria` object. The resulting fully populated business object is returned from the server, and we return it as a result of our `Fetch()` method.

Update

The `Update()` method is similar again, but it doesn't get a `Criteria` object as a parameter. Instead, it gets passed the business object itself. This way, it can pass the business object to the server-side `DataPortal`, which can then call the object's `DataPortal_Update()` method, causing the object to save its data to the database. Here's the code:

```
Public Shared Function Update(ByVal obj As Object) As Object

  If IsTransactionalMethod(GetMethod(obj.GetType, "DataPortal_Update")) Then
    Return ServicedPortal().Update(obj, GetPrincipal())
  Else
    Return Portal().Update(obj, GetPrincipal())
  End If

End Function
```

The basic structure of the implementation remains the same, but we're working with the business object rather than a `Criteria` object, so there are some minor changes. First, we get the `MethodInfo` object for the business object's `DataPortal_Update()` method, and check to see if it has the `<Transactional()>` attribute:

```
If IsTransactionalMethod(GetMethod(obj.GetType, "DataPortal_Update")) Then
```

This is a bit easier than with a `Criteria` object – since we have the business object itself, we can just use its `GetType()` method to retrieve its `Type` object. We can then call the `Update()` method on either the transactional or the non-transactional server-side `DataPortal`, as appropriate. The business object and the result from our `GetPrincipal()` method are passed as parameters.

When the server-side `DataPortal` is done, it returns the updated business object back to us, and we then return it as a result.

It's important to realize that if the server-side `DataPortal` is running in-process, the updated business object that we get as a result of calling `Update()` will be the *same object* we started with. If the server-side `DataPortal` is accessed via remoting, however, the result of the `Update()` call will be a *new object* that contains the updated data.

As a general practice, then, we should always write our code to assume that we get a new object as a result of calling `Update()`. If we do that, then our code will work regardless of whether we get a new object or the original, shielding us from any future configuration changes that cause the server-side `DataPortal` to switch from being in-process to being remote, or vice versa.

> **`Update()` will be called by UI code via the business object's `Save()` method, so this implies that any UI code written to call `Save()` should always assume that it will get a new object as a result of doing so.**

By always returning the updated business object back to the client, we simplify the business developer's life quite a lot. It means that the business developer can make changes to the object's state during the update process without worrying about losing those changes. Essentially, we're ensuring that anywhere within the business class, the business developer can change the object's variables and those changes are consistently available – regardless of whether the changes occurred when the object was on the client or on the server.

Delete

The final client-side `DataPortal` method is `Delete()`, which is virtually identical to `Create()` and `Fetch()`. It also receives a `Criteria` object as a parameter, which it uses to get a `Type` object for the business class, and so forth.

```
Public Shared Sub Delete(ByVal Criteria As Object)

  If IsTransactionalMethod( _
        GetMethod(Criteria.GetType.DeclaringType, "DataPortal_Delete")) Then

    ServicedPortal().Delete(Criteria, GetPrincipal)
  Else
    Portal().Delete(Criteria, GetPrincipal)
  End If

End Sub
```

The `Delete()` method exists to support the *immediate* deletion of an object, without having to retrieve the object first. Instead, it accepts a `Criteria` object that identifies which object's data should be deleted. Ultimately, the server-side `DataPortal` calls the business object's `DataPortal_Delete()` method to perform the delete operation.

Nothing is returned from this method, as it doesn't generate a business object. If the delete operation itself fails, it should raise an error, which will be returned to the client as an indicator of failure.

CSLA.Server.DataPortal

At this point, the client-side `DataPortal` is complete. We can move on to create the non-transactional and transactional server-side `DataPortal` classes, which reside in a pair of new assemblies. In fact, it turns out that the *transactional* `DataPortal` is the simpler of the two, since it's designed simply to run in Enterprise Services to start the transactional processing, and then to delegate all its method calls into the non-transactional `DataPortal`. We discussed this in Chapter 2 when we designed the `DataPortal` mechanism.

What this means is that all the real work of the server-side `DataPortal` only has to be written once, in the `Server.DataPortal` class. From there, it can be called directly by the client-side `DataPortal`, or it can be called by the transactional `DataPortal` after the transactional context has been set up. The following diagram shows how everything is related:

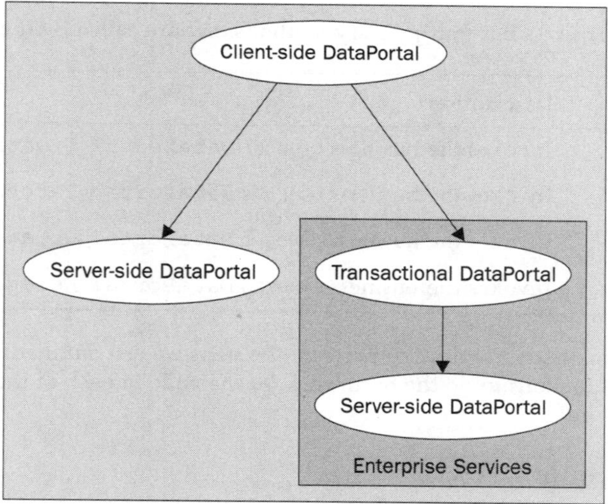

The magic here is that the regular server-side `DataPortal` will automatically run within the COM+ transactional context when it's created by the transactional `DataPortal`. We discussed how and why this works in Chapter 3.

When called directly from the client, `Server.DataPortal` will not run within a COM+ transaction, so our data access code in the business object will (if necessary) implement its own transactions using ADO.NET or stored procedures. This is ideal when we're updating tables within the same database, since our code will run about twice as fast using manual transactions as it will using Enterprise Services.

When called from the transactional `DataPortal`, however, `Server.DataPortal` will be loaded into the COM+ transaction context. In this case, our business object's data access code can rely on COM+ to handle the transactional details – we just need to raise an error if we want the transaction to fail. This is ideal when we're updating tables in multiple databases, since Enterprise Services will ensure that all the database updates are combined into one larger distributed transaction.

The `Server.DataPortal` class is relatively complex. For any data access request, it needs to perform a series of steps that ultimately culminate in the use of reflection to invoke the appropriate method on the business object itself. The server-side `DataPortal` must:

- Impersonate the client security (if using our custom, table-based security)
- Create an instance of the business object (for the create, retrieve, and delete operations)
- Call the appropriate method on the business object
- Return any result to the client-side `DataPortal`

Let's implement this functionality now.

Server.DataPortal

The server-side `DataPortal` has four primary methods that are called by the client-side `DataPortal`:

Method	Description
`Create()`	Invokes the business object's `DataPortal_Create()` method
`Fetch()`	Invokes the business object's `DataPortal_Fetch()` method
`Update()`	Invokes the business object's `DataPortal_Update()` method
`Delete()`	Invokes the business object's `DataPortal_Delete()` method

Within each of these methods, we need to perform the steps we just outlined. As is our tradition, we'll create a set of helper functions to do the hard work, so the code in each of the four methods will be relatively straightforward.

Creating the assembly

The server-side `DataPortal` resides in its own assembly. This is because we may or may not want to deploy the code to the client, so we don't want it to be part of the `CSLA` assembly itself. Add a new Class Library project to our solution, and name it `CSLA.Server.DataPortal`.

We need to change a couple of project properties. First, as with our other projects, set Option Strict to On under the Build tab. Next, notice how the Root namespace under the General tab defaults to the name of the assembly. In this case, that's not quite what we're after – we want the namespace to be `CSLA.Server`, rather than `CSLA.Server.DataPortal`:

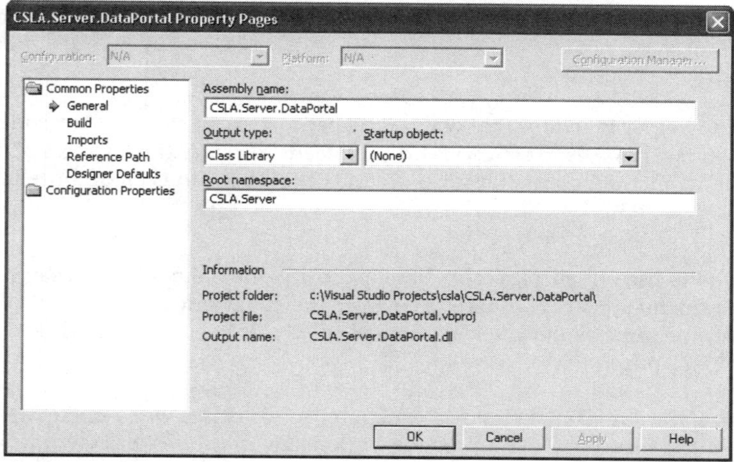

We also need to give the assembly a strong name. In Chapter 3, we discussed the use of Enterprise Services, and how any assembly loaded into Enterprise Services required a strong name. It turns out that any assembly *referenced* by an assembly loaded into Enterprise Services also requires a strong name. We know that we'll be referencing `Server.DataPortal` from our transactional `DataPortal`, which will be running in Enterprise Services. Therefore, the current assembly also needs a strong name.

To give an assembly a strong name, we need a key file. If you already have a key file for your organization, then use that. Otherwise, you can use the `sn.exe` command line utility to create a key file, as discussed in Chapter 3. Then, open the `AssemblyInfo.vb` file and add the following code (changing the path to point to your particular key file):

```
' Strong name
<Assembly: AssemblyKeyFile("mykey.snk")>
```

Next time the assembly is built, it will have a strong name, so it can be referenced by our transactional `DataPortal` project as it runs within Enterprise Services. That means we're all set to start writing code.

Creating the DataPortal class

At this point, we can create the `DataPortal` class itself. The `CSLA.Server.DataPortal` project started with a default class called `Class1`, so rename `Class1.vb` to `DataPortal.vb`, and we can start coding. First, change the class name:

```
Public Class DataPortal

End Class
```

The whole point of the server-side `DataPortal` is to have an object that will run on the server – or more accurately, an object that's *anchored* to the server, as we discussed in Chapter 1. To create an anchored object, we inherit from `MarshalByRefObject`:

```
Public Class DataPortal
  Inherits MarshalByRefObject

End Class
```

This ensures that the `Server.DataPortal` object, once created, will always run on the same machine.

Helper functions

Now let's write the helper functions that will do the hard work. In essence, our code needs to perform three basic operations: it needs to set up security; it needs to create the business object (if appropriate); and it needs to call a method on the business object. Let's deal with each of those in order.

Handling security

If we're configured to use our custom table-based security, the method on the server-side `DataPortal` will be passed a principal object as a parameter from the client-side `DataPortal`. To ensure that our security context is the same as the client's, we need to set this value into our thread's `CurrentPrincipal` property.

On the other hand, if we're using Windows' integrated security, we won't do anything special – the assumption is that the security configuration on both client and server has automatically handled impersonation of the user's identity on our behalf.

Before we get started, let's reference the appropriate .NET security namespace:

```
Imports System.Security.Principal
Imports System.Configuration

Public Class DataPortal
```

The first thing we need to do is to retrieve the security setting from the application configuration file. Then we can write a function to return the configuration value:

```
#Region " Security "

  Private Function AUTHENTICATION() As String
    Return ConfigurationSettings.AppSettings("Authentication")
  End Function

#End Region
```

Keep in mind that the .NET runtime automatically reads and caches the configuration file on its first access. This means that we aren't really reading the file each time we check this value – we're simply retrieving the value from .NET's in-memory cache.

This is the same configuration value that we specified when creating the client-side `DataPortal` to control the type of security we're using. An entry in the configuration file to make our application use the custom, table-based security might appear as:

```
<add key="Authentication" value="CSLA" />
```

Technically this isn't required, because CSLA security is the default. However, it's good practice to include the specific setting in the configuration file for documentation purposes. By putting this line in the application configuration file, we clearly indicate that we're expecting to use CSLA security, rather than Windows' integrated security.

Assuming that we're using our custom security, the real work happens in the `SetPrincipal()` method. We're passed a principal object that contains the user's identity from the client. This object needs to be placed into our thread's `CurrentPrincipal` value. Add the following code to the same region:

```
Private Sub SetPrincipal(ByVal Principal As Object)
  If AUTHENTICATION() = "Windows" Then

    ' When using integrated security, Principal must be Nothing
    If Principal Is Nothing Then

      ' Set .NET to use integrated security
      AppDomain.CurrentDomain.SetPrincipalPolicy( _
                                    PrincipalPolicy.WindowsPrincipal)
      Exit Sub
    Else
      Throw New Security.SecurityException( _
        "No principal object should be passed to DataPortal " & _
        "when using Windows integrated security")
    End If
  End If

  ' We expect Principal to be of type BusinessPrincipal, but we can't enforce
  ' that since it causes a circular reference with the business library.
  ' Instead we must use type Object for the parameter, so here we do a check
  ' on the type of the parameter
  If Principal.ToString = "CSLA.Security.BusinessPrincipal" Then

    ' See if our current principal is different from the caller's principal
    If Not ReferenceEquals(Principal, _
                      System.Threading.Thread.CurrentPrincipal) Then

      ' The caller had a different principal, so change ours to match the
      ' caller's, so all our objects use the caller's security
      System.Threading.Thread.CurrentPrincipal = CType(Principal, IPrincipal)
    End If
  Else
    Throw New Security.SecurityException( _
      "Principal must be of type BusinessPrincipal, not " & _
                                             Principal.ToString)
  End If
End Sub
```

The first thing we do here is to determine whether we're using Windows or CSLA security. If we're using Windows security, we make sure that we weren't passed a principal object by mistake. This is done primarily to simplify debugging, since this would indicate that the client-side configuration is different from the server-side configuration:

```
Throw New Security.SecurityException( _
  "No principal object should be passed to DataPortal " & _
  "when using Windows integrated security")
```

Assuming that we're using CSLA security, we then need to make sure that the principal object that was passed as a parameter is our specific type of principal object (which we'll create later in the chapter) – it will be called `CSLA.Security.BusinessPrincipal`. Now, normally we'd check its type with code such as:

```
If Principal Is CSLA.Security.BusinessPrincipal Then
```

However, this would require that our `CSLA.Server.DataPortal` assembly must have a reference to the `CSLA` assembly – and we already know that the `CSLA` assembly needs a reference to `CSLA.Server.DataPortal`. This type of circular reference between assemblies is not legal, and will prevent our code from compiling properly.

To avoid this issue, we can instead compare the *text* data type of the object to a `String` value, achieving the same result without requiring a reference back to the `CSLA` assembly:

```
If Principal.ToString = "CSLA.Security.BusinessPrincipal" Then
```

At this point, we know we're using CSLA security, and that we have the right type of principal object. We can move on to make it our `CurrentPrincipal`. First, we make sure that it isn't already the current value:

```
If Not ReferenceEquals(Principal, _
                        System.Threading.Thread.CurrentPrincipal) Then
```

This can happen in two scenarios. If `Server.DataPortal` is running in the client process, then obviously it will already have the same principal object. It's also possible that `Server.DataPortal` is running via remoting, and by chance we've already made a data access call that set the security value to our value. This can only happen if no other users have used that same server thread in the meantime, since they obviously would have changed the value to match their own principal object.

If we make it through all those checks, the final step is to set our principal object as 'current':

```
System.Threading.Thread.CurrentPrincipal = CType(Principal, IPrincipal)
```

The `SetPrincipal()` method can be called by each of our four data access methods before doing any other work, thus ensuring that the server's security context is the same as the client's.

In Chapter 7, we'll see how security is used within our business objects, and in Chapters 8 through 10 we'll see how it's used in the UI. In each case, the business developer will use standard .NET Framework techniques to access security information about the user. What we're doing here takes place entirely behind the scenes.

Creating the business object

Create, retrieve, and delete operations must all create a new business object on the server. (For an update operation, we are passed a pre-existing business object from the client, so we don't need to worry about it.) Of course, creating an object is typically very straightforward – we just use the `New` keyword:

```
Dim obj As New BusinessObject()
```

However, as we discussed in Chapter 2, we'll be using the 'class in charge' model for our business objects. This means that the creation, retrieval, or deletion of an object will be handled through a `Shared` method on the business class.

What we're really doing is utilizing an **object factory** design pattern, where the object is not created directly by the client code, but rather is created by a factory and returned to the client code. This scheme protects the client code (the UI code in our case) from knowing exactly how the object was created – it just happens.

To *ensure* that the UI code doesn't directly create a business object, all of our business objects will have a `Private` constructor:

```
Private Sub New()
  ' Prevent direct creation
End Sub
```

With this constructor, we effectively prevent the UI code from using the `New` keyword to create an instance of our object, forcing them to call our `Shared` methods instead. Of course, this would also appear to prevent our server-side `DataPortal` code from creating an instance of the object, but luckily we can use reflection to get around the problem!

> *Obviously, the UI developer could also use reflection to create an instance of our object directly. There's no practical way to prevent a developer from going out of their way to break the rules – at some point, we have to assume that the UI developer isn't malicious, and won't go out of their way to misuse our objects.*

We discussed reflection in Chapter 3; before we use it here, we should import its namespace:

```
Imports System.Reflection
Imports System.Security.Principal
Imports System.Configuration
```

After all that, the `CreateBusinessObject()` method itself isn't too complex:

```
#Region " Creating the business object "

  Private Function CreateBusinessObject(ByVal Criteria As Object) As Object

    ' Get the type of the actual business object
    Dim businessType As Type = Criteria.GetType.DeclaringType

    ' Create an instance of the business object
    Return Activator.CreateInstance(businessType, True)

  End Function

#End Region
```

Since this method will only be used for create, retrieve, and delete operations, we will always have a `Criteria` object passed as a parameter from the client-side `DataPortal`. We can use it to find the data type of the actual business class:

```
Dim businessType As Type = Criteria.GetType.DeclaringType
```

Given a Type object corresponding to the business class itself, we can then use reflection to create an instance of the class:

```
Return Activator.CreateInstance(businessType, True)
```

The second parameter to CreateInstance() indicates that we want to create the object even if it only has a Private constructor.

Calling a method

The final operation our code needs to perform is to call the appropriate DataPortal_xxx() method on the business object itself. Normally, calling a method is trivial, but in this case we know that the DataPortal_xxx() methods on our business objects are non-Public. Typically, they are Protected in scope, meaning that they can't be called through conventional means.

This is intentional, since we don't want the UI developer (or some other business object) to call DataPortal_xxx() methods on our business object – only the server-side DataPortal should call these methods. By making them non-Public, we effectively make them unavailable for accidental invocation, but we do need a way for the server-side DataPortal code to invoke them. Again, reflection comes to the rescue.

The first thing we need in order to call a method through reflection is a MethodInfo object that describes the method. We can get a MethodInfo object for a method by using reflection, just as we did for the client-side data portal:

```
#Region " Calling a method "

  Private Function GetMethod(ByVal ObjectType As Type, _
                             ByVal Method As String) As MethodInfo

    Return ObjectType.GetMethod(Method, BindingFlags.FlattenHierarchy Or _
                                        BindingFlags.Instance Or _
                                        BindingFlags.Public Or _
                                        BindingFlags.NonPublic)
  End Function

#End Region
```

We can now create a function to call the method on the business object by using our GetMethod() function:

```
  Private Function CallMethod(ByVal obj As Object, _
                              ByVal method As String, _
                              ByVal ParamArray params() As Object) As Object

    ' Call a private method on the object
    Dim info As MethodInfo = GetMethod(obj.GetType, method)
    Dim result As Object
```

```
    Try
      result = info.Invoke(obj, params)
    Catch e As Exception
      Throw e.GetBaseException
    End Try

    Return result

  End Function
```

First, we get the MethodInfo object corresponding to the method by calling our GetMethod() function:

```
    Dim info As MethodInfo = GetMethod(obj.GetType, method)
```

Then we attempt to invoke the method in a Try...Catch block:

```
    Try
      result = info.Invoke(obj, params)
    Catch e As Exception
      Throw e.GetBaseException
    End Try
```

If there's an error, all we do to process it is to raise another error. This is of key importance, however, because the error we'll get as a result of calling the Invoke() method on a MethodInfo object is *not* the error that occurred within the method itself (if any).

The error we'll get from an Invoke() call is to tell us that the Invoke() call failed! This means that the Exception object we get describing the error is virtually useless, but thankfully Exception objects can contain other Exception objects, and that's what happens here.

The Exception object we get to tell us that Invoke() failed contains a base Exception object that represents the real error that occurred *within* the function that was invoked. All we're doing in our code is catching the first error, and then raising the more meaningful error it contains. The end result is that the calling code gets an error that contains information about whatever caused the code in the method itself to fail – exactly the same error that would have been returned had the method been invoked using normal means rather than reflection.

Data access methods

At this point, we've got all the helper functions we need, and we can implement the four core data access methods that are called by the client-side DataPortal.

Create

The Create() method will set security, and then create an instance of the business object and call its DataPortal_Create() method. The newly created and populated business object is then returned to the client as a result:

```
#Region " Data Access "

  Public Function Create(ByVal Criteria As Object, _
                         ByVal Principal As Object) As Object
```

```
    SetPrincipal(Principal)

    ' Create an instance of the business object
    Dim obj As Object = CreateBusinessObject(Criteria)

    ' Tell the business object to fetch its data
    CallMethod(obj, "DataPortal_Create", Criteria)

    ' Return the populated business object as a result
    Return obj

  End Function

#End Region
```

Since we did all the hard work in the helper functions, this code should be straightforward and easy to read.

Note that this code contains no error handling; this is intentional. The only reason to catch an exception is if we can do something about it, or if we want to wrap it within another exception of our own making. Within this method, there's nothing we can do to resolve or address an exception that the business object throws as part of its data access routine. Also, there is little value to be added by wrapping the exception within a new exception of our own making.

In fact, were we to wrap the exception within some new exception, we'd reduce the business developer's ability to work easily with the exception in their business code. Right now, we can't predict the type of exception that might be raised by the business object's data access – we might get a generic `Exception`, an `ApplicationException`, a `SecurityException`, or one of any number of others, depending on exactly what went wrong.

If we wrap the detailed exception into some generic exception that we re-throw from within our code, then the poor business developer will be unable to utilize structured error handling to handle the detailed exceptions. Right now, the business developer could write something like this in their `Shared` factory method:

```
Public Shared Function NewResource(ByVal ID As String) As Resource
  Try
    Return DataPortal.Create(New Criteria(ID))

  Catch ex As SecurityException
    ' Deal with the security exception

  Catch ex As SqlException
    ' Deal with the SQL data exception

  Catch ex As Exception
    ' Deal with the generic exception
  End Try
End Function
```

But if we catch and re-throw the exception in the server-side `DataPortal` code, then the business developer loses the ability to differentiate between the various types of exception object that might have been thrown by the underlying data access code.

Fetch

The `Fetch()` method is similar to the `Create()` method. It also sets security and creates a business object, but then calls its `DataPortal_Fetch()` method. The resulting fully populated business object is returned as a result:

```
Public Function Fetch(ByVal Criteria As Object, _
                      ByVal Principal As Object) As Object

  SetPrincipal(Principal)

  ' Create an instance of the business object
  Dim obj As Object = CreateBusinessObject(Criteria)

  ' Tell the business object to fetch its data
  CallMethod(obj, "DataPortal_Fetch", Criteria)

  ' Return the populated business object as a result
  Return obj

End Function
```

As with the `Create()` method, the business object will be returned as a simple object reference if the server-side `DataPortal` is running in-process, or it will be copied by value across the network to the client if the server-side `DataPortal` is running on a separate server via remoting. Those details are handled automatically by .NET on our behalf.

Update

The `Update()` method is a bit simpler, since it gets passed the business object, rather than a `Criteria` object, as a parameter. All it needs to do is set security and then call `DataPortal_Update()` on the object:

```
Public Function Update(ByVal obj As Object, _
                       ByVal Principal As Object) As Object

  SetPrincipal(Principal)

  ' Tell the business object to update itself
  CallMethod(obj, "DataPortal_Update")
  Return obj

End Function
```

Remember that `DataPortal_Update()` might very well alter the object's data, so we need to return the object in order that the client gets that updated data. If the server-side `DataPortal` is running in-process, this isn't strictly necessary, but it's a requirement if we're using remoting. By always coding for the more complex case, we ensure that our framework will operate just fine in either case.

Delete

Finally, we can implement the `Delete()` method. It sets security, creates an instance of the business object, and then calls the `DataPortal_Delete()` method:

```
Public Sub Delete(ByVal Criteria As Object, ByVal Principal As Object)

  SetPrincipal(Principal)

  ' Create an instance of the business object
  Dim obj As Object = CreateBusinessObject(Criteria)

  ' Tell the business object to delete itself
  CallMethod(obj, "DataPortal_Delete", Criteria)

End Sub
```

Since there's no data resulting from a delete operation, this routine doesn't return anything as a result. If the delete operation fails, the error raised by our `DataPortal_Delete()` method is simply returned to the client.

Updating the CSLA project

At this point, the `Server.DataPortal` class is complete. Our client-side `DataPortal` code requires a reference to this class, so we should return to the `CSLA` project and add a reference to the `CSLA.Server.DataPortal` project:

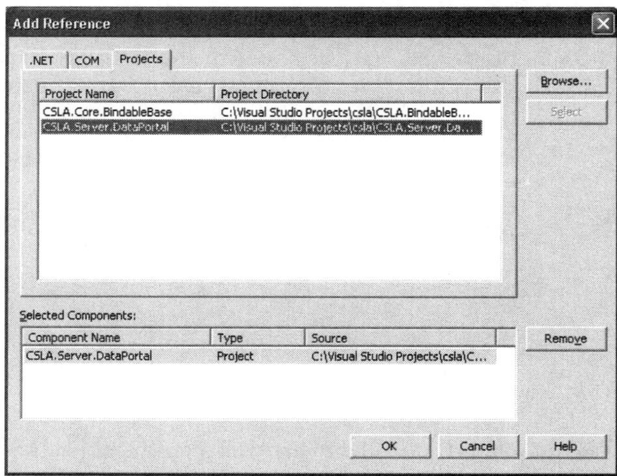

We're almost at a point where our code compiles. Once we complete the transactional `DataPortal`, we should be ready to build.

CSLA.Server.ServicedDataPortal

As far as the data portal mechanism goes, we've done all the hard work at this point. The client-side and server-side `DataPortal` classes we've created take care of all the details around properly invoking the `DataPortal_xxx()` methods in our business objects. All that remains is to provide two-phase transactional support via Enterprise Services (COM+).

In fact, we've already started this process in our implementation of the client-side `DataPortal`, where we detect whether each `DataPortal_xxx()` method on a business object has the `<Transactional()>` attribute. If a method *does* have this attribute, the client-side `DataPortal` invokes a transactional server-side `DataPortal` – which is what we'll write in this section.

The transactional server-side `DataPortal` class is relatively trivial to create because it relies on the `Server.DataPortal` class we've already written to do all the real work. In fact, the only thing that the transactional `DataPortal` class does is to delegate method calls to `Server.DataPortal`!

What makes the whole thing work is that the transactional `DataPortal` object is running as a serviced component in Enterprise Services – its methods will have attributes to set up a transactional context *before* delegating the calls to `Server.DataPortal`. Because the transactional context is already set up, this means that `Server.DataPortal` and our business object code will run within that same context, enjoying all the protection of two-phase transactions.

Of course, it also means that our business logic to do data access will suffer the performance penalties that come with two-phase transactions. It's important to weigh the arguments we made in Chapter 3 against each other to determine what will work best in your application environment.

Transactional DataPortal

The transactional `DataPortal` has the same four methods as `Server.DataPortal`:

Method	Description
`Create()`	Invokes `Server.DataPortal's Create()` method
`Fetch()`	Invokes `Server.DataPortal's Fetch()` method
`Update()`	Invokes `Server.DataPortal's Update()` method
`Delete()`	Invokes `Server.DataPortal's Delete()` method

Prior to delegating each call to `Server.DataPortal`, each of these methods uses Enterprise Services attributes to configure a transactional context within COM+.

Creating the assembly

Because this code will run in COM+, it needs to be in a separate assembly. We don't want or need to force the rest of our framework code or our business objects to be registered within COM+ – only this one class requires this extra step. The following diagram shows all our framework assemblies, and which ones depend on which:

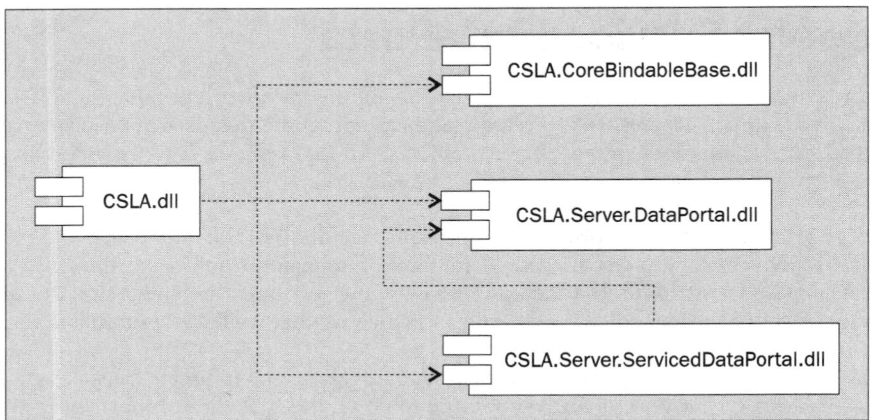

The fact that we can avoid registering the remainder of our framework (and more importantly, our business DLLs) in COM+ is really nice. Where COM+ (or MTS) was somewhat helpful in managing and deploying COM-based code, it complicates the deployment of .NET code, so the fewer assemblies we need to put into COM+, the better.

Add a new project to the solution, and name it `CSLA.Server.ServicedDataPortal`. As with our other projects, use its properties window to change **Option Strict** to **On** under the **Build** tab.

We know that we'll be running in Enterprise Services, and therefore that we'll need a strong name, so add the following lines to `AssemblyInfo.vb`, changing the file name to point to your particular key file:

```
' Strong name
<Assembly: AssemblyKeyFile("mykey.snk")>
```

Since our code will be delegating to `Server.DataPortal`, we need a reference to that project. We'll also need a reference to the Enterprise Services library within .NET. Add both of these using the Add Reference dialog:

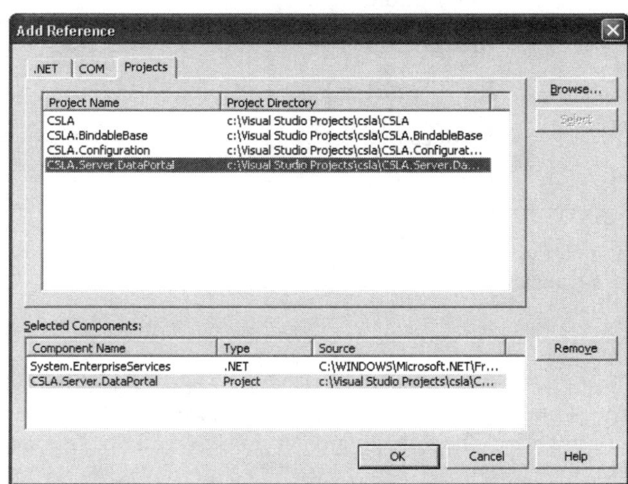

To integrate properly with Enterprise Services, we need to add some attributes to the `AssemblyInfo.vb` file. (These attributes were discussed in Chapter 3.) First, we need to import the Enterprise Services namespace:

```
Imports System.EnterpriseServices
```

Then we can add the attributes:

```
' Enterprise Services settings
<Assembly: ApplicationName("CSLA DataPortal")>
<Assembly: Description("CSLA .NET data portal")>
<Assembly: ApplicationActivation(ActivationOption.Library)>
<Assembly: ApplicationAccessControl(True)>
```

> *Note the use of the `ApplicationAccessControl` attribute, which indicates that COM+ security should be enabled for this assembly. This attribute is not required in .NET 1.0, but in .NET 1.1 we'll get a warning when attempting to register our assembly with COM+ if we omit it. The default is to have security enabled, so by adding this attribute we don't change anything, but we avoid the warning in .NET 1.1.*

The assembly now is configured to run in a COM+ Library Application, which offers optimal performance.

> *In the world of COM and VB6, we usually avoided using Library Applications because of stability issues. By running in the same process as the host, a COM component could destabilize the host process due to bugs in the component. This issue isn't nearly as big in .NET. First, the ASP.NET environment includes self-healing technologies so that if an assembly such as our transactional* `DataPortal` did *have a bug that crashed the host, it would automatically recover. Second, .NET code is far less likely to destabilize the host than COM code was, so there is less chance of this happening in the first place.*

When using the transactional `DataPortal`, we'll typically be invoking via remoting, so the transactional `DataPortal` will be running within our remoting host application (that is, IIS, as implemented later in this chapter). By being set as a Library Application, it means that our code will run in that same process, but within a transactional context. This offers the best performance, since it avoids any extra cross-process communication on the server.

It's also possible to use the transactional `DataPortal` in the client process, assuming that the client is running on a machine where COM+ is installed (Windows 2000 or higher). Again, being configured to use a Library Application avoids any extra cross-process communication, and offers the best possible performance.

Creating the DataPortal class

At this point, our assembly is ready to go, and we can create the transactional `DataPortal` class. Rename `Class1.vb` to `DataPortal.vb`. Next, to run in Enterprise Services, we must inherit from `ServicedComponent`. Change the code in the class to the following:

```
Imports System.EnterpriseServices

Public Class DataPortal
  Inherits ServicedComponent

End Class
```

This is the basic structure of *any* class that will run within Enterprise Services. The `ServicedComponent` base class already inherits from `MarshalByRefObject`, so any class we create for Enterprise Services will create anchored objects that always run on the machine where they are created.

We use attributes on the class and its methods to control which of the Enterprise Services are to be used. In our case, we'll be specifying that we want transactional behaviors:

```
Imports System.EnterpriseServices

<Transaction(TransactionOption.Required), EventTrackingEnabled(True)> _
Public Class DataPortal
  Inherits ServicedComponent

End Class
```

The `<Transaction()>` attribute allows us to tell Enterprise Services that we require a transaction. Notice that we are not requiring a *new* transaction, so we can participate in an existing transaction if one is already underway. However, if no transaction exists, COM+ will always create one before running any code.

The `<EventTrackingEnabled()>` attribute tells Enterprise Services that our object should provide tracking events to COM+. What this means is that our object will display usage information in the Component Services management console, so we can tell how many objects are active, and so forth.

Data access methods

All that remains now is to implement the four methods, which are almost identical to one another: they merely create a `Server.DataPortal` object, and delegate the method call to that object.

Each of our delegating methods has an `<AutoComplete()>` attribute, telling COM+ that the method should be assumed to succeed unless it raises an error. In other words, the only way COM+ will roll back the transaction is if an error is raised by our code. If that doesn't happen, it will commit the transaction.

The magic here is that the `Server.DataPortal` object is created within our pre-existing transactional context. In other words, `Server.DataPortal` is protected by transactions. When it then calls methods on our business object, those methods are *also* protected by transactions. If our business object raises an error, the transaction will be rolled back by COM+.

Here are the four methods:

```
<AutoComplete(True)> _
Public Function Create(ByVal Criteria As Object, _
                       ByVal Principal As Object) As Object

  Dim Portal As New CSLA.Server.DataPortal()
  Return Portal.Create(Criteria, Principal)

End Function

<AutoComplete(True)> _
Public Function Fetch(ByVal Criteria As Object, _
                      ByVal Principal As Object) As Object
```

```
    Dim Portal As New CSLA.Server.DataPortal()
    Return Portal.Fetch(Criteria, Principal)

  End Function

  <AutoComplete(True)> _
  Public Function Update(ByVal obj As Object, _
                         ByVal Principal As Object) As Object

    Dim Portal As New CSLA.Server.DataPortal()
    Return Portal.Update(obj, Principal)

  End Function

  <AutoComplete(True)> _
  Public Sub Delete(ByVal Criteria As Object, _
                    ByVal Principal As Object)

    Dim Portal As New CSLA.Server.DataPortal()
    Portal.Delete(Criteria, Principal)

  End Sub
```

Updating the CSLA project

As with `Server.DataPortal`, our client-side `DataPortal` code makes use of `ServicedDataPortal.DataPortal`, so we need to return to the `CSLA` project and add a reference:

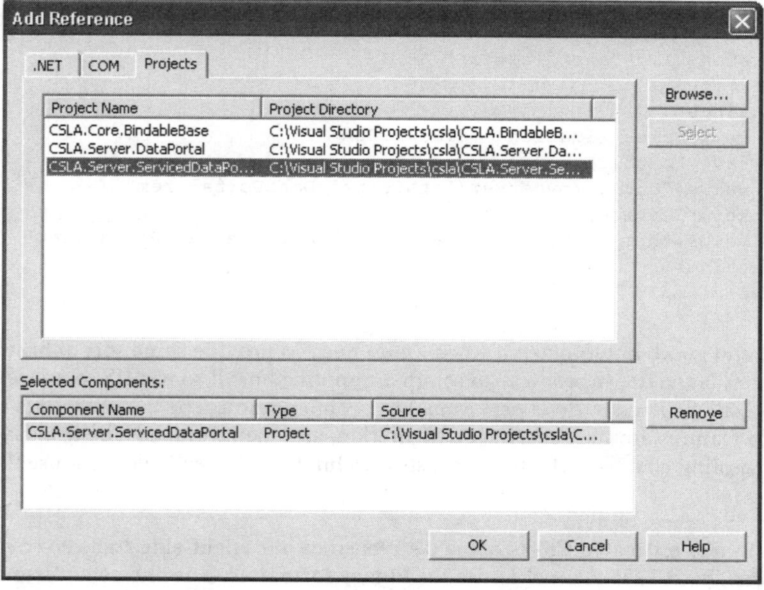

With this reference, our solution should compile. At this point, we have a basically functional framework, though we're obviously not done yet. We still need to create a remoting host in which the server-side DataPortal objects can run if we're configured to use remoting. We also need to implement the custom table-driven security objects, and we'll wrap up by creating a generic, read-only name-value collection object for use by business applications.

DataPortal remoting host

Now that we have both Server.DataPortal and ServicedDataPortal.DataPortal built, we need a place for them to run. One option is to have them run in-process with the client code, and that will work right now, with no new code or configuration file required. If we feel the need to have a configuration file at all, it might look like this:

```
<?xml version="1.0" encoding="utf-8" ?>
<configuration>
  <appSettings>
    <add key="Authentication" value="CSLA" />
  </appSettings>
</configuration>
```

By not providing URLs for the server-side DataPortal objects, we've told the CSLA .NET framework to run them within the client process.

The other option is to put entries in the client application's configuration file that provide URLs for a remote server where the server-side DataPortal objects will run. This might appear like so:

```
<?xml version="1.0" encoding="utf-8" ?>
<configuration>
  <appSettings>
    <add key="Authentication" value="CSLA" />
    <add key="PortalServer"
         value="http://myserver/DataPortal/DataPortal.rem" />
    <add key="ServicedPortalServer"
         value="http://myserver/DataPortal/ServicedDataPortal.rem" />
  </appSettings>
</configuration>
```

This is all well and good, but to make it work we do need to provide some sort of host application that will run on the server. Now, the easiest way to set up a remoting host is to use IIS, because it's basically all ready to do so – all we need to do is perform a little configuration. The benefit to this approach is that we gain a lot of IIS features around security, configuration, and management. The drawback is that we can't use the TCP remoting channel, which is the fastest technology. Instead, we must use the HTTP channel.

> **We've already mitigated this to some degree, since our client-side DataPortal configures the HTTP channel to use the binary formatter. The choice of formatter is far more important than the choice of channel.**

The IIS host will be configured to provide access to both `Server.DataPortal` and `ServicedDataPortal.DataPortal`, via remoting. The `Server.DataPortal` assembly will run directly in the host process. The `ServicedDataPortal.DataPortal` assembly will *also* run in the host process, but also within COM+. This is because we configured it to use a COM+ Library Application.

Because both assemblies will run in the same process, we should get very good performance. Calls from the client need to make a network hop to get to the server, but once on the server, there are no further cross-process or cross-network calls required, which is ideal.

It is important to note that each business application may have its own IIS remoting host configured. All the business objects we host within a single `DataPortal` host will run under the same user account, with the same `Web.config` file, and so forth. This means they basically share the same environment, configuration and security.

In many cases, we'll want to isolate different business applications from each other, so they have different database access, different application-specific configuration files, and so forth. To accomplish this, we'll end up creating a `DataPortal` host for each business application. The following steps discuss how to create such a host. To create other hosts, follow the same steps, but name the IIS project differently and set up the client-side application configuration files so that their URLs point to the appropriate virtual root.

Server-side DataPortal host

Creating a remoting host using IIS is not difficult. Add a new Empty Web Project to our solution, and name it `DataPortal`. This creates a virtual root on our server that is virtually empty – the project includes no web forms, no web services, no style sheets, nothing. Not even a `Web.config` file is created – you get a completely clean slate.

> *We've now got a lot of things named `DataPortal`! We have the client-side `DataPortal` class, the transactional and non-transactional `DataPortal` objects that provide most of our functionality, and the new `DataPortal` host. While this can seem confusing, it's important to remember that the business developer only ever sees the client-side `DataPortal` class. All the rest of the mechanism is hidden within our framework, so the use of the data portal mechanism as a whole is very straightforward.*

Reference CSLA assemblies

The first thing we need to do is add references to all our CSLA projects. As usual, use the Add Reference dialog:

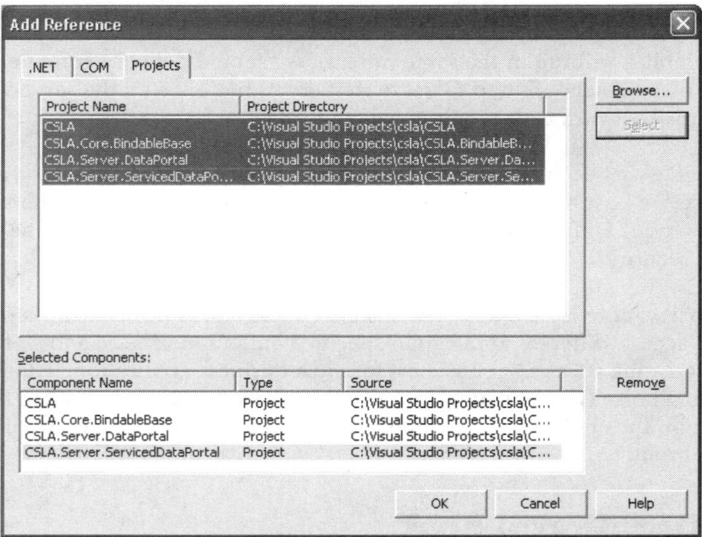

This makes these assemblies available to the project, so that we can expose them via remoting. We will only be *directly* exposing `CSLA.Server.DataPortal` and `CSLA.Server.ServicedDataPortal`, but any business DLLs that we need for our business application will require `CSLA.dll`, and it in turn requires `CSLA.Core.BindableBase.dll`.

Add a Web.config file

To do the job of exposing our assemblies via remoting, we need to do some preparatory work. In a web application, this means using a `Web.config` file, so use the Project | Add New Item menu option to add one that contains some default settings. The next step is to make a couple of changes.

Turn off debugging

For performance reasons, we don't want debugging turned on in this project, so change the `debug` setting to `false`:

```
<compilation defaultLanguage="vb" debug="false" />
```

Even if `debug` is set to `true`, it doesn't really help in a remoting host, because we won't be debugging any web pages or web services. This setting won't allow us to debug the DLLs that are being hosted via remoting in any case, so by setting the value to `false`, we allow ASP.NET to avoid any debugging overhead.

Turn off session state

The default in a new `Web.config` file is that session state is configured to be stored in-process. In our case, however, we don't *need* session state, because we're not trying to host any web pages (or anything else that would require the concept of session state).

Having session state enabled incurs some overhead on each request from a client, so we want to turn it off. This can be done by changing the `<sessionState>` element in the `Web.config` file so that its `mode` setting is `Off`:

```
<sessionState
        mode="Off"
```

This turns off session state entirely, avoiding any overhead on each request.

Configure remoting

To make our server-side `DataPortal` objects available via remoting, we need to add a `<system.runtime.remoting>` element to the `Web.config` file. This element will include all the information necessary to configure remoting for these classes; notice that it's *outside* the existing `<system.web>` element:

```
<?xml version="1.0" encoding="utf-8" ?>
<configuration>

  <system.runtime.remoting>
    <application>
      <service>
        <wellknown mode="SingleCall"
                   objectUri="DataPortal.rem"
                   type="CSLA.Server.DataPortal, CSLA.Server.DataPortal" />
        <wellknown mode="SingleCall"
                   objectUri="ServicedDataPortal.rem"
                   type="CSLA.Server.ServicedDataPortal.DataPortal,
                                     CSLA.Server.ServicedDataPortal" />
      </service>
    </application>
  </system.runtime.remoting>

  <system.web>
```

We're configuring two different classes through the use of two `<wellknown>` elements, which you first saw being used in Chapter 3. The first configures the non-transactional `Server.DataPortal`:

```
<wellknown mode="SingleCall"
           objectUri="DataPortal.rem"
           type="CSLA.Server.DataPortal, CSLA.Server.DataPortal" />
```

First, this tells remoting to use `SingleCall` semantics, so a new server-side `DataPortal` object will be created for each client method call to the server. Then, the `objectUri` attribute tells remoting that the class can be accessed at the URI `DataPortal.rem`. This means that the complete URL for the class is http://myserver/DataPortal/DataPortal.rem. This is the URL we'd put into a client-side configuration file to use this object via remoting.

Finally, the `type` attribute describes how remoting should find the class. It indicates that the class to find is named `CSLA.Server.DataPortal`, and that it can be found in an assembly named `CSLA.Server.DataPortal`. Remoting will therefore look in the `bin` directory for either `CSLA.Server.DataPortal.dll` or `CSLA.Server.DataPortal.exe` to find the class. Since we've referenced the `CSLA.Server.DataPortal` project, its DLL will automatically be copied into the `bin` directory by VS.NET.

We do the same thing for the transactional `DataPortal`:

```
<wellknown mode="SingleCall"
           objectUri="ServicedDataPortal.rem"
           type="CSLA.Server.ServicedDataPortal.DataPortal,
                           CSLA.Server.ServicedDataPortal" />
```

The fact that this class is running in Enterprise Services makes no difference to our configuration settings, but it *does* require an extra step to register the DLL with COM+.

Registering ServicedDataPortal

Before our host can call the `ServicedDataPortal` object, we need to register it in COM+. The .NET runtime will attempt to register any serviced component (such as our `ServicedDataPortal`) with COM+ automatically, the first time it is accessed. Unfortunately, the ASP.NET account doesn't have enough security rights to actually do this. That means that any attempt to use the transactional `DataPortal` will result in an error indicating that the component couldn't be registered in COM+.

We can resolve this by manually registering the assembly with COM+, using the `regsvcs.exe` command line utility that we discussed in Chapter 3. Open a Visual Studio command prompt window, and navigate to the `DataPortal` host website's `bin` directory. Then run `regsvcs.exe` to register the assembly:

```
> regsvcs CSLA.Server.ServicedDataPortal.dll
```

This will register the assembly in COM+, making it available for use by the `DataPortal` host, and thus by any client applications via remoting.

Testing remoting

At this point, we should be able to test to see whether our configuration is correct. Build the solution to compile all the assemblies. This will also result in copies of our CSLA DLLs being placed into the `bin` directory of our web application.

We can then open a browser and navigate to the remoting services to get their XML descriptions, or WSDL. This can be done by going to the following URLs:

```
http://localhost/dataportal/dataportal.rem?wsdl
http://localhost/dataportal/serviceddataportal.rem?wsdl
```

In both cases, we should get back an XML description of the service, including a list of all the methods it exposes, and their parameter expectations. If we've somehow misconfigured remoting, then we'll get an error, and we can proceed to debug until the WSDL result is visible in the browser.

Making the DataPortal useful

At this point, we have a working `DataPortal` host, but it can't really do anything useful because it has no knowledge of any business DLLs or databases. (We'll create a business DLL in Chapter 7.)

Also, as it stands, it's configured to use our custom, table-based security (which is the default in our framework), but there is no security database. At the very least, we'll want to provide configuration regarding the security database, or change the security to use Windows' integrated security.

We'll also want to provide the DataPortal host with access to our business DLLs at some stage.

Configuring CSLA

First, let's look at how we might configure the CSLA framework for security, and indicate the location of databases that will be used by the framework and/or our business DLLs. In the DataPortal host's Web.config file, we can add an <appSettings> element that will contain our configuration settings. This element is a top-level element, just like <system.web> or <system.runtime.remoting>.

We can configure the server to use Windows' integrated security like this:

```
<?xml version="1.0" encoding="utf-8" ?>
<configuration>

  <appSettings>
    <add key="Authentication" value="Windows" />
  </appSettings>
```

Alternatively, we can use CSLA security, in which case we should provide a connection string to a security database. We'll be using this database entry later in the chapter, when we implement the custom table-based security, so let's put it into Web.config:

```
  <appSettings>
    <add key="Authentication" value="CSLA" />
    <add key="DB:Security"
         value="data source=(local);initial catalog=Security;
                                           integrated security=SSPI" />
  </appSettings>
```

We'll create the Security *database later in the chapter, and you may need to change this connection string to point to the right database server, etc.*

Database connection strings

As we add business DLLs to our solution, they will likely make use of other databases, and so we'll likely add other database connection string elements to the configuration file over time. In Chapter 7, for example, we'll add an entry for our example application's database:

```
    <add key="DB:PTracker"
         value="data source=localhost;initial catalog=PTracker;
                                             integrated security=SSPI" />
```

Keep in mind that when using CSLA security and remote, server-side DataPortal objects, all the code in the server-side DataPortal will run under the ASP.NET user account. If we then use integrated security to access the database (as shown here), the ASP.NET user account will need security permissions to access the various databases, tables, and stored procedures that will be used by our code.

As an alternative to the above, we can use specific user ID and password combinations in the connection string to access the database, rather than integrated security. This allows us to avoid opening the databases up for use by any ASP.NET application on the server. The unfortunate side-effect is that the username and password are stored in plain text in the Web.config file.

If we use Windows' integrated security *without* anonymous access, all the server-side `DataPortal` code will run under the impersonated user identity from the client. Microsoft Knowledge Base article 306158 discusses the details of setting up impersonation in ASP.NET. If we use integrated security to access the database, then each user will need the appropriate database permissions.

Microsoft Knowledge Base article 306158 also includes directions for impersonating a *specific* user account for all ASP.NET worker code – which would include our server-side `DataPortal` code and our business object code. This requires changes to `Web.config`, adding a user account to the server, and either changing the ASP.NET user account privileges or changing the account under which all ASP.NET code runs. This approach would allow us to control directly the user account under which all our data access code runs, thus allowing us to set up database security for that particular user account.

In any case, the only way we'll get database connection pooling is if we have some sort of central user ID, be that the ASP.NET account, or a specific user ID and password in the connection string. When using per-user logins, we'll get virtually no database connection pooling, which will likely result in poor application performance. The following table summarizes the options:

Database access option	**IIS configuration**	**Consequences**
Integrated security	Anonymous access (no impersonation)	All database access is done under the ASP.NET account. We get database connection pooling, but the ASP.NET account needs access to our databases. No password values are stored in clear text. *Note that the `SERVER\ASPNET` account is a local account, so this option will not work if the database is on a separate machine from the web server.*
Integrated security	Windows security (impersonation)	All database access is user-specific, so each client identity is used to access the database. We get no real database connection pooling, and database permissions must be granted to the end user identities that are using the application. No password values are stored in clear text.
Specific user IDs and passwords in connection strings	Either anonymous access or Windows security	Database access is done under the specific user IDs. We get database connection pooling and have better control over which applications can access which databases. Password values are stored in clear text.
Integrated security	Anonymous access (impersonating specific user)	Database access is done under the specific user ID we provide. We get database connection pooling and have better control over which applications can access which databases. *Note that the `SERVER\ASPNET` account doesn't have permissions to impersonate a specific user by default. Configuration of this option is complex – see KB article 306158.*

Which configuration is appropriate depends on your specific application and environment. As a general rule, I prefer to use specific user ID and password values in my connection strings, since that provides the highest level of control and flexibility, while still enabling database connection pooling for performance.

> *It is not advisable to use the `sa` user ID in this case. We should always create application-specific user IDs that have limited access to our database, and use those for application data access.*

Throughout the code in this book, however, we'll be using integrated security. This is Microsoft's recommended approach, since it avoids putting user IDs and password values into a clear text file.

Referencing or installing business DLLs

As we build business applications, we'll be building DLLs that contain our business classes. If we have a `Customer` object, its class will be in a DLL – perhaps named `Customer.dll`.

The server-side `DataPortal` needs access to these business class DLLs. Remember: `Server.DataPortal` ultimately creates instances of our business objects, and calls the appropriate `DataPortal_xxx()` methods on the object. In order to do this, the business DLL containing the business object's code *must* be available to our server-side `DataPortal` object.

> *Of course, this only applies if we're running the server-side `DataPortal` remotely. If we're running the server-side `DataPortal` objects locally in the client process, then the business DLLs only need to be in the local client application's directory. This is the directory where the Windows Forms executable (or, in a web environment, the `bin` directory of the Web Forms client) resides.*

What this means in practical terms is that the business DLL must reside in the `bin` directory of the `DataPortal` host website. All code running in the website, including `Server.DataPortal`, will always look in the `bin` directory to find any assemblies.

At runtime, we can always copy business DLLs into the `bin` directory to make them available to the server-side `DataPortal`. This can be done using Windows drag-and-drop, `xcopy` from the command line, or any other means you choose. Alternatively, we can reference the business project from our `DataPortal` host web project. When the web project is built, it will automatically copy the DLLs into the `bin` directory – just like we did with the CSLA assemblies.

As a general rule, this second technique is not a practical solution for business application development, because we don't want our business developers to have the CSLA framework projects open in their individual business application solutions. This will almost certainly lead to unintentional framework changes that might affect (read: cause bugs in) other applications that also use the framework.

> **When a business DLL is created or updated, it should therefore be copied into the `DataPortal` host web application's `bin` directory. At the same time, the client machines or web servers using the business DLL must be updated to the same version as the `DataPortal`, or the application will fail.**

When we pass business objects by value across the network, the *same version* of the DLL must exist at both ends of the link. The .NET remoting and serialization technologies perform version checking to make sure they match – if they don't, we'll get a run-time error. Because of this, it's important to synchronize the update of any business DLL so that the `DataPortal` host and any clients are updated at the same time.

If we are using no-touch deployment to install the application on our client workstations, this is relatively easy to arrange. All we need to do is copy the new versions of the DLLs into the `DataPortal` host's `bin` directory at the same time as we copy them into our server directory for no-touch deployment. (See Appendix A for more information about no-touch deployment.) If we have Web Forms clients, all we have to do is copy the new DLLs into the `DataPortal` host's `bin` directory at the same time as we copy them into the Web Forms client's `bin` directory.

The data portal mechanism and data access infrastructure for our framework is now complete and ready for use. We'll make use of it first as we implement the custom table-based security objects in our framework. Then, we'll move on to create the generic name-value collection object that we talked about earlier.

CSLA.Security

As we've been implementing the client-side and server-side `DataPortal` code, we've talked quite a bit about the idea of our custom, table-based security model. We also discussed the design of the security objects in Chapter 2, and the way .NET handles security in Chapter 3, so you should have a fairly good understanding of the concepts behind principal and identity objects. In this section, we'll implement a custom principal object by implementing the `IPrincipal` interface. We'll also implement an identity object by implementing `IIdentity`.

Of the two that we'll create, the more interesting is probably the `BusinessIdentity` object, since it will require data access in order to validate the user's password and retrieve the list of roles to which the user belongs. To do this, we'll make use of our `DataPortal` technology by making `BusinessIdentity` inherit from `ReadOnlyBase`. Essentially, we are about to create our first business object!

Security table

Before we create `BusinessPrincipal` and `BusinessIdentity`, however, let's create the security database with which they'll interact. In it, we'll need two tables. The first will be a list of the users in our system, including their user ID and password information. The second will be a list of the roles to which each user belongs.

> *You may already have a similar database, or you may be using LDAP or some other mechanism to validate and group your users. If so, you can skip the creation of this database and alter the data access methods in the `BusinessIdentity` object implementation to use your security data store instead of this one.*

Obviously, it's possible to get much more complex with security, but we'll keep it simple here so that it's easier for you to adapt these concepts to fit into your own environment. This philosophy extends to storing our password values in a text field within the database – normally, we'd use a one-way hash to convert the password into a numeric value, so that no one could look into the table to get anyone's password.

> *We'll be writing our code in this book to work with SQL Server 2000. If you have a different database, you can adapt the table structures and stored procedures to fit your environment.*

Some versions of VS.NET include the concept of a Database Project. This type of project can be useful any time developers must work with databases, and especially when working with stored procedures. The scripts to create the database, its tables, and its stored procedures are kept in the Database Project, outside of the database itself. This makes it very easy to use source control or other tools against these scripts.

At the same time, the script files in the project can easily be applied to our database by right-clicking on them in the Solution Explorer window and choosing Run. That will run the script against the database to which the project is linked, updating the database with any required changes.

Database Projects work with SQL scripts, and it's often easier to use the Server Explorer tool within VS.NET to create and edit databases, tables, and stored procedures directly, because we can do all our work using graphical design tools. The trouble is that this approach doesn't easily allow us to use source control, or to share the database design scripts with other developers.

The ideal, therefore, is to use a combination of the Server Explorer to create and edit our database objects, and a Database Project to maintain our SQL scripts, enabling source control and database design sharing. That's what we'll do here; the Database Project is available in the code download associated with this book.

> *Use of a Database Project is not required to use SQL Server, or for this book. You can use the tool or approach of your choice to create the databases described in this chapter and in Chapter 6.*
>
> *If your version of VS.NET doesn't support Database Projects, or if you are using a database server that isn't supported by Database Projects, you'll find SQL Server scripts to create the database and tables in the code download for the book.*

Creating the database

The one thing a Database Project requires before it can do anything else is a link to the database on which it will operate. We'll create ours using the Server Explorer in VS.NET, so right click on the Data Connections entry, and choose Create New SQL Server Database. This brings up a dialog allowing us to enter our server name, the new database name, and a user ID and password to use. Enter an appropriate server name along with other valid data, as shown:

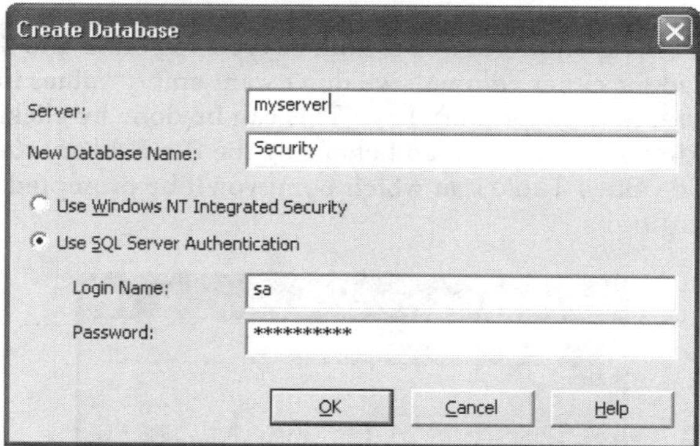

Depending on your options, you may be prompted to provide security information to log into the database, but the end result should be that the database is created and listed in the Server Explorer:

Adding tables

As stated above, our database will have two tables; one for the list of users, and the other containing a list of roles for each user.

Users table

The `Users` table will have just two columns, for storing the user ID and password respectively. In the Server Explorer, open the node for our `Security` database, right-click on Tables, and choose New Table. This will bring up a designer in VS.NET where we can define the columns, keys, and other information about the table.

Add columns called `Username` and `Password`, both as type `varchar` and length 20. Make sure that Allow Nulls is not checked for either column - we don't want empty values in this table. Then, select the `Username` column, and set it as the primary key. (This can be done by clicking the key icon on the toolbar, or by right-clicking on the column and choosing the Set Primary Key option.) Save the designer by choosing File | Save Table1, at which point you'll be prompted to provide a meaningful name for the table. Enter `Users`:

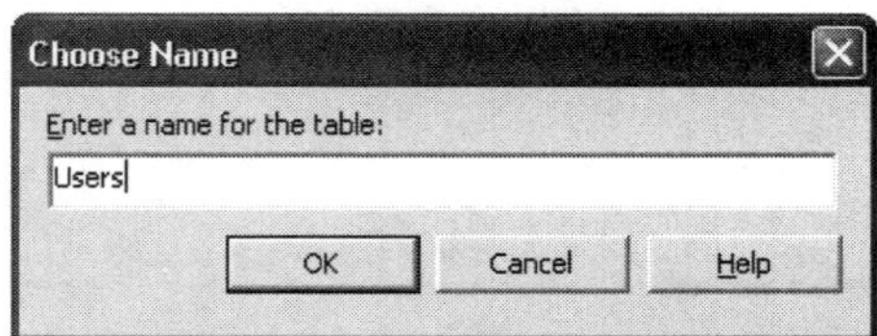

Roles table

We'll do pretty much the same thing to create the `Roles` table, which will associate a list of roles with a specific user. There's a one-to-many relationship from `Users` to `Roles`. Right-click on the Tables entry for our database, and choose New Table. This table will have two columns: `Username` and `Role`. Once again, both are `varchars` of length 20, and neither should allow nulls.

Select both columns at the same time, and set them together as the primary key. This will ensure that there are never duplicate roles for the same user.

We'll also want to add an index for the `Username` column to speed up the login process. When we log in a user, we'll first retrieve their record from the `Users` table, and then we'll retrieve their list of roles from the `Roles` table. This index will speed up that second step. Adding an index is done by right-clicking and choosing the **Indexes/Keys** menu option, or by clicking on the appropriate icon on the toolbar. We can then click the **New** button to add a new index for `Username`:

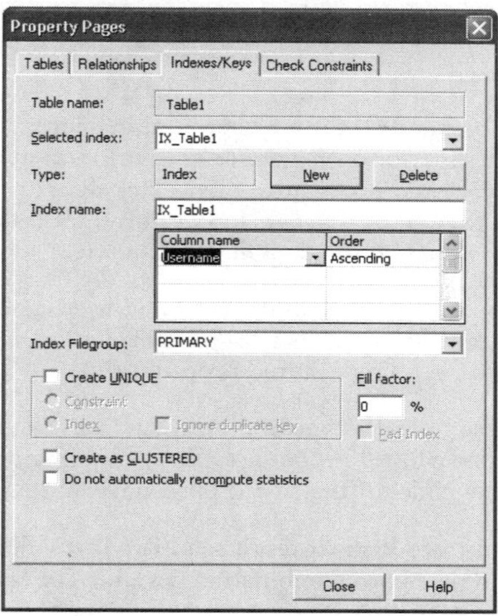

Now save the table and give it the name `Roles`. At this stage, we can add a relationship between our two tables by clicking on the **Relationships** icon on the toolbar and setting up a one-to-many relationship:

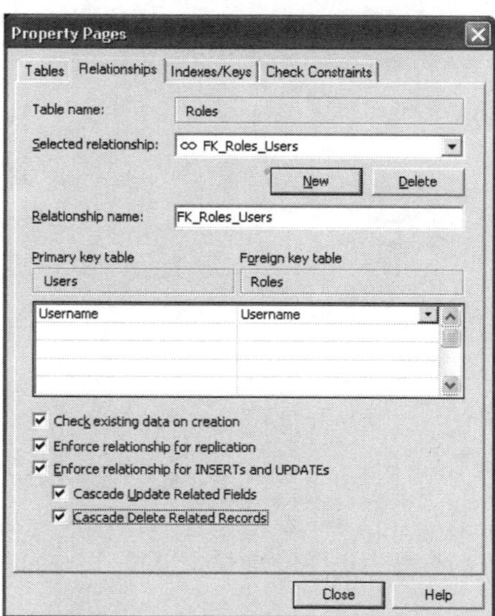

With this done, save the table again. You'll get a warning dialog indicating that this will also update the `Users` table, which makes sense since we're creating a cross-table relationship.

> *I am intentionally oversimplifying this database, acting under the assumption that most organizations already have data stores containing their list of users and their associated roles. You can adapt the data access code we'll write in the `BusinessIdentity` class to use your own specific data store. If you do opt to use the security database we're discussing here, you may wish to add a separate table that contains a list of available roles, and then use it to create a many-to-many relationship between users and roles. I've opted to avoid that here for simplicity.*

Adding a stored procedure

Ideally, all data access should be handled through stored procedures. In SQL Server, stored procedures are pre-compiled, so they offer superior performance over the dynamic SQL statements that we might write in our code. Additionally, stored procedures offer extra security, because we can avoid giving our users access to any tables – all they need is access to the stored procedures to do their work. This helps us to control *exactly* what can be done to the data in the database.

In our case, the application needs to verify that it has a valid username and password combination. If the combination is valid, the application needs a list of the roles to which the user belongs. We can provide both functions from within a single stored procedure.

Under the node for our database in the Server Explorer window is an entry for Stored Procedures. Right-click on it and choose New Stored Procedure. This will bring up a stored procedure designer in VS.NET where we can write the code for the stored procedure.

Our stored procedure will return two distinct result sets. The first will contain the `Username` in the case that the supplied username and password combination is valid. The second will contain a list of the roles to which the user belongs.

> *We could create two stored procedures to perform these operations separately. By doing them in a single stored procedure, however, we're able to have the application make a single call to the database to get all the data it needs. We'll see how to use ADO.NET to process multiple result sets as we implement `BusinessIdentity` a little later on.*

Enter the following code into the designer:

```
CREATE PROCEDURE Login
  (
    @User varchar(20),
    @pw varchar(20)
  )
AS
  SELECT Username
  FROM Users
  WHERE Username=@User AND Password=@pw;

  SELECT R.Role
  FROM Users AS U INNER JOIN Roles AS R ON
    R.UserName = U.UserName
  WHERE U.Username = @User and U.Password = @pw

  RETURN
```

Our data access code within `BusinessIdentity` will use this stored procedure to populate itself with data.

Configuring database permissions

The last thing we need to do here is set up permissions so that the user account under which our server-side `DataPortal` code runs can access the `Login` stored procedure. We discussed the various security options earlier, so your circumstances may vary from what we're showing in this book.

In our case, we'll be using integrated security to talk to the database, and we'll be using anonymous login to IIS. This means that all database access will be done under the ASP.NET user account, so this account needs access to the `Security` database and the `Login` stored procedure.

Unfortunately, security is one of the few areas where the Server Explorer window doesn't help. Instead, we need to use the Enterprise Manager tool for SQL Server to manage the security permissions on a database, or else you can use the following SQL statement (changing `SERVER` to the name of your server):

```
If Not Exists (SELECT * FROM master.dbo.syslogins
               WHERE loginname = N'SERVER\ASPNET')
  EXEC sp_grantlogin N'SERVER\ASPNET'
  EXEC sp_defaultdb N'SERVER\ASPNET', N'master'
  EXEC sp_defaultlanguage N'SERVER\ASPNET', N'us_english'
GO

If Not Exists (SELECT * FROM dbo.sysusers
               WHERE name = N'SERVER\ASPNET' AND uid < 16382)
  EXEC sp_grantdbaccess N'SERVER\ASPNET', N'SERVER\ASPNET'
GO
```

To do this graphically, open Enterprise Manager and navigate to the `Security` database. Under the database is a node for **Users**, on which we can right-click and choose **New Database User**. Select the ASP.NET user, and click **OK**:

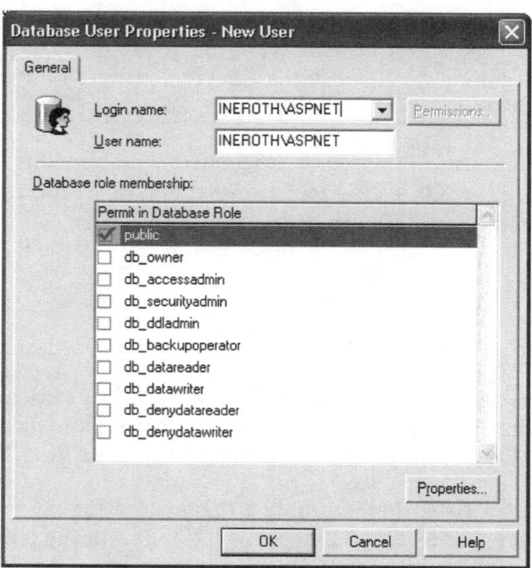

> *If the ASP.NET user is not listed as an option in this dialog, you'll need to add the ASP.NET account as a general user of SQL Server. This is done under the* Security *node for the database server, which has a* Logins *node. You can right-click on* Logins *and choose* New Login *to add a new user account to SQL Server. This dialog allows you to select users from the Windows security environment, including the ASP.NET account.*

Once the user has been added to the `Security` database, the ASP.NET account will be listed under the Users node. However, while the account has access to the database, it has no access to any of the objects within the database, so it can't do anything at this point. We need to allow it to execute the `Login` stored procedure.

Double-click on the ASP.NET user entry to bring up its properties window, and then click the Permissions button. This brings up a window where we can specify what objects the account can access within the database. Select the option to give the account EXEC access to the `Login` stored procedure:

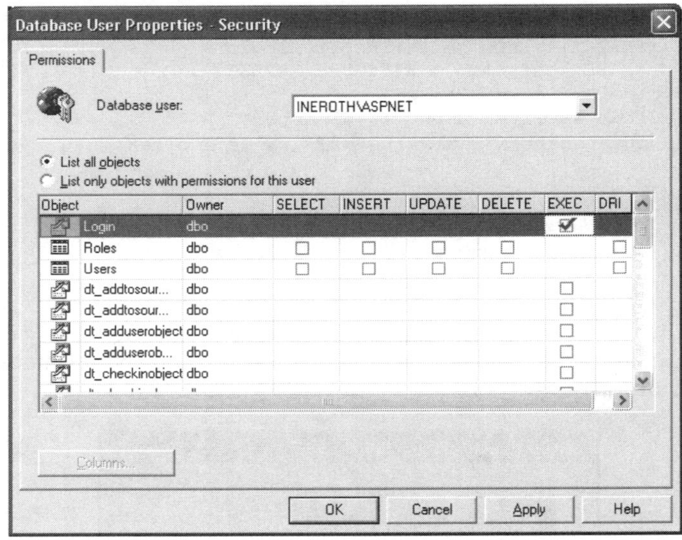

The ASP.NET account can now run this stored procedure, which means that our `BusinessIdentity` code (running under ASP.NET) will be able to retrieve the data it requires. This change in access rights can also be accomplished with the following stored procedure call:

```
Grant Execute On Login To "SERVER\ASPNET"
```

Creating the database project

The `Security` database is complete at this point. However, all its information is 'locked away' within the SQL Server RDBMS where we created it. If we want to share the database structure, or include the structure in source control, we should create a Database Project in VS.NET.

Adding a Database Project to our solution is simply a matter of using the File | Add Project menu – the Database Project type is located under the Other Projects option in the left-hand pane. Name the project `SecurityDB`, hit OK, and you'll be prompted to choose the database to which this project will be linked. Choose the database we just created, and you should find that the project is listed in the Solution Explorer:

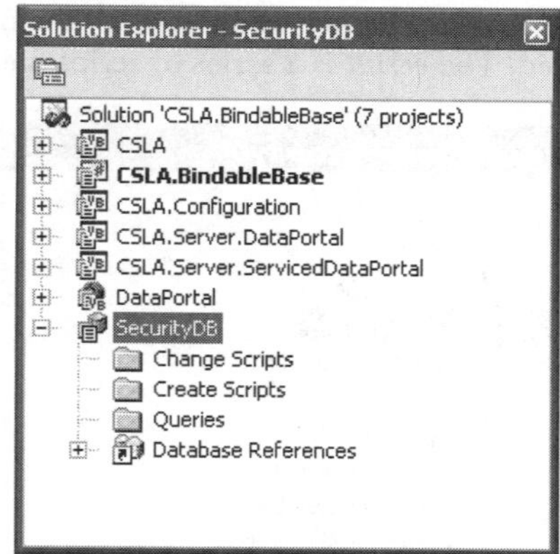

By default, the project includes folders where we can place SQL scripts to change or create database objects, and a folder where we can place query scripts. If we have a pre-existing database with tables and stored procedures, we can drag-and-drop them from the Server Explorer into the folders of this project, and SQL scripts will be automatically created. That's what we'll do in this case, since we already have our tables and stored procedures in the database.

> *This feature requires that the client tools for SQL Server be installed on the development workstation. Remember: this step is not crucial to the running of the sample code in this book.*

We can just drag the **Tables** node from Server Explorer to the **Create Scripts** folder in the `SecurityDB` project. This will bring up a dialog (after possibly asking for login information) where we can select which database objects are to be scripted. In our case, we want all of them scripted, so select that option:

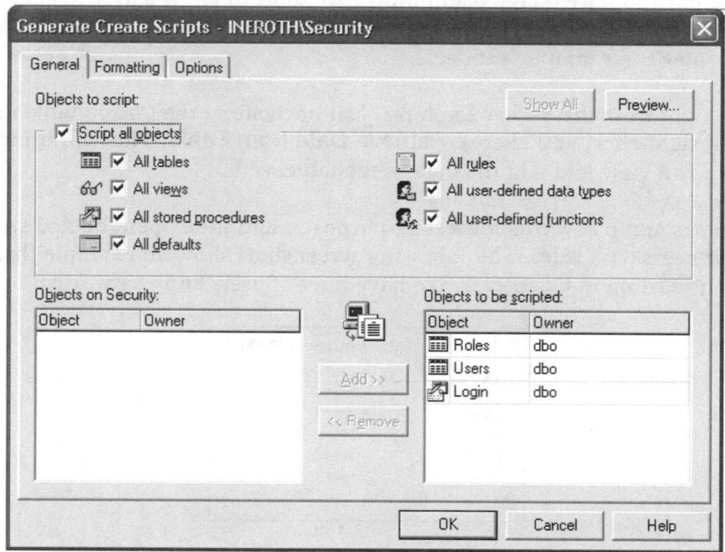

When we click **OK**, VS.NET will confirm that we want to script the objects to the **Create Scripts** folder, and then the scripts will be created. The result is a series of script files in our project:

These files are now all subject to source control, and can be shared with other developers. To recreate the database on a new server, simply highlight all the script files in the Solution Explorer window, right-click on them, and choose the **Run On** menu option. We'll be prompted for the database server on which the scripts should be run, and they'll be executed against that server.

Providing test data

In a production application, we'd create administrative tools to allow a user to add, remove, and edit users and their roles. For our testing purposes, we'll simply use the built-in capabilities of VS.NET to edit the tables to enter some simple test data.

This can be done right from the Server Explorer. Just navigate to the `Users` table under our database connection object, right-click, and choose **Retrieve Data from Table**. This will bring up a VS.NET designer where we can view and edit the data in the table.

Add some usernames and passwords for testing purposes, and then open the `Roles` table for editing, and associate your users with roles. The following screenshots show an example that we'll use in our sample application, starting in Chapter 6. We have a set of users and passwords:

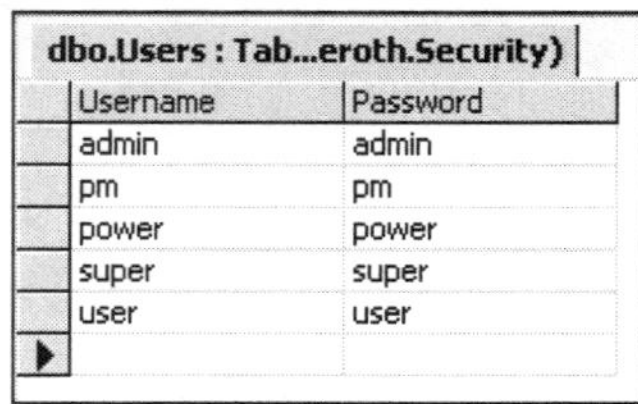
dbo.Users : Tab...eroth.Security)

Username	Password
admin	admin
pm	pm
power	power
super	super
user	user

And we have a set of roles associated with those users:

dbo.Roles : Tab...eroth.Security)

Username	Role
admin	Administrator
pm	ProjectManager
power	Administrator
power	ProjectManager
power	Supervisor
power	User
super	Supervisor
user	User

Notice that we have a power user who is a member of all roles, while the other users have more limited roles. When we build our example application, we'll use these roles to control which users can perform which functions. Since we have several users in different roles, we can use them for testing purposes.

BusinessIdentity

Now that the Security database has been created, we can move on to create our principal and identity objects. The core of the security mechanism is really the identity object, since this is what encapsulates the concept of a user. It's a read-only concept, in that the identity object isn't intended to allow the user to edit their username, password, or roles. To fit into the .NET security framework, an identity object must implement the IIdentity interface.

We'll implement our custom BusinessIdentity object as a regular business object by having it inherit from ReadOnlyBase. This will result in a read-only business object that can be populated with data by using our existing DataPortal mechanism. It will also implement the IIdentity interface, so that it works with the .NET security infrastructure.

Add a new class to the CSLA project and name it BusinessIdentity. This class will be implementing security functionality and interacting with the database, so we can import some namespaces to make that easy:

```
Imports System.Data.SqlClient
Imports System.Security.Principal
```

We also want this class to be in the CSLA.Security namespace, rather than CSLA. To this end, we'll enclose the class in a Namespace block:

```
Namespace Security

  Public Class BusinessIdentity

  End Class

End Namespace
```

Since namespaces are additive, and the project is already in the CSLA namespace, the result is that our class has the full type name CSLA.Security.BusinessIdentity.

Creating a business object

To make `BusinessIdentity` into a business object, we must make it `<Serializable()>`, have it inherit from `ReadOnlyBase`, and implement a `Private` constructor:

```
<Serializable()> _
Public Class BusinessIdentity
  Inherits ReadOnlyBase

#Region " Create and Load "

  Private Sub New()
    ' Prevent direct creation
  End Sub

#End Region

End Class
```

Business objects have other obligations as well. Specifically, they need to provide `Shared` methods through which the object can be created, and they must implement the appropriate `DataPortal_xxx()` methods. In the case of a read-only object, this means overriding `DataPortal_Fetch()`. They must also implement a nested `Criteria` object that can be passed to the `DataPortal_Fetch()` method.

Criteria class

The `Criteria` class contains the information needed to load the object from the database. For this object, that means the `Username` and `Password` fields (which will be provided by the UI) that must be validated against the database.

To create a nested `Criteria` class, we must declare it *inside* the `BusinessIdentity` class – but in all other respects, it's just a normal class. To keep things orderly, we'll implement it within the *Create and Load* region, and mark it as `<Serializable()>` so that it can be passed by value via remoting:

```
#Region " Create and Load "

    <Serializable()> _
    Public Class Criteria
      Public Username As String
      Public Password As String

      Public Sub New(ByVal Username As String, ByVal Password As String)
        Me.Username = Username
        Me.Password = Password
      End Sub
    End Class

    Private Sub New()
      ' Prevent direct creation
    End Sub

#End Region
```

As you can see, the class includes `Public` variables, which is typically a Bad Thing because the data is externalized, breaking encapsulation. In this case, however, we're merely passing the object between our business object and itself, so the coding simplicity that comes from marking the variables as `Public` is worth it. Otherwise, we'd have to implement `Property` methods that did nothing but expose the value – extra code for no value in this case.

Technically, there's no need for a parameterized constructor either, but having it simplifies our code in `BusinessIdentity` quite a lot, so it's worth implementing.

Creation methods

Now that we have a `Criteria` class nested within `BusinessIdentity`, we can create a `Shared` method to allow client code to create an instance of `BusinessIdentity`. This flows from the 'class in charge' scheme that we discussed in Chapter 2.

In the particular case of `BusinessIdentity`, the *only* valid client code will be our `BusinessPrincipal` object. Identity objects are *always* contained within principal objects, so we don't want the UI or arbitrary business object code creating an identity object by themselves – they *must* go through the `BusinessPrincipal` object.

To make sure this works, we'll scope our `Shared` method as `Friend`, so it won't be available outside the `CSLA` project. Given our `Private` constructor as well, this ensures that the object can't be created by either UI or business code. Add the method to the same region:

```
    Friend Shared Function LoadIdentity( _
      ByVal UserName As String, ByVal Password As String) As BusinessIdentity

      Return CType(DataPortal.Fetch(New Criteria(UserName, Password)), _
                                                        BusinessIdentity)
    End Function
```

The method accepts a username and password as parameters, and then uses them to create a new `Criteria` object. This `Criteria` object is then passed to the `Fetch()` method of the client-side `DataPortal`, which in turn calls the server-side `DataPortal` object's `Fetch()` method, which in turn calls our object's `DataPortal_Fetch()` method.

The `DataPortal` mechanism returns a fully populated `BusinessIdentity` object, which we then return as a result of this `Shared` method. We'll see how this is called when we implement the `BusinessPrincipal` class.

DataPortal_Fetch

Though we've now created the `Shared` method to load our object with data, we have not yet implemented a meaningful `DataPortal_Fetch()` method. As it stands, the server-side `DataPortal` will execute the `DataPortal_Fetch()` we implemented in `ReadOnlyBase`, which simply returns an error. To implement our own data access code, we need to override this method.

First though, we need some instance variables in our class into which we can load the data we'll be retrieving:

```
<Serializable()> _
Public Class BusinessIdentity
  Inherits ReadOnlyBase

  Private mUsername As String
  Private mRoles As New ArrayList
```

These variables will store the information that we'll get from our data access code. If the username and password combination was valid, then we have the username value to put into `mUsername`. We'll also have a list of roles to which the user belongs that we can use to populate the `mRoles` `ArrayList` object. Now we can implement the `DataPortal_Fetch()` method itself:

```
#Region " Data access "

  Protected Overrides Sub DataPortal_Fetch(ByVal Criteria As Object)

    Dim crit As Criteria = CType(Criteria, Criteria)
    Dim cn As New SqlConnection(DB("Security"))
    Dim cm As New SqlCommand()

    mRoles.Clear()

    cn.Open()
    Try
      cm.Connection = cn
      cm.CommandText = "Login"
      cm.CommandType = CommandType.StoredProcedure
      cm.Parameters.Add("@user", crit.Username)
      cm.Parameters.Add("@pw", crit.Password)

      Dim dr As SqlDataReader = cm.ExecuteReader()
      Try
        If dr.Read() Then
          mUsername = crit.Username

          If dr.NextResult Then
            While dr.Read
              mRoles.Add(dr.GetString(0))
            End While
          End If

        Else
          mUsername = ""
        End If

      Finally
        dr.Close()
      End Try

    Finally
      cn.Close()
    End Try

  End Sub

#End Region
```

The Criteria object is passed in as a parameter of type Object, so we first cast it to a variable specific to our Criteria object's data type:

```
Dim crit As Criteria = CType(Criteria, Criteria)
```

Then we open a connection to the database:

```
Dim cn As New SqlConnection(DB("Security"))
Dim cm As New SqlCommand()
cn.Open()
```

Notice here the use of the DB() method that we implemented in ReadOnlyBase to retrieve the connection string for the database. Now that the database is open, we go into a Try...Finally block so that we're sure to close the connection regardless of whether we get any errors. We can then call the Login stored procedure by setting up and executing a SqlCommand object:

```
cm.Connection = cn
cm.CommandText = "Login"
cm.CommandType = CommandType.StoredProcedure
cm.Parameters.Add("@user", crit.Username)
cm.Parameters.Add("@pw", crit.Password)
Dim dr As SqlDataReader = cm.ExecuteReader()
```

The processing of the SqlDataReader is also in a Try...Finally block, so that we're sure to close the object when we're done. The first thing we do is see if the username and password matched and returned a row of data:

```
If dr.Read() Then
  mUsername = crit.Username
```

If so, we store the username into our object for later reference. On the other hand, if no record was returned, we take a different route to indicate that the user isn't valid by setting the mUsername field to an empty string:

```
Else
  mUsername = ""
```

If the user *is* valid, we also need to retrieve the roles for the user. This is done by moving to the next result set from SQL Server (remember that our stored procedure returns *two* result sets) and copying its values into our ArrayList:

```
If dr.NextResult Then
  While dr.Read
    mRoles.Add(dr.GetString(0))
  End While
End If
```

For performance reasons, all of this is done using a SqlDataReader rather than a DataSet object. A DataSet object is loaded from a data reader object, so if we'd used a DataSet, our data would have taken the following path:

Database → data reader → DataSet → BusinessIdentity

As it is, we avoid copying the data an extra time by using the data reader directly:

Database → data reader → BusinessIdentity

Thanks to this approach, retrieving a BusinessIdentity object should be roughly as fast as retrieving a DataSet with the same data.

At the end of the DataPortal_Fetch() method, we've populated our object with appropriate data from the database. The DataPortal mechanism then returns the BusinessIdentity object back to the client code – our BusinessPrincipal object in this case.

Implementing IIdentity

To operate properly within the .NET security infrastructure, our BusinessIdentity class must implement the IIdentity interface, which exposes some of the data in our object:

```
<Serializable()> _
Public Class BusinessIdentity
  Inherits ReadOnlyBase
  Implements IIdentity
```

This forces us to implement the properties defined by the interface. These are:

Property	Description
IsAuthenticated	Returns a Boolean indicating whether this identity was successfully authenticated
AuthenticationType	Returns a String indicating the type of authentication used to authenticate the identity
Name	Returns a String containing the name of the authenticated user

Given the variables we've already defined and loaded in our object, these are easily implemented:

```
#Region " IIdentity "

    Public ReadOnly Property IsAuthenticated() As Boolean _
        Implements IIdentity.IsAuthenticated
      Get
        Return Len(mUsername) > 0
      End Get
    End Property

    Public ReadOnly Property AuthenticationType() As String _
        Implements IIdentity.AuthenticationType
      Get
        Return "CSLA"
      End Get
    End Property
```

```
    Public ReadOnly Property Name() As String _
        Implements IIdentity.Name
      Get
        Return mUsername
      End Get
    End Property

  #End Region
```

Each property defined on the interface is implemented here by returning the appropriate value from our data. In the case of `AuthenticationType`, we return the value `"CSLA"` to indicate that the identity was authenticated using our custom, table-based scheme.

Exposing the roles

There's one last bit of information in our object that we have yet to make available: the list of roles for the current user. As we mentioned in Chapter 3, the `IsInRole()` method exists on the `IPrincipal` interface rather than on `IIdentity`, so we somehow need to make the list of roles available to our `BusinessPrincipal` object. This can be done by exposing our own `IsInRole()` method at `Friend` scope, so it's not available to UI or business object code:

```
    Friend Function IsInRole(ByVal Role As String) As Boolean
      Return mRoles.Contains(Role)
    End Function
```

The `IsInRole()` method that we'll implement in `BusinessPrincipal` can make use of this method in its implementation.

That completes the `BusinessIdentity` object, which is our first business object based on the framework. We can now move on to create the `BusinessPrincipal` object that will manage `BusinessIdentity`.

BusinessPrincipal

The principal object's role is to provide the start point for .NET security queries. It implements the `IPrincipal` interface, which comprises the `IsInRole()` method and an `Identity` property to provide access to the underlying identity object. `IsInRole()` can be used from any of our code, in the UI or in business objects, to determine whether the current user belongs to any given role.

It is also the job of the principal object to manage the login process. Our UI code will get the username and password from the user, and provide it to the `BusinessPrincipal` object, which will manage the process of finding out whether the username and password combination is valid. Most of the hard work in this regard was done by our custom `BusinessIdentity` object, but `BusinessPrincipal` does include some interesting code that enables it to integrate properly with the .NET security infrastructure.

In the `CSLA` project, add a new class named `BusinessPrincipal`. During its implementation, we'll be interacting with the security and threading infrastructure of the .NET Framework, so import these namespaces:

```
  Imports System.Security.Principal
  Imports System.Threading
```

As with BusinessIdentity, we want this class to be in the CSLA.Security namespace, so we'll wrap it in a Namespace block. We'll also make the class <Serializable()>, so that it can be passed by value via remoting:

```
Namespace Security

  <Serializable()> _
  Public Class BusinessPrincipal

  End Class

End Namespace
```

Implementing IPrincipal

To help with implementing IsInRole() and Identity, we'll declare a variable to hold a reference to our BusinessIdentity object:

```
  <Serializable()> _
  Public Class BusinessPrincipal
    Implements IPrincipal

    Private mIdentity As BusinessIdentity

#Region " IPrincipal "

    Public ReadOnly Property Identity() As IIdentity _
        Implements IPrincipal.Identity
      Get
        Return mIdentity
      End Get
    End Property

    Public Function IsInRole(ByVal Role As String) As Boolean _
        Implements IPrincipal.IsInRole

      Return mIdentity.IsInRole(Role)
    End Function

#End Region
```

Notice how the IsInRole() method simply delegates the call to the IsInRole() method that we implemented in BusinessIdentity. This allows the BusinessIdentity object to maintain all user-specific data, and us to implement the IsInRole() method as required by IPrincipal.

Of course, we haven't yet implemented any code to get hold of a BusinessIdentity object. That will be handled by the login process.

Login process

The process of logging in has two parts: integrating with .NET security, and creating the BusinessIdentity object.

To integrate properly with .NET security, we must insert our new `BusinessPrincipal` object as the thread's `CurrentPrincipal`. (We discussed the relationship between the principal and identity objects in Chapter 3; these are standard .NET security concepts that are common to all applications.) Unfortunately, the process of setting the principal object for our thread is a bit complex, and I'll try to explain it in some detail to make it clear.

Once that's done, however, we can take the username and password provided by the UI, and use them to create a `BusinessIdentity` object. We've already implemented the details behind that process, so we know that it will result in a `BusinessIdentity` object that will indicate whether the username and password combination was valid.

The entire process will be launched from the UI by calling a `Shared` method named `Login()`:

```
#Region " Login Process "

    Public Shared Sub Login(ByVal Username As String, _
                            ByVal Password As String)

      Dim p As New BusinessPrincipal(Username, Password)
    End Sub

#End Region
```

This method looks a bit odd, since it's creating an instance of our `BusinessPrincipal` object, and then doing nothing with the resulting variable! That's all right, though, because our constructor will be ensuring that the current thread's `CurrentPrincipal` property points to the new `BusinessPrincipal` object. Though we have no use for the reference, there's no way to use the `New` keyword without assigning its result to some variable.

All the interesting work happens in the `Private` constructor. This is where we do the following:

- Create the `BusinessPrincipal` object
- Set our `BusinessPrincipal` as the current thread's principal object, thus making it the active security context
- Attempt to set our `BusinessPrincipal` as the default object for threads created in the future (which can fail if this has ever been done in our application domain before)
- Load the `BusinessIdentity` object with the user's identity and roles

Insert the constructor into the *Login Process* region:

```
    Private Sub New(ByVal Username As String, ByVal Password As String)

      Dim currentdomain As AppDomain = Thread.GetDomain()
      currentdomain.SetPrincipalPolicy(PrincipalPolicy.UnauthenticatedPrincipal)

      Dim OldPrincipal As IPrincipal = Thread.CurrentPrincipal
      Thread.CurrentPrincipal = Me
```

```
    Try
      If Not TypeOf OldPrincipal Is BusinessPrincipal Then
        currentdomain.SetThreadPrincipal(Me)
      End If

    Catch
      ' Failed, but we don't care because there's nothing
      ' we can do in this case
    End Try

    ' Load the underlying identity object that tells whether we are really
    ' logged in. If so, will contain the list of roles we belong to
    mIdentity = BusinessIdentity.LoadIdentity(Username, Password)

  End Sub
```

The first step is to get a reference to our current application domain. Each application domain has a security policy that controls how any thread in the domain gets its principal object. Since we're implementing custom security, we want the policy to avoid doing any automatic authentication, so we set the value to use an `UnauthenticatedPrincipal`:

```
Dim currentdomain As AppDomain = Thread.GetDomain
currentdomain.SetPrincipalPolicy(PrincipalPolicy.UnauthenticatedPrincipal)
```

Obviously, the `BusinessPrincipal` will be authenticated *in the end*, but this setting avoids the potential overhead of doing Windows authentication first, only to discard that result as we perform our own authentication.

The next step is to get a reference to the old principal object, and then set the thread with our new `BusinessPrincipal`:

```
Dim OldPrincipal As IPrincipal = Thread.CurrentPrincipal
Thread.CurrentPrincipal = Me
```

At this point, any code running on our thread will rely on our `BusinessPrincipal` to provide all security information about the user's identity and roles.

The next bit of code is potentially a bit confusing. Though we've set our current thread to use the right principal object, it's possible that other threads will be created within this application domain in the future. Ideally, they'd automatically get this same `BusinessPrincipal` object when they're created. That's what this code does:

```
Try
  If Not TypeOf OldPrincipal Is BusinessPrincipal Then
    currentdomain.SetThreadPrincipal(Me)
  End If

Catch
  ' Failed, but we don't care because there's nothing
  ' we can do in this case
End Try
```

The thing is, this can only happen *once* during the lifetime of an application domain. For a Windows Forms application, this means we can only set it once each time the application is run. For a Web Forms application, the rules are more complex: we can get a new application domain any time ASP.NET resets our website, and this happens any time `Web.config` is changed, or a new file is copied into the directory, or ASP.NET detects that our website has deadlocked or is having trouble.

Because we can't always know what the UI code might have done previously, we can't assume that this code will work. If it *doesn't* work, there's not a whole lot we can do. If it was of critical importance, we could perhaps raise an error that forced the application domain itself to terminate, kicking the user out of the application entirely. This would only work in a Windows UI, however. In a Web Forms UI, we're running in an application domain created by ASP.NET, and this code is almost guaranteed to fail.

Due to these issues, if this causes an error, we simply ignore it and continue with our processing. At this point, it's up to the business developer to realize that they're running in a pre-secured environment, and they'll have to ensure manually that any new threads created for this user get the same `BusinessPrincipal` object.

> *In reality, this is almost never an issue, since most server-side code is single-threaded. The only time we're likely to be spinning up extra threads is on a Windows Forms client, and in that case the application domain default should be set to our* `BusinessPrincipal`*.*

The final step in the process is to create the `BusinessIdentity` object. This is easily done by calling the `Shared` method we implemented earlier:

```
      mIdentity = BusinessIdentity.LoadIdentity(Username, Password)
```

This illustrates how virtually all of our business objects are created. We call the `Shared` method on the class, which returns a fully populated business object for our use. In this case, the resulting `BusinessIdentity` object will contain information to indicate whether the user was successfully authenticated. If so, it will contain the user name, and the list of roles for the user.

At this point, our custom, table-based security infrastructure is complete. Any of our UI or business object code can now use code similar to the following to log into the system:

```
' Login (done once at the beginning of the app)
CSLA.Security.BusinessPrincipal.Login("username", "password")
```

Then we can determine whether the user is in a given role anywhere in our code:

```
If System.Threading.Thread.CurrentPrincipal.IsInRole("role") Then

  ' They are in the role
Else

  ' They are _not_ in the role
End If
```

We'll make use of this capability as we implement our sample application in Chapters 7 thru 10.

Utility classes

We'll wrap up this chapter by creating a couple more utility classes that may be generally useful in application development. The first is `SafeDataReader` – a wrapper around any ADO.NET data reader object that automatically handles any null values that might come from the database. The second is `NameValueList`, which will implement a generic read-only name-value collection object that can be loaded from a database table.

SafeDataReader

Null values should only be allowed in database columns for two reasons. The first is when we care about the difference between a value that was never entered, and a value that is zero (or an empty string). In other words, we actually care about the difference between "" and `Null`, or between 0 and `Null`. There are applications where this matters – where the business rules revolve around whether a field ever had a value (even an empty one), or never had a value at all.

The second reason for using a null value is where a data type doesn't intrinsically support the concept of an empty field. The most common example is the SQL `DateTime` data type, which has no way to represent an empty date value – it *always* contains a valid date. In such a case, we can allow null values in the column specifically so that we can use `Null` to indicate an empty date.

Of course, these two reasons are mutually exclusive. If we're using null values to differentiate between an empty field and one that never had a value, we need to come up with some other scheme to indicate an empty `DateTime` field. The solution to this problem is outside the scope of this book – but thankfully, the problem itself is quite rare.

The reality is that very few applications ever care about the difference between an empty value and one that was never entered, so the first scenario seldom applies. If it *does* apply, then dealing with null values at the database level isn't an issue – all variables in the application must be of type `Object`, so that they can hold a null value. Obviously, there are negative performance implications here, but if the business requirements dictate that "" or 0 are different from `Null`, then this is the answer.

For *most* applications, the only reason for using null values is the second scenario – and this one is quite common. Any application that uses date values, and where an empty date is a valid entry, will likely use `Null` to represent an empty date.

Unfortunately, a whole lot of poorly-designed databases allow null values in columns where *neither* scenario applies, and we developers have to deal with them. These are databases from which we might retrieve a `Null` value even if we don't care about it, and didn't want it. Writing defensive code to guard against tables where null values are erroneously allowed can quickly bloat our data access code and make it hard to read. To avoid this, we'll create a `SafeDataReader` class that will take care of these details on our behalf.

As a rule, data reader objects are `NotInheritable` (sealed), meaning that we can't simply subclass an existing data reader class such as `SqlDataReader` and extend it. However, we *can* do what we did in Chapter 4 to create our `SmartDate` class: we can encapsulate or 'wrap' a data reader object.

Creating the SafeDataReader class

To ensure that we can wrap *any* data reader object, we'll be working with the root IDataReader interface that's implemented by all data reader objects. Also, since we want to *be* a data reader object, we'll implement that interface as well.

> *Because IDataReader is a very large interface, we won't include all the code for the class in the book's text. The complete class is available in the code download associated with the book.*

Create the class

Add a new class to the CSLA project and name it SafeDataReader. Let's start with the following code:

```
Imports System.Data

Namespace Data

  Public Class SafeDataReader

    Implements IDataReader

    Private mDataReader As IDataReader

    Public Sub New(ByVal DataReader As IDataReader)
      mDataReader = DataReader
    End Sub

  End Class

End Namespace
```

We put the class within a Namespace block, so its full type name is CSLA.Data.SafeDataReader. This helps keep the class organized within our framework.

We start by declaring that we'll implement the IDataReader interface ourselves in this class. The class also defines a variable to store a reference to the *real* data reader that we'll be encapsulating, and we have a constructor that accepts that data reader object as a parameter.

In order to create an instance of SafeDataReader, we need to start with an existing data reader object. This is pretty easy – it means that our ADO.NET code might appear as:

```
Dim dr As New SafeDataReader(cm.ExecuteReader)
```

A command object's ExecuteReader() method returns a data reader object that we can use to initialize our wrapper object. The remainder of our data access code can use our SafeDataReader object just like a regular data reader object, because we've implemented IDataReader.

The implementation of IDataReader is a lengthy business – it contains a lot of methods – so we're not going to go through all of it here. However, we should look at a couple of methods to get a feel for how the thing works.

GetString

All the methods that return column data are 'null protected' with code like this:

```
Public Function GetString(ByVal i As Integer) As String _
    Implements IDataReader.GetString

  If mDataReader.IsDBNull(i) Then
    Return ""
  Else
    Return mDataReader.GetString(i)
  End If

End Function
```

If the value in the database is `Null`, we return some more palatable value – typically, whatever passes for 'empty' for the specific data type. If the value is not `Null`, we simply return the value from the underlying data reader object.

There really are a lot of these methods – there has to be one for each data type that we might get from the database!

GetDateTime and GetSmartDate

Most types have 'empty' values that are obvious, but two are problematic: `DateTime` and `Boolean`. The former, for instance, has no 'empty' value:

```
Public Function GetDateTime(ByVal i As Integer) As Date _
    Implements System.Data.IDataReader.GetDateTime

  If mDataReader.IsDBNull(i) Then
    Return Date.MinValue
  Else
    Return mDataReader.GetDateTime(i)
  End If

End Function
```

Here, we are arbitrarily assigning the minimum date value to be the 'empty' value. This hooks into all the issues that we discussed in Chapter 4, when we created the `SmartDate` class. We'll provide an alternative method in `SafeDataReader` that utilizes the `SmartDate` class:

```
Public Function GetSmartDate(ByVal i As Integer, _
    Optional ByVal EmptyIsMin As Boolean = True) As SmartDate

  If mDataReader.IsDBNull(i) Then
    Return New SmartDate(EmptyIsMin)
  Else
    Return New SmartDate(mDataReader.GetDateTime(i), EmptyIsMin)
  End If

End Function
```

Our data access code can now choose either to accept the minimum date value as being equivalent to 'empty', or to retrieve a `SmartDate` object that is more intelligent:

```
Dim myDate As SmartDate = dr.GetSmartDate(0)
```

GetBoolean

Likewise, there is no 'empty' value for the `Boolean` type:

```
Public Function GetBoolean(ByVal i As Integer) As Boolean _
    Implements System.Data.IDataReader.GetBoolean

  If mDataReader.IsDBNull(i) Then
    Return False
  Else
    Return mDataReader.GetBoolean(i)
  End If

End Function
```

As you can see, we arbitrarily return a `False` value in this case; you may need to alter the return value of `GetBoolean()` (or indeed `GetDateTime()`) to suit your specific application requirements.

Other methods

The `IDataReader` interface also includes a number of methods that don't return column values, such as the `Read()` method:

```
Public Function Read() As Boolean Implements IDataReader.Read
  Return mDataReader.Read
End Function
```

In these cases, we simply delegate the method call down to the underlying data reader object for it to handle. Any return values are passed back to the calling code, so the fact that our wrapper is involved is entirely transparent.

The `SafeDataReader` class can be used to simplify our data access code dramatically, any time we're working with tables in which null values are allowed in columns where we really don't want them or care about them. If your application *does* care about the use of null values, you can simply use the regular data reader objects instead.

We'll make use of `SafeDataReader` in Chapter 7 as we implement our business objects.

NameValueList

The last class we'll implement in this chapter – and in the business framework! – is `NameValueList`. This is a base class on which we can easily build name-value lists for our applications.

Many, if not most, applications need read-only name-value lists to populate combo box controls, list box controls, etc. Typically, these lists come from relatively static configuration tables that are separately managed. Examples of such lists might be a list of product types, customer categories, valid shipping methods, and so forth.

Rather than putting in a lot of effort to implement specific read-only collection objects for each type of list in an application, it would be nice if there was an easy way to create them quickly – preferably with little or no code. We won't achieve *no* code here, but by implementing the `NameValueList` base class, we'll be able to implement read-only name-value list objects with very little code indeed. The `NameValueList` class will provide core functionality:

- Retrieve a value, given a name
- Retrieve a name, given a value
- Retrieve a copy of the entire list as a `NameValueCollection`
- Implement generic data access to populate the list
- Data access can be overridden with custom code, if needed

This functionality should be sufficient to provide most of the name-value collection behaviors that we need in business applications. To create a specific name-value collection object, we can subclass `NameValueList`, provide an object-specific `Criteria` class and a `Shared` creation method, and we're pretty much done. All the hard work will be done by the base class we're about to create.

Our end goal is to make it so that the business developer can create a name-value list class with very little code. When we're done, they'll be able to create a typical name-value list like this:

```
<Serializable()> _
Public Class MyDataList
  Inherits NameValueList

#Region " Shared Methods "

  Public Shared Function GetMyDataList() As MyDataList
    Return CType(DataPortal.Fetch(New Criteria), MyDataList)
  End Function

#End Region

#Region " Constructors "

  Private Sub New()
    ' Prevent direct creation
  End Sub

  ' This constructor overload is required because the base class
  '  (NameObjectCollectionBase) implements ISerializable
  Private Sub New( _
        ByVal info As System.Runtime.Serialization.SerializationInfo, _
        ByVal context As System.Runtime.Serialization.StreamingContext)
    MyBase.New(info, context)
  End Sub

#End Region

#Region " Criteria "
```

```
  <Serializable()> _
  Private Class Criteria
    ' Add criteria here
  End Class

#End Region

#Region " Data Access "

  ' Called by DataPortal to load data from the database
  Protected Overrides Sub DataPortal_Fetch(ByVal Criteria As Object)
    SimpleFetch("myDatabase", "myTable", "myNameColumn", " myValueColumn")
  End Sub

#End Region

End Class
```

The resulting business object will be similar to a read-only version of a regular .NET `NameValueCollection`. It will load itself with data from the database, table, and columns specified.

> *The extra `Private` constructor is a bit odd. It turns out that when a class implements the `ISerializable` interface, any class that inherits from it must implement a special constructor, as shown here. The `NameObjectCollectionBase` class from which we'll ultimately inherit implements `ISerializable`, forcing us to write this extra code. Presumably, the default serialization provided by `<Serializable()>` was insufficient for `NameObjectCollectionBase`, so Microsoft had to implement `ISerializable`, leaving us to deal with this unfortunate side-effect.*

While we already have a `ReadOnlyCollectionBase` class on which we can build read-only collections, it's not particularly useful when we want to build a name-value object. A name-value collection is different from a basic collection, because it not only stores values like a collection, but it stores names associated with each of those values. Because `ReadOnlyCollectionBase` is a subclass of `CollectionBase`, it is not well suited to acting as a name-value collection.

However, by creating a subclass of `NameObjectCollectionBase` that integrates with our CSLA .NET framework, we can easily create a base class that provides read-only name-value data that can be loaded from data in a database table. We can think of `NameValueList` as being a peer to `ReadOnlyCollectionBase` within our framework.

Creating NameValueList

Add a new class to the `CSLA` project, and name it `NameValueList`. As usual, we'll be using a number of namespaces, so let's import them now:

```
Imports System.Data.SqlClient
Imports System.Collections.Specialized
Imports System.IO
Imports System.Runtime.Serialization
Imports System.Runtime.Serialization.Formatters.Binary
Imports System.Configuration
```

Then we can start creating the class, which will be very like the `ReadOnlyBase` and `ReadOnlyCollectionBase` classes from Chapter 4. It will be serializable, and it will implement the `ICloneable` interface. To get all the pre-built collection behaviors to track both names and values, we'll inherit from `NameObjectCollectionBase`:

```
<Serializable()> _
Public MustInherit Class NameValueList
  Inherits NameObjectCollectionBase

  Implements ICloneable

#Region " Clone "

  ' All business objects _must_ be serializable and thus
  '  can be cloned - this just clinches the deal
  Public Function Clone() As Object Implements ICloneable.Clone
    Dim buffer As New MemoryStream
    Dim formatter As New BinaryFormatter

    formatter.Serialize(buffer, Me)
    buffer.Position = 0
    Return formatter.Deserialize(buffer)
  End Function

#End Region

End Class
```

Making the data read-only

The `NameObjectCollectionBase` provided by .NET is a lot like the other collection base classes, in that it manages the collection of data internally, leaving it up to us to implement methods such as `Item()` and `Add()`. In fact, `NameObjectCollectionBase` is even nicer, because it *doesn't* automatically expose methods like `Remove()`, `RemoveAt()`, or `Clear()`, so we don't have to write extra code to make our object read-only.

Add the following code to the class:

```
#Region " Collection methods "

  Default Public ReadOnly Property Item(ByVal Index As Integer) As String
    Get
      Return CStr(MyBase.BaseGet(Index))
    End Get
  End Property

  Default Public ReadOnly Property Item(ByVal Name As String) As String
    Get
      Return CStr(MyBase.BaseGet(Name))
    End Get
  End Property
```

```
    Public ReadOnly Property Key(ByVal Item As String) As String
      Get
        Dim keyName As String
        For Each keyName In Me
          If Me.Item(keyName) = Item Then
            Return keyName
          End If
        Next

        ' We didn't find a match - throw an exception
        Throw New ApplicationException("No matching item in collection")
      End Get
    End Property

    Protected Sub Add(ByVal Name As String, ByVal Value As String)
      MyBase.BaseAdd(Name, Value)
    End Sub

  #End Region
```

Here, we've implemented two `Item()` properties so that we can retrieve a value based either on its text key value, or by its numeric location in the list. This mirrors the behavior of the .NET `NameValueCollection`.

We've also implemented a `Key()` property that returns the text of the key that corresponds to a specific value. The rationale behind this is that we often load a list control with values and allow the user to select one. When that happens, we need to convert that value back to the key, since it's typically the key that's important to the database. The value itself is typically human-readable text, which is nice for display, but useless for storage.

If an invalid value is supplied to `Key()`, we'll throw an exception. This is a powerful validation tool, because it means that we can write very simple code to validate user entry. The business logic might look like this:

```
mKey = myList.Key(mUserInput)
```

If the user input isn't a valid item in our list, this will result in an exception being thrown.

Finally, we included an `Add()` method. Notice that this is `Protected` in scope, so only subclasses based on our base class can add data to the collection. We don't want to allow other business objects or the UI to change the data in the collection – it should be loaded from the database, and then be read-only.

Constructor methods

We need to implement two constructor methods, which is a bit different from what we've see so far. We'll explain them following the code:

```
  #Region " Create and Load "

    Protected Sub New()
      ' prevent public creation
    End Sub
```

```
    Protected Sub New(ByVal info As SerializationInfo, _
                      ByVal context As StreamingContext)
      MyBase.New(info, context)
    End Sub

  #End Region
```

The first constructor is a default one that allows the business developer to inherit from our base class. Normally, we don't include default constructors like this, because the VB.NET compiler creates them for us. However, if we write a parameterized constructor, the compiler won't generate a default – so we must add it explicitly.

The second constructor is required because, as stated earlier, the `NameObjectCollectionBase` class implements the `ISerializable` interface. When a class implements this interface, it must provide a special constructor that the serialization infrastructure can call to deserialize the object. Unfortunately, this also means that any classes that inherit from a class that implements `ISerializable` must *also* implement this specific constructor, delegating the call to the base class itself.

Standard data access methods

As with all our other business base classes, we must provide the `DataPortal_xxx()` methods. Since we're creating a base for read-only objects, the only method we need to make non-`Private` is `DataPortal_Fetch()`. That's the only one the business developer needs to worry about overriding:

```
  #Region " Data Access "

    Private Sub DataPortal_Create(ByVal Criteria As Object)
      Throw New NotSupportedException("Invalid operation - create not allowed")
    End Sub

    Protected Overridable Sub DataPortal_Fetch(ByVal Criteria As Object)
      Throw New NotSupportedException("Invalid operation - fetch not allowed")
    End Sub

    Private Sub DataPortal_Update()
      Throw New NotSupportedException("Invalid operation - update not allowed")
    End Sub

    Private Sub DataPortal_Delete(ByVal Criteria As Object)
      Throw New NotSupportedException("Invalid operation - delete not allowed")
    End Sub

    Protected Function DB(ByVal DatabaseName As String) As String
      Return ConfigurationSettings.AppSettings("DB:" & DatabaseName)
    End Function

  #End Region
```

Now the business developer can provide an implementation of `DataPortal_Fetch()` to load the collection with name-value pairs from their database, or from some other data store (such as an XML file).

A data access helper

The code to load a list with name-value pairs is often very generic. Rather than forcing the business developer to write the same basic code over and over, we'll implement a helper function that they can use to do most name-value list data access. This means that the implementation of `DataPortal_Fetch()` in a list object will often be just one line of code that calls into the base class code we'll implement here. For instance:

```
Protected Overrides Sub DataPortal_Fetch(ByVal Criteria As Object)
  SimpleFetch("myDatabase", "myTable", "myNameColumn", " myValueColumn")
End Sub
```

For cases where this generic helper routine *can't* retrieve the data, the business developer will need to write their own data access code in `DataPortal_Fetch()`. This approach allows total customization of data access, if that's what's required, while allowing most list objects to contain virtually no data access code at all.

The generic helper function, `SimpleFetch()`, will retrieve a list of name-value data. It accepts the name of the database and the table from which the data will come as parameters. It also accepts the column names for the name and value columns. Given this information, it connects to the database, and runs a simple `SELECT` query to retrieve the two columns from the specified table.

Add the following code to the class within the *Data Access* region:

```
Protected Sub SimpleFetch( _
      ByVal DataBaseName As String, ByVal TableName As String, _
      ByVal NameColumn As String, ByVal ValueColumn As String)

  Dim cn As New SqlConnection(DB(DataBaseName))
  Dim cm As New SqlCommand

  cn.Open()
  Try
    With cm
      .Connection = cn
      .CommandText = _
        "SELECT " & NameColumn & "," & ValueColumn & " FROM " & TableName
      Dim dr As New Data.SafeDataReader(.ExecuteReader)
      Try
        While dr.Read()
          Add(CStr(dr.GetValue(0)), CStr(dr.GetValue(1)))
        End While

      Finally
        dr.Close()
      End Try

    End With

  Finally
    cn.Close()
  End Try

End Sub
```

This is pretty straightforward ADO.NET code. We use the database name to retrieve a connection string from the application's configuration file and open the connection:

```
Dim cn As New SqlConnection(DB(DataBaseName))
Dim cm As New SqlCommand

cn.Open()
```

Using this connection, we set up a `SqlCommand` object to retrieve the name-value columns from the specified table:

```
    .Connection = cn
    .CommandText = _
      "SELECT " & NameColumn & "," & ValueColumn & " FROM " & TableName
```

Notice that we are not using parameters in the SQL statement here. This is because the values we're providing are the *actual* names of columns and the table, not of data values, so there's no way to make them parameter driven.

The remainder of the code simply uses a `SafeDataReader` to retrieve the data and populate the list. By using `SafeDataReader`, we don't need to worry about the possibility that a null value might be in one of the retrieved columns – it will simply be treated as an empty value.

Also note that we aren't using the strongly typed `GetString()` method to retrieve the data. Rather, we're calling `GetValue()` and then using `CStr()` to convert the value to a `String`. The reason for this is that we can't be *sure* that the underlying database column type is a `String` – it could be numerical, or a date for instance. By using this technique, we ensure that we can read the value and convert it to a `String` representation regardless of the underlying data type of the database column.

Remember that if we need more sophisticated data access than is provided by `SimpleFetch()`, we'd just implement our own code rather than calling into the base class.

Conclusion

In this chapter, we created the business framework classes that enable data access. First, we updated our four base classes on which business objects will be built to include the idea of data access. Mostly, this revolves around the four `DataPortal_xxx()` methods:

- `DataPortal_Create()`
- `DataPortal_Fetch()`
- `DataPortal_Update()`
- `DataPortal_Delete()`

We then moved on to implement the client-side `DataPortal` that abstracts the use of remoting. The end result is that a configuration setting controls whether the actual data access code will run locally in the client process, or remotely on another machine. The client-side `DataPortal` calls into a server-side `DataPortal` object that contains code to create new business objects if needed, and to call the four `DataPortal_xxx()` methods.

We also created a second, transactional, server-side `DataPortal` that runs within Enterprise Services (COM+). While `Server.DataPortal` is faster, and can implement transactions using ADO.NET or stored procedures, the `ServicedDataPortal.DataPortal` runs within COM+, where we get the benefits of two-phase transactions. This is critical when updating two or more databases within a single transaction, but there is a performance penalty for its use.

Once the data access infrastructure was complete, we used it to create principal and identity objects that provide custom table-driven security. This security integrates into the .NET security framework, and also integrates into our business framework – including handling impersonation so that our server-side data access code runs in the same user context as the client-side code.

Finally, we wrapped up by creating a couple of utility classes. The `SafeDataReader` class automatically handles null values in data from a database, converting any null values to an appropriate 'empty' value. The `NameValueList` class is a base class that simplifies the creation of read-only name-value collection objects in our applications. We'll see how this is used in Chapter 7 as we create business classes for our example application.

This chapter completes the creation of the CSLA .NET framework. Through the remainder of the book, we'll be focusing on how to use the framework to create business objects and a variety of UIs for those objects including Windows Forms, Web Forms, and XML Web Services.

CHAPTER 6

6

Object-oriented application design

In Chapters 1 and 2, we discussed the concepts behind distributed, object-oriented systems, and the .NET technologies that make them possible to implement. Then, in Chapters 3 thru 5, we designed and implemented CSLA .NET, a framework upon which we can build distributed, object-oriented applications, avoiding the complexities of the .NET technologies as we create each business class or user interface.

In Chapters 6 and 7, we'll design and implement a set of sample business objects on which we can base an application to track projects and resources assigned to projects. In Chapter 8, we'll implement a Windows Forms UI, and in Chapter 9 we'll implement a Web Forms UI based on these objects. In Chapter 10, we'll implement some XML Web Services to provide an application interface to the business objects so that they can be used by other applications through the standard SOAP protocol.

This chapter will focus on the object-oriented application design process, using a sample scenario and application that we'll implement through the rest of the book. Our design process in this chapter will result in a design for our business objects, and for an underlying database.

Obviously, the challenge we face in designing and building a sample application in a book like this is that the application must be small enough to fit into the space available, and yet be complex enough to illustrate the key features we need to cover. To start with, let's list the key features that I want to focus on:

- Creation of a business object
- Implementation of business rules
- Transactional and non-transactional data access
- Parent-child relationships between objects

- Many-to-many relationships between objects
- Use of name-value lists
- Use of CSLA .NET security

In this chapter, we'll focus on the design of the application by using some example user scenarios, generally referred to as **use cases**. Based on those use cases, we'll develop a list of potential business objects and relationships. By refining this information, we'll develop a class design for the application. Also based on the scenarios, we'll design a relational database to store the data.

As we saw in Chapter 2, object-oriented design and relational design are not the same process, and we'll see in this case how they result in two different models. To resolve these models, our objects will include object-relational mapping (ORM) when we implement them in Chapter 7. This ORM code will reside in the `DataPortal_xxx()` methods of our business objects, and will translate the data between the relational and object-oriented models as each object is retrieved or updated.

Application requirements

There are many ways to gather application requirements, but in general there are three main areas of focus from which we can choose:

- Data analysis and data flow
- UI design and storyboarding
- Business concept and process analysis

The oldest of the three is the idea that we can design an application by understanding the data it requires, and how that data must flow through the system. While this approach can work, it is not ideal when trying to work with object-oriented concepts, because it focuses less on business ideas and more on raw data. It's often a very good analysis approach when building applications that follow a data-centric architecture.

> *The data-focused analysis approach often makes it hard to relate to users as well. Very few users understand database diagrams and database concepts, so there's a constant struggle as we translate the business language and concepts into and out of our relational, data-oriented language and concepts.*

The idea of basing application analysis around the UI came into vogue in the early- to mid-90s with the rise of RAD (rapid application development) tools such as Visual Basic, PowerBuilder, and Delphi. It was subsequently picked up by the web development world, though in that environment the term "storyboarding" was often used to describe the process. UI-focused analysis has the benefit that it is very accessible to the end user – users find it very easy to relate to the UI and how it will flow.

The drawback to this approach is that there is a tendency for business validation and processing to end up being written directly into the UI. Not that this *always* happens, but it's a very real problem – primarily because UI-focused analysis frequently revolves around a UI prototype, which includes more and more business logic as the process progresses, until we decide just to use the prototype as the base for our application since so much work has already been done.

> *Obviously, people can resist this trend and make UI-focused design work, but it takes a great deal of discipline. The reality is that a lot of great applications end up crippled because this technique was used.*

Another drawback to starting with the UI is that users often see the mocked-up UI in a demonstration, and assume that the application is virtually complete. They don't realize that the bulk of the work comes from the business and data access logic that must still be created and tested *behind* the UI. The result is that we are faced with tremendous and unrealistic time pressure to deliver on the application since, from the user's perspective, it is "virtually complete already".

The third option is to focus on business concepts and process flow. This is the middle road in many ways, since it requires an understanding of how the users will interact with the system, the processes that the system must support, and (by extension) the data that must flow through the system to make it all happen. The benefit of this approach is that it's very business focused, allowing the analyst and the end users all to talk the language of business, avoiding computer concepts and terminology. It also lends itself to the creation of object-oriented designs, since the entities and concepts developed during analysis typically turn into objects within the application.

The drawback to this approach is that it doesn't provide the user with the look and feel of the UI, or the graphical reinforcement of how the system will actually work from their perspective. Nor does it produce a clear database design, leaving the database analyst to do more work in order to design the database.

Personally, I use a blend of the business concept and UI approaches. I place the strongest emphasis on the business concept and process flow, while providing key portions of the UI via a prototype, so that the user can get the feel of the system. Since end users have such a hard time relating to database diagrams, I almost never use data-focused analysis techniques, instead leaving the database design process to flow from the other analysis techniques.

In this chapter, we'll make use of the business concept and process flow techniques. It's difficult to storyboard our application at this stage, because we'll be developing both Windows Forms and Web Forms user interfaces, along with a web service application interface. Our starting point, then, is to create a set of use case descriptions based on how the users (or other applications) will interact with our system.

Use cases

Let's create a set of imaginary use cases for our project tracking system. In a real application, these would be developed by interviewing key users and other interested parties. The use cases here are for illustration purposes.

> *This application is relatively simple. A real project tracking system would undoubtedly be more complex, but we need to have something small enough to implement within the context of this book. Remember that all we're doing here is illustrating how to use CSLA .NET to create business objects, child objects, and so forth.*

Though not mentioned specifically in the following use cases, we'll be designing this system to accommodate large numbers of users. In Chapter 8, for instance, our Windows Forms UI will use the features of CSLA .NET to run the application in a physical n-tier deployment with an application server. This physical architecture will provide for optimum scalability. In Chapter 9, our Web Forms UI will make use of CSLA .NET's ability to run the application's UI, business logic, and data access all on the web server. Again this provides the highest scaling and best performing configuration, because we can easily add more web servers as needed to support more users.

Project maintenance

Since this is a project tracking system, there's no surprise that the application must work with projects. Here are some use cases describing the users' expectations.

Add a project

A project manager can add projects to the system. Projects must track key information, including the project's name, description, start date, and end date. A project can have a unique project number, but this is not required; nor should the project manager have to deal with it. The project's name is the field by which projects are identified by users, so every project must have a name.

The start and end dates are optional. Many projects are added to the system so that we can keep a list of them even though they haven't started yet. Once a project has been started, it should have a start date, but no end date. When the project is complete, the project manager can enter an end date. We'll be using these dates to report on the average length of our projects, so obviously the end date can't be earlier than the start date.

Every project also has a list of the resources assigned to it (see *Assigning a resource*).

Edit a project

Project managers can edit any existing projects. The manager chooses from a list of projects, and can then edit that project. They need the ability to change the project's start and end dates, as well as its description. They also need to be able to change the resources assigned to the project (see *Assigning a resource*).

Remove a project

Project managers or administrators must be able to remove projects. We have no need to keep historical data about deleted projects, so they should be completely removed from the system. The user should just choose from a list of projects, confirm their choice, and the project should be removed.

Resource maintenance

At this point, we know that the system not only tracks projects, but also tracks the resources assigned to each project. For the purposes of our simple example, the only project resources we'll track are the people assigned to the projects. With further questioning of the users, we can develop a set of use cases revolving around the resources, without reference (yet) to the projects in which they may be involved.

Add a resource

We don't want to replicate the HR database, but we can't make use of the HR database because they won't give us access. We just want to be able to keep track of the people we can assign to our projects. All we care about is the person's name, and their employee ID. Obviously, each person must have an employee ID and a valid name.

Resources can be added by project managers or by supervisors. It would be really nice if we could assign a person to a project at the same time as the person is being added to our application (see *Assigning a resource*).

Edit a resource

Sometimes, a name is entered wrongly and needs to be fixed, so project managers and supervisors need to be able to change the name.

Remove a resource

When an employee is let go or moves to another division, we want to be able to remove them from our system. Project managers, supervisors, and administrators should be able to do this. Once they're gone, we don't need any historical information, so they should be totally removed.

Assigning a resource

As we were talking to the users to gather the previous use cases, they walked through the requirements for assigning resources to projects. Since this process is common across several other processes, we can centralize it into a use case that's referenced from the others.

The project managers and supervisors need to be able to assign a resource to a project. When we do this, we need to indicate the role that the resource is playing in the project. We have a list of the roles, but we might need to change the list in the future. We also want to know when the resource was assigned to the project.

Sometimes, a resource will switch from one role to another, so we need to be able to change the role at any time. Equally, a resource can be assigned to several projects at one time. (We often have people working part-time on several projects at once.)

Lastly, we need to be able to remove an assignment. This happens when an employee is let go or moves to another division (see *Remove a resource* above), but we often move people around from project to project. There's no need to keep track of who used to be on a project, as we only use this system for tracking current projects and the resources assigned to them right now.

External access

During conversations with users, we discovered that a number of them are highly technical, and are already skeptical of our ability to create all the UI options they desire. They indicated high interest in having programmatic access to the database, or to our business objects. In other words, we have some power users who are used to programming in Access and a bit of VB6, and they want to write their own reports, and maybe their own data entry routines.

> *This same scenario would play out if we wanted to provide access to our application to business partners, customers, vendors, or any external application that is outside of our immediate control.*

Obviously, there are serious issues with giving other people access to our database – especially read-write access. Unless we want to put *all* our business logic in stored procedures – meaning that we get to write all the logic in SQL – we can't safely provide this sort of access.

Likewise, there are issues with providing access to our objects. This is safer in some ways, because our objects implement the business logic and validation, but it is problematic from a maintenance perspective. If other people are writing code to interact directly with our objects, then we can't change our objects without breaking their code. Since they're outside of our control, we're basically forced to say that we'll never change our object model.

Of course, this is totally unrealistic, since we know that there will be future enhancements and requests for changes to the system, which will undoubtedly require changes to our objects. Fortunately, we have web services, which change the equation. If we treat our web services like just another interface (albeit a programmatic one) to our application, we can easily provide access to our application without allowing external programs to interact with our database or our business objects directly.

In Chapter 10, we'll revisit these ideas as we implement a set of web services so that external applications can safely interact with our application.

Object design

At this point, we've gathered the key requirements for our application via the use cases. Based on these use cases, we can create an object-oriented design. There are a variety of techniques used in object-oriented design (you may have heard of CRC cards, decomposition, and many others), and in this chapter we'll use a form of decomposition: identifying the 'nouns' in the use cases, and then narrowing down which of these are actual business objects.

Initial design

The first step in the process, then, is to assemble a list of the nouns in the use case write-ups. By using a bit of judgment, we can eliminate a few nouns that are obviously not objects, but we'll still end up with a good-sized list of potential business objects or entities:

Project manager	Project	Project number
Project name	Start date	End date
Administrator	List of projects	Employee
Resource	Employee name	Employee ID
Supervisor	List of assignments	Role
List of roles	Assignment	Date assigned
List of resources	List of assigned resources	

Using our understanding of the business domain (and probably through further discussion with business users and our fellow designers), we can narrow down the options. Some of these are not objects, but rather are data elements, or security roles. These include:

Project manager

Administrator

Supervisor

This implies that there's already an object to deal with a user's role, and indeed there is: it's the `BusinessPrincipal` *object in the CSLA .NET framework. These security roles should not be confused with the role a resource (person) plays on a project – they are two very different concepts.*

Pulling out these nouns, along with those that are likely to be just data fields (such as Project name and Employee ID), we come up with a smaller list of likely business objects:

Object	Description
Project	An object representing a project in the system
Resource	An object representing a resource (person) in the system
Employee	An object representing an employee in the company
List of projects	A list of the projects in the system
List of resources	A list of the resources in the system
List of assigned resources	A list of the resources assigned to a specific project
List of assignments	A list of the projects to which a resource is assigned
List of roles	A list of the roles a resource (person) might fill on a project
Role	A role that a resource (person) might fill on a project

At this point, we can start creating a basic class diagram in UML. In this diagram, we'll include our potential business objects, along with the data elements that we think belong to each. The diagram should also include relationships between the entities in the diagram. For the most part, these relationships can be inferred from the use case descriptions – for instance, we can infer that a *List of projects* will likely contain *Project* objects; and that a *Project* object will likely contain a *List of assigned resources*, which in turn will likely contain *Resource* objects.

Note that I use the word *likely* here, rather than *will*. We are still very much in a fluid design stage here, so nothing is yet certain. We have a list of potential objects, and we are inferring a list of potential relationships.

As we create the diagram, we'll assign some rather more formal names to our potential objects. The following list shows this:

Project	`Project`
Resource	`Resource`
Employee	`Employee`
List of projects	`ProjectList`
List of resources	`ResourceList`
List of assigned resources	`ProjectResources`
List of assignments	`ResourceAssignments`
List of roles	`RoleList`
Role	`Role`

And the resulting diagram might then appear something like this:

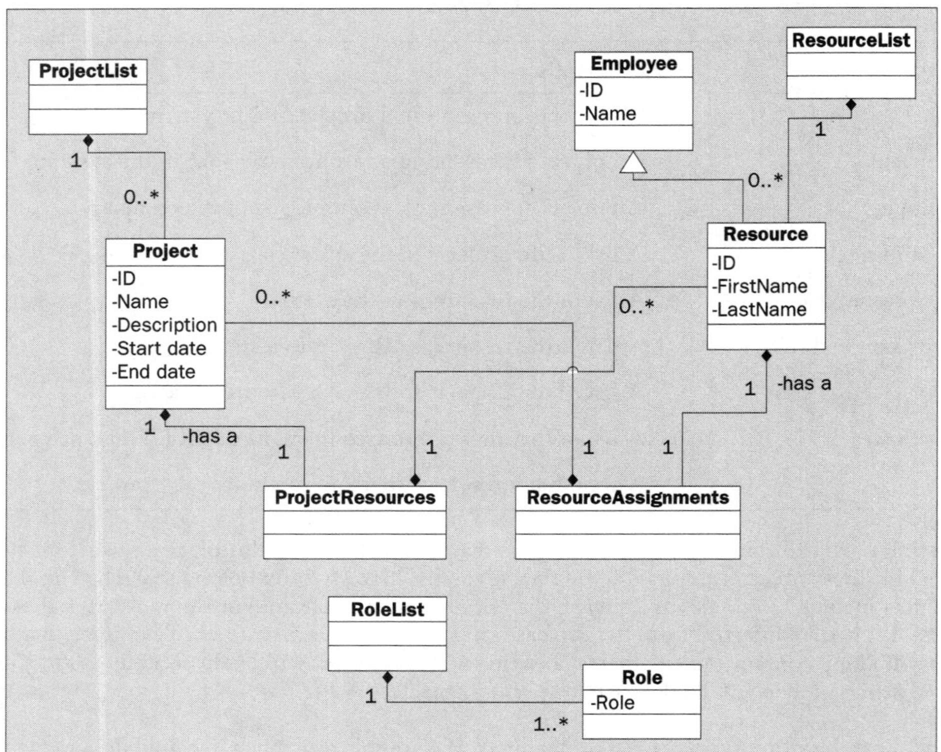

Looking at this diagram, there are some indicators that we have some more work to do. There are several issues that we should look for and address, including duplicate objects, trivial objects, objects that have overly complex relationships in the diagram, and places where we can optimize for performance.

Revising the design

The following list indicates some of the things we need to address:

- `Resource` *is-a* `Employee`, but `Resource` adds nothing to `Employee`, so the two can probably be merged into one class.
- The `RoleList` and `Role` classes aren't used by any other classes. Obviously, they are required by our use cases, but it isn't clear which class should use them in the diagram as it stands.
- The relationship between `Project`, `ProjectResources`, `Resource`, and `ResourceAssignments` is very complex. In fact, it is an infinite loop of containment, which is always a danger sign.
- The use cases for `ProjectList` and `ResourceList` indicate that they are primarily used for selection of objects, not to edit all the projects or resources in the system. Actually loading all the `Project` or `Resource` objects just so that the user can make a simple selection is expensive performance-wise, so this design should be reviewed.

Let's discuss this in a bit more detail.

Duplicate objects

First, we can identify duplicate objects – like `Resource` and `Employee` – that have basically the same data and relationships. Let's eliminate `Employee` in favor of `Resource`, since that's the term most used in our use case descriptions (and thus, presumably, most used by our end users).

In the early stages of *any* object design process there will be duplicate objects, or potential objects that end up being mere data fields in other objects. Usually, a great deal of debate will ensue during the design phase as all the people involved in the design process thrash out which objects are real, which are duplicates, and which should be just data fields. This is healthy and important, though obviously some judgment must be exercised to avoid *analysis paralysis*, where the design entirely stalls due to the debate.

Trivial objects

The `Role` object may not be required either. Fundamentally, a `Role` is just a string value, which means that we can use the `NameValueList` class from the CSLA .NET framework to create a `RoleList` object that maintains a list of the values.

> *This is based on the use cases we assembled earlier. If we intuitively feel that this is overly simplistic or unrealistic, then we should revisit the use cases and our users to make sure that we didn't miss something. For the purposes of this book, we'll assume that the use cases are accurate, and that the* `Role` *field really is a simple* `String` *value.*

Like the process of removing duplicates, the process of finding and removing trivial objects is as much an art as it is a science. It can be the cause of plenty of healthy debate!

Overly complex relationships

While it's certainly true that large and complex applications often have complex relationships between classes and objects, those complex relationships should always be carefully reviewed.

As a general rule, if we have relationship lines crossing each other or wrapping around each other in our UML diagram, we should review those relationships to see if they need to be so difficult. Sometimes, it's just the way things have to be, but often it's a sign that our design needs some work. Though relying on the aesthetics of our diagram may sound a bit odd, it is a good rule of thumb.

In our case, we have a pretty complex relationship between `Project`, `ProjectResources`, `Resource`, and `ResourceAssignments`. What we have, in fact, is a circular containment relationship, where all these objects contain the other objects in an endless chain. In situation like this, we should always be looking for relationships that should be *using*, instead of *containment*. What we'll often find is that we're missing a class in our diagram – one that doesn't necessarily flow directly from the use cases, but is required to make the object model workable.

The specific problem we're trying to deal with is that when we load an object from the database, it will typically also load any child objects it contains – containment relationships will be followed to do the data loading. If we have an endless loop of containment relationships, that poses a rather obvious problem! We need some way to short-circuit the process, and the best way to do this is to introduce a *using* relationship into the mix. Typically, we *won't* follow a using relationship as we load objects.

In our case, what's missing is a class that actually represents the assignment of a resource to a project. There is data described in the use cases that we don't have in our object model: the role of a resource on a particular project, or the date that the resource was assigned to a project. We can't keep these data fields in the `Project`, because a `Project` will have many resources filling many different roles at different times. Similarly, we can't keep these data fields in the `Resource`, because a `Resource` may be assigned to many projects at different times and in different roles.

Adding an assignment class

What we're discovering here is the need for another class to store this data: `Assignment`. If we redraw our UML to include this class, things are a bit different:

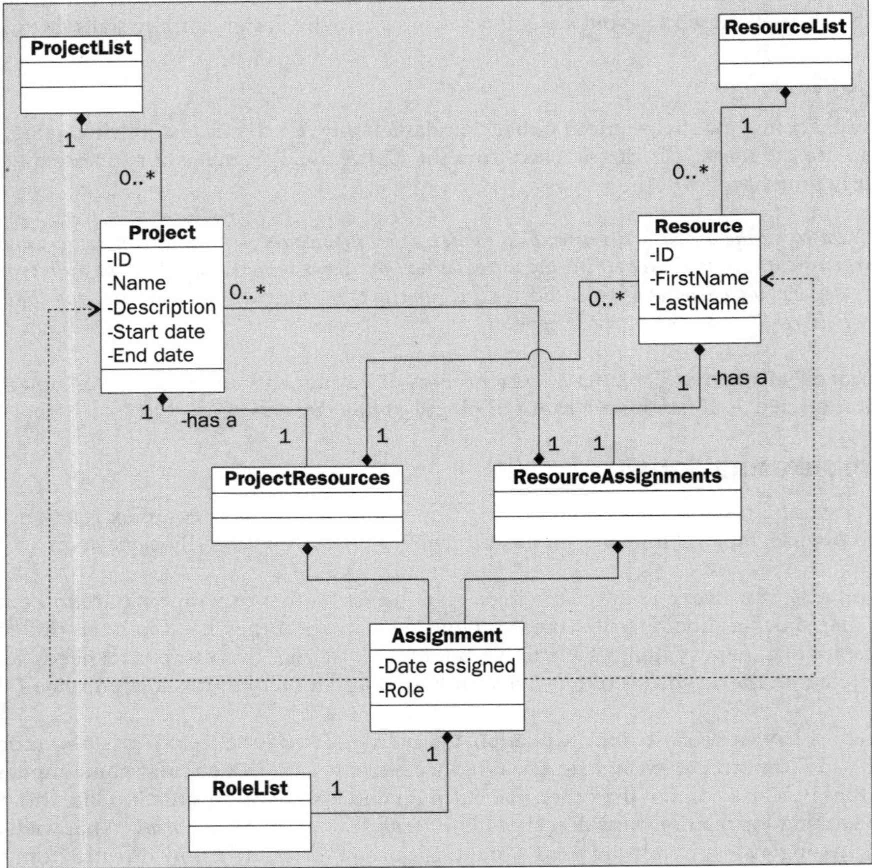

With this change, we've replaced the containment relationships with using relationships, where the new `Assignment` class *uses* both the `Project` and `Resource` classes. The `Assignment` class now also contains our missing data fields: the role and date when the resource was assigned to a project.

However, we're still not done. The `Assignment` class itself just became overly complex, because it's used within two different contexts: from our list of resources assigned to a project, and from the list of projects to which a resource is assigned. This is typically problematic. Having a single object as a child of two different collections makes for very complicated implementation and testing, and should be avoided where possible.

Looking at the diagram, we are also unable to tell when the `Assignment` class is using `Project`, and when it is using `Resource`. Based on our knowledge of the use cases and our overall design, we know that when a `Project` contains a list of `Assignment` objects, the `Assignment` will use a `Resource` to get data about that resource. Likewise, when a `Resource` contains a list of `Assignment` objects, the `Assignment` will use a `Project` to get at project data. But that's not clear from the diagram, and that's not good.

There are two possible solutions. We can combine the list objects into a single list of assignments, or we can have two different `Assignment` objects. To resolve this, we need to think about what we want to accomplish when approaching the object from `Project`, and from a `Resource`.

Assignment from a project perspective

When we list the resources assigned to a project, we'll want to include some useful information, some of which will come from the `Resource` itself. However, it's highly inefficient to load an entire `Resource` object just to get at its `ID` and `Name` properties. It might seem as though the answer to this is to include these fields as part of the other object – in other words, we could include the `Resource`'s `ID` and `Name` fields in `Assignment` – but the problem with that approach is that the business logic associated with those fields exists in the object that owns them.

The logic governing the `ID` and `Name` data for a resource is in the `Resource` class. If we allow users to edit and manipulate those fields in the `Assignment` object, we'd need to replicate that business logic – and that's unacceptable.

An alternative is to 'borrow' the data values, making them read-only fields on other objects. In our `Assignment` object, we can borrow the `Resource`'s `ID` and `Name` fields, exposing them as read-only properties. We don't need to replicate the business logic governing the editing and manipulation of these fields, because we don't allow the fields to be altered. If the user wants to alter or edit the fields, they can do so through the `Resource` object that owns those fields.

> *The exception here is field level security. If our application uses role-based security to restrict who can view certain data elements, we'll have to replicate that business logic anywhere the data fields are made publicly available. If we borrow a data field for display purposes, we'll also have to replicate the business logic that checks to see if the field should be visible. In our particular example, we don't have such field level security requirements, so that's not an issue here.*

Borrowing fields is important for performance, and in most applications it doesn't require replication of business logic across classes. While not ideal from an object-oriented design perspective, it is a compromise that is often necessary to make our applications work in the real world. Using it here would mean that the `Assignment` object needs to look something like this:

Assignment
-Date assigned -Role
+ResourceID (read-only)() +ResourceName (read-only)()

UML doesn't have any provision for indicating that a property method should be read-only, so I'm including it here as a notation.

When an `Assignment` is used from a `Project` perspective, we would borrow the `Resource`'s `ID` and `Name` values, so that it's quickly and easily apparent which `Resource` has been assigned to the `Project`.

Assignment from a resource perspective

Similarly, when we list the projects to which a `Resource` is assigned, we'll want to list some information about the project. This means that the `Assignment` object would need to look something like this:

Assignment
-Date assigned -Role
+ProjectID (read-only)() +ProjectName (read-only)()

Again, we're borrowing fields from another object – a `Project`, in this case – for display purposes within our `Assignment` object.

A combined assignment class

At this stage, we could merge these two `Assignment` classes (from the `Project` and `Resource` perspectives) into a single class:

Assignment
-Date assigned -Role
+ProjectID (read-only)() +ProjectName (read-only)() +ResourceID (read-only)() +ResourceName (read-only)()

The drawback to this approach, however, is that we'd have to populate the fields in this object even when they weren't needed. For instance, when accessing this object from a project, we'd still populate the `ProjectID` and `ProjectName` property values – a total waste, since we already have a `Project` object!

If it doesn't make sense to consolidate these two types of `Assignment`, then we *can't* consolidate the list objects. Instead, we need to create two different types of `Assignment` object. Both represent an assignment of some kind, but each will have some different information.

This is a classic inheritance scenario, since both of our objects will have some data and behaviors in common. The end result is this:

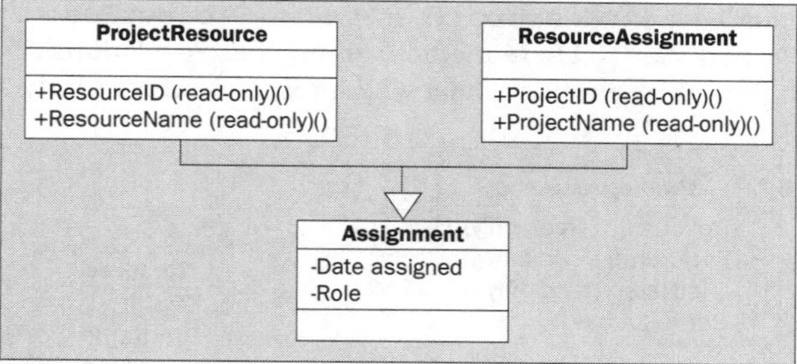

Our two new classes each inherit from `Assignment`, so they contain the core data that makes up an assignment. However, each of them provides read-only data as appropriate to support our application's requirements. The result of this design work is the following:

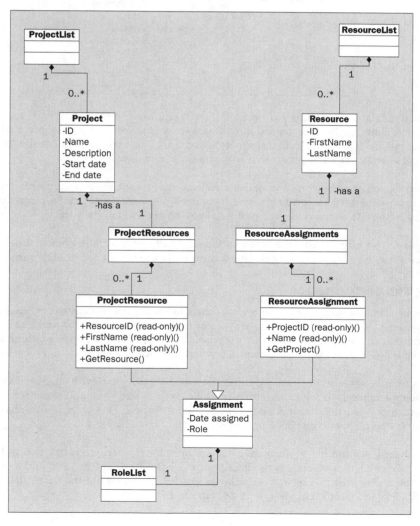

Notice that we've also added a `GetResource()` method to `ProjectResource`, and a `GetProject()` method to `ResourceAssignment`. These methods imply a *using* relationship between these classes and the classes from which they are borrowing data, which resolves things nicely:

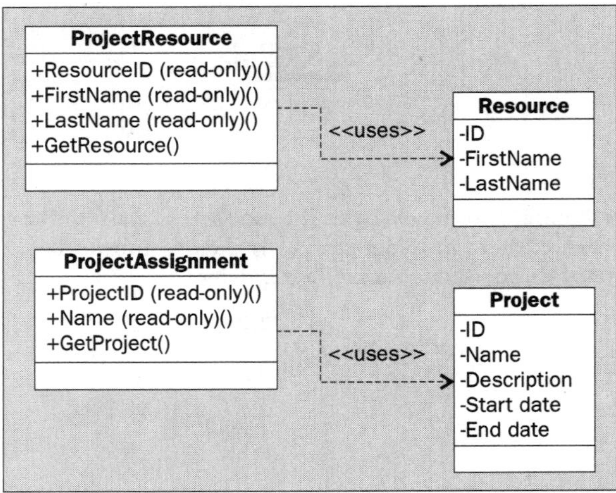

Our `Project` object now contains a collection of `ProjectResource` objects, each of which is useful by itself since it contains the date the assignment was made, the role of the resource, and the resource's `ID` and `Name` values. If we need more information about the resource, we can use the `GetResource()` method to get a real `Resource` object that will contain all the details.

Likewise, our `Resource` object now contains a collection of `ResourceAssignment` objects. Each of these objects contains useful information, and if we need more details about the project itself, we can use the `GetProject()` method to get a real `Project` object with all the data.

We no longer have a circular containment relationship, and our new child objects should have good performance since they are borrowing the most commonly used fields for display purposes.

Optimizing for performance

As part of our object design, we need to review things to ensure that we haven't created a model that will lead to poor performance. This isn't really a single step in the process, as much as something that should be done on a continual basis during the whole process. However, once we think the model is complete, we should always pause to review it for performance issues.

We've already done some performance optimization as the model has evolved. Specifically, we used a field-borrowing technique to take common display fields from `Project` and `Resource` and put them into the `ResourceAssignment` and `ProjectResource` classes. This saves us from having to load entire business objects just to display a couple of common data elements.

We do, however, have another performance issue in our model. Our `ProjectList` and `ResourceList` collection objects, as modeled, retrieve collections of `Project` and `Resource` business objects so that some of their data can be displayed in a list. Based on our use cases, the user then selects one of the objects and chooses to view, edit, or remove that object.

From a purely object-oriented perspective, it's attractive to think that we actually could just load a collection of `Project` objects and allow the user to pick the one they want to edit. However, this could be very expensive, because it means loading all the data for *every* `Project` object, including each project's list of assigned resources, and so forth. As the user adds, edits, and removes `Project` objects, we'd potentially have to maintain our collection in memory too.

Practical performance issues mean that we're better off creating a read-only collection that contains only the information needed to create the user interface. (This is one of the primary reasons why CSLA .NET includes the `ReadOnlyCollectionBase` class, which makes it very easy to create such objects.) We can create `ProjectList` and `ResourceList` collection objects that contain only the data to be displayed, in read-only format. Essentially, this is a variation on the field-borrowing concept: we're creating collection objects that consist entirely of borrowed data. None of this data is editable, and so we typically won't have to replicate any business logic as part of this process.

> *As before, the exception is where we have business rules governing who can see specific data fields. In that case, we'll have to replace that field level security business logic into our read-only collection objects.*

We'll need two read-only collection objects, each with its own structure for the data:

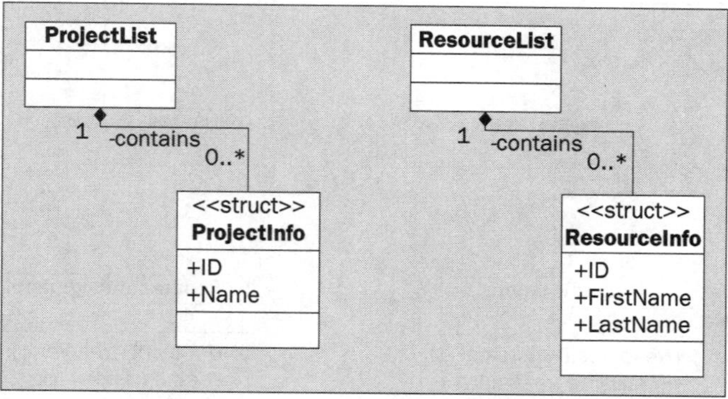

The `ProjectInfo` structure contains fields borrowed from the `Project` class, while `ResourceInfo` contains fields borrowed from `Resource`.

Reviewing the design

The final step in the object design process is to compare our new class diagram with our use case descriptions, to ensure that everything described in each use case can be accomplished through the use of these objects. In doing so, we'll help to ensure that our object model covers all the user requirements. Our complete object model looks like this:

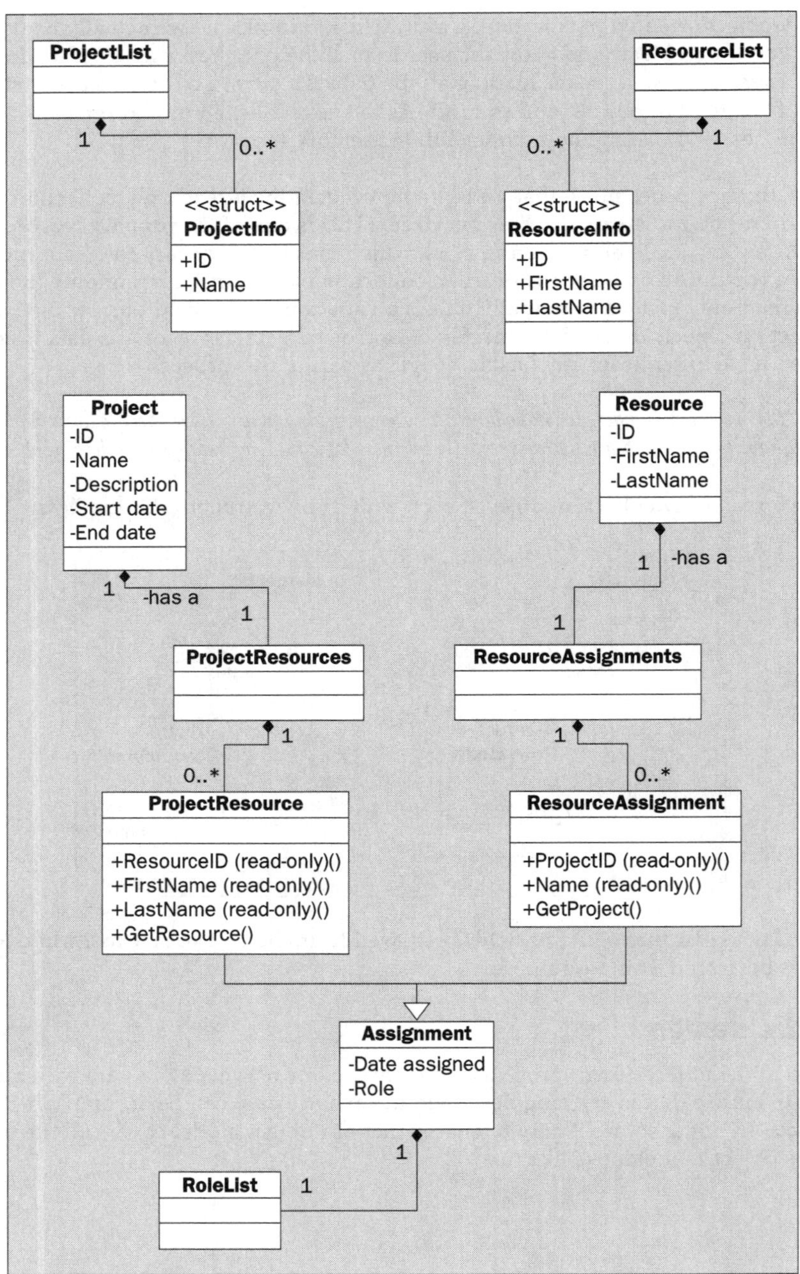

If we review our use cases, we should find that we'll be able to use our objects to accomplish all of the tasks and processes described.

- Users can get a list of projects
- Users can add a project
- Users can edit a project
- Users can remove a project
- Users can get a list of resources
- Users can add a resource
- Users can edit a resource
- Users can remove a resource
- Users can assign a resource to a project (or vice versa)
- When a resource is assigned to a project, users can specify the role the resource will play on the project

At this point, we can consider our object model to be complete.

Using CSLA .NET

The class diagrams that we've created so far have focused entirely on the business domain – which is a good thing. Ideally, we should always start by focusing on business issues, deferring much of the technical design to a later stage in the process. Users typically don't understand (or care about) the technical issues behind the scenes, such as how we're going to implement the Cancel buttons, or how we're going to retrieve data from the database.

Of course, *we* care about these issues, but they can be dealt with after the basic object modeling is complete, so that we have a good understanding of the business issues, and confidence that our model can meet the requirements laid out in the use cases.

In our case, we also have the significant advantage of having designed and built a business framework. What this means for us is that we don't need to spend time figuring out how to design or implement the features we've included in the framework. By relying on CSLA .NET, we gain the following:

Feature	Description
Smart data	Business data is encapsulated in objects along with its associated business logic, so we are never working with raw, unprotected data, and all our business logic is centralized for easy maintenance.
Easy object creation	We use standard .NET object-oriented programming techniques to create business objects.
Flexible physical configuration	Data access runs locally or on an application server, without changing business code.
Object persistence	Clearly defined methods contain all data access code.

Table continued on following page

Feature	Description
Optimized data access	Objects only persist themselves if their data has been changed.
	It's easy to select between high-performance manual transactions, or two-phase distributed transactions for multi-database updates.
	High-performance binary data transfer links between client and server.
Optional n-level undo capabilities	Support for complex Windows Forms interfaces is easy, while also supporting high-performance web interfaces.
Business rule tracking	Reduces the code required to implement business rules.
Simple UI creation	With full support for both Windows Forms and Web Forms data binding, minimal code is required to create sophisticated user interfaces (see Chapters 8 and 9).
Web service support	We can readily create a web service interface to our application, so that other applications can directly tap into both our data and our business logic with minimal effort on our part (see Chapter 10).
Role-based security	Makes it easy to select between Windows' integrated security and CSLA .NET's table-based security.
	It's also easy to customize CSLA .NET's table-based security to use pre-existing security databases.
	Full compliance with standard .NET security objects.

To use CSLA .NET, we merely need to determine which base classes to inherit from as we create each of our business classes. For example, some of our business objects will be editable objects that can be loaded directly by the user. These need to inherit from `BusinessBase`:

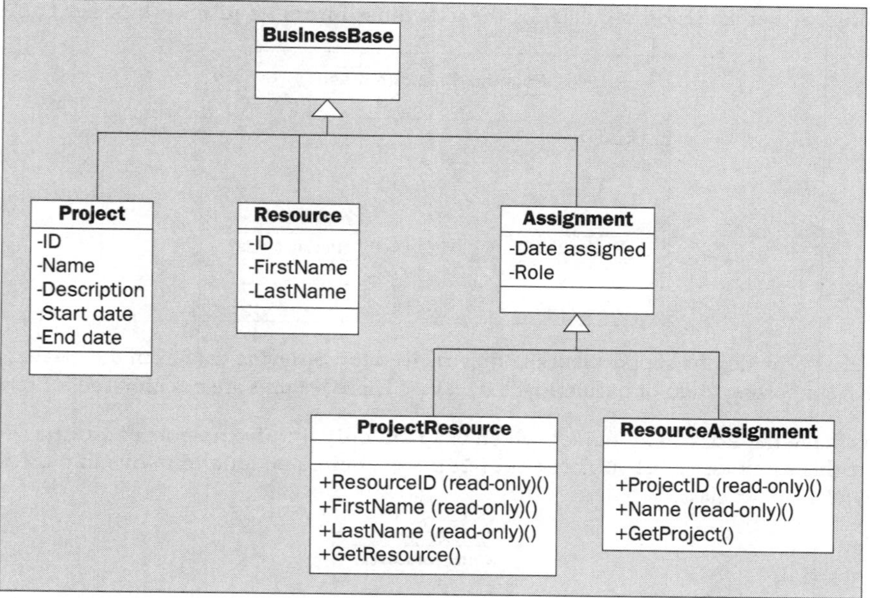

By subclassing `BusinessBase`, all of these objects gain the full set of business object capabilities that we implemented in Chapters 4 and 5.

We also have some objects that are *collections* of business objects, so they should inherit from `BusinessCollectionBase`:

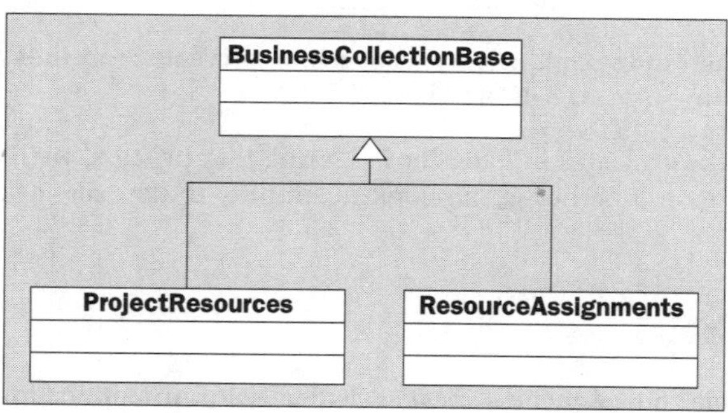

`BusinessCollectionBase` supports the undo capabilities that we implemented for `BusinessBase` – the two classes work hand-in-hand to provide this functionality.

The two objects that list read-only data for the user inherit from `ReadOnlyCollectionBase`:

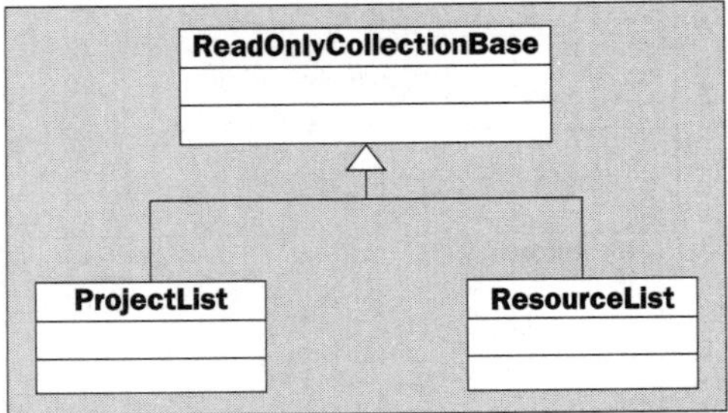

This base class provides the support that our objects need for retrieving data from the database *without* the overhead of supporting undo or business rule tracking. Those features are not required for read-only objects.

Finally, we have the `RoleList` object, which is a read-only list of simple `String` data. While we *could* implement this using `ReadOnlyCollectionBase`, we built a better alternative into the framework – the `NameValueList` class:

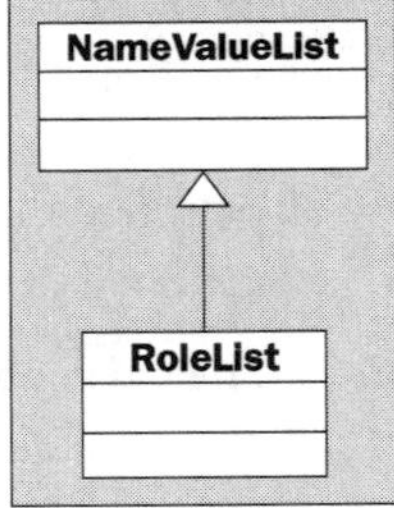

This base class is designed to make it as easy as possible to create read-only lists of text values, so it's ideal for use when building our `RoleList` class.

We'll implement all of these classes in Chapter 7. During that process, we'll see how to use the CSLA .NET framework that we built earlier in the book to simplify the process of creating business objects.

Database design

It's a rare thing to be able to design a database specifically for an application. More often than not, the databases already exist, and we must deal with their existing design. At best, we might be able to add some new tables or columns.

This is one reason why object-relational mapping is a key concept for object-oriented development. We have developed an object model that matches the business requirements without giving any consideration to the database design. It's up to us to create code that translates the data from our databases into our objects, and vice versa. We'll do that in Chapter 7 as we implement our business objects.

In *this* chapter, we'll create a database for use by our project tracking application. One thing to note is that even though we're creating the database specifically for this application, our data model will not match the object model exactly. A good relational model and a good object model are almost never the same thing.

Speaking of good relational models, I strongly recommend that database design be done by a professional DBA, not by software developers. While many of us are reasonably competent at database design, there are many optimizations and design choices that are better made by a DBA. The database design shown here is that of a software developer, and I am sure a DBA would see numerous ways to improve or tweak the result to work better in a production setting.

We'll create this database in SQL Server 2000, along with some stored procedures that we can use to interact with the database.

If you're using an RDBMS other than SQL Server 2000, you should translate the table creation and stored procedures to fit with your environment.

As in Chapter 5, when we created the `Security` database, we'll make use of the Server Explorer in Visual Studio .NET to create our database, tables, and stored procedures. We'll need to use SQL Server's Enterprise Manager to make some security changes once the database has been created. If you don't have access to these tools, the code download for this book also includes SQL scripts that you can run to create the database in SQL Server or MSDE.

Creating the database

To create the database, open the Server Explorer in VS.NET and navigate to the SQL Server where the database is to be created. Right-click on the SQL Server node and choose New Database. When prompted for the database name, enter `PTracker`, and provide appropriate security information. The result is a new, empty database on the server:

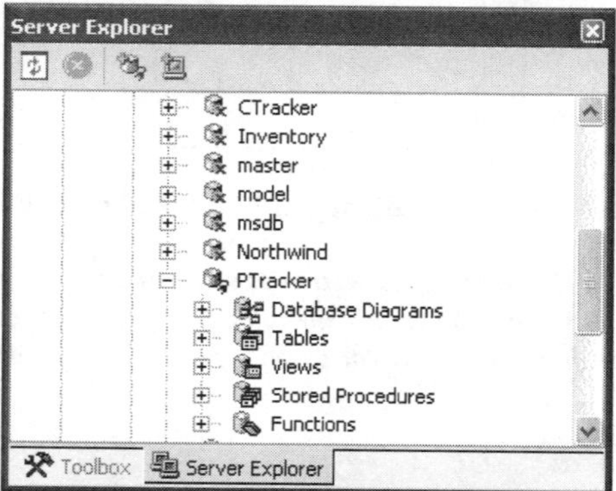

Tables

Table creation can also be done within the Server Explorer: just right-click on the Tables node under the database, and choose New Table. This will bring up a table designer in VS.NET where we can define the columns for the new table.

Once the columns, keys, and indexes have been set up, we need to save the changes by closing the designer or clicking the Save button in the toolbar. At this point, we'll be prompted to provide a name for the table, and it will be added to the database. Follow this process to add each of the following four tables to the database.

Roles

The `Roles` table will store the list of possible roles a resource can fill when assigned to a project – it simply contains an ID value and the name of the role. The following diagram shows the VS.NET designer with these columns added, and the ID column configured as the primary key:

dbo.Table1 : Ta...roth.PTracker)*

Column Name	Data Type	Length	Allow Nulls
ID	int	4	
Name	varchar	50	

Notice that neither column allows null values. With this data, we don't have any need to differentiate between an empty value and one that was never entered, so null values would make no sense.

Though a full-blown application would include maintenance screens for the list of roles, we won't create those screens, or any of the additional plumbing that would be necessary. Instead, we'll simply add some sample roles to the table using VS.NET.

Double-click on the Roles node in the Server Explorer window to bring up a designer in VS.NET that allows us to edit the contents of the table. Add some sample roles, such as those shown in the following figure:

dbo.Roles : Tab...eroth.PTracker)

ID	Name
1	Project Manager
2	System Architect
3	Application Architec
4	Developer
5	QA
6	Technical writer

This is the data that will be used to populate our read-only `RoleList` business object.

> *Remember that these roles are different from the security roles we added to our* `Security` *database in Chapter 5. The roles we're setting up here are the roles that a* `Resource` *can hold when assigned to a* `Project`*, and have nothing to do with the security roles of users that are using our application.*

Projects

The `Projects` table will contain the data for each project in the system. The columns for this table are shown in the following diagram:

dbo.Table1 : Ta...roth.PTracker)*

Column Name	Data Type	Length	Allow Nulls
ID	uniqueidentifier	16	
Name	varchar	50	
Started	datetime	8	✓
Ended	datetime	8	✓
Description	text	16	

The `ID` column is set up as the primary key, and it is of type `uniqueidentifier`, which is a GUID value.

There are many ways to create primary key columns in tables, including the use of auto-incrementing numeric values, or user-assigned values. However, the use of a `uniqueidentifier` is particularly powerful when working with object-oriented designs. Other techniques don't assign the identifier until the data is added to the database, or they allow the user to provide the value, which means that we can't tell if it collides with an existing key value until the data is added to the database. With a `uniqueidentifier`, however, we can assign the primary key value to an object as the object is created – we don't have to wait until it is updated into the database to get or confirm the value. If we don't assign it ahead of time, the database will supply the value.

What we get is the best of both worlds. If we want to assign the value in our object, we can do that and the database will honor our key value. If we *don't* assign the value in our object, the database will assign a key value as the row is added to the table.

Notice that the two `datetime` fields allow null values. We are intentionally 'misusing' the null value here to indicate an empty value for a date. No other fields allow null values, since they have empty value representations, and we don't care to differentiate between an empty value and one that was never entered by the user.

The `Description` column is of type `text`, so that it can hold a blob of text data. We are using this to provide the user with the ability to enter a lengthy description of the project, if so desired. Even though the `Length` shows as 16, this is just the length of the internal data structure – our data itself can be thousands of characters long.

Resources

The `Resources` table will hold the data for the various resources that can be assigned to a project. The columns for this table are shown in the following figure:

dbo.Table1 : Ta...roth.PTracker)*

Column Name	Data Type	Length	Allow Nulls
ID	varchar	10	
LastName	varchar	50	
FirstName	varchar	50	

Once again, the `ID` column is the primary key – it is a `varchar` that will hold a user-entered value. Though I prefer to use `uniqueidentifier` primary key values, this is not always possible. By giving this table a user-assigned primary key, we can explore how to support this concept within our business objects.

> *Many, if not most, pre-existing databases will not have a* `uniqueidentifier` *as a primary key. The* `uniqueidentifier` *concept is only a few years old, and most databases predate its introduction. Moreover, different DBAs have different preferences as to what type of primary key is optimal, and we may not have a say in the matter (depending on our DBA's viewpoints, and how reasonable they are).*

None of the fields allows null values – we don't need to differentiate between empty values and those that were never entered.

Assignments

Finally, we can create the `Assignments` table. There is a many-to-many relationship between projects and resources – a project can have a number of resources assigned to it, and a resource can be assigned to a number of projects.

The way this is represented relationally is to create a **link table** that contains the primary keys of both tables. In our case, it will also include information about the relationship, including the date of the assignment, and the role that the resource plays in the project:

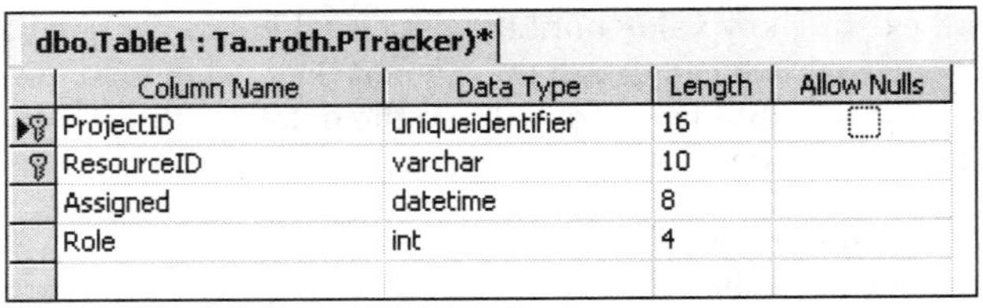

dbo.Table1 : Ta...roth.PTracker)*

	Column Name	Data Type	Length	Allow Nulls
🔑	ProjectID	uniqueidentifier	16	☐
🔑	ResourceID	varchar	10	
	Assigned	datetime	8	
	Role	int	4	

The first two columns here are the primary keys from the `Projects` and `Resources` tables, and combined they make up the primary key in our link table.

Though the `Assigned` column is a `datetime` type, we're not allowing null values. This is because this value can't be empty – a valid date is always required.

The `Role` column is also a foreign key, linking back to the `Roles` table.

The data in this table will be used to populate the `ProjectResource` and `ResourceAssignment` objects, both of which inherit from the `Assignment` class that manages the data from this table.

This really drives home the fact that a relational model is not the same as an object-oriented model. The many-to-many relational design doesn't match up to the object model that represents much of the same data. The objects are designed around behaviors and usage patterns, while the data model is designed around relational theory and the avoidance of redundant data.

Database diagram

The Server Explorer in VS.NET supports the creation of database diagrams, which are stored in SQL Server. These diagrams not only illustrate the relationships between our tables, but also tell SQL Server how to enforce and work with those relationships.

Under our database in the Server Explorer, there is a node for Database Diagrams. Right-click on this entry and choose New Diagram. VS.NET will prompt for the tables to be included in the diagram. Highlight all of them, and click Add and Close:

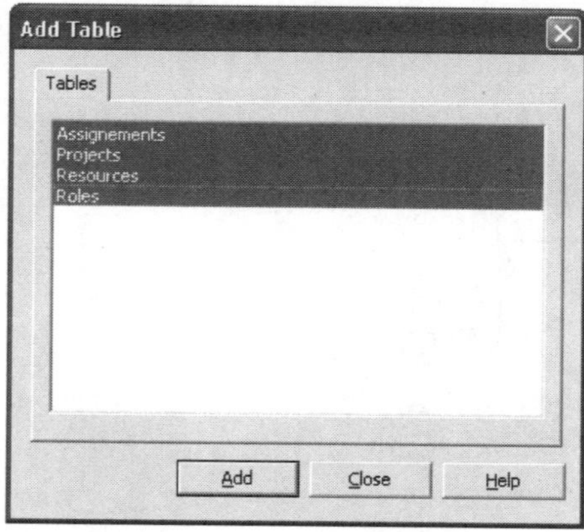

We are then presented with a designer window in which our tables are shown as a diagram. We can drag-and-drop columns from our primary tables to other tables in order to indicate relationships. For example, drag-and-drop the `ID` field from `Projects` to the `ProjectID` field in the `Assignments` table. This will bring up a dialog where we can specify the nature of this relationship:

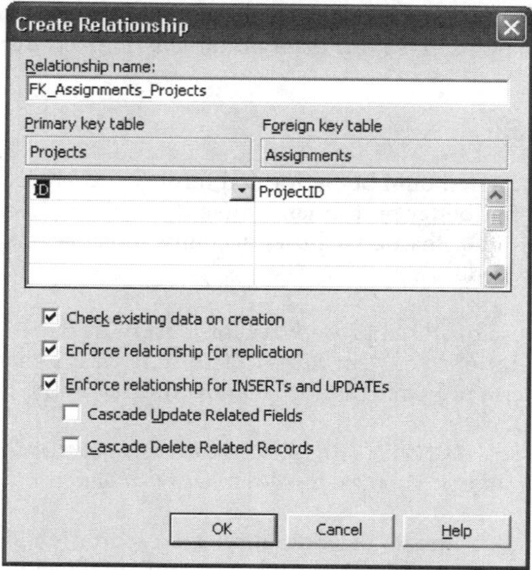

Click OK to create the relationship.

> *Lengthy debates can take place on the subject of whether to have the database automatically cascade updates and deletes. By default, these boxes are unchecked, and I personally like to handle the deletion process manually, in my stored procedures. You may opt to check these boxes, in which case you'll need to alter the stored procedures we'll create later in the chapter.*

Do the same to link the `Resources` table to `Assignments`. We can also link the `Roles` table's `ID` column to the `Role` column in `Assignments`, allowing the database to ensure that only valid roles can be added to the table.

The resulting diagram should appear similar to the following:

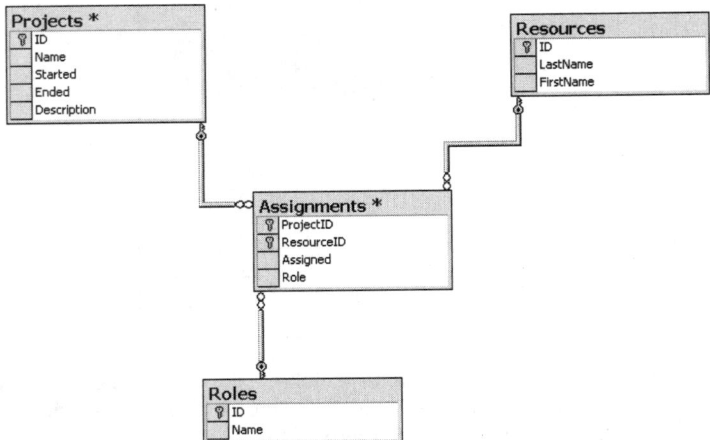

Save the diagram to the database, naming it `PTrackerRelationships`. VS.NET will then ask whether we are sure that we want to update our tables. Remember that these relationships are reflected as formal constraints within the database itself, so this diagram directly impacts our database design.

Stored procedures

Where possible, database access should be performed through stored procedures. As we've discussed before, stored procedures offer better performance than dynamic SQL statements, and powerful security control over the database. Rather than giving user accounts direct access to tables, we can provide access only to the stored procedures.

Our application will make use of stored procedures for most of its database interaction; the exception is when we are retrieving the list of roles. Our `NameValueList` class dynamically generates a `SELECT` statement based on the criteria provided, and we'll allow this read-only access to the `Roles` table.

> *The `NameValueList` base class could be updated to include an overloaded `SimpleFetch()` method that invokes a stored procedure, but we won't make that optimization here.*

In our table design, we opted to handle deletion of related records (child records) manually. This means that we'll need to include code to handle these deletions in the following stored procedures:

- `deleteProject`
- `deleteResource`

We can use the Server Explorer to add the stored procedures to the database by right-clicking on the **Stored Procedures** node under our database, and choosing **New Stored Procedure**. This will bring up a designer window where we can write the stored procedure code. When we close the designer, the stored procedure will be added to the database.

getProjects

The `getProjects` procedure will return the project data to populate the `ProjectList` object:

```
CREATE PROCEDURE getProjects
AS
  SELECT ID, Name
  FROM Projects

  RETURN
```

It simply returns basic data about all of the projects in the system. Our use cases didn't specify details about the order in which the projects should be listed in a project list, so we haven't included an `ORDER BY` clause here. We may have to do so during the testing process, as users typically add such requirements during that phase.

getProject

The `getProject` procedure retrieves the information for a single project. This is a relatively complex proposition, since we need to retrieve not only the core project data, but also the list of resources assigned to the project.

This *could* be done by making two stored procedures and calling both of them to populate the business objects, but we can reduce this to a single database call by putting both `SELECT` statements in a single stored procedure. The stored procedure will then return two result sets, which we can read within our VB.NET code:

```
CREATE PROCEDURE getProject
  (
    @ID uniqueidentifier
  )
AS
  SELECT id,name,started,ended,description
  FROM Projects
  WHERE ID=@ID

  SELECT resourceid,lastname,firstname,assigned,role
  FROM Resources, Assignments
  WHERE ProjectID='" & Criteria.ID.ToString & "' AND ResourceID=ID

  RETURN
```

Notice how the second `SELECT` statement merges data from both the `Assignments` table and the `Resources` table. Remember that our `ProjectResource` object will expose some resource data as read-only properties, so we need to return that data here.

To some degree, we're putting object-relational mapping (ORM) logic in our stored procedures by designing them to make it easy for our VB.NET data access code to populate the objects. This isn't essential – we could write more complex code in VB.NET – but it *is* a good idea, when you can do it.

> *In many cases, we must build applications where we don't have the option of altering the structure of the database or its stored procedures. When that happens, all of the ORM logic must be written within our business objects. The end result is the same; it's merely a matter of where the ORM logic resides.*

addProject

The addProject procedure is called to add a record to the Projects table:

```
CREATE PROCEDURE addProject
  (
    @ID uniqueidentifier,
    @Name varchar(50),
    @Started datetime,
    @Ended datetime,
    @Description text
  )
AS
  INSERT INTO Projects
  (ID,Name,Started,Ended,Description)
  VALUES
  (@ID,@Name,@Started,@Ended,@Description)

  RETURN
```

Note that this only adds the record to the Projects table; a separate stored procedure adds records to the Assignments table.

updateProject

Not only do we need to add records to the Projects table, but also we need to allow them to be changed. The updateProject procedure provides this capability:

```
CREATE PROCEDURE updateProject
  (
    @ID uniqueidentifier,
    @Name varchar(50),
    @Started datetime,
    @Ended datetime,
    @Description text
  )
AS
  UPDATE Projects
  SET
    Name=@Name,
    Started=@Started,
    Ended=@Ended,
    Description=@Description
  WHERE ID=@ID

  RETURN
```

Again, this procedure only updates the record in the Projects table; the related records in the Assignments table are updated separately.

deleteProject

The deleteProject procedure deletes the appropriate record from the Projects table, and also removes any related records in the Assignments table. (This requirement comes as a result of our choice not to have the database automatically cascade deletes to related tables.)

```
CREATE PROCEDURE deleteProject
  (
    @ID uniqueidentifier
  )
AS
  DELETE Assignments
  WHERE ProjectID=@ID

  DELETE Projects
  WHERE ID=@ID

  RETURN
```

Though this procedure updates multiple tables, we are *not* including transactional code here. While we *could* manage the transaction at this level, we gain flexibility by leaving it to our VB.NET code.

Within our CSLA .NET framework, we have the option of running our code within a COM+ transaction, or using ADO.NET to manage the transaction. If we opt to use Enterprise Services transactions, we don't want transactional statements in the stored procedures, since the work will be handled by COM+. If we opt instead to handle the transactions manually, we can choose to put the transactional statements here in the stored procedure, or use an ADO.NET `Transaction` object within our VB.NET code.

addAssignment

When we add or edit a project or a resource, we may also add or change the associated data in the `Assignments` table. The `addAssignment` procedure allows us to add a new record:

```
CREATE PROCEDURE addAssignment
  (
    @ProjectID uniqueidentifier,
    @ResourceID varchar(10),
    @Assigned datetime,
    @Role int
  )
AS
  INSERT INTO Assignments
  (ProjectID,ResourceID,Assigned,Role)
  VALUES
  (@ProjectID,@ResourceID,@Assigned,@Role)

  RETURN
```

This procedure may be called during the adding or editing of either a `Project` or a `Resource` object in our application.

updateAssignment

Likewise, we need to be able to *update* records in the `Assignments` table:

```
CREATE PROCEDURE updateAssignment
  (
    @ProjectID uniqueidentifier,
    @ResourceID varchar(10),
```

```
    @Assigned datetime,
    @Role int
  )
AS
  UPDATE Assignments
  SET
    Assigned=@Assigned,
    Role=@Role
  WHERE ProjectID=@ProjectID AND ResourceID=@ResourceID

  RETURN
```

As with addAssignment, this may be called when updating data from either a Project or a Resource object.

deleteAssignment

As part of the process of updating a project or resource, we will also need to be able to delete a specific record from the Assignments table. An assignment is a child entity beneath a project or resource, and a user can remove a resource from a project, or a project from a resource. In either case, we'll need to be able to remove that specific assignment record from the database:

```
CREATE PROCEDURE deleteAssignment
  (
    @ProjectID uniqueidentifier,
    @ResourceID varchar(10)
  )
AS
  DELETE Assignments
  WHERE ProjectID=@ProjectID AND ResourceID=@ResourceID

  RETURN
```

This completes the operations we can perform on the Assignments data, and note that there's no getAssignments procedure. This is because assignments are always children of a project and a resource. We'll never retrieve just a list of assignments, except as part of retrieving a project or a resource. The getProject procedure, for instance, also retrieves a list of assignments associated with the project – *that's* how we retrieve assignment data.

getResources

Our ResourceList object needs to be able to retrieve a list of basic information about all the records in the Resources table:

```
CREATE PROCEDURE getResources
AS
  SELECT id, LastName, FirstName
  FROM Resources

  RETURN
```

This information will be used to populate the read-only ResourceList business object.

getResource

We also need to be able to get detailed information about a specific record in the `Resources` table, along with its associated data from the `Assignments` table. This is very similar to what we did earlier with the `getProject` procedure. Here, too, we'll return two result sets from the stored procedure:

```
CREATE PROCEDURE getResource
  (
    @ID varchar(10)
  )
AS
  SELECT id,lastname,firstname
  FROM Resources
  WHERE ID=@ID

  SELECT projectid,name,assigned,role
  FROM Projects, Assignments
  WHERE ResourceID=@ID AND ProjectID=ID

  RETURN
```

The second `SELECT` returns data not only from the `Assignments` table, but also from the `Projects` table. This data will be provided as read-only properties in our `ResourceAssignment` object, which inherits from the `Assignment` class. By combining the two `SELECT` statements into a single stored procedure, we can make a single database call to retrieve all the data pertaining to a given `Resource` object.

Now, it might seem that we could combine these two `SELECT` statements into a single `SELECT` using a `JOIN`. That choice would allow us to retrieve the data we need, but at a high cost. First of all, every row of data would include the core `Resource` data, and we'd get a row of data for each assignment. This would result in the database returning a lot of redundant data over the network. Secondly, we'd have to write more complex code in our `Resource` business object, because we'd have to parse the `Resource` data out of a row to load our `Resource` object, and then parse the specific assignment data to populate our collection of `ResourceAssignment` objects. As we'll see in Chapter 7, the code in our business object is very simple and elegant when we return two separate result sets, as we do here.

addResource

When a new `Resource` object is created and saved, its data needs to be inserted into the `Resources` table:

```
CREATE PROCEDURE addResource
  (
    @ID varchar(10),
    @LastName varchar(50),
    @FirstName varchar(50)
  )
AS
  INSERT INTO Resources
  (ID, LastName, FirstName)
  VALUES
  (@ID, @LastName, @FirstName)

  RETURN
```

We've already created the `addAssignment` procedure that can be used to add related records to the `Assignments` table.

updateResource

Likewise, we need to be able to update data in the `Resources` table:

```
CREATE PROCEDURE updateResource
  (
    @ID varchar(10),
    @LastName varchar(50),
    @FirstName varchar(50)
  )
AS
  UPDATE Resources
  SET
    LastName=@LastName,
    FirstName=@FirstName
  WHERE ID=@ID

  RETURN
```

This procedure will be called when an existing `Resource` object is edited and saved.

deleteResource

Finally, we need to be able to remove a `Resource` object from the system. This means removing not only the record from the `Resources` table, but also the associated records from the `Assignments` table:

```
CREATE PROCEDURE deleteResource
  (
    @ID varchar(10)
  )
AS
  DELETE Assignments
  WHERE ResourceID=@ID

  DELETE Resources
  WHERE ID=@ID

  RETURN
```

At this point, we have created stored procedures to do every bit of data access, apart from retrieving the data from the `Roles` table. In Chapter 7, we'll implement data access code using ADO.NET that makes use of these stored procedures from our business objects.

Creating the database project

To allow our database design and stored procedures to be managed via source control, and more easily sharable with other developers, we can create a Database Project within VS.NET. As it was when we created the `Security` database, this step is optional, but it's often a good approach to simplify the management of the database scripts.

The database we created is included in the code download for the book, within a database project.

Open a new Blank Solution by choosing **File | New | Blank Solution** in VS.NET. Name the solution `ProjectTracker`. This solution will contain the business application code that we'll create through the rest of the book. Then, use **File | Add Project | New Project** to add a new Database Project to the solution. Name it `PTrackerDB`:

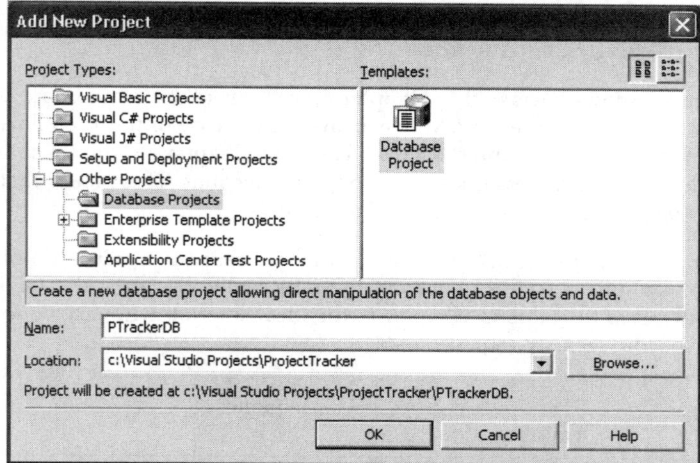

When prompted for a database connection, choose the `PTracker` database. (If it is not in the list, use the dialog to add a new connection, and then choose it.)

Once the project has been created, we can populate it with scripts from our database by simply dragging-and-dropping the **Tables** node from the Server Explorer to the **Create Scripts** node in the `PTrackerDB` project. This will bring up a dialog asking what should be copied. Indicate that we want to copy everything:

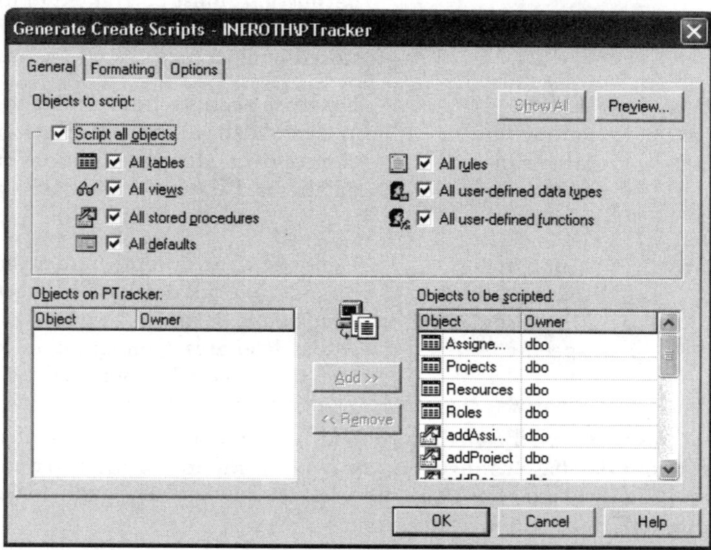

When we click OK and confirm the destination directory, SQL Server will create SQL scripts for all of our database objects, including tables, keys, relationships, and stored procedures. The scripts will be placed into the `PTrackerDB` project.

Database security

The last step in creating the database is to set up security. This can't be done from within VS.NET, so we'll use Enterprise Manager to do the work.

When we build the Windows Forms UI in Chapter 8, we'll make use of a remote `DataPortal`, so the data access code will run under the ASP.NET account. In the case of the Web Forms UI that we'll create in Chapter 9, and the web services interface we'll create in Chapter 10, the UI code and data access code will all run in the same process under the ASP.NET account. This means that the *only* account that will need access to our database is the ASP.NET account.

In a production application, this is not ideal, since it means that any application running under the ASP.NET account would have access to our database. Basically though, we're stuck with the same four options that we laid out in the table in Chapter 5; the ideal solution will vary depending on your environment and specific security requirements:

Database access option	IIS configuration	Consequences
Integrated security	Anonymous access (no impersonation)	All database access is done under the ASP.NET account. We get database connection pooling, but the ASP.NET account needs access to our databases. No password values are stored in clear text.
Integrated security	Windows security (impersonation)	All database access is user-specific, so each client identity is used to access the database. We get no real database connection pooling, and database permissions must be granted to the end user identities that are using the application. No password values are stored in clear text.
Specific user IDs and passwords in connection strings	Either anonymous access or Windows security	Database access is done under the specific user IDs. We get database connection pooling and have better control over which applications can access which databases. Password values are stored in clear text.
Integrated security	Anonymous access (impersonating specific user)	Database access is done under the specific user ID we provide. We get database connection pooling and have better control over which applications can access which databases. Configuration of this option is complex – see KB article 306158.

For the purposes of this book, we'll give the ASP.NET account access to the database, so that we can use integrated security in our database connection string. Open Enterprise Manager and navigate to the `PTracker` database. Right-click on the Users node under the database, and choose New User. In the dialog, select the ASP.NET account for your server:

When we click **OK**, the ASP.NET account will be added as a valid user for the database. However, this act alone doesn't provide the account with access to any database objects. Double-click on the ASP.NET account in the right-hand pane of Enterprise Manager to bring up its properties dialog, and click on the **Permissions** button. The account needs `SELECT` access to the `Roles` table, and `EXEC` access to all our stored procedures:

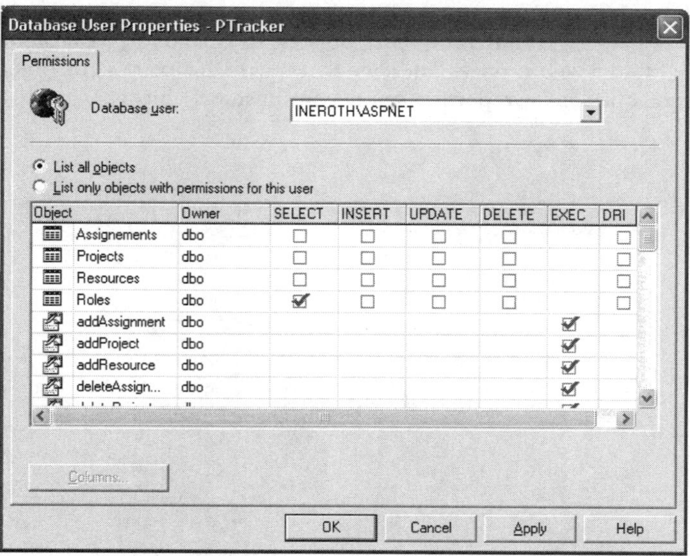

This gives the ASP.NET account, and therefore all of our data access code, the access rights needed to read data from the `Roles` table and to call all the stored procedures we just created.

Conclusion

In this chapter, we started the process of building a sample application that will make use of our CSLA .NET framework. It's a simple project-tracking application that maintains a list of projects and a list of resources, and allows the resources to be assigned to the projects.

To design the application, we used an object-oriented analysis technique that involved creating use cases that described the various ways in which the users need to interact with the system. From those use cases, we created and refined a list of potential business objects.

That object list was then used to create a preliminary class diagram showing the classes, their key data fields, and their relationships. Based on the diagram, our understanding of the business domain, and our use cases, we were able to refine the design until we arrived at a final class diagram describing the business classes that will comprise our application.

We then went through the business classes and determined the appropriate CSLA .NET base classes from which each should inherit. The editable business objects inherit from `BusinessBase`, and the collections of editable child objects inherit from `BusinessCollectionBase`. The lists of read-only data inherit from `ReadOnlyCollectionBase`, and our list of simple name-value data inherits from `NameValueList`.

We also walked through the process of creating a simple relational database to store the data for our application. In most applications, the database already exists, but in this case we had the luxury of creating a database from scratch. Even so, it's interesting to note the differences between our object model and the relational model, highlighting the fact that a good object-oriented model and a good relational model are almost never the same.

In Chapter 7, we'll implement the business objects that we designed in this chapter. Then, in Chapter 8, we'll build a Windows Forms UI based on those objects. In Chapter 9, we'll build a Web Forms UI, and in Chapter 10 we'll build a web services interface that reuses the exact same objects. Finally, in Chapter 11, we'll look at some options for reporting against our business objects.

CHAPTER 7

7

Business object implementation

In this chapter, we will implement the business objects that we designed in Chapter 6, making use of the CSLA .NET framework that we designed and implemented in Chapters 3 thru 5. To a large degree, this chapter will tie together everything that we've discussed in the book so far, illustrating how to write code to create business objects, and making the most of the thought, design, and coding that has gone before.

The business objects that we'll build in this chapter will enjoy all the features and capabilities we built into the CSLA .NET framework, but the great thing is that very little of the code we'll write will have anything to do with them – they'll just be inherited. Instead, almost all the code in our business objects will be business-focused. Each business class will largely consist of three areas:

- UI-focused business properties and methods
- Shared methods to support class-in-charge (as discussed in Chapter 1)
- Data access methods (`DataPortal_xxx()`, as discussed in Chapter 5)

Before we implement the business objects for our sample project tracker application, let's take a look at the life cycle of a business object, and the general code structure for business classes.

Business object lifecycle

Before we get into the code structure for our business objects, it is worth spending some time to understand the lifecycle of those objects. By lifecycle, I mean the sequence of methods and events that occur as the object is created and used. While we can't predict the business properties and methods that might exist on an object, there is a set of steps that occur during the lifetime of *every* business object.

Typically, an object is created by UI code, be that Windows Forms, Web Forms, or a web service. Sometimes, an object may be created by another object, which will happen when we have a *using* relationship between objects, for instance.

Object creation

Whether editable or read-only, all root objects go through the same basic creation process. (Root objects are those that can be directly retrieved from the database, while child objects are retrieved within the context of a root object; never directly.)

As we discussed in Chapter 5, it's up to the root object to invoke methods on its child objects and child collections, so they can load their own data from the database. Usually, the root object actually calls the database and gets all the data back, and then provides that data to the child objects and collections so that they can populate themselves. From a pure OO perspective, it might be ideal to have each object encapsulate the logic to get its own data from the database, but in reality it's not practical to have each object independently contact the database to retrieve one row of data.

Root object creation

Root objects are created by calling a **factory method** – a method that's called in order to create an object – and in our case these will be `Shared` methods on the class. The `Shared` method will either create the object directly, or use the `DataPortal` to load the object with default values.

If we *don't* need to retrieve default values from the database, we can use a simple, fast approach:

- The `Shared` factory method is called
- The `Shared` method creates the object using the `New` keyword, possibly passing parameter values
- The business object does any initialization in the constructor
- The business object is returned

From the business object's perspective, only one method is called:

- `New` (any constructor)

This is illustrated by the following diagram:

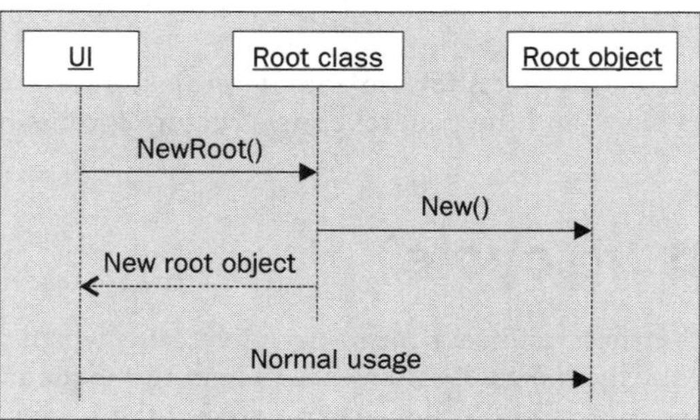

On the other hand, if we *do* need to populate the new object with default values, then we'll use the `DataPortal`'s `Create()` method:

- The `Shared` factory method is called
- The `Shared` method calls `DataPortal.Create()` to get the business object
- `DataPortal.Create()` creates the object using reflection
- The business object can do basic initialization in the constructor
- The `DataPortal_Create()` method is called, and this is where the business object implements data access code to load its default values
- The business object is returned

From the business object's perspective, two methods are called:

- `New` (default constructor)
- `DataPortal_Create()`

This is illustrated by the following diagram:

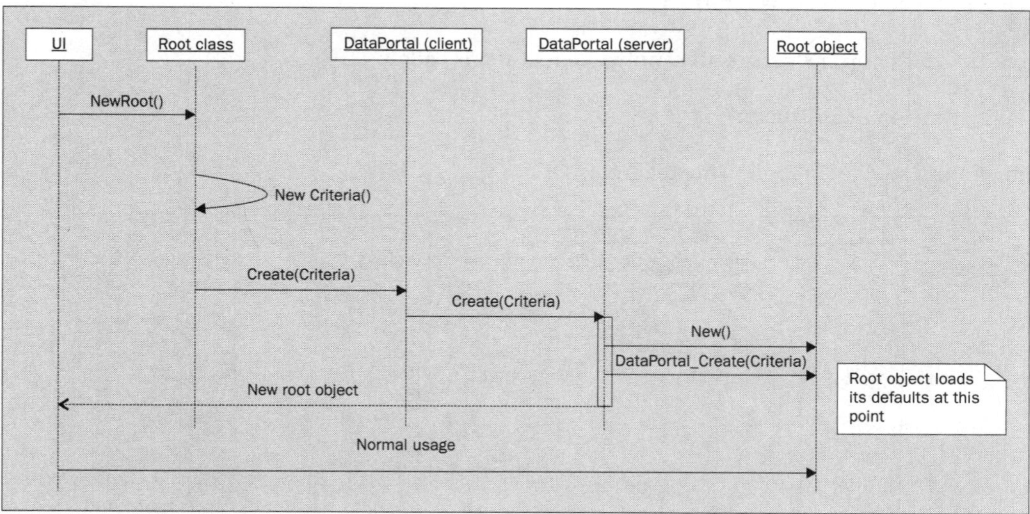

To the UI code, of course, there's no difference: that code just calls the `Shared` factory method, and gets an object back. From the business object's perspective, the primary difference lies in whether `DataPortal_Create()` is called in order to initialize the object.

Child object creation

Child objects are usually created when the UI code calls an `Add()` method on the collection object that contains the child object. Ideally, the child class and the collection class will be in the same project, so the `Shared` factory methods on a child object can be scoped as `Friend`, rather than `Public`. This way, the UI can't directly create the object, but the collection object *can* create the child when the UI calls the collection's `Add()` method.

The framework doesn't actually dictate this approach. Rather, it's a design choice on my part because I feel that it makes the use of the business objects more intuitive from the UI developer's perspective. It is quite possible to allow the UI code to create child objects directly, by making the child factory methods `Public`; the collection's `Add()` method would then accept a pre-built child object as a parameter. I think that's less intuitive, but it's perfectly valid, and you could implement your objects that way if you chose.

As was the situation with the root objects, we may or may not need to load default values from the database when we create a child object.

> *If we don't need to retrieve default values from the database, we could have the collection object create the child object directly, using the `New` keyword. For consistency, however, it's better to stick with the `Shared` factory method approach, so that all objects are created the same way.*

The sequence of steps to create a child object that *doesn't* need default values from the database is:

- The `Shared` factory method (`Friend` scope) is called
- The `Shared` method creates the object locally by using the `New` keyword, possibly passing parameter values
- The child object does any initialization in the constructor method
- The child object is returned

From the child object's perspective, only one method is called:

- `New` (any constructor)

This is illustrated by the following diagram:

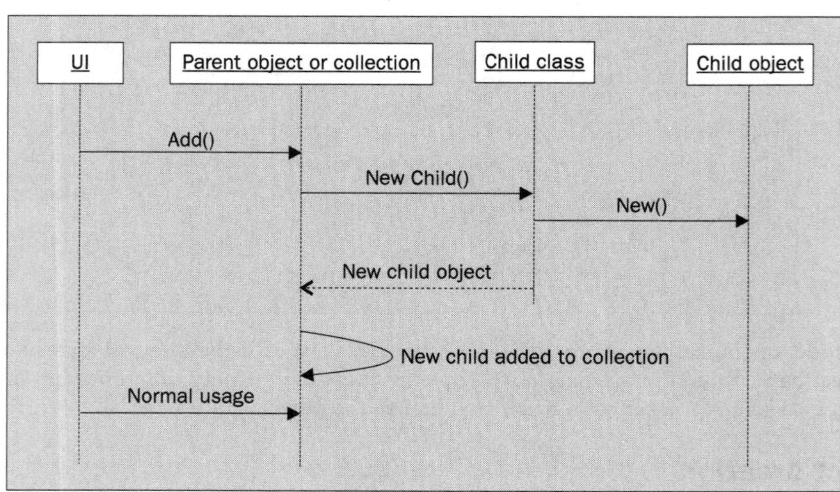

Once the child object has been created and added to the parent, the UI code can access the child via the parent's interface. Typically, the parent will provide an `Item()` property that allows the UI to access child objects directly.

Though the `Shared` factory method is called by the collection object rather than the UI code, this is the same *process* that's used to create a root object. The same is true if we need to retrieve default values from the database:

- The `Shared` factory method (`Friend` scope) is called
- The `Shared` method calls `DataPortal.Create()` to get the business object
- `DataPortal.Create()` creates the object using reflection
- The child object can do basic initialization in the constructor method
- The `DataPortal_Create()` method is called, and this is where the child object implements data access code to load its default values
- The child object is returned

Again, the `Shared` factory method is called by the collection object rather than the UI, but the rest of the process is the same as with a root object. From the child object's perspective, two methods are called:

- `New` (default constructor)
- `DataPortal_Create()`

This is illustrated by the following diagram:

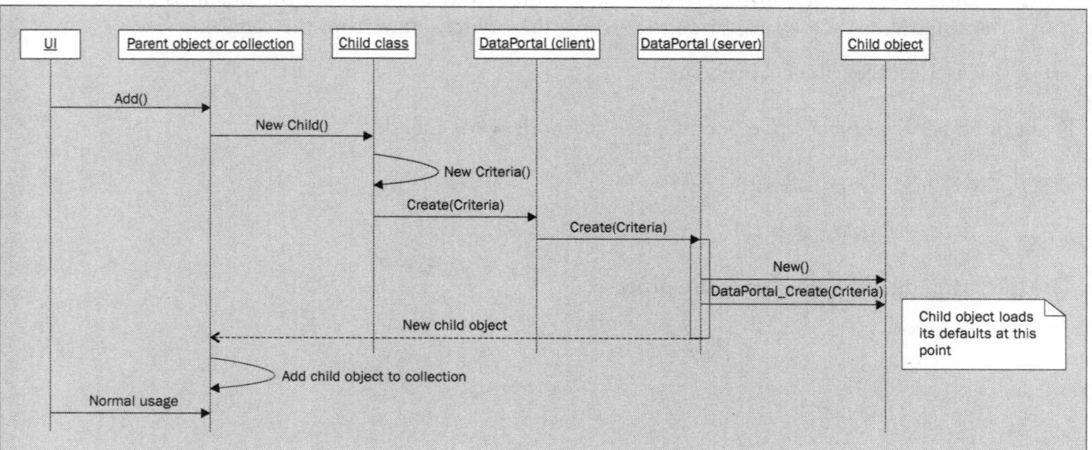

> **Note that this requires the child object to have a nested `Criteria` class. Normally, child objects don't contain a `Criteria` class, since they can't be retrieved directly from the database. In this case, however, they need the `Criteria` class so that the `DataPortal` can properly call the `DataPortal_Create()` method.**

Note that in either of these cases, the UI code is the same: it calls the `Add()` method on the parent object, and then interacts with the parent's interface to get access to the newly added child object. The UI is entirely unaware of how the child object is created (and possibly loaded with default values).

Also note that the *parent* object is unaware of the details. All it does is call the `Shared` factory method on the child class, and receive a new child object in return. All the details about *how* the child object got loaded with default values are encapsulated within the child class.

Object retrieval

Retrieving an existing object from the database is similar to the process of creating an object that requires default values from the database. Only a root object can be retrieved from the database directly by code in the user interface. Child objects are retrieved along with their parent root object, not independently.

Root object retrieval

To retrieve a root object, our UI code simply calls the `Shared` factory method on the class, providing the parameters that identify the object to be retrieved. The `Shared` factory method calls `DataPortal.Fetch()`, which in turn creates the object and calls `DataPortal_Fetch()`:

- The `Shared` factory method is called
- The `Shared` method calls `DataPortal.Fetch()` to get the business object
- `DataPortal.Fetch()` creates the business object using reflection
- The business object can do basic initialization in the constructor method
- The `DataPortal_Fetch()` method is called, and this is where the business object implements data access code to retrieve the object's data from the database
- The business object is returned

From the business object's perspective, two methods were called:

- `New` (default constructor)
- `DataPortal_Fetch()`

The following diagram illustrates the process:

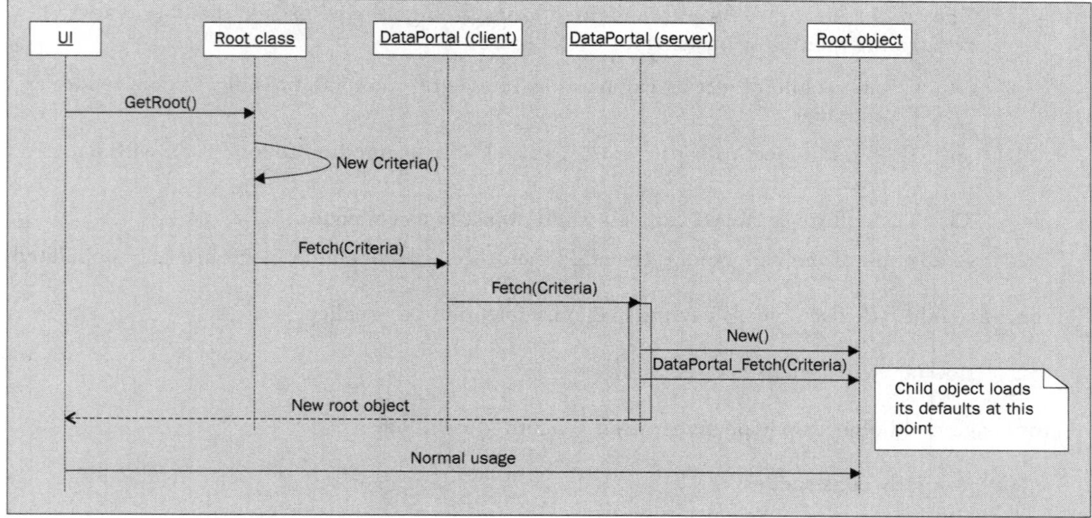

It's important to note that the root object's `DataPortal_Fetch()` is responsible not only for loading the business object's data, but also for starting the process of loading the data for its child objects.

In Chapter 6, we implemented our stored procedures so that they return the root object's data *and also all the child object data* – two result sets from a single stored procedure. This means that when the root object calls the stored procedure to retrieve its data, it will also get the data for its child objects, so it must cause those to be created as well.

The key thing to remember is that the data for the *entire* object, including its child objects, is retrieved when `DataPortal_Fetch()` is called. This avoids having to go back across the network to retrieve each child object's data individually. Though the root object gets the *data*, it is up to each child object to populate itself based on that data. Let's dive one level deeper and discuss how child objects load their data.

Child object retrieval

The retrieval of a child object is quite different from the retrieval of a root object, because the `DataPortal` isn't directly involved. Instead, as stated above, the root object's `DataPortal_Fetch()` method is responsible for loading not only the root object's data, but also the data for all child objects. It then calls methods on the child objects, passing the pre-loaded data as parameters so the child objects can load their variables with data.

The sequence of events goes like this:

- The root object's `DataPortal_Fetch()` creates the child *collection* using a `Shared` factory method on the collection class, passing a data reader object as a parameter
- The child collection implements a `Private Fetch()` method to load its data. This method uses the data reader provided as a parameter

- The child collection's `Fetch()` method loops through the records in the data reader, performing the following steps for each record:
    - Create a child object by calling a Shared factory method, passing the data reader as a parameter
    - The child object calls its own `Private Fetch()` method to load itself with data from the data reader
    - The collection object adds the child object to its collection
- At the end of the data reader, the child collection and all child objects are fully populated

From the child *collection* object's perspective, only one method is called:

- `New` (any constructor)

From each child object's perspective, only one method is called:

- `New` (any constructor)

The following sequence diagram illustrates how this works. Note that this diagram occurs *during the process of loading the root object's data.* This means that this diagram is really an expansion of the previous sequence diagram for retrieving a root object!

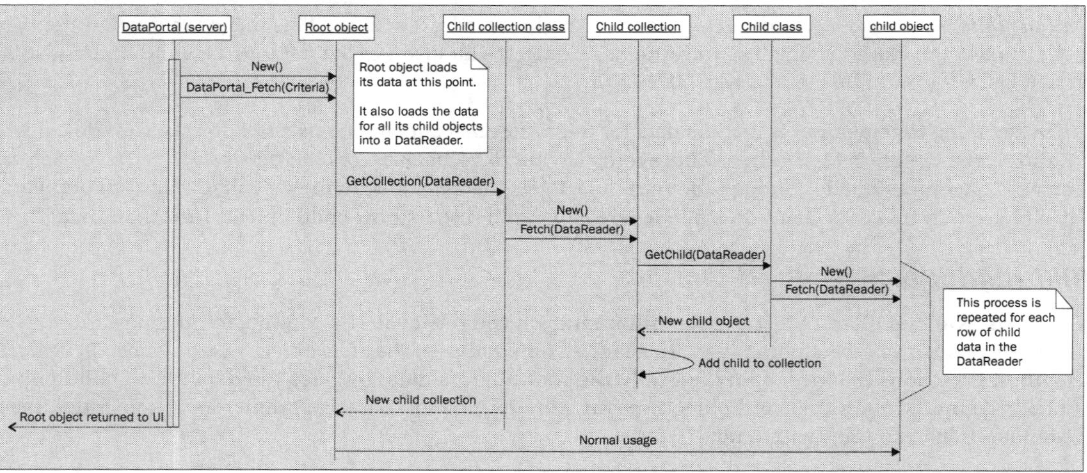

Updating editable objects

For read-only objects, all we need to worry about is retrieval, but for our editable business objects and editable collections (those deriving from `BusinessBase` and `BusinessCollectionBase`) we also need to think through the process of updating the objects into the database. The process is the same for adding or editing an object, and for deleting child objects. As we'll see, deleting a root object is a bit different.

Adding and editing root objects

After an object is created or retrieved, the user will work with the object, changing its values by interacting with the user interface. At some point, the user may click the OK or Save button, triggering the process of updating the object into the database. The sequence of events at that point is this:

- The UI calls the `Save()` method on our business object
- The `Save()` method calls `DataPortal.Update()`
- `DataPortal.Update()` calls the `DataPortal_Update()` method on the business object, which contains the data access code needed to insert or update the data into the database
- During the insert or update process, the business object's data may change
- The updated business object is returned as a result of the `Save()` method

From the business object's perspective, two methods are called:

- `Save()`
- `DataPortal_Update()`

The following diagram illustrates this process:

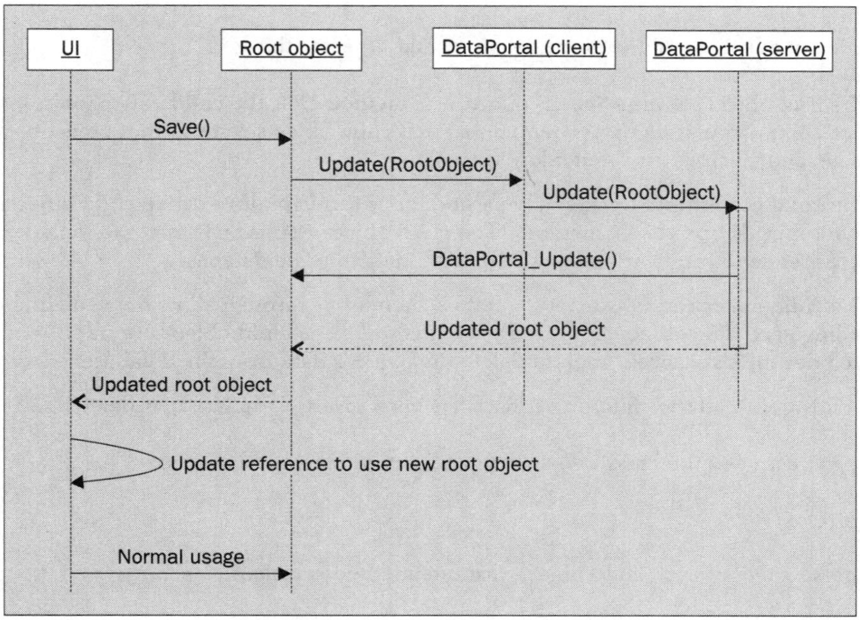

The `Save()` method is implemented in `BusinessBase` and `BusinessCollectionBase`, and typically requires no change or customization. Remember that the framework's `Save()` method includes checks so that we can only save an object if it has no broken rules in the `BrokenRules` collection, and that the object will only be saved if `IsDirty` is `True`. This helps to optimize our data access by preventing the update of invalid or unchanged data.

If we don't like this behavior, our business class can override the framework's `Save()` method and replace that logic with other logic.

All the data access code to handle saving the object is located in `DataPortal_Update()`.

> **It is important to recall that when the server-side `DataPortal` is remote, the updated root object returned to the UI is a *new* object. The UI *must* update its references to use this new object in lieu of the original root object.**

Note that `DataPortal_Update()` is responsible not only for saving the object's data, but also for starting the process of saving all the *child object* data. Child objects are *not* saved by calling the `DataPortal`; they are saved because their root parent object directly calls `Friend`-scoped `Update()` methods on each child collection or object, causing them to save their data.

Adding, editing, and deleting child objects

Child objects are inserted, updated, or deleted as part of the process of updating a root parent object. To support this concept, child collections and child objects implement a `Friend` method named `Update()`, which can be called by the root object during the update process. As we've discussed, it's helpful for related root, child, and child collection classes to be placed in the same project (assembly) so that they can use `Friend` scope in this manner.

The sequence of events to add, edit, or delete a child object is this:

- The root object's `DataPortal_Update()` method calls the child collection's `Update()` method, passing itself as a parameter so that child objects can use root object property values as needed (such as for foreign key values).
- The child collection's `Update()` method loops through all its active child objects, calling each child object's `Update()` method. (The child object's `Update()` method includes the data access code to insert or update the object's data into the database.)
- The child collection's `Update()` method then loops through all its deleted child objects, calling each deleted object's `Update()` method. (The child object's `Update()` method includes the data access code to delete the object's data from the database.)
- At this point, all the child object data has been inserted, updated, or deleted as required.

From the perspective of the child *collection* object, just one method is called:

- `Update()`

From the perspective of each child object, just one method is called:

- `Update()`

The following diagram illustrates this process. Remember that this diagram is connected with the previous diagram showing the update of a root object. The events depicted in this diagram occur as a result of the root object's `DataPortal_Update()` being called, as shown in the previous diagram:

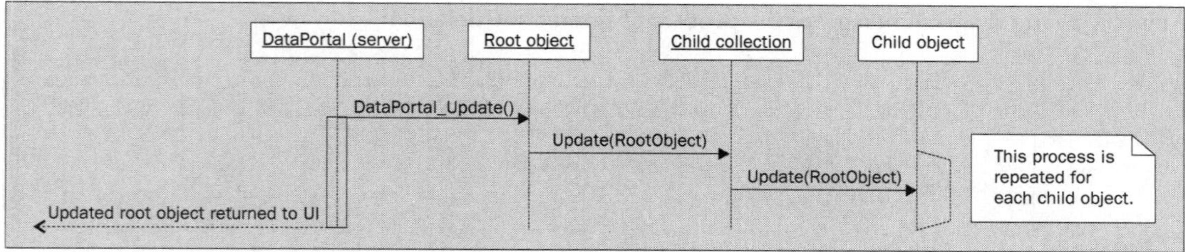

The `Update()` methods often accept parameters. Typically, the root object's primary key value is a required piece of data when we save child objects (since it would be a foreign key in the table), and so we'll typically pass a reference to the root object as a parameter to the `Update()` method. Passing a reference to the root object is better than passing any specific property value, because it helps to decouple the root object from the child object. Using a reference means that the root object doesn't know or care what actual data is required by the child object during the update process – that information is encapsulated within the child class.

Also, if we're implementing transactions manually using ADO.NET, rather than using Enterprise Services, then the ADO.NET transaction object will also need to be passed as a parameter, so that each child object can update its data within the same transaction as the root object.

> *As we implement our sample application, we'll create examples using both Enterprise Services and ADO.NET transactions, to illustrate how each is coded.*

Deleting root objects

While child objects are deleted within the context of the root object that's being updated, we implemented the `DataPortal` so that it supports the idea of *immediate* deletion of a root object, based on criteria. This means that the UI code can call a `Shared` delete method on the business class, providing it with parameters that define the object to be deleted – typically, the same criteria that would be used to retrieve the object.

The sequence of events flows like this:

- The `Shared` delete method is called
- The `Shared` delete method calls `DataPortal.Delete()`
- `DataPortal.Delete()` creates the business object using reflection
- `DataPortal.Delete()` calls the `DataPortal_Delete()` method on the business object, which contains the code needed to delete the object's data (and any related child data, etc.)

From the business object's perspective, two methods are called:

- `New`
- `DataPortal_Delete()`

The following diagram illustrates the process of immediate deletion:

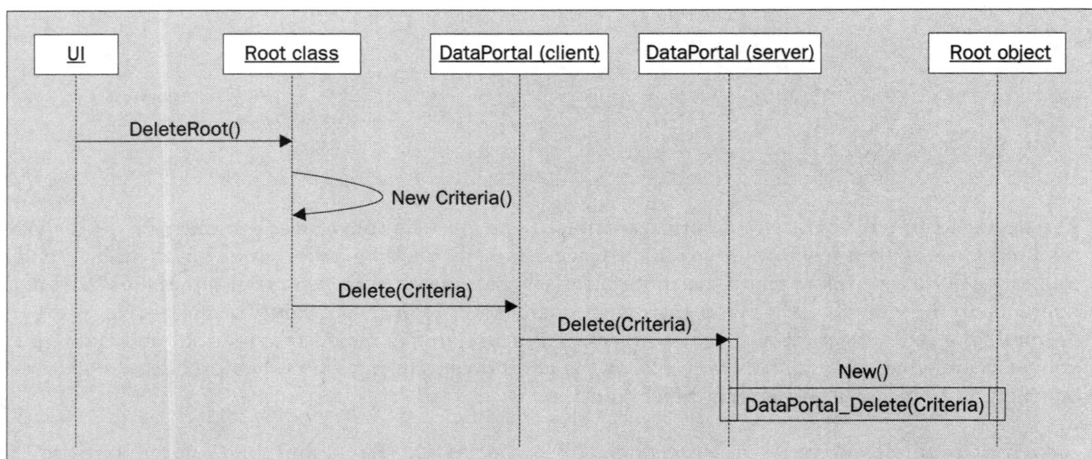

Since this causes the deletion of a root object, the delete process must also remove any data for child objects. This can be done through our ADO.NET data access code, through a stored procedure, or by the database (if cascading deletes are set up on the relationships). In our example application, we'll be deleting the child data within our stored procedures. We created these procedures in Chapter 6.

Disposing and finalizing objects

Most business objects contain moderate amounts of data in their variables. For these, .NET's default garbage collection behavior, in which we don't know exactly when an object will be destroyed, is fine – we don't really care if the object is destroyed immediately we release our reference to it, or later on. The time we *do* care is when we create objects that hold onto 'expensive' resources until they are destroyed.

'Expensive' resources include things like open database connections, open files on disk, very large chunks of memory, and so forth. These are things that need to be released as soon as possible in order to prevent our application from wasting memory, or blocking other users who might need to access a file or reuse a database connection. If we write our objects properly, most of these concerns should go away: our data access code should *never* keep a database connection open for any length of time, and the same is true for any files we might open on disk. However, there are cases where our business object can legitimately contain an expensive resource – something like a multi-megabyte image in a variable, perhaps.

Implementing IDisposable

In such a case, we should implement the `IDisposable` interface in our business class, which will allow the UI code to tell our business object to release its resources. It is then up to us to write the `Dispose()` method to actually release those resources:

```
<Serializable()> _
Public Class MyBusinessClass
  Inherits BusinessBase
  Implements IDisposable

  Public Sub Dispose() Implements IDisposable.Dispose
```

```
        ' Release expensive resources here
    End Sub

  End Class
```

The UI code can now call the `Dispose()` method on our class when it is done using our object, at which point our object will release its expensive resources – such as our hypothetical image.

Note, however, that were we to retrieve a business object using a *remote* `DataPortal` configuration, the business object would be created and loaded on the server. It is then returned to the client via remoting, leaving a copy in memory on the server. The server-side `DataPortal` code is finished when we execute the `Return` statement that returns the object:

```
    Return obj
```

Because of this, there's no way to call the `Dispose()` method on the server. To avoid this scenario, any time that the `DataPortal` may be configured to run outside of the client process (via remoting), our object designs *must* avoid any requirement for a `Dispose()` method. Happily, this is almost never an issue with a properly designed business object, since all database connections or open files should be closed in the same method from which they were opened.

> **If you're calling the `DataPortal` via remoting, you must avoid object designs that require `IDisposable`.**

Implementing a Finalize method

If, for some reason, our business object holds an expensive resource (such as a database connection or a file) that must be closed when the object is destroyed, we need to implement a `Finalize()` method. However, this is generally a poor solution, for at least two reasons.

The `Finalize()` method is called by the garbage collector immediately before our object is destroyed. If our object implements a `Finalize()` method, it will take longer for the garbage collector to destroy our object, because objects with `Finalize()` methods are put into a separate list and processed later than simpler objects.

Also, if our process is shut down, the garbage collector won't call `Finalize()`. It assumes that since we're shutting down, there's no need – but this can leave our resources in an indeterminate state after the application is gone, since we didn't explicitly close or release them.

> **Implementing a `Finalize()` method in a business object to release expensive resources is a last-ditch attempt to solve a problem that would have been better solved through a different design.**

This scenario should not occur in objects created for the CSLA .NET framework. Waiting until `Finalize()` runs doesn't guarantee the release of the resource, and it may happen seconds or minutes after the object was de-referenced. The only situation in which a `Finalize()` method makes sense is in conjunction with implementing `IDisposable`. As we discussed in the previous section, CSLA .NET is not very friendly to the idea of implementing `IDisposable`, and it won't work at all if we are running the `DataPortal` on a server, via remoting.

When designing business objects for CSLA .NET, all expensive resources such as database connections and open files should be closed and released in the same method from which they were opened. Typically, this is in the `DataPortal_xxx()` methods where we are retrieving or saving object data.

Business class structure

As we've seen, business objects follow the same sequence of events as they are created, retrieved, or updated. Because of this, there's a structure and a set of features that's common to all of them. While the structure and features are common, however, the actual code will vary for each business object – all we can do is provide some foundations that make it easier for the business developer to know what needs to be done.

Also, there are differences between editable and read-only objects, and between root and child objects. After we've discussed the features common to all business objects, we'll create 'templates' to illustrate the structure of each type of business object that we can create based on CSLA .NET.

Common features

There are some common features or conventions that must be followed as we code any business classes that will inherit from the CSLA .NET base classes. These are:

- The `<Serializable()>` attribute
- Common regions
- `Private` default constructor
- Nested `Criteria` class

Let's briefly discuss each of these requirements.

The Serializable attribute

All business objects must be unanchored so that they can move across the network as needed. This means that they must be marked as serializable by using the `<Serializable()>` attribute:

```
<Serializable()> _
Public Class MyBusinessClass

End Class
```

This is required for all business classes that inherit from any of the CSLA .NET base classes. It's also required for any objects that our business objects reference. If we reference an object that is not serializable, then we must be sure to mark its variable with the `<NonSerialized()>` attribute to prevent the serialization process from attempting to serialize that object. If we don't do this, the result will be a run-time exception from the .NET Framework.

Common regions

When writing code in VS.NET, we can make use of the `#Region` directive to place our code into collapsible regions. This helps organize our code, and allows us to look only at the code pertaining to a specific type of functionality. All our business classes will have a common set of regions:

- *Business Properties and Methods*
- *System.Object Overrides*
- *Shared Methods*
- *Constructors*
- *Criteria*
- *Data Access*

The *Business Properties and Methods* region will contain the methods that are used by UI code (or other client code) to interact with our business object. This includes any properties that allow retrieval or changing of values in the object, as well as methods that operate on the object's data to perform business processing.

The *System.Object Overrides* region will contain overrides for at least the `ToString()` and `Equals()` methods from `System.Object`. By overriding `ToString()`, we ensure that our business objects will return some meaningful data any time we attempt to convert the object to text. By overriding and/or overloading the `Equals()` method, we provide a standardized mechanism by which two of our business objects can be tested for equality.

The *Shared Methods* region will contain the `Shared` factory methods to create or retrieve our objects, along with the `Shared` delete method (if our object is an editable root object). It will also contain the nested `Criteria` class used by the creation, retrieval, and delete operations, and any constructor methods for our class.

The *Constructors* region will contain the constructor methods for the class. At a minimum, each class will contain a default constructor so that it can be created by the server-side `DataPortal`.

The *Criteria* region will contain the `Criteria` class used by the data portal mechanism to load the class. Many child classes won't include this region, but we'll include it in our template for completeness.

The *Data Access* region will contain the `DataPortal_xxx()` methods.

This means that the skeletal structure of a business object, with these regions, is as follows:

```
<Serializable()> _
Public Class MyBusinessClass
  Inherits CSLA.baseclass

#Region " Business Properties and Methods "

#End Region

#Region " System.Object Overrides "

#End Region

#Region " Shared Methods "

#End Region
```

```
#Region " Constructors "

#End Region

#Region " Criteria "

#End Region

#Region " Data Access "

#End Region

End Class
```

To reiterate, all of the business objects in this chapter will follow this basic region scheme.

Private default constructor

All business objects will be implemented to make use of the 'class-in-charge' scheme that we discussed in Chapter 1. Factory methods are used in lieu of the `New` keyword, which means that it's best if we prevent the use of `New`, forcing the UI developer to use our `Shared` factory methods instead.

> *The concept of an object factory is a common design pattern, and is discussed in the 'Gang of Four' design patterns book,* Design Patterns*, ISBN 0201633612.*

We also know, from Chapter 5, that the `DataPortal` mechanism requires our classes to include a default constructor. As we reviewed the create, fetch, update, and delete processes for each type of object earlier in this chapter, each sequence diagram showed how the server-side `DataPortal` created an instance of our business object. Because this is done through reflection, we must provide a default constructor for the server-side `DataPortal` to invoke.

By making this constructor `Private`, we ensure that UI code must use our `Shared` factory method to get an instance of any object. These two facts together mean that every business object will have a `Private` default constructor:

```
<Serializable()> _
Public Class MyBusinessClass
  Inherits CSLA.baseclass

#Region " Business Properties and Methods "

#End Region

#Region " System.Object Overrides "

#End Region

#Region " Shared Methods "

#End Region

#Region " Constructors "
```

```
  Private Sub New()
    ' Prevent direct creation
  End Sub

#End Region

#Region " Criteria "

#End Region

#Region " Data Access "

#End Region

End Class
```

This constructor both prevents the `New` keyword from working, and provides the `DataPortal` with the ability to create the object via reflection. As we'll see later, our classes might also include other constructors, but this one is required for all objects.

Nested criteria class

Any object that can be retrieved from the database must have a nested `Criteria` class. Also, any object that loads default values from the database (including root and child objects) must have a nested `Criteria` class.

The `Criteria` class simply contains the data required to identify the specific object to be retrieved, or to identify the default data to be loaded. Since it is passed by value to the `DataPortal`, this class must be marked as `<Serializable()>`.

> *Technically, the `Criteria` class can have* any *name, as long as it is `<Serializable()>` and nested within the business class. In some cases, we might have two `Criteria` classes – one defining the data to retrieve an object, the other to define the data needed to find the right default values to load when creating an object.*

Since this class is no more than a way to ferry data to the `DataPortal`, it doesn't need to be fancy. Typically, it is implemented with a constructor to make it easier to create and populate the object all at once. For example, here's a `Criteria` class that includes an `EmployeeID` field:

```
<Serializable()> _
Public Class MyBusinessClass
  Inherits CSLA.baseclass

#Region " Business Properties and Methods "

#End Region

#Region " System.Object Overrides "

#End Region
```

```
#Region " Shared Methods "

#End Region

#Region " Constructors "

  Private Sub New()
    ' Prevent direct creation
  End Sub

#End Region

#Region " Criteria "

  <Serializable()> _
  Private Class Criteria
    Public EmployeeID As String

    Public Sub New(ByVal EmployeeID As String)
      Me.EmployeeID = EmployeeID
    End Sub

  End Class

#End Region

#Region " Data Access "

#End Region

End Class
```

All `Criteria` classes are constructed using a similar scheme. The class is scoped as `Private` because it's only needed within the context of our business class. Even though we'll pass the `Criteria` object through the data portal mechanism, it is passed as type `Object`, so the `DataPortal` code doesn't need access to the object's code. This is ideal, because it means that UI developers, or other business object developers, won't see the `Criteria` class, thus improving our business object's overall encapsulation.

The `Criteria` class will typically contain `Public` fields containing the criteria data needed to identify our specific type of business object. A `Project`, for instance, is uniquely identified by its ID, so the `Criteria` class for our `Project` class will look like this:

```
' Criteria for identifying existing object
<Serializable()> _
Private Class Criteria
  Public ID As Guid

  Public Sub New(ByVal ID As Guid)
    Me.ID = ID
  End Sub
End Class
```

Several times so far, we've noted that exposing fields as `Public` is bad practice. The reason we're doing it here is that we want to make the `Criteria` class as easy to create as possible. While we could declare `Private` variables and create `Public` property methods, this is a lot of extra work to force on the business developer. The reason a `Public` field is acceptable here is because the class itself is `Private` – this class and its fields can *only* be used by code within our `Project` class. Though we're breaking encapsulation of the `Criteria` class, we're *not* breaking it for the `Project` class, which is what really counts in this case.

We are also including a constructor that accepts the criteria data value. This is done to simplify the code that will go into the `Shared` factory methods. Rather than forcing the business developer to create a `Criteria` object and then load its values, this constructor allows the `Criteria` object to be created and initialized in a single statement. In many cases, this means that our `Shared` factory methods will contain just one line of code!

Many `Criteria` classes will contain a single value (as in our examples here), but they can be more complex, providing for more control over the selection of the object to be retrieved. If we have a root collection where we are directly retrieving a collection of child objects, the `Criteria` class may not define a single object, but rather act as a search filter that returns the collection populated with all matching child objects.

In other cases, we may have no criteria data at all. In that case, we still need a `Criteria` class, but it would be empty:

```
<Serializable()> _
Public Class Criteria

End Class
```

We can still create an instance of this class and pass it to the `DataPortal`; it simply provides no criteria data. This is typically used when retrieving a root collection object where we want all the child objects in the database returned at all times. We'll use this technique when we create our `ProjectList` and `ResourceList` collection classes later in the chapter.

Class structures

At this point in the chapter, we've walked through the lifecycle of our business objects, so we know the sequence of events that will occur as they are created, retrieved, updated, and deleted. We've also discussed the code concepts and structures that are common to all business classes. Now let's dive in and look at the specific coding structure for each type of business class that we can create based on the CSLA .NET framework. These include:

- Editable root
- Editable child
- Editable, 'switchable' (that is, root or child) objects
- Editable root collection
- Editable child collection
- Read-only object

- Read-only collection
- Name-value lists

For each of these object types, we'll create the basic starting code that belongs in the class. In a sense, these are the templates from which our business classes can be built.

Ideally, we'd put these templates directly into VS.NET, so that they're available as true templates. Unfortunately, this is a much more difficult prospect now than it was in VB6, requiring the use of Enterprise Templates or the manual editing of cryptic configuration files. Due to this complexity, and the relatively small amounts of template code involved, we won't make these into true VS.NET templates.

Editable root business objects

The most common type of object will be the editable root business object, since any object-oriented system based on CSLA .NET will have at least one root business object or root collection. (Examples of this type of object include our own `Project` and `Resource` objects.) These objects often contain collections of child objects as well as their own object-specific data.

As well as being common, an editable object that's also a root object is the most complex object type, so its code template is the largest we'll be creating. The basic structure for an editable root object is as follows:

Class header and instance variables

```
<Serializable()> _
Public Class EditableRoot
  Inherits BusinessBase

  ' Declare variables here to contain object state

  ' Declare variables for any child collections here
```

We start by declaring the instance variables for our object – the variables that will contain the data used by the object itself. This also means declaring variables to hold any collections of child objects that might be contained by our business object.

Business properties and methods

```
#Region " Business Properties and Methods "

  ' Implement properties and methods here so the UI or
  ' other client code can interact with the object

#End Region
```

In the *Business Properties and Methods* region, we will write the business-specific properties and methods for our object. These properties and methods typically interact with the instance variables, performing validation, calculations, and other manipulation of the data, based on our business logic. We might also include properties to expose our child collections for use by the UI or other client code.

System.Object overrides

```
#Region " System.Object Overrides "

  Public Overrides Function ToString() As String
    ' Return text describing our object
  End Function

  Public Overloads Function Equals(ByVal obj As MyBusinessClass) As Boolean
    ' Implement comparison between two of our type of object
  End Function

  Public Overrides Function GetHashCode() As Integer
    ' Return a hash value for our object
  End Function

#End Region
```

In the *System.Object Overrides* region, we should override `ToString()`, `Equals()`, and `GetHashCode()`.

The `ToString()` method is used throughout .NET to convert an object to a text representation, and we should override it to provide a meaningful text representation for our object. In many cases, this will be the object's primary identifying data – such as the ID field for a `Project` object:

```
Public Overrides Function ToString() As String
  Return mID.ToString
End Function
```

The `Equals()` method is used throughout .NET to compare two objects to each other. The `System.Object` base class defines a generic comparison, but it may not be as efficient or accurate as one we could create here. In most cases, we'll determine whether two objects of the same type are equal by simply comparing their primary identifying data, such as the ID field for a `Project` object:

```
Public Overloads Function Equals(ByVal Project As Project) As Boolean
  Return mID.Equals(Project.ID)
End Function
```

The `GetHashCode()` method is used by the .NET Framework whenever we add our object to a `Hashtable` (or some other hash table-based collection). Like the `Equals()` method, the default behavior of this method as provided by `System.Object` is not particularly accurate or useful. We should override it to return a hash code based on our object's primary identifying data. This would be the ID field for a `Project` object, for instance:

```
Public Overrides Function GetHashCode() As Integer
  Return mID.GetHashCode
End Function
```

Shared methods

```
#Region " Shared Methods "

  Public Shared Function NewEditableRoot() As EditableRoot
    Return CType(DataPortal.Create(New Criteria()), EditableRoot)
  End Function

  Public Shared Function GetEditableRoot() As EditableRoot
    Return CType(DataPortal.Fetch(New Criteria()), EditableRoot)
  End Function

  Public Shared Sub DeleteEditableRoot()
    DataPortal.Delete(New Criteria())
  End Sub

#End Region
```

In the *Shared Methods* region, we see a set of `Shared` methods to create, retrieve, and delete the object. Of course, these are just skeletons that must be fleshed out as appropriate. Typically, these methods will accept parameters so that client code can indicate which object is to be retrieved or deleted. That parameter data would then be used to populate the `Criteria` object, as discussed earlier in the chapter.

Constructors

```
#Region " Constructors "

  Private Sub New()
    ' Prevent direct creation
  End Sub

#End Region
```

We place our constructors in the *Constructors* region. As noted earlier, all business objects at least declare a `Private` default constructor to prevent the UI code from directly creating an instance of our object. By including this method, we ensure that they will use our `Shared` factory methods to create the object.

We also ensure that the class has a default constructor, which is required by the server-side `DataPortal` when it uses reflection to create instances of our class.

Criteria

```
#Region " Criteria "

  <Serializable()> _
  Private Class Criteria
    ' Add criteria here
  End Class

#End Region
```

In our template code, the `Criteria` class is empty; it will need to be customized for each business class so that it contains the criteria values required to identify a specific business object.

Data access

```
#Region " Data Access "

  Protected Overrides Sub DataPortal_Create(ByVal Criteria As Object)
    Dim crit As Criteria = CType(Criteria, Criteria)

    ' Load default values from database
  End Sub

  Protected Overrides Sub DataPortal_Fetch(ByVal Criteria As Object)
    Dim crit As Criteria = CType(Criteria, Criteria)

    ' Load object data from database
  End Sub

  Protected Overrides Sub DataPortal_Update()

    ' Insert or update object data into database
  End Sub

  Protected Overrides Sub DataPortal_Delete(ByVal Criteria As Object)
    Dim crit As Criteria = CType(Criteria, Criteria)

    ' Delete object data from database
  End Sub

#End Region

End Class
```

Finally, in the *Data Access* region, we have the four `DataPortal_xxx()` methods. These methods must include the code to load defaults, to retrieve object data, to update object data, and to delete object data, as appropriate. In most cases, this will be done through ADO.NET, but this code could just as easily be implemented to read or write to an XML file, or to any other data store you can imagine.

> *Many organizations use an abstract, metadata-driven data access layer. In environments like this, the business objects don't use ADO.NET directly. This works fine with CSLA .NET, since the data access code in our `DataPortal_xxx()` methods can interact with an abstract data access layer just as easily as it can interact with ADO.NET directly.*

The key thing to note about this code template is that there is very little code in the class that's not related to the business. Most of the code in an editable root business class will be the business logic that we implement, or the business-related data access code that we write. The bulk of the non-business code is already implemented in the CSLA .NET framework.

Object creation without defaults

The template code shows `NewEditableRoot()` using `DataPortal.Create()` to load default values from the database, which is great if that's what we need, but an unnecessary overhead if we don't. For objects that *don't* need to load default values, we can change the `Shared` factory method:

```
Public Shared Function NewEditableRoot() As EditableRoot
  Return New EditableRoot()
End Function
```

This also means that we can remove the implementation of `DataPortal_Create()`, because it will never be called:

```
'  Protected Overrides Sub DataPortal_Create(ByVal Criteria As Object)
'    Dim crit As Criteria = CType(Criteria, Criteria)
'
'     ' Load default values from database
'  End Sub
```

This approach is faster because it avoids the overhead of using the data portal, but of course it doesn't provide us with any way to load defaults from a database. We can, however, set defaults in the default constructor:

```
Private Sub New()
  ' Prevent direct creation

  ' Set any default values here
End Sub
```

Immediate or deferred deletion

As implemented in the template, we can delete the object by calling the `Shared` delete method and providing the criteria to identify the object to be deleted. As you know, however, the `BusinessBase` class also defines a `Delete()` method which provides for *deferred* deletion, where the object must be retrieved, marked as deleted, and then updated in order for it to be deleted. The object's data is then deleted as part of the update process.

If we only want to support deferred deletion, we can simply remove the `Shared` delete method:

```
'  Public Shared Sub DeleteEditableRoot()
'    DataPortal.Delete(New Criteria())
'  End Sub
```

Then, the only way to delete the object is by calling the `Delete()` method and updating the object to the database.

Editable child business objects

Most applications will have some editable child objects, or even grandchild objects. Examples of these include our `ProjectResource` and `ResourceAssignment` objects. In many cases, the child objects are contained within a child collection object, which we'll discuss later. In other cases, the child object might be referenced directly by the parent object. Either way, the basic structure of a child object is the same; in some ways, this template is very similar to the editable root:

Class header and variable declarations

```
<Serializable()> _
Public Class EditableChild
  Inherits BusinessBase

  ' Declare variables here to contain object state

  ' Declare variables for any child collections here
```

We start out by declaring our variables, along with any collections of child objects (which would be grandchild objects at this point).

Business properties and methods

```
#Region " Business Properties and Methods "

  ' Implement properties and methods here so the UI or
  ' other client code can interact with the object

#End Region
```

The *Business Properties and Methods* region will contain the properties and methods used by client code, such as the UI, to interact with our object. This is no different from what we would do in a root object.

System.Object overrides

```
#Region " System.Object Overrides "

  Public Overrides Function ToString() As String
    ' Return text describing our object
  End Function

  Public Overloads Function Equals(ByVal obj As MyBusinessClass) As Boolean
    ' Implement comparison between two of our type of object
  End Function

  Public Overrides Function GetHashCode() As Integer
    ' Return a hash value for our object
  End Function

#End Region
```

Again, as in a root object, we override key `System.Object` methods. This is even more important when dealing with child objects, as they are very likely to be contained in collections. It is *critical* that the `Equals()` method should operate efficiently and accurately, as it will be used by the collection classes to determine whether the collection contains a specific child object.

Shared factory methods

```
#Region " Shared Methods "

  Friend Shared Function NewEditableChild() As EditableChild
```

```
    Return CType(DataPortal.Create(New Criteria()), EditableChild)
  End Function

  Friend Shared Function GetEditableChild(dr as IDataReader) As EditableChild
    Dim obj As New EditableChild()
    obj.Fetch(dr)
    Return obj
  End Function

#End Region
```

The *Shared Methods* region differs from the root object. We need to support creation of a new child object, but that `Shared` method is now scoped as `Friend`. This way, only the parent object or collection can create an instance of the child object – not client code such as the UI.

We also include a `GetEditableChild()` method, which is called by the parent object or collection during the fetch process. As we discussed earlier in the object lifecycle discussion, the parent object calls this method passing it a data reader object, so that our child object can load its data.

> *If we're obtaining our data from somewhere other than ADO.NET, we might pass a different type of object here. For instance, if we're loading our data from an XML document, we might pass an* `XmlNode` *instead of a data reader.*

Constructors

```
#Region " Constructors "

  Private Sub New()
    ' Prevent direct creation

    ' Tell CSLA .NET that we are a child object
    MarkAsChild()
  End Sub

#End Region
```

Like all business classes, editable child classes include a `Private` default constructor. This constructor includes a call to `MarkAsChild()` to tell CSLA .NET that this is a child object. This call is required – if it weren't there, the framework would view this object as being an editable root object, rather than a child object.

Criteria

```
#Region " Criteria "

  <Serializable()> _
  Private Class Criteria
    ' Add criteria here
  End Class

#End Region
```

We also include a `Criteria` class, but this is only required if we want to load default values from the database as new child objects are created.

Data access

```
#Region " Data Access "

  Protected Overrides Sub DataPortal_Create(ByVal Criteria As Object)
    Dim crit As Criteria = CType(Criteria, Criteria)

    ' Load default values from database
  End Sub

  Private Sub Fetch(ByVal dr As IDataReader)

    ' Load object data from database
  End Sub

  Friend Sub Update(ByVal Parent As EditableRoot)

    ' Insert or update object data into database
  End Sub

#End Region

End Class
```

The biggest difference from a root object comes in the *Data Access* region. We implement `DataPortal_Create()` to support the loading of default values from the database on the creation of a new child object, but otherwise all retrieval and updating of child objects is handled directly by the parent object. To support this concept, we include a `Private` method named `Fetch()` that is called from our `Shared` factory method, and a `Friend` method named `Update()` that will be called by the parent object or collection.

Typically, the parent object calls our `Shared` factory method, passing it a populated data reader. The `Shared` factory method calls our `Private Fetch()` method, which takes the data from the data reader and populates the object with the values.

> *We could also implement* `Fetch()` *so that each child object retrieves its own data from the database. In that case, the parameters to the method would be the key values needed to find the right child object. This approach is usually less efficient than having the parent or collection object retrieve all the data at once, however, so the template's approach is recommended in most cases.*

The `Update()` method is called by the parent or collection object when we should insert, update, or delete our data from the database. This method typically accepts a parameter containing a reference to our parent object, so we can get any property values from it as needed. Each child object usually calls the database directly to save its data.

As an example, our `ProjectResource` child object will need the ID property from its parent `Project` object so that it can store it as a foreign key in the database. By getting a reference to its parent `Project` object, the `ProjectResource` gains access to that value as needed.

Object creation without defaults

As implemented, the template uses `DataPortal.Create()` to load the child object with default values from the database. As we discussed earlier, if our object doesn't *need* to load default values from the database, we can provide a more efficient implementation by changing the `Shared` factory method to create the child object directly. Then we can remove the `Criteria` class and the `DataPortal_Create()` method (since they won't be used), and use the default constructor to set any default values that are hard-coded into the class.

Switchable objects

It's possible that our projects will contain classes that are to be instantiated as root objects on some occasions, and as child objects on others. This can be handled by conditionally calling `MarkAsChild()`, based on how the object is being created.

Typically, this *can't* be done in the default constructor, because there's no way to determine there whether we're being created as a root or a child object. Instead, we need to go back to our object's lifecycle to see where we *can* make this decision. In fact, since the default is for an object to be a root object, all we need to do is determine the paths by which a child object can be created, and make sure to call `MarkAsChild()` only in those cases.

The template for creating a 'switchable' object is the same as the editable root template, with the following exceptions.

Object creation

Our `Criteria` class must include a flag to indicate whether we are being created as a root or a child object (this is in addition to any object-specific criteria fields that we would also have in this class):

```
<Serializable()> _
Private Class Criteria
  Public IsChild As Boolean

  Public Sub New(ByVal IsChild As Boolean)
    Me.IsChild = IsChild
  End Sub
End Class
```

Then, instead of a single `Shared` factory method to create the object, we'll have two methods – one `Public`, the other `Friend`:

```
Public Shared Function NewSwitchable() As Switchable
  Return CType(DataPortal.Create(New Criteria(False)), Switchable)
End Function

Friend Shared Function NewSwitchableChild() As Switchable
  Return CType(DataPortal.Create(New Criteria(True)), Switchable)
End Function
```

Fetching the object

Likewise, our Shared factory fetch methods will be doubled:

```
Public Shared Function GetSwitchable() As Switchable
  Return CType(DataPortal.Fetch(New Criteria(False)), Switchable)
End Function

Friend Shared Function GetSwitchableChild() As Switchable
  Return CType(DataPortal.Fetch(New Criteria(True)), Switchable)
End Function
```

Immediate deletion

And if we support immediate deletion, we'll adapt the Shared delete method as well:

```
Public Shared Sub DeleteSwitchable()
  DataPortal.Delete(New Criteria(False))
End Sub
```

Data access methods

Then, in our DataPortal_Create() method, we can use the flag:

```
Protected Overrides Sub DataPortal_Create(ByVal Criteria As Object)
  Dim crit As Criteria = CType(Criteria, Criteria)

  If crit.IsChild Then
    MarkAsChild()
  End If

  ' Load default values from database

End Sub
```

We'll also implement *both* DataPortal_Fetch() and Fetch(), and DataPortal_Update() and Update() methods. The Private Fetch() method is responsible for calling MarkAsChild() to mark the object as a child, since it is being loaded via the child process:

```
Private Sub Fetch(ByVal dr As IDataReader)
  ' Load object data from database
  MarkAsChild()
End Sub
```

When we're doing updates, we don't need to worry about calling MarkAsChild() (because the object already exists), but we still need to support both *styles* of update, since DataPortal_Update() will be used if we're in root mode, and the Friend Update() method will be used if we're in child mode.

Object creation without defaults

If we're creating the object using the New keyword instead of calling DataPortal.Create(), we can simply alter the Shared factory method to call MarkAsChild() as shown here:

```
Friend Shared Function NewSwitchableChild() As Switchable
  Dim obj As New Switchable
  obj.MarkAsChild()
  Return obj
End Function
```

From the parent object's perspective, there's no difference – it just calls the `Shared` method – but this approach is faster because it doesn't load default values from the database.

Editable root collection

There will be times when we want to retrieve a collection of child objects directly – that is, where the collection itself is the root object. For instance, we may have a Windows Forms UI consisting of a `DataGrid` control, in which we want to display a collection of `Contact` objects. By making the root object a collection of fully populated `Contact` objects, we can simply bind the collection to the `DataGrid`, and the user can do in-place editing of the objects within the grid.

The benefit of this approach is that we start with a *collection* of fully populated and editable child objects. The user can interact with all of them, and save them all at once when all edits are complete. However, this is only subtly different from having a regular root object that has a collection of child objects. The following diagram shows the regular root object approach on the left, and the collection root approach on the right:

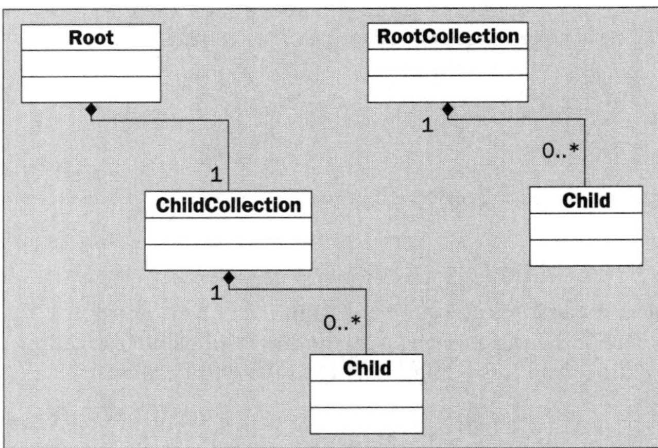

This approach is not recommended when there are large numbers of potential child objects, as the retrieval process can become too slow, but it can be very useful in cases where we can specify criteria to limit the number of objects returned. To create an editable root collection object, we can use a template like this:

```
<Serializable()> _
Public Class EditableRootCollection
  Inherits BusinessCollectionBase
```

```
#Region " Business Properties and Methods "
  Default Public ReadOnly Property Item(ByVal Index As Integer) As EditableChild
    Get
      Return CType(List.Item(Index), EditableChild)
    End Get
  End Property

  Public Sub Add(ByVal Data As String)
    List.Add(EditableChild.NewEditableChild(Data))
  End Sub

  Public Sub Remove(ByVal Child As EditableChild)
    List.Remove(Child)
  End Sub

#End Region
```

The *Business Properties and Methods* region includes the typical collection behaviors: retrieving a specific item, adding an item, and removing an item. Our `BusinessCollectionBase` class already implements other features like a `Count` property.

Whenever we implement a collection object, we need to overload the `Contains()` and `ContainsDeleted()` methods from `BusinessCollectionBase` to provide type-specific comparisons of our child objects. This is placed in a *Contains* region:

```
#Region " Contains "

  Public Overloads Function Contains( _
      ByVal item As EditableChild) As Boolean

    Dim child As EditableChild

    For Each child In list
      If child.Equals(item) Then
        Return True
      End If
    Next

    Return False

  End Function

  Public Overloads Function ContainsDeleted( _
      ByVal item As EditableChild) As Boolean

    Dim child As EditableChild

    For Each child In deletedList
      If child.Equals(item) Then
        Return True
      End If
    Next

    Return False

  End Function

#End Region
```

It seems like this ought to be unnecessary, because the .NET base collection code should properly compare our child objects. Unfortunately, this is not the case – the default .NET behavior *doesn't* call the `Equals()` methods that we implemented in our child objects. This means that we must implement type-specific comparisons within our business collection classes to ensure our `Equals()` methods are invoked.

There is no *System.Object Overrides* region in this template. While there may be a few collection objects in which these overrides would be of value, in most cases the collection object can't be consolidated into something simple enough to be represented by a simple line of text, or easily compared to another collection in an `Equals()` method.

```
#Region " Shared Methods "

  Public Shared Function NewCollection() As EditableRootCollection
    Return New EditableRootCollection()
  End Function

  Public Shared Function GetCollection() As EditableRootCollection
    Return CType(DataPortal.Fetch(New Criteria()), EditableRootCollection)
  End Function

  Public Shared Sub DeleteCollection()
    DataPortal.Delete(New Criteria())
  End Sub

#End Region
```

The *Shared Methods* section includes a method to create an empty collection. While this *could* call `DataPortal.Create()`, it's very unlikely that a collection object will have default values that need retrieving from the database. (If your collection object does require this functionality, call `DataPortal.Create()` and implement a `DataPortal_Create()` method.) There are also methods for retrieving and deleting the collection. The former calls `DataPortal.Fetch()`, and triggers the process of creating and returning all the child objects belonging to the collection. The latter triggers the process of deleting all the data for all child objects belonging to the collection.

The template also includes *Constructor* and *Criteria* regions, just like those in the `EditableRoot` template.

```
#Region " Data Access "

  Protected Overrides Sub DataPortal_Fetch(ByVal Criteria As Object)
    Dim crit As Criteria = CType(Criteria, Criteria)

    ' Retrieve all child data into a data reader
    ' then loop through and create each child object
    While dr.Read
      List.Add(EditableChild.GetEditableChild(dr))
    End While
  End Sub

  Protected Overrides Sub DataPortal_Update()
    ' Loop through each deleted child object and call its Update() method
    For Each child As EditableChild In deletedList
```

```
      child.Update(Me)
    Next

    ' Then clear the list of deleted objects because they are truly gone now
    deletedList.Clear()

    ' Loop through each non-deleted child object and call its Update() method
    For Each child As EditableChild In list
      child.Update(Me)
    Next
  End Sub

  Protected Overrides Sub DataPortal_Delete(ByVal Criteria As Object)
    Dim crit As Criteria = CType(Criteria, Criteria)

    ' Delete all child object data that matches the criteria
  End Sub

#End Region

End Class
```

Finally, the data access methods for collections are somewhat different from those for simple editable objects. The `DataPortal_Fetch()` method is responsible for getting the data from the database, typically via a data reader. It then calls the `Shared` factory method of the child class for each row in the data reader, allowing each child object to load its data. As we've seen, the `Shared` factory method in the child class calls its own `Private Fetch()` method to actually load the data from the data reader.

The `DataPortal_Update()` method must loop through all the child objects contained in the collection, calling each object's `Update()` method in turn. We must run through the list of deleted child objects and the list of non-deleted child objects.

It is critical that the *deleted* child objects be processed first.

It is quite possible for the user to delete a child object from the collection, and then add a new child object *with the same primary key value.* This means that we'll have the original child object marked as deleted in our list of deleted child objects, and the new child object in our list of non-deleted objects. This new object will have its `IsNew` property set to `True`, because it is a new object. If we don't first delete the original child object, the insertion of the new child object will fail.

Thus, in the template, we first process the list of deleted child objects, and then move on to process the list of non-deleted child objects.

Editable child collection

The most common type of collection is one where we have a collection of child objects, like `ProjectResources` and `ResourceAssignments` in our sample application.

Note that the parent object here might be a root object, or it might be a child itself – child objects can be nested, if that's what's required by our business object model. In other words, we support not only root-child, but also child-grandchild and grandchild-great grandchild relationships.

A child collection class inherits from BusinessCollectionBase and calls MarkAsChild() during its creation process to indicate that it's operating in child mode. This also means that it won't be directly retrieved or updated by the DataPortal, but instead will be retrieved or updated by its parent object.

Class header and collection behaviors

The basic code structure is as follows:

```
<Serializable()> _
Public Class EditableChildCollection
  Inherits BusinessCollectionBase

#Region " Business Properties and Methods "

  Default Public ReadOnly Property Item(ByVal Index As Integer) As EditableChild
    Get
      Return CType(List.Item(Index), EditableChild)
    End Get
  End Property

  Public Sub Add(ByVal Data As String)
    List.Add(EditableChild.NewEditableChild(Data))
  End Sub

  Public Sub Remove(ByVal Child As EditableChild)
    List.Remove(Child)
  End Sub

#End Region
```

The *Business Properties and Methods* are no different from those for a root collection. As with any collection, we expose strongly typed Item(), Add(), and Remove() methods.

Contains methods

The *Contains* region is no different from that for a root collection, either:

```
#Region " Contains "

  Public Overloads Function Contains(ByVal item As EditableChild) As Boolean

    Dim child As EditableChild

    For Each child In list
      If child.Equals(item) Then
        Return True
      End If
    Next

    Return False

  End Function
```

```
    Public Overloads Function ContainsDeleted( _
        ByVal item As EditableChild) As Boolean

      Dim child As EditableChild

      For Each child In deletedList
        If child.Equals(item) Then
          Return True
        End If
      Next

      Return False

    End Function

  #End Region
```

Again, we must implement type-specific methods so the overloaded `Equals()` methods of our child objects are properly invoked.

Shared methods and constructors

The *Shared Methods* and *Constructors* regions, however, are quite different. Here's the former:

```
  #Region " Shared Methods "

    Friend Shared Function NewEditableChildCollection() As EditableChildCollection
      Return New EditableChildCollection
    End Function

    Friend Shared Function GetEditableChildCollection( _
                    ByVal dr As IDataReader) As EditableChildCollection
      Dim col As New EditableChildCollection
      col.Fetch(dr)
      Return col
    End Function

  #End Region
```

Since only a parent object can create or fetch an instance of this class, the `Shared` factory methods are scoped as `Friend`. The `Shared` method to create an object simply returns a new collection object. As with the `EditableChild` template, our constructor will call `MarkAsChild()` to indicate that this is a child object. Likewise, the `Shared` method to load the child collection with data creates a new collection object and then calls its `Private Fetch()` method – just like we did in the `EditableChild` template.

The constructor looks like this:

```
  #Region " Constructors "

    Private Sub New()
      ' Prevent direct creation
      MarkAsChild()
    End Sub

  #End Region
```

The constructor method calls `MarkAsChild()` to mark this as a child collection object. This is the same as our code in the `EditableChild` class template.

Since there's virtually never a reason to load a child collection with default values, we don't include a *Criteria* region or `Criteria` class. If you have a need to load the child collection with default values, you can add that region, alter the `Shared` factory method, and add a `DataPortal_Create()` method, as we discussed for the `EditableChild` class template.

Data access

```
#Region " Data Access "

  Private Sub Fetch(ByVal dr As IDataReader)
    ' Create a child object for each row in the data source
    While dr.Read
      List.Add(EditableChild.GetEditableChild(dr))
    End While
  End Sub

  Friend Sub Update(ByVal Parent As EditableRoot)
    ' Loop through each deleted child object and call its Update() method
    For Each child As EditableChild In deletedList
      child.Update(Parent)
    Next

    ' Then clear the list of deleted objects because they are truly gone now
    deletedList.Clear()

    ' Loop through each non-deleted child object and call its Update() method
    For Each child As EditableChild In List
      child.Update(Parent)
    Next
  End Sub

#End Region

End Class
```

The `Fetch()` method is very similar to that in the `EditableChild` template. It accepts a data reader (or some other data source) as a parameter and then loops through the data, creating a child object for each row and then adding that child object to the collection.

The `Update()` method is similar to the `DataPortal_Update()` in our `EditableRootCollection`. It loops through the list of deleted child objects calling their `Update()` methods, and then does the same for the non-deleted child objects.

Read-only business objects

Sometimes, we may need an object that provides data in a read-only fashion. If we want a list of read-only data, we'll create a read-only collection; but if we want a single object containing read-only data, we'll inherit from `ReadOnlyBase`. This is one of the simplest types of object to create, since it does nothing more than retrieve and return data:

```
<Serializable()> _
Public Class ReadOnlyObject
  Inherits ReadOnlyBase

  ' Declare variables here to contain object state

  ' Declare variables for any child collections here

#Region " Business Properties and Methods "

  ' Implement read-only properties and methods here so the UI or
  ' other client code can interact with the object

  'Public ReadOnly Property Data() As String
  '  Get
  '
  '  End Get
  'End Property

#End Region

#Region " System.Object Overrides "

  Public Overrides Function ToString() As String
    ' Return text describing our object
  End Function

  Public Overloads Function Equals(ByVal obj As MyBusinessClass) As Boolean
    ' Implement comparison between two of our type of object
  End Function

  Public Overrides Function GetHashCode() As Integer
    ' Return a hash value for our object
  End Function

#End Region

#Region " Shared Methods "

  Public Shared Function GetReadOnlyObject() As ReadOnlyObject
    Return CType(DataPortal.Fetch(New Criteria), ReadOnlyObject)
  End Function

#End Region

#Region " Constructors "

  Private Sub New()
    ' Prevent direct creation
  End Sub

#End Region
```

```
#Region " Criteria "
  <Serializable()> _
  Private Class Criteria
    ' Add criteria here
  End Class

#End Region

#Region " Data Access "

  Protected Overrides Sub DataPortal_Fetch(ByVal Criteria As Object)
    Dim crit As Criteria = CType(Criteria, Criteria)
    ' Load object data from database
  End Sub

#End Region

End Class
```

Like other business objects, a read-only object will have instance variables that contain its data. It will typically also have read-only properties or methods that allow client code to retrieve values. As long as they don't change the state of the object, these may even be calculated values.

In the *Shared Methods* region, we have a `Shared` factory method that retrieves the object by calling `DataPortal.Fetch()`. This means that we also have a `Criteria` class, which should be modified to contain the criteria data needed to select the correct object for retrieval.

The *Data Access* region just contains `DataPortal_Fetch()`, which is the only `Overridable` method from the base class. Of course, there is no need to support updating or deleting a read-only object.

Read-only collections of objects

We may also need to retrieve a *collection* of read-only objects. When we implemented the CSLA .NET framework, we created the `ReadOnlyCollectionBase` class, which is a read-only collection. It throws an exception any time we attempt to change which items are in the collection by adding or removing objects.

However, there is no way for the collection object to stop client code from interacting with the child objects themselves. Typically, the items in the collection will be derived from `ReadOnlyBase`, so they too are read-only. If we put read-write objects into the collection, client code will be able to alter their data. A read-only collection only guarantees that objects can't be added or removed from the collection.

The code for a typical read-only collection object looks like this:

```
<Serializable()> _
Public Class ReadOnlyCollection
  Inherits ReadOnlyCollectionBase

#Region " Business Properties and Methods "

  Default Public ReadOnly Property Item( _
                              ByVal Index As Integer) As ReadOnlyObject
    Get
```

```
      Return CType(List.Item(Index), ReadOnlyObject)
    End Get
  End Property

#End Region
```

The only valid operation on a read-only collection is to retrieve items, so we have an `Item()` property, but no methods to add or remove elements. We also overload the `Contains()` method to provide a type-specific version that invokes the overloaded `Equals()` method on our child class:

```
#Region " Contains "

  Public Overloads Function Contains(ByVal item As ReadOnlyObject) As Boolean

    Dim child As ReadOnlyObject

    For Each child In list
      If child.Equals(item) Then
        Return True
      End If
    Next

    Return False

  End Function

#End Region
```

In the *Shared Methods* region, we have a `Shared` factory method to return a collection loaded with data. It calls `DataPortal.Fetch()`, and so we have a `Criteria` class as well as a `Private` constructor. This is no different from the classes we've looked at already:

```
#Region " Shared Methods "

  Public Shared Function GetCollection() As ReadOnlyCollection
    Return CType(DataPortal.Fetch(New Criteria), ReadOnlyCollection)
  End Function

#End Region

#Region " Constructors "

  Private Sub New()
    ' Prevent direct creation
  End Sub

#End Region

#Region " Criteria "

  <Serializable()> _
  Public Class Criteria
```

```
    End Class

  #End Region
```

Finally, we have `DataPortal_Fetch()`, where we set the `Locked` flag to `False`, then load the data from the database, and then restore its value to `True`. While `Locked` is set to `True`, any attempt to add or remove items from the collection will result in an exception being thrown, so we need to set it to `False` for long enough to load the data from the database and insert all the appropriate child objects into the collection:

```
  #Region " Data Access "

    Protected Overrides Sub DataPortal_Fetch(ByVal Criteria As Object)
      Locked = False

      Dim crit As Criteria = CType(Criteria, Criteria)

      ' Retrieve all child data into a data reader
      ' then loop through and create each child object
      While dr.Read()
        List.Add(ReadOnlyObject.GetReadOnlyObject(dr))
      End While

      Locked = True
    End Sub

  #End Region

  End Class
```

Name-value list objects

Perhaps the simplest business object that we can create is a name-value list that inherits from the `NameValueList` class in the CSLA .NET framework. The base class provides virtually all the functionality we need, including basic data access and the `Shared` factory method, so all we need to do is provide a `Criteria` class and a `DataPortal_Fetch()` method. It turns out that the *only* code specific to each list is the implementation of `DataPortal_Fetch()`.

Basic name-value code

Here's the code for almost any name-value list object:

```
  <Serializable()> _
  Public Class MyDataList
    Inherits NameValueList

  #Region " Shared Methods "

    Public Shared Function GetMyDataList() As MyDataList
      Return CType(DataPortal.Fetch(New Criteria), MyDataList)
    End Function
```

```
#End Region

#Region " Constructors "

  Private Sub New()
    ' Prevent direct creation
  End Sub

  ' This constructor overload is required because the base class
  '  (NameObjectCollectionBase) implements ISerializable
  Private Sub New( _
        ByVal info As System.Runtime.Serialization.SerializationInfo, _
        ByVal context As System.Runtime.Serialization.StreamingContext)
    MyBase.New(info, context)
  End Sub

#End Region

#Region " Criteria "

  <Serializable()> _
  Private Class Criteria
    ' Add criteria here
  End Class

#End Region

#Region " Data Access "

  ' Called by DataPortal to load data from the database
  Protected Overrides Sub DataPortal_Fetch(ByVal Criteria As Object)
    SimpleFetch("myDatabase", "myTable", "myNameColumn", " myValueColumn")
  End Sub

#End Region

End Class
```

To customize this for almost any data from a single table, simply change the database, table, and column names specified in the `DataPortal_Fetch()` implementation:

```
' Called by DataPortal to load data from the database
Protected Overrides Sub DataPortal_Fetch(ByVal Criteria As Object)
  SimpleFetch("database", "table", "namecolumn", "valuecolumn")
End Sub
```

This will populate the object with the appropriate columns from the specified table in the specified database. The database must have a corresponding entry in the application configuration file so that the `DataPortal` code can retrieve the connection string, as we discussed in Chapter 5.

Complex name-value data retrieval

In some cases, it may not be possible to retrieve the name-value data using the simple retrieval method provided by the `NameValueList` base class – perhaps a table join or some other sophisticated scheme is required; or perhaps the list must be filtered, so that some criteria are required to support the retrieval process.

This can be handled by changing the `Shared` factory method to accept criteria data, enhancing the class to store that data and implementing our own data access code in `DataPortal_Fetch()` rather than calling the `SimpleFetch()` method, just like we did in the `EditableRoot` class template.

At this point, we've examined the basic structure of the code for each type of business object or collection that we can create based on the CSLA .NET framework. Let's move on now and implement our sample project tracker application classes.

Project tracker objects

In Chapter 6, we created an object model for our sample project tracking application. This object model includes some editable root business objects (`Project` and `Resource`), some editable child objects (`ProjectResource` and `ResourceAssignment`), some collections of child objects (`ProjectResources` and `ResourceAssignments`), and a name-value list (`RoleList`). It also includes two read-only collections (`ProjectList` and `ResourceList`).

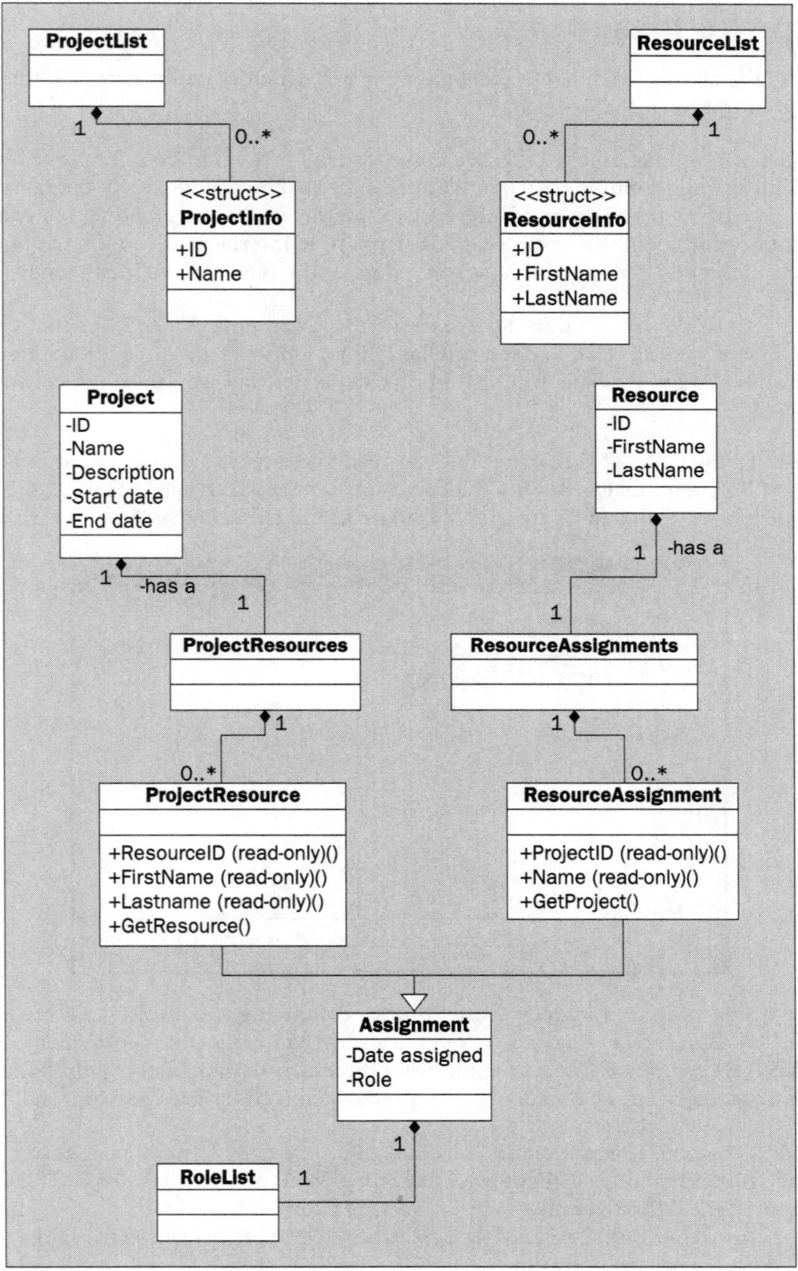

By implementing these objects, we should get a good feel for the practical process of taking the class templates we've just examined and applying them to the creation of real business classes.

Setting up the project

Before creating the classes, we need to create a project in which to build them. On this occasion, this will be a Class Library project, or DLL.

By putting our business classes in a DLL, we make it easy for them to be referenced by various different 'front ends'. This is important for our example, because we'll be using exactly the same DLL to support the Windows Forms, Web Forms, and web services interfaces we'll be creating. It's equally important in 'real world' applications, since they too often have multiple interfaces. Even if an application starts with a single interface, the odds are good that at some time in the future, it will need a new one.

Open the `ProjectTracker` solution that we created in Chapter 6. At the moment, it only contains the `PTrackerDB` database project, so add a new Class Library project and give it a name of `ProjectTracker.Library`. This will be a library of classes that we can use to construct the project tracker application.

Since we'll be using the CSLA .NET framework, we need to reference `CSLA.dll`. As usual, this is done through the Add Reference dialog, so click the **Browse** button and navigate to the `CSLA\bin` directory, where we created the assembly in Chapters 3-5. Choose all the DLLs in the directory, as shown in the figure:

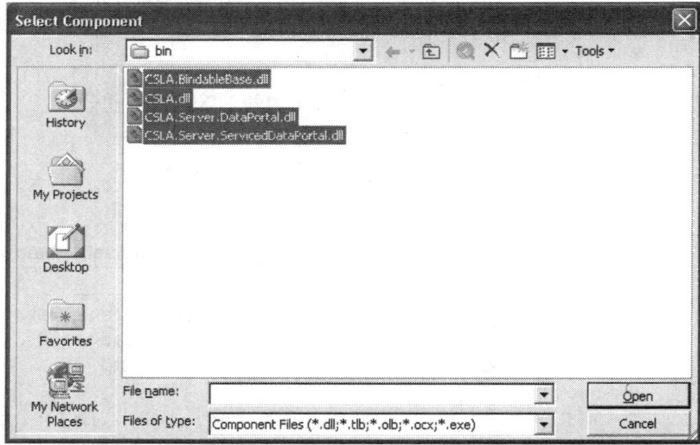

Technically, we only need to reference those libraries containing classes that `CSLA.dll` inherits from – which is just `CSLA.BindableBase.dll` – but we also need to consider deployment. Referencing a DLL causes VS.NET to copy it into our application directory automatically, simplifying deployment because we can just copy our application's `bin` directory to a client machine to install the application.

As a result, `CSLA.Server.DataPortal.dll` and `CSLA.Server.ServicedDataPortal.dll` are referenced and will end up on the client workstations of Windows Forms clients. This might appear to be a problem for workstations running Windows 98, ME, or NT 4.0, since `CSLA.Server.ServicedDataPortal.dll` requires COM+. However, these DLLs won't be accessed (or even loaded into memory) unless they are used.

> **If we plan to run the server-side `DataPortal` on older client workstations, we must not use the `<Transactional()>` attribute on our data access methods.**

As long as we don't use the <Transactional()> attribute on our DataPortal_xxx() methods, none of our code will use transactional components, and so CSLA.Server.ServicedDataPortal.dll will never be loaded into memory. If we *do* use the <Transactional()> attribute and attempt to run the server-side DataPortal code under an older operating system, we'll get run-time exceptions due to the lack of COM+ support on such machines.

If we need the two-phase distributed transactional support provided by Enterprise Services, then we must ensure that the server-side DataPortal code runs on machines with Windows 2000 or higher, where COM+ is available. If we are using older client workstations, then we'll typically do this by running the server-side DataPortal remotely on a Windows 2000 application server.

In the Build tab of the project's properties window, change the Option Strict setting to On. Also, use the Imports tab to add a global import of the CSLA and CSLA.Data namespaces:

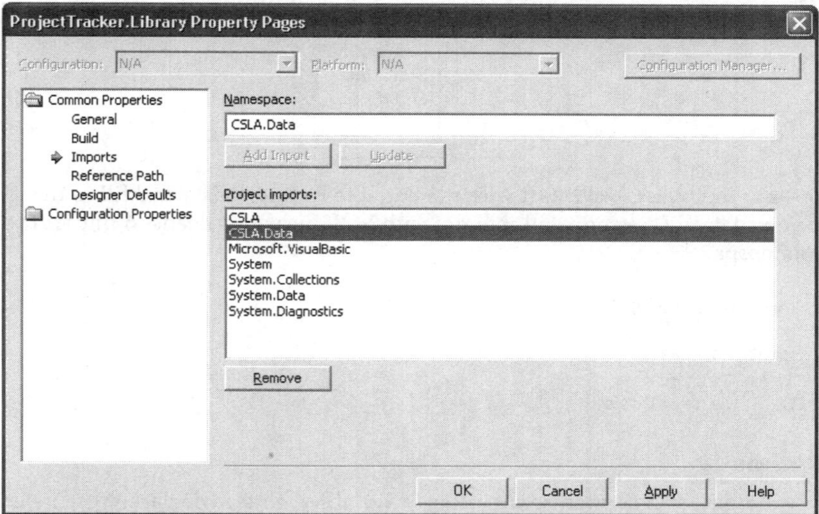

Since virtually every class in this project will be inheriting from some base class in the CSLA .NET framework, adding these global imports makes sense. It means that we don't need to add an Imports statement at the top of every class file in the project to make the base class available.

Finally, delete Class1.vb from the project – we'll add our own classes as needed. At this point, we're all ready to create our business classes.

Business class implementation

The business classes that we'll implement here follow the object-oriented design we created in Chapter 6. In that chapter, we came up with not only the classes to be created, but also their major data elements. Furthermore, we identified which CSLA .NET base classes each one will subclass.

In this section, we'll walk through the first few classes in detail. The other classes will be very similar, so for those we'll discuss only the key features. Of course, the complete code for all classes is available in the code download for this book.

The Project class

The `Project` class is an editable root class that represents a single project in our application. It will follow the `EditableRoot` template, as we discussed earlier in the chapter. This means that it inherits from `BusinessBase`:

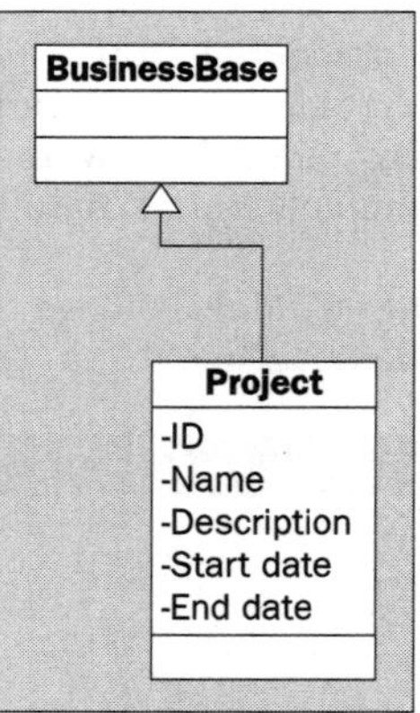

To create the `Project` class, we'll start with the editable root template and fill in the specific code for a project. Since our data access code will interact with SQL Server, it needs to import the `SqlClient` namespace:

```
Imports System.Data.SqlClient

<Serializable()> _
Public Class Project
  Inherits BusinessBase
```

Variable declarations

We know that our class will contain some instance variables, so let's declare those next:

```
  Private mID As Guid = Guid.NewGuid
  Private mName As String = ""
  Private mStarted As New SmartDate(False)
  Private mEnded As New SmartDate
  Private mDescription As String = ""
```

These correspond to the data fields that we described in our object model in Chapter 6.

Notice that the date values are of type `SmartDate`, rather than just `Date`. We're taking advantage of our `SmartDate` class that understands empty dates – and in fact, we're specifying that `mStarted` should treat an empty date as the maximum possible date value, while `mEnded` will treat it as the minimum value.

> **All instance variables should be initialized with a default value as they are declared due to a bug (should that be 'feature'?) in Windows Forms data binding, which throws a run-time exception if attempting to data bind against an object that *doesn't* have its instance variables initialized.**

Our `Project` objects will also contain a collection of `ProjectResource` child objects. Since we haven't yet created the child collection class, this will result in an error at the moment, but we'll add the declaration regardless:

```
  Private mResources As ProjectResources = _
    ProjectResources.NewProjectResources()
```

Business properties and methods

Next up is the *Business Properties and Methods* region, where we implement the bulk of our business logic as well as exposing appropriate data and functionality to any client code. Let's start with the `ID` property:

```
#Region " Business Properties and Methods "

  Public ReadOnly Property ID() As Guid
    Get
      Return mID
    End Get
  End Property

#End Region
```

Since this is the primary key for the data in the database, and the unique ID field for the object, it is a read-only property. Making the property read-only is possible because the value is a GUID, and we can easily generate a unique value when the object is initialized. As we'll see when we implement the `Resource` class, things are more complex when a non-GUID value is used.

Now let's try something a bit more interesting. In Chapter 6, we walked through some use cases that described the application we're now building. Included in the use cases were descriptions of the data the users required, and several rules governing that data. Included in the description of a project was a required `Name` field.

The `Name` property is not only read-write, but it includes some business rule checking, so we'll make use of the `BrokenRules` functionality that we built into our base class. Add this to the same region:

```
  Public Property Name() As String
    Get
      Return mName
    End Get

    Set(ByVal Value As String)
      If mName <> Value Then
        mName = Value
        MarkDirty()

        BrokenRules.Assert("NameLen", "Name too long", _
                           Len(Value) > 50)
        BrokenRules.Assert("NameRequired", "Project name required", _
                           Len(Value) = 0)
      End If
    End Set
  End Property
```

When a new value is provided for the `Name` property, we first check to see if the provided value actually *is* new – if it's the same as the value we already have, then there's no sense doing any work. After that, we check a couple of business validation rules, such as whether the length of the value exceeds our maximum length:

```
BrokenRules.Assert("NameLen", "Name too long", _
                   Len(Value) > 50)
```

If the length exceeds 50, an entry will be added to our list of broken rules. If it is 50 or less, any matching entry in the broken rules list will be removed.

The same is done if the length of the value is zero. Since this is a required field, a zero length results in a broken rule, while a non-zero length is acceptable.

In any case, we update our internal value (`mName`) with the value provided. This might put our object into an invalid state, but that's all right – our base class provides the `IsValid` property, which would then return `False` to indicate that our object is currently invalid. The `IsValid` property is automatically maintained by the CSLA .NET framework as we mark rules as broken or unbroken via the `Assert()` method.

This also ties into the implementation of the `Save()` method in the base class, which prevents any attempt at updating the database when the object is in an invalid state.

When we change the value of the `mName` variable, we also make this call:

```
mName = Value
MarkDirty()
```

This tells the CSLA .NET framework that our object has been altered. If we don't make this call, our object may not be updated into the database properly, and Windows Forms data binding will not work properly.

> **Whenever we change the value of one of our instance variables, we *must* call `MarkDirty()`. In fact, we should call it anywhere that our instance variables are changed, whether that be in a property like this, or within a method that implements business logic that updates our object's values.**

Moving on, the two `SmartDate` fields also include business validation:

- The started date must be prior to the ended date, or the ended date must be empty
- The ended date can be empty, or it must be after the started date
- If there is an ended date, there must be a started date

By storing the date fields in `SmartDate` objects, this becomes easy to implement. We expose the date fields as `String` properties so that they can be easily bound to controls in either Windows Forms or Web Forms interfaces, but behind the scenes we're using the `SmartDate` data type to manage the date values:

```
Public Property Started() As String
  Get
    Return mStarted.Text
  End Get

  Set(ByVal Value As String)
    If mStarted.Text <> Value Then
      mStarted.Text = Value
      MarkDirty()

      If mEnded.IsEmpty Then
        BrokenRules.Assert("DateCol", "", False)
      Else
        BrokenRules.Assert("DateCol", _
                          "Start date must be prior to end date", _
                          mStarted.CompareTo(mEnded) > 0)
      End If
    End If
  End Set
End Property

Public Property Ended() As String
  Get
    Return mEnded.Text
  End Get

  Set(ByVal Value As String)
    If mEnded.Text <> Value Then
      mEnded.Text = Value
      MarkDirty()

      If mEnded.IsEmpty Then
        BrokenRules.Assert("DateCol", "", False)
      Else
        If mStarted.IsEmpty Then
          BrokenRules.Assert("DateCol", _
                            "Ended date must be later than start date", _
                            True)
        Else
          BrokenRules.Assert("DateCol", _
                            "Ended date must be later than start date", _
                            mEnded.CompareTo(mStarted) < 0)
        End If
      End If
    End If
  End Set
End Property
```

These business rules are a bit more complex, since they affect not only the field being updated, but also the 'other' field. Notice the use of the features that we built into the `SmartDate` data type as we check to see if each field is empty, and then do comparisons to see which is greater than the other. Remember that an empty date can represent either the largest or the smallest possible date, which helps keep our code relatively simple.

The user can easily set either date to be empty by clearing the text field in the Windows Forms or Web Forms UI. Remember that our `SmartDate` code considers an empty `String` value to be equivalent to an empty `Date` value.

As with the `Name` property, the calls to `Assert()` automatically add and remove entries from the list of broken rules, potentially moving our object into and out of a valid state as the data changes.

We also have a `Description` property:

```
Public Property Description() As String
  Get
    Return mDescription
  End Get

  Set(ByVal Value As String)
    If mDescription <> Value Then
      mDescription = Value
      MarkDirty()
    End If
  End Set
End Property
```

Since this is an optional text field that can contain almost unlimited amounts of text, there is no real need for any business validation in this property.

The final business property we need to implement in this region provides client code with access to our child objects (this code will initially be displayed as an error because we have not yet implemented the child collection):

```
Public ReadOnly Property Resources() As ProjectResources
  Get
    Return mResources
  End Get
End Property
```

We don't want the client code to be able to replace our collection object with a new one, so this is a read-only property. Because the collection object itself will be editable, however, the client code will be able to add and remove child objects as appropriate.

Overriding IsValid and IsDirty

We need to do one last bit of work before moving on to the remaining code regions. Since this is a parent object that has a collection of child objects, the default behavior for `IsValid` and `IsDirty` won't work.

> **The default `IsValid` and `IsDirty` properties must be enhanced for all objects that subclass `BusinessBase` and contain child objects.**

A parent object is invalid if its own variables are in an invalid state *or* if any of its child objects is in an invalid state. Likewise, a parent object is dirty if its own data has been changed, or if any of its child objects or collections have been changed. To handle this properly, we need to override the `IsValid` and `IsDirty` properties, and provide a slightly more sophisticated implementation of each:

```
Public Overrides ReadOnly Property IsValid() As Boolean
  Get
    Return MyBase.IsValid AndAlso mResources.IsValid
  End Get
End Property

Public Overrides ReadOnly Property IsDirty() As Boolean
  Get
    Return MyBase.IsDirty OrElse mResources.IsDirty
  End Get
End Property
```

In both cases, we first see if the `Project` object itself is invalid or dirty. If so, we can simply return `True`. Otherwise, we check the child collection to see if it (and by extension, any of its child objects) is invalid or dirty.

The key here is the use of the `OrElse` keyword. If `MyBase.IsValid` returns `True`, there's no need to go through all the work of checking the child objects – we can simply return `True`. The `OrElse` keyword understands this and short-circuits the check, avoiding the extra call when appropriate.

System.Object overrides

To be good .NET citizens, our objects should at least override the `ToString()` method and provide a meaningful implementation of the `Equals()` method. These are placed in our *System.Object Overrides* region:

```
#Region " System.Object Overrides "

  Public Overrides Function ToString() As String
    Return mID.ToString
  End Function

  Public Overloads Function Equals(ByVal Project As Project) As Boolean
    Return mID.Equals(Project.ID)
  End Function

  Public Overrides Function GetHashCode() As Integer
    Return mID.GetHashCode()
  End Function

#End Region
```

Since a `Project` object's unique identifying field is its GUID, we can return that value in `ToString()`, thus providing a meaningful text value that identifies our object. Likewise, to compare two `Project` objects for equality, all we really need to do is see if their GUIDs match. If they do, then the two objects represent the same project.

Shared methods

We can now move on to create our `Shared` factory methods:

```
#Region " Shared Methods "

  ' Create new object
  Public Shared Function NewProject() As Project
    Return CType(DataPortal.Create(New Criteria(Guid.Empty)), Project)
  End Function

  ' Load existing object by ID
  Public Shared Function GetProject(ByVal ID As Guid) As Project
    Return CType(DataPortal.Fetch(New Criteria(ID)), Project)
  End Function

  ' Delete object
  Public Shared Sub DeleteProject(ByVal ID As Guid)
    DataPortal.Delete(New Criteria(ID))
  End Sub

#End Region
```

We need to support the creation of a brand new `Project` object. This can be done in two ways: either by calling `DataPortal.Create()` to load default values from the database, or by using the `New` keyword to create the object directly.

Though in our application, our `Project` objects won't load any defaults from the database, we've implemented the `NewProject()` method so that it calls `DataPortal.Create()`, just to illustrate how it's done. Since the `DataPortal.Create()` method requires a `Criteria` object, we create one with a dummy GUID. When we implement our `DataPortal_Create()` method, we'll load the object with a set of default values.

We also implement the `GetProject()` `Shared` factory method to retrieve an existing `Project` object, populated with data from the database. This method simply calls `DataPortal.Fetch()`, which in turn ends up creating a new `Project` object and calling its `DataPortal_Fetch()` method to do the actual data access. The `Criteria` object is passed through this process, so our data access code will have access to the GUID key.

Finally, we include a `Shared` method to allow immediate deletion of a project. Our `Project` object also supports deferred deletion (where the client code calls the `Delete()` method on the object, then calls the `Save()` method to update the object and complete the deletion process), but this `Shared` method provides for a more direct approach. The client code provides the GUID key, and the project's data is removed from the database directly, without the overhead of having to retrieve the object first.

Constructors

As we noted earlier, all business objects must include a default constructor:

```
#Region " Constructors "

  Private Sub New()
    ' Prevent direct instantiation
  End Sub

#End Region
```

This is straight out of the template we discussed earlier in the chapter. It ensures that client code must use our `Shared` factory methods to create or retrieve a `Project` object, and it provides the `DataPortal` with a constructor that it can call via reflection.

Criteria

Next, let's create our `Criteria` class. The unique identifier for a project, in both the database and our object model, is its GUID `ID` value. Since the GUID value will always identify a single project, it is the criterion that we'll use to retrieve a `Project` object. Add it in the *Criteria* region:

```
#Region " Criteria "

  ' Criteria for identifying existing object
  <Serializable()> _
  Private Class Criteria
    Public ID As Guid

    Public Sub New(ByVal ID As Guid)
      Me.ID = ID
    End Sub
  End Class

#End Region
```

As we've discussed before, the sole purpose of a `Criteria` object is to pass data from the client to the `DataPortal` in order to select the right object. To make our `Shared` factory methods easier to implement, we include a constructor that accepts the criterion as a parameter. To make a `Criteria` object easy to use during the data creation, retrieval, and delete processes, we store the criterion value in a `Public` variable that can be directly accessed by our data access code.

At this point, we've completed the business properties and methods, and the `Shared` factory methods. All that remains is to implement the data access logic so that the object can be created, retrieved, updated, and deleted.

Data access

In the *Data Access* region, we'll implement the four `DataPortal_xxx()` methods that support the creation, retrieval, updating, and deletion of a `Project` object's data. In our sample application, the data access code is relatively straightforward. Keep in mind, however, that these routines could be much more complex, interacting with multiple databases, merging data from various sources, and doing whatever is required to retrieve and update data in your business environment.

For the `Project` object, we'll make use of Enterprise Services' transactional support by using our `<Transactional()>` attribute on the `DataPortal_Update()` and `DataPortal_Delete()` methods. With the `Resource` object, we'll go the other way, using the faster ADO.NET transactional support.

> *Remember that using Enterprise Services transactions has a big performance impact – our data access code will run roughly 50% slower than when using ADO.NET transactions. If we're updating multiple databases, we* must *use Enterprise Services to protect our data with transactions. If we're updating a single database (as in our sample application), such transactions are not required, but they can simplify our code – they free us from dealing manually with ADO.NET transaction objects.*

As a general rule, I recommend using manual ADO.NET transactions when updating a single database, as I consider the performance impact of Enterprise Services transactions to be too high.

As we go through this code, notice that we never actually *catch* any exceptions. We use `Try...Finally` blocks to ensure that database connections and data reader objects are closed properly, but we don't catch any exceptions. The reasons for this are twofold:

- First, we're using the `<Transactional()>` attribute, which causes our code to run within COM+ using auto-complete transactions. An exception causes the transaction to be rolled back, which is exactly what we want to have happen. If we caught exceptions, then the transaction wouldn't be rolled back by COM+, and our application would misbehave.
- Second, if an exception occurs, we don't want normal processing to continue. Instead, we want the client code to know that the operation failed – and why. By allowing the exception to be returned to the client code, we are allowing the client code to know that there was a problem during data access. The client code can then choose how to handle the fact that the object couldn't be created, retrieved, updated, or deleted.

DataPortal_Create

The `DataPortal_Create()` method is called by the `DataPortal` when we are creating a brand new `Project` object that needs to have default values loaded from the database. Though our example is too simple to need to load such values, we're implementing this scheme to illustrate how it would work. The `DataPortal_Create()` implementation here simply loads some default, hard-coded values rather than talking to the database:

```
#Region " Data Access "

  ' Called by DataPortal so that we can set defaults as needed
  Protected Overrides Sub DataPortal_Create(ByVal Criteria As Object)
    Dim crit As Criteria = CType(Criteria, Criteria)
    mID = Guid.NewGuid
    Started = CStr(Today)
    Name = ""
  End Sub

#End Region
```

There are a couple of things to notice here. First, we're directly altering the instance variable of our object's ID value by setting `mID` to a new GUID value. Since the `ID` property is read-only, this is the only way to load the `ID` property with a new value.

However, the `Started` and `Name` properties are set via their property accessors. This allows us to take advantage of any business validation that exists in those methods. For instance, in this case the `Name` property is required, so by setting the empty value into the property we've triggered our business validation code, and our object is now marked as being invalid by the framework's `BrokenRules` functionality.

In a more complex object, where default values come from the database, this method would contain ADO.NET code that retrieved those values and used them to initialize the object's variables. The implementation shown here is not ideal, because we're incurring the overhead of the `DataPortal` *to initialize values that could have been initialized in a constructor method. We'll see an example of that implementation when we create the* `Resource` *class.*

DataPortal_Fetch

More interesting and complex is the `DataPortal_Fetch()` method, which is called by the `DataPortal` to tell our object that it should load its data. We get a `Criteria` object as a parameter, which contains the criteria data we need to identify the data to load:

```
' Called by DataPortal to load data from the database
Protected Overrides Sub DataPortal_Fetch(ByVal Criteria As Object)

  ' Retrieve data from db
  Dim crit As Criteria = CType(Criteria, Criteria)
  Dim cn As New SqlConnection(DB("PTracker"))
  Dim cm As New SqlCommand

  cn.Open()
  Try
    With cm
      .Connection = cn
      .CommandType = CommandType.StoredProcedure
      .CommandText = "getProject"
      .Parameters.Add("@ID", crit.ID)

      Dim dr As New SafeDataReader(.ExecuteReader)
      Try
        dr.Read()
        With dr
          mID = .GetGuid(0)
          mName = .GetString(1)
          mStarted = .GetSmartDate(2, mStarted.EmptyIsMin)
          mEnded = .GetSmartDate(3, mEnded.EmptyIsMin)
          mDescription = .GetString(4)

          ' Load child objects
          .NextResult()
           mResources = ProjectResources.GetProjectResources(dr)
        End With

      Finally
        dr.Close()
      End Try
    End With
    MarkOld()

  Finally
    cn.Close()
  End Try
End Sub
```

We use the `DB()` method from our base class to retrieve the database connection string and open a connection to the database:

```
Dim cn As New SqlConnection(DB("PTracker"))
```

Then, within a `Try...Finally` block, we initialize and execute a `SqlCommand` object to call our `getProject` stored procedure:

```
.Connection = cn
.CommandType = CommandType.StoredProcedure
.CommandText = "getProject"
.Parameters.Add("@ID", crit.ID)

Dim dr As New SafeDataReader(.ExecuteReader)
```

The interesting thing here is that we're creating and using an instance of our `SafeDataReader` class, rather than the normal `SqlDataReader`. This way, we get automatic protection from errant null values in our data, and we also get support for the `SmartDate` data type.

Once we've got the data reader object, we use its data to populate our object's variables:

```
With dr
  mID = .GetGuid(0)
  mName = .GetString(1)
  mStarted = .GetSmartDate(2, mStarted.MinIsEmpty)
  mEnded = .GetSmartDate(3, mEnded.MinIsEmpty)
  mDescription = .GetString(4)
```

Since we're using a `SafeDataReader`, we can use its `GetSmartDate()` method to retrieve `SmartDate` values rather than simple date values, thereby automatically handling the translation of a null value into the appropriate empty date value.

Also notice that we're using numeric indexing to get the appropriate column from the data reader object. While this reduces the readability of our code, it is the fastest data access option.

After the `Project` object's variables are loaded, we also need to create and initialize any child objects. While we haven't created the child and child collection classes yet, we know the basic structure that we want to follow, which is to call the `Fetch()` method on the child collection, passing it the data reader object with the child object data:

```
  ' Load child objects
  .NextResult()
  mResources.ProjectResources.GetProjectResources(dr)
End With
```

Remember that our stored procedure returns *two* result sets – the first with the project's data; the second with the data for the child objects. The `NextResult()` method of the data reader moves us to the second result set, so the child collection object can simply loop through all the rows, creating a child object for each.

The rest of the code simply closes the data access objects, with the exception of a call to `MarkOld()`. This is important, however, as it changes our object from being a new object to being an old object – an object that reflects a set of data stored in our database. The `MarkOld()` method also turns the dirty flag to `False`, indicating that the values in the object have not been changed, but rather reflect the actual values stored in the database.

DataPortal_Update

The `DataPortal_Update()` method handles adding, updating, and removing `Project` objects and their child objects. The decision of whether to do an add, an update, or a delete is driven by the `IsNew` and `IsDeleted` flags from our base class:

```
' Called by DataPortal to delete/add/update data into the database
<Transactional()> _
Protected Overrides Sub DataPortal_Update()

  ' Save data into db
  Dim cn As New SqlConnection(DB("PTracker"))
  Dim cm As New SqlCommand

  cn.Open()
  Try
    With cm
      .Connection = cn
      .CommandType = CommandType.StoredProcedure
      If Me.IsDeleted Then

        ' We're being deleted
        If Not Me.IsNew Then

          ' We're not new, so get rid of our data
          .CommandText = "deleteProject"
          .Parameters.Add("@ID", mID)
          .ExecuteNonQuery()
        End If

        ' Reset our status to be a new object
        MarkNew()
      Else

        ' We're not being deleted, so insert or update
        If Me.IsNew Then

          ' We're new, so insert
          .CommandText = "addProject"
        Else

          ' We're not new, so update
          .CommandText = "updateProject"
        End If

        .Parameters.Add("@ID", mID)
        .Parameters.Add("@Name", mName)
        .Parameters.Add("@Started", mStarted.DBValue)
        .Parameters.Add("@Ended", mEnded.DBValue)
        .Parameters.Add("@Description", mDescription)
        .ExecuteNonQuery()

        ' Make sure we're marked as an old object
        MarkOld()
```

```
        End If
      End With
    Finally
      cn.Close()
    End Try

    ' Update child objects
    mResources.Update(Me)

  End Sub
```

There's a lot going on here, so let's break it down. The method is marked as `<Transactional()>`, so we don't need to deal manually with transactions in the code itself – it will be running within the context of a COM+ transaction:

```
<Transactional()> _
Protected Overrides Sub DataPortal_Update()
```

This will cause the client-side `DataPortal` to invoke the `ServicedDataPortal` on the server automatically, so our code will run within the context of a COM+ transaction. Technically, we could just use ADO.NET or stored procedure transactions for this purpose, but this illustrates how to make a method use COM+ transactions through the CSLA .NET framework.

> **Because this method is marked as `<Transactional()>` our data access code *must* run on a machine that has COM+, which means Windows 2000 or higher.**

The first thing we do is find out if the `IsDeleted` flag is True. If it is, then we know that the object should be deleted from the database – if it already exists. If the `IsNew` flag is also set, then we don't need to do any real work, otherwise we call the `deleteProject` stored procedure:

```
      If Me.IsDeleted Then

        ' We're being deleted
        If Not Me.IsNew Then

          ' We're not new, so get rid of our data
          .CommandText = "deleteProject"
          .Parameters.Add("@ID", mID)
          .ExecuteNonQuery()
        End If

        ' Reset our status to be a new object
        MarkNew()
```

In any case, after the object has been deleted from the database, it no longer reflects data *in* the database, and so it is technically 'new'. To signal this, we call the `MarkNew()` method. If `IsDeleted` was `True`, we're all done at this point – the database connection is closed, and the data portal mechanism will return our updated object back to the client.

Since the `DataPortal` mechanism returns our object by value to the client, we don't have to worry about having the `DataPortal_Update()` method return any values. All it needs to do is update the database, and any object variables. Once that's done, the server-side `DataPortal` will return the object by value to the client-side `DataPortal`, which returns it to the UI.

If `IsDeleted` was `False`, on the other hand, then we know that we're either adding or updating the object. This is determined by checking the `IsNew` flag and setting ourselves up to call either the `addProject` or the `updateProject` stored procedure, as appropriate:

```
' We're not being deleted, so insert or update
If Me.IsNew Then

  ' We're new, so insert
  .CommandText = "addProject"
Else

  ' We're not new, so update
  .CommandText = "updateProject"
End If
```

Either way, we add the appropriate parameter values, and execute the stored procedure:

```
.Parameters.Add("@ID", mID)
.Parameters.Add("@Name", mName)
.Parameters.Add("@Started", mStarted.DBValue)
.Parameters.Add("@Ended", mEnded.DBValue)
.Parameters.Add("@Description", mDescription)
.ExecuteNonQuery()
```

Whether we're adding or updating, we now know that our object represents data stored in the database and that our data fields are the same as those in the database. To mark this, we call `MarkOld()`, which ensures that both `IsNew` and `IsDirty` are `False`.

The final step in the process, after we've closed the database connection, is to tell our child collection to update the child objects as well:

```
' Update child objects
mResources.Update(Me)
```

Since we're using Enterprise Services transactions, the child updates can be handled on their own database connections, which will automatically be enrolled in the same overall transactional context.

DataPortal_Delete

If the client code calls our `Shared` deletion method, the `DataPortal` will create a `Project` object, and then call our `DataPortal_Delete()` method to delete the appropriate data. A `Criteria` object is passed as a parameter, so we'll have the GUID key of the project to be deleted. Then, it's just a matter of calling our `deleteProject` stored procedure:

```
<Transactional()> _
Protected Overrides Sub DataPortal_Delete(ByVal Criteria As Object)
  Dim crit As Criteria = CType(Criteria, Criteria)
  Dim cn As New SqlConnection(db("PTracker"))
  Dim cm As New SqlCommand

  cn.Open()

  Try
    With cm
      .Connection = cn
      .CommandType = CommandType.StoredProcedure
      .CommandText = "deleteProject"
      .Parameters.Add("@ID", crit.ID)
      .ExecuteNonQuery()
    End With

  Finally
    cn.Close()
  End Try
End Sub
```

Like `DataPortal_Update()`, this method is marked as `<Transactional()>` so that it will run within Enterprise Services and be protected by a COM+ transactional context. We just open the database connection, configure the `SqlCommand` object to call the `deleteProject` stored procedure, and we're all done.

Security

The final functionality that we need to implement in the `Project` object is security. According to our use cases in Chapter 6, not all users can add, edit, or remove a `Project` object. Only a project manager can add or edit a `Project`, and only project managers or administrators can remove them.

When you think about it, security checks are just another form of business logic. Who can do what with our objects is a business decision that's driven by business requirements, and so these checks *must* be implemented in our objects.

In reality, these security checks are the last defense. The UI developer should incorporate security checks directly into the UI, and hide (or at least gray out) the buttons, menu options, or links so that users are physically unable to add, update, or delete objects if they aren't in the right role. Sometimes, however, these details are missed in the UI, or a later UI is written without full understanding of the business requirements. In cases like these, including the security checks in the business objects ensures compliance.

Our CSLA .NET framework supports either Windows' integrated security or our custom, table-driven security model. Either way, the security implementation relies on the underlying .NET security model, which is based on principal and identity objects. To do role checking, we use the principal object. Our business code is the same regardless of which type of security is being used behind the scenes.

This means that we can easily enhance the `Shared` method that creates a new `Project` object to do a security check:

```
' Create new object
Public Shared Function NewProject() As Project
  If Not Threading.Thread.CurrentPrincipal.IsInRole("ProjectManager") Then
    Throw New System.Security.SecurityException( _
      "User not authorized to add a project")
  End If
  Return CType(DataPortal.Create(New Criteria(Guid.NewGuid)), Project)
End Function
```

If the user is not in the `ProjectManager` role, we throw a security exception to indicate that the user can't add a new project. If we're using Windows' integrated security, the user would need to be in a Windows group named `ProjectManager`. If we're using our custom, table-based security, the user would need to have an entry in the `Roles` table indicating they have the role of `ProjectManager`.

Notice that our code here doesn't care which type of security we're using – it relies on the .NET framework to handle those details. The thread's `Principal` object could be of type `WindowsPrincipal` or our own `BusinessPrincipal`, but we don't care which it is. Both implement the `IPrincipal` interface, which is what we're relying on in our code.

We do the same thing for the `Shared` deletion method, where we need to ensure that the user is either a `ProjectManager` or an `Administrator`:

```
' Delete object
Public Shared Sub DeleteProject(ByVal ID As Guid)
  If Not Threading.Thread.CurrentPrincipal.IsInRole("ProjectManager") _
     AndAlso _
     Not Threading.Thread.CurrentPrincipal.IsInRole("Administrator") Then
    Throw New System.Security.SecurityException( _
      "User not authorized to remove a project")
  End If
  DataPortal.Delete(New Criteria(ID))
End Sub
```

Controlling the edit process is a bit different. Presumably, all users can *view* a `Project`; it's the update process that needs to be secured. We can check the update process in a couple of places, either by overriding the `Save()` method, or by putting our checks in the `DataPortal_Update()` method.

Overriding the `Save()` method is nice, because it means that the security check occurs before the `DataPortal` is invoked – the check will occur on the client, and be faster. We need to keep in mind, however, that `Save()` is called for adding, updating, *and deleting* the object. Add this override to the *Shared Methods* region:

```
Public Overrides Function Save() As BusinessBase
  If IsDeleted Then
    If Not Threading.Thread.CurrentPrincipal.IsInRole("ProjectManager") _
       AndAlso _
       Not Threading.Thread.CurrentPrincipal.IsInRole("Administrator") Then
      Throw New System.Security.SecurityException( _
        "User not authorized to remove a project")
    End If
```

```
    Else
      ' No deletion - we're adding or updating
      If Not Threading.Thread.CurrentPrincipal.IsInRole("ProjectManager") Then
        Throw New System.Security.SecurityException( _
          "User not authorized to update a project")
      End If
    End If

    Return MyBase.Save
  End Function
```

We have to implement two different security checks: one if `IsDeleted` is `True`, and the other if it is `False`. This way, we can follow the use case requirements regarding who can do what. After the security checks are complete – and assuming the user met the criteria – we call `MyBase.Save()`, which performs the normal behavior of the `Save()` method. By calling the `Save()` method of the base class, we ensure that the normal checks to ensure that the object is valid and is dirty occur before the update process starts.

This completes the code for the `Project` class, which now contains business properties and methods, along with their associated business rules. (In a more complex object, we'd have implemented additional business processing such as calculations or other data manipulations.) It also contains the `Shared` methods, `Criteria` class, and constructor method that are required to implement the 'class-in-charge' model, and to work with the `DataPortal`. Finally, it includes the four `DataPortal_xxx()` methods that the `DataPortal` will call to create, retrieve, update, and delete our `Project` objects.

RoleList

Before we get into the creation of the child objects for a `Project`, we need to create a supporting object that they'll use: the `RoleList`. This object contains a read-only name-value list of the possible roles that a `Resource` can hold when assigned to a `Project`. Because we have a powerful `NameValueList` base class in the CSLA .NET framework, this object is quite easy to implement.

Add a new class to the project, and name it `RoleList`. Then add the following code, based on the template that we discussed earlier:

```
<Serializable()> _
Public Class RoleList
  Inherits NameValueList

#Region " Shared Methods "

  Public Shared Function GetList() As RoleList
    Return CType(DataPortal.Fetch(New Criteria), RoleList)
  End Function

#End Region

#Region " Constructors "

  Private Sub New()
    ' Prevent direct creation
  End Sub
```

```
  ' This constructor overload is required because the base class
  '   (NameObjectCollectionBase) implements ISerializable
  Private Sub New( _
        ByVal info As System.Runtime.Serialization.SerializationInfo, _
        ByVal context As System.Runtime.Serialization.StreamingContext)
    MyBase.New(info, context)
  End Sub

#End Region

#Region " Criteria "

  <Serializable()> _
  Private Class Criteria
    ' Add criteria here
  End Class

#End Region

#Region " Data Access "

  ' Called by DataPortal to load data from the database
  Protected Overrides Sub DataPortal_Fetch(ByVal Criteria As Object)
    SimpleFetch("PTracker", "Roles", "id", "name")
  End Sub

#End Region

End Class
```

Since the names and values for this object are coming from a single table in our database (`Roles`), we can make use of the `SimpleFetch()` method in the `NameValueList` base class, providing it with the name of the database, the name of the table, and the two columns from which to read the data:

```
SimpleFetch("PTracker", "Roles", "id", "name")
```

The base class takes care of the rest of the work, so we're all done.

Resource

Our other primary root object is `Resource`. Like `Project`, a `Resource` object can be directly created, retrieved, or updated. It also contains a list of child objects.

Since we've already walked through the creation of an editable root business object in detail, there's no need to do the same for the `Resource` class. Simply get hold of the `Resource.vb` code from the download, and add it to the project using the Add | Add Existing Item option. However, there are two aspects that we need to examine in a little detail.

Object creation

The first process we'll consider is the creation of a new `Resource` object. When we created the `Project` class, we called `DataPortal.Create()` to initialize the object with default values, illustrating how this technique would allow such values to be loaded from a database. For many other objects, however, the default values are simply the empty values of the underlying data type – an empty string for a `String` variable, for instance. In other cases, we can simply hard-code the defaults into our code. In these last two scenarios, we don't need to invoke `DataPortal.Create()`, and we can use a more efficient technique.

In the *Shared Methods* region of the `Resource` class, we have a `NewResource()` method that doesn't call `DataPortal.Create()`, but rather creates an instance of the `Resource` class directly:

```
' Create new object
Public Shared Function NewResource(ByVal ID As String) As Resource
  If Not Threading.Thread.CurrentPrincipal.IsInRole("Supervisor") _
     AndAlso _
     Not Threading.Thread.CurrentPrincipal.IsInRole("ProjectManager") Then
    Throw New System.Security.SecurityException( _
       "User not authorized to add a resource")
  End If

  Return New Resource(ID)
End Function
```

Notice that we're calling a constructor that accepts parameters, rather than the default constructor. This not only allows us to provide criteria data to the creation process, but also keeps the construction of a new object with default values separate from the default construction process used by `DataPortal`. The constructor sets the default values of the object as it's created:

```
#Region " Constructors "

  Private Sub New(ByVal ID As String)
    mID = ID
  End Sub

  Private Sub New()
    ' prevent direct instantiation
  End Sub

#End Region
```

These values can't come from the database like those in a `DataPortal_Create()` method, but we can provide any hard-coded or algorithmic default values here.

Data access

The other thing we need to look at is data access. In the `Project` class, we used the `<Transactional()>` attribute for our data access, which provides for simple code that's capable of updating multiple databases within a transaction, but at a substantial performance cost. If we're only updating a single database, it's often preferable to use ADO.NET transactions instead. They provide much better performance, and require only slightly different coding.

> *Details on the performance difference between manual ADO.NET transactions and Enterprise Services transactions can be found in the MSDN Library* (msdn.microsoft.com) *in an article entitled* Performance Comparison: Transaction Control.

The following table may help you to determine whether to use Enterprise Services (COM+) transactions or ADO.NET manual transactions:

	Enterprise Services	ADO.NET Manual
Updating two or more databases	Yes	No
Simpler code	Yes	No
Optimal performance	No	Yes
Requires Windows 2000 or higher	Yes	No

Since we've already implemented code using Enterprise Services and our `<Transactional()>` attribute in the `Project` class, for the `Resource` class we'll demonstrate the use of ADO.NET manual transactions.

To implement ADO.NET manual transactions, we need to call the `BeginTransaction()` method on our open database connection object. This will return a `SqlTransaction` object representing the transaction. If we get through all the database updates without any exceptions, we need to call the `Commit()` method on the `SqlTransaction` object; otherwise we need to call the `Rollback()` method.

The `BeginTransaction()` method of the `SqlConnection` object optionally takes a parameter to indicate the level of isolation for our transaction, which we should specify appropriately for our application requirements. The `IsolationLevel` options are shown in the following table:

Isolation Level	Description
`Chaos`	The pending changes from more highly isolated transactions cannot be overwritten.
`ReadCommitted`	Shared locks are held while the data is being read to avoid dirty reads, but the data can be changed before the end of the transaction, resulting in non-repeatable reads or phantom data.
`ReadUncommitted`	A dirty read is possible, meaning that no shared locks are issued, and no exclusive locks are honored.
`RepeatableRead`	Locks are placed on all data that is used in a query, preventing other users from updating the data. Prevents non-repeatable reads, but phantom rows are still possible.
`Serializable`	A range lock is placed on the data, preventing other users from updating or inserting rows into the dataset until the transaction is complete.
`Unspecified`	A different isolation level than the one specified is being used, but the level cannot be determined.

Each option provides a different level of isolation, ensuring that the data we read or update is more or less isolated from other concurrent users of the system. The more isolated our transaction, the more expensive it will be in terms of performance and database server resources.

The typical default isolation level is `ReadCommitted`, though if we're using the `OdbcTransaction` object, the default will depend on the underlying ODBC driver's default, and that can vary from driver to driver. The `Serializable` isolation level provides complete safety when updating data, as it ensures that no one can interact with data that we're updating until our transaction is complete. This is often desirable, though it can reduce performance and increase the chance of database deadlocks in higher volume applications.

DataPortal_Fetch

When we read data, we often don't think about using transactions. However, if we're concerned that another concurrent user might change the data we're reading in the middle of us doing the read operation, then we *should* use a transaction to protect our data retrieval. In many applications, this is not a substantial concern, but we'll use such a transaction here to illustrate how it works.

The structure of `DataPortal_Fetch()` with manual transactions is very similar to the `DataPortal_Fetch()` that we implemented for `Project`:

```
' Called by DataPortal to load data from the database
Protected Overrides Sub DataPortal_Fetch(ByVal Criteria As Object)
  Dim crit As Criteria = CType(Criteria, Criteria)
  Dim cn As New SqlConnection(DB("PTracker"))
  Dim cm As New SqlCommand
  Dim tr As SqlTransaction

  cn.Open()
  Try
    tr = cn.BeginTransaction(IsolationLevel.ReadCommitted)
    With cm
      .Connection = cn
      .Transaction = tr
      .CommandType = CommandType.StoredProcedure
      .CommandText = "getResource"
      .Parameters.Add("@ID", crit.ID)

      Dim dr As New SafeDataReader(.ExecuteReader)
      Try
        dr.Read()
        With dr
          mID = .GetString(0)
          mLastName = .GetString(1)
          mFirstName = .GetString(2)
        End With

        ' Load child objects
        dr.NextResult()
        mAssignments = ResourceAssignments.GetResourceAssignments(dr)

      Finally
        dr.Close()
      End Try
    End With

    MarkOld()
```

```
        tr.Commit()

      Catch ex As Exception
        tr.Rollback()
        Throw ex

      Finally
        cn.Close()
      End Try
    End Sub
```

We declare a `SqlTransaction` variable, and then create a transaction after the database connection has been opened:

```
        tr = cn.BeginTransaction(IsolationLevel.ReadCommitted)
```

In this case, we're opting for minimal transactional protection, but this will prevent any dirty reads – that is, where a row of data is in the middle of being changed while we read that same data. If we need to read some data that is currently being updated, our query will block until a clean read of the data is possible.

Each command object must be linked to the transaction object before it is executed:

```
            .Transaction = tr
```

Failure to do this will result in a run-time error, since all command objects associated with our database connection object *must* have an associated transaction, as a result of the `BeginTransaction()` call.

The rest of the code to set up and execute the command is very typical ADO.NET code. However, notice that we call the `Commit()` method of the transaction object if everything's going well, and we have a `Catch` block that calls `Rollback()` in the event of an exception:

```
        tr.Commit()

      Catch ex As Exception
        tr.Rollback()
        Throw ex
```

The key here is that our call to the `Fetch()` method of our child collection is *inside* the `Try` block, meaning that retrieval of the child objects is protected by the same transaction as the `Resource` data itself.

Also notice that the `Catch` block not only rolls back the transaction, but also re-raises the exception. This allows client code to get the exception, so it knows what went wrong, and can take appropriate steps. It also provides the client code with exactly the same behavior as with a COM+ transactional implementation – the client code has no idea (and doesn't care) whether a COM+ transaction or manual transaction was used.

Our child object code, on the other hand, will need access to this same database connection and transaction object in order to ensure that the child database updates are handled within the same transaction. We'll see how this works later when we implement the `ResourceAssignment` class.

DataPortal_Update

The DataPortal_Update() method of the Resource class works in very similar fashion. Again, we begin a transaction and ultimately commit or roll back that transaction depending on whether an exception occurs. The big difference is that we must pass the SqlTransaction object to the Update() method of our child collection, so that each child object can link its SqlCommand objects to this transaction. We'll see how that's done from the child's point of view when we implement the Assignment class shortly.

The salient bits of code in this method include the creation of the SqlTransaction object and linking it to the SqlCommand object for the Resource update:

```
cn.Open()
Try
  tr = cn.BeginTransaction(IsolationLevel.Serializable)
  With cm
    .Connection = cn
    .Transaction = tr
    .CommandType = CommandType.StoredProcedure
```

In this case, we're using a higher level of isolation to protect our update process against collisions with other users more carefully.

After we update the core Resource data, we call the Update() method on the child collection, passing the SqlTransaction object as a parameter:

```
      ' Update child objects
      mAssignments.Update(tr, Me)
```

This code is *inside* the Try block, so if any child object throws an exception, we can catch it and roll back the transaction.

The Try...Catch block itself exists so that we call either the Commit() or the Rollback() method on the transaction, just like we did in DataPortal_Fetch():

```
  tr.Commit()

Catch ex As Exception
  tr.Rollback()
  Throw ex
```

The end result is that with very little extra code, we've implemented a manual transaction scheme that will run nearly twice as fast as if we'd used COM+ transactions. It's only applicable if we're working with a single database, but it's an option that should be seriously considered due to the performance benefits it brings.

DataPortal_Delete

The same changes from the Project code apply to the simpler DataPortal_Delete() method. Again, we start the transaction and link our SqlCommand object to the SqlTransaction object:

```
      cn.Open()
      Try
        tr = cn.BeginTransaction(IsolationLevel.Serializable)
        With cm
          .Connection = cn
          .Transaction = tr
```

We then either commit the transaction, or in the case of an exception we roll it back within a `Catch` block:

```
        tr.Commit()

      Catch ex As Exception
        tr.Rollback()
        Throw ex
```

Again, with very little extra code, we've used manual transactions instead of using COM+ transactions.

Assignment

The child object of a `Project` is a `ProjectResource`. The `ProjectResource` object contains read-only information about a `Resource` that's been assigned to the `Project`, as well as basic information about the assignment itself.

The assignment information includes the date of assignment, and the role that the resource will play in the project. This information is common to both the `ProjectResource` and `ResourceAssignment` business objects, and as we discussed in Chapter 6 when we were creating our object model, this is an appropriate place to use inheritance. We can create an `Assignment` class that contains the common functionality, and we can then reuse this functionality in both `ProjectResource` and `ResourceAssignment`. Add a new class to the project, and name it `Assignment`.

This class is an implementation of an editable child object, so it will inherit from `BusinessBase`, but it will call `MarkAsChild()` during creation so that it will operate as a child object.

We'll go through most of this code relatively quickly, since the basic structure was discussed earlier in the chapter, and we've already walked through the creation of two business objects in some detail. First, let's import the data namespace, set up the class properly, and declare our variables:

```
Imports System.Data.SqlClient

<Serializable()> _
Public MustInherit Class Assignment
  Inherits BusinessBase

  Protected mAssigned As New SmartDate(Now)
  Protected mRole As Integer = 0

End Class
```

The class is declared using the `MustInherit` keyword. Client code can never create an `Assignment` object – only the derived `ProjectResource` and `ResourceAssignment` objects can be instantiated.

The variables are all assigned values as they are declared. The `mAssigned` variable is a `SmartDate`, and is given the current date. Notice that the variables are declared as `Protected`, which allows them to be accessed and modified by `ProjectResource` and `ResourceAssignment` objects at runtime.

Only the values that are common across both `ProjectResource` and `ResourceAssignment` are declared here. The other values that are specific to each type of child class will be declared in the respective child classes when we create them later.

Handling roles

Each assignment of a `Resource` to a `Project` has an associated `Role`, and this value must be one of those from the `RoleList` object that we just created. In order to ensure that the `Role` value is in this list, our `Assignment` objects will need access to the `RoleList`.

However, we don't want to load the `RoleList` from the database every time we create a new `Assignment` object. Since the list of roles won't change very often, we should be able to use a caching mechanism to keep a single `RoleList` object on the client during the lifetime of our application.

> *If our underlying data changes periodically, we may be unable to use this type of caching approach. Alternatively, we can use a `Timer` object to refresh the cache periodically.*

One approach to this is to use the `System.Web.Caching` namespace, which provides powerful support for caching objects in .NET. This is the technology used by ASP.NET to implement page caching, and we can tap into it from our code as well. However, there is an easier solution available to us in this case: we can simply create a `Shared` variable in the `Assignment` class to store a `RoleList` object. This `RoleList` object will then be available to all `Assignment` objects in our application, and it will only be loaded once, when the application first accesses the `RoleList` object.

While it's not as sophisticated as using the built-in .NET caching infrastructure, this approach is simple to code, and works fine for our purposes. We'll put this code in a special region to keep it separate from the rest of our work:

```
#Region " Roles List "

  Private Shared mRoles As RoleList

  Shared Sub New()
    mRoles = RoleList.GetList()
  End Sub

  Public Shared ReadOnly Property Roles() As RoleList
    Get
      Return mRoles
    End Get
  End Property

  Protected Shared ReadOnly Property DefaultRole() As String
    Get
      ' Return the first role in the list
      Return Roles.Item(0)
    End Get
  End Property

#End Region
```

We are using a Shared constructor method to retrieve the RoleList object:

```
Shared Sub New()
  mRoles = RoleList.GetList()
End Sub
```

The Shared constructor method is always called before *any* other method on the Assignment class (or an Assignment object). Any interaction with the Assignment class, including the creation of an Assignment object, will cause this method to be run first. This guarantees that we'll have a populated RoleList object before any other Assignment class code is run.

We then expose the RoleList object by implementing a Roles() property. Since this property is Shared, it is available to any code in our application, and in any Assignment objects. We have basically created a globally shared cache containing the list of valid roles.

We also expose a DefaultRole() property that returns the name of the first role in the RoleList object. This will be useful as we create a user interface, since it provides a default value for any combo box (or other list control) in the UI.

Business properties and methods

Next, we can create the business functionality for an Assignment object:

```
#Region " Business Properties and Methods "

  Public ReadOnly Property Assigned() As String
    Get
      Return mAssigned.Text
    End Get
  End Property

  Public Property Role() As String
    Get
      Return Roles.Item(CStr(mRole))
    End Get
    Set(ByVal Value As String)
      If Role <> Value Then
        mRole = CInt(Roles.Key(Value))
        MarkDirty()
      End If
    End Set
  End Property

#End Region
```

The only editable field here is the Role property. The Assigned property is set as the object is first created, leaving only the Role property to be changeable. In fact, Role is quite interesting, since it validates the user's entry against the RoleList object we're caching:

```
Set(ByVal Value As String)
  If Role <> Value Then
    mRole = CInt(Roles.Key(Value))
    MarkDirty()
  End If
End Set
```

The client code has no idea that the `Role` value is an integer – all the client or UI code sees is that this is a text value. The UI can populate a combo box (or any other list control) with a list of the roles from the `RoleList` object, and as the user selects a text value from the list, it can be used to set the value of our property.

Inside the `Set` block, we attempt to convert that text value to its corresponding key value by retrieving the `Name()` from the `RoleList` object. If this succeeds, we'll have the key value; if it fails, it will raise an exception indicating that the client code provided us with an invalid text value. We get both validation and name-value translation with very little code.

Constructors

Since `Assignment` is a child object, it doesn't have `Public` methods to allow creation or retrieval. In fact, this is a base class that we can't create an instance of directly at all. However, we will implement a constructor method that marks this as a child object:

```
#Region " Constructors "

  Protected Sub New()
    MarkAsChild()
  End Sub

#End Region
```

This way, our `ProjectResource` and `ResourceAssignment` classes don't need to worry about this detail. Since this is the default constructor, it will automatically be invoked by the .NET runtime as the objects are created.

ProjectResource

With the base `Assignment` class built, we can move on to create the child class for the `Project` object: `ProjectResource`. A `ProjectResource` is an `Assignment`, plus some read-only values from the `Resources` table for display purposes. `ProjectResource` objects will be contained in a child collection object, which we'll create shortly.

We won't walk through the creation of this class, which you'll find in the code download as `ProjectResource.vb`. Add it as an existing item, and we'll then look at its most important features. First of all, since it inherits from `Assignment` (and therefore, indirectly, from `BusinessBase`), `ProjectResource` starts out with all the data and behaviors we built into the `Assignment` class. All we need to do is add the data items specifically required for a child of a `Project`:

```
Imports System.Data.SqlClient

<Serializable()> _
Public Class ProjectResource
  Inherits Assignment

  Private mResourceID As String = ""
  Private mLastName As String = ""
  Private mFirstName As String = ""
```

Business properties and methods

We then implement business properties and methods that return these specific values:

```
#Region " Business Properties and Methods "

  Public ReadOnly Property ResourceID() As String
    Get
      Return mResourceID
    End Get
  End Property

  Public ReadOnly Property LastName() As String
    Get
      Return mLastName
    End Get
  End Property

  Public ReadOnly Property FirstName() As String
    Get
      Return mFirstName
    End Get
  End Property

#End Region
```

Remember that these values *must* be read-only in this object. The data values 'belong' to the `Resource` object, not to this object. We're just 'borrowing' them for display purposes.

Since the `ProjectResource` object provides `Resource` information, it's a good idea to have it provide an easy link to the actual `Resource` object. This can be done by including a `GetResource()` method in our *Business Properties and Methods* region:

```
  Public Function GetResource() As Resource
    Return Resource.GetResource(mResourceID)
  End Function
```

This method is easy to implement, since our `ProjectResource` object already has the ID value for the `Resource` object. All we need to do is call the `Shared` factory method on the `Resource` class to retrieve the appropriate `Resource` object.

Implementing this method simplifies life for the UI developer. This way, they don't need to grab the right ID value and retrieve the object for themselves. More importantly, this method directly and specifically indicates the nature of the *uses* relationship between a `ProjectResource` and its related `Resource` object. We have just implemented a form of self-documentation in our object model.

System.Object overrides

Since this object represents a specific `Resource` that has been assigned to our `Project`, we can implement `ToString()` to return some useful information – in this case, the name of the `Resource`. Also, we should always overload the `Equals()` method to handle our specific class:

```
#Region " System.Object Overrides "

  Public Overrides Function ToString() As String
    Return mLastName & ", " & mFirstName
  End Function

  Public Overloads Function Equals(ByVal Assignment As ProjectResource) _
     As Boolean

    If mResourceID = Assignment.ResourceID Then
      Return True
    Else
      Return False
    End If

  End Function

  Public Overrides Function GetHashCode() As Integer
    Return mResourceID.GetHashCode
  End Function

#End Region
```

Since a ProjectResource object basically represents a specific Resource assigned to our project, the test of whether it's equal to another ProjectResource object is whether the objects have the same ResourceID value.

Shared methods

The Assignment class was marked as MustInherit, so there was no way to create an Assignment object directly. Our ProjectResource class *can* be used to create objects, however, so it must provide appropriate methods for this purpose.

We could directly implement Friend constructor methods that can be called by the parent collection object. In the interests of consistency, however, it's better to use the Shared factory method scheme that's used in our other business objects, so that the creation of any business object is always handled the same way.

When a ProjectResource object is created, it is *being* created to reflect the fact that a Resource is being assigned to the current Project object to fill a specific role. This should be reflected in our factory methods.

We have a Shared factory method that exposes this functionality to the parent collection object:

```
Friend Shared Function NewProjectResource( _
        ByVal Resource As Resource, ByVal Role As String) As ProjectResource

  Return New ProjectResource(Resource, Role)
End Function
```

There are a couple of variations on this theme that might be useful as well:

```
  Friend Shared Function NewProjectResource( _
          ByVal ResourceID As String, ByVal Role As String) As ProjectResource

    Return New ProjectResource(Resource.GetResource(ResourceID), Role)
  End Function

  Friend Shared Function NewProjectResource( _
          ByVal ResourceID As String) As ProjectResource

    Return New ProjectResource(Resource.GetResource(ResourceID), DefaultRole)
  End Function
```

These two implementations might be viewed as optional. After all, the parent collection object could include the code to retrieve the appropriate `Resource` object to pass in as a parameter. It's good practice, however, for our business objects to provide this type of flexible functionality. When we implement the `ProjectResources` collection object, we'll see how these methods are used, and why they are valuable.

We also implement a factory method that can be used by our parent object during the fetch process. In that case, our parent `Project` object will have created a data reader with our data that will be passed to the `ProjectResources` collection as a parameter. The `ProjectResources` collection loops through the data reader, creating a `ProjectResource` object for each row of data. We are passed the data reader, with its cursor pointing at the row of data we should use to populate this object:

```
  Friend Shared Function GetProjectResource( _
            ByVal dr As SafeDataReader) As ProjectResource

    Dim child As New ProjectResource
    child.Fetch(dr)
    Return child
  End Function
```

We'll come to the `Fetch()` method implementation momentarily – it will be responsible for actually loading our object's variables with data from the data reader.

Constructors

Like all our constructors, these are scoped as `Private`. The actual creation process occurs via the `Shared` factory methods.

```
#Region " Constructors "

  Private Sub New(ByVal Resource As Resource, ByVal Role As String)
    With Resource
      mResourceID = .ID
      mLastName = .LastName
      mFirstName = .FirstName
      mAssigned.Date = Now
      mRole = CInt(Roles.Name(Role))
    End With
  End Sub
```

```
    Private Sub New()
      ' Prevent direct creation of this object
    End Sub

  #End Region
```

The first constructor accepts both a `Resource` object and a `Role`, which are then used to initialize the `ResourceProject` object with its data. These parameters directly reflect the business process that we're emulating, where a resource is being associated with our project.

We also include the obligatory default constructor to prevent our class from being instantiated directly.

Data access

As with any editable business class, we must provide methods to load our data from the database, and to update our data into the database.

In the case of `ProjectResource`, we retrieve not only the core assignment data, but also some fields from the `Resources` table. We get this data via a pre-loaded data reader object that was created by the `DataPortal_Fetch()` method in the `Project` object. Our code simply pulls the values out of the current row from the data reader, and puts them into the object's variables:

```
  #Region " Data Access "

    Private Sub Fetch(ByVal dr As SafeDataReader)
      With dr
        mResourceID = .GetString(0)
        mLastName = .GetString(1)
        mFirstName = .GetString(2)
        mAssigned = .GetSmartDate(3)
        mRole = .GetInt32(4)
        MarkOld()
      End With
    End Sub

  #End Region
```

This method is scoped as `Private` because it is called by our `Shared` factory method, rather than directly by the parent collection object.

There's no transaction handling, database connections, or anything complex here at all. We are provided with a data reader that points to a row of data, and we simply use that data to populate our object.

Since the object now reflects data in the database, it meets the criteria for being an 'old' object, so we call the `MarkOld()` method that sets `IsNew` and `IsDirty` to `False`.

When a `Project` object is updated, its `DataPortal_Update()` method calls the `Update()` method on its child collection object. The child collection object's `Update()` method will loop through all the `ProjectResource` objects it contains, calling each object's `Update()` method in turn. In order to ensure that the child object has access to the parent object's ID value, the parent `Project` object is passed as a parameter to the `Update()` method.

The `Update()` method itself must open a connection to the database and call the appropriate stored procedure to delete, insert, or update the child object's data. We don't need to worry about transactions or other object updates, because those details are handled by Enterprise Services. All we need to do is ensure that any exceptions that occur are not trapped – that way, they'll trigger an automatic rollback by COM+.

In general, this `Update()` method is structured very like the `DataPortal_Update()` method we created in the `Project` object:

```
Friend Sub Update(ByVal Project As Project)

  ' If we're not dirty then don't update the database
  If Not Me.IsDirty Then Exit Sub

  ' Do the update
  Dim cn As New SqlConnection(DB("PTracker"))
  cn.Open()

  Try
    Dim cm As New SqlCommand()
    With cm
      .Connection = cn
      .CommandType = CommandType.StoredProcedure
      If Me.IsDeleted Then
        If Not Me.IsNew Then

          ' We're not new, so delete
          .CommandText = "deleteAssignment"
          .Parameters.Add("@ProjectID", Project.ID)
          .Parameters.Add("@ResourceID", mResourceID)
          .ExecuteNonQuery()

          MarkNew()
        End If
      Else

        ' We are either adding or updating
        If Me.IsNew Then

          ' We're new, so insert
          .CommandText = "addAssignment"
        Else

          ' We're not new, so update
          .CommandText = "updateAssignment"
        End If

        .Parameters.Add("@ProjectID", Project.ID)
        .Parameters.Add("@ResourceID", mResourceID)
        .Parameters.Add("@Assigned", mAssigned.DBValue)
        .Parameters.Add("@Role", mRole)
        .ExecuteNonQuery()
```

```
            MarkOld()
          End If
        End With
      Finally
        cn.Close()
      End Try
    End Sub
```

Note that we *don't* use the <Transactional()> attribute here – that attribute only has meaning on a DataPortal_xxx() method of a root object. Our Update() method will automatically run in the transaction started by DataPortal_Update() in the Project object.

In this method, we first see if the object's data has changed. If it's not dirty, we don't need to update the database at all. If it *is* dirty, we open a connection to the database, and proceed to call the appropriate stored procedure.

If IsDeleted is True and IsNew is False, we call the deleteAssignment stored procedure to delete the Assignment data. Otherwise, we call either addAssignment or updateAssignment, depending on the value of IsNew.

In the end, we've deleted, added, or updated the data for this particular Assignment object.

ResourceAssignment

The ResourceAssignment class provides us with the child objects for our Resource object. These objects are the counterparts to the child objects of a Project, and they also inherit from the Assignment base class.

> *The code for the ResourceAssignment class is supplied in the code download.*

The architecture of the ResourceAssignment class is virtually identical to that of ProjectResource. The difference is that a ResourceAssignment class contains read-only data from the Projects table, in addition to the core assignment data.

Because it reflects a Project that's associated with the current Resource, it includes a GetProject() method that provides comparable functionality to the GetResource() method in the ProjectResource class:

```
Public Function GetProject() As Project
  Return Project.GetProject(mProjectID)
End Function
```

The class also includes specific Shared factory methods for creating the child object. In this case, we're a child of a Resource object, and we need to provide the Project object and Role to which this Resource will be assigned. This is reflected in the constructor:

```
Private Sub New(ByVal Project As Project, ByVal Role As String)
  mProjectID = Project.ID
  mProjectName = Project.Name
  mAssigned.Date = Now
  mRole = CInt(Roles.Name(Role))
End Sub
```

This is a mirror image of the constructor in the ProjectResource class, and there are corresponding Shared factory methods as well – just like in ProjectResource.

Data access

Also, we have a Fetch() method that accepts a data reader object pointing to the row that contains our data. This data reader comes from the DataPortal_Fetch() method of the Resource object:

```
#Region " Data Access "

  Private Sub Fetch(ByVal dr As SafeDataReader)
    With dr
      mProjectID = .GetGuid(0)
      mProjectName = .GetString(1)
      mAssigned = .GetSmartDate(2)
      mRole = .GetInt32(3)
      MarkOld()
    End With
  End Sub

#End Region
```

Once again, this is basically the same as ProjectResource, but with slightly different data.

Predictably, we also have an Update() method, but let's look at this in a bit more detail (we're using manual ADO.NET transactions rather than COM+ transactions, which makes things just a bit different). The vast majority of the code is similar to that in ProjectResource, but we assume responsibility for managing the transaction, just like we did in the Resource class.

In this case, the Resource object's DataPortal_Update() opens the connection to the database and starts a transaction on that connection. This means that we have a SqlTransaction object that represents the transaction and connection. It is passed to the child collection's Update() method, which loops through all the child ResourceAssignment objects, passing the transaction object to each child object in turn.

A reference to the parent Resource object is also passed to the Update() method, so that we have access to the parent object's data values as needed. In our particular case, we need the ID value from the Resource object, but by passing the entire object as a parameter we ensure that neither Resource nor the ResourceAssignments collection knows what data we're using. This is good because it means our objects are more loosely coupled.

As we'll see when we implement the DataPortal_Update() method in the Resource class, the transaction is committed or rolled back based on whether an exception occurs during the update process. If no exception occurs, the transaction is committed; otherwise, it is rolled back. This means that the Update() methods in our child objects don't need to worry about committing or rolling back the transaction – they just need to do the update and allow any exceptions to flow back up to DataPortal_Update() to cause a rollback to occur.

This keeps the structure of the method very simple, and virtually identical to the COM+ approach. The biggest difference is that we don't open or close the database connection in a child object, because we passed the transaction in. The state of the database is therefore handled by the root Resource object:

```
Friend Sub Update(ByVal tr As SqlTransaction, _
                  ByVal Resource As Resource)

  ' If we're not dirty then don't update the database
  If Not Me.IsDirty Then Exit Sub

  ' Do the update
  Dim cm As New SqlCommand()
  With cm
    .Connection = tr.Connection
    .Transaction = tr
    .CommandType = CommandType.StoredProcedure

    If Me.IsDeleted Then
      If Not Me.IsNew Then

        ' We're not new, so delete
        .CommandText = "deleteAssignment"
        .Parameters.Add("@ProjectID", mProjectID)
        .Parameters.Add("@ResourceID", Resource.ID)
        .ExecuteNonQuery()

        MarkNew()
      End If
    Else

      ' We are either adding or updating
      If Me.IsNew Then

        ' We're new, so insert
        .CommandText = "addAssignment"
      Else

        ' We're not new, so update
        .CommandText = "updateAssignment"
      End If

      .Parameters.Add("@ProjectID", mProjectID)
      .Parameters.Add("@ResourceID", Resource.ID)
      .Parameters.Add("@Assigned", mAssigned.DBValue)
      .Parameters.Add("@Role", mRole)
      .ExecuteNonQuery()

      MarkOld()
    End If
  End With
End Sub
```

The `SqlTransaction` object that we're passed provides us with the connection to use, and allows us to link our `SqlCommand` object with the transaction:

```
  Dim cm As New SqlCommand
  With cm
    .Connection = tr.Connection
    .Transaction = tr
    .CommandType = CommandType.StoredProcedure
```

The code to call the `deleteAssignment`, `addAssignment`, or `updateAssignment` stored procedures is the same as in the previous implementation, but notice that we don't close the database connection. That must remain open, so that the remaining child objects can use that same connection and transaction. The connection will be closed by the code in the root `Resource` object's `DataPortal_Update()` method, which also deals with committing or rolling back the transaction.

Again, in a real-world application, you'd pick *either* the COM+ *or* the manual transaction approach. In other words, you'd write only one of these implementations, rather than both of them.

ProjectResources

At this point, we have our `Project` class, and we have its child `ProjectResource` class. The only thing we're missing is the child collection class that manages the `ProjectResource` objects. We'll also have a similar collection class for the `ResourceAssignment` objects.

Since this is our first business collection class, we'll walk through it in some detail. `ProjectResources` starts out like any business class, importing the data namespace, being marked as `<Serializable()>`, and inheriting from the appropriate CSLA .NET base class:

```
Imports System.Data.SqlClient

<Serializable()> _
Public Class ProjectResources
  Inherits BusinessCollectionBase

End Class
```

Since this is a collection object, we typically don't need to declare any instance variables – that's all taken care of by `BusinessCollectionBase`.

Business properties and methods

What we *do* need to do is implement an `Item` property to retrieve items from the collection, and a `Remove()` method to remove items from the collection:

```
#Region " Business Properties and Methods "

  Default Public ReadOnly Property Item(ByVal Index As Integer) _
      As ProjectResource
    Get
      Return CType(List.Item(Index), ProjectResource)
    End Get
  End Property

  Default Public ReadOnly Property Item(ByVal ResourceID As String) _
      As ProjectResource
    Get
      Dim child As ProjectResource
      For Each child In List
        If child.ResourceID = ResourceID Then
          Return child
        End If
```

```
      Next
      Return Nothing
    End Get
  End Property
```

In fact, there are *two* `Item` properties. The basic one is easily implemented by simply returning the item from our internal collection, `List`. The reason why this `Item` property has to be implemented here, rather than in the base class, is that it's strongly typed – it returns an object of type `ProjectResource`.

The second `Item` property provides more usability in some ways, because it allows the UI developer to retrieve a child object based on that object's unique identification value, rather than a simple numeric index. In the case of a `ProjectResource`, we can always identify the child object by the `ResourceID` field.

We have two `Remove()` methods in order to provide flexibility to the UI developer.

```
  Public Sub Remove(ByVal Resource As ProjectResource)
    List.Remove(Resource)
  End Sub

  Public Sub Remove(ByVal ResourceID As String)
    Dim r As ProjectResource
    For Each r In List
      If r.ResourceID = ResourceID Then
        Remove(r)
        Exit For
      End If
    Next
  End Sub

#End Region
```

The easy case is where we're given a `ProjectResource` object to remove, since we can use the base class functionality to do all the work. More complex is the case where we're given the `ResourceID` of the `ProjectResource` object. Then, we have to scan through the list of child objects to find the matching entry; after that, we can have the base class remove it.

The other functionality we need to implement is the ability to add new `ProjectResource` child objects to the collection. We specifically designed our `ProjectResource` class so that the UI developer can't directly create instances of the child object – they need to call methods on our collection to do that.

Looking at it from above, what we're doing here is adding a resource to our project to fill a certain role. In the `ProjectResource` class, we implemented a number of `Shared` factory methods that make it easy to create a child object, given a `Resource` object or a `ResourceID`. The assignment can be made to a specific role, or we can use a default role value.

Because all the hard work of creating and initializing a new child object is already handled by the methods we wrote in the `ProjectResource` class, the only thing we need to worry about in our collection class is getting the new object into the collection properly. The trick is to ensure that we don't add duplicate objects to the collection, which we can handle with the following method, which you should place inside the *Business Properties and Methods* region:

```
Private Sub DoAssignment(ByVal Resource As ProjectResource)
  If Not Contains(Resource) Then
    List.Add(Resource)
  Else
    Throw New Exception("Resource already assigned")
  End If
End Sub
```

This method checks the lists of active objects to see if any of them already represent this particular resource. If one does, we raise an exception; otherwise, the new child object is added to the active list.

Then all we need to do is create the set of methods that the UI code can use to add a new child object. Add these three methods to the same region:

```
Public Sub Assign(ByVal Resource As Resource, ByVal Role As String)
  DoAssignment(ProjectResource.NewProjectResource(Resource, Role))
End Sub

Public Sub Assign(ByVal ResourceID As String, ByVal Role As String)
  DoAssignment(ProjectResource.NewProjectResource(ResourceID, Role))
End Sub

Public Sub Assign(ByVal ResourceID As String)
  DoAssignment(ProjectResource.NewProjectResource(ResourceID))
End Sub
```

These methods allow the UI developer to provide us with a `Resource` object and a role, or just a resource ID value, and provide an option in between. Notice how we're using the `Shared` factory methods from the `ProjectResource` class to create the child object, keeping the code here in our collection class relatively simple.

Contains

As we noted when we built our collection templates, whenever we implement a collection object we need to overload the `Contains()` and `ContainsDeleted()` methods from `BusinessCollectionBase` to provide type-specific comparisons of our child objects:

```
#Region " Contains "

  Public Overloads Function Contains( _
      ByVal Assignment As ProjectResource) As Boolean

    Dim child As ProjectResource

    For Each child In List
      If child.Equals(Assignment) Then
        Return True
      End If
    Next

    Return False
  End Function
```

```
    Public Overloads Function ContainsDeleted( _
      ByVal Assignment As ProjectResource) As Boolean

      Dim child As ProjectResource

      For Each child In deletedList
        If child.Equals(Assignment) Then
          Return True
        End If
      Next

      Return False

    End Function

  #End Region
```

In our case, we'll also implement another variation on the `Contains()` and `ContainsDeleted()` methods in this region, to accept ID values rather than objects. This will come in very handy when we implement our Web Forms UI, as it will allow us to determine quickly if the collection contains a child object, when all we know is the child object's ID value:

```
    Public Overloads Function Contains(ByVal ResourceID As String) As Boolean

      Dim r As ProjectResource

      For Each r In List
        If r.ResourceID = ResourceID Then
          Return True
        End If
      Next

      Return False

    End Function

    Public Overloads Function ContainsDeleted( _
      ByVal ResourceID As String) As Boolean

      Dim r As ProjectResource

      For Each r In deletedList
        If r.ResourceID = ResourceID Then
          Return True
        End If
      Next

      Return False

    End Function
```

As we'll see in Chapter 9 when we build the Web Forms UI, we sometimes have cases where the UI knows the ID value of a child object, but we haven't yet loaded the child object from the database. By allowing this check, we can find out if the child object can be added to the collection *before* going to the expense of loading the object from the database.

Shared methods

In our *Shared Methods* region, we'll have two methods to create a new collection and to load the collection with data during the fetch operation:

```
#Region " Shared Methods "

  Friend Shared Function NewProjectResources() As ProjectResources
    Return New ProjectResources
  End Function

  Friend Shared Function GetProjectResources( _
              ByVal dr As SafeDataReader) As ProjectResources

    Dim col As New ProjectResources
    col.Fetch(dr)
    Return col
  End Function

#End Region
```

With these functions, the `Project` object can now easily create an instance of the child collection using our standard factory method approach.

Constructors

We also have the standard `Private` constructor method that calls `MarkAsChild()` so that our collection object acts like a child:

```
#Region " Constructors "

  Private Sub New()
    ' Disallow direct creation
    ' Mark us as a child collection
    MarkAsChild()
  End Sub

#End Region
```

Data access

Finally, we need to create the data access methods. In a child object or child collection, we implement `Friend` methods that are called by the parent object. We'll have a `Fetch()` method that's called by our factory method, which in turn is called by the `Project` object's `DataPortal_Fetch()`. The `Fetch()` method is passed a `SafeDataReader` object from the `Project`. All it needs to do is move through the rows in the former, adding a new `ProjectResource` object for each row:

```
#Region " Data Access "

  ' Called by Project to load data from the database
  Private Sub Fetch(ByVal dr As SafeDataReader)
    While dr.Read()
      List.Add(ProjectResource.GetProjectResource(dr))
    End While
  End Sub
```

In `Project.DataPortal_Fetch()`, we loaded the data reader with data, and got it pointed at the right result set from the `getProject` stored procedure. This means that our code here can simply use the data provided – it doesn't need to worry about retrieving it. The `ProjectResource` class includes a special factory method – GetProjectResource`()` – that accepts a data reader object as a parameter specifically to support this scenario.

We also need to implement an `Update()` method that's called from `Project.DataPortal_Update()`. Since the latter includes the `<Transactional()>` attribute, our data updates here will automatically be protected by a COM+ transaction. The interesting thing here is that we need to call `Update()` on the child objects in both the active *and* deleted lists:

```
  ' Called by Project to delete/add/update data into the database
  Friend Sub Update(ByVal Project As Project)
    Dim obj As ProjectResource

    ' Update (thus deleting) any deleted child objects
    For Each obj In deletedList
      obj.Update(Project)
    Next

    ' Now that they are deleted, remove them from memory too
    deletedList.Clear()

    ' Add/update any current child objects
    For Each obj In List()
      obj.Update(Project)
    Next

  End Sub

#End Region
```

Each child object is responsible for updating itself into the database. We pass a reference to the root `Project` object to each child, so that it can retrieve any data it requires from that object. In our case, each child object needs to know the ID of the `Project` to use as a foreign key in the database.

Once the deleted objects have been updated into the database, we clear the deleted list. Since these objects are physically out of the database at this point, we don't need to retain them in memory either. Then we update the list of non-deleted child objects. The end result is that our collection and all its child objects are an exact copy of the data in the underlying database.

ResourceAssignments

As you'd expect, the ResourceAssignments class is very similar to ProjectResources. The biggest differences between the two come because we're illustrating the use of Enterprise Services transactions with the ProjectResources object, but manual ADO.NET transactions with ResourceAssignments. In this section, we'll just focus just on the parts dealing with the transactional code, so add the existing class from the download.

In the *Data Access* region, we have the Fetch() method. By the time execution gets here, the Resource object's DataPortal_Fetch() method has retrieved our data from the getResource stored procedure within the context of a transaction. It passes the populated data reader to our collection so that we can read the data as we create each child object.

Our collection code doesn't need to worry about committing or rolling back the transaction, as that's handled by DataPortal_Fetch(). We're just responsible for reading the data:

```
' Called by Resource to load data from the database
Private Sub Fetch(ByVal dr As SafeDataReader)
  While dr.Read()
    List.Add(ResourceAssignment.GetResourceAssignment(dr))
  End While
End Sub
```

This code is no different, regardless of whether we use COM+ or manual transactions.

The story is a bit different with the Update() method, however. In this case, DataPortal_Update() in the Resource object opened a database connection and started a transaction on that connection. Our update code needs to use that same connection and transaction in order to be protected too. This means that we get the SqlTransaction object passed as a parameter. This also gives us the underlying connection object, since that's a property of the SqlTransaction object.

The primary difference between the resulting Update() method and the one in our earlier ProjectResources class is that we pass the SqlTransaction object to each child object so that it can use the same connection and transaction to update its data:

```
' Called by Resource to delete/add/update data into the database
Friend Sub Update(ByVal tr As SqlTransaction, ByVal Resource As Resource)

  Dim obj As ResourceAssignment

  ' Update (thus deleting) any deleted child objects
  For Each obj In deletedList
    obj.Update(tr, Resource)
  Next

  ' Now that they are deleted, remove them from memory too
  deletedList.Clear()

  ' Add/update any current child objects
  For Each obj In list
    obj.Update(tr, Resource)
  Next

End Sub
```

The differences between using COM+ and manual transactions when updating a collection are very minor. Most of the changes occur in the child class (`Assignment`), which we discussed earlier in the chapter.

ProjectList

The final two classes that we need to create are the read-only lists containing project and resource data. As with most applications, we need to present the user with a list of items. From that list of items, the user will choose which one to view, edit, delete, or whatever.

We *could* simply retrieve a collection of `Project` objects and display their data, but that would mean retrieving a lot of data for `Project` objects that the user may never use. Instead, it is more efficient to retrieve a small set of read-only data for display purposes, and then retrieve an actual `Project` object once the user has chosen which one to use.

> *In VB6, we'd probably have used a disconnected* `Recordset` *object for this purpose. In VB.NET, however, we'll often get better performance using this object-oriented implementation as opposed to using a* `DataSet`*, because our implementation will have less overhead in terms of metadata.*

The CSLA .NET framework includes the `ReadOnlyCollectionBase` class, which is designed specifically to support this type of read-only list. Add a new class called `ProjectList`, and add the following three lines:

```
Imports System.Data.SqlClient

<Serializable()> _
Public Class ProjectList
  Inherits CSLA.ReadOnlyCollectionBase

End Class
```

As with any other class, we'll implement business properties, shared methods, and data access, though the implementations will be comparatively simple.

Data structure

The easiest way to implement this type of class is to define a `Structure` containing the data fields we want to display. As a value type, rather than a reference type, a `Structure` requires less overhead than an object, so this approach will perform better as well.

Normally, we'd define a `Structure` like this:

```
<Serializable()> _
Public Structure ProjectInfo
  Public ID As Guid
  Public Name As String
End Structure
```

The catch here is that we want to support data binding. Windows Forms data binding will bind just fine to a `Structure` that has `Public` fields, like the one we've shown above. Unfortunately, Web Forms data binding won't bind to fields, but only to `Property` methods. This means that we need to make our fields `Private` and implement `Public` properties instead:

```
Imports System.Data.SqlClient

<Serializable()> _
Public Class ProjectList
  Inherits CSLA.ReadOnlyCollectionBase

#Region " Data Structure "

  <Serializable()> _
  Public Structure ProjectInfo
    ' This has private members, public properties because
    ' ASP.NET can't data bind to public members of a structure...
    Private mID As Guid
    Private mName As String

    Public Property ID() As Guid
      Get
        Return mID
      End Get

      Set(ByVal Value As Guid)
        mID = Value
      End Set
    End Property

    Public Property Name() As String
      Get
        Return mName
      End Get

      Set(ByVal Value As String)
        mName = Value
      End Set
    End Property

    Public Overloads Function Equals(ByVal info As ProjectInfo) As Boolean
      Return mID.Equals(info.ID)
    End Function

  End Structure

#End Region

End Class
```

The end result is the same: we have a `Structure` with `ID` and `Name` values, but by exposing the values via `Property` methods, we allow both Web Forms and Windows Forms to data bind to the `Structure`. We also overload the `Equals()` method so that we can provide strongly typed comparisons.

Business properties and methods

Since we're a read-only collection, the only business property we need to expose is an `Item` property:

```
#Region " Business Properties and Methods "

  Default Public ReadOnly Property Item(ByVal Index As Integer) As ProjectInfo
    Get
      Return CType(list.Item(Index), ProjectInfo)
    End Get
  End Property

#End Region
```

This is the same kind of code we use to implement any strongly typed `Item` property in a collection object.

Contains

As with our other collections, we overload the `Contains()` method:

```
#Region " Contains "

  Public Overloads Function Contains( _
    ByVal item As ProjectInfo) As Boolean

    Dim child As ProjectInfo

    For Each child In List
      If child.Equals(item) Then
        Return True
      End If
    Next

    Return False

  End Function

#End Region
```

This ensures that the overload `Equals()` method on our child structures will be invoked.

Shared methods

We then need to implement a `Shared` factory method that returns a populated `ProjectList` object:

```
  Public Shared Function GetProjectList() As ProjectList
    Return CType(DataPortal.Fetch(New Criteria), ProjectList)
  End Function
```

This method simply calls `DataPortal.Fetch()`, so that the `DataPortal` can create an instance of the `ProjectList` class and call its `DataPortal_Fetch()` method.

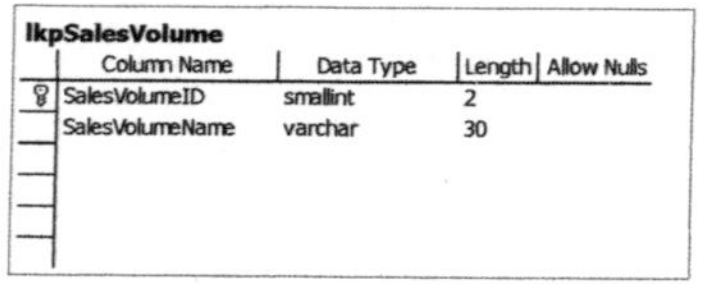

lkpSalesVolume

	Column Name	Data Type	Length	Allow Nulls
🔑	SalesVolumeID	smallint	2	
	SalesVolumeName	varchar	30	

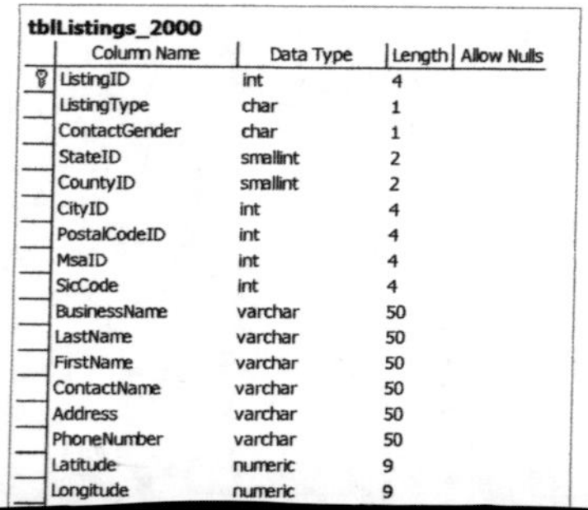

tblListings_2000

	Column Name	Data Type	Length	Allow Nulls
🔑	ListingID	int	4	
	ListingType	char	1	
	ContactGender	char	1	
	StateID	smallint	2	
	CountyID	smallint	2	
	CityID	int	4	
	PostalCodeID	int	4	
	MsaID	int	4	
	SicCode	int	4	
	BusinessName	varchar	50	
	LastName	varchar	50	
	FirstName	varchar	50	
	ContactName	varchar	50	
	Address	varchar	50	
	PhoneNumber	varchar	50	
	Latitude	numeric	9	
	Longitude	numeric	9	

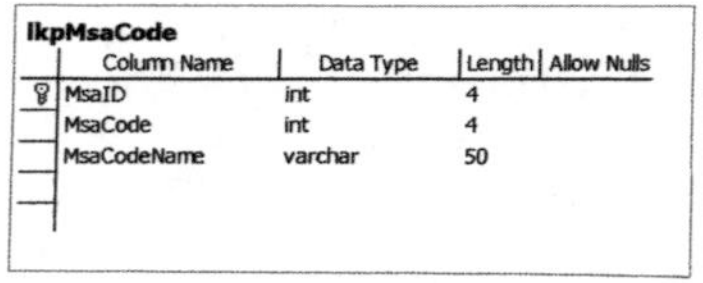

lkpMsaCode

	Column Name	Data Type	Length	Allow Nulls
🔑	MsaID	int	4	
	MsaCode	int	4	
	MsaCodeName	varchar	50	

lkpSicCode

Column Name	Data Type	Length	Allow Nulls
SicCode	int	4	
SicCodeName	varchar	50	

Column Name	Data Type	Length	Allow Nulls
SalesVolumeID	smallint	2	
MedianIncome	int	4	
MeanHousingValue	int	4	

lkpEmployeeSize

Column Name	Data Type	Length	Allow Nulls
EmployeeSizeID	smallint	2	
EmployeeSizeName	varchar	30	

Criteria and constructors

As with any business object that interacts with the DataPortal, we need a Private constructor and a nested Criteria class. In this case, we'll always be retrieving all the project data, so there's no criteria data. We still need a Criteria class to drive the DataPortal, however:

```
#Region " Criteria "

  <Serializable()> _
  Public Class Criteria
    ' No criteria - we retrieve all projects
  End Class

#End Region

#Region " Constructors "

  Protected Sub New()
    ' Prevent direct creation
  End Sub

#End Region
```

In many cases, we would use criteria to filter the result set, since it's not wise to return large amounts of data in a distributed application. To do this, we'd simply add fields to the Criteria class, as we have in the previous business classes in this chapter.

Data access

Since this is a read-only object, the only method we can implement for data access is DataPortal_Fetch(). This method is relatively straightforward – it involves calling the getProjects stored procedure and then creating a ProjectInfo Structure for each row of data returned:

```
#Region " Data Access "

  Protected Overrides Sub DataPortal_Fetch(ByVal Criteria As Object)
    Dim cn As New SqlConnection(DB("PTracker"))
    Dim cm As New SqlCommand()

    cn.Open()
    Try
      With cm
        .Connection = cn
        .CommandType = CommandType.StoredProcedure
        .CommandText = "getProjects"

        Dim dr As New SafeDataReader(.ExecuteReader)
        Try
          While dr.Read()
            Dim info As ProjectInfo
            info.ID = dr.GetGuid(0)
            info.Name = dr.GetString(1)
            innerlist.Add(info)
          End While
```

```
          Finally
            dr.Close()
          End Try
        End With
      Finally
        cn.Close()
      End Try
    End Sub

  #End Region
```

This method follows the same basic pattern as all the other `DataPortal_Fetch()` methods we've implemented so far. The end result is that the `ProjectList` collection contains one `ProjectInfo` entry for each project in our database.

ResourceList

The `ResourceList` class is very similar to `ProjectList`. The entire class is available with the code download for the book; it has its own `Structure` to represent the appropriate `Resource` data:

```
#Region " Data Structure "

  <Serializable()> _
  Public Structure ResourceInfo
    ' This has private members, public properties because
    ' ASP.NET can't databind to public members of a structure...
    Private mID As String
    Private mName As String

    Public Property ID() As String
      Get
        Return mID
      End Get
      Set(ByVal Value As String)
        mID = Value
      End Set
    End Property

    Public Property Name() As String
      Get
        Return mName
      End Get
      Set(ByVal Value As String)
        mName = Value
      End Set
    End Property

    Public Overloads Function Equals(ByVal info As ResourceInfo) As Boolean
      Return mID = info.ID
    End Function

  End Structure

#End Region
```

And its `DataPortal_Fetch()` method calls the `getResources` stored procedure and populates the collection based on that data:

```
#Region " Data Access "

  Protected Overrides Sub DataPortal_Fetch(ByVal Criteria As Object)
    Dim cn As New SqlConnection(DB("PTracker"))
    Dim cm As New SqlCommand

    cn.Open()
    Try
      With cm
        .Connection = cn
        .CommandType = CommandType.StoredProcedure
        .CommandText = "getResources"

        Dim dr As New SafeDataReader(.ExecuteReader)
        Try
          While dr.Read()
            Dim info As ResourceInfo
            info.ID = dr.GetString(0)
            info.Name = dr.GetString(1) & ", " & dr.GetString(2)
            innerlist.Add(info)
          End While

        Finally
          dr.Close()
        End Try
      End With
    Finally
      cn.Close()
    End Try
  End Sub

#End Region
```

Notice how the `Name` property in the `Structure` is populated by concatenating two values from the database. This illustrates how business rules and formatting can be incorporated into the business object to provide the most useful set of return data for display.

At this stage, and as you'd probably hope, the `ProjectTracker` solution will compile without error, and we're ready to move on and write code that actually uses it.

Conclusion

In this chapter, we discussed the basic concepts and requirements for all business classes based on CSLA .NET. We discussed the lifecycle of business objects, walking through the creation process, the retrieval process, the update process, and the delete process.

We then looked at the basic structure of our business classes. There are common elements, including making all the classes `<Serializable()>`, a common set of `Region` blocks for clarity of code, a `Private` constructor, and having a nested `Criteria` class. There are also specific structures or templates for each type of business object, including:

- Editable root
- Editable child
- Switchable object
- Editable root collection
- Editable child collection
- Read-only object
- Read-only collection
- Name-value list

Using this background information and the basic class structures, we walked through the implementation of the classes for our 'project tracker' sample application. The end result is the `ProjectTracker.Library` assembly, which we'll use to create the Windows Forms, Web Forms, and web services interfaces in the next three chapters.

CHAPTER 8

8

Windows Forms UI

To this point, we've been focused on the server side of our application, as we've designed and created objects and business logic. Now let's shift gears and look at how we can create a user interface based on our business objects. In this chapter, we'll build a Windows Forms interface.

Windows Forms is a flexible technology that can be used to create a great many types of UI, as testified by the fact that there are entire books on Windows Forms UI development. We won't rehash that sort of material in this book; what we want to focus on here is how to make effective use of our business objects and collections as we create Windows Forms displays and entry forms.

As we created the CSLA .NET framework, we put in quite a bit of effort to allow our business objects to support Windows Forms development. Though our business objects themselves are focused around modeling the business process described in the use cases from Chapter 6, our objects gained quite a few important features that we'll use as we create the UI in this chapter. Most importantly, we added support for data binding to Windows Forms controls. While we could certainly write our own code to move the data between our object properties and the controls on our forms, it's far easier to use data binding where possible.

As for a user interface style, we'll create a multiple document interface (MDI) application – perhaps the most commonly used style when building business applications. It provides the user with a single, unified view of the application, while allowing the application to interact with the user in a complex and powerful manner. Since our business objects already implement all business logic, including validation, manipulation, and data access, the code in our UI will be very focused on user interaction.

Windows Forms interface

We'll create the UI application within the existing ProjectTracker solution. Open the solution (if you ever got around to closing it) and add a new project using **File | Add Project | New Project**. Make it a Windows Application project, and name it PTWin.

We'll be using the ProjectTracker.Library assembly, so we need to reference it. Because that assembly also requires the four CSLA .NET assemblies, we'll need to reference those as well. Use the Add Reference dialog to get the job done:

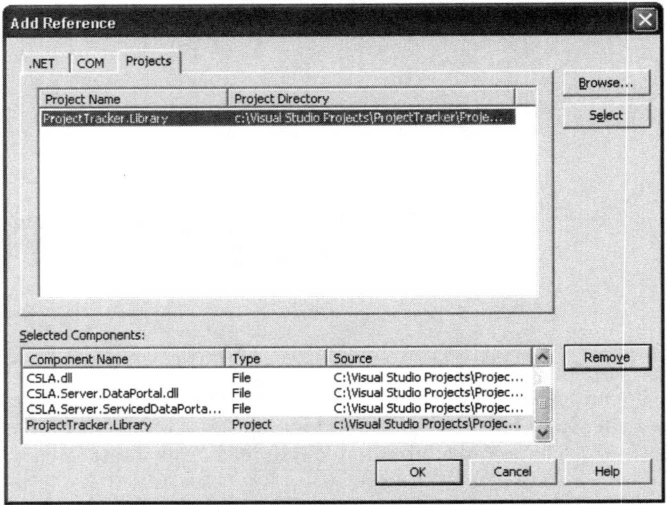

We can use the **Projects** tab to add the reference to ProjectTracker.Library, but we need to click the **Browse** button and navigate to the ProjectTracker.Library\bin directory to reference the CSLA assemblies. (We could alternatively navigate to the CSLA bin directory, but it's safer to get them from the ProjectTracker.Library's directory, since we know that these are the actual files being used by the ProjectTracker.Library assembly.)

As usual, bring up the project's properties window and change **Option Strict** to **On** in the **Build** pane. Also, add a global import of ProjectTracker.Library to the list of imports:

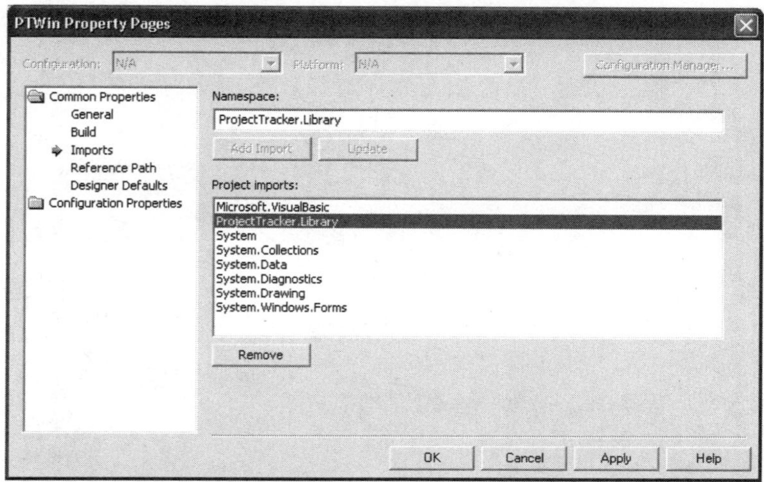

Next, remove `Form1` from the project – we'll add our own forms as we need them. Finally, right-click on the project in Solution Explorer, and set it as the startup project. This way, we can easily use the debugger to test our work as we go along.

Application configuration

Before we create any forms or interact with the business objects, we need to provide some basic configuration information to the application, via the application's configuration file. (This is also done through the `DataPortal` server configuration file if we are running the `DataPortal` on a separate machine via remoting.)

Application configuration file

In the client application configuration file, we can either provide connection strings so that the application can interact with the database directly, or we can provide URLs so that the application can interact with a remote `DataPortal` server via remoting. We discussed this in Chapter 5 when we set up our `DataPortal` host application in IIS.

In Chapter 1, we discussed the tradeoffs between performance, scalability, fault tolerance, and security that come with various physical n-tier configurations. As we said then, the most scalable solution for an intelligent client UI is to use an application server to run our data access tier. That's what we'll do here by configuring our client application to access the server-side `DataPortal` via remoting.

This is controlled by the application's configuration file. To add such a file, choose Project | Add New Item, and then choose the Application Configuration File option:

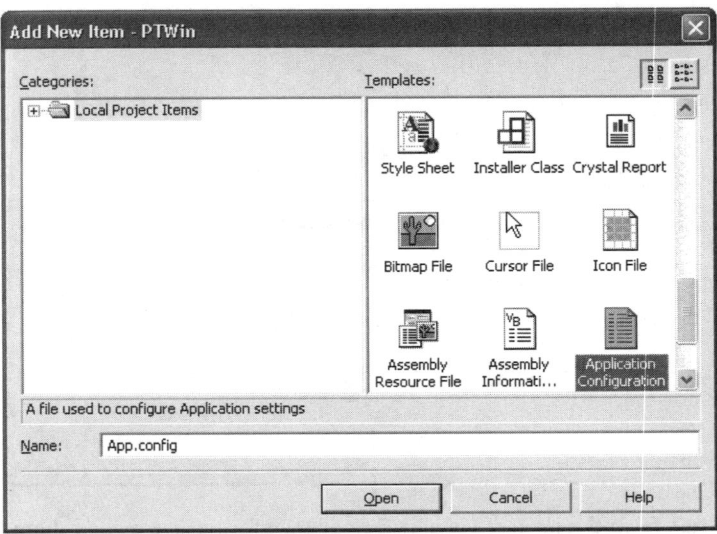

> **Leaving the file name as `App.config` is important. VS.NET will automatically copy the file into our `bin` directory, changing the name to match that of our program. In our case, it will change the name to `PTWin.exe.config` as it copies it into the `bin` directory. This occurs each time we build the project in VS.NET.**

Considering `App.config`, if we wanted to have our client application interact directly with the database, we'd use the following (with "`server`" changed to the name of your database server):

```
<?xml version="1.0" encoding="utf-8" ?>
<configuration>
  <appSettings>
    <add key="DB:PTracker"
         value="data source=server;initial catalog=PTracker;
                                   integrated security=SSPI" />
    <add key="DB:Security"
         value="data source=server;initial catalog=Security;
                                   integrated security=SSPI" />
  </appSettings>
</configuration>
```

However, we want to demonstrate best practices, so we'll configure the application to use a remote `DataPortal` instead. While this won't perform as well for small numbers of users, it provides the best scalability in most cases:

```
<?xml version="1.0" encoding="utf-8" ?>
<configuration>
  <appSettings>
    <add key="Authentication" value="CSLA" />
```

```
    <add key="PortalServer"
         value="http://localhost/DataPortal/DataPortal.rem" />
    <add key="ServicedPortalServer"
         value="http://localhost/DataPortal/ServicedDataPortal.rem" />
  </appSettings>
</configuration>
```

Here, you need to change "localhost" to the name of your application server on which the DataPortal host is installed (unless it's actually on the local machine, of course).

> *The* App.config *file won't be useful for no-touch deployment. In that case, we need to make a copy of this file and name it* PTWin.exe.remoteconfig*. This then needs to be placed in the same server directory as the application and its DLLs, so that it's available to clients running the program via the* NetRun *utility, as described in Appendix A.*

Notice that we're configuring the application to use our custom CSLA security model. If we wanted to use Windows' integrated security, we could do so by changing the Authentication key to Windows. In that case, we'd need to change the way the DataPortal host is configured as well. We'll discuss those changes when we configure the DataPortal server.

Configuring the DataPortal server

Since we've configured the client application to use a remote DataPortal, we need to make sure that the DataPortal host has access to our ProjectTracker.Library business assembly. Remember that all our data access code will run on the DataPortal server, so the DataPortal server needs our DLL.

Providing access to the DLL is simply a matter of copying the ProjectTracker.Library.dll file from our bin directory to the bin directory of the DataPortal host. By default, that would be a directory such as c:\inetpub\wwwroot\DataPortal\bin. Once it's installed, our framework DataPortal code will automatically load and use the ProjectTracker.Library.dll as needed.

This bin directory may contain business DLLs for many applications. It will automatically invoke the appropriate DLL that corresponds to the business DLL being used by the client application.

> *If this presents a security or application isolation issue in your environment, you can duplicate the* DataPortal *host by creating multiple virtual roots in IIS, each with its own copy of the* DataPortal *server, but only the business DLLs for a specific application. The client-side application configuration file would have URLs that point to the specific virtual root, so the application would be isolated from other applications.*

Note that the business DLL on the client *must* be the same as the one on the server. If they get out of sync, the client will be unable to invoke the server, because our objects won't pass by value. This is a feature of the .NET Framework – it performs version checking to ensure that the DLLs at both ends are the same when an object is passed by value across the network.

> **If we update ProjectTracker.Library.dll, we need to update both the DataPortal server directory and all client workstations at the same time.**

This is why no-touch deployment is so important and powerful. We can easily ensure that anytime a new business DLL is copied into the DataPortal server's bin directory, it is also copied into the appropriate server directory, so that it's automatically deployed to all clients as well.

We also need to provide database connection strings to our server-side code. This is done by editing the Web.config file in the DataPortal host project, adding an <appSettings> child element of <configuration> (if one doesn't already exist):

```
<appSettings>
  <add key="Authentication" value="CSLA" />
  <add key="DB:Security"
       value="data source=server;initial catalog=Security;
                                  integrated security=SSPI" />
  <add key="DB:PTracker"
       value="data source=server;initial catalog=PTracker;
                                  integrated security=SSPI" />
</appSettings>
```

Once again, you should replace "server" with the name of your database server. Also, you'll need to change the security settings if you're using a specific user ID and password instead of relying on integrated security.

I usually use a specific user ID for the application rather than using integrated security – the latter means that data access is handled by the ASP.NET account for all applications on my server, and that's typically unacceptable. Using an application-specific account provides more control over what an application can do or access in the database.

Notice that we're configuring the server to use our custom CSLA security model. This matches what we did in the client configuration file.

The security authentication models on client and server must be the same.

If we wanted to use Windows' integrated security, we could do so by changing the Authentication key to Windows on both client and server. In that case, we'd need to change the DataPortal host's virtual root settings through IIS to disallow anonymous users. We'd also need to add an extra element to the <system.web> section of the DataPortal host's Web.config file:

```
<identity impersonate="true"/>
```

These steps ensure that IIS requires the client to authenticate with the server as it connects, and that the ASP.NET process in which our DataPortal code runs will properly impersonate the user logged into the client workstation. We discussed the theory behind this in Chapter 3 when we covered .NET security, and in Chapter 5 when we implemented our own principal and identity classes.

Now that our client is configured to use a remote DataPortal, and the DataPortal server has access to our business DLL, we can move on to create the UI itself.

Main form

Since we'll be creating an MDI application, we need an MDI container form to start from. Add a new form to the project, and name it `Main`. Change the following properties:

Property	Value
`IsMdiContainer`	`True`
`WindowState`	`Maximized`
`Text`	`Project Tracker`

This form's purpose is to contain all our other forms, and to provide a menu and status for the user.

Make sure to change the project's properties to make the new `Main` form the startup form for the application.

Menu

Drag-and-drop a `MainMenu` control from the Toolbox onto the form. Add menu items to the control by clicking in the control on the form itself and adding the items shown in the following figure:

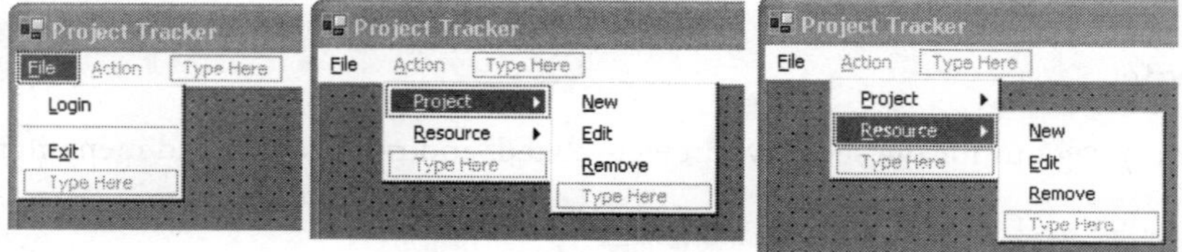

Once this is done, right-click on the menu, and choose the Edit Names menu option. This changes the display so that we can see the names of the menu elements. Change the names of the elements to match those shown in this figure:

Note that we're only assigning names to the menu options we'll be using via code. It wouldn't hurt to assign names to the **File**, **Project**, and **Resource** options, but there's little point since we won't be interacting with them.

We can now double-click on menu items to bring up the code window that enables us to write code to respond when the user clicks the item. To start with, let's double-click on the **File | Exit** option and write the following:

```
Private Sub mnuFileExit_Click(ByVal sender As System.Object, _
                    ByVal e As System.EventArgs) Handles mnuFileExit.Click
  Close()
End Sub
```

Since we'll have a fair amount of code in the main form when we're done, let's put this into a region to keep it organized:

```
#Region " Load and Exit "

  Private Sub mnuFileExit_Click(ByVal sender As System.Object, _
                    ByVal e As System.EventArgs) Handles mnuFileExit.Click

    Close()

  End Sub

#End Region
```

Also, add empty regions for the security, project-related, and resource-related menu items:

```
#Region " Login/Logout/Authorization "

#End Region

#Region " Projects "

#End Region

#Region " Resources "

#End Region
```

We'll add code for the remaining menu items as we create the forms that they will invoke.

The final thing we need to do is to set the initial state of the menus. When the user first runs the application, they won't be validated as a user, so the **Action** menu should be unavailable. Set its `Enabled` property to `False`; we'll set the value to `True` once the user has logged into the application.

Status

An MDI parent window typically also includes a status bar so that the user can see what's happening with the application. Drag and drop a `StatusBar` control onto the form, change its `ShowPanels` property to `True` so that its panels are displayed, and then click the '...' button in the `Panels` entry of the Properties window to bring up a dialog where we can create panels for the control.

We'll create two panels: one to display status information, and the other to display the user ID of the user once they've logged into the application. Add the first of these as shown in the figure:

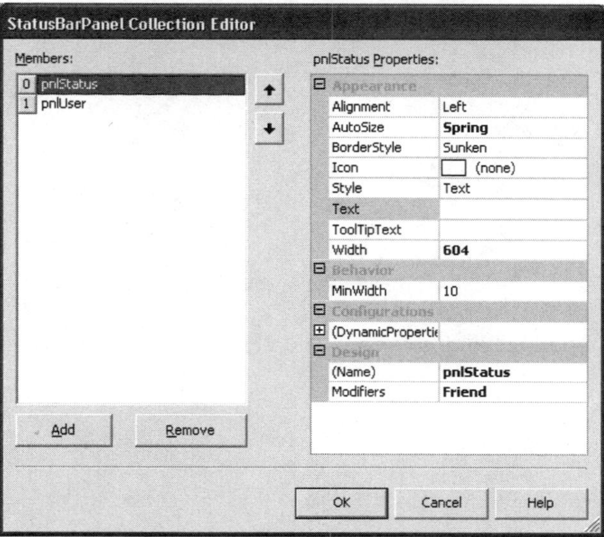

Setting the `AutoSize` property to `Spring` indicates that this panel should consume all the available space in the bar. This will give us as much space as possible to display our status text. Once that's done, you can add the second panel, as shown below:

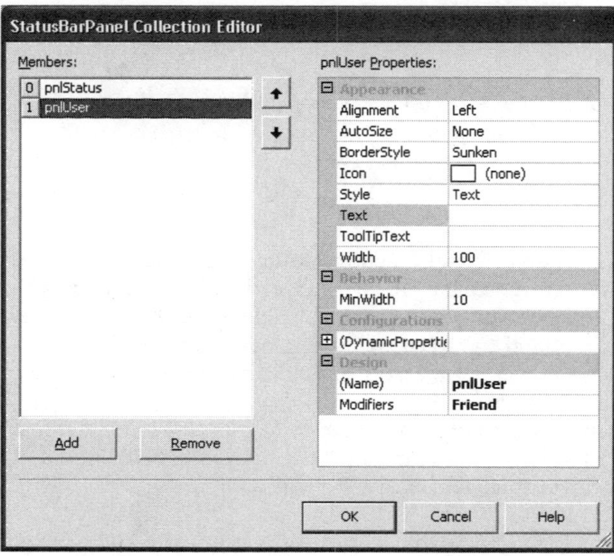

Here, the `AutoSize` property is left at the default value of `None`, indicating that the panel's size is fixed according to the `Width` property value.

We'll use these two panels on a number of occasions as we implement the remainder of the application. To simplify setting the status value from other forms in the UI, add the following code to the `Main` form:

```
#Region " Status "

  Private Shared mMain As Main

  Public Shared Sub Status(ByVal Text As String)

    mMain.pnlStatus.Text = Text

  End Sub

#End Region
```

Notice that this is a `Shared` method, so any code on any form in our UI project can update the status with code like this:

```
mMain.Status("My status text")
```

For this to work, we need a `Shared` variable that points to our form, so add the following to the *Load and Exit* region:

```
  Private Sub Main_Load(ByVal sender As System.Object, _
      ByVal e As System.EventArgs) Handles MyBase.Load

    mMain = Me

  End Sub
```

As the form is loaded, it sets the `Shared mMain` variable to point to the form, thus allowing our `Shared` method to update the status text.

Login form

Before any of our business objects will function, we need to have the user log into the application. Until we've set the `CurrentPrincipal` for the client thread with either a `WindowsPrincipal` or a `BusinessPrincipal` object, our objects won't be able to verify the user's identity or roles. In our case, we've configured the client and `DataPortal` server configuration files to use CSLA table-based security, which means we're using the `BusinessPrincipal` object to manage security.

To use the `BusinessPrincipal` class, we need to call its `Login()` method, providing it with a username and password. `BusinessPrincipal` takes care of verifying the username and password, and loading the associated list of roles (if the user is valid).

To do this, we'll create a login dialog that retrieves the username and password from a user, and we'll call the dialog from the main form as appropriate. The actual login process will be handled by the code in the main form. This keeps the login dialog very simple (and potentially reusable), since it merely prompts the user for a username and password combination.

The login dialog

We can create a simple form to get the username and password from the user. Add a new form to the project and name it `Login`. Set the following properties on the form:

Property	Value
ControlBox	False
FormBorderStyle	FixedSingle
MaximizeBox	False
MinimizeBox	False
ShowInTaskbar	False
StartPosition	CenterParent
Text	Login

Then add two `Labels`, two `TextBoxes`, and two `Button` controls as shown in the figure. In my case, I added a picture as well, but obviously that's an optional extra:

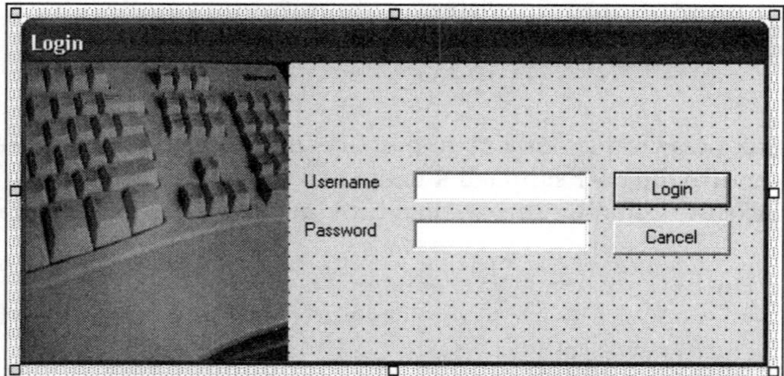

Name the `TextBox` controls `txtUsername` and `txtPassword` respectively. Name the `Button` controls `btnLogin` and `btnCancel`. Set the `PasswordChar` property of `txtPassword` to '*' so that it hides the contents of the field. Set the form's `CancelButton` property to `btnCancel`, and the `AcceptButton` property to `btnLogin`. Also, set `btnLogin` so its `Enabled` property is `False`.

After all that, we can add some code. First, let's declare some variables to hold the results of the dialog:

```
Private mUsername As String
Private mPassword As String
Private mLogin As Boolean
```

Then, add some properties so that our main form can retrieve the results after the dialog has been displayed:

```
Public ReadOnly Property Username() As String
  Get
    Return mUsername
  End Get
End Property
```

```
Public ReadOnly Property Password() As String
  Get
    Return mPassword
  End Get
End Property

Public ReadOnly Property Login() As Boolean
  Get
    Return mLogin
  End Get
End Property
```

Using these properties, our code in the main form can easily determine whether the user clicked the **Login** button. If so, we can retrieve the username and password values.

We'll also add code to enable the **Login** button only if the user has entered a username. Double-click `txtUsername` in the designer, and add the following code:

```
Private Sub txtUsername_TextChanged(ByVal sender As System.Object, _
    ByVal e As System.EventArgs) Handles txtUsername.TextChanged

  btnLogin.Enabled = (Len(txtUsername.Text) > 0)

End Sub
```

Though having a blank password is not a good practice, it does happen, so we're supporting the concept by only checking to ensure the user supplied a name. All that remains then is to handle the button click events. If the user clicks the **Login** button, we can provide the values for retrieval:

```
Private Sub btnLogin_Click(ByVal sender As System.Object, _
                  ByVal e As System.EventArgs) Handles btnLogin.Click
  mUsername = txtUsername.Text
  mPassword = txtPassword.Text
  mLogin = True
  Hide()
End Sub
```

On the other hand, if the user clicks the **Cancel** button, then we don't want to return the values:

```
Private Sub btnCancel_Click(ByVal sender As System.Object, _
                  ByVal e As System.EventArgs) Handles btnCancel.Click
  mUsername = ""
  mPassword = ""
  mLogin = False
  Hide()
End Sub
```

Either way, it's up to the main form to decide what to do with these results – the dialog we've created here is nicely generic and may be reused elsewhere with little or no change.

Doing the login

Now that our login dialog is complete, we can add code to the main form to invoke the dialog and do the actual login process. First, add this code to the main form's *Login/Logout/Authorization* region:

```
Imports CSLA.Security
Imports System.Threading

...

#Region " Login/Logout/Authorization "

  Private Sub DoLogin()
    Dim dlg As New Login
    dlg.ShowDialog(Me)

    If dlg.Login Then
      Cursor = Cursors.WaitCursor
      Status("Verifying user...")
      BusinessPrincipal.Login(dlg.Username, dlg.Password)
      Status("")
      Cursor = Cursors.Default

      If Thread.CurrentPrincipal.Identity.IsAuthenticated Then
        pnlUser.Text = Thread.CurrentPrincipal.Identity.Name
        EnableMenus()
      Else
        DoLogout()
        MsgBox("The username and password were not valid", _
               MsgBoxStyle.Exclamation)
      End If

    Else
      DoLogout()
    End If
  End Sub

#End Region
```

This code displays the `Login` dialog to retrieve the username and password from the user. If the user clicks the **Login** button, we call the `Login()` method on the `BusinessPrincipal` class to perform the actual login verification:

```
BusinessPrincipal.Login(dlg.Username, dlg.Password)
```

Once this call is complete, we can use our thread's `CurrentPrincipal` to determine whether the user was successfully authenticated – if so, we can retrieve the user's identity and check the user's roles using the principal and identity objects and standard .NET security coding techniques.

Note that we make a couple of calls to a `DoLogout()` method. Let's implement that method now:

```
Private Sub DoLogout()

  ' Drop any reference to a Principal
  Thread.CurrentPrincipal = Nothing
  pnlUser.Text = ""
  mnuAction.Enabled = False

End Sub
```

This method ensures that we are no longer logged in by setting the current principal to `Nothing`.

In both `DoLogin()` and `DoLogout()`, we change the `Enabled` properties of our menus – a procedure that's rather more complicated for enabling than for disabling, on account of the different actions that different users are allowed to perform. We need to implement the `EnableMenus()` method for this purpose:

```
Private Sub EnableMenus()
  Dim user As Security.Principal.IPrincipal
  user = Thread.CurrentPrincipal

  mnuAction.Enabled = True

  mnuProjectNew.Enabled = user.IsInRole("ProjectManager")

  mnuProjectRemove.Enabled = user.IsInRole("ProjectManager") OrElse _
                             user.IsInRole("Administrator")

  mnuResourceNew.Enabled = user.IsInRole("ProjectManager") OrElse _
                           user.IsInRole("Supervisor")

  mnuResourceRemove.Enabled = user.IsInRole("ProjectManager") OrElse _
                              user.IsInRole("Supervisor") OrElse _
                              user.IsInRole("Administrator")
End Sub
```

By enabling and disabling the various menu options based on whether the user is logged in and what the user's roles are, we provide immediate and obvious feedback to the user regarding what they can and cannot do within the application.

Updating the menu

Now we're finally ready to make the security dialog and login process occur based on the user's actions. First, when the user starts the application, we'll want to have the login take place immediately. Update the form's `Load` event handler as shown:

```
Private Sub Main_Load(ByVal sender As System.Object, _
                 ByVal e As System.EventArgs) Handles MyBase.Load

  mMain = Me

  DoLogin()
End Sub
```

We also want to allow the user to log in based on the login menu item, so add this to the *Login/Logout/Authorization* region:

```
   Private Sub mnuFileLogin_Click(ByVal sender As System.Object, _
                     ByVal e As System.EventArgs) Handles mnuFileLogin.Click
     DoLogin()
   End Sub
```

At this point, the user is prompted to log in when the application starts, and they can log in or change their identity as needed by using the menu option.

Using Windows' integrated security

If we wanted to use Windows' integrated security, we wouldn't need a login form, because the client workstation already knows the user's identity. Instead, we'd need to add a bit of code to our main menu form so that as it loads, the `CurrentPrincipal` is configured with a `WindowsPrincipal` object.

The following code shows how we can detect the authentication mode and adapt to use either Windows or CSLA security appropriately:

```
Imports CSLA.Security
Imports System.Configuration
Imports System.Security.Principal
Imports System.Threading

...

  Private Sub Main_Load(ByVal sender As System.Object, _
                        ByVal e As System.EventArgs) Handles MyBase.Load

    mMain = Me

    If ConfigurationSettings.AppSettings("Authentication") = "Windows" Then
      mnuFileLogin.Visible = False
      AppDomain.CurrentDomain.SetPrincipalPolicy( _
                  PrincipalPolicy.WindowsPrincipal)
      EnableMenus()

    Else
      DoLogin()
    End If
  End Sub
```

Calling `SetPrincipalPolicy` like this triggers the .NET runtime to create and populate a `WindowsPrincipal` object and make it the current object for our client thread.

Of course, both the client and `DataPortal` server configuration files must be set to use Windows security. Also, the `DataPortal` server host in IIS must be set to disallow anonymous access, forcing the client to provide IIS with the Windows identity from the client workstation via integrated security.

Project list

When the user wants to edit or remove a project from the system, they'll need to be presented with a list of projects. We implemented the `ProjectList` business object for this purpose, so the infrastructure already exists to retrieve the project data. All we need to do is provide a dialog to display the information.

Since this dialog needs to support both edit and removal operations, we'll make the dialog itself generic – it will simply display the list of projects and allow the user to select one. All the intelligence about what to *do* with the selected item will occur in the main form's code.

The biggest challenge we face is that the `ListView` control doesn't support data binding, which is a real shame. The `ListView` control is ideal for displaying a list of data because it's much lighter-weight than a grid control, and users are very familiar with it. Because I like the `ListView` control so much, I created a version that supports data binding. This is described in an article I wrote for MSDN at http://msdn.microsoft.com/library/default.asp?url=/library/en-us/dnadvnet/html/vbnet08262002.asp.

> *The control and its code are included in the download for the book, but for full details about how it works, please refer to the MSDN article.*

The new control is called a `DataListView`, and we'll be using it in several of our forms.

ProjectSelect dialog

Add a new form to the project, and name it `ProjectSelect`. Add a `DataListView` control and two `Button` controls, as shown:

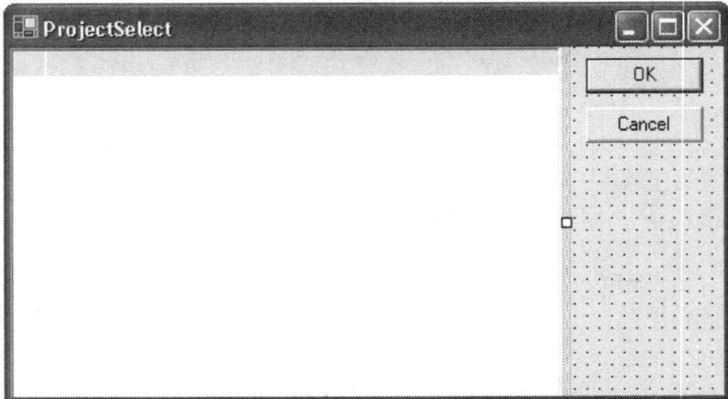

The `DataListView` control is an enhanced `ListView` that supports data binding. It also defaults to a 'detail' view, so it displays data in a grid-like format, and allows the user to select a single row at a time.

Name the `DataListView` control `dvDisplay`, the `Button` controls `btnOK` and `btnCancel` and set the form's `AcceptButton` and `CancelButton` properties to point to the appropriate buttons.

Because our `ProjectList` business object does most of the work, and data binding in the form does most of what's left, we don't have to write very much code. First, declare a variable to hold the user's selection:

```
Private mResult As String
```

Then, create a property so that the main form can retrieve the value:

```
Public ReadOnly Property Result() As String
  Get
    Return mResult
  End Get
End Property
```

When the form loads, we need to get a `ProjectList` object and bind it to the `DataListView` control:

```
Private Sub ProjectSelect_Load(ByVal sender As System.Object, _
                  ByVal e As System.EventArgs) Handles MyBase.Load

  Dim list As ProjectList = ProjectList.GetProjectList()
  With dvDisplay
    .AutoDiscover = False
    .Columns.Add("ID", "ID", 0)
    .Columns.Add("Project name", "Name", dvDisplay.Width)
    .DataSource = list
    .Focus()
  End With

End Sub
```

Retrieving the list of projects is trivial, because the business object does all the work:

```
  Dim list As ProjectList = ProjectList.GetProjectList
```

Once we have the list, we configure the columns to be displayed in the `DataListView` control. First, we tell the control not to discover all the properties on the object automatically, but rather to allow us to control the columns to be displayed. Then we add two columns – one for each data field.

The `ID` column is set to a width of zero, so the value is in the control, but it's not displayed to the user. The project's name, however, *is* displayed. Finally, we set the `DataSource` of the control to our business collection:

```
    .DataSource = list
```

This binds the control to the collection, so the list of project data will be automatically displayed.

All we need to do now is add code behind our buttons. In the case of the OK button, we want to return the value chosen by the user; otherwise, we want to return an empty `String`:

```
Private Sub btnOK_Click(ByVal sender As System.Object, _
                        ByVal e As System.EventArgs) _
                        Handles btnOK.Click, dvDisplay.DoubleClick
```

```
    If dvDisplay.SelectedItems.Count > 0 Then
      mResult = dvDisplay.SelectedItems(0).Text
    Else
      mResult = ""
    End If
    Hide()
  End Sub

  Private Sub btnCancel_Click(ByVal sender As System.Object, _
                              ByVal e As System.EventArgs) _
                              Handles btnCancel.Click

    mResult = ""
    Hide()
  End Sub
```

Either way, the dialog doesn't care what's done with the value – its purpose is solely to allow the user to select a project.

Project edit

To support both adding and editing a project, we'll create a form that allows the user to interact with a `Project` object. Our `Project` business object already implements our business functionality, so once again the form itself can be relatively straightforward, leaving the object to do all validation, manipulation, calculation, and other business operations.

The form is complicated a little because we need to display the list of *resources* assigned to the project – the user needs to be able to add and remove resources too. To manage this display, we'll again use a `DataListView` control so that we can easily use data binding.

ProjectEdit form

Add a new form to the project, named `ProjectEdit`. Add controls as shown in the figure and table:

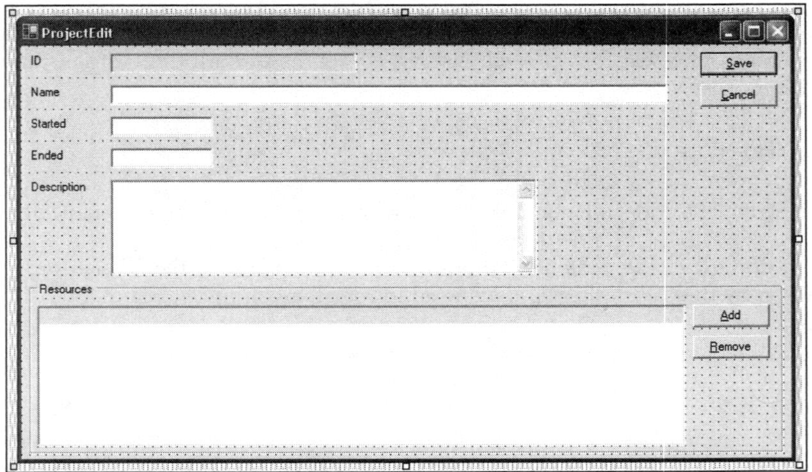

Control	Properties
TextBox	Name=txtID; Text=""; ReadOnly=True
TextBox	Name=txtName
TextBox	Name=txtStarted
TextBox	Name=txtEnded
TextBox	Name=txtDescription; Multiline=True; Scrollbars=Vertical
ContextMenu	Name=mnuRoles
DataListView	Name=dvResources; ContextMenu=mnuRoles
Button	Name=btnSave; Text=Save
Button	Name=btnCancel; Text=Cancel
Button	Name=btnAddResource; Text=Add
Button	Name=btnRemoveResource; Text=Remove

Set the AcceptButton and CancelButton properties of the form to btnSave and btnCancel.

The chkIsDirty control

There's one other control that we need to add, and its requirements are a bit odd. In fact, this is a bit of a hack.

Back in Chapter 4, where we created our CSLA .NET framework code – in particular, the C# BindableBase class – we implemented an IsDirtyChanged event that could be used safely even though our business objects are <Serializable()>. We then designed our MarkDirty() method so that it raises this event any time our object is marked as dirty.

At the time, we remarked that Windows Forms data binding requires that any time a property on the object is changed, a *property*Changed event should be raised by the data source (our business object), where *property* corresponds to the property name. Data binding then receives this event, which triggers a refresh in the display of all data bound controls. Unfortunately, that mechanism requires us to create a C# base class to declare such an event for each and every property – otherwise, we can't use .NET serialization.

> *All this is because the VB.NET compiler doesn't support the* field *target for attributes. Microsoft is aware of this oversight, so hopefully it will be resolved in a future version of VB.NET.*

Fortunately, there's a compromise. It turns out that all we need to do is raise the *same* *property*Changed event any time that *any* property changes. We don't have to raise an event specifically related to the property that was changed. Because any property change on our object will result in MarkDirty() being called, we can use the IsDirtyChanged event to trigger Windows Forms data binding to refresh the changed data for any and all properties on our object.

For this to work, however, the IsDirty property on our object must be bound to a control on the form. There's no reason to display this control to the user, but at the same time, we can't just change its Visible property to False. Unless a control is visible, it won't be data bound. Luckily, there's a way to solve this problem. We can make a control invisible to the user by placing it physically outside the borders of the form. Then, technically it's still 'visible', even though the user can't see it.

So: add a CheckBox control to the form, and name it chkIsDirty. Set its Enabled property to False. While this control is required on the form for data binding to work, we don't want the user interacting with it. We also don't want the user accidentally tabbing into the control. Disabling the control avoids these potential issues.

Now use the Properties window to set its Location property. We want its top location to be some large negative number, putting the control well above the top of the form. A value of -368, 136 works fine, for example. This leaves the control visible according to Windows Forms, but it will never be physically visible to the user because it's off the top of the form.

If you'd prefer, you can also position the control behind another control on your form, or set its size to 0, 0. The whole idea is to ensure that it is not visible to the user, but yet its Visible *property is still* True.

We'll data-bind this control to our object along with the other controls, with the end result being that our IsDirtyChanged event will be automatically caught by the data binding mechanism, so all our controls will refresh their values when a property is changed on the business object.

Getting the Project object

Now we can add code behind the form. First of all, we know that we'll be dealing with a Project object. This object will be provided to our form from the main form, which will create or retrieve the appropriate object on our behalf. We just need to include a variable and a property so that we can get access to the object:

```
Private mProject As Project

Public Property Project() As Project
  Get
    Return mProject
  End Get
  Set(ByVal Value As Project)
    mProject = Value
  End Set
End Property
```

The main form will set this property before displaying the ProjectEdit form.

Loading the form

As the form loads, we'll need to do some security checks, because there are some users who can bring up the form to look at its contents, but can't actually edit a Project object. In these cases, the Save button will need to be disabled.

To determine whether or not to disable the button, we'll use the IsInRole() method of our thread's Principal security object. To simplify access to the Principal object, we'll import the System.Threading namespace:

```
Imports System.Threading
```

Then, as the form loads, we can set the security *and* fill the form based on the data in the Project object:

```
Private Sub ProjectEdit_Load(ByVal sender As System.Object, _
                ByVal e As System.EventArgs) Handles MyBase.Load

  Me.Text = "Project " & mProject.Name
  Dim Role As String
  For Each Role In Assignment.Roles
    mnuRoles.MenuItems.Add(Assignment.Roles.Item(Role))
    AddHandler mnuRoles.MenuItems(mnuRoles.MenuItems.Count - 1).Click, _
       AddressOf mnuRoles_Click
  Next

  If Thread.CurrentPrincipal.IsInRole("ProjectManager") Then

    mProject.BeginEdit()

    ' Only project managers can assign resources
    btnAddResource.Enabled = True
    btnRemoveResource.Enabled = True

  Else
    btnAddResource.Enabled = False
    btnRemoveResource.Enabled = False
  End If

  DataBind()

End Sub
```

First, we change our caption text to reflect the `Project` object:

```
Me.Text = "Project " & mProject.Name
```

Then, we populate the `mnuRoles` control with the list of valid roles for a resource on a project. The `Assignment` business class provides this data, so our UI code doesn't need to worry about where it came from – it can just use the data:

```
Dim Role As String
For Each Role In Assignment.Roles
  mnuRoles.MenuItems.Add(Assignment.Roles.Item(Role))
  AddHandler mnuRoles.MenuItems(mnuRoles.MenuItems.Count - 1).Click, _
     AddressOf mnuRoles_Click
Next
```

We'll be using `mnuRules` as a context menu in the `DataListView` control so that the user can change the role a resource is playing in our project.

We then check the role of the current user to see if they should have access to the buttons for adding and removing a resource from the project:

```
If Thread.CurrentPrincipal.IsInRole("ProjectManager") Then
```

Notice also that we only call `BeginEdit()` in the case that we're allowing editing of the object. This call triggers the object to take a snapshot of its state so that if the user later cancels the form, we can call `CancelEdit()` to restore the object to its original values.

Finally, we call a `DataBind()` method (which we've yet to write) to bind the form to the `Project` object.

Simplifying data binding

The `DataBind()` method will itself make heavy use of a method named `BindField()` that wraps a couple of standard Windows Forms data binding methods in order to keep our code simpler.

Binding a property of a control to a data source is a single call:

```
control.DataBindings.Add( _
    controlPropertyName, dataSource, dataSourcePropertyName)
```

The italicized items in this statement should be replaced with meaningful values. The following table describes the meaning of each:

Item	Description
control	A reference to the control to bind
controlPropertyName	The text name of the property on the control to which we want to bind the value
dataSource	A reference to the data source (our business object)
dataSourcePropertyName	The text name of the property of the data source that is to be bound to the control's property

The `DataBindings` collection exists on all Windows Forms controls, so we can use this technique to bind values from a data source to one or more properties on any control.

Unfortunately, we can get into trouble if we try to re-bind the same property a second time, as this will result in a run-time error. This can happen if we reuse our form to bind against multiple data sources over time. Before we can bind a new data source to our controls, we need to make sure that any pre-existing data bindings are removed.

The `BindField()` method takes care of these details, thus simplifying the code we write in our forms.

To make the `BindField()` method available to all forms in our project, we'll add it to a `Module`. A `Module` is ideal for code-sharing in VB.NET, since any non-`Private` methods we add to a `Module` become new global functions throughout our entire project.

Add a new `Module` to the project, and name it `Util`. Then, add the `BindField()` method to it:

```
Module Util

  Public Sub BindField(ByVal control As Control, _
                       ByVal propertyName As String, _
```

```
                        ByVal dataSource As Object, _
                        ByVal dataMember As String)
    Dim bd As Binding
    Dim index As Integer

    For index = control.DataBindings.Count - 1 To 0 Step -1
      bd = control.DataBindings.Item(index)
      If bd.PropertyName = propertyName Then
        control.DataBindings.Remove(bd)
      End If
    Next
    control.DataBindings.Add(propertyName, dataSource, dataMember)

  End Sub

End Module
```

The DataBind method

Back in the `ProjectEdit` form, we can now add the `DataBind()` method:

```
  Private Sub DataBind()

    If Thread.CurrentPrincipal.IsInRole("ProjectManager") Then
      ' Only project managers can save a project
      BindField(btnSave, "Enabled", mProject, "IsValid")
    Else
      btnSave.Enabled = False
    End If

    BindField(chkIsDirty, "Checked", mProject, "IsDirty")
    BindField(txtID, "Text", mProject, "ID")
    BindField(txtName, "Text", mProject, "Name")
    BindField(txtStarted, "Text", mProject, "Started")
    BindField(txtEnded, "Text", mProject, "Ended")
    BindField(txtDescription, "Text", mProject, "Description")

    With dvResources
      .SuspendLayout()
      .Clear()
      .AutoDiscover = False
      .Columns.Add("ID", "ResourceID", 0)
      .Columns.Add("Last name", "LastName", 100)
      .Columns.Add("First name", "FirstName", 100)
      .Columns.Add("Assigned", "Assigned", 100)
      .Columns.Add("Role", "Role", 150)
      .DataSource = mProject.Resources
      .ResumeLayout()
    End With

  End Sub
```

First, we do a security check to see if the **Save** button should be available or not:

```
If Thread.CurrentPrincipal.IsInRole("ProjectManager") Then
```

Even if the button should be available based on security, we still only want it to be available in the case that the `Project` object is in a valid state. This can be done easily, by binding its `Enabled` property to the `IsValid` property on the object:

```
  BindField(btnSave, "Enabled", mProject, "IsValid")
```

We then bind our other controls to the business object:

```
BindField(chkIsDirty, "Checked", mProject, "IsDirty")
BindField(txtID, "Text", mProject, "ID")
BindField(txtName, "Text", mProject, "Name")
BindField(txtStarted, "Text", mProject, "Started")
BindField(txtEnded, "Text", mProject, "Ended")
BindField(txtDescription, "Text", mProject, "Description")
```

Note that we also bind `chkIsDirty` to the object's `IsDirty` property, even though this control has been placed well above the top of the form and is not visible to the user. By doing this, we ensure that our `IsDirtyChanged` event is available to the data binding infrastructure. When our business logic calls `MarkDirty()`, that in turn calls `OnIsDirtyChanged()`. This raises the `IsDirtyChanged` event, which is automatically handled by the data binding infrastructure because the `IsDirty` property is bound to a control. Data binding then automatically refreshes our controls any time a property changes on our business object.

Finally, we bind the collection of child objects to the `DataListView` control, manually specifying which columns are to be displayed, and what widths should be used for each.

Since Windows Forms data binding is read-write, we've now accomplished the vast majority of the coding that's necessary in our form, and you should notice that our form doesn't include any validation code. The business object takes care of those details, setting its `IsValid` property based on whether its data is valid or not. Since we've bound the **Save** button to `IsValid`, the user can only save the object in the case that it is indeed valid.

> *Also remember that the `Save()` method itself checks the `IsValid` property, and throws an exception if it is called when the object is invalid. Even if the UI code was to allow the **Save** button to be clicked at any time, the object would still have the final say.*

Saving the object

We need to write some code to handle the **Save** button. If the user clicks the **Save** button, we want to save the changes to the database:

```
Private Sub btnSave_Click(ByVal sender As System.Object, _
                  ByVal e As System.EventArgs) Handles btnSave.Click
  Try
    Cursor.Current = Cursors.WaitCursor
    mProject.ApplyEdit()
    mProject = CType(mProject.Save(), Project)
    Cursor.Current = Cursors.Default
```

```
      Catch ex As Exception
        Cursor.Current = Cursors.Default
        MsgBox(ex.ToString)
      End Try

      Hide()
    End Sub
```

First, we call `ApplyEdit()` to commit any changes that the user has made to the object's state. This doesn't save the data to the database, but it does cause the object to resolve its 'undo' stack. We then call the `Save()` method to trigger the actual save to the database. Of course, writing to a database comes with potential dangers – perhaps there's a duplicate key, or some other relational rule gets violated? Because of this, we use a `Try`...`Catch` block to catch the exception and display any problem to the user.

The bigger issue here is that the call to `Save()` returns a new instance of the `Project` object:

```
        mProject = CType(mProject.Save(), Project)
```

Notice that we update the form's `mProject` variable with the new object. If we planned to continue to use the object in the form, we *must* re-bind the data so that our controls are bound to the new object! In this example, we immediately close the form, so rebinding is unnecessary.

> **Were we to leave the form open and allow continued editing of the object, we'd need to call the `DataBind()` method to rebind the form to the new `Project` object we received as a result of the call to the `Save()` method.**

This fact is the reason why `DataBind()` calls `BindField()`. The latter simplifies the process of rebinding the controls to a new object, because it automatically removes the previous (now invalid) binding and replaces it with the new one. If we were to change the Save button *not* to close the form, we'd need to change the code as follows:

```
    Private Sub btnSave_Click(ByVal sender As System.Object, _
                      ByVal e As System.EventArgs) Handles btnSave.Click
      Try
        Cursor.Current = Cursors.WaitCursor
        mProject.ApplyEdit()
        mProject = CType(mProject.Save(), Project)
        Cursor.Current = Cursors.Default
      Catch ex As Exception
        Cursor.Current = Cursors.Default
        MsgBox(ex.ToString)
      End Try

      DataBind()
    End Sub
```

If we don't rebind the form to the new object, our application will not work properly, but it won't crash either. The form would remain bound to the old version of the object, even though we need to be using the new version. Any changes made by the user would be to the old version, but a subsequent click of the Save button would affect the new version. Things can obviously get messy very quickly, so it's *critical* that the form be rebound to the new object, or that the form be closed.

Canceling and closing

We also need to write code to handle the **Cancel** button being clicked. Specifically, we need to tell the `Project` object to cancel any edits. (We need to do the same if the user clicks the close button on the form itself.)

```
Private Sub btnCancel_Click(ByVal sender As System.Object, _
                ByVal e As System.EventArgs) Handles btnCancel.Click

  mProject.CancelEdit()
  Hide()
End Sub

Private Sub ProjectEdit_Closing(ByVal sender As Object, _
   ByVal e As System.ComponentModel.CancelEventArgs) Handles MyBase.Closing

  mProject.CancelEdit()
End Sub
```

The `CancelEdit()` call resets the object to its state when we called `BeginEdit()`.

> *Since we're immediately hiding or closing the form, it might seem like a waste of time to reset the object. However, it's important to remember that other code in our application could have a reference to this object, so resetting it to its original values is important for overall consistency.*
>
> *Consider Microsoft Outlook, for instance. Within Outlook, it is quite possible to have several different windows open to view or interact with the same e-mail at the same time. All those windows refer to the same underlying object, so it's important to keep that object consistent, even when one of the windows is done with it.*

Adding child objects

As with everything else in our user interface, we rely on the business objects to handle the details of working with child objects. *Displaying* the child objects – in this case, the list of resources assigned to this project – is handled by binding the child collection to the `DataListView` control. All we need to do is put a bit of code behind the **Add** and **Remove** buttons, and allow the user to right-click on a resource to change its role in the project.

Behind the **Add** button, we can implement code so that the user can select a resource, and then assign it to the project. Though we haven't done so yet, we will be creating a `ResourceSelect` dialog that's just like the `ProjectSelect` dialog we created earlier. The click event handler for the button looks like this:

```
Private Sub btnAddResource_Click(ByVal sender As System.Object, _
                ByVal e As System.EventArgs) Handles btnAddResource.Click

  Dim dlg As New ResourceSelect()
  dlg.Text = "Assign resource"
  dlg.ShowDialog(Me)
  Dim ID As String = dlg.Result

  If Len(ID) > 0 Then
    dvResources.SuspendLayout()
    dvResources.DataSource = Nothing
```

```
      Try
        mProject.Resources.Assign(ID)

      Catch ex As Exception
        MsgBox(ex.Message)

      Finally
        dvResources.DataSource = mProject.Resources
        dvResources.ResumeLayout()
      End Try
    End If
  End Sub
```

First, we show the ResourceSelect dialog to get the right resource from the user:

```
Dim dlg As New ResourceSelect()
dlg.Text = "Assign resource"
dlg.ShowDialog(Me)
Dim ID As String = dlg.Result
```

If the user selected a resource, then we assign it to the project:

```
mProject.Resources.Assign(ID)
```

You may remember that we implemented several variations on the Assign() method. This one assigns the resource to the project with the default Role value.

Notice that there's some other code in the method. The calls to SuspendLayout() and ResumeLayout() are there for performance reasons – they stop the DataListView control from refreshing its display as we update its underlying data. More importantly, we're unbinding and rebinding the control to the list of child objects to ensure that it reflects the new item we've added. If we don't do this, the list control won't reflect the changes, even though the underlying child collection will.

Removing child objects

Removing a child object is simpler than adding a new one, since we don't need to arrange for the user to select a new resource. They just select an item from our DataListView control, and then click the Remove button:

```
  Private Sub btnRemoveResource_Click(ByVal sender As System.Object, _
     ByVal e As System.EventArgs) Handles btnRemoveResource.Click

    Dim ID As String = dvResources.SelectedItems(0).Text

    If MsgBox("Remove resource " & ID & " from project?", _
              MsgBoxStyle.YesNo, "Remove resource") = MsgBoxResult.Yes Then
      dvResources.SuspendLayout()
      dvResources.DataSource = Nothing
      mProject.Resources.Remove(ID)
      dvResources.DataSource = mProject.Resources
      dvResources.ResumeLayout()
    End If

  End Sub
```

We retrieve the selected resource ID from the control, and ask the user if they're sure about the operation they're about to perform. If they say yes, then we suspend the update of our control, unbind the control, remove the child, and rebind the control to the child collection.

Remember that when both adding and removing child objects, the database itself isn't changed until the user clicks the Save button and the `Project` object (along with its child objects) is updated to the database. Nothing we're doing here is permanent until the `Save()` method on the `Project` object is called.

Setting the role

The final operation that we can perform on a child object is to change its role. Here, we're allowing the user to do that via a right-click context menu on the child item list.

In the form's `Load` event handler, we populated the context menu with the list of roles:

```
Dim Role As String
For Each Role In Assignment.Roles.GetCollection
  mnuRoles.MenuItems.Add(Assignment.Roles.Item(Role))
  AddHandler mnuRoles.MenuItems(mnuRoles.MenuItems.Count - 1).Click, _
     AddressOf mnuRoles_Click
Next
```

Notice that we not only add the name of each role to the menu control, but also use the `AddHandler()` method to link each new menu item to a click event handler. This means that any time the user clicks on an item in the menu, the click event will be routed to the `mnuRoles_Click()` method.

Setting the `ContextMenu` property of the `dvDisplay` control to `mnuRoles` attached the menu to the control, and .NET now automatically takes care of bringing up the context menu when the user right-clicks on it. All we need to do is handle the selection by the user. As we noted above, we've linked the click events of all items in the menu to the `mnuRoles_Click()` method, so that's what we need to write:

```
  Private Sub mnuRoles_Click(ByVal sender As System.Object, _
                             ByVal e As System.EventArgs)

    Dim Item As MenuItem = CType(sender, MenuItem)
    If dvResources.SelectedItems.Count > 0 Then
      Dim ID As String = dvResources.SelectedItems(0).Text

      dvResources.SuspendLayout()
      dvResources.DataSource = Nothing
      mProject.Resources.Item(ID).Role = Item.Text
      dvResources.DataSource = mProject.Resources
      dvResources.ResumeLayout()
    End If

  End Sub
```

When the user clicks an option in the context menu, we determine which value they selected. We also determine which (if any) child object was selected. If the user did right-click on a valid item in the list, we then change the child object's `Role` property to match the value selected by the user.

Again, notice that we unbind and rebind the control to the child collection to ensure that it reflects the changes we've made to the child objects.

Opening a resource

Another behavior a user expects from a list is that if they double-click on an item, something useful will happen. In our case, we can bring up the selected `Resource` object for editing if a user double-clicks on a `ProjectResource` child object.

We haven't implemented the `ResourceEdit` form yet, but we'll invoke it from here nonetheless. When the user double-clicks on an assigned resource, the details about that resource will be displayed:

```
Private Sub dvResources_DoubleClick(ByVal sender As Object, _
    ByVal e As System.EventArgs) Handles dvResources.DoubleClick

  Dim ID As String = dvResources.SelectedItems(0).Text
  Cursor.Current = Cursors.WaitCursor
  Dim frm As New ResourceEdit()
  frm.MdiParent = Me.MdiParent
  frm.Resource = Resource.GetResource(ID)
  Cursor.Current = Cursors.Default
  frm.Show()

End Sub
```

By implementing both `ProjectEdit` and `ResourceEdit` so that the calling code provides the business object, rather than making the forms retrieve the object themselves, the forms become highly reusable. We can invoke them from the main menu form, or from any other form, as long as we can provide a valid `Project` or `Resource` business object for them to display or edit.

Displaying BrokenRules

The last thing we should discuss here is how we can display the list of broken rules as the user interacts with the business object. (This is entirely optional, but many readers of my VB6 Business Objects book contacted me to say that they got a lot of value out of displaying the list of broken rules to their users through the UI.)

We designed the `BrokenRules` object in the CSLA .NET framework to support this concept, so implementing it in the UI by using data binding is quite easy. Add a `ListBox` control to the form, under the Cancel button and to the right of the `Description` control. Name it `lstRules`:

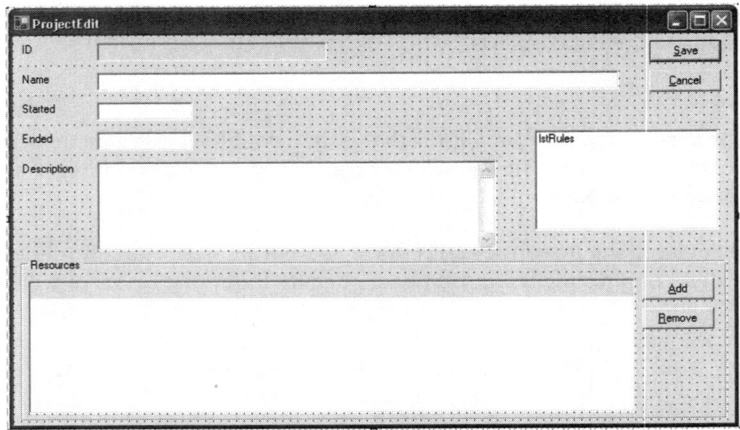

To make this control display the list of broken rules, all we need to do is add a couple of lines to the `DataBind()` method:

```
Private Sub DataBind()

  If Thread.CurrentPrincipal.IsInRole("ProjectManager") Then

    ' Only project managers can save a project
    BindField(btnSave, "Enabled", mProject, "IsValid")
  Else
    btnSave.Enabled = False
  End If

  BindField(chkIsDirty, "Checked", mProject, "IsDirty")
  BindField(txtID, "Text", mProject, "ID")
  BindField(txtName, "Text", mProject, "Name")
  BindField(txtStarted, "Text", mProject, "Started")
  BindField(txtEnded, "Text", mProject, "Ended")
  BindField(txtDescription, "Text", mProject, "Description")

  lstRules.DataSource = mProject.GetBrokenRulesCollection()
  lstRules.DisplayMember = "Description"

  With dvResources
    .SuspendLayout()
    .Clear()
    .AutoDiscover = False
    .Columns.Add("ID", "ResourceID", 0)
    .Columns.Add("Last name", "LastName", 100)
    .Columns.Add("First name", "FirstName", 100)
    .Columns.Add("Assigned", "Assigned", 100)
    .Columns.Add("Role", "Role", 150)
    .DataSource = mProject.Resources
    .ResumeLayout()
  End With

End Sub
```

The `GetBrokenRulesCollection()` method exists on all CSLA .NET business objects, and it returns a read-only collection that reflects the list of broken rules for that object. In this case, we're telling the `ListBox` control to display the `Description` property of each rule, so that the user gets a human-readable description of all broken rules. This list is automatically updated by data binding, so as the user alters the data in the form and rules are broken and unbroken, their status will be updated in this control.

Updating the menu

To make the `ProjectEdit` form available to the user, we need to enhance the main form a little. Specifically, we need to include code that invokes the `ProjectEdit` form to add a new `Project` and to edit an existing `Project`.

To add a new `Project`, write the following code in the `Projects` region of `Main.vb`:

```
Private Sub mnuProjectNew_Click(ByVal sender As System.Object, _
    ByVal e As System.EventArgs) Handles mnuProjectNew.Click

  Cursor.Current = Cursors.WaitCursor
  Dim frm As New ProjectEdit()
  frm.MdiParent = Me
  frm.Project = Project.NewProject()
  Cursor.Current = Cursors.Default
  frm.Show()

End Sub
```

The line of interest here is the one where we call the `NewProject()` method on the `Project` class to get a brand new `Project` object:

```
  frm.Project = Project.NewProject()
```

This method initializes the new object with any default values, and gets it ready for use. All of the details surrounding loading and setting default values are handled by the business class, so our UI code doesn't need to worry about that – it simply gets the new object and provides it to the `ProjectEdit` form.

Editing an existing `Project` is handled in a similar fashion. We use the `ProjectSelect` dialog so that the user can select the object to be edited; we retrieve an instance of that particular `Project` object; and then we open a `ProjectEdit` form so the user can interact with the object:

```
Private Sub mnuProjectEdit_Click(ByVal sender As System.Object, _
    ByVal e As System.EventArgs) Handles mnuProjectEdit.Click

  Dim dlg As New ProjectSelect()
  dlg.Text = "Edit Project"
  dlg.ShowDialog(Me)

  Dim Result As String = dlg.Result
  If Len(Result) > 0 Then
    Try
      Cursor.Current = Cursors.WaitCursor
      Dim ID As Guid = New Guid(Result)
```

```
        Dim obj As Project = Project.GetProject(ID)

        Dim frm As New ProjectEdit()
        frm.MdiParent = Me
        frm.Project = obj
        Cursor.Current = Cursors.Default
        frm.Show()

      Catch ex As Exception
        Cursor.Current = Cursors.Default
        MsgBox("Error loading project " & vbCrLf & ex.Message)
      End Try
    End If

  End Sub
```

First we use our `ProjectSelect` dialog to show the users a list of existing `Project` objects. For instance:

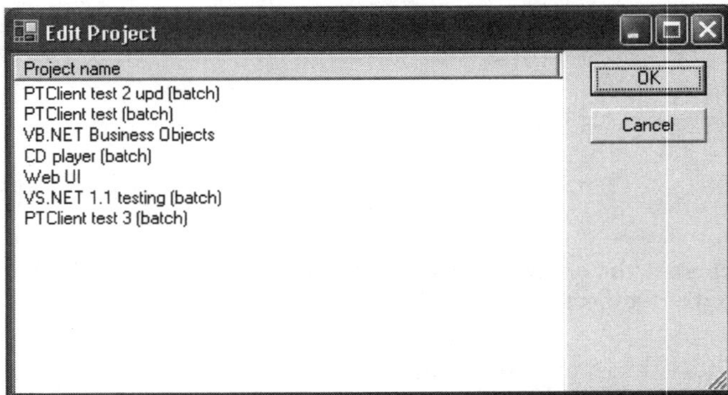

If the user selects a project and clicks **OK**, we'll get the project's ID value as a result. The main processing then occurs when we ask the `Project` class to get the right `Project` object for us, based on the user's selection:

```
        Dim ID As Guid = New Guid(Result)
        Dim obj As Project = Project.GetProject(ID)
```

This fully populated object is then provided to the `ProjectEdit` form, which displays it to the user.

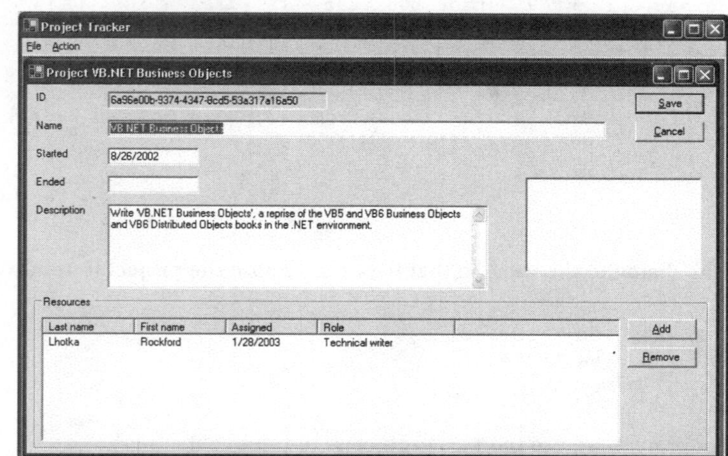

Removing a project

In our main form, we also have a menu option to remove a project from the system. When the user selects this menu option, we'll display the `ProjectSelect` dialog. If the user then chooses a project, we'll remove it. This is relatively simple, because the `Project` class provides us with a `DeleteProject()` method to remove a project based on its ID value.

In the *Projects* region, add the event handler for the appropriate menu item with this code:

```
Private Sub mnuProjectRemove_Click(ByVal sender As System.Object, _
                ByVal e As System.EventArgs) Handles mnuProjectRemove.Click

    Dim dlg As New ProjectSelect()
    dlg.Text = "Remove Project"
    dlg.ShowDialog(Me)

    Dim Result As String = dlg.Result
    If Len(Result) > 0 Then
      If MsgBox("Remove project " & Result, _
          MsgBoxStyle.YesNo, "Remove project") = MsgBoxResult.Yes Then
        Try
          Cursor.Current = Cursors.WaitCursor
          pnlStatus.Text = "Deleting project..."

          Dim ID As Guid = New Guid(Result)
          Project.DeleteProject(ID)

          Cursor.Current = Cursors.Default
          MsgBox("Project deleted")
```

```
          Catch ex As Exception
            Cursor.Current = Cursors.Default
            MsgBox("Error deleting project" & vbCrLf & ex.ToString)
          Finally
            pnlStatus.Text = ""
          End Try
        End If
      End If

    End Sub
```

First, we display the dialog to the user, so that they can choose the project to remove:

```
      Dim dlg As New ProjectSelect()
      dlg.Text = "Remove Project"
      dlg.ShowDialog(Me)
```

If the user selects a project, we use the Project class to remove it:

```
          Dim ID As Guid = New Guid(Result)
          Project.DeleteProject(ID)
```

Since a project's ID is a GUID, we first need to convert the value from the ProjectSelect dialog into a GUID, which we can then pass to the DeleteProject() method of the Project class. This method includes the appropriate code to contact the DataPortal and invoke the DataPortal_Delete() method of the business object to delete the project from the database.

Our method also includes error-handling code, and some other code that sets the cursor and status display so that the user has visual feedback that the application is busy while deletion is taking place.

Resource list

At this point, we're well over halfway done with the Windows Forms UI. The remaining two forms, ResourceSelect and ResourceEdit, are conceptually the same as the ProjectSelect and ProjectEdit forms that we've already built. We'll go through these new forms a little more quickly, since the design and concepts behind them should be familiar.

ResourceSelect dialog

The ResourceSelect form is a dialog that will be used to select resources. It will be used to edit and remove Resource objects, and it's also used from the ProjectEdit form when we want to add a new resource to a project.

Add a new form to the project and name it ResourceSelect. Add a DataListView and two Button controls, as shown:

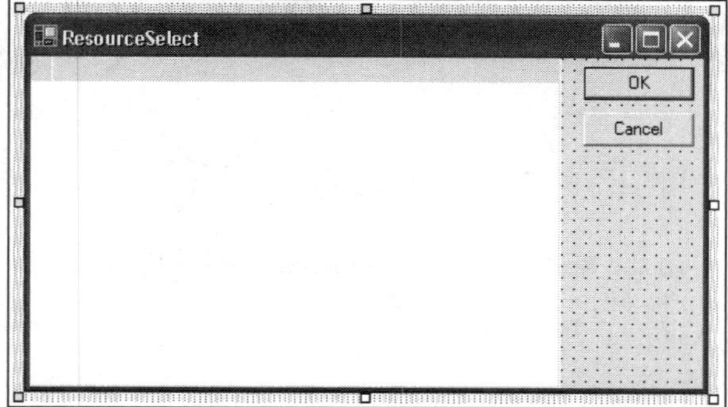

Name the `Button` controls `btnOK` and `btnCancel`, the `DataListView` `dvDisplay`, and set the form's `AcceptButton` and `CancelButton` properties accordingly. Then, as with the `ProjectSelect` dialog, we'll declare a variable and a `Property` method so that the dialog can return its result to the calling code:

```
Private mResult As String

Public ReadOnly Property Result() As String
  Get
    Return mResult
  End Get
End Property
```

As you'd expect, we'll have the **OK** and **Cancel** buttons set and reset this value:

```
Private Sub btnOK_Click(ByVal sender As System.Object, _
   ByVal e As System.EventArgs) Handles btnOK.Click, dvDisplay.DoubleClick

  If dvDisplay.SelectedItems.Count > 0 Then
    mResult = dvDisplay.SelectedItems(0).Text
  Else
    mResult = ""
  End If
  Hide()
End Sub

Private Sub btnCancel_Click(ByVal sender As System.Object, _
   ByVal e As System.EventArgs) Handles btnCancel.Click

  mResult = ""
  Hide()
End Sub
```

And as the form is loaded, we'll retrieve and display the list of resources:

```
Private Sub ResourceSelect_Load(ByVal sender As System.Object, _
   ByVal e As System.EventArgs) Handles MyBase.Load

  Dim list As ResourceList = ResourceList.GetResourceList()
  With dvDisplay
    .AutoDiscover = False
```

```
      .Columns.Add("ID", 0)
      .Columns.Add("Name", dvDisplay.Width)
      .DataSource = list
      .Focus()
    End With

  End Sub
```

Again, since we can rely on the ResourceList business object to do the hard work, all we need to do here is bind the collection to our control so that it's displayed.

Removing a resource

Back in the main form, we can now enable the menu option for removing a resource:

```
#Region " Resources "

  Private Sub mnuResourceRemove_Click(ByVal sender As System.Object, _
     ByVal e As System.EventArgs) Handles mnuResourceRemove.Click

    Dim dlg As New ResourceSelect()
    dlg.Text = "Remove Resource"
    dlg.ShowDialog(Me)

    Dim Result As String = dlg.Result
    If Len(Result) > 0 Then
      If MsgBox("Remove resource " & Result, _
          MsgBoxStyle.YesNo, "Remove resource") = MsgBoxResult.Yes Then
        Try
          Cursor.Current = Cursors.WaitCursor
          pnlStatus.Text = "Removing resource..."

          Resource.DeleteResource(Result)
          Cursor.Current = Cursors.Default
          MsgBox("Resource deleted")

        Catch ex As Exception
          Cursor.Current = Cursors.Default
          MsgBox("Error deleting resource" & vbCrLf & ex.ToString)

        Finally
          pnlStatus.Text = ""
        End Try
      End If
    End If

  End Sub

#End Region
```

Since the Resource class implements a DeleteResource() method, our UI code doesn't need to do a whole lot:

```
          Resource.DeleteResource(Result)
```

Most of our coding effort is in updating the status display and the mouse cursor icon, and in handling any possible errors so that the user can be notified of them.

Resource edit

The `ResourceEdit` form will be designed like the `ProjectEdit` form, in that it will have a property enabling calling code to provide us with the `Resource` object we're to display or edit. This provides a high degree of flexibility, allowing our form to be called by the main menu to add a new `Resource`, or edit an existing `Resource`. It also allows the `ProjectEdit` form to call the `ResourceEdit` form to display a `Resource` object, and vice versa.

The ResourceEdit form

Add a new form named `ResourceEdit` to the project, and add controls as described in the figure and table below:

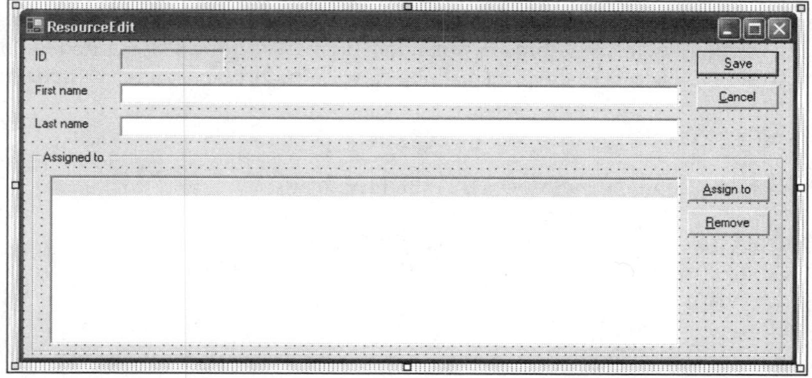

Control	Properties
`TextBox`	`Name=txtID; Text=""; ReadOnly=True`
`TextBox`	`Name=txtFirstName`
`TextBox`	`Name=txtLastName`
`ContextMenu`	`Name=mnuRoles`
`DataListView`	`Name=dvProjects; ContextMenu=mnuRoles`
`Button`	`Name=btnSave; Text="Save"`
`Button`	`Name=btnCancel; Text="Cancel"`
`Button`	`Name=btnAssignProject; Text="Assign to"`
`Button`	`Name=btnRemoveProject; Text="Remove"`
`CheckBox`	`Name=chkIsDirty; Location= -368, 136`

Set the form's `AcceptButton` and `CancelButton` properties to `btnSave` and `btnCancel` respectively.

The Resource object

Since we expect the calling code to provide us with a `Resource` object, we need to create a property and a variable for that object, which will be used by the rest of our code:

```
Private mResource As Resource

Public Property Resource() As Resource
  Get
    Return mResource
  End Get
  Set(ByVal Value As Resource)
    mResource = Value
  End Set
End Property
```

Loading the form

As the form is loaded, we'll do some initialization based on the `Resource` object and the user's roles. As in `ProjectEdit`, we'll use the current thread's principal object's `IsInRole()` method to do our authorization. To simplify access to the principal object, we'll import the `System.Threading` namespace:

```
Imports System.Threading
```

Then we can perform the initialization work as the form loads:

```
Private Sub ResourceEdit_Load(ByVal sender As System.Object, _
   ByVal e As System.EventArgs) Handles MyBase.Load

  Me.Text = "Resource " & mResource.LastName & ", " & mResource.FirstName

  Dim Role As String
  For Each Role In Assignment.Roles
    mnuRoles.MenuItems.Add(Assignment.Roles.Item(Role))
    AddHandler mnuRoles.MenuItems(mnuRoles.MenuItems.Count - 1).Click, _
       AddressOf mnuRoles_Click
  Next

  If Thread.CurrentPrincipal.IsInRole("ProjectManager") OrElse _
     Thread.CurrentPrincipal.IsInRole("Supervisor") Then

    mResource.BeginEdit()

    ' Only project managers or supervisors can assign projects
    btnAssignProject.Enabled = True
    btnRemoveProject.Enabled = True
  Else
    btnAssignProject.Enabled = False
    btnRemoveProject.Enabled = False
  End If

  DataBind()

End Sub
```

This is very similar to the Load event handler in ProjectEdit. We set the form's caption text, load the list of Role data into mnuRoles, enable/disable some buttons based on the user's security role, and call the DataBind() method, which binds the form to the business object:

```
Private Sub DataBind()

  If Thread.CurrentPrincipal.IsInRole("ProjectManager") OrElse _
     Thread.CurrentPrincipal.IsInRole("Supervisor") Then

    ' Only project managers or supervisors can save a resource
    BindField(btnSave, "Enabled", mResource, "IsValid")
  Else
    btnSave.Enabled = False
  End If

  BindField(chkIsDirty, "Checked", mResource, "IsDirty")
  BindField(txtID, "Text", mResource, "ID")
  BindField(txtLastname, "Text", mResource, "LastName")
  BindField(txtFirstname, "Text", mResource, "FirstName")

  With dvProjects
    .SuspendLayout()
    .Clear()
    .AutoDiscover = False
    .Columns.Add("ID", "ProjectID", 0)
    .Columns.Add("Project", "ProjectName", 200)
    .Columns.Add("Assigned", "Assigned", 100)
    .Columns.Add("Role", "Role", 150)
    .DataSource = mResource.Assignments
    .ResumeLayout()
  End With

End Sub
```

The btnSave control is only bound if the user's role allows them to edit a resource. The other fields on the form – including chkIsDirty – are always bound to the Resource object, so that the data binding reflects updates made to the object's data. The DataListView control is bound to the list of projects to which this resource is assigned, and we manually set the columns and their widths so that the display looks good.

Save, cancel, and close

When the user clicks the **Save** button, we need to tell the object to apply any changes, committing them inside the object itself. This mirrors the call to BeginEdit() that we made as the form was loaded. With that done, we then call the Save() method to save the object to the database:

```
Private Sub btnSave_Click(ByVal sender As System.Object, _
   ByVal e As System.EventArgs) Handles btnSave.Click

  Try
    Cursor.Current = Cursors.WaitCursor
    mResource.ApplyEdit()
    mResource = CType(mResource.Save(), Resource)
```

```
      Cursor.Current = Cursors.Default

    Catch ex As Exception
      Cursor.Current = Cursors.Default
      MsgBox(ex.ToString)
    End Try

    Hide()

  End Sub
```

Remember: if we don't close the form here, we need to call `DataBind()` to bind the form to the new instance of the `Resource` object that's returned from the `Save()` method.

> **Failure to re-bind to the new object, or to close the form, will result in hard-to-debug errors in the application.**

If the user clicks the Cancel button or closes the form by clicking the form's close button, we need to tell the object to cancel any edit process:

```
  Private Sub btnCancel_Click(ByVal sender As System.Object, _
      ByVal e As System.EventArgs) Handles btnCancel.Click

    mResource.CancelEdit()
    Hide()

  End Sub

  Private Sub ResourceEdit_Closing(ByVal sender As Object, _
      ByVal e As System.ComponentModel.CancelEventArgs) Handles MyBase.Closing

    mResource.CancelEdit()

  End Sub
```

This resets the object to the state it was in when we called `BeginEdit()`.

Adding child objects

When we add a child object, we're adding a `ResourceAssignment`. To do this, however, we need to have the user select a project to which the resource will be assigned. Fortunately, we designed the `ProjectSelect` form as a reusable dialog, so we can simply call it here to ask the user to select a project:

```
  Private Sub btnAssignProject_Click(ByVal sender As System.Object, _
     ByVal e As System.EventArgs) Handles btnAssignProject.Click

    Dim dlg As New ProjectSelect()
    dlg.Text = "Assign to project"
    dlg.ShowDialog(Me)
    Dim Result As String = dlg.Result
```

```
    If Len(Result) > 0 Then
      dvProjects.SuspendLayout()
      dvProjects.DataSource = Nothing
      Dim ID As Guid = New Guid(Result)
      Try
        mResource.Assignments.AssignTo(ID)

      Catch ex As Exception
        MsgBox(ex.Message)

      Finally
        dvProjects.DataSource = mResource.Assignments
        dvProjects.ResumeLayout()
      End Try
      dvProjects.DataSource = mResource.Assignments
      dvProjects.ResumeLayout()
    End If

  End Sub
```

Assuming that the user picks a project from the list, we call our `AssignTo()` method to assign this resource to that project:

```
Dim ID As Guid = New Guid(Result)
mResource.Assignments.AssignTo(ID)
```

This particular implementation of `AssignTo()` assigns the resource to the project using the default `Role` value.

Removing child objects

We can also remove a project from the list, which would mean that this resource is no longer assigned to the project we've removed:

```
  Private Sub btnRemoveProject_Click(ByVal sender As System.Object, _
     ByVal e As System.EventArgs) Handles btnRemoveProject.Click

    Dim ID As Guid = New Guid(dvProjects.SelectedItems(0).Text)
    Dim Name As String = dvProjects.SelectedItems(0).SubItems(0).Text

    If MsgBox("Remove from project " & Name & "?", _
       MsgBoxStyle.YesNo, "Remove assignment") = MsgBoxResult.Yes Then

      dvProjects.SuspendLayout()
      dvProjects.DataSource = Nothing
      mResource.Assignments.Remove(ID)
      dvProjects.DataSource = mResource.Assignments
      dvProjects.ResumeLayout()
    End If

  End Sub
```

First, we prompt the user to make sure they want to do this. If they say yes, then we remove the project from the list:

```
mResource.Assignments.Remove(ID)
```

Remember that neither this nor the addition of a child object actually updates the database. Our operation here is only affecting the `Resource` object in memory on the client. When the `Save()` method of the `Resource` object is called, both the `Resource` object and its child objects are updated to the database.

Changing roles

Another option is to change the role of the resource on a project. As before, this is done through a context menu that appears when the user right-clicks on the `DataListView` control and chooses a role from the pop-up menu. Most of the work is done by .NET or our business object, so all we need to do is catch the menu's click event:

```
Private Sub mnuRoles_Click(ByVal sender As System.Object, _
                           ByVal e As System.EventArgs)

  Dim Item As MenuItem = CType(sender, MenuItem)
  If dvProjects.SelectedItems.Count > 0 Then
    Dim ID As Guid = New Guid(dvProjects.SelectedItems(0).Text)

    dvProjects.SuspendLayout()
    dvProjects.DataSource = Nothing
    mResource.Assignments.Item(ID).Role = Item.Text
    dvProjects.DataSource = mResource.Assignments
    dvProjects.ResumeLayout()
  End If

End Sub
```

All we do is take the role value selected from the menu, and store it in the child object selected by the user:

```
mResource.Assignments.Item(ID).Role = Item.Text
```

The fact that the role value is stored as a numeric ID, rather than as a human-readable text value, is invisible to the UI code. This is nice because it means that the UI code deals with the same text values that the user sees. The business object completely encapsulates the code to translate between the cryptic numeric value and our text value. Perhaps more importantly, the business object validates the value, ensuring that only a valid role is specified.

Displaying a project

Finally, we can support a double-click operation on a child item. If the user double-clicks on a `ResourceAssignment` in our `DataListView`, we can bring up the `ProjectEdit` form with the corresponding project so that the user can view or edit that project's details:

```
Private Sub dvProjects_DoubleClick(ByVal sender As Object, _
   ByVal e As System.EventArgs) Handles dvProjects.DoubleClick

  Dim ID As Guid = New Guid(dvProjects.SelectedItems(0).Text)
  Cursor.Current = Cursors.WaitCursor

  Dim frm As New ProjectEdit()
  frm.MdiParent = Me.MdiParent
  frm.Project = Project.GetProject(ID)
  Cursor.Current = Cursors.Default
  frm.Show()

End Sub
```

Again, this is possible – and quite simple – primarily because we designed the `ProjectEdit` form so that it doesn't load the `Project` object itself. Rather, it expects our code to load the `Project` object first, and *then* open the form. Because of this design, we can get a great deal of reuse out of the `ProjectEdit` form.

Updating the menu

The `ResourceEdit` form is now complete, so we can return to the main menu form and enable the menu options to add and edit a resource.

To add a resource, we simply create a new `Resource` object and open a `ResourceEdit` form. Because the ID value for a resource is not a GUID, we can't randomly generate it. In this case, we'll prompt the user to enter the new ID value, and then bring up the `ResourceEdit` form. Put this code in the *Resources* region:

```
Private Sub mnuResourceNew_Click(ByVal sender As System.Object, _
    ByVal e As System.EventArgs) Handles mnuResourceNew.Click

  Dim ID As String = InputBox("Resource ID", "New resource")
  If Len(ID) > 0 Then
    Cursor.Current = Cursors.WaitCursor
    Dim obj As Resource = Resource.NewResource(ID)
    Dim frm As New ResourceEdit
    frm.MdiParent = Me
    frm.Resource = obj
    Cursor.Current = Cursors.Default
    frm.Show()
  End If

End Sub
```

To allow the user to edit an existing `Resource` object, we use the `ResourceSelect` dialog so that the user can select an existing item. We then use that item's ID to load a `Resource` object and open a `ResourceEdit` form:

```
Private Sub mnuResourceEdit_Click(ByVal sender As System.Object, _
    ByVal e As System.EventArgs) Handles mnuResourceEdit.Click
```

```
    Dim dlg As New ResourceSelect()
    dlg.Text = "Edit Resource"
    dlg.ShowDialog(Me)

    Dim Result As String = dlg.Result
    If Len(Result) > 0 Then
      Try
        Cursor.Current = Cursors.WaitCursor
        Dim obj As Resource = Resource.GetResource(Result)
        Dim frm As New ResourceEdit()
        frm.MdiParent = Me
        frm.Resource = obj
        Cursor.Current = Cursors.Default
        frm.Show()

      Catch ex As Exception
        Cursor.Current = Cursors.Default
        MsgBox("Error loading resource" & vbCrLf & ex.Message)
      End Try
    End If

  End Sub
```

First, we display the `ResourceSelect` dialog so the user can select a resource from the list:

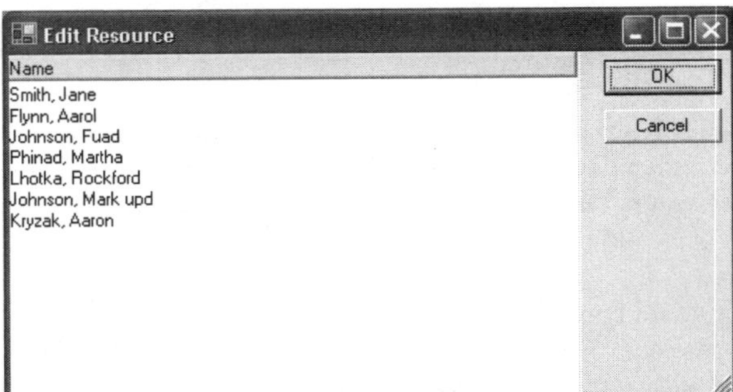

If the user selects a resource and clicks OK, we'll get the resource's ID value as a result. We then use that ID value as a parameter to the `GetResource()` factory method on the `Resource` class to get back a fully populated `Resource` object that we can pass to the `ResourceEdit` form:

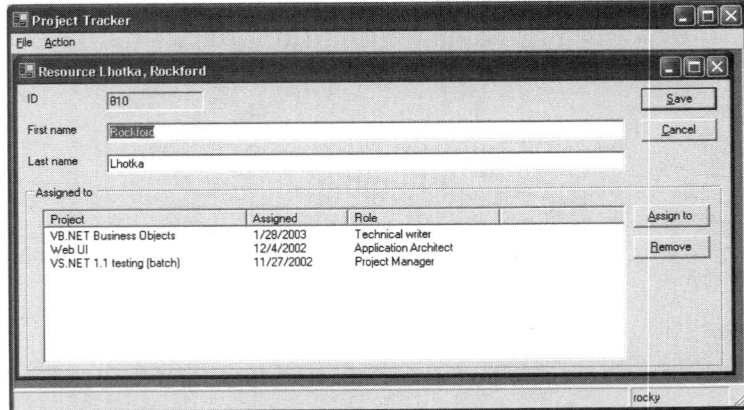

At this point, our Windows Forms UI is complete. We can use it to add, edit, and remove projects and resources. It also allows us to assign resources to projects and set their roles.

Notice that nowhere in this UI did we deal with database concepts, SQL statements, or even ADO.NET. We allow the business objects to take care of all those details, so that we can focus on the user experience.

Conclusion

In this chapter, we've walked through the process of creating a basic Windows Forms UI based on our business objects. Obviously, there are many ways to create a UI using Windows Forms, and this particular implementation is not the only one where our objects will come in useful.

Because of the way we designed our objects to support nested `BeginEdit()` calls, we can support very sophisticated user experiences based on nested child windows, or a simpler experience like the one we've implemented here. Since we support full data binding from our objects and collections, we can use the `DataGrid` control to edit objects or child objects if we need to. The possibilities are very broad.

The key point to take from this chapter is that when we use the business objects, the UI developer doesn't need to worry about business rules, data access, or most other complex issues. The UI developer can focus on the UI itself, the user experience, the look and feel of the application, and so forth. We achieve a high degree of separation between the logical UI tier and the logical business tier through the use of objects in this manner.

At the same time, because the objects use the `DataPortal` mechanism to retrieve and update data, we have good separation between the logical business tier and the logical data access tier. Better still, we can simply change the application configuration file to switch between various *physical* n-tier configurations as needed to meet our performance, scalability, reliability, and security requirements.

In Chapter 9, we'll implement a Web Forms UI based on the same set of business objects. While there are obvious differences between the Windows Forms and Web Forms environments, we'll achieve total reuse of our business logic and data access code as we move from one UI type to the next.

CHAPTER 9

9

Web Forms UI

In Chapter 8, we built a Windows Forms UI based on our Project Tracker business objects. But Visual Basic .NET also supports web development, through ASP.NET and the Web Forms technology. We can use our business objects to create a Web Forms interface in a similar manner to the way we built the Windows Forms interface.

Web Forms can be used to create many different user interfaces, and this chapter is not intended to act as a tutorial on web development in ASP.NET. Instead, we'll focus on how business objects are used within a web application, including state management and data binding.

> *ASP.NET is the .NET web server component that hosts Web Forms, web services, and other server-side handlers in IIS. ASP.NET is a very broad and flexible technology. Web Forms are hosted within ASP.NET, and provide us with 'normal' web development capabilities.*

Before we get into the development of the Web Forms UI, we need to discuss some of the basic concepts around the use of business objects in web development.

Web development and objects

Historically, the world of web development has been strongly resistant to the use of 'stateful' objects behind web pages, and not without reason. In particular, using such objects without careful forethought can be very bad for web site performance. Sometimes, however, it's suggested that instead of a stateful object, we should use a `DataSet` – which itself is a very large, stateful object! Most people don't think twice about using one of those for web development.

Clearly then, stateful objects aren't inherently bad – it is how they're designed and how we use them that matters. Business objects can be very useful in web development; we just need to look carefully at how such objects are conceived and employed.

> **Objects *can* work very well in web development, if they are designed and used properly.**

In Chapter 3, we discussed ADO.NET, including data reader and `DataSet` objects. As part of that discussion, we covered how web applications can choose from three basic data access models:

- Data reader → page
- Data reader → `DataSet` → page
- Data reader → business object → page

Using the data reader directly can be very beneficial if our data set is relatively small and the page processing is fast, because it allows us to take the data directly from the database and put it into our page. We don't *need* to copy the data into an in-memory container (such as a `DataSet` or business object) before putting it into the page output.

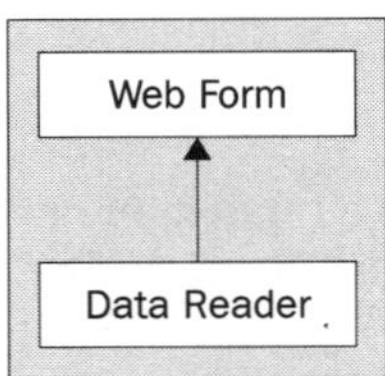

However, if our data set is large or the page processing is slow, using a data reader becomes a less attractive option. Using one requires the database connection to remain open for longer, causing an increase in the number of database connections required on the server overall, and thereby decreasing scalability.

Direct use of a data reader also typically leads to code that's harder to maintain. A data reader doesn't offer the ease of use of the `DataSet` or a business object. Nor does it provide any business logic or protection for the data, leaving it up to the UI code to provide all validation and other business processing.

> **In most cases, use of the `DataSet` or a business object will offer better scalability when compared to direct use of a data reader, and result in code that's easier to maintain.**

Having discounted the use of a data reader in all but a few situations, the question we're faced with is whether to use the `DataSet` or a business object as our stateful, in-memory data container. These options are similar, in that the data is loaded from a data reader into the stateful object, and from there into the page:

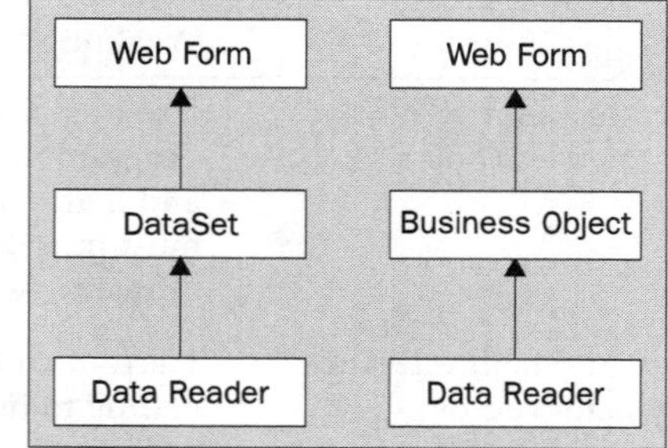

This means that in general, we can expect similar performance characteristics from `DataSets` and business objects. However, our business objects are actually *lighter weight* than the ADO.NET `DataSet` object. This is because our objects are specific to the data they contain, and don't need to retain all the metadata required by the `DataSet` object.

Better yet, our business objects provide access not only to the application's data, but also to its *business logic*. As we discussed in Chapter 1, business objects can be thought of as *smart data*. They encapsulate the business logic and the data, so the UI doesn't need to worry about potential data misuse.

Overall, business objects provide the high scalability characteristics of the `DataSet`, without the overhead. They offer better use of database connections than the data reader, though at the cost of some performance in some situations. When compared to both other technologies, business objects enable a much higher level of reuse and easier long-term maintenance, making them the best choice overall.

State management

The Achilles heel of web development is state management. The original design of web technology was merely for document viewing, not for the myriad purposes for which it is used today. Because of this, the issue of state management was never thought through in a methodical way. Instead, state management techniques have evolved over time in a relatively ad hoc manner.

Through this haphazard process, some workable solutions have evolved, though each requires tradeoffs in terms of performance, scalability and fault-tolerance. The primary options at our disposal are:

- State is maintained on the web server
- State is transferred from server to client to server on each page request
- State is stored in temporary files or database tables

Whether we use a `DataSet`, a data reader, or business objects to retrieve and update our data is actually immaterial here. Ultimately, we're left to choose one of these three state management strategies. The following table summarizes the strengths and weaknesses of each:

Approach	Strengths	Weaknesses
State stored on web server	Easy to code and use. Works well with business objects.	Use of global variables/data is poor programming practice. To get scalability and fault tolerance via a web farm, we must introduce complexity of infrastructure.
State transferred to/from client	Scalability and fault tolerance are easily achieved by implementing a web farm.	Hard to code, requires a lot of manual coding to implement. Performance can be a problem over slow network links.
State stored in file/database	Scalability and fault tolerance are easily achieved by implementing a web farm. We can efficiently store a lot of state data or very complex data.	Increased load on database server since we retrieve/store state on each page hit. Requires manual coding to implement. Data cleanup must be implemented to deal with abandoned state data.

As you can see, all of these solutions have more drawbacks than benefits. Unfortunately, in the seven or more years that the Web has been a mainstream technology, no vendor or standards body has been able to provide a comprehensive solution to the issue of dealing with state data. All we can do is choose the solution that has the least negative impact on our particular application.

Let's go into some more detail on each of these techniques, in the context of using business objects behind our web forms.

State on the web server

First, we can choose to keep state on the web server. This is easily accomplished through the use of the ASP.NET `Session` object, which is a name-value collection of arbitrary data or objects. ASP.NET manages the `Session` object, ensuring that each user has a unique `Session`, and that the `Session` object is available to all our Web Forms code on any page request.

This is by far the easiest way to program web applications. The `Session` object acts as a global repository for almost any data that we need to keep from page to page. By storing state data on the web server, we enable the type of host-based computing that has been done on mainframes and minicomputers for decades.

> *In ASP and COM, there were a number of limitations on the* `Session` *object, the most significant of which was that we couldn't put VB6 objects into* `Session` *without incurring serious performance penalties. The ASP.NET* `Session` *object and VB.NET objects do not have these issues, so it's perfectly acceptable to store VB.NET objects in* `Session` *in ASP.NET.*

As we've already expressed, however, there are drawbacks. `Session` is a *global* repository for our user, but as any experienced programmer knows, the use of global variables is very dangerous and can rapidly lead to code that's hard to maintain. If we choose to use `Session` to store state, we must be disciplined in its use to avoid these problems.

The use of `Session` also has scalability and fault tolerance ramifications.

Using a web farm in ASP.NET

To achieve scalability and fault tolerance, we typically implement a web farm – two or more web servers that are running exactly the same application. It doesn't matter which server handles each user page request, because all the servers run the same code. This effectively spreads the processing load across multiple machines, thus increasing scalability. We also gain fault tolerance, since if one machine goes down, user requests will simply be handled by the remaining server(s).

What I just described is a fully load-balanced web farm. However, because state data is often maintained directly on each web server, the above scenario is not possible. Instead, web farms are often configured using 'sticky sessions', so once a user starts using a specific server, they remain on that server because that's where their data is located. This provides *some* scalability, because our processing load is still spread across multiple servers, but it provides very limited fault tolerance. If a server goes down, all the users attached to that server also go down.

To enable a fully load-balanced web farm, *no* state can be maintained on *any* web server. As soon as user state is stored on a web server, our users become attached to that server, to the extent that only that server can handle their web requests. By default, the ASP.NET `Session` object runs on our web server in our ASP.NET process. This provides optimal performance, because the state data is stored in-process with our code, but this approach doesn't allow us to implement a fully load-balanced web farm.

Instead, the `Session` object can be run in a separate process on our web server. This can help improve fault tolerance, since the ASP.NET process can restart, and users won't lose their state data. However, this still doesn't help us to implement a fully load-balanced web farm, so it doesn't help with scalability. Also, there is a performance cost, because the state data must be serialized and transferred from the state management process to the ASP.NET process (and back again) on every page request.

As a third option, ASP.NET allows us to run the `Session` object on a dedicated, separate server, rather than on any specific web server. This **state server** can maintain the state data for all users, making it equally accessible to all web servers in a web farm. This *does* mean that we can implement a fully load-balanced web farm, in which each user request is routed to the least loaded web server. No user is ever 'stuck' on a specific web server:

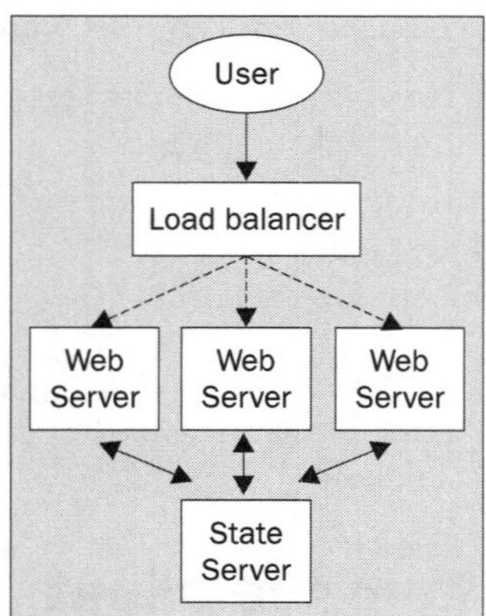

With this arrangement, we can lose a web server with minimal impact. Obviously, users in the middle of having a page processed on that particular server will be affected, but all other users should be redirected to the remaining live servers transparently. All of their `Session` data will remain available.

As with the out-of-process option that we discussed previously, the `Session` object is serialized so that it can be transferred to the state server machine efficiently. This means that all objects referenced by `Session` are also serialized – which is not a problem for our business objects, since they are marked as `<Serializable()>`.

> **When using this approach, all state *must* be maintained in `<Serializable()>` objects.**

In this arrangement, our fault tolerance is significantly improved, but if the state server itself goes down, then all user state is lost. To help address *this*, we can put the `Session` objects into a SQL Server database (rather than just into memory on the state server), and then use clustering to make the SQL Server fault tolerant as well.

Obviously, these solutions are becoming increasingly complex and costly, and they also worsen performance. By putting our state on a separate state server, we now incur network overhead on each page request, since the user's `Session` object must be retrieved from the state server by the web server so that our Web Forms code can use the `Session` data. Once our page is complete, the `Session` object is transferred back across the network to the state server for storage.

The following table summarizes our options:

Location of state data	Performance, scalability, and fault tolerance
`Session` in process	High performance Low scalability Low fault tolerance Web farms must use sticky sessions; fully load-balanced web farms not supported
`Session` out of process	Decreased performance Low scalability Improved fault tolerance (ASP.NET process can reset without losing state data) Web farms must use sticky sessions; fully load-balanced web farms not supported
`Session` on state server	Decreased performance High scalability High fault tolerance

In conclusion, while storing state data on the web server (or in a state server) provides the simplest programming model, it makes some obvious sacrifices with regard to complexity and performance in order to achieve scalability and fault tolerance.

Transferring state to/from the client

The second of the options we're considering is to transfer all state from the server to the client, and back to the server again, on each page request. The idea here is that the web server never maintains any state data – it gets all state data along with the page request, works with the data, and then sends it back to the client as part of the resulting page.

This approach provides high scalability and fault tolerance with very little complexity in our infrastructure: since the web servers never maintain state data, we can implement a fully load balanced web farm without worrying about server-side state issues. On the other hand, there are some drawbacks.

First of all, we are now transferring all the state data over what is typically the slowest link in our system: the link between the user's browser and the web server. Moreover, we are transferring that state *twice* for each page – from the server to the browser, and then from the browser back to the server. Obviously, this can have serious performance implications over a slow network link (like a modem), and can even affect an organization's overall network performance, due to the volume of data being transferred on each page request.

The other major drawback is the complexity of our *code*. There's no automatic mechanism that puts all our state data into each page – we must do that by hand. Often, this means creating hidden fields on our pages in which we can store state data that's required, but which the user shouldn't see. Our pages can quickly become very complex as we add these extra fields.

This can also be a security problem. When we send state data to the client, that data becomes potentially available to the end user. In many cases, our state data will include internal information that's not intended for direct consumption by the user. Sometimes, this information may be sensitive, so sending it to the client could create a security loophole in our system. While we could encrypt this data, that incurs extra processing overhead and increases the size of our data, so performance is decreased.

To avoid such difficulties, applications often minimize the amount of data stored in the page by re-retrieving it from the original database on each page request. All we need to keep in the page then is the key information to retrieve the data, and any data values that we've changed. Any other data values can always be reloaded from the database. This solution can dramatically increase the load on our database server, but continues to avoid keeping any state on the web server.

In conclusion, while this solution offers good scalability and fault tolerance, it can be quite complex to program, and can often result in a lot of extra code to write and maintain. Additionally, it can have negative performance impact, especially if our users connect over low speed lines.

State in a file or database

The final solution to consider is the use of temporary files (or database tables of temporary data) in which we can store state data. Such a solution offers further other alternatives, including the creation of data schemas where we can store state data such that it can be retrieved in parts, reported against, and so forth. Typically, these activities aren't important for state data, but they *can* be important if we want to keep the state data for a long period of time.

Most state data just exists between page calls, or at most for the period of time during which the user is actively interacting with our site. Some applications, however, keep state data for longer periods of time, allowing the user's 'session' to last for days, weeks, or months. Persistent shopping carts and wish lists are examples of long-term state data that's typically stored in a meaningful format in a database.

Whether we store our state as a single blob of data or in a schema, storing it in a file or a database provides good scalability and fault tolerance. It can also provide better performance than sending the state to and from the client workstation, since communicating with a database is typically faster than communicating with the client. In situations like these, the state data isn't kept on the client or the web server, so we can create fully load-balanced web farms:

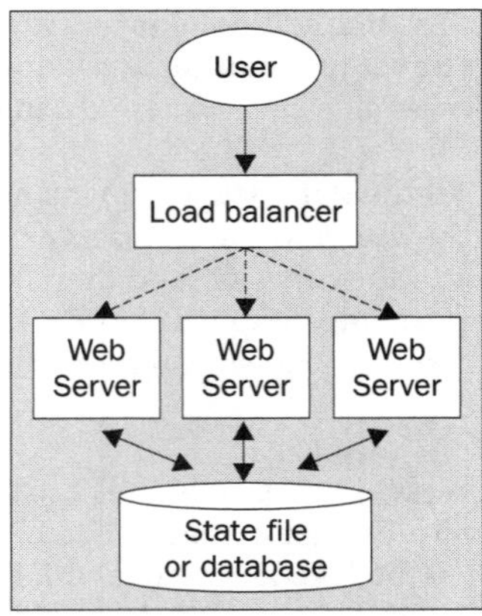

> *As we mentioned earlier, one way to accomplish this is to use the ASP.NET `Session` object, and configure it such that the data is stored in a SQL Server database. If we just want to store arbitrary state data as a single chunk of data in the database, then this is probably the best solution.*

The first thing you'll notice is that this diagram is virtually identical to the state server diagram that we discussed earlier, and it turns out the basic model and benefits are indeed consistent with that approach. We get scalability and fault tolerance because we can implement a web farm, where state is retrieved from the central database by the web server handling each page request. Once the page request is complete, the data is stored back in the central state database. Using clustering technology, we can make the database server itself fault tolerant, minimizing it as a single point of failure.

In conclusion, while this approach offers a high degree of scalability and fault tolerance, if we implement the retrieval and storage of the state data by hand it increases the complexity of our code. There are also performance implications, since all our state data is transferred across a network and back for each page request – and then there's the cost of storing and retrieving the data in the database itself.

In the final analysis, determining which of the three solutions to use depends on the specific requirements of your application and environment. For most applications, using the ASP.NET `Session` object to maintain state data will offer the easiest programming model and the most flexibility. We can get optimal performance by running it in-process with our pages, or optimal scalability and fault tolerance by having the `Session` object stored in a SQL Server database on a clustered database server – and there are shades of compromise in between.

The key is that our business objects are `<Serializable()>`, so the `Session` object can serialize them as needed. Even if we choose to implement our own blob-based file or data storage approach, the fact that our objects are `<Serializable()>` means that we too can easily convert our objects to a byte stream that can be stored as a blob. If our objects were not `<Serializable()>`, our options would be severely limited.

For our sample application, we'll use the `Session` object to help manage our state data – but we'll use it sparingly, because overuse of global variables is a cardinal sin!

Web Forms interface

We'll create our Web Forms interface within the existing `ProjectTracker` solution, and you'll soon see that most of the steps necessary to set up a Web Forms application are very similar to those we made in Chapter 8 to set up our Windows Forms application. In the `ProjectTracker` solution, choose **File | Add Project | New Project**. Make it an ASP.NET Web Application, and name it `PTWeb`:

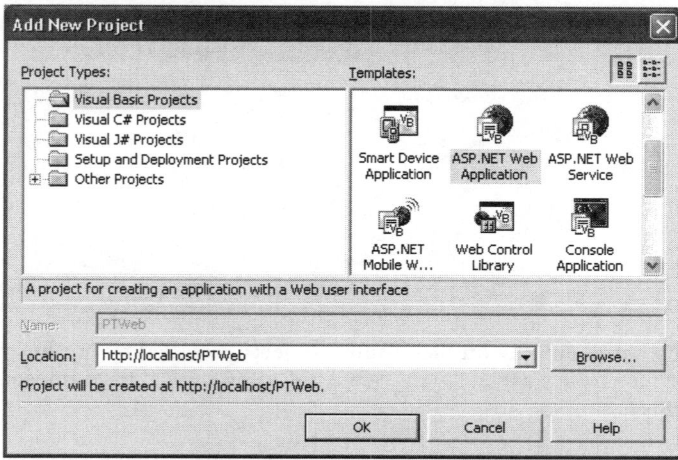

As with our Windows Forms application, we need to reference the `ProjectTracker.Library` assembly and the CSLA .NET framework assemblies by using the Add Reference dialog. Add the former via the **Projects** tab, and use the **Browse** button to navigate to the `ProjectTracker.Library` project's `bin` directory and select the CSLA .NET assemblies from there:

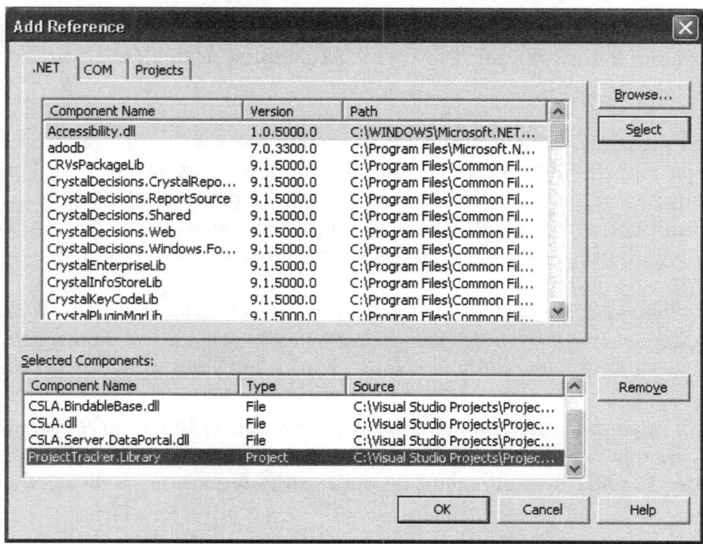

Also, add a global import of `ProjectTracker.Library` to the list of imports:

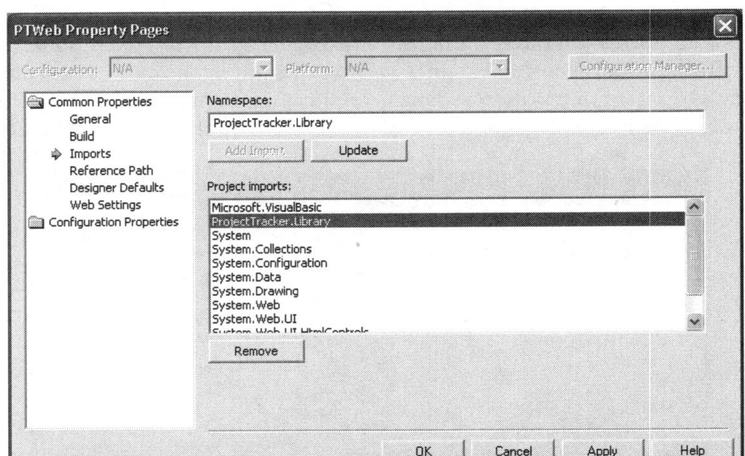

Since our UI will be based entirely on the business objects provided by our business assembly, it makes sense to import the namespace project-wide. We *could* opt to import the namespace manually at the top of each page, but this is simpler.

Lastly, remove `WebForm1.aspx` from the project – we'll add our own forms as we need them – and right-click on the project in Solution Explorer to set it as the startup project. This way, we can easily use the debugger to test our work as we go along.

Application configuration

In our Windows Forms application, we added an `App.config` file and used it to provide configuration data for our client application. We need to do the same thing in the `Web.config` file of our Web Forms client application.

As we've discussed previously, the optimal configuration for a web application is to run the `DataPortal` server and the data access code in the same process as our Web Forms. The whole reason for using a *remote* `DataPortal` is so that we can get all our data access code on a server and exploit database connection pooling. In a web environment, we are *already* on a server, so we can get database connection pooling with no need to go across yet another network boundary.

> *Sometimes, performance is trumped by security requirements, which mandate that the web server must talk to an application server behind a second firewall to do any data access. In that case, we know that we'll take a performance hit of about 50%, but we are potentially increasing our security.*

In this chapter, we'll implement the optimal 2-tier configuration, with the server-side `DataPortal` running in the same process as our Web Forms UI. We'll also discuss how to configure the application to use a remote `DataPortal` server, so you can easily adjust if your security requirements dictate that approach.

The Web.config file

When we create a web application project, a `Web.config` file is created for us automatically. Open that file, and add an `<appSettings>` section to it, as shown:

```
<?xml version="1.0" encoding="utf-8" ?>
<configuration>
  <appSettings>
    <add key="Authentication" value="CSLA" />
    <add key="DB:Security" value="data source=server;initial catalog=Security;
                              integrated security=SSPI" />
    <add key="DB:PTracker" value="data source=server;initial catalog=PTracker;
                              integrated security=SSPI" />
  </appSettings>

  <system.web>

  ...
```

Notice that `<appSettings>` is inside the `<configuration>` element, but not inside the `<system.web>` element.

By specifying the database connection strings here, rather than supplying the location of the remote `DataPortal`, we're configuring the CSLA .NET framework to run the `DataPortal` server code in our local process. Since it's the `DataPortal` server that invokes our business objects to run their data access code, this means that our data access code will also run in-process.

This provides optimal performance, since the data is retrieved from the database directly into our process, and is immediately available to our UI code. No object serialization or network data transfers occur. Also, since all our users are sharing the web server, all of the data access code will run on this server. Since we've configured the connection strings to use integrated security, and our website allows anonymous users, all connections will be made under the ASP.NET user account. This means that we'll get database connection pooling.

Typically, I use an application-specific username and password rather than using integrated security. Having all applications on the web server use the ASP.NET account means that all applications would have access to each other's data, which is often unacceptable. By using a specific user account and password, we restrict the data each application can access.

We're configuring the client to use CSLA .NET security, which is appropriate if we're allowing anonymous access to our website. If we want to use Windows' integrated security, we should change the configuration file shown here, and also change the IIS configuration to disallow anonymous access, forcing users to authenticate using NT security credentials. We'll discuss security further when we implement our login form as part of the user interface.

A note about Enterprise Services

With these configuration settings, our server-side `DataPortal` code will run in the ASP.NET process along with our Web Forms UI code and our business objects. This includes not only `Server.DataPortal`, but also `Server.ServicedDataPortal.DataPortal`.

The reason why `ServicedDataPortal` will also run in-process is because it's configured to run in COM+ within a Library Application, and code in a Library Application runs within the host process that calls the components. This is ideal, since we get the transactional protection of COM+ transactions at minimal overhead, since the code is running in-process.

It's important to remember that the ASP.NET account can't register `CSLA.Server.ServicedDataPortal.dll` with COM+ because it doesn't have enough security rights. We must use the `regsvcs.exe` utility to register the DLL in COM+, as we discussed in Chapter 5.

Using a separate DataPortal server

Sometimes, due to security requirements, we can't run data access code directly on the web server. In that case, we need to configure the Web Forms client rather as we configured the Windows Forms client in Chapter 8.

> *This section is for informational purposes only.* Do not *make the following changes to the* `Web.config` *file.*

Instead of specifying the database connection strings in `Web.config`, we need to specify where to find the remote `DataPortal` objects:

```
<?xml version="1.0" encoding="utf-8" ?>
<configuration>
  <appSettings>
    <add key="Authentication" value="CSLA" />
    <add key="PortalServer"
         value="http://server/DataPortal/DataPortal.rem" />
    <add key="ServicedPortalServer"
         value="http://server/DataPortal/ServicedDataPortal.rem" />
  </appSettings>

  <system.web>
```

Obviously, you should change '`server`' to your application server's name or address. You may also specify a different port, since these application servers are often configured to listen on a non-standard port:

```
http://server:8123/DataPortal/DataPortal.rem
```

Then we need to configure the `DataPortal` server as described in Chapter 8, including making sure that the `DataPortal` host has our `ProjectTracker.Library` assembly in its `bin` directory.

> **If we update `ProjectTracker.Library.dll`, we need to update both the `DataPortal` server directory and the web UI directory at the same time.**

As we discussed in Chapter 8, the `DataPortal` server needs the database connection strings and the `ProjectTracker.Library` assembly in order to provide appropriate data access services to our client code. By making these simple changes to the Web Forms client's `Web.config` file and configuring a `DataPortal` host on another server, we switch our application from running everything in-process on the web server, to running the data access code on a separate server.

Again, we'll stick with the higher-performance approach in this chapter, running the server-side `DataPortal` in process with the UI and business objects in ASP.NET.

UI overview

The Web Forms interface we'll create in this chapter is straightforward – we'll focus on how to use business objects from Web Forms more than on how to create fancy Web Forms displays. By and large, the UI mirrors what we did in Chapter 8 with the Windows Forms UI, so we'll have two primary edit forms:

- `ProjectEdit`
- `ResourceEdit`

And two list forms, where the user can select a project or resource to edit or delete:

- `ProjectList`
- `ResourceList`

A resource can be assigned to a project, or a project can be assigned to a resource (depending on whether we are editing a project or a resource to start with). To accommodate this, we'll have two assignment forms:

- `AssignResource`
- `AssignToProject`

We also need a way to change the role a resource plays on a project. To do this, we'll create another form:

- `ChooseRole`

Since we're configured to use CSLA table-based security, we need to prompt the user for a username and password. To ensure that they provide this information, we'll use ASP.NET forms-based security, but we have to create the form to get the user's credentials:

- `Login`

And finally, we need a main menu page. This is the default page where the user starts interacting with our application:

- `Default`

Let's start with the last item in this list, by creating the default menu page.

Default form

Web sites typically have a default page that's accessed when the user navigates to our virtual directory in their browser. This default page often provides menu or navigation support so that the user can easily access the functions provided by our application.

Add a new Web Form by using the Project | Add Web Form menu option, and name it `Default`. IIS is configured to look for a file named `Default.aspx` as the default page for a Web Forms application.

Property	Value
`pageLayout`	`FlowLayout`
`enableViewState`	`False`

By setting the `pageLayout` property to `FlowLayout`, we allow the controls on the page to position themselves automatically as we place them on the form. Also, since this form has no data entry fields, we have no need to maintain page state, so we set `enableViewState` to `False`. This minimizes the amount of data sent to and from the browser.

Add text and controls as shown in the diagram:

The controls are:

Control	Properties
`Label`	`ID=lblName; Text=User`
`HyperLink`	`Text=Work with Projects; NavigateUrl=Projects.aspx`
`HyperLink`	`Text=Work with Resources; NavigateUrl=Resources.aspx`

The only code we'll add to this page is in the page's `Load` event handler, where we'll set the value of `lblName` by using the user's identity:

```
Private Sub Page_Load(ByVal sender As System.Object, _
                      ByVal e As System.EventArgs) Handles MyBase.Load
  lblName.Text = User.Identity.Name
End Sub
```

Notice that this is *not* the same code that we used in the Windows Forms interface to retrieve the user's name for display in our `StatusBar` control. The ASP.NET environment provides its own principal object, separate from the thread's principal object. Any code within a Web Form can make use of the `User` property of the current page (or the `HttpContext` object) to get at the principal object. This is standard ASP.NET security code to retrieve the identity of the currently logged-in user, and it works whether the user was authenticated using CSLA .NET security or Windows' integrated security.

When we implement our CSLA .NET security, we'll make sure that both the current thread *and* the `HttpContext` have the correct principal object. This way, our web code can use the `User` property on each page, and our business objects can use the principal from the current thread.

In any case, everything we've just talked about implies that the user was authenticated prior to reaching our default page (or indeed any other page in the application). Let's implement that next.

Login form and security configuration

ASP.NET supports the concept of forms-based security, which means that users will be automatically redirected to a login form before being allowed to access any other pages in our application. Better still, this is relatively easy to implement, especially since we already have a `BusinessPrincipal` class that does the actual work of authenticating the user.

> *We wouldn't implement a login form when using Windows' integrated security. In that case, anonymous access to our site is disallowed by IIS, so IIS itself ensures that the user provides Windows credentials before it allows the user to access any of our application's forms.*

Changing the Web.config file

Before we create the login form, we should update `Web.config` to turn on forms-based security. It contains an `<authentication>` element that you should change, as shown here:

```
<authentication mode="Forms">
  <forms name="login" loginUrl="login.aspx" protection="All" timeout="60" />
</authentication>
```

We're indicating that the authentication mode is `Forms`, which turns on forms-based security. Then, we provide the name of our login form, so that ASP.NET knows where to redirect any unauthenticated users who attempt to access our pages.

The `protection` attribute indicates that we're protecting all of the content in our site, and the `timeout` attribute indicates that the user's authentication remains valid for up to 60 minutes after their last access to the site.

> *ASP.NET security is flexible and has many options that we're not addressing here. Please refer to* Professional ASP.NET *for more detailed information about ASP.NET security.*

If we wanted to use Windows' integrated security instead of CSLA .NET security, we'd set the authentication mode here to `Windows`, and also alter the configuration in `<appSettings>`, and change IIS to disallow anonymous access to our site. This will cause IIS to authenticate the user, and our thread's principal and identity objects will be `WindowsPrincipal` and `WindowsIdentity` objects.

We also need to update the `<authorization>` element in `Web.config`:

```
<authorization>
  <deny users="?" /> <!-- Deny unauthorized users -->
</authorization>
```

By default, all users are allowed to use our pages, but we want to deny all users access unless they are authenticated. This change ensures that only users who have been authenticated through our login form will be able to access the pages in our application.

Login form

When using forms-based security, we need to implement a login form. All users are redirected here by ASP.NET to be authenticated. If we authenticate them successfully, then they can continue to use our site. If not, they continue to be redirected to this page.

Add a new Web Form to the project, naming it `Login`. Change the form's properties as shown:

Property	Value
`pageLayout`	`FlowLayout`

With its elements added, the form should look like this:

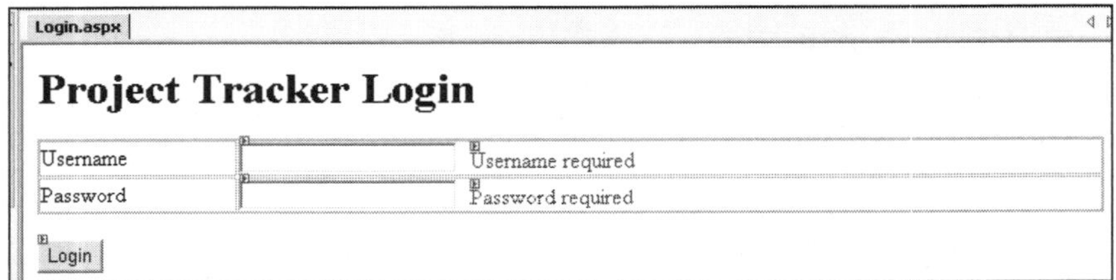

The title is simple text, while the input controls are in a standard HTML table so that they line up nicely. The controls themselves are as follows:

Control	Properties
`TextBox`	`ID=txtUsername`
`RequiredFieldValidator`	`ErrorMessage=Username required` `ControlToValidate=txtUsername`
`TextBox`	`ID=txtPassword` `TextMode=Password`
`RequiredFieldValidator`	`ErrorMessage=Password required` `ControlToValidate=txtPassword`
`Button`	`ID=btnLogin` `Text=Login`

Given that our business objects provide business rules, including validation, why are we including the `RequiredFieldValidator` controls here to validate the input? Typically, duplication of logic is a bad thing, but when building web interfaces, we are faced with tough choices. Since our business objects can't run on the client in the browser, we can only use the objects to validate input once the user has submitted the form back to the server. That doesn't provide a very responsive or pleasant user experience.

The only realistic way to overcome this issue and provide a responsive user experience is somehow to 'extend' some of the validation processing out to the browser, which means duplicating some business logic. We can't allow the UI to be the final check because our objects service other interfaces and we want to ensure that the rules are enforced constantly – so we duplicate the logic.

This is not ideal, but it's a trade-off. We increase the cost of maintenance and the chance of introducing bugs over time in order to provide the user with a richer experience.

Whether to use this technique depends on your application's requirements, and your willingness to deal with the long-term maintenance issues. In any case, our business objects will validate any data that we attempt to put into the object. In the case of our login form, the business object we'll be using is the `BusinessPrincipal` from the CSLA .NET framework. To make it easier to code, we'll import a couple of namespaces into the form's code:

```
Imports CSLA.Security
Imports System.Threading
```

Then, we can write code to respond when the user clicks the Login button:

```
Private Sub btnLogin_Click(ByVal sender As System.Object, _
                           ByVal e As System.EventArgs) Handles btnLogin.Click
  Dim UserName As String = txtUsername.Text
  Dim Password As String = txtPassword.Text

  ' If we're logging in, clear the current session
  Session.Clear()

  ' Log into the system
  BusinessPrincipal.Login(UserName, Password)

  ' See if we logged in successfully
  If Thread.CurrentPrincipal.Identity.IsAuthenticated Then
    Session("CSLA-Principal") = Threading.Thread.CurrentPrincipal
    HttpContext.Current.User = Session("CSLA-Principal")

    ' Redirect to the page the user requested
    Web.Security.FormsAuthentication.RedirectFromLoginPage(UserName, False)
  End If
End Sub
```

The core of this code is where we do the authentication using `BusinessPrincipal`, and it's the same as our code in the Windows Forms UI:

```
BusinessPrincipal.Login(UserName, Password)
```

This method call causes our CSLA .NET code to check the username and password values against our security database. The result is that the current thread will have a `BusinessPrincipal` object that we can check to see if the user was successfully authenticated or not.

However, there's a lot more going on here in order to deal with the requirements of the Web Forms environment. For example, we may get to this form because the user is just arriving, or we could get here because they were already using the system and navigated here by hand. To ensure that we start with a clean slate, we clear our session state before doing anything else. Then we attempt to log in using `BusinessPrincipal`. If that succeeds, we store the resulting `BusinessPrincipal` object as part of our session state:

```
If Thread.CurrentPrincipal.Identity.IsAuthenticated Then
  Session("CSLA-Principal") = Threading.Thread.CurrentPrincipal
```

This is important, because the `CurrentPrincipal` object contains the list of roles to which the user belongs, and we'll need that information on subsequent pages. There's nothing in the ASP.NET security infrastructure to keep this object around from page to page, so it's up to us to retain it. In this case, we're retaining it in the `Session` object.

> *Though forms-based security* does *keep track of the fact that the user is authenticated, it has no provision for keeping track of extra information (like the user's list of roles).*

By putting the `BusinessPrincipal` object into `Session`, we can easily retrieve it on each page request by adding some code into `Global.asax` – we'll add that code shortly. The key here is that we have a way to restore the `BusinessPrincipal` object before each page request, and `Session` allows us to keep the object around from page to page.

If the user did successfully log in, we also make sure that the ASP.NET environment is using the correct principal object. The ASP.NET environment manages its security via the `HttpContext` object, which is available to all code running within ASP.NET. We need to set its `User` property to our `BusinessPrincipal` object:

```
HttpContext.Current.User = Session("CSLA-Principal")
```

This makes the correct principal object available via `HttpContext.Current.User`, and also via the `User` property in each Web Form.

Finally, now that we know the user is authenticated and we've stored the `BusinessPrincipal` object for later use, we can have the forms-based security mechanism allow the user to continue on to the page they were trying to access:

```
' Redirect to the page the user requested
Web.Security.FormsAuthentication.RedirectFromLoginPage(UserName, False)
```

If the user accessed our login form directly, it redirects them to the default page for the application. It also generates a cookie that contains a user ticket, or hashed key value, that identifies the user to ASP.NET. ASP.NET automatically generates and manages this cookie on our behalf; if it is lost or becomes invalid, ASP.NET automatically redirects the user back to `Login.aspx` to be authenticated again.

> *ASP.NET also provides an option to put the ticket into the URL instead of a cookie. This can be important if we want to support users who turn off cookie support in their browsers. The unfortunate side-effect of this approach is that the URL always contains a chunk of encrypted data, making it difficult for end users to add the URL to their favorites, or to send the URL to another user. In either case, subsequent use of that URL will be invalid because the ticket will be invalid.*

Global.asax

Once the user is logged in, we store the BusinessPrincipal object in Session, thereby making it available to subsequent pages. However, our CSLA .NET framework code is designed to use standard .NET security by accessing the thread's CurrentPrincipal property, not to look at ASP.NET-specific features like Session. Additionally, ASP.NET won't automatically maintain the HttpContext principal object from page to page; it's up to us to make sure it is set properly at the start of each page request.

This means that before the code in our individual Web Forms runs, we should ensure that both the thread's CurrentPrincipal property and the HttpContext User property contain our BusinessPrincipal object. ASP.NET provides a standard mechanism for us to do this through the Global.asax file.

> *If you're using Windows' integrated security, this step is not needed. The thread and* HttpContext *principal objects* will *be automatically set by ASP.NET in that case.*

Global.asax contains methods that respond when events are raised by the ASP.NET environment. We can respond to events indicating that the application has started, that a page request has begun or ended, or that the Session object has been loaded just before page processing begins.

In our case, we want to respond to the last of these. When this event fires, we have access to the Session data, and we know we're running before any code in the Web Form itself. Open the Global.asax file, and add an Imports statement:

```
Imports System.Web
Imports System.Web.SessionState
Imports System.Threading
```

Then, add a method to handle the AcquireRequestState event:

```
  Private Sub Global_AcquireRequestState(ByVal sender As Object, _
     ByVal e As System.EventArgs) Handles MyBase.AcquireRequestState

    ' Set the security principal to our BusinessPrincipal
    If Not Session("CSLA-Principal") Is Nothing Then
      Thread.CurrentPrincipal = Session("CSLA-Principal")
      HttpContext.Current.User = Session("CSLA-Principal")
    Else
      If Thread.CurrentPrincipal.Identity.IsAuthenticated Then
        Web.Security.FormsAuthentication.SignOut()
        Server.Transfer("Login.aspx")
      End If
    End If
  End Sub
```

The first part of this is pretty straightforward: if the Session object contains our BusinessPrincipal, make it the current principal object for the thread and HttpContext:

```
    If Not Session("CSLA-Principal") Is Nothing Then
      Thread.CurrentPrincipal = Session("CSLA-Principal")
      HttpContext.Current.User = Session("CSLA-Principal")
```

The second part isn't so obvious, but it solves a critical problem. If Session is configured to run in-process with our Web Forms (which is the default), and our AppDomain gets reset, then the Session object is destroyed. However, the user's authentication ticket (which is automatically stored in a cookie by ASP.NET) is *not* destroyed, so the user can continue to access the pages of our application.

Of course, without a proper BusinessPrincipal object, we can't check security, and neither can our business objects or the DataPortal. In fact, without a proper BusinessPrincipal object, the application will crash at some point. This means that if we find no BusinessPrincipal in the Session object, but the user is already authenticated, then we know we're in trouble. The solution is to sign the user out and redirect them to the login form so that we can re-authenticate them and get a new BusinessPrincipal object:

```
Web.Security.FormsAuthentication.SignOut()
Server.Transfer("Login.aspx")
```

From the user's perspective, this is rather inconvenient, not to mention confusing. If it happens often, we may want to consider running the Session object in its own process or on a separate state server machine, as discussed earlier in the chapter.

At this point, we should be able to build the project and navigate to the site. We'll be redirected to the login form, where we can provide a valid username and password, after which we'll end up on the default page with our name displayed in the label near the top:

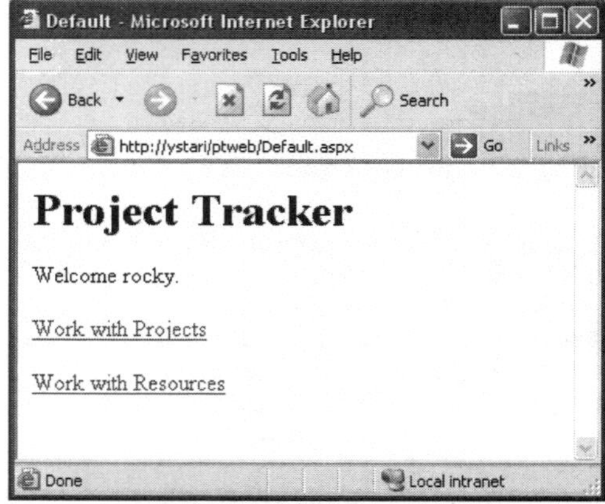

Since we haven't implemented the Projects or Resources forms yet, the links won't work, but we've established that our security infrastructure works, so we can move on.

Projects form

From Default.aspx, the user can choose to work with either projects or resources. If they choose the former, we'll direct them to a form that displays a list of projects. From there, the user can add, remove, or edit projects (assuming they have security clearance to do so).

Setting up the form

Add a new Web Form to the project and name it `Projects`. Set its properties as follows:

Property	Value
`pageLayout`	`FlowLayout`
`enableViewState`	`False`

With the controls added, the form should look like this:

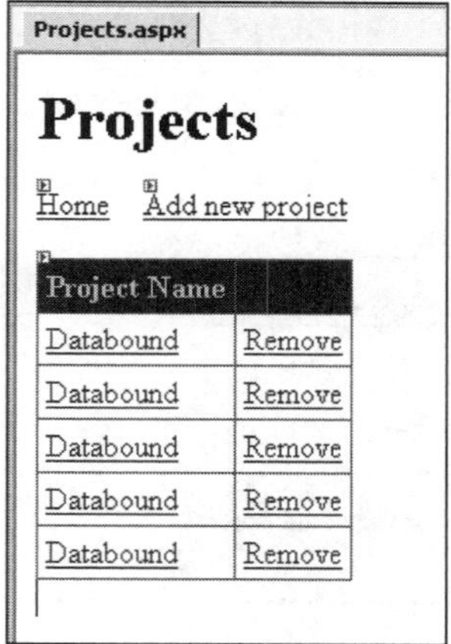

The title is simple text formatted with the Header 1 style. The controls are detailed in the following table:

Control	Properties
`HyperLink`	`Text=Home` `NavigateUrl=Default.aspx`
`LinkButton`	`Name=btnNewProject` `Text=Add new project`
`DataGrid`	`Name=dgProjects` `EnableViewState=False`

We set the `EnableViewState` property of the `DataGrid` control to `False` because we'll rebind it to the `ProjectList` object each time the page is loaded. When displaying potentially large amounts of data in a grid control, it's often better to reload the grid's data from the source than to send a large amount of page state to and from the browser on each page request. This approach also ensures that the user gets current data displayed on each page request, so changes to the data are always reflected in the display.

The `DataGrid` control requires a bit more setup than this, since we'll be using data binding to populate it from our `ProjectList` business object. Right-click on the `DataGrid` control, and select the **Property Builder** option. This brings up a Properties dialog, where you should select the **Columns** tab. This tab allows us to add and manipulate the columns included in the grid control.

First, uncheck the Create columns automatically at run time box, which allows the grid to generate columns dynamically, based on the data source. We want more control over the process. We'll add two columns to the control for the `ID` and `Name` values, and one for a Remove hyperlink. The ID column should look like this:

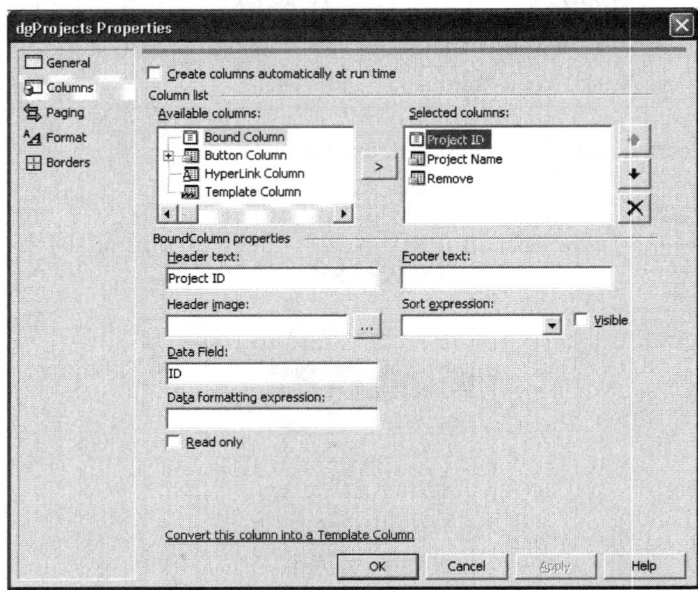

We're creating a simple bound column that's bound to the `ID` property of the data source, but is not visible. We'll need this ID value to implement our code, but the user doesn't need to see our internal GUID values.

The name column is a button column, and should look like this:

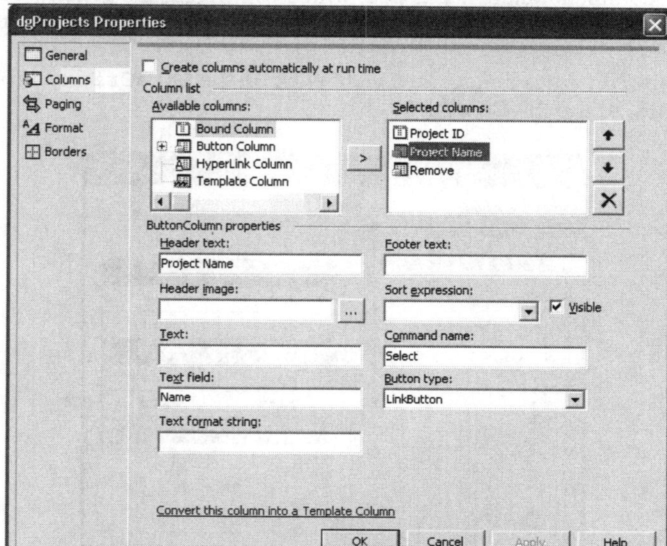

This column doesn't *only* display the `Name` property from the data source – it's also a hyperlink-style button. The `Select` command is special, causing the `DataGrid` to raise the `SelectedIndexChanged` event when an item in this column is clicked. Later on, we'll write code to react to this event and take appropriate action.

The remove column is also a button column:

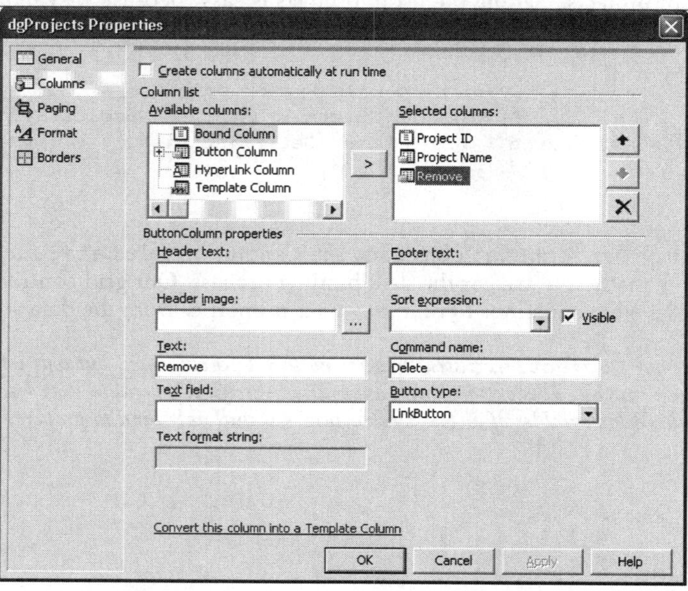

In this case, we're not binding the display to a property, but we *are* providing `Remove` as the constant text to display. The command name is `Delete`, which will trigger the generic `DeleteCommand` event to be raised by the grid control. We can write code in the handler for this event to take appropriate action.

Click **OK** to close the Properties dialog, then right-click on the `DataGrid` control, choose **Auto Format**, and format the control to use the **Colorful 2** scheme:

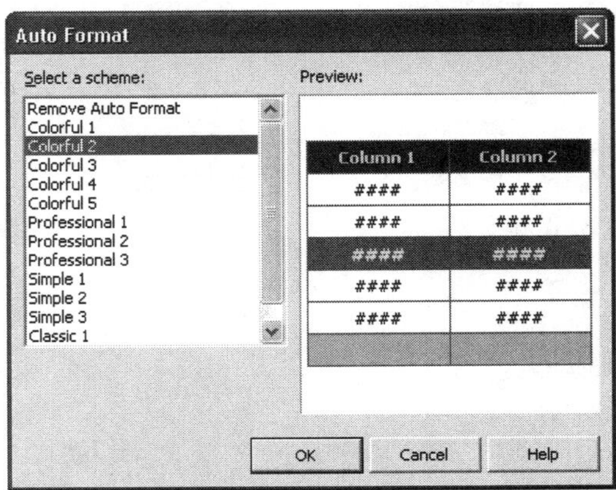

Coding the form

At this point the form is ready, and we can move on to writing the code that makes it work.

Loading data

When the form is first loaded, we need to do a couple of things. First, we need to load the `DataGrid` control with a list of projects. Getting the list of projects is easy, because we can use our `ProjectList` business object. Populating the control is also easy, because we can just use data binding:

```
Private Sub Page_Load(ByVal sender As System.Object, _
                      ByVal e As System.EventArgs) Handles MyBase.Load
  dgProjects.DataSource = ProjectList.GetProjectList()
  DataBind()
End Sub
```

All we do is get a new `ProjectList` object and set it as the control's `DataSource`. We then call the page's `DataBind()` method to trigger the data binding process. Our grid control has predefined columns, so it knows which columns to bind to which properties from the data source.

> *Remember that our `ProjectInfo` structure has no `Public` variables, but was implemented with property methods instead. This extra work was required specifically because Web Forms data binding won't bind to variables of a class or structure – it will only bind to property methods.*

When the page is accessed, the DataGrid will display the list of project data from the ProjectList object:

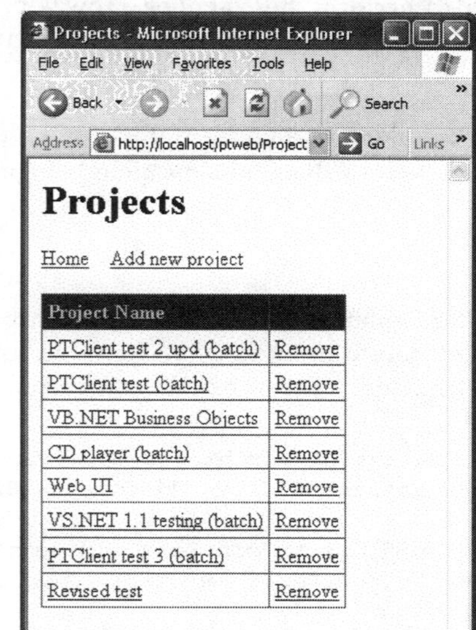

From here we can view, edit, and remove Project objects.

Security

The other thing we need to do as the page is loaded is deal with security. Specifically, we want to ensure that only the appropriate options are displayed, based on the user's role.

> *In web development this is often called **personalization**, but it's the same good UI design practice from Windows development, applied to the web environment.*

Since we've already built all the code to make sure that our thread's security principal object is a valid BusinessPrincipal, we can use standard .NET security code to hide or show the UI elements:

```
Private Sub Page_Load(ByVal sender As System.Object, _
                      ByVal e As System.EventArgs) Handles MyBase.Load

  dgProjects.DataSource = ProjectList.GetProjectList()
  DataBind()

  ' Set security
  btnNewProject.Visible = User.IsInRole("ProjectManager")
  dgProjects.Columns(2).Visible = User.IsInRole("ProjectManager") OrElse _
                                  User.IsInRole("Administrator")

End Sub
```

We set the Visible properties on the link to add a new project, and on the column to remove a project, based on the user's role. This is directly analogous to the security code we put into our Windows Forms UI.

Technically, this code is optional, as the business objects themselves already include code to ensure that the user must be in the right role to perform these actions. However, good UI design dictates that a user should only have the option to do things that they can *actually do*, and so it's good practice to include some security code in the UI to hide or disable invalid options.

Even if we don't implement the security in the UI, or if the user bypasses this security by typing in a URL to navigate directly to a page, our business objects include logic to prevent the user from doing anything invalid.

Selecting a project

The `DataGrid` control has a button column with the `Select` command. If the user clicks an element in this column, we'll get a `SelectedIndexChanged` event from the control. We can handle this event to navigate to another page where the user can view or edit that particular project:

```
Private Sub dgProjects_SelectedIndexChanged(ByVal sender As System.Object, _
   ByVal e As System.EventArgs) Handles dgProjects.SelectedIndexChanged

    Dim id As Guid = New Guid(dgProjects.SelectedItem.Cells(0).Text)
    Session("Project") = Project.GetProject(id)
    Response.Redirect("ProjectEdit.aspx")

End Sub
```

To do this, we need to know the ID value for the project the user selected. The first (invisible) column in the `DataGrid` control contains this value, and we can retrieve it with expressions like the following:

```
dgProjects.SelectedItem.Cells(0).Text
```

The ID value is text representing the GUID for a `Project` object, so we convert it to a `Guid` variable and use it to retrieve the `Project` object. This `Project` object is then placed in `Session` so that it will be available to the next page, which is `ProjectEdit.aspx` (which we'll build shortly). To get there, we use `Response.Redirect()` to cause the user's browser to navigate to that form.

> *We could also use `Server.Transfer()` to navigate to the `ProjectEdit` form, but then the browser would not display the correct URL for the `ProjectEdit` page, which may be confusing for the user. Additionally, `Server.Transfer()` doesn't allow us to pass parameters as part of the URL. Though we're not using that feature here, it's a limitation to be aware of. For these reasons, I'll be using `Response.Redirect()` throughout this application.*

Now, when the user clicks on a project in the `DataGrid`, we'll bring up the `ProjectEdit` form with the selected project displayed for viewing or editing.

Removing a project

Similarly, the user can click on the Remove link in a row, and we need to remove that project from the system in response. When they perform the action, we'll get a `DeleteCommand` event from the control. In our event handler code, we simply remove the selected project:

```
Private Sub dgProjects_DeleteCommand(ByVal source As Object, _
    ByVal e As System.Web.UI.WebControls.DataGridCommandEventArgs) _
    Handles dgProjects.DeleteCommand

  Dim id As New Guid(e.Item.Cells(0).Text)
  Project.DeleteProject(id)

  dgProjects.DataSource = ProjectList.GetProjectList()
  DataBind()

End Sub
```

As before, we use the DataGridCommandEventArgs parameter passed to our code to find the ID value of the selected item:

```
Dim id As New Guid(e.Item.Cells(0).Text)
Project.DeleteProject(id)
```

We then rebind the DataGrid control to a new ProjectList object so that it reflects the fact that the project has been removed from the system:

```
dgProjects.DataSource = ProjectList.GetProjectList()
DataBind()
```

Adding a new project

The final code we need to add is to handle the click event of the LinkButton for adding a new Project object. When this button is clicked, we'll create a new Project object, and then navigate to the ProjectEdit form so the user can edit the new object. Add the following code to the form:

```
Private Sub btnNewProject_Click(ByVal sender As System.Object, _
    ByVal e As System.EventArgs) Handles btnNewProject.Click

  Session("Project") = Project.NewProject()
  Response.Redirect("ProjectEdit.aspx")

End Sub
```

We simply use the NewProject() method of the Project class to create a new Project object. We put this object into Session so that it will be available to the ProjectEdit form – just like we did earlier for editing a Project. Then we navigate to the ProjectEdit page, where the user can add their data to the object.

The Projects form is now complete, and you should be able to build the project and navigate to it to see a list of projects. The **Remove** button on each row will also work. Let's move on to implement the ProjectEdit form, so that we can successfully select a project to view or edit.

ProjectEdit form

`ProjectEdit` is the main form for adding, viewing, and editing projects. We will get here because the user clicked the link to add a new project in `Projects.aspx`, or because they clicked a link in that form to view or edit a specific project. Also, when we're done with the `ResourceEdit` form, they'll have a link from there to view or edit a specific project as well.

Setting up the form

Add a new Web Form and name it `ProjectEdit`. Change its properties as follows:

Property	Value
`pageLayout`	`FlowLayout`

That was easy enough, but this form is actually rather more complex than the ones we've created so far.

Basic layout

We'll use a standard HTML table to organize the columns, so that they line up nicely:

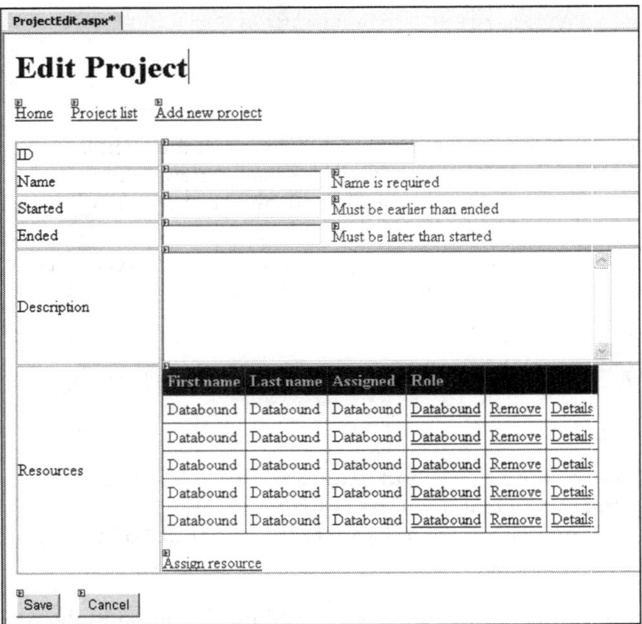

Control details

The controls on the page are as follows:

Control	Properties
HyperLink	Text=Home NavigateUrl=Default.aspx
HyperLink	Text=Project list NavigateUrl=Projects.aspx
LinkButton	ID=btnNewProject Text=Add new project
TextBox	ID=txtID ReadOnly=True
TextBox	ID=txtName
RequiredFieldValidator	ErrorMessage=Name is required ControlToValidate=txtName
TextBox	ID=txtStarted
CompareValidator	ErrorMessage=Must be earlier than ended ControlToCompare=txtEnded ControlToValidate=txtStarted Operator=LessThanEqual
TextBox	ID=txtEnded
CompareValidator	ErrorMessage=Must be later than started ControlToCompare=txtStarted ControlToValidate=txtEnded Operator=GreaterThanEqual
TextBox	ID=txtDescription TextMode=MultiLine
DataGrid	ID=dgResources EnableViewState=False
LinkButton	ID=btnAssignResource Text=Assign resource
Button	ID=btnSave Text=Save
Button	ID=btnCancel Text=Cancel

This sets the basic configuration of all the controls, but we need to take extra steps to set up the `TextBox` controls for data binding, and we need to configure the columns in the `DataGrid` control.

Data binding the controls

Data binding in Web Forms is quite different from data binding in Windows Forms. The biggest functional difference is that data binding in Web Forms is read-only – it can be used to copy values from the data source into the control, but not from the control back into the data source. The dialogs that configure data binding are also quite different.

Each simple Web Forms server control, such as a `TextBox`, has a `DataBindings` property in the Properties window. If we click the '...' button for the property, we'll get a dialog where we can specify what should be bound to the properties of the control.

To see how this works, select the `txtID` control and click the '...' button for `DataBindings`. This dialog is designed to simplify the process of binding the control to a data source. Unfortunately, it doesn't recognize our business objects as being valid data sources, so it isn't of great help to us. However, we *can* use it to specify a custom binding expression:

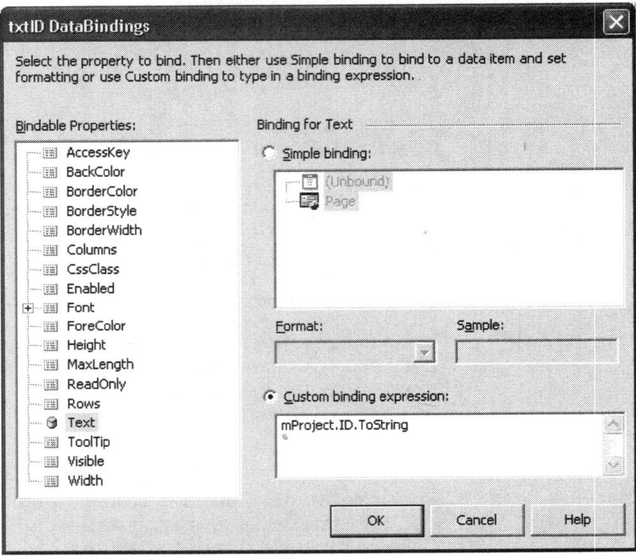

This binding expression can refer to *any* data source available from our page's code, including business objects. For this expression to work, all we need to do is ensure that we expose a variable named `mProject` that has an `ID` property. Since we know that `ID` is a GUID value, we're converting it to a `String` value by including the `ToString()` method.

In the HTML for the page, this translates to the following:

```
<asp:TextBox id="txtID" runat="server" Text="<%# mProject.ID.ToString %>"
             ReadOnly="True" Width="245px" >
```

The `Text` property of the control is set to the data binding expression `<%# mProject.ID.ToString %>`. When our ASPX page is compiled, this will translate into code that retrieves the ID value from a form-level variable named `mProject`.

> *For this to work, we need to declare a form-level variable named* `mProject`*, and ensure that it references an appropriate object before we invoke the data binding mechanism on the page. We'll take care of these details when we get into the code behind the form.*

Use this technique to set up custom binding expressions for the other text controls:

Control	Property	Expression
txtName	Text	mProject.Name
txtStarted	Text	mProject.Started
txtEnded	Text	mProject.Ended
txtDescription	Text	mProject.Description

By setting these properties on the controls, we avoid writing code to load data into the controls manually, or configuring the data binding through code. This is nice, because it means that we can change the layout of the page – including the binding of properties from the Project object to our controls – without having to change the code behind the form.

Configuring the DataGrid columns

As with the DataGrid control on the Projects form, this one requires more setting up in order to configure its columns and appearance. Right-click, choose Auto Format, and select the Colorful 2 scheme to get the appearance right. Then, right-click and choose Property Builder to bring up the Properties dialog so that we can configure the columns to be displayed.

In the Columns tab, unselect the option to create the columns automatically. Then, add the following columns:

Column type	Properties
Bound	Header text=Resource ID; Data Field=ResourceID; Visible=False
Bound	Header text=First name; Data Field=FirstName
Bound	Header text=Last name; Data Field=LastName
Bound	Header text=Assigned; Data Field=Assigned
Button	Text field=Role; Command name=SelectRole
Button	Text=Remove; Command name=Delete
Button	Text=Details; Command name=Select

This configuration provides us with columns to display the name, assigned date, and role for each resource assigned to the project. The data will come from the ProjectResources collection associated with our Project object, so we can just use data binding to populate the grid control.

We've made the Role column into a button column, so the user can click on the role of a resource to indicate that they want to change it. There are also a couple of columns to allow the removal of a resource, and to view or edit the details of a resource.

Coding the form

At this point, we're ready to write the code behind the form. We'll need to load data when the form is loaded, and react to the events that are raised when the user clicks on the various controls on the page.

Loading data

As we noted earlier, this page may be reached from a number of locations within the UI as a whole. We may get here via the Add new project link on the `Projects` page, or because the user clicked a link to edit an existing project. The user could also navigate here directly in their browser, without going through any previous pages. They might even get here by pressing the Back button in their browser.

In the Windows Forms interface, we relied on the form that called into `ProjectEdit` to set up a `Project` object before moving to `ProjectEdit` – and we'll do the same thing here. In our `Projects` page, we included code to load a `Project` object with data and put it in `Session` before navigating to our `ProjectEdit` page. This means that by the time we get here, we've already got a `Project` object ready to edit.

We can also get here and *not* have a `Project` object. This can happen because the user navigated to this page directly, or pressed the Back button in the browser. In the former scenario, we'll assume that the user wants to add a new `Project`. If they used the Back button, we'll try to reload the object they were editing on this page last time they were here.

In any case, we need to remember that all our code will be interacting with a `Project` business object in order to do its work. To make this object available to all the code in our form, we'll declare a form-level variable and load it with the `Project` object each time the form loads. Add this form-level variable declaration:

```
' We make this a page-level variable and then always load it in Page_Load()
' That way, the object is available to all our code at all times
Protected mProject As Project
```

Between pages, we'll store the `Project` object in `Session`, but while the page is being processed we'll put it here for easier access by our code. Notice that this variable is declared with `Protected` scope; there's a good reason for this. You'll remember that we used custom data binding expressions to bind our controls to the `mProject` variable when we designed the form. For this to work, the HTML portion of the page must have access to the `mProject` variable, which means that it must be `Protected`, `Friend`, or `Public`. Good programming practice dictates that we should only expand the scope as much as needed, and the most restrictive scope that still works is `Protected`.

We can now create the `Load` event handler to initialize this variable each time the page loads:

```
Private Sub Page_Load(ByVal sender As System.Object, _
                      ByVal e As System.EventArgs) Handles MyBase.Load

  ' Get the existing Project (if any)
  mProject = Session("Project")

  If mProject Is Nothing Then

    ' Got here via either direct navigation or back button
    If Len(txtID.Text) = 0 Then

      ' Got here via direct navigation so create a new project
      mProject = Project.NewProject()
```

```
    Else
      ' We've returned here via the Browser's back button
      ' Load object based on ID value
      mProject = Project.GetProject(New Guid(txtID.Text))
    End If
    Session("Project") = mProject
  End If

  ' Bind the grid every time (we're not using viewstate to keep it populated)
  dgResources.DataSource = mProject.Resources

  If IsPostBack Then
    dgResources.DataBind()
  Else
    DataBind()
  End If

End Sub
```

The first thing we do is attempt to retrieve the object:

```
' Get the existing Project (if any)
mProject = Session("Project")
```

There are four scenarios we may encounter here:

- The user may have navigated here directly
- The user may have pressed the **Back** button in the browser
- This may be a postback of the current page
- The user may have navigated here from another page

In the first two scenarios, `Session` won't contain a `Project` object. In that case, we can check the value of the `txtID` field to determine if the user navigated here directly, or used the **Back** button. If the latter, the field will contain the ID value of the `Project` object they were editing at that time, so we can attempt to reload it. Otherwise, we'll simply create a new `Project` object for the user to edit:

```
' Got here via either direct navigation or back button
If Len(txtID.Text) = 0 Then

  ' Got here via direct navigation so create a new project
  mProject = Project.NewProject()
Else

  ' We've returned here via the Browser's back button
  ' Load object based on ID value
  mProject = Project.GetProject(New Guid(txtID.Text))
End If
Session("Project") = mProject
```

At this point, we know that we have a `Project` object to work with – either a pre-existing one we're editing, or a new one we're creating. We put that object into `Session` to make sure that it's available on subsequent page requests, and then we bind the `DataGrid` to the object's `Resources` collection:

```
' Bind the grid every time (we're not using viewstate to keep it populated)
dgResources.DataSource = mProject.Resources
```

Notice that this is done regardless of whether this is a postback. The reason for this is that we've set `EnableViewState` to `False` for this control, so that its state is not transferred to and from the browser on each page request. While that cuts down on network traffic, it does mean that we need to rebind the control each time.

> *In doing this, we're trading bandwidth against server processing. We've decreased the size of our HTML output, but we have to reload the control with data on each page request. In almost every case, processing speed is faster than bandwidth, so this is a good tradeoff. If your server is so slow that bandwidth is not the bottleneck, you can change this code to avoid rebinding the data on postback (though if your server is actually that slow, you're probably better off getting a bigger server, or implementing a web farm).*

Finally, we trigger the data binding process to populate the display on the form:

```
If IsPostBack Then
  dgResources.DataBind()
Else
  DataBind()
End If
```

In the case of a postback, our regular controls will already have their values, so only the grid needs to be rebound. Otherwise, this is the first time the user has hit the page, and so we need to populate *all* the controls. For this, we call the page's global `DataBind()` method.

Security

There's one more thing that we need to do as the form is loaded, and that's to set security based on the user's role. While many types of user can use this page to *view* data, only people in the `ProjectManager` role can actually *edit* a `Project` object. We'll check the user's role and (conditionally) hide controls that would allow the user to save any changes to the object.

Add the following code to the bottom of the `Page_Load()` method:

```
    ' Set security
    If Not User.IsInRole("ProjectManager") Then
      btnNewProject.Visible = False
      btnSave.Visible = False
      btnAssignResource.Visible = False
      dgResources.Columns(5).Visible = False
    End If

  End Sub
```

As we did in the `Projects` form, we check the `Principal` object to see if the user is in a valid role. If the user is not in the `ProjectManager` role, we hide all the controls that allow the user to change the `Project` object permanently.

With this done, the form should now load and display either the default values for a new project, or the existing values from a project that was loaded from the database.

Saving the form

If the user clicks the **Save** button, they expect that any changes they've made on the form will be stored in the database. On the surface, this seems like a simple thing, since all we need to do is call the `Save()` method on our `Project` object. However, we need to keep in mind that Web Forms data binding is *read-only*, so it's up to us to copy the values from the form back into the object. To do this, we can create a helper function:

```
Private Sub SaveFormToObject()

  With mProject
    .Name = txtName.Text
    .Started = txtStarted.Text
    .Ended = txtEnded.Text
    .Description = txtDescription.Text
  End With

End Sub
```

This code is not complex: for each value, we simply copy the value from the form into the object. Given this helper method, we can easily implement the code for the **Save** button's `Click` event handler:

```
Private Sub btnSave_Click(ByVal sender As System.Object, _
   ByVal e As System.EventArgs) Handles btnSave.Click

  SaveFormToObject()
  mProject = mProject.Save()
  Session.Remove("Project")
  Response.Redirect("Projects.aspx")

End Sub
```

Here, the form's contents are saved into the object, and the object is then saved into the database by calling its `Save()` method. With that done, we navigate the user back to the `Projects` form. At this point, we no longer need the `Project` object – it has been saved to the database, so we remove it from `Session`. This is good practice because it helps minimize the amount of data in `Session`, improving performance if `Session` is being kept out of process or on a state server machine.

Canceling the form

If the user clicks the **Cancel** button, things are simpler. All we need to do in that case is abandon the `Project` object and navigate the user back to the `Projects` form:

```
Private Sub btnCancel_Click(ByVal sender As System.Object, _
   ByVal e As System.EventArgs) Handles btnCancel.Click

  Session.Remove("Project")
  Response.Redirect("Projects.aspx")
End Sub
```

Here too, we are minimizing the amount of data in Session by removing the object now that we're done with it.

Adding a new project

Just like we had in the Projects form, we have a LinkButton that the user can click if they want to add a new Project object. Unsurprisingly, our code here will be the same as in the Projects form:

```
Private Sub btnNewProject_Click(ByVal sender As System.Object, _
    ByVal e As System.EventArgs) Handles btnNewProject.Click

  Session("Project") = Project.NewProject()
  Response.Redirect("ProjectEdit.aspx")

End Sub
```

We simply create a new Project object by calling the NewProject() method, and then navigate to the ProjectEdit form so that the user can edit this new object.

Adding a resource

Our form also includes a LinkButton control that allows the user to assign a resource to the project that's currently being edited. If the user clicks this button, we'll bring up a form where they can select the resource and indicate the role that the resource will play in the project. This new form will be named AssignResource, and it will act rather like a dialog window.

Before we can navigate from ProjectEdit to the AssignResource dialog form, we need to save the contents of our form into the Project object. If we don't do this, any changes the user has made on our form will be lost, since only the Project object is persistent across pages, through the Session object:

```
Private Sub btnAssignResource_Click(ByVal sender As System.Object, _
   ByVal e As System.EventArgs) Handles btnAssignResource.Click

  SaveFormToObject()
  Response.Redirect("AssignResource.aspx")
End Sub
```

We save the form's contents to the object by calling the SaveFormToObject() method that we created above. That copies the values from the form into mProject, and then updates Session so that it has a reference to the updated object. With that done, we can safely navigate to the AssignResource form.

Selecting a resource

Within the DataGrid control that displays the resources assigned to the project, we included a Details column. If the user clicks on a Details button in the grid, a SelectedIndexChanged event will be raised. We can respond to this event to display details about the resource by navigating to the ResourceEdit form (which we'll create shortly).

When this happens, the user is navigating away from editing a project, and will then be editing a resource. From our point of view, this is a huge shift, and there are various ways we can handle it. For this implementation, we'll say that this action is the same as the user first clicking the **Save** button, and then navigating to ResourceEdit – this way, the user's changes will be retained.

If the user doesn't have security clearance to change a Project object, we'll simply drop the Project object and navigate the user to the ResourceEdit form:

```
Private Sub dgResources_SelectedIndexChanged( _
  ByVal sender As System.Object, _
  ByVal e As System.EventArgs) Handles dgResources.SelectedIndexChanged

  ' Check security
  If User.IsInRole("ProjectManager") Then

    ' Only do save if user is in a valid role
    SaveFormToObject()
    mProject = mProject.Save
  End If

  Session.Remove("Project")

  Dim id As String = dgResources.SelectedItem.Cells(0).Text
  Session("Resource") = Resource.GetResource(id)
  Response.Redirect("ResourceEdit.aspx")
End Sub
```

First, we check to see if the user is a ProjectManager. If so, we save any changes to the Project object:

```
' Check security
If User.IsInRole("ProjectManager") Then

  ' Only do save if user is in a valid role
  SaveFormToObject()
  mProject = mProject.Save
End If
```

When the user clicks on a resource, we're treating it as though they clicked Save or Cancel to exit the ProjectEdit form, and then navigated to a specific resource from the Resources form. Any time the user clicks Save or Cancel on ProjectEdit, we remove the Project object from Session to save memory, so we do that here as well:

```
Session.Remove("Project")
```

Then, whether they're a ProjectManager or not, we navigate the user to the ResourceEdit page so that they can view or edit the selected Resource object:

```
Dim id As String = dgResources.SelectedItem.Cells(0).Text
Session("Resource") = Resource.GetResource(id)
Response.Redirect("ResourceEdit.aspx")
```

Changing a role

The user might also click on the Role column in the grid control to indicate that they want to change the role the resource plays on the project. When this column is clicked, we'll get an ItemCommand event from the grid control, where we can process the request.

ItemCommand is a generic event that can be raised for more than one column in the grid control. When we set up the **Role** column, we specified that the command text was SelectRole. We can check for that in our code:

```
Private Sub dgResources_ItemCommand(ByVal source As Object, _
    ByVal e As System.Web.UI.WebControls.DataGridCommandEventArgs) _
    Handles dgResources.ItemCommand

  If e.CommandName = "SelectRole" Then
    Dim id As String = e.Item.Cells(0).Text
    Session("ProjectResource") = mProject.Resources(id)
    Session("Source") = "ProjectEdit.aspx"
    Response.Redirect("ChooseRole.aspx")
  End If

End Sub
```

If the user clicks an item in the **Role** column, we retrieve the ID value of the item from the grid and use it to locate the specific ProjectResource object from mProject. This value is placed into Session so that the ChooseRole form can tell which object to edit:

```
Session("ProjectResource") = mProject.Resources(id)
```

We also record the name of our current form in Session:

```
Session("Source") = "ProjectEdit.aspx"
```

This is done because ChooseRole will be used not only from ProjectEdit, but also from ResourceEdit. When the user has selected the new role for the resource, the ChooseRole form needs to know which form the user came from so it can return them to that form.

Finally, we navigate to the ChooseRole form, which we'll create later in the chapter.

Removing a resource

The final action that the user might select is to click the **Remove** link in the DataGrid to indicate that they want to remove a resource from the project. When they do this, we'll get a DeleteCommand event, where we can remove the item:

```
Private Sub dgResources_DeleteCommand(ByVal source As Object, _
    ByVal e As System.Web.UI.WebControls.DataGridCommandEventArgs) _
    Handles dgResources.DeleteCommand

  Dim id As String = e.Item.Cells(0).Text
  mProject.Resources.Remove(id)

  ' Rebind grid to update display
  dgResources.DataSource = mProject.Resources
  dgResources.DataBind()

End Sub
```

We retrieve the resource's ID value from the first column of the DataGrid, and use it to call the Remove() method of our Resources collection. This will remove the item from the collection, based on the business logic we wrote in our object. Once this is done, we need to rebind the DataGrid control to the Resources collection so that it reflects the fact that the entry has been removed.

At this point, the ProjectEdit form is functional:

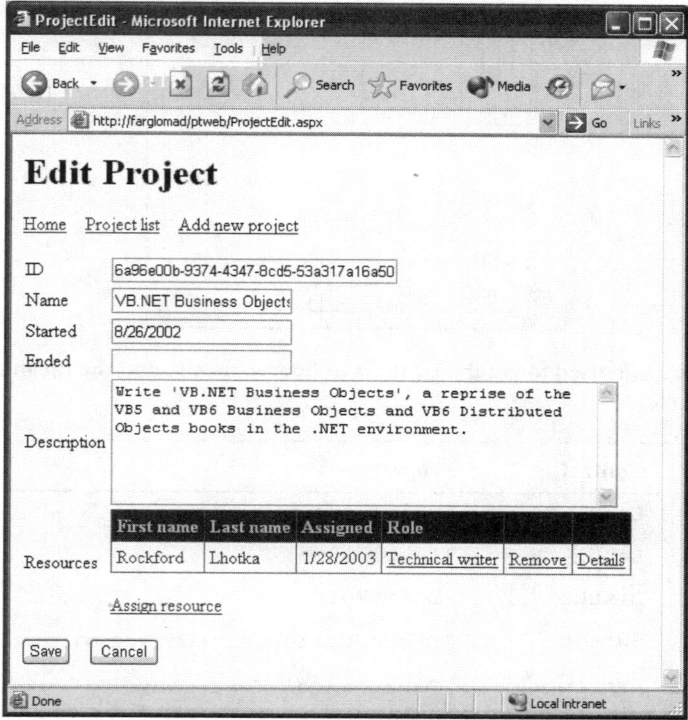

Of course, we still have the not insignificant limitation that the user can't navigate to the ChooseRole, AssignResource, or ResourceEdit forms, because we haven't built them yet!

The ChooseRole form

The ChooseRole form is a 'dialog' form, in that it's intended to be used from the ProjectEdit or ResourceEdit forms so that the user can change the role of a resource on a project. When the user is done with this form, it will navigate them back to the form where they started, so they can continue to edit their project or resource.

> *We've only created ProjectEdit so far, but ResourceEdit will also navigate the user to ChooseRole if they want to change the role of a resource on a project. We'll write code to support both scenarios as we create this form.*

Setting up the form

Add a new Web Form to the project and name it `ChooseRole`. Set its `pageLayout` property to `FlowLayout`, and add a table and controls as shown:

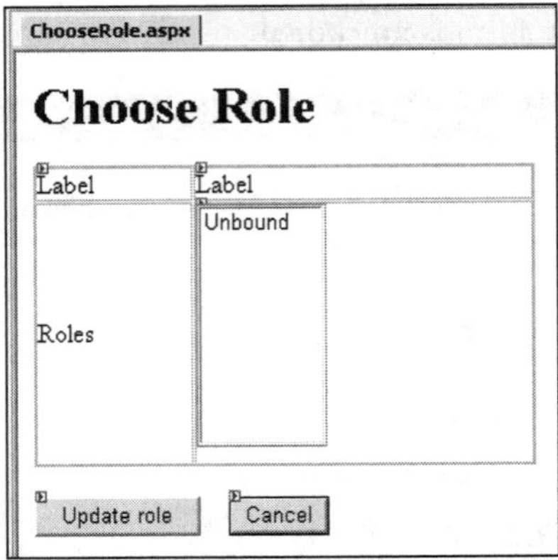

An HTML table is again used to get the controls to line up nicely, and the meaningful controls are listed in the following table:

Control	Properties
`Label`	`ID=lblLabel`
`Label`	`ID=lblValue`
`ListBox`	`ID=lstRoles`
`Button`	`ID=btnUpdate; Text=Update role`
`Button`	`ID=btnCancel; Text=Cancel`

Since this form has no `DataGrid`, that's all there is to the setup of the controls!

Coding the form

The code for this form is not terribly complex, though it might appear that way at first! Remember that the user may reach this form from either `ProjectEdit` or `ResourceEdit`, and so we may be working with a `ProjectResource` or a `ResourceAssignment` child object respectively. This leads to a bit of extra coding, since we need to handle each scenario appropriately.

Loading the roles

When the user first arrives at this page, we need to load the form with data. The `ListBox` control will contain the list of valid roles, and the two `Label` controls at the top will display some context information so that the user knows what they are doing on the form. Let's start by loading the `ListBox` control with the valid roles:

```
Private Sub Page_Load(ByVal sender As System.Object, _
                      ByVal e As System.EventArgs) Handles MyBase.Load
  If Not Page.IsPostBack Then
    Dim role As String
    For Each role In Assignment.Roles
      lstRoles.Items.Add(Assignment.Roles.Item(role))
    Next
  End If
End Sub
```

While it would be nice to use data binding here, we can't bind to a `NameValueCollection`, which is what we get from the `Roles.GetCollection()` method. Instead, we simply loop through the collection, putting each value into the `ListBox` control.

> *This is a case in which we might opt to include a `GetArray()` method in the `Roles` class to provide the data in a bindable format.*

Notice that we only do this the first time the user hits the page – after that, we rely on the page's view state to maintain the list of values. This is important, since we're using the value selected by the user to change the object's value when the user clicks the update button. If we reloaded the `ListBox` control with data on a postback, we'd wipe out the user's selection, preventing the form from functioning properly.

Loading data from the child object

Now we can move on to deal with the actual business object. This isn't complicated, but it does require a security check. Remember that only a `ProjectManager` can edit a `Project` object, and only a `Supervisor` or a `ProjectManager` can edit a `Resource`, so we need to include these checks in here as well:

```
If Not Page.IsPostBack Then
  Dim role As String
  For Each role In Assignment.Roles.GetCollection
    lstRoles.Items.Add(Assignment.Roles.Item(role))
  Next

  If Session("Source") = "ProjectEdit.aspx" Then

    ' We are dealing with a ProjectResource, so check security
    If Not User.IsInRole("ProjectManager") Then

      ' They should not be here
      SendUserBack()
    End If

    Dim obj As ProjectResource = Session("ProjectResource")
    lblLabel.Text = "Resource"
    lblValue.Text = obj.FirstName & " " & obj.LastName
    lstRoles.SelectedValue = obj.Role

  Else

    ' We are dealing with a ResourceAssignment, so check security
    If Not User.IsInRole("Supervisor") AndAlso _
       Not User.IsInRole("ProjectManager") Then
```

```
          ' They should not be here
          SendUserBack()
        End If

        Dim obj As ResourceAssignment = Session("ResourceAssignment")
        lblLabel.Text = "Project"
        lblValue.Text = obj.ProjectName
        lstRoles.SelectedValue = obj.Role
      End If
    End If
```

In either case, if we detect that the user isn't authorized to change the value, we redirect them back to where they came from by calling a `SendUserBack()` method:

```
  Private Sub SendUserBack()
    Dim src As String = Session("Source")
    Session.Remove("Source")
    Response.Redirect(src)
  End Sub
```

This method retrieves the name of the page from which they came and navigates back to that page. You may remember that in `ProjectEdit`, before we navigated to `ChooseRole`, we recorded `ProjectEdit.aspx` in `Session` for this very purpose.

Assuming that the user is in the right role to be here, we get the appropriate business object and use it to populate the display. If they came from `ProjectEdit`, then we're editing a `ProjectResource` object:

```
        Dim obj As ProjectResource = Session("ProjectResource")
        lblLabel.Text = "Resource"
        lblValue.Text = obj.FirstName & " " & obj.LastName
        lstRoles.SelectedValue = obj.Role
```

We retrieve the `ProjectResource` object from `Session`, and then set the two `Label` controls to provide some context for the user. We also change the selected item in the `ListBox` control so that it matches the current `Role` value from the business object.

> *Note that the `SelectedValue` property of this control is a feature of .NET 1.1. If you're using .NET 1.0, you'll need to loop through the control's elements manually to find the numeric index of the correct one, and then set the control's selected index to that value.*

The equivalent procedure is followed if the user came from `ResourceEdit`.

Updating the object

Once the user selects the new role from the `ListBox` control, they may click the **Update** button to indicate that they want to save the change. In that case, we retrieve the correct child object, just like we did in the `Load` event handler. Then we update its `Role` property, and return to the original form – either `ProjectEdit` or `ResourceEdit`, as appropriate:

```
Private Sub btnUpdate_Click(ByVal sender As System.Object, _
    ByVal e As System.EventArgs) Handles btnUpdate.Click
  If Session("Source") = "ProjectEdit.aspx" Then

    ' We are dealing with a ProjectResource
    Dim obj As ProjectResource = Session("ProjectResource")
    obj.Role = lstRoles.SelectedValue
  Else

    ' We are dealing with a ResourceAssignment
    Dim obj As ResourceAssignment = Session("ResourceAssignment")
    obj.Role = lstRoles.SelectedValue
  End If

  SendUserBack()

End Sub
```

For instance, if we're dealing with a `ProjectResource` object from the `ProjectEdit` form, we execute the following code:

```
' We are dealing with a ProjectResource
Dim obj As ProjectResource = Session("ProjectResource")
obj.Role = lstRoles.SelectedValue
```

We retrieve the `ProjectResource` object from `Session`, and then set its `Role` property to the value the user selected in the `ListBox` control. The user is then redirected back to the edit form from which they came by calling the `SendUserBack()` helper function that we created earlier. This procedure is possible because our business object was designed to display and accept human-readable values for the `Role` property. Not only doesn't the user have to see the cryptic ID values for the roles, but the UI developer doesn't need to deal with them either.

The same basic steps occur if the user is working with a `ResourceAssignment` child object.

Canceling the update

If the user clicks the Cancel button, all we need to do is redirect them back to where they came from *without* first updating the business object's value:

```
Private Sub btnCancel_Click(ByVal sender As System.Object, _
    ByVal e As System.EventArgs) Handles btnCancel.Click

  SendUserBack()

End Sub
```

With all of this code in place, the form will now display the list of roles so that user can change the role as required:

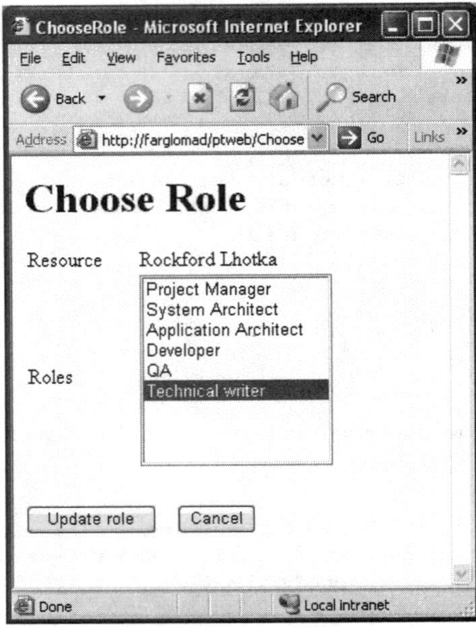

Remember that this form is just editing the business object in memory on the web server. Nothing is stored to the database until the user clicks the Save button on the main edit form.

The AssignResource form

The other 'dialog' form that we need to create for project editing allows the user to assign a new resource to the project. As with `ChooseRole`, the user ends up at this form because they're editing a `Project` object; when they're done on this form, they'll be returned to the `ProjectEdit` form. Unlike `ChooseRole`, however, this particular 'dialog' form *only* deals with `ProjectResource` child objects, so it's somewhat simpler.

Setting up the form

Add a Web Form to the project and name it `AssignResource`. Change its `pageLayout` property to `FlowLayout` and add controls as shown:

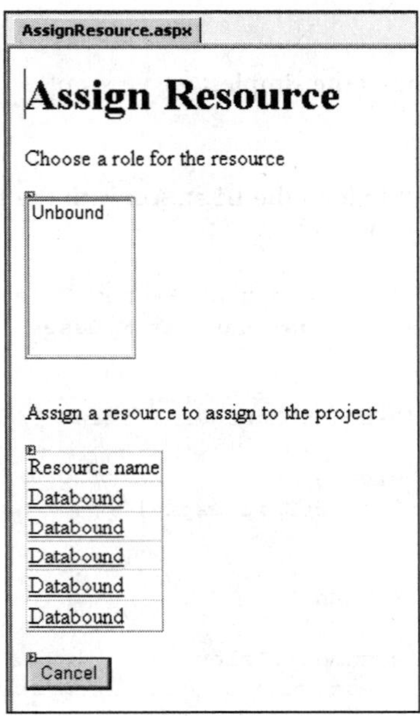

This time, there's no HTML table on this page, as it's simple enough not to need one for organization. The controls are:

Control	Properties
`ListBox`	`ID=lstRoles`
`DataGrid`	`ID=dgResources; EnableViewState=False`
`Button`	`ID=btnCancel; Text=Cancel`

Like our other `DataGrid` controls, this one requires a bit more configuration. Use the Property Builder dialog to turn off auto-generation of columns, and then add the following columns manually:

Column type	Properties
Bound	`Header text=Resource ID; Data Field=ID; Visible=False`
Button	`Header text=Resource name; Text field=Name; Command name=Select`

We'll use the `DataGrid` to display a list of names from the `ResourceList` business object. If the user clicks on one of the names, we'll use the `SelectedIndexChanged` event to indicate that the user wants to assign that resource to the project.

Coding the form

The code behind this form is some of the simplest we've seen!

Loading data

When the form is loaded, we need to load the ListBox with the list of valid roles, and the DataGrid with the list of resources:

```
Private Sub Page_Load(ByVal sender As System.Object, _
    ByVal e As System.EventArgs) Handles MyBase.Load

  ' Check security
  If Not User.IsInRole("ProjectManager") Then

    ' They should not be here
    Response.Redirect("ProjectEdit.aspx")
  End If

  If Not Page.IsPostBack Then
    Dim role As String
    For Each role In Assignment.Roles
      lstRoles.Items.Add(Assignment.Roles.Item(role))
    Next
    If lstRoles.Items.Count > 0 Then lstRoles.SelectedIndex = 0
  End If

  dgResources.DataSource = ResourceList.GetResourceList
  dgResources.DataBind()

End Sub
```

Since we've left EnableViewState set to True for the ListBox this time, we only need to load the list of roles when the page is first accessed. As with the ChooseRole form, this is important, since reloading the list of roles on a postback would prevent us from getting access to the user's selection.

The DataGrid, on the other hand, has EnableViewState set to False, so we need to reload its data on each page access. Assuming that we have a large amount of resources in our database, this is good practice, as it reduces the amount of view state data transferred to and from the browser on each page request.

Assigning a resource

When the user clicks on a role in the ListBox, there is no postback to the page. However, when the user clicks on a resource name in the DataGrid, the page *does* post back, and we receive a SelectedIndexChanged event. In the handler, we can determine the resource selected *and* the role the user clicked on in the ListBox:

```
Private Sub dgResources_SelectedIndexChanged(ByVal sender As System.Object, _
    ByVal e As System.EventArgs) Handles dgResources.SelectedIndexChanged

  Dim project As Project = Session("Project")
  Dim id As String = dgResources.SelectedItem.Cells(0).Text
  project.Resources.Assign(id, lstRoles.SelectedValue)
  Response.Redirect("ProjectEdit.aspx")
End Sub
```

First, we retrieve the `Project` object from `Session` so that we can add the new resource to it. We then use the resource's ID value from the grid and the `Role` value from the `ListBox` as parameters to the `Assign()` method, assigning a new resource to the `Project` object.

Once the resource has been assigned, we redirect the user back to the `ProjectEdit` form, where they can continue to edit the `Project` object.

Canceling the action

If the user clicks the Cancel button, we simply redirect them back to the edit form:

```
Private Sub btnCancel_Click(ByVal sender As System.Object, _
    ByVal e As System.EventArgs) Handles btnCancel.Click

  Response.Redirect("ProjectEdit.aspx")
End Sub
```

This completes all the functionality required in `ProjectEdit`, except for the provision of a `ResourceEdit` form, to allow the editing of a specific `Resource` object. We'll be coming to that shortly.

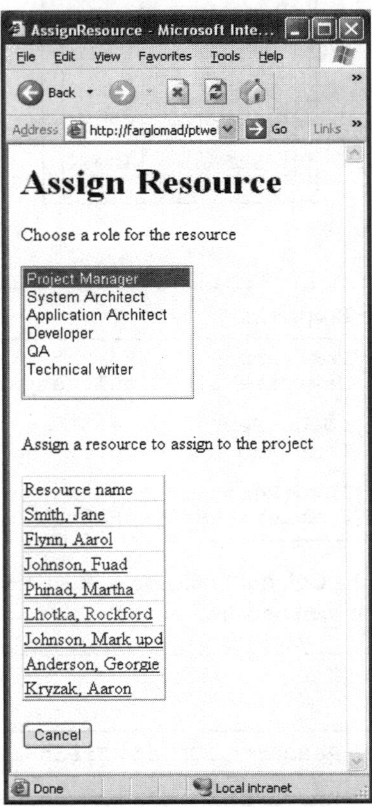

Other than that, the user can add, edit, and view `Project` objects – including assigning resources and changing their roles.

Resources form

We're now most of way through the Web Forms UI, and the three remaining forms – Resources, ResourceEdit, and AssignToProject – are very similar to forms we've already created. Because of this, we'll skim through the creation of these forms quite rapidly.

The Resources form displays a list of the resources currently stored in the system, providing a launching point from which the user can add, edit, or remove resources. Set up the Resources form just like the Projects form:

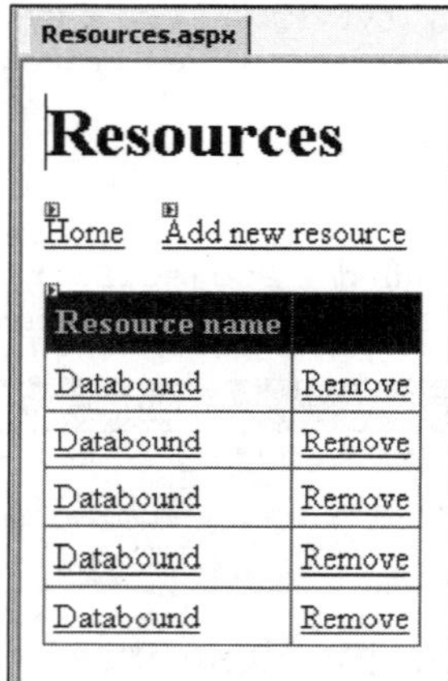

The controls are:

Control	Properties
HyperLink	Text=Home NavigateUrl=Default.aspx
LinkButton	ID=btnNewResource Text=Add new resource
DataGrid	ID=dgResources EnableViewState=False

The DataGrid should be given the Colorful 2 scheme, and automatic column generation should be turned off. Then, configure it with the following columns:

Column type	Properties
Bound	Header text=Resource ID; Data Field=ID; Visible=False
Button	Header text=Resource name; Text field=Name; Command name=Select
Button	Text=Remove; Command name=Remove

As the form loads, we need to populate the DataGrid with data from a ResourceList object. We also need to check the user's role to see if they should be able to add or remove Resource objects:

```
Private Sub Page_Load(ByVal sender As System.Object, _
     ByVal e As System.EventArgs) Handles MyBase.Load

  dgResources.DataSource = ResourceList.GetResourceList
  DataBind()

  ' Set security
  btnNewResource.Visible = User.IsInRole("Supervisor") OrElse _
                           User.IsInRole("ProjectManager")

  dgResources.Columns(2).Visible = User.IsInRole("Supervisor") OrElse _
                                   User.IsInRole("ProjectManager") OrElse _
                                   User.IsInRole("Administrator")
End Sub
```

If the user selects a resource from the list, we can redirect them to the ResourceEdit form by loading a Resource object, putting it in Session, and navigating to ResourceEdit.

```
Private Sub dgResources_SelectedIndexChanged(ByVal sender As System.Object, _
    ByVal e As System.EventArgs) Handles dgResources.SelectedIndexChanged

  Dim id As String = dgResources.SelectedItem.Cells(0).Text
  Session("Resource") = Resource.GetResource(id)
  Response.Redirect("ResourceEdit.aspx")
End Sub
```

If the user clicks the **Add new resource** link at the top of the page, we navigate to the ResourceEdit form. Note that this is different from what we do with ProjectEdit:

```
Private Sub btnNewResource_Click(ByVal sender As System.Object, _
    ByVal e As System.EventArgs) Handles btnNewResource.Click

  ' Make sure there's no active resource
  ' so ResourceEdit knows to add a new object
  Session.Remove("Resource")
  Response.Redirect("ResourceEdit.aspx")
End Sub
```

The difference is that we're not creating a new Resource object before navigating to ResourceEdit. This is because we can't create a new Resource object without first knowing the ID of the new object. The ResourceEdit form will be somewhat different from ProjectEdit in this regard, since it needs to allow the user to enter the ID value for a new Resource manually.

ResourceEdit will assume that we're creating a new Resource if Session doesn't contain one, so here we simply make sure that Session doesn't have a Resource object.

Finally, if the user clicks the **Remove** button on a row, we need to remove that resource from the system:

```
    Private Sub dgResources_DeleteCommand(ByVal source As Object, _
        ByVal e As System.Web.UI.WebControls.DataGridCommandEventArgs) _
        Handles dgResources.DeleteCommand

      Dim id As String = e.Item.Cells(0).Text
      Resource.DeleteResource(id)

      dgResources.DataSource = ResourceList.GetResourceList
      DataBind()
    End Sub
```

Here, the `DataGridCommandEventArgs` parameter provides us with a reference to the row in the `DataGrid` on which the user clicked. We can use the first column in that row to retrieve the ID value, which we can then use to call the `DeleteResource()` method.

The result is a form that lists all the resources in the system:

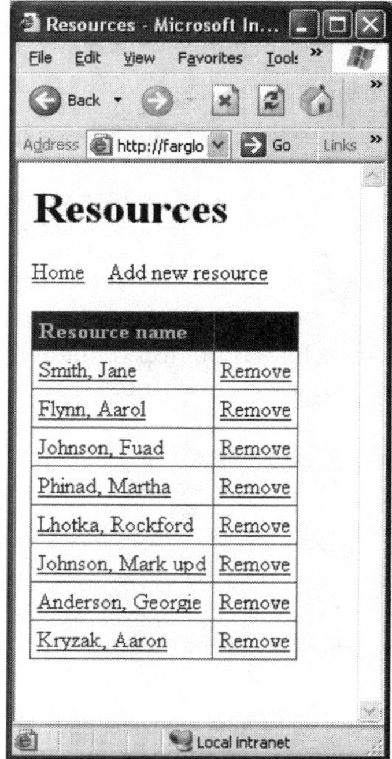

From here, the user can edit or remove resources as needed.

The ResourceEdit form

Like the `ProjectEdit` form, `ResourceEdit` is large and relatively complex. It displays all the data about a `Resource` object, including the list of projects to which the resource is assigned. From this form, the user can edit a `Resource` object as well as adding, removing, or changing the list of project assignments.

As hinted at above, there are some key differences in this form when compared to `ProjectEdit`, because of the way we create `Resource` objects. To create a new `Resource` object we must first have the user-supplied ID value of that object. This complicates matters because it means that we can't create a new `Resource` object until *after* the user has interacted with our form and entered an ID value.

To accommodate this, our form's `Load` event handler will detect whether we're adding a new `Resource`. If we *are* adding a new `Resource`, we'll make the ID control read-write, so that the user can enter a value. Then, before attempting to save the data, we'll create a new `Resource` object using that ID value. Other than this change (and a related change in the **Save** button handler), however, the code in `ResourceEdit` will be very similar to that in `ProjectEdit`.

Setting up the form

Add the `ResourceEdit` form and set it up just like the `ProjectEdit` form above. It should look something like this:

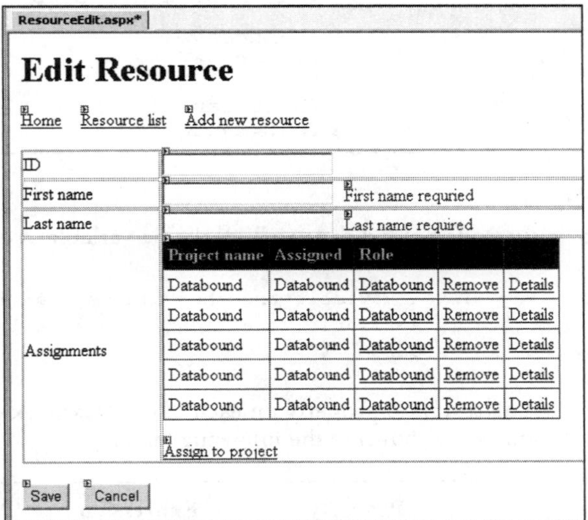

Control properties

The controls themselves are described in the following table:

Control	Properties
`HyperLink`	`Text=Home` `NavigateUrl=Default.aspx`
`HyperLink`	`Text=Resource list` `NavigateUrl=Resources.aspx`
`LinkButton`	`ID=btnNewResource` `Text=Add new resource`
`TextBox`	`ID=txtID` `ReadOnly=True`

Table continued on following page

Control	Properties
RequiredFieldValidator	ErrorMessage=ID Required ControlToValidate=txtID
TextBox	ID=txtFirstName
RequiredFieldValidator	ErrorMessage=First name required ControlToValidate=txtFirstName
TextBox	ID=txtLastName
RequiredFieldValidator	ErrorMessage=Last name required ControlToValidate=txtLastName
DataGrid	ID=dgProjects
LinkButton	ID=btnAssign Text=Assign to project
Button	ID=btnSave Text=Save
Button	ID=btnCancel Text=Cancel

Data binding the controls

As with `ProjectEdit`, in the code-behind page we'll declare a variable to hold our business object:

```
' We make this a page-level variable and then always load it in Page_Load
' That way, the object is available to all our code at all times
Protected mResource As Resource
```

We can then change the `DataBindings` property on each of our `TextBox` controls in order to bind them to the object. The bindings are shown in the following table:

Control	Property	Expression
txtID	Text	mResource.ID
txtFirstName	Text	mResource.FirstName
txtLastName	Text	mResource.LastName

For example, the txtID data bindings dialog would appear as:

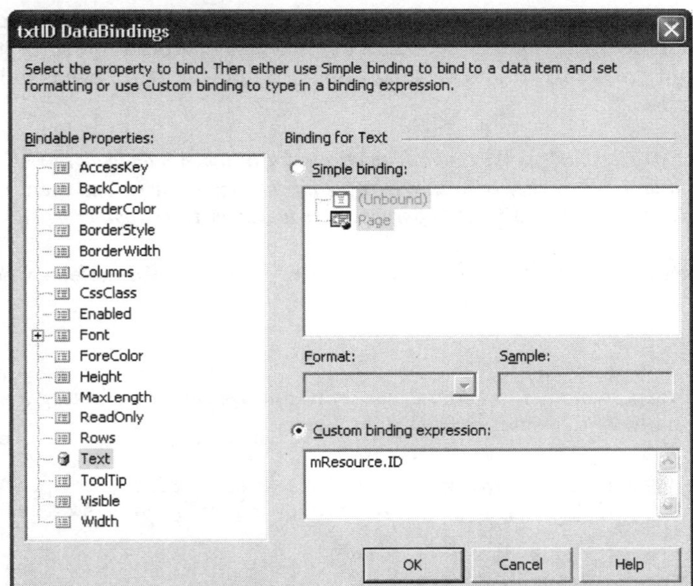

This isolates the display of data from our code, making maintenance of the UI better overall.

Configuring the DataGrid

We also need to finish configuring the DataGrid control. Set its appearance to Colorful 2, and then set up the following columns:

Column type	Properties
Bound	Header text=Project ID; Data Field=ProjectID; Visible=False
Bound	Header text=Name; Data Field=Name
Bound	Header text=Assigned; Data Field=Assigned
Button	Text field=Role; Command name=SelectRole
Button	Text=Remove; Command name=Remove
Button	Text=Details; Command name=Select

As in the ProjectEdit form, we've included a Role column that allows the user to navigate to the ChooseRole form to change the role of this resource on a project. We've already coded that form to handle requests from this form appropriately.

Coding the form

What makes this form different from ProjectEdit is that the ID value of a Resource object is user-supplied, rather than being auto-generated. This complicates matters a bit, since it means that the txtID control is only read-only for an existing Resource object, but it needs to be read-write when we add a new Resource.

> *This is only one possible design. We could do what we did in the Windows Forms UI, and have the user first go to a form where they enter the ID value for the new resource, and* then *navigate to this page. I implemented it using a different approach here to demonstrate another possible variation.*

The primary impact here is on the Page_Load() code, with a few side-effects where we actually save the object.

Loading data

When we load the form, we need to take into account that we may be creating a new Resource – in which case, we won't have a business object right away:

```
Private Sub Page_Load(ByVal sender As System.Object, _
                      ByVal e As System.EventArgs) Handles MyBase.Load

  ' Get the existing Resource (if any)
  mResource = Session("Resource")

  If mResource Is Nothing Then

    ' Either we're adding a new object or the user hit the back button
    If Len(txtID.Text) = 0 Then

      ' We are adding a new resource
      txtID.ReadOnly = False
      btnAssign.Visible = False
    Else
      If txtID.ReadOnly Then

        ' We've returned here via the Browser's back button
        ' Load object based on ID value
        mResource = Resource.GetResource(txtID.Text)
        Session("Resource") = mResource
      Else

        ' We are adding a new resource
        mResource = Resource.NewResource(txtID.Text)
        Session("Resource") = mResource
        txtID.ReadOnly = True
        btnAssign.Visible = True
      End If
    End If
  End If

  If Not mResource Is Nothing Then

    ' We have a resource to which we can bind
    dgProjects.DataSource = mResource.Assignments
```

```
    If IsPostBack Then
      dgProjects.DataBind()
    Else
      DataBind()
    End If
  End If

End Sub
```

If we are to edit a `Resource` object, that object will have been loaded into `Session` by the previous form. This means that if we arrive at this form *without* a `Resource` object in `Session`, we know that one of the following conditions is true:

- The user navigated here directly, and thus wants to add a resource
- The user clicked an **Add new resource** link
- The user clicked the **Back** button

As we did in `ProjectEdit`, we check for these conditions and set up the form appropriately. In this case, we can't simply create a `Resource` object to start with, since we don't yet know its ID value. Instead, if the user is adding a new `Resource`, we change the `txtID` control to be read-write so that the user can enter the ID value.

We can tell whether we're adding a new `Resource` by checking to see if `txtID` contains a value. If it's empty, then we know that this form doesn't represent an existing object:

```
If mResource Is Nothing Then

  ' Either we're adding a new object or the user hit the back button
  If Len(txtID.Text) = 0 Then

    ' We are adding a new resource
    txtID.ReadOnly = False
    btnAssign.Visible = False
```

In this case, we also hide `btnAssign`. Until we've created a `Resource` object, there's no way to assign it to any projects, so the button would be invalid at this stage.

If `txtID` *does* contain a value, then we know that one of two things is true:

- The user hit the **Back** button and returned to this page
- The user is adding a new `Resource`, has entered an ID value, and then clicked the **Save** button, causing a postback of this page to itself

We can tell the difference between *these* two cases by checking whether `txtID` is read-only. If it's read-only and there's a value in `txtID`, then we know that the user pressed the **Back** button to get here. In this case, we use that ID value to reload the appropriate `Resource` object:

```
    If txtID.ReadOnly Then

      ' We've returned here via the Browser's back button
      ' Load object based on ID value
      mResource = Resource.GetResource(txtID.Text)
      Session("Resource") = mResource
```

If there's a value in `txtID` and `txtID` is *not* read-only, then we know that we were in the middle of adding a new `Resource` object and the user clicked the **Save** button. That button click causes a postback to our page so that the click event can be processed, but first we need to create a new `Resource` object by using the ID value in `txtID`:

```
    Else

      ' We are adding a new resource
      mResource = Resource.NewResource(txtID.Text)
      Session("Resource") = mResource
      txtID.ReadOnly = True
      btnAssign.Visible = True
    End If
```

Now that we've determined whether we're editing, adding, or doing the postback after the user clicked **Save**, we can proceed. If we do have a `Resource` object, we need to bind the form's controls to the object, just like we did in `ProjectEdit`:

```
  If Not mResource Is Nothing Then

    ' We have a resource to which we can bind
    dgProjects.DataSource = mResource.Assignments

    If IsPostBack Then
      dgProjects.DataBind()
    Else
      DataBind()
    End If
  End If
```

If we don't have a `Resource` object, we skip the data binding, and the form will be displayed with blank fields so the user can fill them in.

Security

We also need to do some security checks as the form is loaded. Add this to the bottom of the `Page_Load()` method:

```
    ' Set security
    If Not User.IsInRole("Supervisor") AndAlso _
      Not User.IsInRole("ProjectManager") Then
      btnNewResource.Visible = False
      btnSave.Visible = False
      btnAssign.Visible = False
```

```
      dgProjects.Columns(4).Visible = False
    End If

  End Sub
```

In order to edit a Resource object, the user must be either a Supervisor or a ProjectManager. If they are not, we hide the controls that enable the user to save a Resource object. Of course, the user could bypass this by typing a URL directly into their browser, but in that case our business objects themselves would enforce the security constraints, and the user would still be unable to perform invalid actions.

Saving the data

If the user clicks the **Save** button, we need to save the object. First though, we need to copy the data from the form into the object. As before, we can put this functionality into a helper method:

```
  Private Sub SaveFormToObject()

    With mResource
      .FirstName = txtFirstname.Text
      .LastName = txtLastname.Text
    End With

  End Sub
```

This is fundamentally the same as what we did in ProjectEdit. We simply copy the values from the form's controls into the object.

This method is called by the Save() method, which is a bit different from the one in ProjectEdit, because we need to handle the case where the user is adding a new Resource object. The primary change is that we want to leave the user on the ResourceEdit page, so that they can assign the new resource to projects, if so desired:

```
  Private Sub btnSave_Click(ByVal sender As System.Object, _
      ByVal e As System.EventArgs) Handles btnSave.Click

    SaveFormToObject()

    If mResource.IsNew Then
      mResource = mResource.Save
      Session("Resource") = mResource
      Response.Redirect("ResourceEdit.aspx")

    Else
      mResource.Save()
      Session.Remove("Resource")
      Response.Redirect("Resources.aspx")
    End If

  End Sub
```

If mResource is a new object, we save it, put it into Session, and then navigate right back to ResourceEdit. By doing this, the user is left on the ResourceEdit page, with the object loaded into the form for editing. This allows the user to change the object's data, and more importantly assign the resource to projects.

On the other hand, if mResource is *not* new, then we do the same thing as we did in ProjectEdit. We save the object, remove it from Session to save memory, and navigate back to the Resources form.

Canceling the edit

If the user clicks the Cancel button, we return them to the Resources form:

```
Private Sub btnCancel_Click(ByVal sender As System.Object, _
    ByVal e As System.EventArgs) Handles btnCancel.Click

  Session.Remove("Resource")
  Response.Redirect("Resources.aspx")

End Sub
```

As in the Save button handler, we're removing the business object from Session before we leave the edit form, minimizing the memory required on the server and the bandwidth used by Session if it is being stored on a state server.

Selecting an assignment

The user has the option of clicking on a project to which the resource is assigned. In this case, we'll bring up the ProjectEdit page so that they can interact with the project. Before we leave this page, however, we'll save the Resource object (assuming that the user is in the right role):

```
Private Sub dgProjects_SelectedIndexChanged(ByVal sender As System.Object, _
    ByVal e As System.EventArgs) Handles dgProjects.SelectedIndexChanged

  ' Check security
  If User.IsInRole("Supervisor") OrElse User.IsInRole("ProjectManager") Then

    ' Only do save if user is in a valid role
    SaveFormToObject()
    mResource = mResource.Save
  End If

  Session.Remove("Resource")

  Dim id As New Guid(dgProjects.SelectedItem.Cells(0).Text)
  Session("Project") = Project.GetProject(id)
  Response.Redirect("ProjectEdit.aspx")

End Sub
```

This is the same basic functionality as we provided in ProjectEdit.

Changing the role

As in ProjectEdit, when the user clicks on an item in the Role column of the grid, we navigate to the ChooseRole form. Before we navigate there, we get the selected ResourceAssignment object and put it into Session, so the code in ChooseRole knows which object to edit:

```
Private Sub dgProjects_ItemCommand(ByVal source As Object, _
    ByVal e As System.Web.UI.WebControls.DataGridCommandEventArgs) _
    Handles dgProjects.ItemCommand

  If e.CommandName = "SelectRole" Then
    Dim id As New Guid(e.Item.Cells(0).Text)
    Session("ResourceAssignment") = mResource.Assignments(id)
    Session("Source") = "ResourceEdit.aspx"
    Response.Redirect("ChooseRole.aspx")
  End If

End Sub
```

This code is similar to that in `ProjectEdit`, though we're using a `ResourceAssignment` object here instead of a `ProjectResource` object.

Removing an assignment

When the user clicks on the **Remove** button in the `DataGrid`, we need to remove the specified assignment:

```
Private Sub dgProjects_DeleteCommand(ByVal source As Object, _
    ByVal e As System.Web.UI.WebControls.DataGridCommandEventArgs) _
    Handles dgProjects.DeleteCommand

  Dim id As String = e.Item.Cells(0).Text
  mResource.Assignments.Remove(New Guid(id))

  ' Rebind grid to update display
  dgProjects.DataSource = mResource.Assignments
  dgProjects.DataBind()

End Sub
```

At this stage, you've seen enough code like this to know exactly what's going on here!

Adding an assignment

Finally, we need to support the concept of assigning this resource to a new project. We'll create a dialog form named `AssignToProject` where the user can choose the project and role. Here, we simply need to navigate to that form:

```
Private Sub btnAssign_Click(ByVal sender As System.Object, _
    ByVal e As System.EventArgs) Handles btnAssign.Click

  SaveFormToObject()
  Response.Redirect("AssignToProject.aspx")

End Sub
```

Before navigating away, we need to make sure that we copy the values from our form into the business object, or they'll be lost. Remember that Web Forms data binding is read-only, so it is up to us to copy the values from the form's controls back into the object.

You should now be able to view and edit Resource objects (but you can't yet assign a resource to a project – we'll do that next):

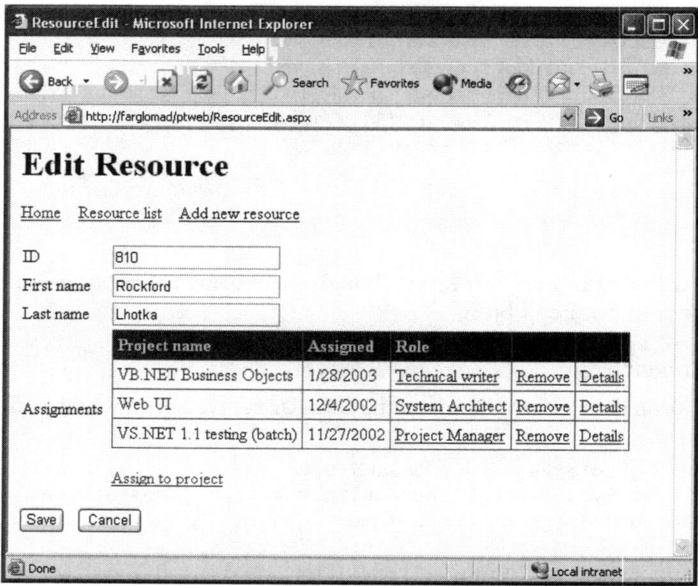

The screenshot above shows the form being used to edit an existing resource.

The AssignToProject form

The final form in our Web Forms UI allows the user to assign a resource to a project. The user needs to pick the role for the resource, and then click on the project. This is virtually identical to the AssignResource form that we created earlier, but here the user selects a project instead of a resource.

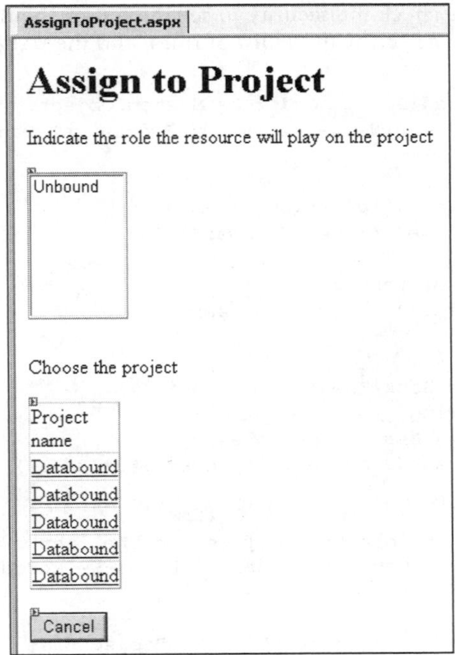

The controls are:

Control	Properties
`ListBox`	`ID=lstRoles`
`DataGrid`	`ID=dgProjects; EnableViewState=False`
`Button`	`ID=btnCancel; Text=Cancel`

Like our other `DataGrid` controls, this one requires a bit more configuration. Use the Property Builder dialog to turn off auto-generation of columns and then add the following columns manually:

Column type	Properties

Bound	`Header text=Project ID`
	`Data Field=ID`
	`Visible=False`

Button	`Header text=Project name`
	`Text field=Name`
	`Command name=Select`

We'll use the `DataGrid` to display a list of projects from the `ProjectList` business object. If the user clicks on one of the names, we'll use the `SelectedIndexChanged` event to indicate that the user wants to assign the resource to that project.

When the form is loaded, we check the security to see if the user should be here. If they are in the right role, we then populate the `ListBox` with the list of roles, and the `DataGrid` with the list of projects:

```
Private Sub Page_Load(ByVal sender As System.Object, _
                      ByVal e As System.EventArgs) Handles MyBase.Load

  ' Check security
  If Not User.IsInRole("Supervisor") AndAlso _
    Not User.IsInRole("ProjectManager") Then

    ' They should not be here
    Response.Redirect("ResourceEdit.aspx")
  End If

  If Not Page.IsPostBack Then
    Dim role As String
    For Each role In Assignment.Roles
      lstRoles.Items.Add(Assignment.Roles.Item(role))
    Next

    ' Set the default role to the first in the list
    If lstRoles.Items.Count > 0 Then lstRoles.SelectedIndex = 0
  End If

  dgProjects.DataSource = ProjectList.GetProjectList
  dgProjects.DataBind()

End Sub
```

When the user clicks on a project in the list, we'll create a new assignment for the `Resource` object based on the selected role and project:

```
Private Sub dgProjects_SelectedIndexChanged(ByVal sender As System.Object, _
  ByVal e As System.EventArgs) Handles dgProjects.SelectedIndexChanged

  Dim resource As Resource = Session("Resource")
  Dim id As Guid = New Guid(dgProjects.SelectedItem.Cells(0).Text)
  resource.Assignments.AssignTo(id, lstRoles.SelectedValue)
  Response.Redirect("ResourceEdit.aspx")
End Sub
```

Finally, if the user clicks the Cancel button, we'll simply return them to the `ResourceEdit` form:

```
Private Sub btnCancel_Click(ByVal sender As System.Object, _
  ByVal e As System.EventArgs) Handles btnCancel.Click

  Response.Redirect("ResourceEdit.aspx")

End Sub
```

At this point, we should be able to assign the current resource to a project:

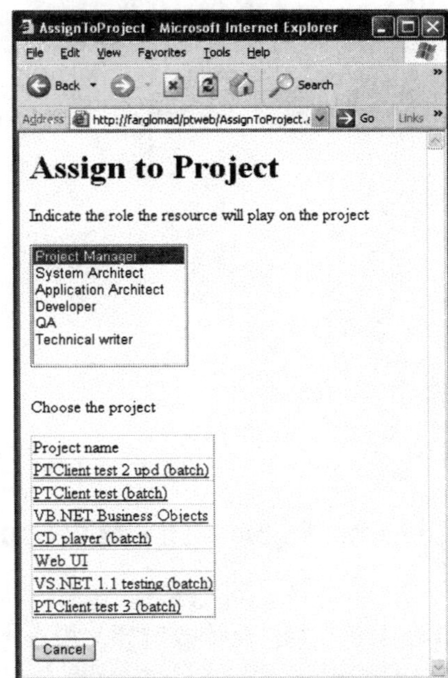

This completes the Web Forms UI. You should now be able to navigate throughout the UI to add, edit, and remove both `Project` and `Resource` objects.

Conclusion

In this chapter, we've created a basic Web Forms UI based on our business objects. As with the Windows Forms technology in Chapter 8, there are many ways to create a Web Forms interface, and the one we've created here is just one option among many.

The key is that we've designed our business objects so that they automatically enforce all business rules and provide business processing, so the UI doesn't need to include any of that code. We have now created two very different user interfaces based on exactly the same set of business objects, data access code, and database design.

As shown here, we configured the application for optimal performance, running the `Session` and the `DataPortal` in the same process as our Web Forms. We could increase scalability and fault tolerance by moving `Session` into its own process, or onto a state server. We could potentially increase security by running the `DataPortal` server on an application server, behind a second firewall. In either case, all we need to do is change some settings in `Web.config` – our UI code and business objects will work in all these scenarios.

In Chapter 10, we'll create another type of interface to our business objects, by using web services.

CHAPTER 10

10

Web services interface

One of the most hyped technologies to be linked with .NET is XML Web Services. Microsoft says that .NET is, "the platform for building and using web services," and there's no doubt that when they're used appropriately, web services are powerful and useful indeed. It's important to realize, however, that web services are fundamentally just a text format for data interchange – they're not designed to simplify the process of creating object-oriented systems.

In my view, web services are just another type of interface to applications. We've already discussed and created Windows Forms and Web Forms interfaces, which allow a user to access our application:

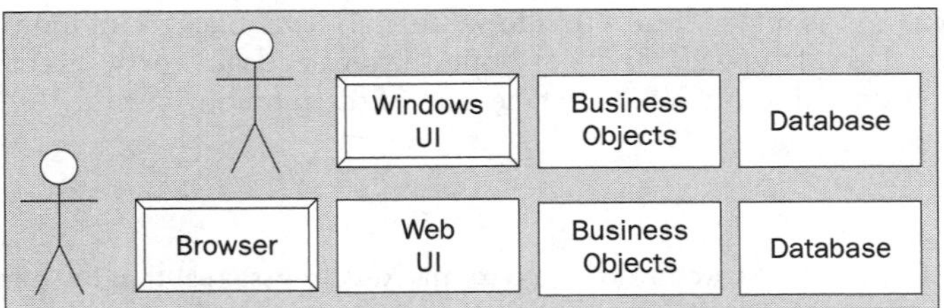

Web services are another type of interface that our application can make available. The primary difference is that a web service interface is designed for use by other *applications*, not directly by users. Another application can use web services to get or update data in our application. This other application that's consuming our data may or may not have users of its own:

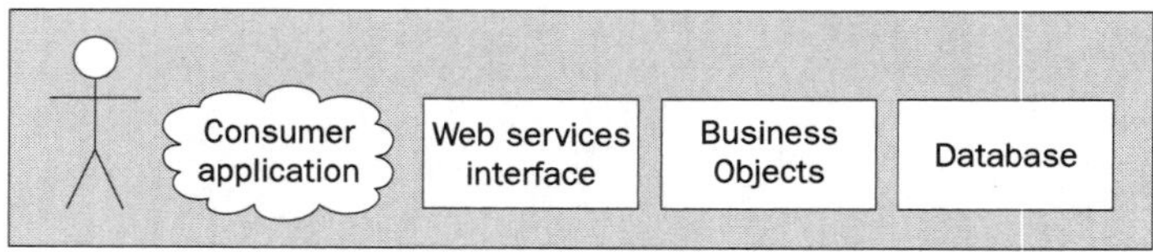

I fully realize that web services are being sold as offering much more than this. We'll discuss my rationale some more before we actually implement the web services in this chapter.

In this chapter, we'll quickly review web services and SOAP technology. Then we'll discuss the various roles that people often associate with web services, to make it clear why they work best if viewed as I've described them here. After that, we'll create a web services interface for our project tracker business objects, to illustrate how our business objects support the creation of web services.

Overview of web services

At an abstract level, web services enable one application to call procedures or methods in another application. On the face of it, this is similar to the aims of RPC (remote procedure calls), DCOM, RMI, IIOP, and .NET remoting – all of these technologies enable one application to invoke procedures in another application.

It's also possible to view these technologies as a way for two components in the same application to interact with each other. While this is definitely a common use for the other technologies I mention, it is not the intended use of web services. Web services are designed for cross-application communication, not cross-component communication. This is because the focus of web services is interoperability. Due to this focus, web services don't offer the same performance or features as the other more platform-specific technologies listed.

More specifically, XML Web Services is an implementation of SOAP (the Simple Object Access Protocol), which uses the HTTP protocol for communication between one application and another.

The following discussion is intended to provide some high level background information on SOAP and web services. As we'll see, a typical .NET developer never needs to worry directly about these details, because the .NET Framework and VS.NET take care of them on our behalf.

SOAP

SOAP defines the format and structure of the data packets (messages) that are sent back and forth between the applications involved. There are two primary types of message:

- A procedure call
- The results of a procedure call

When an application wants to call a procedure or a method in another application, it constructs a SOAP message that describes the method to be called and provides any parameter data. Any results from the procedure are likewise packed up into a SOAP message that's returned to the original application.

SOAP defines a couple of important things that must go into a message:

- The format of the data that's being transferred
- An envelope of metadata around the data that's being transferred

The SOAP data format is designed to be supported by virtually any platform. It defines a rich set of data types, including numbers, text, arrays, and so forth. Data of these types can be encoded into a standard XML format that can be understood by any platform that supports SOAP. The format is designed for interoperability, which means that most platforms will have more complex data types or structures that can't be readily encoded into SOAP XML.

The SOAP envelope contains metadata describing the nature and purpose of the message. We can think of the envelope as being like a 'header' for the actual data, a little like an HTTP header. The envelope can be quite complex, and is extensible. This means that we can add arbitrary additional data into the envelope – a feature we'll use later in the chapter to pass security credentials along with our method call.

Originally, SOAP was conceived as a way to make calls on objects – hence that word "object" in the acronym – but this is not now the case, and the acronym is falling into disuse: SOAP is just SOAP. There need not be any objects anywhere in your system in order to use SOAP – it simply allows one application to call a procedure in another application. Whether that procedure is a method of an object or a routine written in COBOL doesn't matter.

Message-based communication

A key point to remember is that SOAP *only* controls the XML that makes up the message; it doesn't describe how that message should be delivered from one application to another. It's down to some other mechanism to deliver a SOAP-formatted message from one application (the consumer) to the other (the publisher). The publisher application then runs the requested procedure. Any results from that procedure are packaged up into another SOAP-formatted message, which is returned to the consumer:

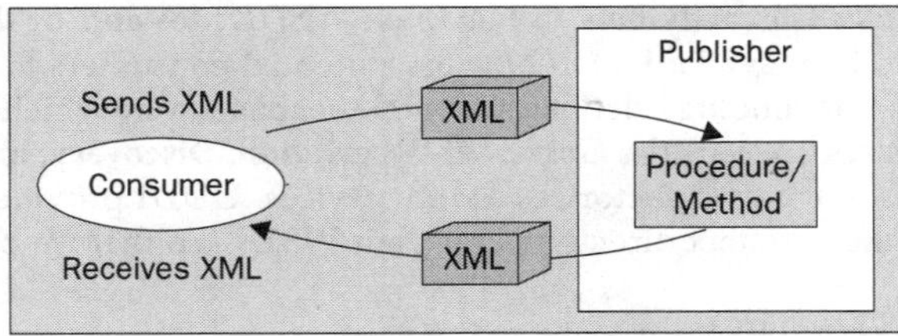

The most common approach today is for the applications to communicate via HTTP, but the SOAP data format can be transferred via e-mail, MSMQ, raw sockets, text files, instant messaging technology, or any other way that you can think of to get the data from one application to the other.

SOAP and web services

This, then, is where web services come into play. Web services allow their consumers to connect to them using the HTTP protocol. Each procedure call is an isolated event in which the consumer connects to the service, makes the call, and gets back the result.

However, using web services over HTTP is about more than just passing SOAP XML messages back and forth. While that's at the core of the process, there are a number of supporting features that are very important, including:

- Describing the nature of a web service
- Generating consumer-side proxies for a web service
- Discovery of the web services on a machine
- Managing directories of web services

Describing a web service means generating a list of all the procedures (often called **web methods**) that are available to consumers, along with the data types of the parameters those procedures require, and the data types of any return values. There is a standard for describing this information: WSDL (Web Services Description Language). WSDL is an XML dialect that *describes* a web service. When we (or VS.NET on our behalf) need information about a web service, we retrieve a WSDL document.

The primary reason for retrieving a WSDL document is to create a consumer-side proxy for the web service: an object on the consumer machine that *looks like* the web service. Any method calls we make on this proxy are automatically packaged into SOAP XML and sent to the publisher application. This is really no different from how we use client-side proxy objects in remoting, DCOM, or any other similar technology.

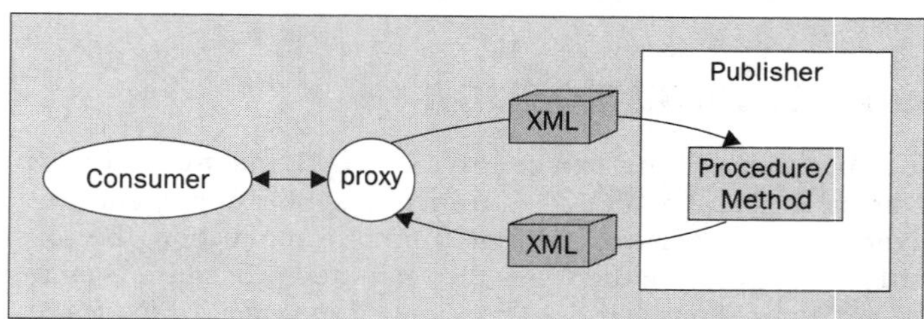

The next challenge we face is exactly how to *find* these WSDL files and/or their associated web services. It's all very well making them available, but how are potential consumers to discover that they exist? Happily, the web services technology defines a formal mechanism by which web services can be discovered. Along with this, there is the **Universal Description, Discovery, and Integration** standard (**UDDI**), which allows us to create directories of web services. UDDI provides an index of available web services, which we can then contact directly to get their WSDL, so that we can create a proxy.

SOAP, web services, and the .NET Framework

As .NET developers, we typically don't think about the creation of SOAP messages and envelopes. Nor do we really think about the details of delivering a SOAP message via HTTP. All this is handled on our behalf by the .NET Framework and its support for web services.

To create a publisher (an application that exposes web services), we simply create an ASP.NET Web Services project and write some code. Alternatively, we can just add a web service to an existing ASP.NET web application. In either case, apart from adding a couple of special attributes to our code, we don't usually have to any difficult work.

For instance, we might write the following code in a web service within an ASP.NET application:

```
<System.Web.Services.WebService( _
  Namespace:="http://ws.lhotka.net/PTService/ProjectTracker")> _
Public Class ProjectTracker
  Inherits System.Web.Services.WebService

  <WebMethod(Description:="Get Resource Name")> _
  Public Function GetResourceName(ByVal ID As String) As String

    Dim name As String

    ' Retrieve name

    Return name

  End Function

End Class
```

When this ASP.NET application is compiled, VS.NET will automatically generate all the extra files needed to provide access to this method via web services. This includes the ability to generate WSDL descriptions for the web service dynamically.

Equally, a typical .NET developer doesn't need to worry about creating consumer-side proxy objects. If we're using VS.NET, we simply add a web reference to the web service. VS.NET then automatically retrieves the WSDL describing the web service and generates the proxy. If we're not using VS.NET, the .NET Framework offers the `soapsuds.exe` command line utility, which can also create the proxy.

Because of the tight integration of web services into the .NET Framework and VS.NET, we can avoid dealing with the details of publishing and consuming web services. This means that we can focus on how to use them in our business applications, rather than worrying about how to make them.

Now that we have a basic understanding of the technologies behind web services, let's discuss where they fit into our overall application architecture.

Web services as an interface

Because web services have received so much publicity, there are a lot of different ideas and opinions about what they are for and how they can best be used. In this section, we'll explore an extreme opinion, before settling down to the idea of using web services as just another interface to our application.

Web services are all about exposing data or functionality to unknown consumers on unknown hardware, written in unknown tools or languages. They are all about providing access to data and functionality in such a way that neither the consumer nor the publisher needs to know anything about the other, beyond that they can send and receive XML.

Our Project Tracker application has no need for web services *internally*, since if we do any network communication, we're using the more efficient and powerful remoting technology. However, it's quite possible that our application's data or functionality could have value to other applications within our organization, or perhaps to our business partners or customers. Clearly, we have no good way of predicting the types of hardware, operating systems, or software that may be used to create these other applications, but nor should we care.

A web service for every tier?

Some people believe that every logical tier in an application should be exposed via web services. This would allow a consumer to use a web service to retrieve or update data directly from the database, or to call middle-tier business objects, or maybe even to call UI functionality. In our five-tier logical model from Chapter 1, the result would look something like this:

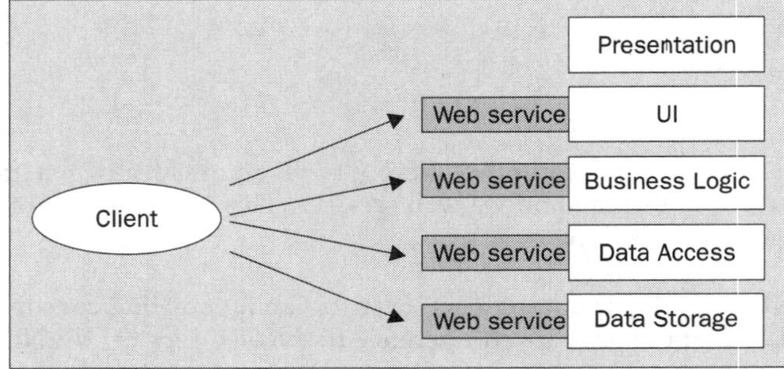

The primary rationale for this approach is that we'd use web services for *all* interaction with each tier of the application, thus gaining reuse. This sounds attractive on the surface, but it gets very ugly very quickly.

Consider what happens to our application if we allow just any consumer to interact directly with the database, via web services. Our data has rules – validation, security, and so forth – that must be enforced. If a consumer can call a web service to update data in the database, then the database itself must have all the business rules available. Typically, this would mean writing all our business logic in something like T-SQL, which is not the most productive or easiest language to use.

Remember: we can't predict what kinds of consumers will be created in the future. Anywhere that we allow these unknown consumers to access our code, we must be defensive. We must assume that they will introduce bugs by skipping validation, bypassing security, or otherwise ignoring the functionality required by the business process that *our* application was intended to address.

> *I'm somewhat adamant on this point, having been the victim of exposing procedures to unknown clients in COM. I exposed a set of low-level COM components to a client application outside of my control, but I hadn't coded my components defensively (they were designed for my application's use). The developer of the new client application misunderstood how data was to be used, and the components didn't enforce the rules, leading to corrupt data.*

What this really means is that our application architecture collapses into something like this:

Presentation
Web service UI
Client
Web service Business Logic Data Storage

Our UI becomes just another client of the database server, where all the business logic and data management occurs.

We've been here before with 2-tier client-server applications, in the early- to mid-1990s. Then, we learned that if the only place where the business logic resides is the database, our user interface has to accept virtually any user input, and then send it to the database to find out whether what the user entered was any good. In response, developers duplicate the business logic in their UI code – but then the two can get out of sync, and then we have bugs. Hopefully, you can begin to see that web services don't change the fundamental reasons why we use the n-tier designs that I've been advocating in this book!

A web service as the 'user interface'

Instead of the approach presented in the previous section, the way to view web services is that they provide 'just another' interface to our application. We can tie this idea back to our n-tier model from Chapter 2:

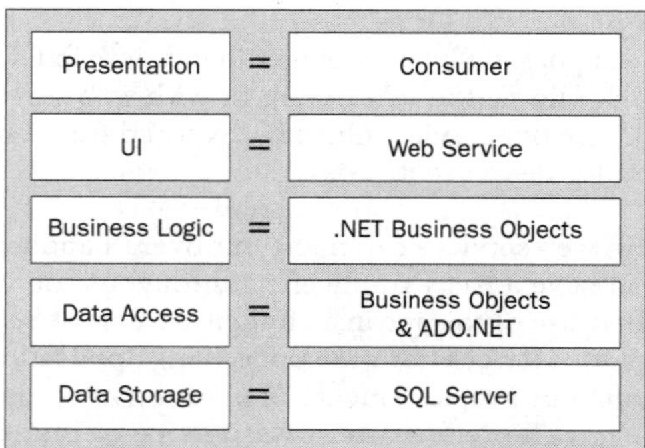

Notice that the web service and the consumer have clearly defined roles in this model: the consumer has become responsible for handling presentation, and any other details of that sort. From the point of view of a web service, all of that is out of our scope. All we care is that we're providing the Presentation tier with what it needs to do its work.

As always, it's for the UI tier to interact with the business logic, and for the Data Access tier to retrieve, process, and update data on behalf of the Presentation tier. In a Web Forms UI, this revolves around the creation and processing of HTML, while with web services it's all about XML. In many ways, this is a pretty minor difference.

By taking this view of web services, we provide access not only to our data, but also to the combination of data and functionality within the context of our existing application. This is much more powerful, because it means that we automatically gain access to all our existing business logic, including validation, manipulation, security, and so forth. If another application wants to use our data, we want to perform security checks to see if that's OK. If another application wants to update our data, we want to perform security and validation checks, *and* apply any other business processing or rules.

The end result is that we'll write a set of web services that provide the same basic functionality as our Windows Forms or Web Forms interfaces, but without any consideration for the presentation. The web services code will interact with our existing business objects to retrieve, manipulate, update, or delete data. Since our objects provide not only the data, but also all related business functionality, we're guaranteed to have the same business rules enforced as with our other two interfaces.

Web services and contracts

Perhaps the most important thing to remember about web services is that after we publish a web service and consumers start using it, the web service interface can no longer be changed without breaking those consumers.

This is the same issue we faced with COM components: after you publish the interface to a component (or a web service), you can never change it without compatibility issues.

For this reason, we have to view the interface of each web service method as a contract. Once we publish the web service, the contract is finalized, and we can only change it by paying up on the huge penalty clause built into that contract. In our case, the penalty clause translates to irate calls from all the users and authors of all the consumers that use our web service!

With web services, this issue is potentially even bigger than it was in COM – and it was big enough in COM. (Remember DLL hell?) The reason *why* it's bigger with web services is that we can't predict what consumers may be created to use our service. Once it's exposed from our server, almost any programmer out there might decide to use it.

If we're not careful, the use of web services can make our overall application architecture very fragile. A change to our application can have a nasty ripple effect throughout our organization, or those of our partners or our customers. Because of this intrinsic fragility, we must be incredibly careful to separate the *interface* exposed by our web services from the underlying application. We want to be able to change, enhance, and maintain our Project Tracker application over time, while at the same time minimizing the possibility that we'll break existing web service consumers.

This is another reason why exposing every tier of our application via web services would be problematic. As soon as we expose a web service, we lose almost all flexibility in terms of implementing changes or enhancements. The interface for our tier becomes locked in place. By exposing web services as a form of interface on top of our application, we can largely shield our application itself from these effects, meaning that we can change and enhance the application and still provide a consistent set of web services.

At heart, a web service is just a collection of methods that accept parameters and return results. The parameters and results are just data that's passed between consumer and service. If we can clearly define these parameters and results up front, we'll have gone a long way toward defining the contract by which we must live.

A very easy way to define this data contract clearly is to use `Structure` types in our web service code. When we define a `Public Structure` in a web service, that data structure is exposed as part of our SOAP interface. This means that any consumer has easy access to the specific layout of the data structure we've defined.

Tools such as VS.NET take this data structure definition and use it to create consumer-side proxy classes that mirror the data structure automatically. This makes it very easy for the consumer developer to format data to be sent to our web service properly, and to understand any complex data that our web service returns to the consumer.

While we might use other techniques (such as an XML document) to transfer complex data, the use of a `Structure` provides the most automated and self-documenting interface with the least amount of work on our part, so that is what we'll do in this book.

> *We could also define a class and use an object to expose the data in a defined way – from the perspective of a consumer the end result would be no different from using a* `Structure`*. However, a* `Structure` *is much faster to create and destroy than an object, because a* `Structure` *is a value type. Since we'll be creating and destroying a* `Structure` *on each web service, we'll get better performance than if we did the same thing with an object.*

Now that we've discussed some of the core concepts – most notably, the view that web services are just another type of interface to our application, and that this interface is an immutable contract – we can move on to implement a set of web services for our sample application.

Implementing a web services interface

In many ways, a web service interface is easier to construct than a Windows Forms or Web Forms interface, because we don't need to worry about any issues of presentation, or display, or user interaction. Those are the responsibility of the consumer. All we need to worry about is providing an interface that allows the developer of a consumer to access the information and functionality provided by our application's business logic and data.

Web service design

In designing a web service, there are four primary issues that we must face:

- What web methods (procedures) do we want to expose?
- How will we organize the web methods into web services?
- What data do we want to expose and accept?
- What are our security requirements?

Deciding on web methods

It's possible to subdivide our Project Tracker application's functionality in many different ways. For example, we could be very specific and provide a set of discrete services, such as:

Add project	Get project	Remove project	Change project name
Change project start date	Change project end date	Add resource	Get resource
Remove resource	Change resource first name	Change resource last name	Get list of projects
Get list of resources	Change project description	Add resource to project	Remove resource from project
Add project to resource	Remove project from resource	Change role of resource on project	...and so on and so on.

Following this approach, we could end up writing a rather large number of web methods! While it's perfectly possible to do that, we might instead consider consolidating some of these operations into web methods with broader functionality:

- Get a list of projects
- Get details for a project
- Add or update a project
- Delete a project
- Get a list of resources
- Get details for a resource
- Add or update a resource
- Delete a resource

This is a smaller list of discrete operations – and by having fewer operations, we have less code to maintain. Moreover, we provide a higher level of abstraction: a consumer has no idea what happens when they request details for a project, and over time we may change how that process works without having any impact on our consumers.

Grouping web methods into web services

Under the .NET Framework, web methods are grouped together within a URL such as http://server/root/projecttracker.asmx, where `projecttracker.asmx` is the page or file that contains our web service. Within a given virtual root on a given web server, there can be any number of such web service pages, each with their own set of web methods.

This, then, is a decision point in our design: should we put all our web methods into a single web service file, or put each web method in its own web service, or something in between? Unfortunately, there is no hard-and-fast rule to guide our decision.

At the time of writing, web services technology is too new for best practices to have evolved, and there are conflicting views that may drive your particular design choices. Are web services an API technology, a messaging technology, a component technology, or an EAI (Enterprise Application Integration) or BPI (Business Process Integration) technology? Web services can be viewed as any one of these, and each has its own set of best practices that guide how to group procedures or functions together. The one you favor will color your decisions in terms of design.

In this context, one way to view a web service is as a component that we happen to be accessing via Internet technologies. A component is a container for similar groupings of functionality (COM or .NET components typically contain a group of related classes), so likewise a web service 'component' should contain a group of related web methods. Of course, we know that all of our functionality is related in some way; the question is whether we should break it up into multiple web services – perhaps one for project-related tasks, and one for resource-related tasks?

However, there's another angle to this question that we need to consider before making our decision, and that's the consumer. Consumers don't reference an entire virtual root; they reference a specific web service (ASMX file). The more granular we make our web services, the more different references the developer of the consumer will need to make in order to use our web methods.

Because of this, I prefer to group related web methods into web services based on the likely usage pattern of consumer developers. Since the web methods will all be related within the context of the Project Tracker application, we're following basic component design concepts; and since we're creating an *interface* to our application, we're also taking into account the needs of the end user (the consumer developer).

For our Project Tracker sample application, this means putting all our web methods into a single web service. They are all related to each other, so they naturally fit into a component. More importantly, it's likely that any consumer will be dealing with both projects and resources, and there's no sense in forcing the consumer developer to establish two separate references to our server just to use our web methods.

Returning our data

The next issue we need to consider is how to return our complex business data. Our data exists in our business objects, but it needs to be returned to the consumer via SOAP-formatted XML.

In many sample web services, the web methods return simple data types such as `Integer` or `String`, but that doesn't match the needs of most applications. In our example, we need to return complex data, such as an array or collection of project data. And the project data itself isn't a simple data type – it consists of multiple data fields.

There are a couple of approaches we might consider:

- Returning the business objects directly
- Defining formal data structures and returning the data via those structures

As we'll see, the more formal approach is superior, but to be thorough, let's discuss the first option too.

Returning business objects directly

It may seem tempting to return a business object (or an array of business objects) as a result of a web method. Why should we go through the work of copying the data from our business object into some formal data structure, just so that data structure can be converted into XML to be returned to the consumer? After all, the .NET web services infrastructure can automatically examine our business class and expose all the `Public` read-write `Property` methods and `Public` variables of our object:

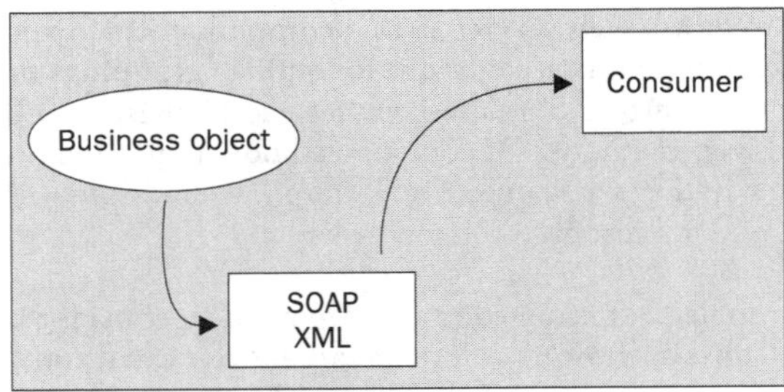

Unfortunately, there are two flaws with this approach that make it untenable. First and most important is the fact that doing this restricts our ability to change, enhance, and maintain our business objects over time. If we expose the business object directly, then the object's interface becomes part of the web service interface. This means the object's interface is part of the contract that we are establishing by publishing the web service. This is almost never acceptable – we need to retain the ability to alter and enhance the interface of our business objects over time without impacting other applications that use our web service.

Secondly, make careful note of the fact that only the `Public`, read-write `Property` methods and `Public` fields are exposed. Non-public properties are not exposed. Read-only properties (such as `ID` on the `Project` and `Resource` objects) are not exposed. Unless we are willing to compromise our object design specifically to accommodate the requirements of web service design, we won't be able to expose the data we choose via web services.

Beyond this, we must also expose a `Public` default constructor on any class exposed directly via web services. If we don't provide a `Public` default constructor, we'll get a run-time exception when attempting to access the web service. The design of CSLA .NET business objects specifically precludes the use of `Public` default constructors, as we always use `Shared` factory methods to create instances of our business objects.

Due to these drawbacks, directly exposing our objects is not a good practice. The answer instead is to create a façade around the business objects that can separate the public interface of our web service from the interface of our business objects. We can construct this façade such that its properties and fields are always available for serialization into XML.

Returning formal data structures

We can easily create a formal data structure to define the external interface of our web service by using a `Structure` or user-defined type. This data structure will define the public interface of our web service, meaning that the web service interface is separate from our business object interface. The web service and this data structure form a façade so that consumers of the web service don't know or care about the specific interface of our business object.

For instance, we can define a `Structure` that describes the data for a project like this:

```
Public Structure ProjectInfo
  Public ID As String
  Public Name As String
  Public Started As String
  Public Ended As String
  Public Description As String
End Structure
```

Then, we can have our project-related web methods return a result of this type – or even an array of results of this type. When this is returned as a result of our web method, its data will be converted into SOAP-formatted XML that's returned to the consumer. What we're talking about doing here is illustrated by the following diagram:

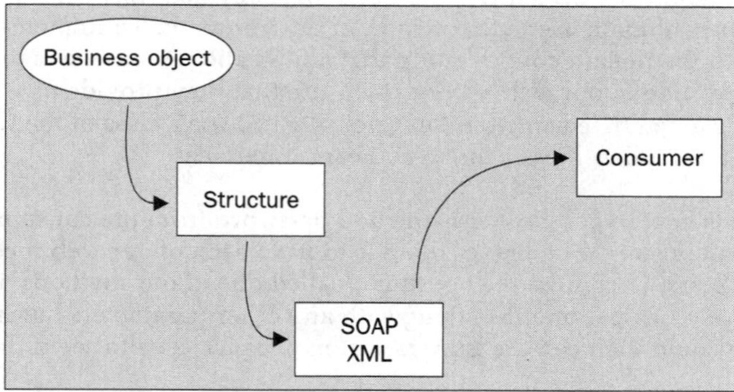

When consumers reference our web service, they'll gain access to the definition of this type via the WSDL data that's associated with the service. This means that the consumer will have information about the data we're returning in a very clear and concise format.

When we come to creating a consumer for the web service, Visual Studio .NET uses this information to create a proxy class that mirrors the data structure. This gives consumer developers the benefits of IntelliSense, so that they can easily understand what data we require or return from our web methods.

Security

The final consideration is security. Of course, there are many types and layers of security, but what we're concerned with here is how to use either CSLA .NET or Windows' integrated security to identify the users and their roles.

Even though the 'user' in this case is a remote application, that application must still identify itself so that we can apply appropriate security-related business rules and processing. In our case, this means that only someone in the `ProjectManager` role can add or edit a project, for example.

Whether the remote consumer uses a hard-coded username and password, or prompts its actual user for credentials, isn't up to us. All we can do is ensure that the consumer provides *our* application with valid credentials.

If we opt to use Windows' integrated security, we'll configure IIS to disallow anonymous access to the virtual root containing our web service ASMX file. We'll also add an `<identity impersonate="true" />` element into the `<system.web>` section of the site's `Web.config` file, so that ASP.NET knows to impersonate the user's account. This will force the consumer to provide valid Windows credentials in order to interact with our web service.

No extra work is required in our code, other than ensuring that the `Web.config` file in our web service application has the `<appSettings>` entry to configure CSLA .NET to use Windows security.

> *Windows' integrated security is probably* not *a viable option in most cases. It is relatively unlikely that unknown clients on unknown platforms will be authenticated within our Windows domain. While our architecture does support this option, using it would mean that consumers must start out with valid Windows domain accounts with which they can authenticate to our server.*

CSLA .NET security requires a bit more work, but avoids any necessity for the remote consumer (or its users) to have Windows domain user accounts in our environment. To implement CSLA .NET security, IIS should be left with the default configuration that allows anonymous users to access our virtual root. We must then include code in our web service to ensure that they provide us with a username and password, which we can validate using the `BusinessPrincipal` class in the CSLA .NET framework – just like we did in the Windows Forms and Web Forms interfaces.

The harder question is how to get the username and password from the consumer, and there are two basic approaches to an answer. The first of these is to have each of our web methods include username and password parameters. Each time the consumer called one of our methods, it would then have to provide values for these two parameters (along with any other parameters our method requires). Within our web method, we could then call the `BusinessPrincipal` class to see if the combination is valid.

While this works, it pollutes the parameter lists of all our methods. Each method ends up with these two extra parameters that really have nothing to do with the method itself. This is far from ideal.

The other approach is to use the SOAP header to pass the information from consumer to server *outside* the context of the method, but as part of the same exchange of data. In other words, the username and password information will piggy-back on the method call, but won't be part of the method call.

This is a standard technique for passing extra information along with method calls. It's supported by the SOAP standard, and therefore by all SOAP-compliant client development tools. What this means is that it's a perfectly acceptable approach – in fact, it's the preferred approach. We'll use it as we develop our sample interface.

Web service implementation

Visual Studio .NET makes the creation of web methods and web services very easy. Of course, the *development* of a web method is all about the business code we write – and that can be quite complex. Fortunately, we already have business objects that implement all the data access and business logic, so our code will be pretty straightforward!

Creating the project

In the existing `ProjectTracker` solution, add a new project using File | Add Project | New Project. Make it an ASP.NET Web Service project, and name it `PTService`:

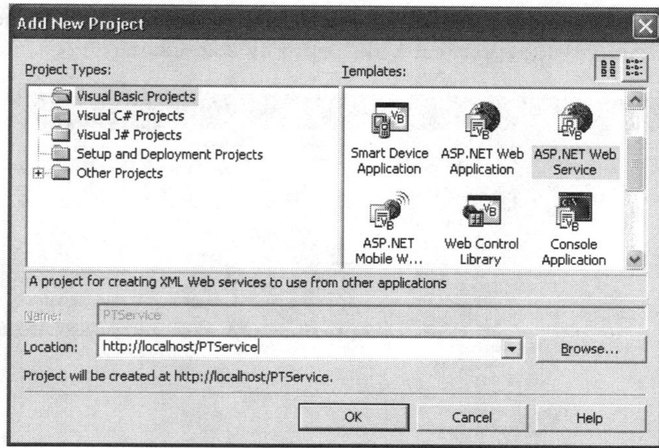

VS.NET will automatically create a new virtual root for our web service application, so any web services that we create will have a URL similar to this:

```
http://server/PTService/myservice.asmx
```

Of course, '*server*' will be the name of your web server, and `myservice.asmx` will be the name of the actual web service file we'll create.

Referencing and importing assemblies

Since our code will be making use of the business objects from Chapter 7, we need to add a reference to the `ProjectTracker.Library` project. That in turn relies on the CSLA .NET framework DLLs, so we'll need to reference those as well by using the **Browse** button, just as we did for the Windows Forms and Web Forms interfaces:

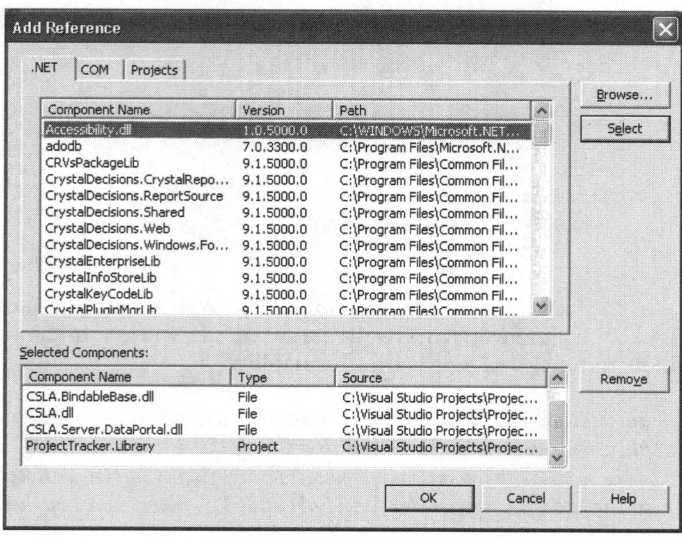

Since we'll be using the `ProjectTracker.Library` classes throughout our code, let's again use the project's properties dialog to add a project-wide `Imports` statement:

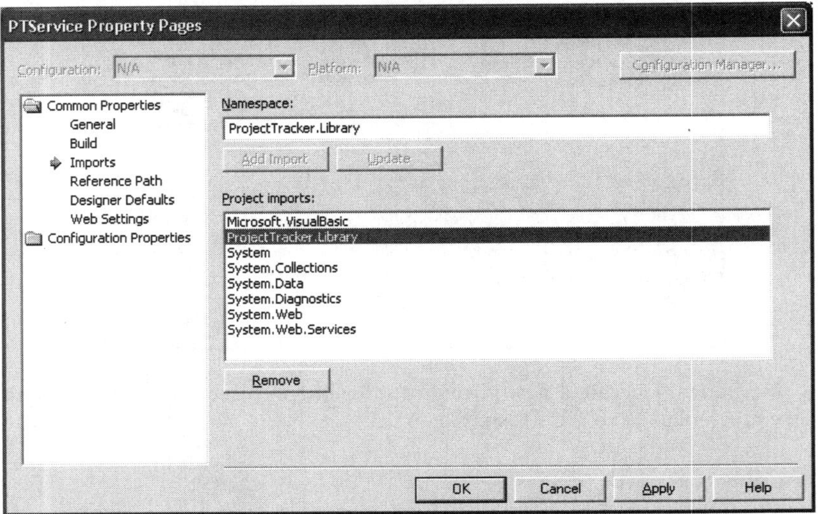

Configuring the application

As with our other interfaces, we need to provide application configuration information through a configuration file. Since a web service is just another type of web application, its configuration file is `Web.config`, and one is automatically added to our project. Open that file and add the following `<appSettings>` block:

```
<?xml version="1.0" encoding="utf-8" ?>
<configuration>

  <appSettings>
    <add key="Authentication" value="CSLA" />
    <add key="DB:Security"
         value="data source=server;initial catalog=Security;
                integrated security=SSPI" />
    <add key="DB:PTracker"
         value="data source=server;initial catalog=PTracker;
                integrated security=SSPI" />
  </appSettings>
```

Note that this is *exactly* the same as our configuration for the Web Forms interface. Again, we've configured the CSLA .NET framework so that the `DataPortal` will run in the same process as our web service code, providing optimal performance and scalability.

> *As with any web application, your security environment may dictate that the data access must be handled by an application server behind a second firewall. If this is the case, change this configuration to be the same as the* Windows *Forms interface from Chapter 8. Keep in mind that doing this will result in a performance reduction of about 50% – a cost that's often paid to gain increased security.*

Since web services don't typically use the concept of a `Session`, we should turn that off as well. This is an entry in the `<system.web>` section of `Web.config`:

```
<sessionState
   mode="Off"
   stateConnectionString="tcpip=127.0.0.1:42424"
   sqlConnectionString="data source=127.0.0.1;Trusted_Connection=yes"
   cookieless="false"
   timeout="20"
/>
```

This reduces the amount of overhead for the application because it doesn't have to worry about `Session` objects that we won't be using anyway.

Creating the web service

VS.NET starts us with a default web service file named `Service1.asmx`. Remove it now, and use Project | Add Web Service to add a new web service named `ProjectTracker`:

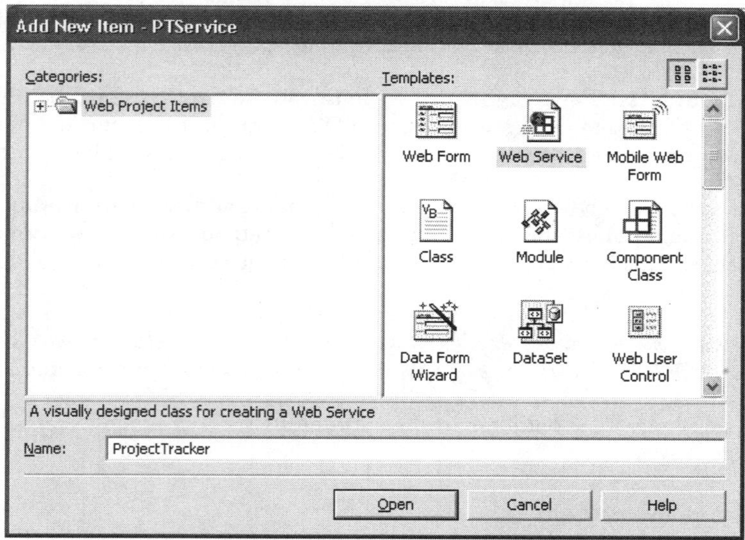

We'll be writing all our code in this new file.

> *While it's technically possible to rename `Service1.asmx` to `ProjectTracker.asmx`, and then to do a mass substitution of `Service1` for `ProjectTracker` within the pre-built code, it's often simpler just to delete the default file and create a new one with the right name.*

Web services exist in a 'namespace' that's fairly similar to the .NET concept of the same name. For web services, however, the namespaces are global on the Internet, and they are typically identified by our organization's domain name. By default, web services created in VS.NET are configured to use a diagnostic namespace, and we should change this to a namespace that's appropriate to our organization.

This is done by opening the code window for ProjectTracker.asmx and changing the Namespace value in the <WebService()> attribute. For instance:

```
<System.Web.Services.WebService( _
   Namespace:="http://ws.lhotka.net/PTService/ProjectTracker")> _
Public Class ProjectTracker
  Inherits System.Web.Services.WebService
```

Notice that the domain name of the namespace is now a meaningful value that corresponds to a specific organization. You should use your organization's domain here instead of ws.lhotka.net.

Handling security on the server

Notice that our <appSettings> configuration includes the line:

```
<add key="Authentication" value="CSLA" />
```

So we're using our table-based CSLA .NET security model.

> *We could also use the Windows' integrated security model, as described above. However, if we decide to go down that route, we* must not *implement the security code we're about to create.*

When we use the CSLA .NET security model, we must call the Login() method of the BusinessPrincipal class to authenticate the user. This requires username and password values, which means that we need to get those values from the consumer that's calling our web service.

As we discussed earlier, we could do this by putting username and password parameters on all our web methods, but that would pollute the parameter lists of our methods. Instead, we can use a SOAP header to transfer the values. This is a standard SOAP concept, and it's easily implemented in our .NET code (on both the server and consumer).

> *Note that the username and password will be passed in clear text in the SOAP envelope. You may want to use the .NET Framework's cryptography support to encrypt this data for additional security.*

Before we write this code, we should import the appropriate security namespaces into our code for ProjectTracker.asmx:

```
Imports System.Web.Services
Imports System.Web.Services.Protocols
Imports CSLA.Security
```

The System.Web.Services.Protocols namespace includes functionality that we'll need in order to implement SOAP header that contains the username and password values. The CSLA.Security namespace includes the BusinessPrincipal class that we'll use to authenticate the user.

There are three steps required in order to set up and use the SOAP header for our security credentials:

- Implement a SoapHeader class that defines the data we require from the consumer
- Implement a method that takes the username and password values, and uses them to authenticate the user and set up the principal object on the current thread.

- Apply a `<SoapHeader()>` attribute to *all* our web methods as we write them, indicating that the web method requires our particular SOAP header

We'll follow these steps as we create the rest of our code.

Creating the SoapHeader class

`SoapHeader` is just a class that defines some fields of data that are to be included in the XML header data of a SOAP message that we talked about earlier. In our case, we need two values – username and password – to be passed in the SOAP header along with every method call. Our `SoapHeader` class will clearly define this requirement. In the `ProjectTracker` class, add the following code:

```
#Region " Security "

  Public Class CSLACredentials
    Inherits SoapHeader

    Public Username As String
    Public Password As String
  End Class

  Public Credentials As New CSLACredentials

#End Region
```

Note that this code is *inside* the existing `ProjectTracker` web service class; we are creating a nested class named `CSLACredentials`. By nesting it within our web service class, we ensure that it is properly exposed to the consumers via our WSDL definition.

The class itself is very simple – it just defines the two data fields we require:

```
Public Username As String
Public Password As String
```

More important is the fact that it inherits from `SoapHeader`:

```
Inherits SoapHeader
```

Not surprisingly, it's this line that turns our class into a `SoapHeader`. It means that its values will be automatically populated by the .NET runtime, based on the data in the SOAP header that's provided as part of each method call.

The `CSLACredentials` class is also `Public` in scope, so it will be included as part of our web service definition in our WSDL. This means that any consumers that reference our web service will have full access to the type information that we've defined here, so they will clearly see that we require username and password values.

If we're creating the consumer with VS.NET, it will automatically create a consumer-side proxy class for `CSLACredentials`*, dramatically simplifying the process of providing the data. We'll see an example of this later in the chapter.*

We also declare a variable based on this class:

```
Public Credentials As New CSLACredentials
```

This step is required, as it will be into this object that the actual data values are placed. There's no magic here – we'll just use the `<SoapHeader()>` attribute on each method call to indicate that the SOAP header data should be loaded into this object.

Using the <SoapHeader()> attribute

Now that we've defined a `SoapHeader` class, any consumer that references our web service will have a clearly defined structure into which it can place username and password values. By default, web methods don't require SOAP headers, but we can use the `<SoapHeader()>` attribute on a web method to indicate that it does. This attribute accepts a parameter that we can use to link the SOAP header to a specific `SoapHeader` object in our code – in this case, to the `Credentials` object that we declared to be of type `CSLACredentials`.

This means that our web methods will be declared like this:

```
<WebMethod(Description:="A sample method"), SoapHeader("Credentials")> _
Public Sub SampleMethod()

End Sub
```

When this method is invoked by a consumer, the .NET runtime uses reflection to find a variable within our code called `Credentials`. It then uses reflection against that `Credentials` variable to discover its type. Based on that type information, it looks at the SOAP header data to find the SOAP header that matches that type, and takes the appropriate data out of the SOAP header.

This SOAP XML might look something like this (with our header highlighted):

```
POST /PTservice/projecttracker.asmx HTTP/1.1
Host: localhost
Content-Type: text/xml; charset=utf-8
Content-Length: length
SOAPAction: "http://ws.lhotka.net/PTService/ProjectTracker/GetResourceList"

<?xml version="1.0" encoding="utf-8"?>
<soap:Envelope xmlns:xsi="http://www.w3.org/2001/XMLSchema-instance"
xmlns:xsd="http://www.w3.org/2001/XMLSchema"
xmlns:soap="http://schemas.xmlsoap.org/soap/envelope/">
  <soap:Header>
    <CSLACredentials xmlns="http://ws.lhotka.net/PTService/ProjectTracker">
      <Username>string</Username>
      <Password>string</Password>
    </CSLACredentials>
  </soap:Header>
  <soap:Body>
    <GetResourceList xmlns="http://ws.lhotka.net/PTService/ProjectTracker" />
  </soap:Body>
</soap:Envelope>
```

That data is loaded into our `Credentials` object, and then the web method itself is called.

> **Note that the `<SoapHeader()>` attribute indicates a *required* SOAP header, so our method can *only* be called by a consumer that provides this information.**

This means that by the time our web method code is running, the `Credentials` object will be loaded with the username and password values provided by the consumer, via the SOAP header.

Implementing a Login method

Now that we have a way of requiring the consumer to provide a username and a password, and of making those values automatically available to our code, we can move on to implement a method to authenticate the user based on those values.

As part of this process, the current thread's principal object will be set to a valid `BusinessPrincipal` object, meaning that our business objects, the CSLA .NET framework objects, and our web service code can all use standard .NET security code to check whether the user was authenticated, and to determine the user's roles.

Since each method will need to perform this login step, we'll create a single method within the `ProjectTracker` class to take care of the details. Then, our web methods can just call this one method to do the work. Add the following method within the *Security* region in our code:

```
Public Sub Login()

  If Len(Credentials.Username) = 0 Then
    Throw New System.Security.SecurityException( _
      "Valid credentials not provided")
  End If

  With Credentials
    BusinessPrincipal.Login(.Username, .Password)
  End With

  Dim principal As System.Security.Principal.IPrincipal = _
   Threading.Thread.CurrentPrincipal

  If Not principal.Identity.IsAuthenticated Then

    ' The user is not valid, raise an exception
    Throw New Exception("Invalid user or password")
  End If

End Sub
```

Since the `Credentials` object is automatically populated by the .NET runtime, we can simply write code to use it. First, we check to make sure the consumer provided us with a username that actually contains data. If we get past that check, we just call the `Login()` method of our `BusinessPrincipal` class.

`BusinessPrincipal.Login()` attempts to authenticate the username and password against our security database, and creates a `BusinessPrincipal` object that reflects the success or failure of that effort. That object is automatically set to be the thread's current principal object, so all our code has easy access to the information using standard .NET security coding techniques.

Once this is done, we ensure that the user was successfully authenticated:

```
Dim principal As System.Security.Principal.IPrincipal = _
   Threading.Thread.CurrentPrincipal

If Not principal.Identity.IsAuthenticated Then

  ' The user is not valid, raise an exception
  Throw New Exception("Invalid user or password")
End If
```

If the user credentials weren't valid, we raise an exception that's automatically returned to the consumer by the .NET runtime. Thanks to this, the consumer will know that their method call failed due to a security violation.

All of this work ensures that only valid, authenticated users gain access to our web methods, provided that those methods have the following structure:

```
<WebMethod(Description:="A sample method"), SoapHeader("Credentials")> _
Public Sub SampleMethod()

  Login()

  ' Web method implementation code goes here
End Sub
```

Now we can move on to defining the data structures and implementing the web methods that form the contract we're making with our consumers.

Defining data structures

Earlier in the chapter, we discussed the dangers involved in exposing business objects directly via web services, and decided that we are best served by creating clearly defined data structures that are independent of our actual business objects. These structures will be exposed to consumers, forming a large part of the contract that we agree to uphold once our web service has been published.

If we define these `Structure` types with `Public` scope within our `ProjectTracker` class, they will automatically become part of our web service definition (as defined in the WSDL), so consumers have easy access to the descriptions of the structures. Add the following to the `ProjectTracker` class:

```
#Region " Data Structures "

  Public Structure ProjectInfo
    Public ID As String
    Public Name As String
```

```
    Public Started As String
    Public Ended As String
    Public Description As String
    Public Resources() As ProjectResourceInfo
  End Structure

  Public Structure ProjectResourceInfo
    Public ResourceID As String
    Public FirstName As String
    Public LastName As String
    Public Assigned As String
    Public Role As String
  End Structure

  Public Structure ResourceInfo
    Public ID As String
    Public Name As String
    Public Assignments() As ResourceAssignmentInfo
  End Structure

  Public Structure ResourceAssignmentInfo
    Public ProjectID As String
    Public Name As String
    Public Assigned As String
    Public Role As String
  End Structure

#End Region
```

For the most part, these `Structure` types mirror our business objects, and you might think that this is not particularly surprising. The real benefit here, however, is that our business objects can change over time without risk of breaking these data structures. We might add new values to `Project` or `Resource` as our application's requirements change over time, but our web service interface can remain consistent.

> **The reality is that we'll probably need to update our web service interface over time as well, but this split allows us to keep application updates and web service updates largely independent of one another.**

The `ProjectInfo` data structure defines the basic data for a project, including an array containing data about the resources assigned to the project. The `ResourceInfo` data structure provides similar information for a resource.

Notice that the data here is all of type `String`. This is not required – the web services infrastructure supports many common data types, including `Integer`, `Date`, and so forth – but in our case we're supporting the concept of a blank date value, and a `String` allows us to represent this more readily than a `Date` value could. We also have the project ID values, which are internally of type `Guid`. Not all client platforms have native support for a GUID data type, so it's better to leave them as type `String` too.

Even if we do *set up our variables to use* `Date` *or* `Guid` *data types, remember that the data is ultimately converted into XML text anyway. All we're doing here is dictating the way .NET converts the text data into and out of our local variables.*

When we turn to look at the `ProjectResourceInfo` data structure, we see that it includes both read-only and read-write data fields. Remember that some of the fields in our `ProjectResource` object are read-only because they are 'borrowed' from the `Resource` object – in reality, only the `Role` field can be changed.

For better or worse, we have no way of conveying this sort of information to consumers. The SOAP standard is not expressive enough to allow us to define some things as read-only, and others as read-write. All we can do is provide data in a generic form for consumers to use as they see fit.

What this means is that documentation is important. It's not enough simply to publish a web service and expect the WSDL to be a sufficient documentation tool. WSDL contains a lot of valuable information, but it doesn't replace human-readable documentation describing other requirements or restrictions on our data.

WSDL doesn't convey semantic information about the meaning of data, either. Though we don't have anything in our sample application that's semantically complex, most business applications do. If we expose a `ProductID` *field, what is the* meaning *of that field? Is it a simple ID, or is it one in which the first two characters indicate one thing, the next four indicate another thing, and the digits at the end indicate something else? None of these subtleties is part of WSDL, which means that we need to provide good documentation for the users of our web services.*

By defining these data structures, we've clarified half of the contract we're creating with consumers. The rest of the interface comes in the form of our web methods themselves. The name of each web method, its parameter list, and its return values comprise the remainder of the interface we're creating, so let's move on to create them.

Get a project list

.NET makes the creation of a basic web method very easy: you simply apply the `<WebMethod()>` attribute to a method in a web service, and you're all set. The trickier part is implementing the logic *within* the web method.

Fortunately for us, our business objects do most of the work. All we need to do is take the data from our business objects, and put it into the data structures we've defined as part of our web service's interface – or vice versa.

For instance, let's look at what is probably the simplest case: retrieval of a list of projects. We already have a `ProjectList` business object that retrieves basic project information. Using that object, we can just loop through each project to populate our `ProjectInfo` data structure. Since this is our first web method, we'll walk through it in some detail:

```
#Region " Projects "

  <WebMethod(Description:="Get list of projects"), SoapHeader("Credentials")> _
  Public Function GetProjectList() As ProjectInfo()

    Login()
```

```
    Dim list As ProjectList = ProjectList.GetProjectList()
    Dim info(list.Count - 1) As ProjectInfo
    Dim project As ProjectList.ProjectInfo
    Dim index As Integer

    For Each project In list
      With info(index)

        ' ProjectList only returns 2 of our data fields
        .ID = project.ID.ToString
        .Name = project.Name
      End With
      index += 1
    Next

    Return info

  End Function

#End Region
```

Here we have the standard declaration of a web method, which includes our `<SoapHeader()>` attribute so that we get security credentials:

```
<WebMethod(Description:="Get list of projects"), SoapHeader("Credentials")> _
Public Function GetProjectList() As ProjectInfo()
```

Notice that the return type from the method is an array of `ProjectInfo` data structures. From our perspective as web service authors, this is very simple, readable code. It is also easily understood by development tools that might be used to create a consumer.

Next, the `Login()` method is called to authenticate the user and get a valid `BusinessPrincipal` object into our thread's current principal slot:

```
Login()
```

Once we're past this call, we know that the user has been successfully authenticated, so we can move on to do our work. If the authentication process fails, it throws an exception, which is automatically returned to the consumer by the .NET runtime.

We don't need to include code to check the user's role (which affects their ability to perform certain operations) because our business objects already perform those checks. In our Windows Forms and Web Forms interfaces, we checked those roles to enable or disable various UI components. With a web services interface, all we can do is throw an exception in the case of failure – and our business objects already have that functionality implemented.

After logging in, we retrieve a `ProjectList` object:

```
Dim list As ProjectList = ProjectList.GetProjectList()
```

Then we can use the information from this collection object to dimension and populate our array of `ProjectInfo` data structures:

```
Dim info(list.Count - 1) As ProjectInfo
Dim project As ProjectList.ProjectInfo
Dim index As Integer

For Each project In list
  With info(index)

    ' ProjectList only returns 2 of our data fields
    .ID = project.ID.ToString
    .Name = project.Name
  End With
  index += 1
Next
```

This is simply a matter of copying the values from each element in the `ProjectList` collection into an element in our array. Once the values have been copied, we simply return the array as a result:

```
Return info
```

Even if our business objects change over time, we can preserve the web service interface just by updating the code here to accommodate the new business object or model. Any consumers will continue to get a consistent, predictable result.

Get a project

Almost as a variation on the theme, we can provide a web method that returns detailed information about a specific project, based on the ID value. This is no more complex, because we're still just copying data from business objects into data structures. In this case, we can return all the data about a project, since we have a full-blown `Project` object rather than the lighter-weight data from the `ProjectList` object:

```
<WebMethod(Description:="Get detailed data for a specific project"), _
 SoapHeader("Credentials")> _
Public Function GetProject(ByVal ID As String) As ProjectInfo

  Login()

  Dim info As ProjectInfo
  Dim project As Project = project.GetProject(New Guid(ID))

  With info
    .ID = project.ID.ToString
    .Name = project.Name
    .Started = project.Started
    .Ended = project.Ended
    .Description = project.Description

    ' Load child objects
```

```
      ReDim .Resources(project.Resources.Count - 1)
      Dim idx As Integer
      For idx = 0 To project.Resources.Count - 1
        .Resources(idx).ResourceID = project.Resources(idx).ResourceID
        .Resources(idx).FirstName = project.Resources(idx).FirstName
        .Resources(idx).LastName = project.Resources(idx).LastName
        .Resources(idx).Assigned = project.Resources(idx).Assigned
        .Resources(idx).Role = project.Resources(idx).Role
      Next
    End With

    Return info

  End Function
```

Here, we retrieve the requested `Project` object based on its ID value:

```
Dim project As Project = project.GetProject(New Guid(ID))
```

Again, all the hard work is done in a single line of code – all we do now is copy the values from the populated business object into the data structure:

```
With info
  .ID = project.ID.ToString
  .Name = project.Name
  .Started = project.Started
  .Ended = project.Ended
  .Description = project.Description
```

Because the business object and the data structure have clearly defined elements, we get full IntelliSense support while typing the code, and the result is very clear, readable, and thus maintainable.

What makes the function more interesting is that we're loading not only the basic information, but also an array with all the resources that are assigned to the project. To get the array to the right size, we use a `ReDim` statement:

```
  ' Load child objects
  ReDim .Resources(project.Resources.Count - 1)
```

After that, it's just a matter of looping through all the items in the business collection, copying the data from each into an element of the array:

```
  Dim idx As Integer
  For idx = 0 To project.Resources.Count - 1
    .Resources(idx).ResourceID = project.Resources(idx).ResourceID
    .Resources(idx).FirstName = project.Resources(idx).FirstName
    .Resources(idx).LastName = project.Resources(idx).LastName
    .Resources(idx).Assigned = project.Resources(idx).Assigned
    .Resources(idx).Role = project.Resources(idx).Role
  Next
```

Again, the code is quite readable because the data structure and the business object have clearly defined properties.

Add or update a project

The two web methods that we've implemented so far merely retrieve data. However, there's nothing stopping us from providing a web method that allows a consumer to add or update project data. All we need to do is accept a `ProjectInfo` data structure as a parameter, copy its values into a `Project` object, and ask the object to save itself.

Since the business object already contains all our business logic – including validation logic – the only thing we need to figure out is whether the project is to be added or updated. We can do this by checking to see if the consumer passed us an ID value for the project. If they did, we'll assume that they mean to update a project; otherwise, it will be considered to be an add operation. Here's the complete code:

```
<WebMethod(Description:="Add or update project"), SoapHeader("Credentials")> _
Public Function UpdateProject(ByVal Data As ProjectInfo) As String

  Login()

  Dim project As Project
  If Len(Data.ID) = 0 Then

    ' No ID so this is a new project
    project = project.NewProject()
  Else

    ' They provided an ID so we are updating a project
    project = project.GetProject(New Guid(Data.ID))
  End If

  With project
    .Name = Data.Name
    .Started = Data.Started
    .Ended = Data.Ended
    .Description = Data.Description

    ' Load child objects
    Dim idx As Integer
    For idx = 0 To UBound(Data.Resources)
      If .Resources.Contains(Data.Resources(idx).ResourceID) Then

        ' Update existing resource
        ' Of course only the Role field can be changed...
        .Resources(idx).Role = Data.Resources(idx).Role
      Else

        ' Just add new resource
        .Resources.Assign( _
           Data.Resources(idx).ResourceID, Data.Resources(idx).Role)
      End If
    Next
  End With
```

```
    project = project.Save
    Return project.ID.ToString

  End Function
```

The first thing we do is to decide whether they're adding or updating a project:

```
    Dim project As Project
    If Len(Data.ID) = 0 Then

     ' No id so this is a new project
      project = project.NewProject()
    Else

      ' They provided an ID so we are updating a project
      project = project.GetProject(New Guid(Data.ID))
    End If
```

If we're provided with an ID value, we use it to retrieve the existing `Project` object. Otherwise, we create a new `Project` object (automatically preloaded with any default values, of course).

Then, we simply copy the values from the `ProjectInfo` data structure into the business object – including any resource assignments. That's a little tricky, because we need to determine if a particular resource assignment is new, or the user just wants to change the `Role` property of an existing one. Fortunately, we implemented a `Contains()` method on our `ProjectResources` collection object, so it's easy to determine whether a specific resource has already been assigned to the project:

```
        If .Resources.Contains(Data.Resources(idx).ResourceID) Then
```

If our collection already contains the resource, we simply update the `Role` property. If not, we call the `Assign()` method to assign the resource to the project.

Once all the data fields have been copied from the data structure into our business objects, we just call the `Save()` method to update the database:

```
    project = project.Save
```

The nice thing about the use of business objects in this case is that we don't need to worry about enforcing business rules, validation, or security. These rules and any other business processing are handled by the objects, and are therefore totally consistent across our Windows Forms, Web Forms, and web services interfaces.

If the consumer attempts to do anything invalid, our business objects will detect that, and throw an exception. The exception is returned to the consumer so that they know their action was invalid.

Delete a project

The only other major operation that we should support is the ability to remove a project from the system. As with our other web methods, this is easily accomplished through the use of our business objects. In fact, for a delete operation, it's just one line of code:

```
<WebMethod(Description:="Remove a project from the system"), _
 SoapHeader("Credentials")> _
Public Sub DeleteProject(ByVal ProjectID As String)

  Login()

  Project.DeleteProject(New Guid(ProjectID))
End Sub
```

All security checks are handled by the business object code, so we can simply call the `DeleteProject()` method and let the magic happen.

Resource web services

There's a corresponding set of four web methods to deal with resources as well. The `GetResourceList()`, `GetResource()`, and `DeleteResource()` methods are virtually identical to the code we've just seen, so we won't go through them here. The code for those methods is included in the code download for this book.

There are some slight differences in the `UpdateResource()` method, however, because the ID value for a resource is not a GUID, but a user-supplied value. Because of this, in `UpdateResource()` we need to use a different strategy for determining whether we are adding or updating a `Resource` object.

Rather than checking for a blank ID value, we *always* require an ID value. To find out if that corresponds to an existing `Resource` object, we attempt to load the object. If there's no corresponding `Resource` object, we'll get an exception, which we can catch:

```
Dim Resource As Resource
Try
  Resource = Resource.GetResource(Data.ID)
Catch ex As Exception

  ' Failed to retrieve resource, so this must be new
  Resource = Resource.NewResource(Data.ID)
End Try
```

If an error occurs, we simply create a new, empty `Resource` object (which will automatically be loaded with default values by our business logic).

From this point forward, the functionality is virtually identical to what we saw in `UpdateProject()`. We simply copy the data from the data structure into the `Resource` object, and then call its `Save()` method to update the database. The object contains the code to do an insert or update operation, as appropriate.

At this point, our web service is complete. We have a set of web methods that allow any consumer using SOAP to interact with our application's business logic and data. These consumers may be running on any hardware platform or OS, and may be written in virtually any programming language – we can't know and don't care. What we do know is that they are interacting with our data *through* our business logic, including validation and security, making it difficult for a consumer to misuse our data or functionality.

Web service consumer implementation

The thing about creating web services is that it's not a very satisfying experience. There's nothing to see – no visual reinforcement that we've accomplished anything. Fortunately, ASP.NET includes functionality to generate a test page for web services automatically.

We can simply use the browser to navigate to the ASMX file. Enter http://*server*/PTService/ProjectTracker.asmx into the address box, for example, and you'll get an informational display about the web service and its capabilities:

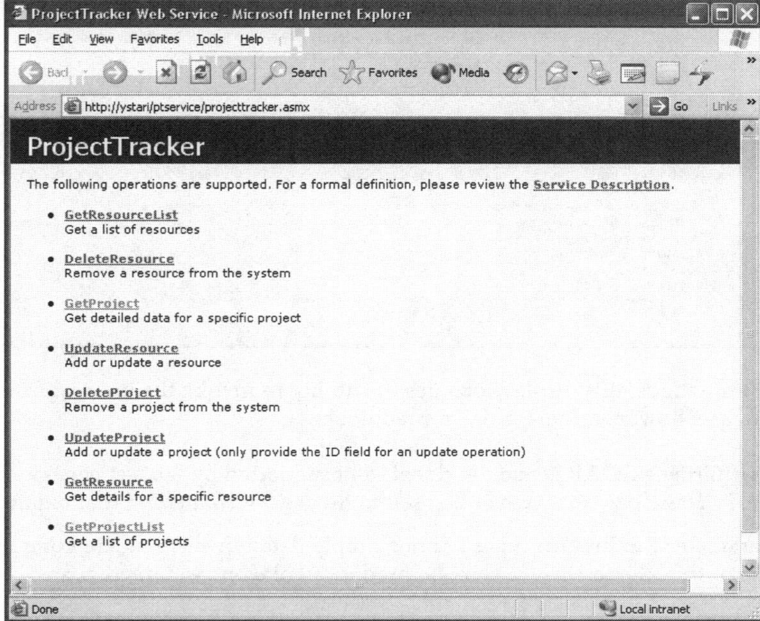

If we then click on one of the links for a web method, we'll get details about that method. For instance, clicking on the `GetResourceList()` method brings up a display similar to the one overleaf:

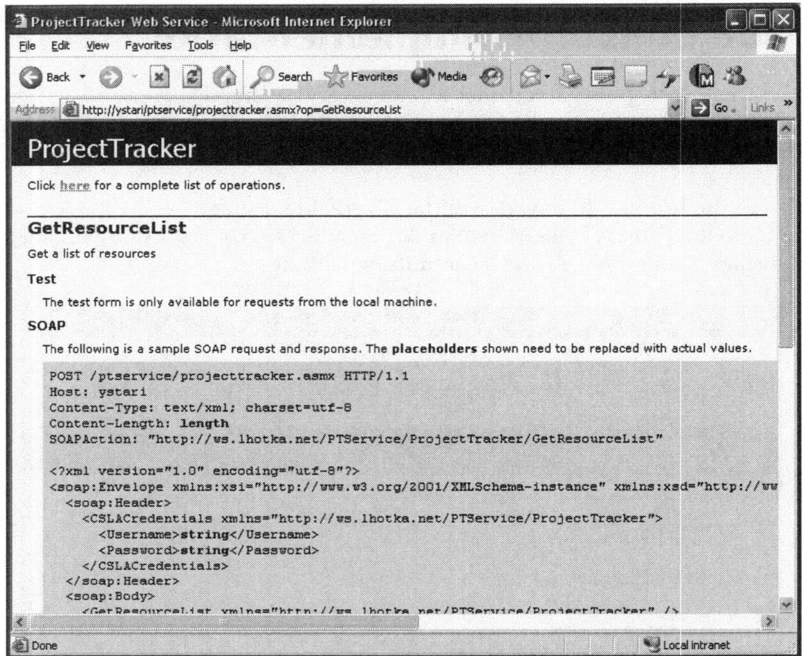

With simple web methods, this display includes the ability to invoke the method from within the browser. In our case, however, there are two roadblocks:

- We're requiring a SOAP header, and that's not supported by the test pages generated by ASP.NET. These pages can never be used to invoke a web method that requires a SOAP header.
- Our parameters and return types are not simple data types – they are complex structures. Because of this, the test pages can't be used to invoke our web methods.

What this means is that in order to test our web service, or to get any visual feedback that our methods work, we need to create a test application. We'll use VS.NET to create this test application, so it will be very easy to do. However, there's nothing to prevent the creation of similar applications using other tools on other hardware platforms or operating systems.

Creating the project

Open a new project in a new solution – make it a Windows Application, and call it `PTClient`. We'll keep this very simple, since all we're trying to do is illustrate that we can write code to call each of our methods and have them work as planned.

The first thing we need to do is add a web reference so that we can make use of our `ProjectTracker` service. Choose **Project | Add Web Reference** to bring up the Add Web Reference dialog. Navigate to our web service, either by using the links in the dialog display, or by entering the URL directly into the URL text box:

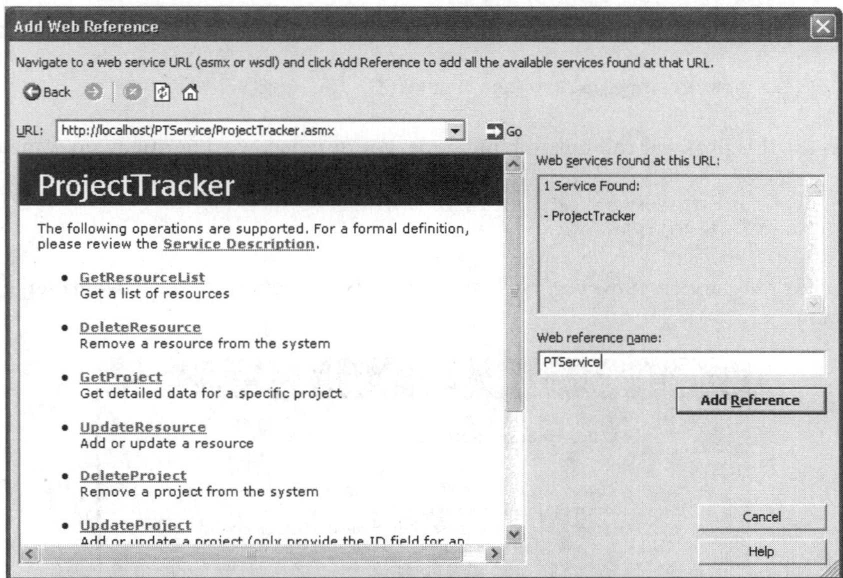

Notice that we've changed the **Web reference name** field here to `PTService`. This defaults to the name of the web server that's hosting the service, but that's typically not very descriptive or meaningful. Web servers can host many web services, so it's better to provide a more memorable name.

When we click the **Add Reference** button, VS.NET will add a reference to the web service. What then goes on behind the scenes is fairly extensive. VS.NET uses the WSDL description for our web service to determine all the types it exposes – including `CSLACredentials`, `ProjectInfo`, and our other data structures; and the `ProjectTracker` class that contains our web methods. VS.NET uses this information to create consumer-side proxy classes for all these types, so we can use them in our consumer code as though they were local classes.

> *Note that all of these types – including the `Structures` – become classes. A web services consumer has no way of knowing what is or isn't an object on the server. For all the consumer knows, the web service is written entirely in classic ASP, and hasn't got a class or an object anywhere. In the end, it really doesn't matter.*

Handling security on the consumer

Now that the web reference has been set up, we can move on to code our test consumer. Essentially, calling a web service from within VB.NET is easy – almost trivial, in fact. However, in our case we've added a bit of a wrinkle, because our web methods require a custom SOAP header: a `CSLACredentials` object.

As you'd expect, .NET fully supports this concept. We've already seen the server-side support, and there's also consumer-side support that makes the use of SOAP headers relatively painless.

When we want to call a web service, we create an instance of the consumer-side proxy object that represents it. In the case of our sample application, the proxy is called `PTService.ProjectTracker`.

The following line of code creates an instance of the proxy:

```
Dim svc As New PTService.ProjectTracker()
```

And we then use this proxy to call our web methods. For instance, we'd normally do something like this:

```
Dim proj() As PTService.ProjectInfo
proj = svc.GetProjectList()
```

If we try this for our service, however, we'll get a security exception, because we haven't provided the SOAP header:

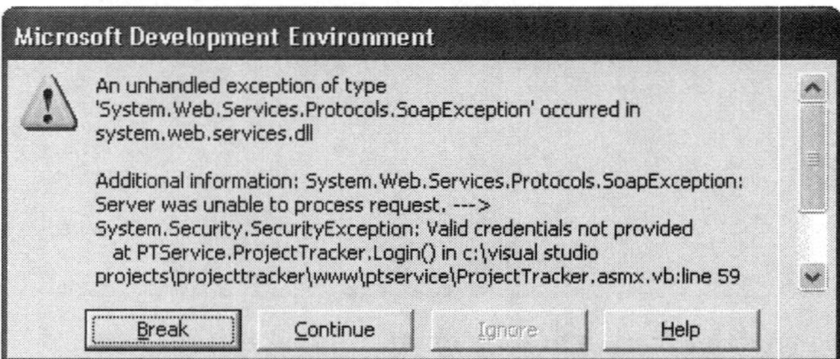

To supply a SOAP header, we need to create an instance of the `SoapHeader` class – in our case, `CSLACredentials` – and then attach that object to the consumer-side proxy for our web service. For instance:

```
' Create the security credentials
Dim cred As New PTService.CSLACredentials()
cred.Username = "rocky"
cred.Password = "lhotka"

' Provide the credentials to the service proxy
svc.CSLACredentialsValue = cred
```

Because the `CSLACredentials` class was exposed by our web service, VS.NET automatically created a consumer-side proxy class for it that we can use to create and populate a `CSLACredentials` object. The WSDL definition for our web service also indicated that we have web methods that require this as a SOAP header, so VS.NET automatically added a `CSLACredentialsValue` property to our consumer-side proxy. To pass a `CSLACredentials` object to the server as a SOAP header, all we need to do is set this `CSLACredentialsValue` property!

Despite all of Visual Studio .NET's assistance, this is quite a lot of code to write each time we want to call a web method. We can encapsulate it into a single method that creates the consumer-side proxy and configures it appropriately. To make this a bit more efficient, we'll also cache the consumer-side proxy object so that it's only created on the first call.

Open the code window for `Form1`, and add the following code within the form:

```
#Region " Security "

  Private mService As PTService.ProjectTracker
  Private Function WebService() As PTService.ProjectTracker

    If mService Is Nothing Then

      ' Create the web service proxy
      mService = New PTService.ProjectTracker()

      ' Create the security credentials
      Dim cred As New PTService.CSLACredentials()
      cred.Username = "rocky"
      cred.Password = "lhotka"

      ' Provide the credentials to the service proxy
      mService.CSLACredentialsValue = cred

      ' Return the service proxy for use
      Return mService
    Else

      ' We had a cached proxy - return it
      Return mService
    End If

  End Function

#End Region
```

First, we see if we already have a consumer-side proxy object:

```
    If mService Is Nothing Then
```

If we don't already have one, then we create it, create a `CSLACredentials` object, link the two and return the fully configured consumer-side proxy object as a result:

```
      ' Create the web service proxy
      mService = New PTService.ProjectTracker()

      ' Create the security credentials
      Dim cred As New PTService.CSLACredentials()
      cred.Username = "rocky"
      cred.Password = "lhotka"

      ' Provide the credentials to the service proxy
      mService.CSLACredentialsValue = cred

      ' Return the service proxy for use
      Return mService
```

On the other hand, if we *did* already have a consumer-side proxy, we simply return that pre-existing value:

```
Else

  ' We had a cached proxy - return it
  Return mService
End If
```

Now our code can simply call the `WebService()` method any time that it needs a reference to the web service – all the details of security and SOAP headers are nicely encapsulated.

Calling web services

Since we've already taken care of the SOAP header details, calling methods on our web service is pretty straightforward.

To see how this works, add a button named `btnGetProject` to the form, and then double-click it to bring up the code window. Enter this code:

```
Private Sub btnGetProject_Click(ByVal sender As System.Object, _
   ByVal e As System.EventArgs) Handles btnGetProject.Click

  Dim proj() As PTService.ProjectInfo
  proj = WebService().GetProjectList()
  MsgBox(UBound(proj))

End Sub
```

This code retrieves a list of project data from the server, and then brings up a message box to display the number of projects retrieved. First, we declare an array of type `ProjectInfo` to store the results:

```
Dim proj() As PTService.ProjectInfo
```

Since the `ProjectInfo` data structure was exposed as `Public` in our web service, its definition was included in the WSDL. When we added the web reference, VS.NET automatically created a proxy class that mirrors the server-side structure, so we can just use that pre-built proxy here.

We then invoke the web method to retrieve the array of project data:

```
proj = WebService().GetProjectList()
```

We use the `WebService()` method we created earlier, so all the SOAP header and security credentials are handled transparently. The result is an array of `ProjectInfo` objects, populated with the data returned from the server.

In the code download for this book, the `PTClient` application includes examples of calling all the other web methods in our `ProjectTracker` web service. Obviously, this is done just for testing – a real consumer would presumably be doing other business operations, and would need access to our project or resource data within that context.

Conclusion

Web services are an exciting and powerful technology. By using a distributed, object-oriented model for our application, we can tap into this new technology and still reuse our existing business objects, logic, and data.

In this chapter, we discussed a way of viewing web services technology as a useful tool in creating an interface to our business objects. This is just another type of interface, on a level with a Windows Forms or Web Forms interface, but instead of being targeted directly at the end user, a web services interface is targeted at other applications.

We also discussed the fact that a web service interface, once published, must be viewed as an immutable contract between us and an unknown and unpredictable number of consumers. Any change to our web method names, parameters, or return types will break consumers. This is complicated when we're dealing with complex data types, because our contract then extends beyond the methods to include the layout of the data we are sending and receiving.

An easy way to define the data layouts for complex data is to use user-defined types, or `Structure` types. These are easy to create, easy to read, and are automatically exposed as part of our web service. This means that consumers can easily determine the data layouts, based on the WSDL definition for our service.

Using all these concepts, coupled with a custom SOAP header to handle security, we implemented a web service containing web methods that expose all the functionality of our business system. Because all of our business logic, including validation and security, is in our business objects, the web methods themselves contain relatively little code.

In Chapter 11, we'll close the book by discussing some ways to do reporting and batch processing operations in a distributed, object-oriented environment.

CHAPTER 11

11

Reporting and batch processing

To this point in the book – and although you may not have realized it – our focus has been around **online transaction processing** (**OLTP**) applications. We've discussed how to create business objects that model entities within our problem domain, and how to use them to retrieve and update data from a data store. This is all very important, and most real-world applications have a great deal of OLTP functionality.

However, most real-world applications *also* have functionality that is *not* OLTP, and that's the focus of this final chapter. For example, most applications provide some form of report generation. End users often want to view or print lists of data or groups of data, or to have huge amounts of data compressed into summaries. Retrieving and manipulating all the data required to generate reports is often very complex and resource intensive.

Similarly, many applications need to do batch processing, which typically also involves manipulation of large amounts of data as part of a single process. For instance, most sales systems have end-of-day processing, where they take all the sales transactions for the day and post that data into the accounting system. Most manufacturing systems have daily or weekly processing that recalculates projected manufacturing schedules based on future sales orders.

In truth, it is the rare enterprise application that *doesn't* have some large reporting or processing task that runs against large amounts of data. This type of task is fundamentally different from OLTP. An OLTP task typically involves the retrieval and update of small, discrete amounts of data. Each such update is relatively isolated from any other OLTP task.

When we discuss report generation or batch processing, however, we're talking about a single task that reads and/or updates large sets of data all as part of one large process. Where the time to do an OLTP task is often measured in milliseconds, the time to generate a report or run a batch process is often measured in minutes, and sometimes even hours.

What's not to like?

For most developers, report generation and batch processing are the two least enjoyable parts of any application. Much of this dislike flows from the fact that they are both rather complex to implement. Our development tools and the .NET platform itself provide powerful support for the creation of rich user interfaces and OLTP processing. Unfortunately, they offer comparatively little support for report generation or the development of batch processing systems.

The complexity is amplified if we have developed our application to run in a distributed environment. This is because both report generation and batch processing interact with large amounts of data. The simple act of moving large amounts of data from the database server across the network to a web server or a client workstation can cause huge performance problems in our application. And yet to generate a report or perform a batch process, we need to interact with large amounts of data.

The fact that we're basing our application on the use of business objects can also increase complexity. When we code a batch processing job, we are usually very careful only to retrieve the very minimum data we need. Then we are very careful to optimize any data updates to minimize the impact on the database. We *have* to be very careful, because we're often interacting with thousands and thousands of rows of data, so retrieval of even one extra field can radically decrease performance.

Contrast this to a typical business object that's designed to support user interaction in an OLTP setting. In that case, we often retrieve extra data because we don't know what the user might want to see. We simply retrieve everything that the user might want, because it's cheaper to get all the data at once than to go back to the database over and over to get more data.

The use of business objects is also problematic in terms of report generation. This is because the commercial report generation products on the market aren't designed to generate reports based on objects. Rather, they are designed to directly interact with a database in order to retrieve their data.

In this chapter, we'll discuss some of the key issues surrounding reporting and batch processing. Then we'll create some tools that can simplify our development efforts. In some cases, these tools may provide the answer to reporting or batch processing when creating distributed, object-oriented applications. In other cases, they may provide the base on which a more comprehensive solution can be built. Specifically, we'll be creating the following:

- A simple, server-based batch processing engine
- A converter to generate a `DataSet` from an object or a collection of objects

The batch processing engine is quite complex, even though it's a relatively simple implementation of the concept. The object-to-`DataSet` converter is a relatively straightforward application of reflection and ADO.NET code. I'm assuming by this point in the book that you have become quite comfortable with .NET technologies such as remoting, serialization of objects, and reflection, so we'll make use of them without a great deal of discussion. The batch queue processor will also be multi-threaded, so we're assuming some basic knowledge of threads and how they work too.

Dealing with distributed environments

Whether we're generating a report based on thousands or millions of rows of data, or we're running a batch process that affects or analyzes billions of rows of data, distributed environments are problematic. This is true whether we're using data-centric or object-oriented application architectures.

We're in an area where mainframe- and minicomputer-based applications have always excelled, because there the application generating the report or doing the batch process is on *the same machine* as the data. Of course, it doesn't hurt that both mainframe and minicomputer operating systems come with powerful queued processing engines, so reports and batch processing can be run in the background, at scheduled times, and so forth.

Conversely, we're in an area where PC and web-based computing have always been very weak, primarily because of their distributed nature. Moving those thousands or millions of rows across the network from the database server to a client machine, application server, or web server is incredibly expensive. It almost always results in very inferior results when compared to centralized computing systems. It doesn't help that neither PC nor web environments include queued processing engines, so we almost always resort to the user launching these tasks manually, or trying to hack something together by using the Windows `AT` command or SQL Server's job launcher.

The keys to success are twofold. First, we need to avoid moving massive amounts of data as much as possible. Second, we need some mechanism by which report generation and batch processing tasks can be run automatically – probably from a queue processing engine of some sort.

Avoiding data transfer

In most environments, the database server is already a bottleneck, so running additional processing on that machine is often taboo. Yet that is *exactly* the ideal solution when we're dealing with large volumes of data. If we can avoid transferring the data across the network, we can come close to the power of the mainframe/minicomputer environments.

More likely, however, we'll have to move the data across the network at least once to get it onto a machine where we can process the information without tying up yet more database server resources. Of course, the simple act of copying thousands or millions of rows of data across the network is problematic in terms of performance, regardless of the actual processing activity we are performing.

The point here is that we have a classic trade-off between using database server resources and taking a performance hit by moving the data across the network. If you *can* run the processing on the database server, you can gain some serious benefits; otherwise, you'll have to pay the data transfer cost.

The most important point here is that the data shouldn't be transferred any further than absolutely necessary. Ideally, our report generation and batch processing will occur on a server machine that's physically near the database server, and which is connected by the highest speed network connection possible. The worst thing we can do is transfer all that data out to some client workstation, across who knows how much network infrastructure.

Providing background processing

Another significant issue when trying to do report generation and batch processing on a server machine is that we don't have any standard mechanism by which to launch or control such processing. The Windows and .NET environments don't include the kind of queue processing engines that you'd find on a mainframe or minicomputer.

So, what *do* we have? Well, there's the Windows `AT` command, which provides some primitive abilities to schedule tasks for processing. And then there's SQL Server's job scheduler, which many people use (or misuse) for this purpose. There's MSMQ, but that has no provisions for *scheduling* jobs – just for queuing and running them as fast as possible. None of these solves all the core issues we face:

- Allowing the user to request and/or schedule a task on a server
- Allowing a user to remove a pending task from a server
- Monitoring and viewing the scheduled, pending, and active tasks on a server
- Hosting (running) the task in a process on the server

There are a variety of freeware, shareware, and commercial batch processing engines available for the Windows environment. However, most organizations that require this kind of functionality end up creating their own batch processing mechanism – and following that trend, we'll be creating a basic one for .NET later in this chapter.

> *I recommend looking at commercial alternatives – creating a comprehensive batch processing engine is not trivial. The one we'll create in this chapter provides minimum functionality. If you need something more comprehensive, it could be more cost effective to purchase a commercial product.*

Dealing with object-oriented applications

Whether we're in a distributed environment or not, the use of an object-oriented application architecture poses different sets of challenges for reporting and batch processing, which we can take a look at in turn.

Reporting and objects

Before we get into the details of report generation and objects, we need to divide the idea of report generation into two groups: small reports and large reports.

Many ERP (enterprise resource planning) and MRP (manufacturing resource planning) systems make exactly this distinction: small reports are often called **lists**, while large reports are called **reports**. Lists can be generated at any time and are displayed immediately on the client, while reports are typically generated in the background and are later displayed through a viewer, or printed out.

Of course, the exact delineation between a 'small' and a 'large' report varies. Ultimately, small reports require small enough amounts of data that it's reasonable to transfer that data to the client immediately upon a user request. Large reports require too much data to transfer to the client immediately, or they take too long to generate to have the user's machine (or browser) tied up waiting for it to complete.

The problem of sheer data volume affects both large reports *and* batch processing, so we'll discuss it (and a potential solution) in the next section. In this section, we'll deal with a problem that affects large and small reports alike: report generation tools lack support for objects.

The Windows Forms and Web Forms environments both provide solid support for UI creation when using objects. As we've seen, we can use data binding to bind UI controls to the properties of our objects, just as we can with data sources such as the ADO.NET `DataSet`. In fact, this support is comprehensive enough that we haven't used a single `DataSet` object in this entire book – until now.

The problem we face with reporting is that none of the major report engine tools supports data binding against custom objects. Reports generated with popular tools such as Crystal Reports or Active Reports can only be generated against ADO.NET object such as the `DataSet`.

> *To be fair, these report engines also work in an "unbound" mode, where we have the opportunity to supply the data to populate the report manually. This technique can certainly be used with business objects. We can write code to pull the data out of our objects, and provide that data to the report engine as it generates the report. The trouble is that this is a lot of work, especially when compared to just binding the report to a* `DataSet`.

Ideally, in the future, one of the major report engine vendors will support data binding against objects just like Windows Forms and Web Forms do, but that's not the case today. Today, we can either generate the report from a `DataSet`, or use the engines in unbound mode and provide the data manually.

To help address this for now, we can create a compromise solution: a converter to load a `DataSet` with data from objects. If we can convert an object into a `DataSet`, we can then generate reports in standard report engines such as Crystal Reports or Active Reports by using that `DataSet`.

Batch processing and objects

While the primary problem with reporting and objects is lack of support from the tools, there is another issue. In fact, this issue is the primary problem we face when implementing batch processing with objects: data volume.

If we're interacting with thousands or millions of rows of data to generate a report or to perform a batch process, this could mean creating thousands or millions of objects in memory. There is overhead involved with each object we create. It takes processor power and memory to create an object, memory is consumed as long as the object is alive, and processor power is consumed to destroy the object. In the case of our CSLA .NET business objects, there's additional overhead in storing `IsDirty`, `IsDeleted`, `BrokenRules`, and other state data for each object.

In most applications, we don't even think about this overhead, because the creation of a few dozen or even a few hundred objects is pretty inconsequential – the overhead is tiny. This all changes if we're proposing to create a few hundred thousand objects, or a few million. The tiny overhead of each object, multiplied by these huge numbers, becomes a lot of overhead that can be very problematic.

Obviously, there's a certain amount of processing and memory usage that's unavoidable – we have to at least load the raw data that we're going to work on! The issue here is that wrapping that data in objects increases the overhead – and with huge data volumes, this is a big issue.

> **This isn't a new concept, or one that's unique to .NET, or to our implementation of business objects. This issue has been plaguing object-oriented development since its inception.**

The most common solution to this problem is to avoid the use of conventional objects when implementing large data processing applications. This isn't to say that we don't use object-oriented concepts and techniques, but it *is* to say that classic, 'stateful' objects don't have much application when building large batch processing or reporting systems.

One possible object-oriented solution is described by the *Flyweight* design pattern, where a small number of objects are created. Each of these objects points to a particular data element while that element is in use, and then to other elements as they are used. The key is that a *Flyweight* object contains little or no internal state. Instead, it gets its state data as a parameter to each method, so the state data exists outside the object itself.

> *The* Flyweight *design pattern is discussed in* Design Patterns*, ISBN 0201633612.*

Even after considering a technique like this, though, the reality is that large reports and large batch processing is often best done without the use of objects. Instead, large reports are usually best generated by using ADO.NET to retrieve the data, and feeding that data directly into the report engine. Large batch processes are usually best implemented by reading the data directly from a data reader, and doing the updates by calling stored procedures directly through a command object. We can encapsulate this code into a class or object, but ultimately the process is a linear, procedural one.

Batch queue server

Now that we've discussed some of the key issues that we face when doing reporting or batch processing in distributed, object-oriented environments, let's move on to provide some solutions – or at least, the basis from which you can develop complete solutions for your specific requirements.

Since we don't have a batch queue processing service available as part of .NET, we'll create one here. While this really is just a basic implementation, it will allow users to schedule tasks to be run on a batch server machine – one that should have a very high-speed connection to the database server so that it can interact with large data volumes efficiently. We'll be able to use this to generate reports or run batch processing on the server.

The batch queue service will be multithreaded, allowing multiple batch jobs to run concurrently on different threads. We'll provide a setting through which the system administrator can specify the maximum number of batch jobs to run at any one time.

Mainframe and minicomputer operating systems have pretty much always included powerful batch processing engines, allowing users to submit tasks for background processing. These tasks are queued up and processed either as soon as possible, or at a scheduled time. Users can get a list of the pending tasks, and remove tasks from the list if they wish.

> *In many cases, a lot of other features are also provided, such as the ability to suspend a task, reschedule it, and so forth. The infrastructure to support batch processing is typically quite extensive in these environments.*

The lack of such concepts in the .NET environment is a big drawback, especially if we need to generate large reports or perform long-running batch processing tasks, or if we need to schedule tasks to run in the middle of the night when no user is around to launch them manually.

CSLA.BatchQueue design

In creating our batch queue processor, we'll use a design similar to that of our `DataPortal`: there will be a client-side `BatchQueue` class that has `Shared` methods so that client code can easily interact with the batch queue mechanism. The client-side `BatchQueue` class will use remoting to communicate with a server-side `BatchQueue` object, and this server-side object will actually interact with the queue processor, `Server.BatchQueueService`. The entire scheme is shown in the following class diagram:

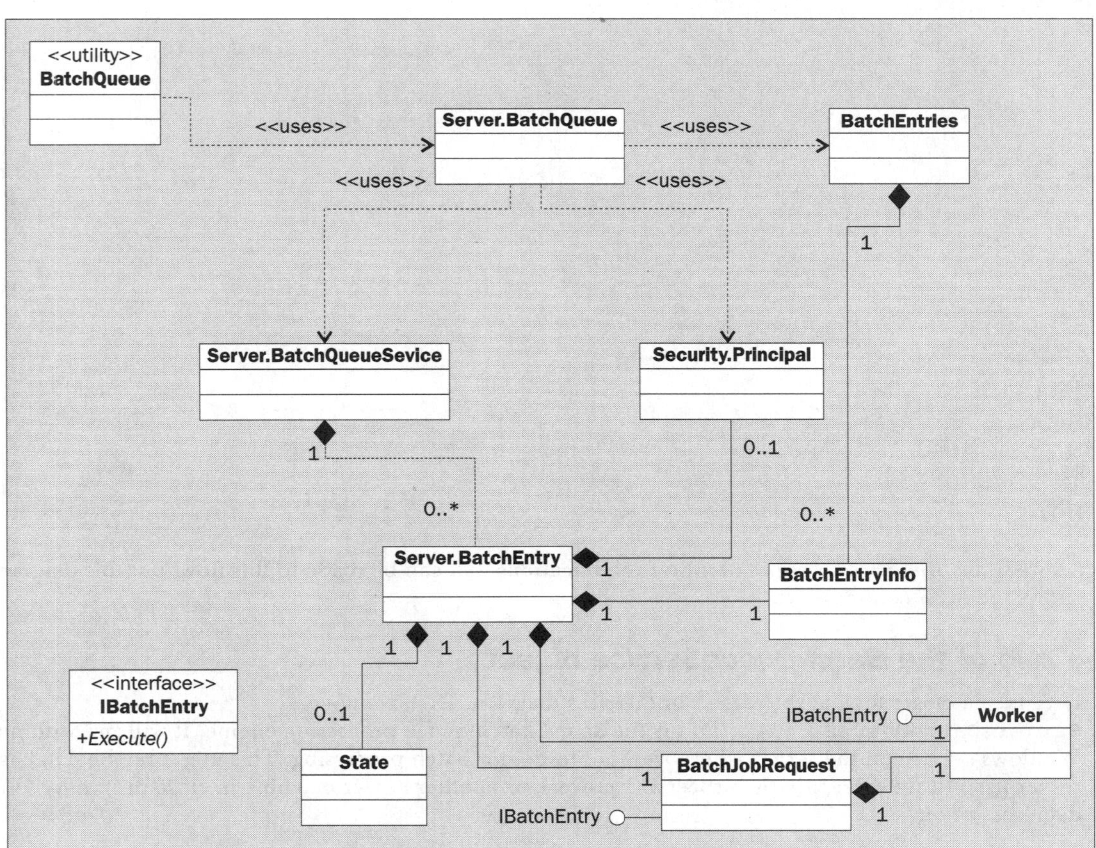

Needless to say, there's a lot going on here, so let's break it down a bit. When a client wants to submit a batch job, the following process occurs:

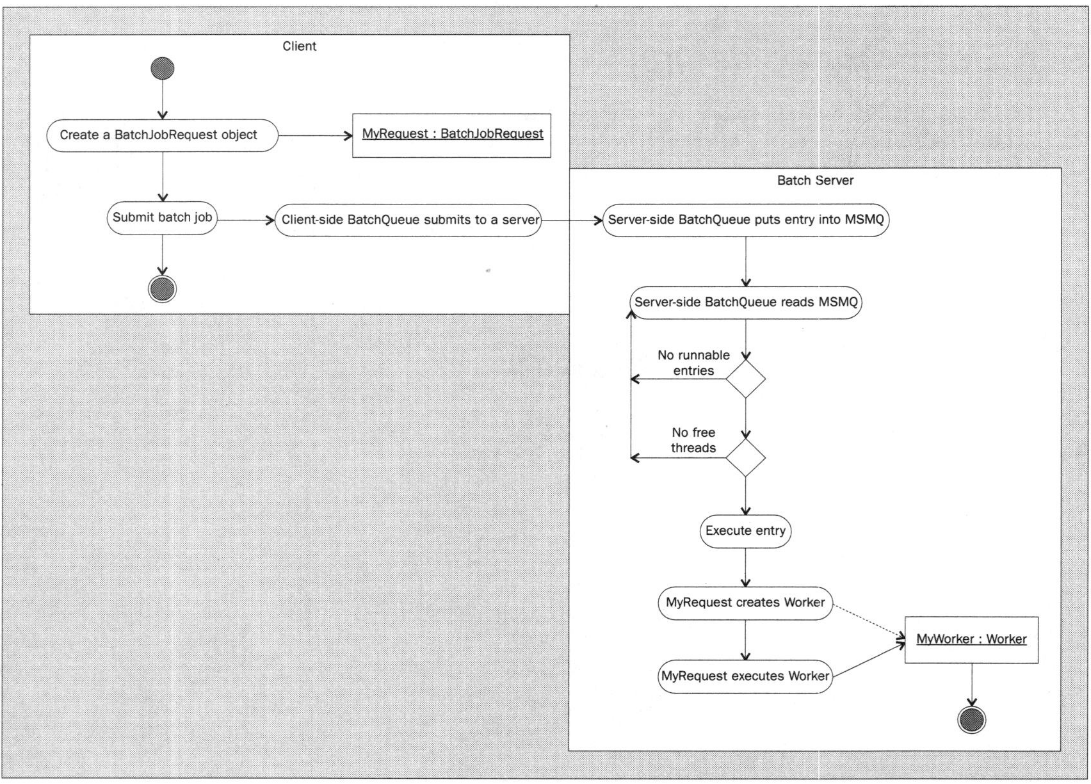

As we'll see, there are a couple of minor modifications that can be made to this flow, but this diagram shows the most common process.

The role of the BatchQueueService object

Let's take a closer look at the classes in the class diagram. First, we have `Server.BatchQueueService`. This is the actual batch queue processing engine. It will run within a Windows service on the server where we want to do our batch processing. This might be the database server itself (if we can spare the processing power), or another server machine in close proximity to the database server.

The `BatchQueueService` object uses an MSMQ queue to queue up all its tasks. Each task is represented by a `Server.BatchEntry` object which contains all the information about the task, including the priority of the job and when it should start, the requesting user's identity, any parameter data, and the worker object that actually implements the batch job. `BatchEntry` doesn't *implement* the batch job code; it merely contains all the information that our batch job object will need to do its work.

This means that BatchQueueService just manages a collection of BatchEntry objects that are waiting to be processed:

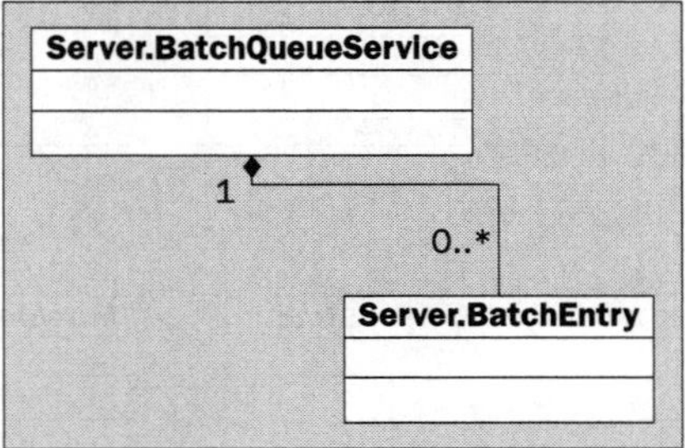

The role of the BatchEntry object

Each BatchEntry object contains basic information about the entry in a BatchEntryInfo object, and the worker object that will perform the actual task (see the next figure). This object can be created in two different ways, but either way the worker class must implement IBatchEntry so that the batch processing system can invoke the object.

One possibility is for the task object to be created on the client machine and sent to the batch server through remoting. This requires the DLL containing the task code to be installed on both the client and the batch server machines – the object is created on the client, and then passed by value to the server.

Alternatively, the client can create a BatchJobRequest object, which contains the assembly and type name of a class in a DLL on the batch server. The BatchJobRequest object will dynamically load this class on the server, and then invoke it so that it performs the batch task. This approach is nice because the DLL containing the batch task object only needs to exist on the batch server – the client never creates the task object, and doesn't need that DLL.

> *The DLL containing the* BatchJobRequest *class itself must then be installed on both client and server, but it will be part of our batch framework, so that shouldn't be a problem. The batch framework DLL will contain the code needed on the client in order to use the batch processor, and it will contain the code needed on the server for the server to run.*

Either way, a Server.BatchEntry object contains a number of things:

- a BatchEntryInfo object
- a batch task object (either BatchJobRequest, or the worker object itself)
- an optional State object containing parameter data from the client (this can be any <Serializable()> object that we want to pass to the batch job)
- the user's BusinessPrincipal object (if we're using CSLA .NET security)

This is illustrated by the following diagram:

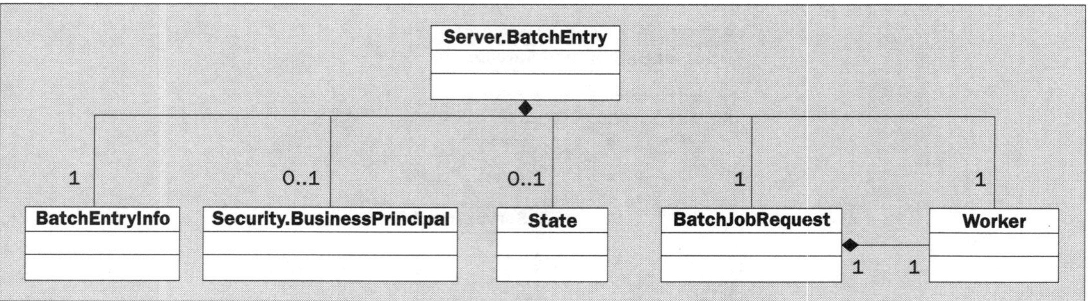

All of these objects will be serialized into an MSMQ `Message` object and then stored in an MSMQ queue on the batch server. By storing these objects in an MSMQ queue, we avoid having to track them ourselves. Also, MSMQ automatically sorts the entries by priority, so we don't need to worry about that either. Finally, by storing the entries in MSMQ we don't need to worry about recording them in a file or a database. Even if we stop and restart our batch service, MSMQ continues to retain any entries queued for processing.

When it's time to process an entry, `Server.BatchQueueService` deserializes the `BatchEntry` object (and all the objects it contains) into memory on the server. It then executes the entry on a thread from the .NET thread pool.

The role of the BatchEntryInfo object

The `BatchEntryInfo` object contains information about the user that submitted the request, as well as the date and time that the task is to be executed, and its priority within the queue. This information is not only used by the batch processor itself, but can also be retrieved by the client. The client might want a list of all the pending and active batch jobs in the queue. In this case, we return a collection of `BatchEntryInfo` objects in a `BatchEntries` object:

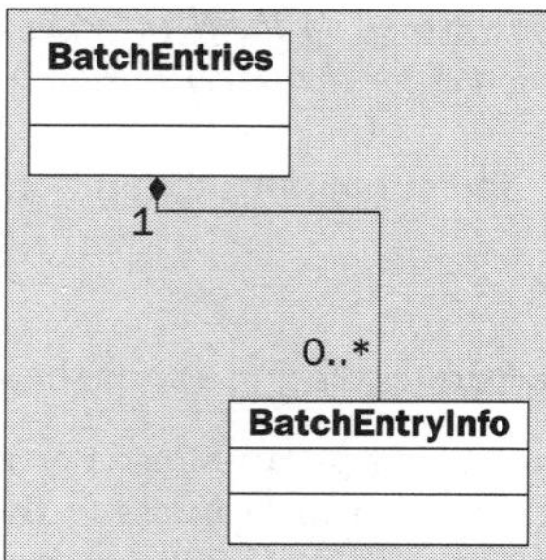

When this is requested, the batch server creates a `BatchEntries` collection object and populates it with the `BatchEntryInfo` objects for all active (currently running) and pending batch tasks. The collection is then returned by value (through remoting) back to the client, where it can be displayed to the user.

Security and user identities

You may have noticed that the main UML diagram also includes the `Security.Principal` class from the core CSLA .NET implementation. When we implemented the `DataPortal`, we passed the user's `BusinessPrincipal` object to the server so that the server could impersonate the user, ensuring that our business objects would have the same security context on the server as on the client. We will do the same thing here in the batch processing environment.

The caveat is that this won't work with Windows' integrated security. Unfortunately, there's no easy way to have our Windows service impersonate an actual Windows user when the batch task is invoked. While we can impersonate the user when the task is *submitted*, we can't preserve the user's `WindowsPrincipal` object for use when the task is actually invoked.

> *This is* technically *possible – COM+, for example, is able to do this sort of thing. However, it is non-trivial to implement, requiring extensive and in-depth knowledge of the deepest parts of Windows security and its related APIs.*
>
> *One solution (if our server is running Windows Server 2003) is to have the user enter their password, so that we can pass their user name and password to the server. We could then call a .NET method to impersonate the user, providing the user name and password as credentials to the Windows security subsystem. Even then, this is problematic because we'd need to protect the clear-text password entered by the user, which is a big security risk.*

Because of the complexity of trying to do Windows impersonation, our implementation will provide impersonation only when CSLA .NET table-based security is used. In such a case, the `Server.BatchEntry` object will contain not only a `BatchEntryInfo` object and the task object, but also contain the user's `BusinessPrincipal` object.

If we set our authentication to `"Windows"`, we will get no security. All batch-processing code will run under the account that's running the Windows service on the server.

Creating the BatchQueue assembly

We'll implement the `CSLA.BatchQueue` component as a new assembly. Clearly, not all applications will make use of batch queuing, in which case they won't need this functionality. By putting it into a separate assembly, we make it optional. This is particularly important when no-touch deployment is used, since it minimizes the amount of code that must be downloaded to the client workstations.

Open the `CSLA` solution and add a new Class Library project to it. Name it `CSLA.BatchQueue`, and set its Option Strict property to On in the project's properties dialog.

Next, we'll be using the `BusinessPrincipal` class that's located in `CSLA.dll`, so add a reference to the `CSLA` project. Also, we'll be using remoting to communicate between client and server, and MSMQ to manage our queued tasks, so add references to `System.Runtime.Remoting` and `System.Messaging.dll` too. Finally, remove `Class1.vb`, as we'll be adding our own classes as we create them.

To implement the `CSLA.BatchQueue`, we'll start with the simpler classes, saving `BatchQueueService` for last – it's the most complex class, and it ties everything together.

IBatchEntry interface

It's up to the business developer to implement the worker code that will run in the batch process; all that our framework can reasonably do is to manage the process of launching that code on the server.

With this in mind, the worker code must be written in a class that implements a specific interface, so that our batch processing engine knows how to invoke it. Once the class has been created within a DLL, that DLL can be installed on the batch server, and we can use a `BatchJobRequest` object to queue it up for processing. Alternatively, we can deploy the DLL on both client *and* server, and pass the object by value to the batch server for processing.

The following diagram shows these two options:

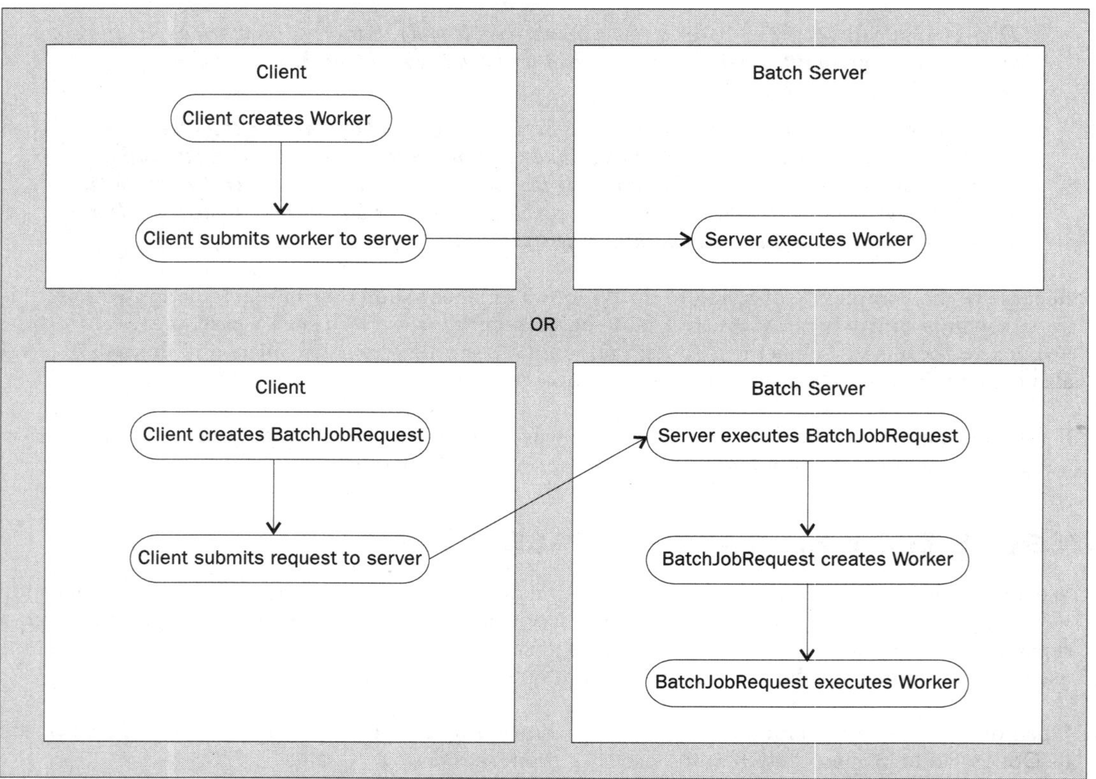

In either case, the worker object containing the business code must ultimately be executed by our batch processing framework. To make this practical, add a new class to the project named `IBatchEntry`, and change it to define an interface:

```
Public Interface IBatchEntry
   Sub Execute(ByVal State As Object)
End Interface
```

Any business class can implement this interface by providing a method that takes a single `Object` parameter. Our batch processing framework will pass this 'state' object from the client to the server, allowing the client to pass arbitrary information to the batch processing method. Typically, this will be used to pass criteria so that the batch job does the work requested by the user, but that's all up to the business developer, not our framework code.

BatchEntryInfo class

Each batch job will include a set of information that includes data about the user that submitted the request, and the request itself. For the latter, we need to know the job's ID, the priority of the job in the queue, the date and time it is scheduled to run, and its current status. Status is one of:

- `Active`: an entry that's currently executing
- `Pending`: an entry that's waiting to execute, and will as soon as there's a free thread in the queue
- `Holding`: an entry that's scheduled to run at a future time

All of this data will be kept in a `BatchEntryInfo` object associated with the task. By keeping the data in a separate object, we simplify the process of retrieving a list of all entries in the batch queue. As we described above, all we need to do is loop through all queued entries, and make a collection of their `BatchEntryInfo` objects.

Add a new class named `BatchEntryInfo` to the project; this will be a simple informational class. A `BatchEntryInfo` object is created on the client when the business application submits a job to the batch processing framework. As the object is created, we'll gather information about the user's identity and the client computer. Add the following code:

```
Imports System.Environment

Public Enum BatchEntryStatus
  Pending
  Holding
  Active
End Enum

<Serializable()> _
Public Class BatchEntryInfo
  Private mID As Guid = Guid.NewGuid()
  Private mSubmitted As Date = Now
  Private mUser As String = System.Environment.UserName
  Private mMachine As String = System.Environment.MachineName
  Private mPriority As Messaging.MessagePriority = _
     Messaging.MessagePriority.Normal
  Private mMsgID As String
  Private mHoldUntil As Date = Date.MinValue
  Private mStatus As BatchEntryStatus = BatchEntryStatus.Pending

  Public ReadOnly Property ID() As Guid
    Get
      Return mID
    End Get
  End Property
```

```
Public ReadOnly Property Submitted() As Date
  Get
    Return mSubmitted
  End Get
End Property

Public ReadOnly Property User() As String
  Get
    Return mUser
  End Get
End Property

Public ReadOnly Property Machine() As String
  Get
    Return mMachine
  End Get
End Property

Public Property Priority() As Messaging.MessagePriority
  Get
    Return mPriority
  End Get
  Set(ByVal Value As Messaging.MessagePriority)
    mPriority = Value
  End Set
End Property

Public ReadOnly Property MessageID() As String
  Get
    Return mMsgID
  End Get
End Property

Friend Sub SetMessageID(ByVal ID As String)
  mMsgID = ID
End Sub

Public Property HoldUntil() As Date
  Get
    Return mHoldUntil
  End Get
  Set(ByVal Value As Date)
    mHoldUntil = Value
  End Set
End Property

Public ReadOnly Property Status() As BatchEntryStatus
  Get
    If mHoldUntil > Now AndAlso mStatus = BatchEntryStatus.Pending Then
      Return BatchEntryStatus.Holding
    Else
      Return mStatus
    End If
  End Get
```

```
    End Property
    Friend Sub SetStatus(ByVal Status As BatchEntryStatus)
      mStatus = Status
    End Sub

  #Region " System.Object overrides "

    Public Overrides Function ToString() As String
      Return mUser & "@" & mMachine & ":" & mID.ToString
    End Function

    Public Overloads Function Equals(ByVal Info As BatchEntryInfo) As Boolean
      Return mID.Equals(Info.ID)
    End Function

    Public Overrides Function GetHashCode() As Integer
      Return mID.GetHashCode()
    End Function

  #End Region

  End Class
```

In this quite long but fairly straightforward listing, we define an enumerated value to indicate the status of the entry, followed by the `BatchEntryInfo` class itself. Notice that the latter is marked as `<Serializable()>` so that it can be passed by value across the network, and also so that it can be serialized into an MSMQ message body on the server.

Many of these properties, such as the name of the client machine, are set automatically as the object is first created, and so they are read-only. Others, such as the ID and status of the MSMQ message, are to be set only by our framework – so they are read-only properties with `Friend` methods to set the values. Still others, such as `HoldUntil`, can be set by business code, so they are read-write properties.

The bulk of the code here just stores and exposes data about the user and machine where the entry was submitted, and about the entry's priority, status, and so forth. We also override some `System.Object` methods so that our object behaves in a friendly manner.

BatchEntries class

A feature that we particularly want to enable is the ability for a client application to request a list of all the entries in the queue, regardless of their current status (holding, pending, or active). Since all pertinent information about each entry is in that entry's `BatchEntryInfo` object, all we need to do is create a collection of those objects on the server, and then return that collection to the client.

Such a collection is easily implemented as a custom collection object. Add a `BatchEntries` class to the project with the following code:

```
  Imports System.Messaging
  Imports System.Runtime.Serialization.Formatters.Binary
```

```
<Serializable()> _
Public Class BatchEntries
  Inherits CollectionBase

  Default Public ReadOnly Property Entry(ByVal index As Integer) _
      As BatchEntryInfo
    Get
      Return CType(List.Item(index), BatchEntryInfo)
    End Get
  End Property

  Default Public ReadOnly Property Entry(ByVal ID As Guid) As BatchEntryInfo
    Get
      Dim obj As BatchEntryInfo
      For Each obj In List
        If obj.ID.Equals(ID) Then
          Return obj
        End If
      Next
    End Get
  End Property

  Friend Sub New()

    ' Prevent direct creation
  End Sub

  Friend Sub Add(ByVal Value As BatchEntryInfo)
    List.Add(Value)
  End Sub

End Class
```

Since we'll be passing this collection from the server back to the client via remoting, we have marked it as `<Serializable()>`. Also note that its constructor is scoped as `Friend`, so the object can't be created directly by client code. The only way a client can get an object of this type is by requesting it from our queue processing framework, which ensures that we can create and populate the object on the server and then return it to the client.

Lastly, notice the `Add()` method. This will be used by our server-side code to populate the collection with the `BatchEntryInfo` objects that are currently in the queue. Client code can use this collection of `BatchEntryInfo` objects to display a list of entries in the queue to the user, or for whatever other purpose makes sense for the client application in question.

Client-side BatchQueue class

Our client code needs an easy way to interact with the batch processing server, so we'll provide a client-side class named `BatchQueue` for this purpose. Each `BatchQueue` object will represent a connection to a specific batch queue server process. This allows an enterprise environment to have many batch processing servers running, and allows a client to create `BatchQueue` objects to interact with each of them as needed.

We'll be using remoting to communicate with the batch queue server processes, so we'll use the remoting URL for the server process as an identifier for that server. When we create a `BatchQueue` object, we'll provide it with the URL of the server with which it should communicate. If no URL is provided, we'll have the `BatchQueue` object read the application's configuration file to find the default queue URL.

Add a `BatchQueue` class to the project. We'll start with the following code to construct the object:

```
Imports System.Runtime.Remoting.Channels
Imports System.Runtime.Remoting.Channels.Tcp

Public Class BatchQueue
  Private mQueueURL As String
  Private mServer As Server.BatchQueue

#Region " Constructors and Initialization "

  Public Sub New()
    mQueueURL = ConfigurationSettings.AppSettings("DefaultBatchQueueServer")
  End Sub

  Public Sub New(ByVal QueueServerURL As String)
    mQueueURL = QueueServerURL
  End Sub

  Private Function QueueServer() As Server.BatchQueue
    If mServer Is Nothing Then
      mServer = CType(Activator.GetObject(GetType(Server.BatchQueue), _
                mQueueURL), Server.BatchQueue)
    End If

    Return mServer
  End Function

#End Region

End Class
```

We provide two constructors: one where the client supplies the URL for the server, and the other where we read it from the configuration file. We also implement a `QueueServer()` method that caches the remoting proxy object for the server, so we only have to create it once. This is similar to the code we implemented for the client-side `DataPortal` class.

Also similar to `DataPortal` is the need to pass our `BusinessPrincipal` object to the server, in the case that the security model is set to `CSLA`. Add the following helper methods to make this easy:

```
#Region " Security "

  Private Function AUTHENTICATION() As String
    Return ConfigurationSettings.AppSettings("Authentication")
  End Function
```

```
    Private Function GetPrincipal() As System.Security.Principal.IPrincipal
      If AUTHENTICATION() = "Windows" Then

        ' Windows integrated security
        Return Nothing
      Else

        ' We assume using the CSLA framework security
        Return System.Threading.Thread.CurrentPrincipal
      End If
    End Function

  #End Region
```

Following .NET best practices, we'll override the `System.Object` methods `ToString()`, `Equals()`, and `GetHashCode()`. You can see the details of this in the code download.

Now, the primary purposes of the `BatchQueue` object are to allow client code to submit jobs to the queue, to get a list of jobs in the queue, and to remove jobs from the queue. Of course, all the real work happens on the server, but we need to implement methods to make these activities available to the client.

> *As implemented in this chapter, any user can remove any entry in the queue. You may choose to enhance this implementation to restrict which users can remove entries.*

There are many possible variations on submitting a job to the queue – the code download includes eight different implementations. The following list should provide a sample of the types of options available:

- The client creates a worker object (which implements `IBatchEntry`) and submits it
- The client creates a worker object (which implements `IBatchEntry`) and submits it, along with a 'state' object
- As an option to the above, the client may specify the priority of the entry in the queue
- As an option to the above, the client may specify a date and time when the entry should start

These are handled by providing overloaded `Submit()` methods. All of them will work in more-or-less the same way, but we'll examine a couple of variations here. This is the simplest:

```
    Public Sub Submit(ByVal Entry As IBatchEntry)
      QueueServer().Submit(New Server.BatchEntry(Entry))
    End Sub
```

In this case, the user is supplying us with a reference to an object they've created, which must be `<Serializable()>` and implement the `IBatchEntry` interface. We use it to initialize a `BatchEntry` object, which is then submitted to the server via remoting. The `Submit()` method is running on the server, so this new `BatchEntry` object, along with the user-supplied object, is passed by value to the server.

The most complex version of `Submit()` is the one where the client specifies *everything*:

```
Public Sub Submit(ByVal Entry As IBatchEntry, _
                  ByVal State As Object, _
                  ByVal HoldUntil As Date, _
                  ByVal Priority As Messaging.MessagePriority)

  Dim job As Server.BatchEntry = New Server.BatchEntry(Entry, State)
  job.Info.HoldUntil = HoldUntil
  job.Info.Priority = Priority
  QueueServer().Submit(job)
End Sub
```

Here, the client provides us with not only a reference to their worker object, but also a 'state' object that we'll pass through to the worker object's `Execute()` method when we run it on the server. The client is also providing a priority for the entry in the queue, and a date and time when the entry should be run.

You can refer to the code download for other overloaded implementations of the `Submit()` *method.*

The client may also want to get a list of the entries in the queue on the server. The result is a `BatchEntries` collection object containing `BatchEntryInfo` objects for each entry in the queue. This collection object is created and populated on the server, so it contains the list of batch entries in the order they will be executed. It is then returned to the client, so all we need to do is provide a simple method to invoke the server functionality:

```
Public ReadOnly Property Entries() As BatchEntries
  Get
    Return QueueServer().GetEntries(GetPrincipal)
  End Get
End Property
```

The end result is that the client has a collection of `BatchEntryInfo` objects that can be used to display the list to the user, or in any other way that's deemed appropriate.

We also provide a `Remove()` method:

```
Public Sub Remove(ByVal Entry As BatchEntryInfo)
  QueueServer().Remove(Entry)
End Sub
```

The client must provide us with the `BatchEntryInfo` object corresponding to an entry in the queue on the server. We simply pass this off to the server so that it can remove the entry from the queue.

Though our current implementation uses ID values to identify entries, we require the entire object to be passed. This helps keep the overall system more abstract. Because the entire object is passed, we could change the way that entries are identified in the future without risk of breaking client code. The client has no idea what information we need out of the `BatchEntryInfo` object, so there's no dependency here.

Server-side BatchQueue class

Much of the code in the client-side `BatchQueue` class was making method calls to a server-side `BatchQueue` object. This is very similar in style to the client and server `DataPortal` objects, which were also designed to interact with each other in this way.

Add a new class *file* named `BatchQueueServer` to the project. This class will be exposed via remoting, so that the client-side `BatchQueue` object can interact with it. This means that it needs to inherit from `MarshalByRefObject`. Since it will be running on the server, we'll put it into a `Server` namespace as well:

```
Imports System.Security.Principal
Imports CSLA.Security

Namespace Server

  ' This is the entry point for all queue requests from the client via remoting
  Public Class BatchQueue
    Inherits MarshalByRefObject

  End Class

End Namespace
```

The full type name for this class is `CSLA.BatchQueue.Server.BatchQueue`, and it's available via remoting as an anchored object. Since we've already implemented the client-side `BatchQueue` code that calls this object, we already know that we need to implement `Submit()`, `GetEntries()`, and `Remove()` methods:

```
    Public Sub Submit(ByVal Entry As BatchEntry)
      BatchQueueService.Enqueue(Entry)
    End Sub

    Public Sub Remove(ByVal Entry As BatchEntryInfo)
      BatchQueueService.Dequeue(Entry)
    End Sub

    Public Function GetEntries(ByVal Principal As IPrincipal) As BatchEntries
      SetPrincipal(Principal)
      Dim entries As New BatchEntries()
      BatchQueueService.LoadEntries(entries)
      Return entries
    End Function
```

The `Submit()` and `Remove()` methods merely ask the `BatchQueueService` class to do the actual submission and removal of the entry from the queue. The `BatchQueueService` class contains all the code to manage and interact with the queue – which is good, because that code is multithreaded, and therefore relatively complex, as we'll see when we implement it.

The `GetEntries()` method creates an instance of the `BatchEntries` collection object and then has the `BatchQueueService` class populate the collection with the current list of entries in the queue. Again, we are totally encapsulating all the interaction with the queue inside the `BatchQueueService` class itself.

The `Server.BatchQueue` class in the download also includes copies of the `AUTHORIZATION()` and `SetPrincipal()` methods from the `DataPortal` server. Notice that the `GetEntries()` method calls `SetPrincipal()` before executing, ensuring that we have access to the user's identity as our code runs. In this case, we're not using that information, but we *could* set up roles so that only certain users can submit, remove, or view the entries in the queue.

BatchEntry class

Each entry in the queue is contained within a `BatchEntry` object. Put another way, the `BatchEntry` object is a container for the worker object, the state object, the `BatchEntryInfo` object, and the `BusinessPrincipal` object (if we're using CSLA .NET security).

Being a container for these objects isn't hard. However, the `BatchEntry` object is *also* responsible for managing the execution of the batch task when it is invoked. This code is a bit more complex, since it includes setting up the security context before the worker object is executed, and then ensuring that the `BatchQueueService` knows when the job is complete, so the next batch job can be started.

Let's start by creating the `BatchEntry` class and adding the code to contain the four other objects:

```
Imports System.Security.Principal

Namespace Server

  <Serializable()> _
  Public NotInheritable Class BatchEntry
    Private mInfo As New BatchEntryInfo()
    Private mPrincipal As IPrincipal = GetPrincipal()
    Private mWorker As IBatchEntry
    Private mState As Object

    Public ReadOnly Property Info() As BatchEntryInfo
      Get
        Return mInfo
      End Get
    End Property

    Public ReadOnly Property Principal() As IPrincipal
      Get
        Return mPrincipal
      End Get
    End Property

    Public Property Entry() As IBatchEntry
      Get
        Return mWorker
      End Get
      Set(ByVal Value As IBatchEntry)
        mWorker = Value
      End Set
    End Property

    Public Property State() As Object
      Get
        Return mState
      End Get
      Set(ByVal Value As Object)
        mState = Value
      End Set
    End Property

  End Class

End Namespace
```

We also have a couple of constructors that are used by the client-side `BatchQueue` object to create and initialize the `BatchEntry` object:

```
#Region " Constructors "

    Friend Sub New(ByVal Entry As IBatchEntry)
      mWorker = Entry
    End Sub

    Friend Sub New(ByVal Entry As IBatchEntry, ByVal State As Object)
      mWorker = Entry
      mState = State
    End Sub

#End Region
```

Note that these are scoped as `Friend`, so the client can't create a `BatchEntry` object directly – it must use the client-side `BatchQueue` object to create the `BatchEntry` as it is being submitted.

The real work in this class is done when we execute the batch job. It's up to the `BatchQueueService` to determine that our entry should be run, based on its priority and whether it's being held to run at a specific time. `BatchQueueService` then delegates the work of actually launching the job to our `BatchEntry` code. The `BatchQueueService` runs our `BatchEntry` object's `Execute()` method on a background thread (actually a thread out of the thread pool), so this `Execute()` method will always be running on some background thread.

Quite a lot happens as part of this process. Here's the complete code:

```
#Region " Batch execution "

    ' This will run in a background thread in the thread pool
    Friend Sub Execute(ByVal State As Object)

      Dim oldPrincipal As IPrincipal
      Try
        ' Set this thread's principal to our user
        oldPrincipal = Threading.Thread.CurrentPrincipal
        SetPrincipal(mPrincipal)

        Try
          ' Now run the user's code
          mWorker.Execute(mState)

          Dim sb As New Text.StringBuilder()
          With sb
            .Append("Batch job completed")
            .Append(vbCrLf)
            .AppendFormat("Batch job: {0}", Me.ToString)
            .Append(vbCrLf)
            .AppendFormat("Job object: {0}", CType(mWorker, Object).ToString)
            .Append(vbCrLf)
          End With
```

```
        System.Diagnostics.EventLog.WriteEntry( _
          BatchQueueService.Name, sb.ToString, EventLogEntryType.Information)

      Catch ex As Exception
        Dim sb As New Text.StringBuilder()
        With sb
          .Append("Batch job failed due to execution error")
          .Append(vbCrLf)
          .AppendFormat("Batch job: {0}", Me.ToString)
          .Append(vbCrLf)
          .AppendFormat("Job object: {0}", CType(mWorker, Object).ToString)
          .Append(vbCrLf)
          .Append(ex.ToString)
        End With

        System.Diagnostics.EventLog.WriteEntry( _
          BatchQueueService.Name, sb.ToString, EventLogEntryType.Warning)
      End Try

    Finally
      BatchQueueService.Deactivate(Me)

      ' Reset the thread's principal object
      Threading.Thread.CurrentPrincipal = oldPrincipal
    End Try

  End Sub

#End Region
```

We start by calling `SetPrincipal()`, which works just like the `SetPrincipal()` method in the server-side `DataPortal` – that is, it checks if we're using CSLA .NET security, and if so it sets the user's `BusinessPrincipal` as the current principal object for the thread.

Remember that this particular thread is from the thread pool, so we don't know what principal object it used to have – we just need to ensure that it has *our* principal object for the duration of the process. However, we store the original principal value first, and restore the thread's `CurrentPrincipal` to its original value when we're done. This way, we're only impersonating our specific user for as long as we're running this particular entry.

When we go to execute the job itself, we're calling the worker object's `Execute()` method via the `IBatchEntry` interface, passing it the 'state' object as a parameter. Notice that nowhere in our framework do we care what is in this 'state' object – it is passed from the client to the worker object unchanged, allowing the client to pass parameter values or criteria to the worker as it needs.

Also notice that the worker object's `Execute()` call is wrapped in a `Try`...`Catch` block. If it succeeds, we write an entry to the system's application event log indicating success; otherwise we catch the exception and write a failure message to the log. Since our batch queue processor is running as a Windows service, we can't show dialogs or otherwise inform the user of status, so the application event log is an appropriate place to do so.

> *By writing this information to the system's application event log, we enable management of the system. There are commercial tools available that allow monitoring and reporting against entries in the event log, and these can be used to track whether jobs succeed or fail.*
>
> *Alternatively, we might choose to write this information to a table in a database. We could then create utilities so that the user could easily generate reports on that data to see whether their batch entries succeeded or failed.*

The `BatchEntry` class also includes the `AUTHORIZATION()`, `GetPrincipal()`, and `SetPrincipal()` security methods. We also follow .NET best practices by overriding the standard `System.Object` methods `ToString()`, `Equals()`, and `GetHashCode()`. Refer to the code download for the implementations of all these methods.

BatchJobRequest class

To submit a job to the batch processor, the client code must supply a worker object that implements the `IBatchEntry` interface. One way to do this is to have the client create such an object, in which case it will be passed by value from the client to the batch server. A simple worker class looks like this:

```
Public Class MyWorker
  Implements IBatchEntry

  Public Sub Execute(ByVal State As Object) Implements IBatchEntry.Execute
    ' Do batch processing work here
  End Sub

End Class
```

Then we could submit the worker to the queue like this:

```
Dim worker As New MyWorker()
Dim queue As New BatchQueue()

queue.Submit(worker)
```

This is a very elegant approach, since it means that the client can create and initialize the worker object before sending it to the batch server. As we discussed earlier, though, the drawback to this approach is that the DLL containing the worker code must be installed on both client and server, which can complicate deployment.

An alternative is for the client to create a `BatchJobRequest` object, which contains the assembly and type name of a class on the batch server that is to be run. The client merely supplies the assembly name and class name as `String` values – the actual worker object is dynamically loaded on the server. This approach means that the client *can't* initialize the worker object, since it never physically exists on the client machine – all parameter or criteria data must be passed via the 'state' object instead. The benefit, however, is that the DLL containing the worker code only needs to be installed on the batch server, not on the client. This can simplify deployment quite a lot.

In this case, the worker class would be the same as above, but its DLL would only be installed on the batch server. The client code to submit the job is quite different (assuming the `MyWorker` class is compiled into `Worker.dll`):

```
Dim worker As New BatchJobRequest("Worker.MyWorker", "Worker")
Dim queue As New BatchQueue()

queue.Submit(worker)
```

The client creates our generic `BatchJobRequest`, providing it with the type and assembly information necessary to load the worker object on the server dynamically.

A `BatchJobRequest` object is also a worker object, and it therefore implements `IBatchEntry`. It is special, however, because what it does when executed on the server is to load the *real* worker object to do the actual work. Add a `BatchJobRequest` class to the project with the following code:

```
<Serializable()> _
Public Class BatchJobRequest

  Implements IBatchEntry

  Private mAssembly As String = ""
  Private mType As String = ""

  Public Sub New(ByVal Type As String, ByVal [Assembly] As String)
    mAssembly = [Assembly]
    mType = Type
  End Sub

  Public Property Type() As String
    Get
      Return mType
    End Get
    Set(ByVal Value As String)
      mType = Value
    End Set
  End Property

  Public Property [Assembly]() As String
    Get
      Return mAssembly
    End Get
    Set(ByVal Value As String)
      mAssembly = Value
    End Set
  End Property

  ' This method runs on the server - it is called by BatchEntry,
  ' which is called by Server.BatchQueueService
  Public Sub Execute(ByVal State As Object) _
      Implements IBatchEntry.Execute

    ' Create an instance of the specified object
    Dim job As IBatchEntry
    job = CType(AppDomain.CurrentDomain.CreateInstanceAndUnwrap( _
              mAssembly, mType), IBatchEntry)
```

```
      ' Execute the job
      job.Execute(State)

    End Sub

  #Region " System.Object overrides "

    Public Overrides Function ToString() As String
      Return "BatchJobRequest: " & mType & "," & mAssembly
    End Function

  #End Region

  End Class
```

The constructor, variables, and properties of this class interact so that the client code can set the assembly name and class name of the actual worker class. This is pretty much what we do when we configure remoting, for instance – in the configuration file, we provide the assembly and type name of the class to be exposed via remoting, and that class is dynamically loaded. We're doing the same thing here, but we're writing the code to load the class dynamically.

The `Execute()` method is run on the server when our entry is invoked. Of course, we have no business logic here – we simply use the assembly and type names to load the real worker object and then call its `Execute()` method:

```
      ' Create an instance of the specified object
      Dim job As IBatchEntry
      job = CType(AppDomain.CurrentDomain.CreateInstanceAndUnwrap( _
                  mAssembly, mType), IBatchEntry)

      ' Execute the job
      job.Execute(State)
```

The `CreateInstanceAndUnwrap()` method dynamically loads the assembly into memory, and then creates an instance of the class based on its name.

This is analogous to the `CreateObject()` method that's used to create COM objects dynamically, but this approach is used to create .NET objects dynamically.

We then use `CType()` so that we're accessing the object via its `IBatchEntry` interface, and then we call its `Execute()` method.

Note that there's no exception handling here. We already implemented error handling in `BatchEntry`, so if any exceptions occur here, they'll be caught by `BatchEntry`, which will record the failure into the system's application event log.

BatchQueueService class

We've saved the best, and most complex, for last. At this point, we have all the parts necessary to create a batch entry, to retrieve batch information, and so forth. What we're lacking is the actual batch queue processing service itself.

This queue processor is tricky. It must put new entries into MSMQ, retrieve entries from MSMQ when they are to be run or removed, and ensure that entries are only run when they are scheduled, based on the `HoldUntil` property in the `BatchEntryInfo` object. On top of that, we may want to configure the processor to run more than one entry at a time, so it must have a way to launch up to a set number of entries simultaneously.

As if all that wasn't enough, we are in a multithreaded environment. The Windows service itself will run on one thread, each remoting request will automatically run on a different thread, and each of our jobs should execute on yet another thread, so that they don't block each other, remoting, or the Windows service.

Creating multithreaded code is almost always quite difficult. Any time when more than one thread can interact with a single variable or object, we need to add code to ensure that the threads don't conflict with each other. Unfortunately, as soon as we start blocking one thread while another is running, we have to worry about issues like deadlocks (where threads block each other and get stuck forever) and performance (threads can block each other unnecessarily and thus cause performance problems).

Windows service best practices

Another thing to consider is that we'll ultimately be creating a Windows service... so why then are we putting all the code to implement the service into our DLL, rather than into the service project itself? It turns out that this is a best practice implementation because it simplifies debugging and testing of our service code.

If we create the service code directly in a Windows Service project, then the only way to execute that code is by installing and starting the service. Unfortunately, it's somewhat difficult to use the VS.NET debugger to step through a Windows service. This means that we typically end up debugging the code by writing a lot of application event log entries!

However, if we put all the actual service code into a DLL, we can easily call the code from a Windows Service project. More importantly we can *also* create a Console Application project that calls the DLL – and of course we *can* use the VS.NET debugger to debug a console application. Once we've fully debugged and tested our code from the console, we can run it from the Windows service application.

Creating the class

Let's start by adding a `BatchQueueService` class to the project and writing some basic code, including the `Imports` statements for all the namespaces we'll be using:

```
Imports System.Messaging
Imports System.Runtime.Remoting
Imports System.Runtime.Remoting.Channels
Imports System.Runtime.Remoting.Channels.Tcp
Imports System.IO
Imports System.Runtime.Serialization.Formatters.Binary

Namespace Server

  Public Class BatchQueueService

    Private Shared mChannel As TcpServerChannel
    Private Shared mQueue As MessageQueue
    Private Shared mMonitor As Threading.Thread
```

```
    Private Shared WithEvents mTimer As New System.Timers.Timer
    Private Shared mRunning As Boolean
    Private Shared mActiveEntries As Hashtable = _
      Hashtable.Synchronized(New Hashtable)

    Private Shared mSync As New Threading.AutoResetEvent(False)
    Private Shared mWaitToEnd As New Threading.ManualResetEvent(False)

    Public Shared ReadOnly Property Name() As String
      Get
        Return LISTENER_NAME()
      End Get
    End Property

  End Class

End Namespace
```

We'll create the `LISTENER_NAME()` *function later on; for now it's enough to know that it retrieves the URL on which our queue processor will listen for remoting client calls from a configuration file.*

Notice that *everything* is marked as `Shared`. The code in this class will be invoked by the Windows service and our `Server.BatchQueue` objects, and by 'sharing' everything, we make it very easy to use from any other code in our component.

Moving on to specifics, we declare a `TcpServerChannel` variable, which will handle inbound remoting requests from clients. This is different from when we created the server-side `DataPortal` host, because in this case we are not using IIS to host our code. Since we're creating our own remoting host as a Windows service, we need to configure remoting to listen for requests manually. With the `DataPortal`, we were able to allow IIS to handle those details.

We also declare a `MessageQueue` variable that will provide us with access to our underlying MSMQ queue.

One rule about Windows service creation is that the main thread can never be blocked – it must always be free to interact with the Windows service manager. This means that *our* 'main' thread must be a background thread – and so we declare the `mMonitor` variable, which will be the thread on which we do all our work.

We also have a `System.Timers.Timer` object that raises its events on a background thread from the thread pool. We'll be using it to wake up our process to run entries that are being held until a specific time. Since we're creating a Windows service, we can't use any 'busy wait' techniques – instead, we need to suspend our threads any time they are not doing productive work. The timer will fire at the time when our next entry should be processed, and it will unblock the 'main' thread in our service so that it can launch the batch entry.

For more information on multi-threading in .NET, please refer to Visual Basic .NET Threading Handbook *(1-861007-13-2).*

The `mRunning` variable is used to indicate whether we're trying to exit. When creating multi-threaded applications, it can be very difficult to shut the application down properly, since we need to allow all our threads to terminate before we're completely done. We'll be using this variable as a flag to indicate that we're trying to shut down.

The `mActiveEntries` variable points to a synchronized `Hashtable` object:

```
Private Shared mActiveEntries As Hashtable = _
   Hashtable.Synchronized(New Hashtable)
```

`mActiveEntries` will contain references to the `BatchEntry` objects that are currently executing. It will be accessed by multiple threads, which can be awkward – we can't actually allow multiple threads to *alter* the data in the `Hashtable` at the same time. Fortunately, the .NET Framework takes this into account, and provides a synchronized wrapper for the `Hashtable` object. We can use Microsoft's code rather than trying to implement our own!

> *This is true for most objects in the `System.Collections` namespace, so we can easily get synchronized wrappers for `Queue`, `Stack`, and other collection objects as well.*

Finally, we have the `mSync` and `mWaitToEnd` variables that point to synchronization objects that we'll use to block our 'main' thread when it's not doing productive work. For instance, if there's nothing in the queue to process, the 'main' thread will block on `mSync`. When a new entry is placed into the queue, the `Enqueue()` method (running on a background thread through remoting) will signal the `mSync` object, thus unblocking our 'main' thread so that it can process the new entry.

> *Remember that this code will be running on a background thread, not on the primary thread for our Windows service. Because we can't block the primary thread, we are creating our own 'main' thread that will run our code and can block as needed.*

The use of all these variables will become clearer as we implement the remainder of our service code.

Starting the service

When our service first starts up (either from a Windows service or from a console application, for debugging) it needs to do quite a bit of setup work. We need to open our MSMQ queue (and create it if necessary). Then, the main processing thread needs to be started so that it can read entries from the queue and process them. Finally, we need to configure remoting so that clients can call our `Server.BatchQueue` object to submit, remove, or list the entries in the queue.

All of this will be done in a `Start()` method, which can be called by the Windows service as it starts up, or by a test console application for debugging purposes:

```
Public Shared Sub Start()

  mTimer.AutoReset = False

  ' Open and/or create queue
  If MessageQueue.Exists(QUEUE_NAME) Then
    mQueue = New MessageQueue(QUEUE_NAME)
  Else
    mQueue = MessageQueue.Create(QUEUE_NAME)
  End If

  mQueue.MessageReadPropertyFilter.Extension = True
```

```
    ' Start reading from queue
    mRunning = True
    mMonitor = New Threading.Thread(AddressOf MonitorQueue)
    mMonitor.Name = "MonitorQueue"
    mMonitor.Start()

    ' Start remoting for Server.BatchQueue
    If mChannel Is Nothing Then

      ' Set application name (virtual root name)
      RemotingConfiguration.ApplicationName = LISTENER_NAME()

      ' Set up channel
      Dim properties As New Hashtable()
      properties("name") = "TcpBinary"
      properties("port") = CStr(PORT())
      Dim svFormatter As New BinaryServerFormatterSinkProvider

      ' This line required for .NET 1.1 only
      svFormatter.TypeFilterLevel = _
         Runtime.Serialization.Formatters.TypeFilterLevel.Full

      mChannel = New TcpServerChannel(properties, svFormatter)
      Channels.ChannelServices.RegisterChannel(mChannel)

      ' Register our class
      RemotingConfiguration.RegisterWellKnownServiceType( _
         GetType(Server.BatchQueue), _
         "BatchQueue.rem", _
         WellKnownObjectMode.SingleCall)

    Else
      mChannel.StartListening(Nothing)
    End If

  End Sub
```

First, we open (and/or create) the MSMQ queue where we'll store all pending and scheduled entries:

```
    ' Open and/or create queue
    If MessageQueue.Exists(QUEUE_NAME) Then
      mQueue = New MessageQueue(QUEUE_NAME)
    Else
      mQueue = MessageQueue.Create(QUEUE_NAME)
    End If
```

The name of the queue is loaded from the application configuration file via the `QUEUE_NAME()` method:

```
  Private Shared Function QUEUE_NAME() As String
    Return ".\private$\" & ConfigurationSettings.AppSettings("QueueName")
  End Function
```

Notice that we're using a private queue here – only our service code will ever interact with the queue, so there's no need for it to be public. Using a private queue is more flexible, because we don't need to have Active Directory installed in our environment – we just need to have the messaging subsystem installed on our server.

```
mQueue.MessageReadPropertyFilter.Extension = True
```

We'll be using the Extension property on our queued messages to store the execution time of our tasks. The Extension property is a Byte array that we can use to store application-specific information. By default, this value is not retrieved when a message is read from the queue, so we specifically indicate that we want this value to be retrieved.

Now that the queue is open, we can start the background thread that runs our main code to process messages in the queue:

```
' Start reading from queue
mRunning = True
mMonitor = New Threading.Thread(AddressOf MonitorQueue)
mMonitor.Name = "MonitorQueue"
mMonitor.Start()
```

We set the mRunning variable to True, indicating that we want to continue running. Setting it to False indicates that we're trying to shut down and that our code should exit.

We then create a new thread object that will execute our MonitorQueue() method (which we'll create shortly), give the thread a meaningful name for debugging purposes, and start it. At this point, the main thread starts reading entries from the MSMQ queue and executing them.

The final step during startup is to configure remoting so that we can accept client requests. We start by configuring our TcpServerChannel object (if necessary):

```
' Start remoting for Server.BatchQueue
If mChannel Is Nothing Then

  ' Set application name (virtual root name)
  RemotingConfiguration.ApplicationName = LISTENER_NAME()

  ' Set up channel
  Dim properties As New Hashtable
  properties("name") = "TcpBinary"
  properties("port") = CStr(PORT())
  Dim svFormatter As New BinaryServerFormatterSinkProvider

  ' This line required for .NET 1.1 only
  svFormatter.TypeFilterLevel = _
     Runtime.Serialization.Formatters.TypeFilterLevel.Full

  mChannel = New TcpServerChannel(properties, svFormatter)
  Channels.ChannelServices.RegisterChannel(mChannel)
```

Under .NET 1.0, this wasn't quite so complex, but under 1.1 we need to set the `TypeFilterLevel` property on the formatter object, which requires a bit of extra code. If we don't set this property, remoting will prevent any system objects (such as collections) from being transferred across the network by value – and we count on that functionality. This change was made by Microsoft to tighten the default security of the .NET Framework.

Notice that the name (virtual root) of our remoting object and the port on which we listen come from the application configuration file, via the `LISTENER_NAME()` and `PORT()` methods:

```
Private Shared Function LISTENER_NAME() As String
  Return ConfigurationSettings.AppSettings("ListenerName")
End Function

Private Shared Function PORT() As Integer
  Return CInt(ConfigurationSettings.AppSettings("ListenerPort"))
End Function
```

By reading these values from the configuration file, we provide for flexible deployment and configuration of the service. When this service is installed on a server, an administrator can ensure that there are no port or virtual root collisions on the server by adjusting these values.

Once we have a channel configured, we can register our `Server.BatchQueue` class so that it's available:

```
      ' Register our class
      RemotingConfiguration.RegisterWellKnownServiceType( _
         GetType(Server.BatchQueue), _
         "BatchQueue.rem", _
         WellKnownObjectMode.SingleCall)

    Else
      mChannel.StartListening(Nothing)
    End If
```

At this point, remoting is configured, and our service will accept inbound requests from clients. Each inbound request will cause the creation of a `Server.BatchQueue` object running on a background thread from the thread pool.

Stopping the service

Because we're running in a multithreaded environment in which our 'main' processing is on one background thread, remoting requests are on other threads, and our batch jobs are executing on yet other threads, stopping the service is somewhat complex. Before we can close, we need to ensure that all these threads have completed – and while we're waiting for them to complete, we need to ensure that new threads aren't started up!

Fortunately, we can use various thread synchronization objects and techniques to simplify the coding of all this. The trouble is that any simple mistake in this code can cause our service to shut down improperly, or to remain running indefinitely! The `Stop()` method is called by the Windows service or a console application:

```
Public Shared Sub [Stop]()

  ' Stop remoting for Server.BatchQueue
  mChannel.StopListening(Nothing)

  ' Signal to stop working
  mRunning = False
  mSync.Set()
  mMonitor.Join()

  ' Close queue
  mQueue.Close()

  If mActiveEntries.Count > 0 Then

    ' Wait for work to end
    mWaitToEnd.WaitOne()
  End If

End Sub
```

First, we stop listening for client requests via remoting, thus preventing clients from submitting new entries:

```
' Stop remoting for Server.BatchQueue
mChannel.StopListening(Nothing)
```

Then, we tell our main processing thread to stop by setting `mRunning` to `False`. Of course, that thread might be blocked by the `mSync` object, so we set the `mSync` object to unblock the thread. It may still take some time for that thread to stop, and we don't want to go any further until it does, so we call the `Join()` method on that thread – which suspends our *current* thread until the `mMonitor` thread terminates:

```
' Signal to stop working
mRunning = False
mSync.Set()
mMonitor.Join()

' Close queue
mQueue.Close()
```

Once the queue-reading thread is terminated, we can close the MSMQ queue, since nothing will be interacting with it.

At this point, we're no longer accepting new client requests, and our queue-reading thread is terminated, so we won't start any new batch jobs. However, there might still be active batch jobs running, and we're not done until they're complete too:

```
If mActiveEntries.Count > 0 Then
  ' Wait for work to end
  mWaitToEnd.WaitOne()
End If
```

If there are active jobs running, then we wait on the `mWaitToEnd` synchronization object. When the last job completes, it will signal this object, unblocking our thread so that we can terminate.

Processing queued entries

When our service starts up, it creates a background thread to run a `MonitorQueue()` method. This method is responsible for reading messages from the MSMQ queue and launching batch entries when appropriate. While this process is fairly complex, we'll break it down into smaller parts, starting with the core loop:

```
' This will be running on a background thread
Private Shared Sub MonitorQueue()

  While mRunning
    ScanQueue()
    mSync.WaitOne()
  End While

End Sub
```

This loop will run until the service shuts down by having `mRunning` set to `False`. Notice that when we're not scanning the queue for entries to process, we're blocked on the `mSync` object due to the call to its `WaitOne()` method. The `WaitOne()` method blocks our thread until some other thread signals the `mSync` object by calling its `Set()` method.

The `mSync` object is signaled in several cases:

- When a new entry is submitted by a client
- When the timer object fires to indicate that a schedule entry should be run
- When an active batch entry completes
- When we are shutting down and the `Stop()` method wants us to terminate

In the first three cases, when we wake up we'll immediately call the `ScanQueue()` method, which scans the queue to see if there are any entries that should be executed. Now, in normal MSMQ code, we'd simply call the `MessageQueue` object's `Receive()` method to read the next entry in the queue. Unfortunately, this won't work in our case.

The trouble here is that MSMQ has no concept of scheduled messages. It understands priorities, and always processes the highest priority messages first, but it has no way of leaving messages in the queue if they are not ready for processing. Because of this, we can't simply call the `Receive()` method to read the next message from the queue. Instead, we need to scan the queue manually to see if any entries should actually be processed at this time.

While we're doing this, we also need to see if there are any entries that are scheduled for future processing. If there are, then we need to find out when the next one is to be executed so that we can set our timer object to fire at that time:

```
    ' This is called by MonitorQueue
    Private Shared Sub ScanQueue()
      Dim msg As Message
      Dim holdUntil As Date
      Dim nextWake As Date = Date.MaxValue

      Dim en As MessageEnumerator = mQueue.GetMessageEnumerator()
      While en.MoveNext()
        msg = en.Current
        holdUntil = CDate(Text.Encoding.ASCII.GetString(msg.Extension))
        If holdUntil <= Now Then
          If mActiveEntries.Count < MAX_ENTRIES() Then
            ProcessEntry(mQueue.ReceiveById(msg.Id))
          Else

            ' The queue is busy, block the thread
            Exit Sub
          End If
        ElseIf holdUntil < nextWake Then

          ' Find the minimum holduntil value
          nextWake = holdUntil
        End If
      End While

      If nextWake < Date.MaxValue AndAlso nextWake > Now Then
        ' We have at least one entry holding, so set
        ' the timer to wake us when it should be run
        mTimer.Interval = nextWake.Subtract(Now).TotalMilliseconds
        mTimer.Start()
      End If

    End Sub
```

Manually scanning through the entries in the queue is actually pretty easy. We simply create a `MessageEnumerator` object, which is like a collection of entries in the queue. This object can be used to loop through all the entries by calling its `MoveNext()` method:

```
      Dim en As MessageEnumerator = mQueue.GetMessageEnumerator()
      While en.MoveNext()
```

We're using the `Extension` property of each MSMQ `Message` object to store the date and time when the entry should be processed. For each message, we take this value and convert it to a `Date` object so that we can easily see if its date/time is in the future:

```
        msg = en.Current
        holdUntil = CDate(Text.Encoding.ASCII.GetString(msg.Extension))
        If holdUntil <= Now Then
```

If the message is scheduled to run now (or in the past), then we'll execute it immediately (assuming the queue isn't busy):

```
If mActiveEntries.Count < MAX_ENTRIES() Then
  ProcessEntry(mQueue.ReceiveById(msg.Id))
Else

  ' The queue is busy, block the thread
  Exit Sub
End If
```

The `MAX_ENTRIES()` function returns the maximum number of worker threads that we can run, based on a configuration file setting:

```
Private Shared Function MAX_ENTRIES() As Integer
  Return CInt(ConfigurationSettings.AppSettings("MaxmActiveEntries"))
End Function
```

Note that the configuration file settings are read once, *when the Windows service starts up. They are then cached in memory by the .NET runtime. To change these settings, we need to stop and restart the service.*

If the number of active jobs is less than the maximum, then we call `ProcessEntry()` to execute the entry. Otherwise, we can exit the entire method because the queue is busy. As soon as one of the active entries completes, it will signal the `mSync` object, thus causing our thread to scan the queue again and run any pending entries.

If we do want to process the entry, we call `ProcessEntry()`, passing it the `Message` object from the queue. Notice that here we *are* calling a "receive" method – `ReceiveById()`. This not only gives us the `Message` object, but also removes the message from the queue.

On the other hand, if this particular entry is scheduled for future execution, we see if its scheduled date is the soonest we've seen, and if so we record its date/time:

```
ElseIf holdUntil < nextWake Then

  ' Find the minimum holduntil value
  nextWake = holdUntil
End If
```

After we've looped through all the entries in the queue, we check to see if there are entries scheduled in the future. If there are, then we set our timer object to fire when the next entry is to be run:

```
If nextWake < Date.MaxValue AndAlso nextWake > Now Then

  ' We have at least one entry holding, so set
  ' the timer to wake us when it should be run
  mTimer.Interval = nextWake.Subtract(Now).TotalMilliseconds
  mTimer.Start()
End If
```

When the timer fires, we simply signal the `mSync` object, releasing our main thread to scan the queue so that it can process the entry:

```
' This runs on a threadpool thread
Private Shared Sub mTimer_Elapsed(ByVal sender As Object, _
  ByVal e As System.Timers.ElapsedEventArgs) Handles mTimer.Elapsed

  mTimer.Stop()
  mSync.Set()
End Sub
```

Notice that the timer's `Stop()` method is called, so it won't fire again unless it is reset by the `ScanQueue()` method. If we have no entries scheduled for future processing, then there's no sense having the timer fire, so we just turn it off.

In the case that `ScanQueue()` did find an entry to execute, it calls the `ProcessEntry()` method. This actually does the work of launching the entry on a background thread from the thread pool:

```
Private Shared Sub ProcessEntry(ByVal msg As Message)

  ' Get entry from queue
  Dim entry As BatchEntry
  Dim formatter As New BinaryFormatter
  entry = CType(formatter.Deserialize(msg.BodyStream), BatchEntry)

  ' Make active
  entry.Info.SetStatus(BatchEntryStatus.Active)
  mActiveEntries.Add(entry.Info.ID, entry.Info)

  ' Start processing entry on background thread
  Threading.ThreadPool.QueueUserWorkItem(AddressOf entry.Execute)
End Sub
```

The first thing we do is to deserialize the `BatchEntry` object out of the MSMQ `Message` object:

```
' Get entry from queue
Dim entry As BatchEntry
Dim formatter As New BinaryFormatter
entry = CType(formatter.Deserialize(msg.BodyStream), BatchEntry)
```

> *The `Body` property of a `Message` object uses XML formatters, like those for web services. In our case, we're doing deep serialization using the `BinaryFormatter`, so we get a complete copy of the object, rather than a copy of just a few of its properties. This requires that we use the `BodyStream` property instead, so that we can read and write our own binary data stream into the `Message` object.*

Once we have the `BatchEntry` object, we also have access to the four objects it contains: the worker, 'state', `BatchEntryInfo` and `BusinessPrincipal` objects.

The next thing we need to do is mark this entry as being active. Remember that the `Message` object is no longer in the MSMQ queue at this stage, so it's up to us to keep track of it as it runs. That's why we created the `mActiveEntries` `Hashtable` object:

```
' Make active
entry.Info.SetStatus(BatchEntryStatus.Active)
mActiveEntries.Add(entry.Info.ID, entry.Info)
```

Since this is a synchronized `Hashtable`, we don't have to worry about threading issues as we add the entry to the collection. The `Hashtable` object takes care of any synchronization issues for us.

Because our active entries are only stored in an in-memory `Hashtable`, if the Windows service or server machine crashes during the processing of a batch job, that batch job will be lost. Solving this is a non-trivial problem. Though we could easily keep a persistent list of the active jobs, there's no way to know if it is safe to re-run them when the service comes back online. We have no way of knowing if they were halfway through a task, or if restarting that task would destroy data.

The final step is to execute the `BatchEntry` object, which in turn will execute the worker object. We want this to run on a background thread so that it doesn't tie up any of our existing threads.

While we could manually create a thread each time we want to run a background task, this is somewhat expensive. There's quite a bit of overhead involved in creating threads, so it's best to reuse existing threads when possible. In fact, it would be ideal to have a pool of existing threads to which we could assign tasks when needed. Luckily, the .NET Framework includes a `ThreadPool` class that manages exactly such a thread pool on our behalf. We can simply add our `BatchEntry` object's `Execute()` method to the list of tasks to be processed by a thread in the pool:

```
' Start processing entry on background thread
Threading.ThreadPool.QueueUserWorkItem(AddressOf entry.Execute)
```

Note that the `ThreadPool` class maintains its own queue of tasks to perform; this pool is shared across our entire Windows process, and is used by remoting, timer objects, and various other .NET runtime code, as well as being available for our use. As soon as a thread is available from the thread pool, it will be used to execute our code.

The number of threads in the thread pool is managed by the .NET runtime. The maximum number of threads in the pool defaults to 25 per processor on the machine. This can be changed if desired – refer to the online help for details at:
ms-help://MS.VSCC.2003/MS.MSDNQTR.2003FEB.1033/cpref/html/frlrfSystemThreadingThreadPoolClassTopic.htm.

At this point, the batch task will run on the background thread in the thread pool, and our main thread can go back to scanning the queue for other entries that are ready to run.

Marking an entry as complete

Earlier, we wrote code to implement the `BatchEntry` object. In its `Execute()` method, it invokes the actual worker object via its `IBatchEntry` interface:

```
' Now run the user's code
mWorker.Execute(mState)
```

This code is wrapped in a `Try...Finally` block, guaranteeing that when the worker is done processing, we will call a method on the `BatchQueueService` to indicate that the entry is complete:

```
    Finally
      Server.BatchQueueService.Deactivate(Me)
```

This `Deactivate()` method is responsible for removing the entry from the list of active tasks. It also signals the `mSync` object to release the main thread so that the latter scans the queue to see if another entry should be executed:

```
' Called by BatchEntry when it is done processing so we know
' that it is complete and we can start another job if needed
Friend Shared Sub Deactivate(ByVal entry As BatchEntry)

  mActiveEntries.Remove(entry.Info.ID)
  mSync.Set()

  If Not mRunning AndAlso mActiveEntries.Count = 0 Then
    ' Indicate that there are no active workers
    mWaitToEnd.Set()
  End If

End Sub
```

It also checks to see if we are trying to close down the service. If we *are* trying to do that (`mRunning` is `False`), and this was the last active entry, we signal the `mWaitToEnd` object to indicate that it's safe to exit the entire service:

```
    If Not mRunning AndAlso mActiveEntries.Count = 0 Then
      ' Indicate that there are no active workers
      mWaitToEnd.Set()
    End If
```

Remember that in the `Stop()` method, we block on `mWaitToEnd` if there are any active tasks. This code therefore ensures that when the last task completes, we notify the main service thread that everything is complete, so the service can terminate. Of course, the service will only terminate if the server machine is shutting down, or if the user has requested that the service be stopped by using the management console.

Enqueue/Dequeue/LoadEntries

The `Server.BatchQueue` object also accepts requests from clients to submit, remove, and list batch entries. In all three cases, the `Server.BatchQueue` object calls into our `BatchQueueService` class to enqueue, dequeue, or list the entries in the queue. The `Enqueue()` method adds a new entry to the queue:

```
Friend Shared Sub Enqueue(ByVal Entry As BatchEntry)

  Dim msg As New Message
  Dim f As New BinaryFormatter

  With msg
    .Label = Entry.ToString
    .Priority = Entry.Info.Priority
    .Extension = Text.Encoding.ASCII.GetBytes(CStr(Entry.Info.HoldUntil))
    Entry.Info.SetMessageID(.Id)
```

```
            f.Serialize(.BodyStream, Entry)
        End With

        mQueue.Send(msg)
        mSync.Set()

    End Sub
```

Here, we set some members of the Message object, including its Label, Priority, and Extension properties. In our case, we want to store the date/time when the entry should run, so we convert that value to a Byte array and put it into the property:

```
            .Label = Entry.ToString
            .Priority = Entry.Info.Priority
            .Extension = Text.Encoding.ASCII.GetBytes(CStr(Entry.Info.HoldUntil))
```

Then we put the Message object's Id property value into our BatchEntryInfo object for later reference:

```
            Entry.Info.SetMessageID(.Id)
```

Finally, we serialize the BatchEntry object (and thus the objects it contains) into a binary format, which is loaded into the MSMQ Message object's BodyStream property:

```
            f.Serialize(.BodyStream, Entry)
```

Once the Message object is all configured, we submit it to MSMQ:

```
        mQueue.Send(msg)
```

MSMQ will automatically sort the entries in the queue based on their priority, and our ScanQueue() method will ensure that the entry won't run until its HoldUntil time. Of these two, the HoldUntil value has precedence. In other words, an entry will *never* run before its HoldUntil time. After its HoldUntil time is passed, an entry will be changed from Holding to Pending status in the queue, and will run in priority order along with any other Pending entries in the queue at that time.

It's very likely that the main queue reader thread is blocked on the mSync object, so we need to wake it up so that it can process our new entry in the queue. We do this by calling the Set() method on the mSync object:

```
        mSync.Set()
```

At this point, the queue will be scanned and our entry will be launched – assuming, of course, that it isn't scheduled for future processing, and the queue isn't already busy.

The client can also remove an entry from the queue. We implement this in the `Dequeue()` method, which finds the queue entry based on its `Label` value, and removes it from the MSMQ queue:

```
Friend Shared Sub Dequeue(ByVal Entry As BatchEntryInfo)

  Dim label As String
  Dim msg As Message
  Dim msgID As String

  label = Entry.ToString
  Dim en As MessageEnumerator = mQueue.GetMessageEnumerator
  mQueue.MessageReadPropertyFilter.Label = True

  While en.MoveNext()
    If en.Current.Label = label Then

      ' We found a match
      msgID = en.Current.Id
      Exit While
    End If
  End While

  If Len(msgID) > 0 Then
    mQueue.ReceiveById(msgID)
  End If

End Sub
```

Remember that the `Message` object's label is set to the `ToString()` value of our `BatchEntryInfo` object. That value contains the unique GUID we assigned to the `BatchEntry` when it was created, so it's a good value to use when searching for a specific entry in the queue.

We create a `MessageEnumerator` object and use it to scan through all the entries in the queue. If we find one with a matching `Label` value, we record the `Message` object's `Id` property and exit the loop. Finally, if we got a `Message Id` value, we remove the message from the queue based on its `Id`:

```
  If Len(msgID) > 0 Then
    mQueue.ReceiveById(msgID)
  End If
```

The last bit of functionality that we need to provide is the ability to get a list of the entries in the queue, including the entries that are actively being processed. We'll be populating a `BatchEntries` collection object with this data, but the data itself will come from both our `Hashtable` and the MSMQ queue:

```
Friend Shared Sub LoadEntries(ByVal List As BatchEntries)

  ' Load our list of BatchEntry objects
  Dim msgs() As Message
  Dim msg As Message
  Dim formatter As New BinaryFormatter
  Dim de As DictionaryEntry
  Dim entry As Server.BatchEntry
```

```
      ' Get all active entries
      SyncLock mActiveEntries.SyncRoot
        For Each de In Server.BatchQueueService.mActiveEntries
          List.Add(CType(de.Value, BatchEntryInfo))
        Next
      End SyncLock

      ' Get all queued entries
      msgs = mQueue.GetAllMessages
      For Each msg In msgs
        entry = CType(formatter.Deserialize(msg.BodyStream), Server.BatchEntry)
        entry.Info.SetMessageID(msg.Id)
        List.Add(entry.Info)
      Next

    End Sub
```

First, we scan through the active entries in the `Hashtable`, adding each entry's `BatchEntryInfo` object to the `BatchEntries` collection object:

```
      ' Get all active entries
      SyncLock mActiveEntries.SyncRoot
        For Each de In Server.BatchQueueService.mActiveEntries
          List.Add(CType(de.Value, BatchEntryInfo))
        Next
      End SyncLock
```

Note that we've enclosed this in a `SyncLock` block based on the `Hashtable` object's `SyncRoot` property. The VB.NET `SyncLock` statement is used to synchronize multiple threads, to ensure that only one thread can run the code inside the block structure at any one time. If a thread is running this code, any other thread wishing to run the code is blocked at the `SyncLock` statement until the first thread exits the block.

> *This is a classic implementation of a critical section, which is a common synchronization technique used in multithreaded applications.*

This technique is required any time we want to enumerate through all the entries in a synchronized `Hashtable` object. The `Hashtable` object's synchronization wrapper automatically handles synchronization for adding and removing entries from the collection, but it *doesn't* protect the enumeration process, so we need this `SyncLock` block to make sure that no other threads collide with our code.

Once we have a list of the active entries, we scan the MSMQ queue to get a list of all the pending and future scheduled entries:

```
' Get all queued entries
msgs = mQueue.GetAllMessages
For Each msg In msgs
  entry = CType(formatter.Deserialize(msg.BodyStream), Server.BatchEntry)
  entry.Info.SetMessageID(msg.Id)
  List.Add(entry.Info)
Next
```

Since we're creating a collection of `BatchEntryInfo` objects, we must deserialize the `BatchEntry` objects contained in each of the `Message` objects so that we can get at the `BatchEntryInfo` object. That object is then added to the `BatchEntries` collection object.

The end result is that the `BatchEntries` collection object has a list of all the active, pending, and holding batch entries in our queue. That collection object can then be returned to the client as a result of its remoting call. At this point, our `CSLA.BatchQueue` assembly is complete. We can move on to debugging it via a console application, and then to running it within a Windows service application.

Creating a console application for debugging

Since all the actual work for our service is encapsulated in the `CSLA.BatchQueue` assembly, creating a host application – either a Windows service or a console application – is very easy. All we need to do is reference the appropriate CSLA assemblies, and call the `Start()` and `Stop()` methods on the `CSLA.BatchQueue.Server.BatchQueueService` class as appropriate.

Add a new Console Application named `BatchQueueTest` to the `CSLA` solution. Then, add a reference to the CSLA projects that our code uses (directly or indirectly):

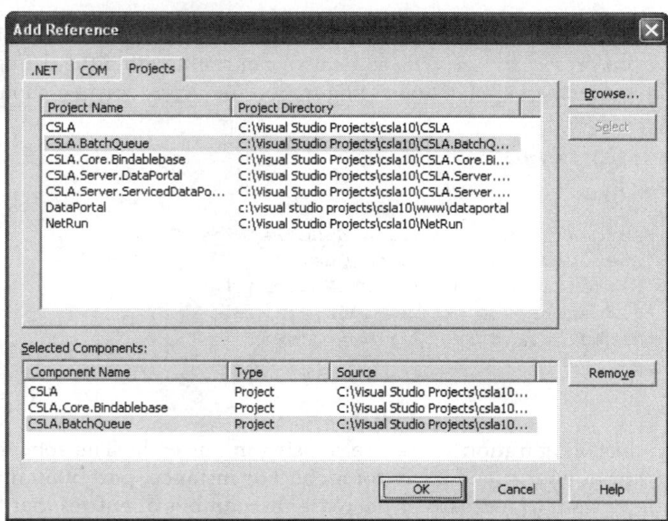

Though we'll only be *using* `CSLA.BatchQueue`, it relies on classes from `CSLA`, and `CSLA` relies on classes from `CSLA.BindableBase`.

Now we can write the code to host our service. Update `Module1` as follows:

```
Imports CSLA.BatchQueue.Server

Module Module1

  Sub Main()

    Console.WriteLine("Server on thread {0}", AppDomain.GetCurrentThreadId)
    Console.WriteLine("Starting...")
    BatchQueueService.Start()
    Console.WriteLine("Started")

    Console.WriteLine("Press ENTER to end")
    Console.ReadLine()

    Console.WriteLine("Stopping...")
    BatchQueueService.Stop()
    Console.WriteLine("Stopped")

  End Sub

End Module
```

In this test, all we need to do is start up the service by calling `BatchQueueService.Start()`, and then wait until the user presses the *Enter* key. At that point, we can call the `Stop()` method to shut down the service.

Our code will run here just like it would in a Windows service, but we have the ability to set our console application as the startup project in VS.NET, so that we can run it within the debugger. We also need to add a new item to the project: an application configuration file. `App.config` should contain the following:

```
<?xml version="1.0" encoding="utf-8" ?>
<configuration>
  <appSettings>
    <add key="Authentication" value="Windows" />
    <add key="QueueName" value="BatchQueue" />
    <add key="ListenerName" value="CSLABatch" />
    <add key="ListenerPort" value="5050" />
    <add key="MaxActiveEntries" value="2" />
  </appSettings>
</configuration>
```

This defines the various configuration values we're using in our code. The specific values may need to be adjusted to work within your specific environment. For instance, port 5050 may already be in use on your server, or you may want to increase or decrease the number of entries that the queue will execute on different threads at any given time.

> **Remember that any DLLs containing worker object code must also reside in the same directory as `BatchQueueTest.exe`.**

At this point, we should be able to run the batch queue service at the console. If we put business DLLs containing our worker objects into the same directory as the console application, we can submit jobs to the queue and have them processed.

In the code download, there's also a Windows client project named `BatchMonitor` that provides a graphic display of the entries in the queue.

Creating the Windows Service project

We can also create a Windows service host for the batch queue processing code. Happily, doing so in VS.NET is pretty straightforward, as it's a standard project type. Add a new Windows Service project to the `CSLA` solution, and name it `BatchQueue`.

Add references to the `CSLA.BindableBase`, `CSLA`, and `CSLA.BatchQueue` projects, just like we did for the console application. Also, add an `App.config` file to the project with the same contents as the console application above.

Rename `Service1` to `BatchQueue` (both the VB file and all references to `Service1` in the file's code – you should find three of them). In that component, import the `CSLA.BatchQueue` namespace:

```
Imports System.ServiceProcess
Imports CSLA.BatchQueue.Server
```

Then all we need to do is call our `Start()` and `Stop()` methods in the service's `OnStart()` and `OnStop()` handlers:

```
  Protected Overrides Sub OnStart(ByVal args() As String)
    BatchQueueService.Start()
  End Sub

  Protected Overrides Sub OnStop()
    BatchQueueService.Stop()
  End Sub
```

And that's all there is to it! Our `BatchQueueService` class contains all the code to make the service work, including ensuring that all the actual work occurs on background threads, so the main service thread remains available for interaction with the operating system and the Windows service manager.

The only other thing we need to do is add an installer class to the project. This is required for all Windows service assemblies, as it contains the information necessary to install and configure the service on the server. This installer object is automatically invoked by the .NET runtime as our service is installed or uninstalled on a system.

> *For a more complete discussion of the installer class and the creation of a Windows service, please refer to* Fast Track VB.NET *(1-861007-12-4).*

Add a new installer class called `BatchQueueInstaller` to the project:

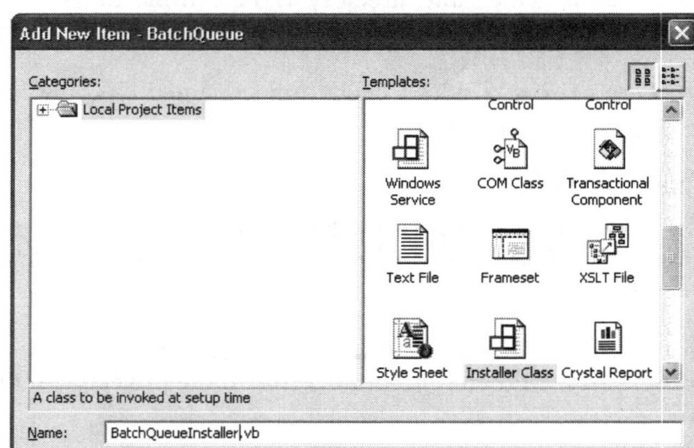

It needs to import the `System.ServiceProcess` namespace:

```
Imports System.ComponentModel
Imports System.Configuration.Install
Imports System.ServiceProcess
```

Within the installer class itself, we need to declare and initialize a couple of variables:

```
  Private mServiceInstaller As New ServiceInstaller
  Private mProcessInstaller As New ServiceProcessInstaller

  Private Sub InitInstaller()
    mProcessInstaller.Account = ServiceAccount.LocalSystem
    mServiceInstaller.StartType = ServiceStartMode.Automatic
    mServiceInstaller.ServiceName = "CSLABatchQueue"
    Installers.Add(mServiceInstaller)
    Installers.Add(mProcessInstaller)
  End Sub
```

The `ServiceInstaller` object is used to specify information about the Windows service, including its startup mode and the name of the service. The `ServiceProcessInstaller` object is used to specify the login credentials for the Windows service process. In this case, we're indicating that the service should run under the local `System` account on the server.

Both of these objects are then added to the `Installers` collection, so that they're available to the installation process.

We need to initialize these variables in three different cases: install, uninstall, and rollback of an install. Each of these cases causes an event to be raised, so all we need to do is handle these events and call the initialization method from each:

```
Private Sub Installer_BeforeInstall(ByVal sender As Object, _
   ByVal e As System.Configuration.Install.InstallEventArgs) _
   Handles MyBase.BeforeInstall

  InitInstaller()
End Sub

Private Sub Installer_BeforeRollback(ByVal sender As Object, _
   ByVal e As System.Configuration.Install.InstallEventArgs) _
   Handles MyBase.BeforeRollback

  InitInstaller()
End Sub

Private Sub Installer_BeforeUninstall(ByVal sender As Object, _
   ByVal e As System.Configuration.Install.InstallEventArgs) _
   Handles MyBase.BeforeUninstall

  InitInstaller()
End Sub
```

This code is run by the .NET runtime as our service is being installed or uninstalled, or during the rollback of an installation. `InitInstaller()` configures .NET Framework objects to provide the information required by the .NET runtime to install or uninstall the service properly. We simply make sure to call this method before any attempt is made to install, rollback the install, or uninstall the service.

At this point, our Windows service is complete, and can therefore be installed on a server by using the `installutil.exe` command line utility:

```
> installutil batchqueue.exe
```

This .NET utility will install the service on the machine by invoking our installer object. To uninstall the service, use the `/u` switch:

```
> installutil batchqueue.exe /u
```

Note that uninstallation won't complete while the Service Management Console is open. If the console is open, it must be closed and reopened to allow uninstallation to complete.

Once the service is installed, we can use the Windows Service Management Console to start, stop, and otherwise interact with the service:

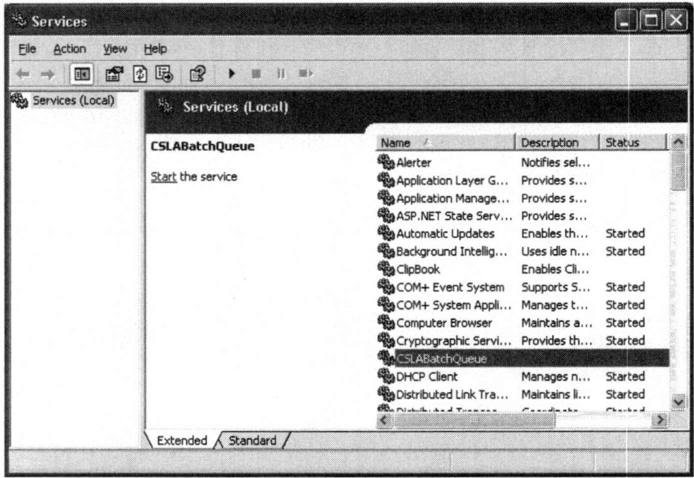

When the service is started, it will open the MSMQ queue and listen for client requests via remoting. At this point, with the service running, we can create batch worker DLLs and then submit them from client applications.

Creating and running batch jobs

Now that we have a batch processing utility, we should walk through the process of actually using it. This comes in two parts: creating code to run in the batch processor, and creating client code to submit the task.

Creating a batch job

To create a batch job, all we need to do is create an assembly that references `CSLA.BatchQueue` and includes a class that implements the `IBatchEntry` interface. What we do beyond that is entirely up to us – we could be generating a report, processing data from a database, or doing virtually any other task that we might want to run on the server.

For instance, in our `ProjectTracker` solution, we can add a new Class Library project named `PTBatch`. Since this code will interact with our CLSA-based `ProjectTracker.Library.dll` assembly, we need to reference the following assemblies:

- `CSLA.dll`
- `CSLA.BindableBase.dll`
- `CSLA.Server.DataPortal.dll`
- `CSLA.Server.ServicedDataPortal.dll`
- `CSLA.BatchQueue.dll`

The first four of these assemblies should be referenced using the **Browse** button in the Add Reference dialog, and they should come from the `ProjectTracker.Library` project's `bin` directory. The `CSLA.BatchQueue.dll` assembly should be referenced from the `bin` directory of the `CSLA.BatchQueue` project. Of course, we also need to reference the `ProjectTracker.Library` project to get access to our business classes.

In this new project, we can add a class named `ProjectJob` with the following code:

```
Imports CSLA.BatchQueue
Imports ProjectTracker.Library

Public Class ProjectJob
  Implements IBatchEntry

  Public Sub Execute(ByVal State As Object) _
     Implements CSLA.BatchQueue.IBatchEntry.Execute

    Dim projects As ProjectList = ProjectList.GetProjectList
    Dim info As ProjectList.ProjectInfo
    Dim project As Project

    For Each info In projects
      project = project.GetProject(info.ID)
      project.Name = project.Name & " (batch)"
      project.Save()
    Next

  End Sub

End Class
```

The class implements the `IBatchEntry` interface, so it can be invoked by our batch processing service. Within the `Execute()` method, we place the code that's to be run on the server. In this case, we're simply getting a list of all the projects in the system, then looping through them to update their `Name` properties.

In fact, this code illustrates a rather poor approach to updating all the `Name` values of our `Project` objects. This sort of thing is probably better done through a stored procedure within the database server itself. If we must do this sort of thing on the application server, we'd be better off using direct ADO.NET code to update the records. I've used this implementation merely as an example of how to construct a batch job that runs on the server to do some business processing, not as an ideal example for large-scale batch processing.

Build this assembly, and then copy the `PTBatch.dll` file from the `bin` directory to the directory containing our `BatchQueue.exe` Windows service file, so that it's available to the batch processing service.

We also need to copy `ProjectTracker.Library.dll` into the batch service directory, as it's required by `PTBatch.dll`.

The caveat here is that our batch code will be using the application configuration file *for the batch processing service*, which means that the configuration file for the service must include any configuration entries that will be used by our batch worker code. In our case, this means that the standard CSLA .NET configuration entries for security, and either database connection strings or `DataPortal` URLs, must be included. We'll have a look at such a file in the next section.

Also be aware that the user account under which the Windows service is running must have access to the databases, and to any other system resources used by our code. The `System` account of the server is rarely ideal for this purpose, so we should create an account specifically for the batch service to run under. This way, we can grant *that* account appropriate database access, and so forth.

Submitting a batch job

We can now create code in our client to submit the batch job. We can do this from Windows, web, or web service interface code, or from other batch job code.

In any case, the client project needs to have a reference to `CSLA.BatchQueue.dll`, and its configuration file needs to have an entry specifying the URL of the default batch server. For instance, add the following line to the `App.config` file in the `PTWin` project:

```
<add key="DefaultBatchQueueServer"
     value="tcp://localhost:5050/cslabatch/batchqueue.rem" />
```

You'll have to change the port and virtual root name to match those from the `BatchQueue` *host application's configuration file.*

With that done, we can create a `BatchQueue` object and call its `Submit()` method to submit a job for processing. In most cases, we'll use the `BatchJobRequest` object to do this, so we don't need to install the worker DLL on the client workstation.

For instance, in our Windows Forms client, we could add a menu option to submit our project batch job like this:

```
Private Sub mnuProjectUpdate_Click(ByVal sender As System.Object, _
   ByVal e As System.EventArgs) Handles mnuProjectUpdate.Click

  Dim batch As New BatchQueue
  batch.Submit(New BatchJobRequest("PTBatch.ProjectJob", "PTBatch"))
End Sub
```

All we have to do is to create an instance of the `BatchQueue` object, and then call its `Submit()` method, passing a worker object as a parameter. In this case, we're passing a `BatchJobRequest` object that's been initialized with the type and assembly name of our `PTBatch.ProjectJob` class.

To see this work, take the following steps:

- Copy `PTBatch.dll` and `ProjectTracker.Library.dll` to the directory containing the batch service application
- Add the CSLA .NET and application-specific configuration file entries to the service configuration file
- Set up the Windows service to run under a user account that has access to our database server

By copying `PTBatch.dll` and `ProjectTracker.Library.dll` to the batch service directory, we make that code available for use by the batch engine. This is important, since the `BatchJobRequest` object we created in `PTWin` contains the type and assembly information to create an instance of our worker class from the `PTBatch.dll` assembly.

Since our worker code will run in the batch server process, it will use the configuration file settings of the batch server application. Because of this, we need to make sure that the configuration file includes the database connection strings required by our code to access the `PTracker` database. The end result is that the configuration file should look like this:

```
<?xml version="1.0" encoding="utf-8" ?>
<configuration>
  <appSettings>
    <add key="Authentication" value="CSLA" />
    <add key="QueueName" value="BatchQueue" />
    <add key="ListenerName" value="CSLABatch" />
    <add key="ListenerPort" value="5050" />
    <add key="MaxActiveEntries" value="2" />

    <add key="DB:PTracker" value="data source=server;
               initial catalog=PTracker;
               integrated security=SSPI" />
    <add key="DB:Security" value="data source=server;
               initial catalog=Security;
               integrated security=SSPI" />
    <add key="DefaultBatchQueueServer"
      value="tcp://localhost:5050/cslabatch/batchqueue.rem" />
  </appSettings>
</configuration>
```

We include not only the settings to configure the batch server, but also the database connection strings for our databases.

Also notice that we've included the `DefaultBatchQueueServer` setting in this file too. This is useful because it allows our worker code to submit new batch entries to the queue, if we so desire. (An example where this could be important is a daily job that needs to resubmit itself to run the next day.)

Before we can run the `PTWin` application and choose the menu option to submit a new entry, the queue service must be running. We can either start the Windows service, or we can run the console application version of the service. Either way, once it is running, the service listens on the port we specified (5050 in the example) for inbound remoting requests.

The `PTWin` client application can then call the `Submit()` method of the client-side `BatchQueue` class, which contacts the server via remoting to submit the job. The end result should be that the batch job runs, all of our `Project` objects' `Name` values are updated, and an entry is written into the application event log indicating success:

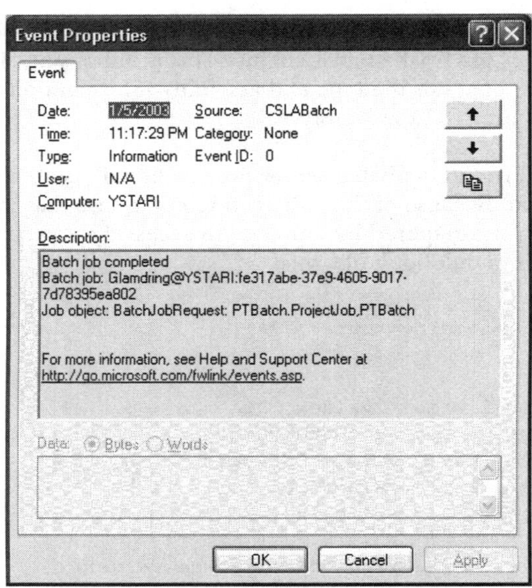

Using this technique, we can easily create and submit almost any type of batch job to the server, including the creation of reports, processing of large data sets, and so forth.

Loading a DataSet from objects

As we discussed earlier, the biggest single problem we face when trying to do reporting in an object-oriented application is that the commercial report generation engines don't support the concept of reporting against objects.

There's also the issue that generating reports against large sets of data would require that we create massive numbers of objects – and there's a lot of overhead involved in that process. The truth is that when we need to create a really large report, we're probably better off simply generating the report directly from the database. For smaller reports or lists, however, it would be nice if we could generate reports based on our objects.

> *Though the code we're about to create is unrelated to the batch processor we just finished, the two can be used in combination: it's quite likely that a batch job will be used to generate a report. In that case, we may use the object-to-`DataSet` converter within that batch job's worker code as we generate the report.*

To overcome the limitations of the reporting tools, we can create a utility that generates a `DataSet` (or more accurately, a `DataTable` in a `DataSet`) based on an object (or a collection of objects). This is not terribly difficult, as we can use reflection to get a list of the properties or fields on the objects, and then to loop through the objects' properties to populate the `DataTable` with their values.

> *This is not a new concept. The `OleDbDataAdapter` object has a `Fill()` method that populates a `DataTable` object from an ADO `Recordset`. We're going to do basically the same thing, but using a business object or collection of objects as a data source, instead of a `Recordset`.*

What we're creating is somewhat similar to a data adapter object such as `OleDbDataAdapter`, in that we'll implement a `Fill()` method that fills a `DataSet` with data from an object or collection.

The ObjectAdapter class

To implement a `Fill()` method that copies data from a source such as a business object into a `DataSet`, we need to support a certain amount of basic functionality. In ADO.NET, data is stored in a `DataTable`, and then that `DataTable` is held in a `DataSet`. This means that what we're really talking about here is copying data from a data source into a `DataTable` object.

So: we need to be able to examine the data source to get a list of the properties, fields, or columns it exposes. That list will be used to define the list of columns we'll be creating in the target `DataTable` object. Alternatively, we'll support the concept of a pre-existing `DataTable` that already contains columns. In that case, we'll attempt to find properties, fields, or columns in our data source that match the columns that already exist in the target `DataTable` object.

Also, rather obviously, we need to be able to retrieve data values from the original data source. To do this, we'll use reflection, as it allows us to create code to retrieve values from the properties or fields of an object dynamically.

Operational scope

The following diagram illustrates the possible data sources we want to support with our `ObjectAdapter` class:

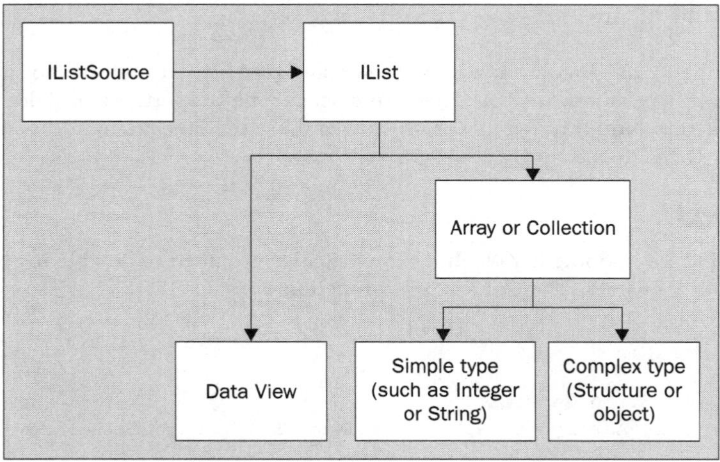

> *We could simplify our code by only supporting binding to an object, but by supporting* any *valid data source (including ADO.NET objects, or arrays of simple values), we are providing a more complete solution.*

Ultimately, we want to be able to retrieve a list of column, property, or field names from a `DataView`, or from the elements contained within an array or collection – and those might be simple types (such as `Integer` or `String`) or complex types (such as a `Structure` or an object).

Helpfully, as you can see, all data sources implement the IList interface that's defined in the .NET Framework. However, sometimes we need to dig a bit to find that interface. Some data source objects, such as a DataSet, don't expose IList directly. Instead, they expose IListSource, which we can use to get an IList. As you'll see, we'll have to allow for these different possibilities as we build our class.

Setting up the class

Add a new class to the CSLA project named ObjectAdapter. This class will contain our code to create a DataTable from an object. To start it off, let's import some namespaces and declare an ArrayList to hold the names of the columns we'll be adding to the DataTable:

```
Imports System.ComponentModel
Imports System.Reflection

Namespace Data

  Public Class ObjectAdapter

    Private mColumns As New ArrayList

  End Class

End Namespace
```

The full type name for this class is CSLA.Data.ObjectAdapter. The mColumns object will be used to maintain a list of the columns of the DataTable that we'll be populating from our object's properties and fields during the fill process.

Before we write the Fill() method, we need to create some helper methods to simplify the process. When we do the fill operation, we'll first need to discover the properties and fields on the source object, and then we'll need to loop through all the objects, and use the object data to populate rows of data in the target DataTable.

GetField method

At the core of what we're doing is reflection. In particular, we need to be able to retrieve a value from the object's property or field. The GetField() function does just that:

```
#Region " GetField "

    Private Function GetField( _
       ByVal obj As Object, ByVal FieldName As String) As String

      If TypeOf obj Is DataRowView Then

        ' This is a DataRowView from a DataView
        Return CType(obj, DataRowView).Item(FieldName).ToString
      ElseIf TypeOf obj Is ValueType AndAlso obj.GetType.IsPrimitive Then

        ' This is a primitive value type
        Return obj.ToString
```

```
      ElseIf TypeOf obj Is String Then
        ' This is a simple string
        Return CStr(obj)
      Else

        ' This is an object or Structure
        Try
          Dim sourcetype As Type = obj.GetType

          ' See if the field is a property
          Dim prop As PropertyInfo = sourcetype.GetProperty(FieldName)

          If prop Is Nothing OrElse Not prop.CanRead Then

            ' No readable property of that name exists - check for a field
            Dim field As FieldInfo = sourcetype.GetField(FieldName)
            If field Is Nothing Then

              ' No field exists either, throw an exception
              Throw New System.Data.DataException( _
                          "No such value exists: " & FieldName)
            Else

              ' Got a field, return its value
              Return field.GetValue(obj).ToString
            End If
          Else

            ' Found a property, return its value
            Return prop.GetValue(obj, Nothing).ToString
          End If

        Catch ex As Exception
          Throw New System.Data.DataException( _
                      "Error reading value: " & FieldName, ex)
        End Try
      End If

    End Function

  #End Region
```

One of the data sources that we said we want to support is an ADO.NET `DataView`. In that case, the object we're dealing with here will be a `DataRowView`:

```
      If TypeOf obj Is DataRowView Then

        ' This is a DataRowView from a DataView
        Return CType(obj, DataRowView).Item(FieldName).ToString
```

Our data source might also be an array of simple values such as `Integer`, in which case we need to detect that and return the simple value:

```
ElseIf TypeOf obj Is ValueType AndAlso obj.GetType.IsPrimitive Then

  ' This is a primitive value type
  Return obj.ToString
```

Similarly, our data source might be an array of `String` data:

```
ElseIf TypeOf obj Is String Then

  ' This is a simple string
  Return CStr(obj)
```

If our data source was none of the above, then it's some more complex type – a `Structure` or an object. In this case, we have more work to do, since we must use reflection to find the property or field and retrieve its value. The first thing we do is get a `Type` object, so that we have access to type information about the source object:

```
  ' This is an object or Structure
  Try
    Dim sourcetype As Type = obj.GetType
```

Then, we try to see if there's a `Property` with the name of the column we're after:

```
    ' See if the field is a property
    Dim prop As PropertyInfo = sourcetype.GetProperty(FieldName)
    If prop Is Nothing OrElse Not prop.CanRead Then
```

If there is no such property (or if the property is not readable), then we must assume we're looking for a field instead. However, if we *do* find a readable property, we can return its value:

```
    Else

      ' Found a property, return its value
      Return prop.GetValue(obj, Nothing).ToString
    End If
```

On the other hand, if we didn't find a readable property, we look for a field:

```
      ' No readable property of that name exists - check for a field
      Dim field As FieldInfo = sourcetype.GetField(FieldName)
      If field Is Nothing Then
```

By supporting `Public` fields, we are conforming to the data binding behavior of Windows Forms. Unfortunately, Web Forms data binding only supports retrieving data from `Property` methods, which makes it quite awkward to use with typical `Structure` data types. By conforming to the Windows Forms behavior, we are providing a more complete solution.

If there's no field by this name, then we're stuck, so we throw an exception indicating that we were unsuccessful:

```
        Throw New System.Data.DataException( _
              "No such value exists: " & FieldName)
```

However, if we *do* find a matching field, we return its value:

```
      Else

        ' Got a field, return its value
        Return field.GetValue(obj).ToString
      End If
```

If we get an error as we try to do any of this, we return the error text as a result, instead of the data value:

```
    Catch ex As Exception
      Throw New System.Data.DataException( _
            "Error reading value: " & FieldName, ex)
    End Try
```

The end result is that the `GetField()` method will return a property or field value from a row in a `DataView`, from an array of simple values, or from a `Structure` or object. We'll use this functionality as we copy the data values from our data source into the `DataTable` object during the fill operation.

Automatic discovery of properties and fields

We will support two ways of deciding which properties and fields should be copied from our data source into the target `DataSet`. One way is that the `DataTable` pre-exists and already has columns defined. In that case, we'll simply attempt to copy values from the data source into those columns.

However, we will also support loading data into a new, empty `DataTable` object. In this case, we want to be able to create the columns in the new `DataTable` dynamically: one column for each property or field in our data source.

This means that we need to get a list of the `Public` properties and fields on the object (or other data source, such as a `DataView`, array, or `Structure`). We can use reflection to do this discovery process.

Getting column names from a DataView

If our data source is a `DataView`, we can implement a simple routine to retrieve the column names from the `DataView` to populate our list:

```
  Private Sub ScanDataView(ByVal ds As DataView)

    Dim field As Integer
    For field = 0 To ds.Table.Columns.Count - 1
      mColumns.Add(ds.Table.Columns(field).ColumnName)
    Next

  End Sub
```

This is the simplest scenario, since the `DataView` object provides us with an easy interface to retrieve the list of columns.

Getting field names from an IList

Our other main option is that we're dealing with an `IList`: either an array or a collection object. Here, we have a couple of scenarios: either the elements in the list are simple data types such as `Integer` or `String`, or they are complex `Structure` or object elements. We can create a `ScanIList()` method to detect these scenarios:

```
Private Sub ScanIList(ByVal ds As IList)

  If ds.Count > 0 Then

    ' Retrieve the first item from the list
    Dim obj As Object = ds.Item(0)

    If TypeOf obj Is ValueType AndAlso obj.GetType.IsPrimitive Then

      ' The value is a primitive value type
      mColumns.Add("Value")
    ElseIf TypeOf obj Is String Then

      ' The value is a simple string
      mColumns.Add("Text")
    Else

      ' We have a complex Structure or object
      ScanObject(obj)
    End If
  End If

End Sub
```

If we have an `IList`, it means that we have a collection of elements. In order to detect the fields and properties, we need to get access to the first element in the list. After that, we assume that all the other elements in the list have the same fields and properties.

> *This is the way Windows Forms and Web Forms data binding work as well: they assume that all elements in an array or collection are of the same data type.*

Once we have a reference to the first element in the list, we can see if it is a simple data type:

```
If TypeOf obj Is ValueType AndAlso obj.GetType.IsPrimitive Then

  ' The value is a primitive value type
  mColumns.Add("Value")
```

We can also check to see if it is a `String` (which is not *actually* a primitive type, but we want to treat it as such):

```
ElseIf TypeOf obj Is String Then

  ' The value is a simple string
  mColumns.Add("Text")
```

If the first element in the list is neither a primitive data type nor a `String`, we'll assume that it's a complex structure or object – in which case, we'll call a `ScanObject()` method that will scan the object to get a list of its properties and fields:

```
      Else

        ' We have a complex Structure or object
        ScanObject(obj)
      End If
```

Getting property and field names from a structure or object

Now we can move on to implementing the routine that scans the object. The `ScanObject()` method will use reflection to scan the object (or `Structure`) for all its `Public` properties and fields:

```
  Private Sub ScanObject(ByVal Source As Object)

    Dim SourceType As Type = Source.GetType
    Dim column As Integer

    ' Retrieve a list of all public properties
    Dim props As PropertyInfo() = SourceType.GetProperties()
    If UBound(props) >= 0 Then
      For column = 0 To UBound(props)
        If props(column).CanRead Then
          mColumns.Add(props(column).Name)
        End If
      Next
    End If

    ' Retrieve a list of all public fields
    Dim fields As FieldInfo() = SourceType.GetFields()
    If UBound(fields) >= 0 Then
      For column = 0 To UBound(fields)
        mColumns.Add(fields(column).Name)
      Next
    End If

  End Sub
```

First, we loop through all the `Public Property` methods on the object, adding the name of each readable property to our list of columns:

```
    ' Retrieve a list of all public properties
    Dim props As PropertyInfo() = SourceType.GetProperties()
    If UBound(props) >= 0 Then
      For column = 0 To UBound(props)
        If props(column).CanRead Then
          mColumns.Add(props(column).Name)
        End If
      Next
    End If
```

Then we loop through all the Public fields on the object and add their names to the list of columns:

```
' Retrieve a list of all public fields
Dim fields As FieldInfo() = SourceType.GetFields()
If UBound(fields) >= 0 Then
  For column = 0 To UBound(fields)
    mColumns.Add(fields(column).Name)
  Next
End If
```

Going through the list of fields is particularly important in supporting Structure types, since they typically expose their data in that way. The end result is that we have a list of all the properties and fields on our data type, whether it is a DataView, an IList of simple types, or a Structure or an object. (In the case of simple types, there's just one column of data.)

Implementing the AutoDiscover method

Now that we have the scanning methods complete, the AutoDiscover() method can be implemented easily. All we need to do is determine if we're dealing with an IListSource, an IList, or a basic object, and call the appropriate scan method:

```
Private Sub AutoDiscover(ByVal source As Object)

  Dim innerSource As Object
  If TypeOf source Is IListSource Then
    innerSource = CType(source, IListSource).GetList
  Else
    innerSource = source
  End If

  If TypeOf innerSource Is DataView Then
    ScanDataView(CType(innerSource, DataView))

  ElseIf TypeOf innerSource Is IList Then
    ScanIList(CType(innerSource, IList))

  Else

    ' They gave us a regular object
    ScanObject(innerSource)
  End If

End Sub
```

The first thing we need to do in our auto-discovery routine is to determine if the data source is an IListSource, which is the case with a DataSet, for instance:

```
Dim innerSource As Object
If TypeOf source Is IListSource Then
  innerSource = CType(source, IListSource).GetList
Else
  innerSource = source
End If
```

At this point, the innerSource variable contains a reference to a DataView, an IList interface, a Structure, or an object. Now we can check the type of the innerSource object to see which it is. If it's a DataView, we can call a routine that scans the DataView to get its list of columns:

```
If TypeOf innerSource Is DataView Then
  ScanDataView(CType(innerSource, DataView))
```

Alternatively, it could be an IList:

```
ElseIf TypeOf innerSource Is IList Then
  ScanIList(CType(innerSource, IList))
```

If the object is neither a DataView nor an IList, then it must be a regular object. We scan it directly:

```
Else
  ' They gave us a regular object
  ScanObject(innerSource)
```

At this point, the mColumn array contains a list of all the columns we'll be using to populate the DataTable, so we can move on to implement the routine that actually does the data copy.

Populating a DataTable from an IList

The core of this process is a method that copies data from the elements in an IList into a DataTable object:

```
Private Sub DataCopyIList(ByVal dt As DataTable, ByVal ds As IList)

  Dim index As Integer
  Dim column As String
  Dim item As String

  ' Create columns if needed
  For Each column In mColumns
    If Not dt.Columns.Contains(column) Then
      dt.Columns.Add(column)
    End If
  Next

  ' Load the data into the DataTable
  dt.BeginLoadData()
  For index = 0 To ds.Count - 1
    Dim dr As DataRow = dt.NewRow
    For Each column In mColumns
      Try
        dr(column) = GetField(ds(index), column)
      Catch ex As Exception
        dr(column) = ex.Message
      End Try
    Next
    dt.Rows.Add(dr)
  Next
  dt.EndLoadData()

End Sub
```

The first thing we do is make sure that the `DataTable` object has columns corresponding to our list of column names in `mColumns`:

```
' Create columns if needed
For Each column In mColumns
  If Not dt.Columns.Contains(column) Then
    dt.Columns.Add(column)
  End If
Next
```

It's possible that the `DataTable` already exists and has some or all of the columns we'll be populating, so we only add columns if they don't already exist.

With that done, we can loop through all the elements in the `IList`, copying the data from each item into a `DataTable` row. To get each value from the object, we use the `GetField()` method we implemented earlier. Since it supports `DataView`, primitive, `String`, and complex data sources, it handles all the details of getting the right type of value from the data source.

Copying the data

We also need to create a method to initiate the data copy process. Like `AutoDiscover()`, this method needs to see if the data source is an `IListSource`, or an `IList`, or something else. Ultimately, we need an `IList` interface, so this method ensures that we have one:

```
Private Sub DataCopy(ByVal dt As DataTable, ByVal source As Object)

  If source Is Nothing Then Exit Sub
  If mColumns.Count < 1 Then Exit Sub

  If TypeOf source Is IListSource Then
    DataCopyIList(dt, CType(source, IListSource).GetList)
  ElseIf TypeOf source Is IList Then
    DataCopyIList(dt, CType(source, IList))
  Else

    ' They gave us a regular object - create a list
    Dim col As New ArrayList
    col.Add(source)
    DataCopyIList(dt, CType(col, IList))
  End If

End Sub
```

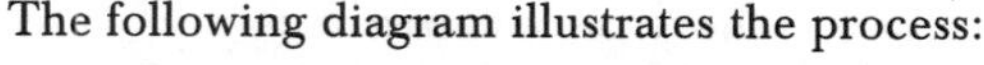

The following diagram illustrates the process:

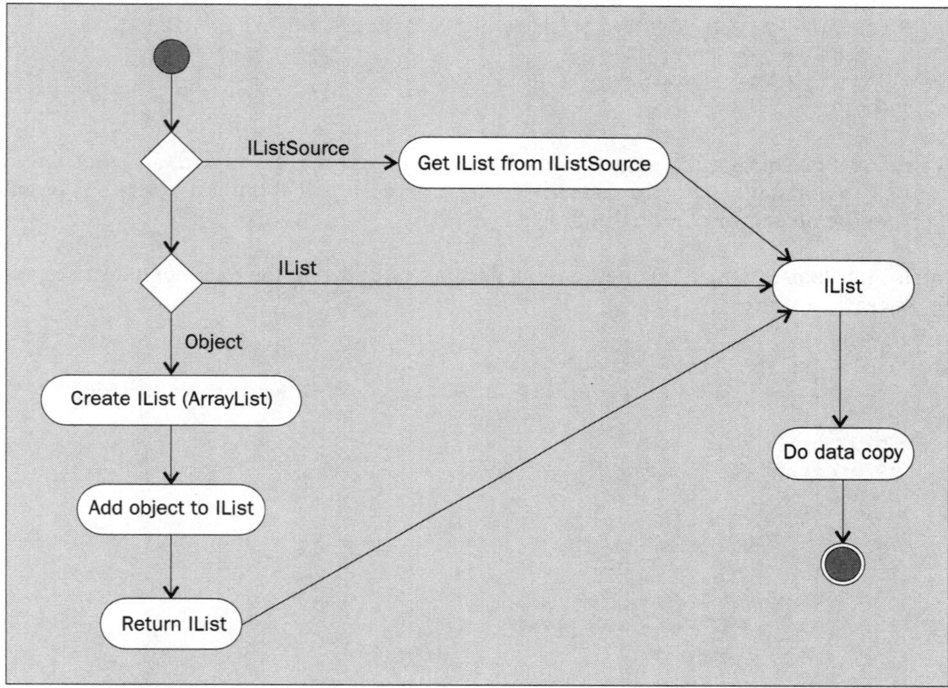

If the data source is an `IListSource`, we use it to get an `IList` reference. If it's already an `IList`, we can use it directly. If the data source is neither of the above, then it's a regular `Structure` or object and so we need to create a collection object – in this case an `ArrayList` – so that we have an `IList` reference:

```
Else

  ' They gave us a regular object - create a list
  Dim col As New ArrayList
  col.Add(source)
  DataCopyIList(dt, CType(col, IList))
End If
```

Ultimately, we have an `IList`, so we can call the `DataCopyIList()` method to copy the values into the `DataTable`.

Implementing the Fill methods

All that remains at this point is to implement the `Fill()` methods that will be used by client code to copy the data into a `DataSet`. We'll model our `Fill()` methods after the `Fill()` methods on ADO.NET data adapter objects – specifically, the `Fill()` method on `OleDbDataAdapter` that allows us to copy the data from an ADO `Recordset` into an ADO.NET `DataSet`.

The most basic Fill() method is the one that copies an object into a DataTable:

```
Public Sub Fill(ByVal dt As DataTable, ByVal source As Object)
  AutoDiscover(source)
  DataCopy(dt, source)
End Sub
```

First, we run AutoDiscover() to generate a list of the columns to be copied, and then we call DataCopy() to initiate the copy process itself. The end result is that the DataTable is populated with the data from the object (or collection of objects).

We can also implement a Fill() method that accepts a DataSet, the name of a DataTable to create, and the object data source:

```
Public Sub Fill(ByVal ds As DataSet, _
                ByVal TableName As String, ByVal source As Object)

  Dim dt As DataTable
  Dim exists As Boolean

  dt = ds.Tables(TableName)
  exists = Not dt Is Nothing

  If Not exists Then
    dt = New DataTable(TableName)
  End If

  Fill(dt, source)

  If Not exists Then
    ds.Tables.Add(dt)
  End If

End Sub
```

In this case, we check to see if a DataTable by this name already exists. If it doesn't exist, then we create it, populate it, and add it to the DataSet. If it *does* already exist, we simply add the object's data to the existing DataTable, merging the new data into the DataTable along with whatever data might already be in the DataTable.

The final variation on the Fill() method is one where we're passed a DataSet and the object, in which case we'll generate a DataTable name based on the type name of the object itself:

```
Public Sub Fill(ByVal ds As DataSet, ByVal source As Object)

  Dim className As String
  className = TypeName(source)
  Fill(ds, className, source)

End Sub
```

Since we've already implemented a `Fill()` method that handles the creation of a `DataTable` by name, we can simply invoke that version of `Fill()`, passing it the table name we've generated here.

At this point, our `ObjectAdapter` is complete. Client code can use our `Fill()` methods to copy data from virtually any object or collection of objects into a `DataTable`. Once the data is in a `DataTable`, we can use commercial reporting engines such as Crystal Reports or Active Reports to generate reports against the data.

Reporting using ObjectAdapter

The actual process of creating a report using Crystal Reports or Active Reports is outside the scope of this book, but it is worth walking through the basic process and some of the key code involved in working with the `ObjectAdapter` to create a report using these tools. In this example, we'll use Crystal Reports, since it is included with many versions of VS.NET.

The complete code for a report is included in the Windows Forms client application for our `ProjectTracker` application. The `ProjectList` form in the `PTWin` project contains the code to generate a Crystal Report based on a `Project` object.

The key steps involved are:

- Manually create a `DataSet` object in the project by using the `DataSet` designer in VS.NET
- Create the report based on the `DataSet` we created in the designer
- Write code to retrieve the business object
- Write code to call `ObjectAdapter` to populate the `DataSet` we created, using the object
- Set the report's data source to the `DataSet` we just populated

The first couple of steps may seem odd: why should we have to create a `DataSet` object manually, using the designer? The answer is that Crystal Reports requires a `DataSet` with information about the 'tables' (and the columns in each 'table') in order to design a report. Without such a `DataSet`, we can't use the graphical designers to create the report itself.

> *Remember that when we say 'table' here, we're really talking about a `DataTable` generated with values from our objects. When we manually create this `DataSet`, we should create 'tables' and 'columns' that match our business objects and their properties and fields, not the structure of any underlying database.*

As long as we create the tables and columns in our `DataSet` based on the object, property, and field names from our business objects, the `ObjectAdapter` will fill the `DataSet` with object data just fine. For instance, in the `PTWin` project you'll find a `Projects.xsd` file, which describes a `DataSet` defined using the VS.NET designer:

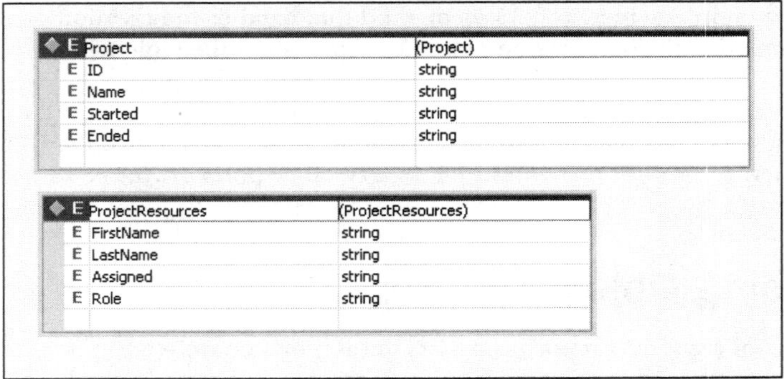

Using this `DataSet`, we can create a Crystal Report using the Crystal Reports designer. In this case, we're creating a simple list that displays basic information about a `Project` object and its `ProjectResources`:

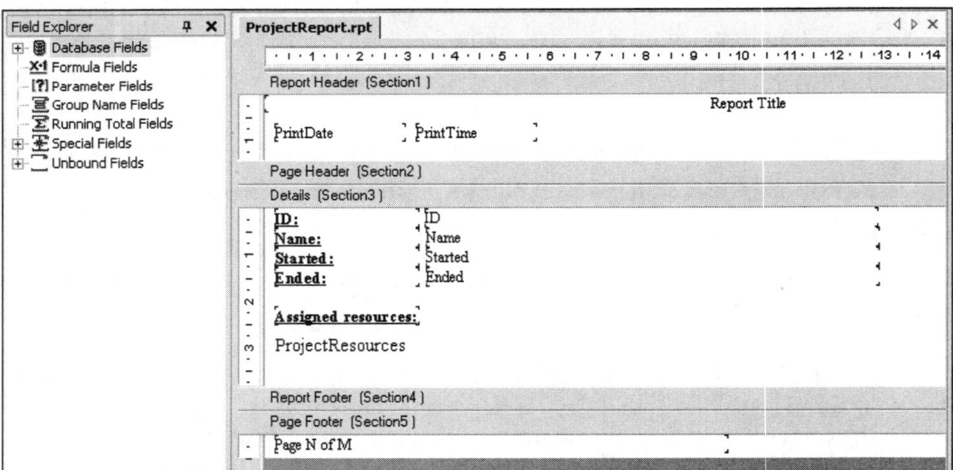

Once the `DataSet` is populated with data via the `ObjectAdapter`, it's a simple matter to tell Crystal Reports to generate the report, using our `DataSet` as its data source. The code to do this, given a pre-loaded `Project` object, is similar to this:

```
Dim da As New CSLA.Data.ObjectAdapter
Dim ds As New Projects
da.Fill(ds, mProject)
da.Fill(ds, mProject.Resources)

projectReport1.SetDataSource(ds)

CrystalReportViewer1.ReportSource = projectReport1
```

We create a new `ObjectAdapter` object and a new `DataSet` based on the `Projects.xsd` file in our project. We then use the `ObjectAdapter` to fill the `DataSet` with the data from the `Project` object, and also from its `Resources` collection.

Once the `DataSet` has been populated with our data, we set the data source of the Crystal Report object to be our `DataSet`, and then we have the Crystal Report Viewer display the report. The end result is a normal Crystal Report, just like we'd get from a database, but instead populated from our business objects:

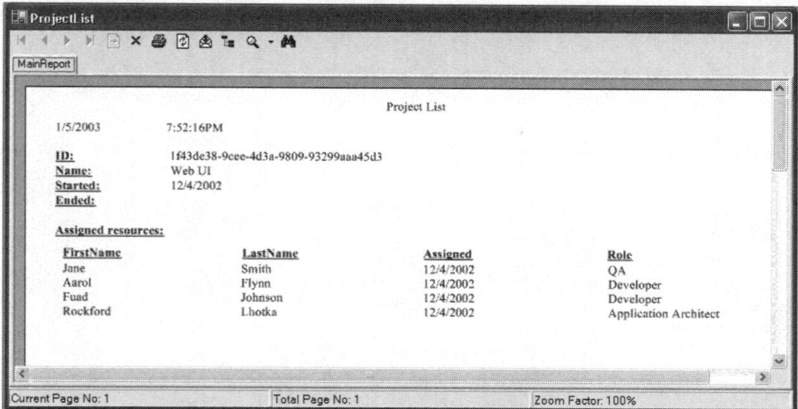

Using the `ObjectAdapter`, we can easily convert our objects and collections into a `DataSet`, which makes virtually any data-centric reporting tool available for our use.

The primary advantage to doing this is, when we want to generate small reports or lists on the client workstation. We already have the ability to retrieve business objects through our `DataPortal` mechanism, and once they're on the client, we can easily copy them to a `DataSet` and generate reports.

If we're creating reports that require access to large volumes of data, however, we should generate the report on a server. In such a case, we might also consider using the batch processing engine that we created in the first half of the chapter!

Conclusion

In this chapter, we've addressed some of the issues surrounding batch processing and report generating in a distributed, object-oriented environment.

What we created in this chapter is a basic-but-functional batch queue processor that allows us easily to submit tasks to be run on a server machine. This batch server might be the database server – thus avoiding the network transfer of large volumes of data – or it might be an application server that has a high-speed network connection to the database server. Either way, it's likely that the processing of batch jobs on such a server will be more efficient than running the same task on a client workstation or web server.

The object-oriented nature of our applications poses particular challenges, especially with reporting. Commercial reporting engines don't support the concept of binding a report to objects, rendering them nearly useless for reporting in an object-oriented environment. While we can use these report engines in unbound mode and manually provide them with data from our objects, that's a lot more work than binding the report to a `DataSet`!

To overcome this, we created the `ObjectAdapter` class, which makes it very easy to populate a `DataSet` with data from an object or collection of objects. Once our object data is loaded into a `DataSet`, we can use the features of standard reporting engines to generate reports based on the data with ease.

APPENDIX

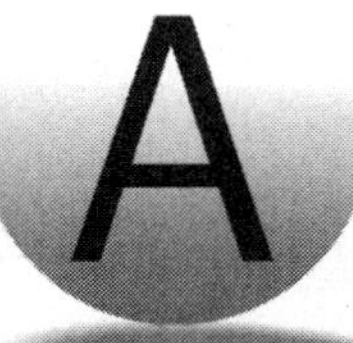

NetRun

Throughout the book we've been making the assumption that the Windows Forms application code might be deployed using **no-touch deployment**. No-touch deployment is a feature of the .NET runtime whereby .NET assemblies can be downloaded to a client workstation automatically, where they are then executed.

Much is made of the XCOPY deployment capabilities of .NET, but the reality is that XCOPY deployment still requires a *manual* copy process to get the code to the client. No-touch deployment is more powerful, because it uses an *automatic* copy process to get the code to the client. Installing or updating an application through no-touch deployment is as simple as copying the EXE and its related DLLs to a virtual directory on a web server!

> *The benefits of no-touch deployment are tremendous. Many business applications are created as browser-based applications because of the sheer cost of deploying Windows applications. With no-touch deployment, the cost of deploying a Windows application is the same as deploying a web application – which means that we can choose between Windows Forms and Web Forms based on features and user requirements, rather than on deployment cost issues.*

No-touch deployment

No-touch deployment flows from reflection. As we saw in Chapter 3, reflection allows us to write code that examines and interacts with .NET assemblies, types, and objects: we can use reflection to load an assembly into memory from a URL (or the hard drive) dynamically; and once the assembly is *in* memory, reflection allows us to interact with it.

We can place .NET assemblies in a virtual directory on a web server, and .NET can download the files to each client machine automatically. On the server, this requires nothing special: just a virtual directory (or some other directory that can be accessed via a URL). Into that directory, we can place all the EXE and DLL files required by our application. It doesn't have to be possible to browse the web directory, and nor does it need any ASPX, ASMX, or other web-related files.

Once the files are accessible via a URL, the client workstation can use them. In fact, it's possible simply to create a web page with a link to the remote EXE. When the user clicks on that link, .NET will automatically download the EXE and run it on the client. If the EXE depends on any DLLs, they will also be automatically downloaded as required.

These automatically downloaded files are placed into a user-specific client-side cache. On subsequent attempts to run the application, the cached version is checked against the server version, and any updated files are downloaded automatically. If updates are not required, the cached version is run.

Of course, such lofty claims are rarely as good as they sound – no-touch deployment really *does* offer us the ability to deploy applications just by copying the code to a web directory, but there are some issues that we need to overcome to make it work the way we want it to. Specifically, we need to address the following:

- No-touch deployed code runs in an *extremely* secure environment that prevents the use of remoting, reflection, and serialization of objects
- There is a bug in .NET that prevents serialization (using the binary formatter or the SOAP formatter) from working in no-touch deployed code
- ASP.NET blocks the download of `.config` files, which typically prevents no-touch deployed code from reading an application configuration file
- When an application is launched from a URL, the browser pops up for a second and then disappears before then the application loads; this is disconcerting to most users

Fortunately, with a little effort, we can overcome all of these issues, allowing us to enjoy the benefits of no-touch deployment to the full. In this appendix, we'll see how they're overcome by a single application – `NetRun.exe` – that needs to be installed once on each client workstation. Once installed, `NetRun` can be used to launch Windows Forms (or console) applications from a web server, via a URL. For instance, we could launch an application with a command line such as:

```
> netrun http://myserver/myroot/myapplication.exe
```

`NetRun` uses the native, no-touch deployment functionality built into the .NET runtime; but it also addresses the issues above. Before we get into the development of `NetRun`, let's discuss those issues in a little more detail.

Security considerations

Code deployed via no-touch deployment runs within a security context defined by the location the code was downloaded from. By default, this is controlled by the security zones that are defined by Internet Explorer, plus a couple of extras. In .NET, the only code that's fully trusted is code that's run from the local computer's hard drives – all other code runs in a much more restrictive environment.

Even code from a network shared drive or an intranet web server will run in the `LocalIntranet_Zone`*, which prevents the use of remoting, reflection, object serialization and a host of other common business application activities. Other zones (such as the* `Internet_Zone` *or the* `Trusted_Zone`*) are even more restrictive.*

Our CSLA .NET framework *relies* on remoting, reflection and object serialization to function, so these default security configurations are always too restrictive for deployment of CSLA-based applications.

> **In fact, remoting requires the highest level of permission: `FullTrust`. Any application that makes use of remoting must be fully trusted by the .NET security infrastructure.**

Changing the default security for whole zones is not recommended. Instead, we'll implement a solution where the security for a specific web directory, based on a URL, is temporarily granted `FullTrust` permissions while our application is running. When the application closes, the `FullTrust` permissions will be revoked.

Using `NetRun`, we'll get `FullTrust` for our business application without granting that permission to any other applications or code.

Object serialization workaround

There's a bug in the .NET runtime that prevents the deserialization of objects in code that has been deployed via no-touch deployment, regardless of the security settings in effect. It only affects serialization using the binary formatter or SOAP formatter, but since that's the type of serialization used by remoting and by our CSLA .NET framework, it's a serious issue for us.

If all we're doing is using the serialization techniques offered by the XML formatter and web services, we don't need to worry about this issue. Of course, these techniques don't make complete copies of our objects, so they're of little use when implementing a distributed, object-oriented application like those based on CSLA .NET.

The problem is that the deserialization process only scans locally loaded code to find the assembly containing the class into which the data should be deserialized. Since our assemblies are loaded via no-touch deployment, the deserialization process fails to find them, and throws an exception.

Luckily, the .NET runtime raises an event prior to failing, and we can handle this event through our code to provide the .NET runtime with a reference to our assembly – even though it was loaded via no-touch deployment. The code to do this is not terribly complex, and by placing it in `NetRun`, we provide a workaround for our entire application, provided that `NetRun` is used to launch it.

Reading application configuration settings

We're likely to use an ASP.NET web server as the source for our code – that is, the server where we'll copy the EXE and any DLLs so that clients can download them. However, ASP.NET security prevents the download of any file ending in a `.config` extension to prevent people from downloading `Web.config` files and breaching web site security. Unfortunately, our application configuration files *also* end in a `.config` extension, which means that ASP.NET will prevent our applications from downloading their configuration settings.

This issue is not a problem if the web server isn't IIS, or if our IIS server doesn't have ASP.NET installed. In those cases, the `.config` file can be downloaded like any other file.

It's possible to alter the security settings on an IIS web server to allow the downloading of `.config` files, but this is not recommended. This could allow the download of `machine.config` or `Web.config` files for web applications on the server, and that's not our intent – the restrictions are there for good reasons. Instead, it's better to leave the server's security intact, and change our client application to read some other type of file.

Altering the security settings on our web server to allow the download of `.config` files is not recommended.

Fortunately, we can build functionality into `NetRun` to choose the name of the configuration file to be downloaded for our particular application. This means that we can request a configuration file with a different file extension from `.config`. In our case, we'll set things up so that our application uses a file ending in a `.remoteconfig` extension.

Preventing browser popup

The final issue is more cosmetic. The no-touch deployment functionality is built into the .NET runtime, and it integrates into Windows and Internet Explorer. This means that it's quite possible to launch a .NET application from the command prompt or from the Start | Run dialog just by providing a URL. For instance:

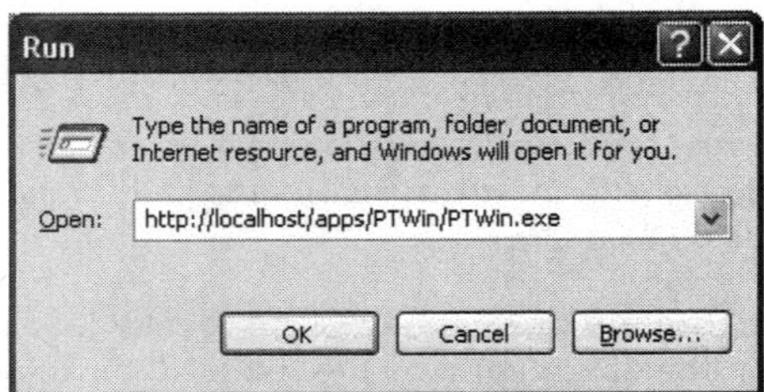

What happens here is that the browser launches, because we've specified an HTTP-based URL. The browser comes up, immediately realizes that it isn't needed, and closes. The result is an annoying (and potentially confusing) 'flicker' of the browser on the screen before our application appears.

We could avoid this little glitch by having the user manually open the browser and then type our URL into the browser's Address field. Alternatively, we could provide the user with a web page that has a link to our application. Still, it seems rather counter-intuitive to force the user to open the browser just so that they can launch a Windows application.

Additionally, launching applications this way means that we can't solve the first three problems we discussed. Without using some type of launcher application, there's no way to run code that resolves those issues before the application itself is launched.

The answer is to use a launcher program – in our case, NetRun – to run the application. The launcher program can directly invoke the .NET runtime to load the remote application code via no-touch deployment, thus avoiding bringing up the browser for no reason. We simply invoke NetRun on the command line instead:

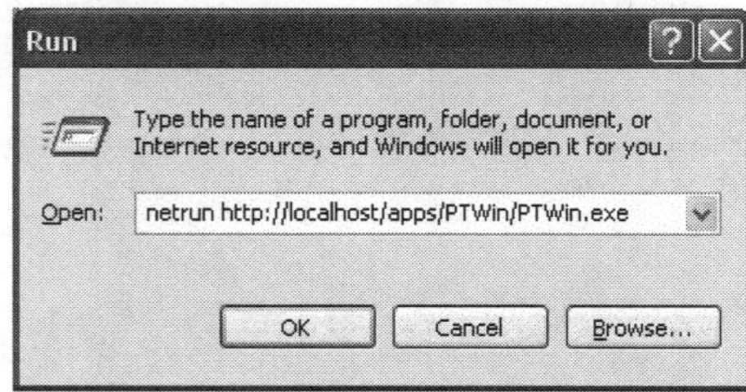

This way, the browser doesn't pop up, and our application launches in an environment where all four of the issues are addressed, so everything works properly. A useful side-effect is that we can put this command into a desktop shortcut or a shortcut in the user's Start menu, so that to the user our application is just another icon they click on to run – just like they do for Excel, Word or any other locally installed application.

NetRun design

The NetRun application is designed to be installed once on each client machine, and then used to launch other .NET applications (either Windows Forms or console applications). It accepts the URL of the application's EXE file as a command line parameter, and it uses that URL to load both the EXE and the .remoteconfig file for the application.

Invoking the .NET runtime's support for no-touch deployment is not difficult. In fact, it can be done in very few lines of code. All the complexity in NetRun comes because we're resolving the first three issues we discussed: security, serialization, and reading the configuration file.

To overcome the security issue, we'll grant FullTrust to the URL of the directory where the EXE resides. Once the application has terminated, we'll revoke FullTrust from that URL, so the system is reset to its starting state.

To overcome the serialization problem in dynamically loaded code, we'll set up an event handler to catch the event from the application domain that indicates there's a problem. In our handler, we'll fix the problem by providing a reference to the correct assembly, so that our objects can be deserialized.

It turns out that the biggest issue is the configuration file. As you know, all .NET code runs inside a .NET application domain, which provides the environment within which our code will run – including knowledge of the configuration file. Inevitably, NetRun itself runs inside an application domain – one that's set up to read from a configuration file named netrun.exe.config that's located in the same directory as NetRun.exe. By the time our NetRun code is running, this is set in stone and cannot be changed.

In order to launch our application, we need to create and initialize a new application domain for it to run in. As we do this, we can specify the name of the configuration file that will be read for any code in the new application domain. This way, we can dictate that we want to read a file with a .remoteconfig extension.

Since we're creating a new application domain in order to specify the configuration file, we need to make sure that the security and serialization issues are resolved *for that application domain*, not for the one that's hosting `NetRun` itself. In other words, we don't need to enhance security or fix serialization for `NetRun`; we need to fix it for the application we're loading dynamically.

This means that the basic flow of `NetRun` goes like this:

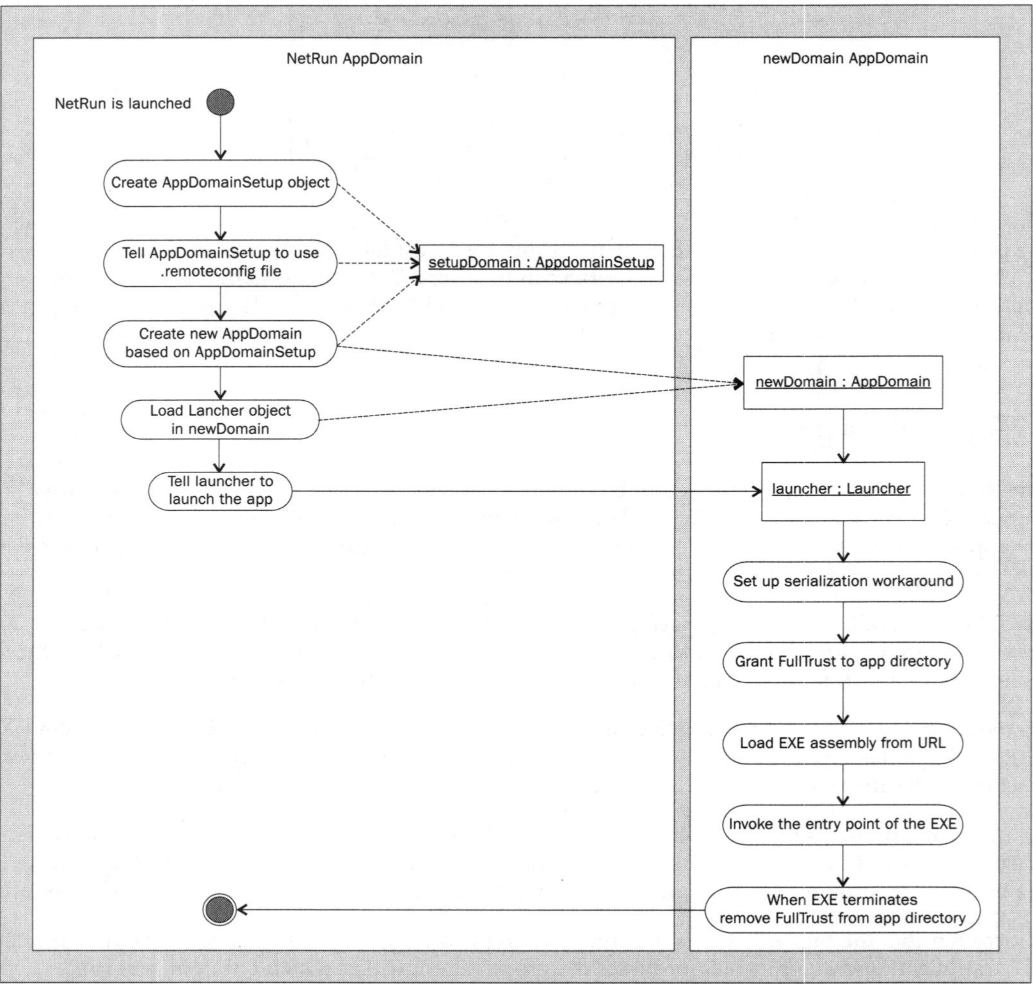

Notice how the main code in `NetRun` just configures a new application domain and loads a `Launcher` object into that domain to do the rest of the work. The `Launcher` class is our code, and it resides in `NetRun.exe`, but it's loaded into and executed in this new application domain.

The `Launcher` object then sets up the event handler for the serialization workaround, grants `FullTrust` to the URL where the EXE resides, and loads the EXE into memory. After that, it invokes the entry point (the special start method) of the application. When the application terminates, `Launcher` revokes `FullTrust` security from the URL, and then `NetRun` also terminates.

NetRun implementation

`NetRun` is a Windows Application, even though it has no UI of its own. Instead of a UI, it has a `Module` named `Main`, with `Main()` as its entry point.

Main module

We import a number of namespaces to provide easy access to the .NET Framework code we use:

```
Imports System.IO
Imports System.Reflection
Imports System.Security
Imports System.Security.Policy
Imports System.Security.Permissions
```

Helper methods

Before we get into the core code, we need some helper functions to parse the URL provided on the command line. As we'll see, we'll need to isolate the application name, and the directory. The URL provided on the command line will always include both of these:

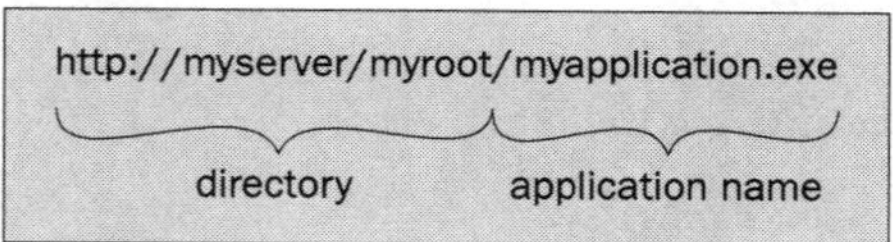

The `GetAppDirectory()` method will parse the URL and return only the directory, while `GetAppName()` will return the application name. Add this code to the `Main` module:

```
#Region " URL parsing functions "

  Public Function GetAppDirectory(ByVal AppURL As String) As String

    ' Get the path without application name
    Dim appURI As New System.Uri(AppURL)
    Dim appPath As String = appURI.GetLeftPart(UriPartial.Path)
    Dim pos As Integer

    For pos = Len(appPath) To 1 Step -1
      If Mid(appPath, pos, 1) = "/" OrElse Mid(appPath, pos, 1) = "\" Then
        Return Left(appPath, pos - 1)
      End If
    Next
    Return ""

  End Function
```

```
    Public Function GetAppName(ByVal AppURL As String) As String
      ' Get the application name without path
      Dim appURI As New System.Uri(AppURL)
      Dim appPath As String = appURI.GetLeftPart(UriPartial.Path)
      Dim pos As Integer

      For pos = Len(appPath) To 1 Step -1
        If Mid(appPath, pos, 1) = "/" OrElse Mid(appPath, pos, 1) = "\" Then
          Return Mid(appPath, pos + 1)
        End If
      Next
      Return ""

    End Function

  #End Region
```

Note that these methods are scoped as `Public`, so they're available to all the code in our `NetRun` project. We'll need these helper methods not only in the `Main` module, but also in the `Launcher` class.

We'll also need to retrieve the directory path of the current application domain – that is, the one in which `NetRun` itself is running. We can get the full path of `NetRun.exe` from the .NET runtime, and then we can simply parse out the directory portion of the path:

```
  #Region " GetCurrentDomainPath "

    Private Function CurrentDomainPath() As String

      ' Get path of current assembly
      Dim currentPath As String = [Assembly].GetExecutingAssembly.CodeBase

      ' Convert it to a URI for ease of use
      Dim currentURI As Uri = New Uri(currentPath)

      ' Get the path portion of the URI
      Dim currentLocalPath As String = currentURI.LocalPath

      ' Return the full name of the path
      Return New DirectoryInfo(currentLocalPath).Parent.FullName

    End Function

  #End Region
```

We'll use these helper functions as we implement the remainder of the code.

Sub Main

`Main()` itself simply provides some top-level exception handling; the actual process of launching the application is handled by another method:

```
Module Main

  Public Sub Main()

    Try
      ' Launch the app based on the URL provided by the user
      RunApplication(Microsoft.VisualBasic.Command)

    Catch ex As Exception
      Dim sb As New System.Text.StringBuilder
      sb.Append("NetRun was unable to launch the application")
      sb.Append(vbCrLf)
      sb.Append(Microsoft.VisualBasic.Command)
      sb.Append(vbCrLf)
      sb.Append(vbCrLf)
      sb.Append(ex.ToString)
      MsgBox(sb.ToString, MsgBoxStyle.Exclamation)
    End Try

  End Sub
```

RunApplication

It's in `RunApplication()` that we set up and create the new application domain in which our application will run. This is implemented as follows:

```
#Region " RunApplication "

  Private Sub RunApplication(ByVal AppURL As String)

    ' Create setup object for the new application domain
    Dim setupDomain As New AppDomainSetup
    With setupDomain

      ' Give it a valid base path
      .ApplicationBase = CurrentDomainPath()

      ' Give it a safe configuration file name
      .ConfigurationFile = AppURL & ".remoteconfig"
    End With

    ' Create new application domain
    Dim newDomain As AppDomain = AppDomain.CreateDomain( _
                     GetAppName(AppURL), Nothing, setupDomain)

    ' Create launcher object in new application domain
    Dim launcher As Launcher = CType(newDomain.CreateInstanceAndUnwrap( _
                     "NetRun", "NetRun.Launcher"), Launcher)

    ' Use launcher object from the new domain
    '  to launch the remote app in that application domain
    launcher.RunApp(AppURL)

  End Sub

#End Region
```

The first step is to create the AppDomainSetup object that will be used to configure the new application domain. The key element here is that we specify the name of the application configuration file. To do this, we get the path of the EXE (which is our URL), and we append a .remoteconfig extension to it:

```
.ConfigurationFile = AppURL & ".remoteconfig"
```

By default, .NET uses the path of the EXE with a .config extension, so all we've really done here is to change it to use a .remoteconfig extension. This way, the download of our configuration file won't be blocked by ASP.NET security.

We then use this AppDomainSetup object to create our new application domain:

```
Dim newDomain As AppDomain = AppDomain.CreateDomain( _
                              GetAppName(AppURL), Nothing, setupDomain)
```

We set the name of the application domain to the name of the application we're dynamically launching. Typically, an application domain's name is the same as that of the EXE that's being run, so this is consistent with default .NET behavior.

To the same method call, we provide a reference to our AppDomainSetup object, so this new domain will be configured using its settings. This means that the .NET Framework code in System.Configuration will read configuration data from the configuration file path we provided.

The next step is to create an instance of the Launcher class *in the new application domain.* When an application domain is first created, it contains no application code. Until we load application code into the application domain, it has nothing to do. We create a Launcher object in the empty application domain like this:

```
Dim launcher As Launcher = CType(newDomain.CreateInstanceAndUnwrap( _
                              "NetRun", "NetRun.Launcher"), Launcher)
```

This code tells the empty application domain to load the NetRun.Launcher class from the NetRun assembly, and then to create an instance of the Launcher class. The result is that our code in the NetRun application domain has a reference to the Launcher class in the new application domain.

Technically, our NetRun code has a remoting proxy object that links to the Launcher object in the new application domain. It's not possible to communicate between application domains directly, so remoting is used. In this case, remoting is automatically configured for us by the .NET runtime.

Our last step is to use this reference to call the RunApp() method on the Launcher object:

```
launcher.RunApp(AppURL)
```

The RunApp() method does the actual work of setting up the serialization workaround, setting security, dynamically loading the EXE, and launching the application. When the application terminates, the RunApp() method makes sure that the FullTrust security is revoked.

Launcher class

As you've probably begun to gather, most of the hard work happens in the `Launcher` class. To start with, though, it's very ordinary. The `Launcher` class imports a number of .NET namespaces to make our coding easier:

```
Imports System.Reflection
Imports System.Security
Imports System.Security.Policy
Imports System.Security.Permissions
```

The class itself is set up as an anchored class by inheriting from `MarshalByRefObject`:

```
Public Class Launcher
  Inherits MarshalByRefObject

End Class
```

We also declare some variables for use by our code:

```
  Private mAppURL As String
  Private mAppDir As String
  Private mAppName As String

  Private mGroupExisted As Boolean
```

The first three of these are used to store the full URL, the directory, and the name of the application to be launched. To generate the latter two values, we'll use the helper methods we created in the `Main` module.

The `mGroupExisted` variable is a flag that we'll use to indicate whether the workstation already had security set up for the application's URL. If the workstation does already have security set up for the application's URL, we won't tamper with it. Otherwise, we'll set it up with `FullTrust` security, and revoke that security when the application terminates.

RunApp

The `RunApp()` method does the following:

- Invokes the workaround for the serialization bug
- Gets and parses the URL for the remote application
- Sets security for the URL to `FullTrust`
- Launches the application
- In case of an error, displays a message box for the user
- Revokes the `FullTrust` security setting

All of the actual work will be done in helper methods, so `RunApp()` just choreographs the process:

```
Public Sub RunApp(ByVal AppURL As String)

  ' Before anything else, invoke the workaround for the serialization bug
  SerializationWorkaround()

  Try
    ' Get and parse the URL for the app we are launching
    mAppURL = AppURL
    mAppDir = GetAppDirectory(mAppURL)
    mAppName = GetAppName(mAppURL)

    SetSecurity()

    ' Load the assembly into our AppDomain
    Dim asm As [Assembly]
    asm = [Assembly].LoadFrom(AppURL)

    ' Run the program by invoking its entry point
    asm.EntryPoint.Invoke(asm.EntryPoint, Nothing)

  Finally
    RemoveSecurity()
  End Try

End Sub
```

The core of the method is where we dynamically load and launch the application. To do this, we ask the .NET runtime to load the EXE from the URL:

```
Dim asm As [Assembly]
asm = [Assembly].LoadFrom(AppURL)
```

This seemingly trivial bit of code triggers the no-touch deployment process. The .NET runtime automatically detects that the path to the EXE is a URL, and downloads the EXE into a user-specific cache on the client workstation.

If the EXE was already in the cache, the .NET runtime does a file date/time check to compare the cached version against the version on the remote server. If they match, the file is not downloaded, and the cached version is used. Otherwise, the new version is downloaded into the cache.

As the code in the EXE runs, it might call code in external DLLs. When that happens, the appropriate DLL is downloaded into the cache. Again, the file date/time comparison is used, so these DLLs are only downloaded if needed.

Note that this means that only DLLs that are *actually used* are downloaded. Our EXE could have references to DLLs containing code that's not called – and in that case, those DLLs are never downloaded to the client.

Similarly, if our code uses an application configuration file, that too is automatically downloaded. The name of the configuration file was specified when the application domain was created, and we made sure that it's looking for a file with a `.remoteconfig` extension so ASP.NET security doesn't block the download.

Once the EXE has been loaded into memory within the application domain, we invoke its entry point:

```
asm.EntryPoint.Invoke(asm.EntryPoint, Nothing)
```

This actually runs the application. All .NET applications (EXEs) have a well-known method called an **entry point**. The compiler creates this when the EXE is created, and the .NET runtime uses it to launch the application. By invoking the entry point method, we're simply emulating what the .NET runtime would normally do.

The call to `Invoke()` is synchronous, which means that it won't return from this call until the client application has terminated. This means that the next line of code, which revokes `FullTrust` security from the URL, won't run until after the application has finished.

Serialization bug workaround

The serialization bug (or more accurately, the *de*serialization bug) occurs because the .NET runtime fails to find our assembly in memory. Our assembly *is* actually in memory, but .NET fails to find it. This is because .NET keeps a couple of lists of the assemblies that are currently loaded – and the dynamically loaded assemblies are in their own list. For some reason, the deserialization process doesn't check that particular list to find assemblies.

Fortunately, when it fails to find an assembly, the runtime raises an `AssemblyResolve` event from the application domain object. We can handle this event and provide the runtime with a reference to the right assembly.

Providing the reference isn't hard – the assembly is already loaded, and the application domain object has a list of all the currently loaded assemblies, so all we need to do is scan through that list of assemblies to find the right one.

The code to implement this comes in two parts. First, there's the `SerializationWorkaround()` method, which just adds a handler for the `AssemblyResolve` event:

```
#Region " Serialization bug workaround "

  Private Sub SerializationWorkaround()

    ' Hook up the AssemblyResolve event so deep serialization works properly
    ' This is a workaround for a bug in the .NET runtime
    Dim currentDomain As AppDomain = AppDomain.CurrentDomain

    AddHandler currentDomain.AssemblyResolve, AddressOf ResolveEventHandler

  End Sub
```

Then there's the event handler itself. This method gets a parameter of type `ResolveEventArgs`, which includes the name of the assembly that the .NET runtime failed to find. All we need to do is get a list of all the assemblies that are currently loaded, and then scan through them to find the one with the matching name:

```
    Private Function ResolveEventHandler( _
        ByVal sender As Object, ByVal args As ResolveEventArgs) _
        As [Assembly]

      ' Get a list of all the assemblies loaded in our application domain
      Dim list() As [Assembly] = AppDomain.CurrentDomain.GetAssemblies()

      ' Search the list to find the assembly that was not found
      '  automatically, and return the assembly from the list
      Dim asm As [Assembly]

      For Each asm In list
        If asm.FullName = args.Name Then
          Return asm
        End If
      Next

    End Function

  #End Region
```

If we find the right assembly, we simply return it as a result, and the .NET runtime will use it to deserialize our object, solving the problem. If we *don't* find the assembly, we return nothing, and the .NET runtime will continue as normal. This means that it will throw an exception indicating that the assembly couldn't be found, and our application will terminate.

Set FullTrust security

The .NET runtime applies code-based security to all the code we run. As we've discussed, code is grouped into zones based on where it came from. Code that comes from our hard drive is fully trusted, code that comes from an intranet location or network drive is more restricted, and code from other locations (such as the Internet) is restricted further still.

> **Altering security settings always comes with some risk. If we alter security for the Internet zone, or even for a single Internet URL, we can allow malicious code to run on our machine with enough permission to do harm.**

This implementation of `NetRun` grants `FullTrust` security – the highest level – to the URL from where our application is being downloaded. This means that any application run via this version of `NetRun` can do pretty much anything it likes on the client machine – just like a regular Windows application or COM component has been able to do for the past decade or more.

In a production environment, you may want to alter `NetRun` so that it only grants `FullTrust` permissions to URLs that are within the `LocalIntranet_Zone`, or where the domain name matches the domain of your organization. This would prevent users from running arbitrary Internet code with `FullTrust` permissions.

Granting `FullTrust` permissions to a URL is done by using some of the security classes built into the .NET Framework. Permissions in .NET are grouped under `Enterprise`, `Machine`, and `User` areas. Within each of these are **code groups** that define the categories or zones for permissions.

This is most easily displayed by using the .NET Framework Configuration tool. For instance:

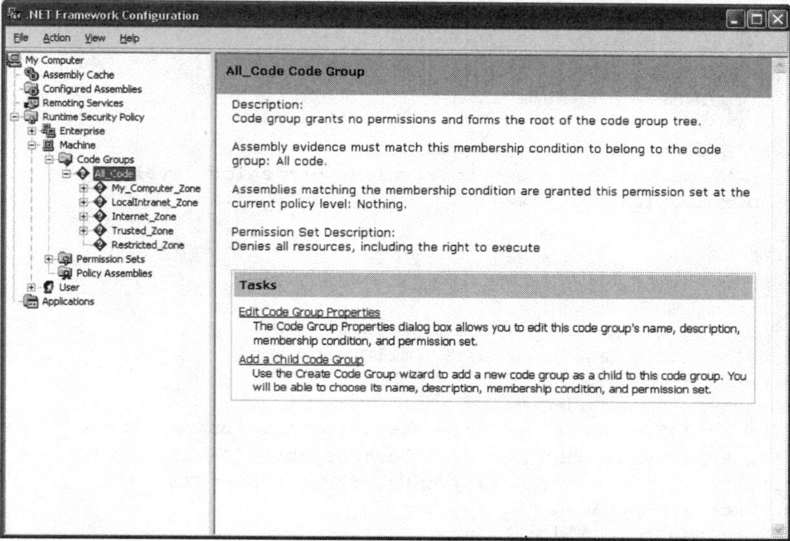

In this screenshot, you can see the zones defined at the `Machine` level for the current computer. Each of these zones has a set of permissions. The `My_Computer_Zone`, for instance, has `FullTrust`, while the `Restricted_Zone` has no permissions at all – that is, no code from that zone will execute.

To grant extra permissions to a URL, we need to add a new code group to this list, and associate that code group with a set of permissions – in our case, the `FullTrust` permission set. That's what `SetSecurity()` does:

```
#Region " SetSecurity to FullTrust "

  Private Sub SetSecurity()

    Dim ph As System.Collections.IEnumerator
    Dim pl As System.Security.Policy.PolicyLevel
    Dim found As Boolean

    ' Retrieve the security policy hierarchy
    ph = SecurityManager.PolicyHierarchy

    ' Loop through to find the Machine level sub-tree
    Do While ph.MoveNext
      pl = CType(ph.Current, PolicyLevel)
      If pl.Label = "Machine" Then
        found = True
        Exit Do
      End If
    Loop
```

```
    If found Then
      ' See if the code group for this application
      '  already exists as a machine-level entry
      Dim cg As CodeGroup
      For Each cg In pl.RootCodeGroup.Children
        If cg.Name = mAppName Then

          ' Code group already exists
          ' We assume it is set to a valid permission level
          mGroupExisted = True
          Exit Sub
        End If
      Next

      ' The code group doesn't already exist, so
      '  we'll add a URL group with FullTrust
      mGroupExisted = False
      Dim ucg As UnionCodeGroup = _
        New UnionCodeGroup(New UrlMembershipCondition(mAppDir & "/*"), _
        New PolicyStatement(New NamedPermissionSet("FullTrust")))
      ucg.Description = "Temporary entry for " & mAppURL
      ucg.Name = mAppName
      pl.RootCodeGroup.AddChild(ucg)
      SecurityManager.SavePolicy()
    End If

  End Sub

#End Region
```

The first step is to retrieve the security policy tree, or hierarchy, and then scan through it to find the `Machine` node (as shown in the previous screenshot):

```
' Retrieve the security policy hierarchy
ph = SecurityManager.PolicyHierarchy

' Loop through to find the Machine level sub-tree
Do While ph.MoveNext
  pl = CType(ph.Current, PolicyLevel)
  If pl.Label = "Machine" Then
    found = True
    Exit Do
  End If
Loop
```

Once we've found the `Machine` node, we can scan the list of child nodes to see if there's already a code group with the same name as our application:

```
  Dim cg As CodeGroup
  For Each cg In pl.RootCodeGroup.Children
    If cg.Name = mAppName Then

      ' Code group already exists
      ' We assume it is set to a valid permission level
      mGroupExisted = True
      Exit Sub
    End If
  Next
```

Using the application name as the code group name is somewhat arbitrary, but it means that the node name is meaningful in case someone should use the .NET Configuration Management while our application is running. It also means that we can manually add a node using that tool, in the case that we want to assign different permissions for a specific application manually. Notice that if our code detects a pre-existing code group, we simply exit and don't modify or update its existing set of permissions.

If no code group exists for our application, then we need to add one. This is done by creating a new code group object that specifies both the URL where our code resides, and the `FullTrust` permission set we want to associate with the group:

```
Dim ucg As UnionCodeGroup = _
  New UnionCodeGroup(New UrlMembershipCondition(mAppDir & "/*"), _
  New PolicyStatement(New NamedPermissionSet("FullTrust")))
```

We then set the new code group's description and name to meaningful values:

```
ucg.Description = "Temporary entry for " & mAppURL
ucg.Name = mAppName
```

Finally, we add the new code group to the security policy tree and then save the policy tree, thereby making the change effective:

```
pl.RootCodeGroup.AddChild(ucg)
SecurityManager.SavePolicy()
```

At this point, any code (EXEs or DLLs) that we run from this URL will do so with `FullTrust` permissions, just as they would if they'd been manually installed on our machine's hard drive.

Revoke FullTrust security

Removing a code group is pretty straightforward. All we need to do is scan through the security policy hierarchy to find the `Machine` node. Then, within that node, we look for the code group we inserted based on the application name. When we find it, we simply remove it.

However, we *only* do this if we actually inserted the code group. If there was a pre-existing code group of this name, we didn't add or alter the code group when we set up security, so we shouldn't remove or alter it here either. The following code takes care of this:

```
#Region " RemoveSecurity "

  Private Sub RemoveSecurity()

    ' If the group existed before NetRun was used, we want
    '  to leave the group intact, so we can just exit
    If mGroupExisted Then Exit Sub

    ' On the other hand, if the group didn't already exist, then we need
    '  to remove it now that the business application is closed
    Dim ph As System.Collections.IEnumerator
    Dim pl As System.Security.Policy.PolicyLevel
    Dim found As Boolean
```

```
    ' Retrieve the security policy hierarchy
    ph = SecurityManager.PolicyHierarchy

    ' Loop through to find the Machine-level sub-tree
    Do While ph.MoveNext
      pl = CType(ph.Current, PolicyLevel)
      If pl.Label = "Machine" Then
        found = True
        Exit Do
      End If
    Loop

    If found Then
      ' See if the code group for this app exists as a Machine-level entry
      Dim cg As CodeGroup
      For Each cg In pl.RootCodeGroup.Children
        If cg.Name = mAppName Then

          ' Code group exists - remove it
          pl.RootCodeGroup.RemoveChild(cg)
          SecurityManager.SavePolicy()
          Exit For
        End If
      Next
    End If

  End Sub

#End Region
```

First, we check to see if the code group existed in the first place. If it did, we simply exit without doing any work:

```
    If mGroupExisted Then Exit Sub
```

The `mGroupExisted` variable was set in our `SetSecurity()` method when we searched for the code group.

Assuming it was `NetRun` that added the code group, we need to find and remove it. First, we scan through the policy hierarchy to find the `Machine` node, just like we did in `SetSecurity()`. Then, we scan through the child nodes looking for the node named the same as our application, just like we did in `SetSecurity()`. If we find such a node, then we remove it:

```
        If cg.Name = mAppName Then

          ' Code group exists - remove it
          pl.RootCodeGroup.RemoveChild(cg)
          SecurityManager.SavePolicy()
          Exit For
        End If
```

We just remove the node from the policy hierarchy and then save the hierarchy, which applies our changes to the system.

At this point, the application has closed and we've cleaned up after ourselves by removing the temporary code group we added. The system is just as it was before we started.

Installing NetRun

`NetRun.exe` must be installed directly on the hard drive of client workstations. It requires `FullTrust` to work, and it solves a set of no-touch deployment issues, so we can't really run `NetRun` itself using no-touch deployment! It must be installed manually, and then *it* can run other applications using no-touch deployment.

`NetRun` can be installed to client workstations using XCOPY deployment, or by creating a setup program or MSI file that users can run. This only needs to be done once to get `NetRun` out there – after that, we'll simply use `NetRun` to launch all our other business applications.

When using `NetRun` as the core deployment strategy for Windows client applications, it's best to view the installation of the .NET runtime and `NetRun.exe` as a pre-condition that all client workstations must meet in order to run our applications.

Ideally, `NetRun.exe` should be installed into a directory that is in the `PATH` on the client machine, so that it can be run directly from any command prompt, the Start | Run dialog, or from within a shortcut icon.. Either install it into a directory that's already in the `PATH`, or alter the `PATH` on the machine to include the directory where `NetRun.exe` resides.

If we don't put `NetRun.exe` in the `PATH`, then the user (or the shortcut) will need to type the full path to `NetRun.exe`, followed by the URL for the program that is to be launched.

Using NetRun

Once `NetRun` is installed on a client workstation, no further work is required on that machine. To deploy an application to the client, all we need to do is copy the application's EXE and associated DLLs to a directory on our web server.

> **If our application uses a `.config` file, we'll also need to rename that file to have a `.remoteconfig` extension.**

For instance, we can deploy our `PTWin` client application for use by `NetRun`. Create a directory on the web server beneath `inetpub\wwwroot`, name it `Apps`, and then create a `PTWin` directory beneath that. Then, copy all files from `PTWin\bin` to our new `inetpub\wwwroot\Apps\PTWin` directory on the web server, and rename `PTWin.exe.config` to `PTWin.exe.remoteconfig`.

The deployment of our application is now complete! Return to the client workstation, and launch the program using NetRun:

```
> netrun http://server/apps/ptwin/ptwin.exe
```

The PTWin application should appear after a brief pause (remember that it had to be downloaded from the server first) and then should run normally.

If we want to deploy a new version of the PTWin application, all we need to do is copy the new version into the web directory on our server. Client applications will automatically download the new versions of the EXE and DLLs the next time the application is launched.

The version checking mechanism used by .NET is the same file data/time check that is used to determine whether a web page is current in the Internet Explorer cache. In other words, the *version* of each assembly is immaterial – it is the file date/time that triggers a client to download a new version of each file.

Conclusion

From a Windows Forms application perspective, no-touch deployment is possibly the most powerful feature of .NET. Unfortunately, no-touch deployment isn't quite as seamless as we'd like it to be, but the NetRun application we've seen here resolves the major issues we face.

Using NetRun and no-touch deployment, we can deploy Windows Forms applications for the same near-zero cost with which we can deploy Web Forms applications. We simply copy the application and its DLLs to a directory on the web server, and it is automatically deployed or updated to all client workstations.

INDEX

Indexes

There are two indexes. One is a general index, the other lists the examples used in this book. Important entries have numbers in **bold** type.

General Index

Symbol

A

B

E

F

G

H

I

K

L

M

N

O

P

Q

R

T

U

Examples Index

A

B

C

D

E

F

G

N

O

P

Q

R

S

T

U